UNPLANNED

UNPLANNED

The snakes and ladders of a life in the City of Westminster

The Autobiography of
Robert Davis MA MBE DL

**Former Lord Mayor of Westminster and
Deputy Leader of Westminster Council**

BROWN
DOG
BOOKS

Published under licence by Brown Dog Books
10b Greenway Farm, Bath Rd, Wick, nr. Bath BS30 5RL

ISBN printed book: 978-1-83952-455-4
ISBN e-book: 978-1-83952-456-1

Cover design by Kevin Rylands
Internal design by Tim Jollands

Printed and bound in the UK

This book is printed on FSC certified paper

MIX
Paper from
responsible sources
FSC
www.fsc.org
FSC® C013604

Contents

	Acknowledgements	7
	Dedication	9
	Prologue	10
1.	Pomp and Ceremony	13
2.	How It All Started	18
3.	My Family and Heritage	20
4.	My Childhood	40
5.	Cilla	58
6.	The Enlightenment	63
7.	Cambridge Conservatives	81
8.	My Oscar	93
9.	Freeman Box	101
10.	Westminster Calls	108
11.	My Life as a Public Servant	116
12.	Scandals at City Hall	130
13.	Amusement Arcades	141
14.	The Westminster Initiative	145
15.	The Day that Changed My Life	151
16.	Realising My Ambition	153
17.	State Visits	124
18.	Mayoral Stories	171
19.	New Leaders and Consequential Changes	176
20.	Managing the City	187
21.	My Marriage	203

22.	My Love of Theatre	208
23.	West End Live	219
24.	Switzerland and the Glockenspiel	229
25.	The London Mayors' Association	243
26.	The Wasting Tales and Other Stories	267
27.	Fascinating People	288
28.	More Westminster Stories	308
29.	The Americans and Tale of the Crispy Duck	334
30.	My Times at the Palace	340
31.	Plaques Galore	351
32.	Mallorca	357
33.	Remembering Simon	371
34.	In Simon's Memory	381
35.	My Charitable and Voluntary Work	391
36.	Honours and Recognition	417
37.	My Downfall . . . or What Goes Up Must Come Down	428
38.	Moving On	470
39.	A Life of Ups and Downs – A Reflection	473
	Index	476

Acknowledgements

The author would like to thank a number of people for their support and assistance in the publication of this book, namely: David Elliott, Mark Galloway, Catriona Durell, Laura and Michael Stadler, Rick Senat, Duncan Rodgers, Jace Tyrrell, Linus Giliomee, Helen Corner-Bryant, Jeffrey Archer, Jeremy Burns, Nica Burns, Larry Moneta, Stanley Lee, the late Stanley Goldstein, the late Frank Burns, Lesley Bennett, Steve Summers, Sybil R, Etty Payne as well as Douglas Walker, Frances Prior-Reeves, Tim Jollands and everyone at Brown Dog Books.

The author would also like to thank and acknowledge the following for the use of their photographs, namely: Hugo Rittson-Thomas (front cover and 'The Royal We' photo), Paul Mellor (many of my photos as a councillor and Lord Mayor as well as those of my wedding), Marc Brenner (photo of *Evita* at the Open Air Theatre), David Jensen (photo of *Pride and Prejudice* at the Open Air Theatre), Andrew Dunsmore of the Picture Partnership (photos at Westminster Abbey), Annie Walker and the Past Overseers Society of Saint Michael and Saint John the Evangelist (photos of the society's silver), C Ford (photo of the Astoria theatre), Jon Bushell (photo with Princess Anne), Anwar Hussein (photo of The Queen and Nelson Mandela), Chiko Photography (my niece's wedding photo), Aylesford School, Kent, and The Royal Academy of Culinary Arts 'Adopt a School' for their photos of the work supported by the Savoy Educational Trust, Simon Thomas and Ian Haworth of the Hippodrome Casino (photo of Boris Johnson opening the Hippodrome).

With regard to the photographs included in this work, no copyright infringement is intended.

Dedication

This book is dedicated
to the love of my life

Hoopie

(known to everyone else as the late Sir Simon Milton)

Prologue

They say that if a butterfly flaps its wings, it can affect someone on the other side of the world. So, when in the early spring of 1982, General Leopoldo Galtieri decided to invade two (then) unknown British dependencies in the South Atlantic, thousands of miles away from me sitting watching TV in my flat in Paddington, I was not to know that this was going to dramatically change my life.

Six months earlier, I had decided to stand for election to Westminster City Council as a Conservative and, as a twenty-four-year-old novice, after a struggle to get selected by the Conservative Party to fight a seat, I was eventually given a ward that we were expected to lose. It was two years into Thatcher's rule as Prime Minister and despite her resounding victory in May 1979, she was now widely disliked.

The 1978 local elections in London had been a great success for the Conservatives, as they happened at a time when the Labour government's handling of the economy was widely criticised, culminating months later in the Winter of Discontent, with crippling strikes affecting every walk of life, rubbish piling six-foot-high in Leicester Square and bodies not being buried. This eventually brought down the Government of James Callaghan.

While in the 1978 election, the Conservatives had won many seats for the first time, it was feared that we would lose most of them back to Labour in an anti-government swing in the ensuing 1982 local election. So, as the young and naïve activist, I was selected for a seat won surprisingly by the Conservatives in 1978 but which we expected to lose in the forthcoming election. Two of the three sitting councillors for the ward (including Francis Maude, later a cabinet minister in the Major government) had moved to safer seats with the third councillor for the ward deciding to stand down. Two candidates had been selected for the three-councillor ward, Neil Heywood and Simon Mabey. I was honoured to be selected to complete the slate.

Canvassing was very depressing over that cold and wet winter, especially when you announced yourself as a Conservative. The resultant abuse directed at Mrs Thatcher and her policies was quite overwhelming.

When news broke on the morning of 2nd April 1982 of the invasion of the Falkland Islands, followed later by the invasion of South Georgia, most of us had never heard of them, let alone taken any serious interest. But as the days passed, the seriousness of what had happened dawned on us and with Thatcher making it clear we would send our troops and an entire naval task force thousands of miles away, to reclaim the islands for the British, we knew this was going to affect the election.

The initial view was that Thatcher would be blamed for having taken her eyes off the ball and so orders from Conservative Central Office were to stop canvassing so as not to antagonise the electorate.

But with our troops gathering at Portsmouth and the fleet setting sail, the mood in the country changed and Thatcher moved from villain to heroine, almost overnight.

Accordingly, our orders changed and we were back on the doorstep. This time, however, we were greeted with hugs and thumbs up. 'You can rely on my vote' and 'We love Mrs Thatcher' were just some of the responses we received. Thatcherism was on the up and, irrespective of my views or my limited experience, everyone was pledging their support for Thatcher and for me and my colleagues.

Within weeks, on 7th May 1982 (coincidently my mother's birthday) with my mother at my side, I attended the post-election count in the Porchester Hall in Bayswater, the venue where she had held her wedding reception 26 years earlier, to see me duly elected, one of the youngest new councillors in the City of Westminster, with a large majority. My life would change for ever.

When, almost fourteen years later, I was elected Lord Mayor of Westminster, in my inaugural speech I told the assembled councillors, officers and guests that 'I have one person to thank for me being here today, former President Galtieri of Argentina'.

It was through my membership of the City Council that I was introduced to Jeremy Freeman and Trevor Box, who invited me to join their legal firm and subsequently become a partner and it was through the Council that I met the love of my life, my husband and friend, Sir Simon Milton.

And as I stood there, accepting office following my election as the youngest ever Lord Mayor of Westminster and Westminster's First Citizen, I could not help but feel proud that the descendant of poor immigrants from impoverished small 'Fiddler-on-the-Roof' style villages in Eastern Europe had reached the echelons of the British Establishment.

But how did I get there and why? And as they say, everything that goes up must come down. So, this is my story of the snakes and ladders of being a politician in modern day London.

The Right Worshipful The Lord Mayor of Westminster 1996–1997 Councillor Robert Davis in full civic state photographed in the Wallace Collection.

Chapter 1

Pomp and Ceremony

No one does pomp and ceremony like the British. And to be at the centre of it is like being in a magical dream.

An Official Welcome

I stood there in my royal blue damask flowing robes embroidered with extensive gold thread, with a white lace jabot around my neck on which lay the heavy historic chains and badge of office, on the stage of the majestic Royal Pavilion that had been erected on Horse Guards Parade specially for the occasion. I looked ahead to see the Guard of Honour comprising row after row of red tunicked guards from the First Battalion of the Irish Guards, all wearing their black fur Bearskins, lined up facing the Royal Pavilion. Behind them were The Queen's Colour and the Band of the Irish Guards. To my left were the Sovereign's Escort of the Household Cavalry, the Life Guards and the Blues and Royals, in their silver-plated armoury and white or red plumed helmets, mounted on magnificent black horses, awaiting to escort Her Majesty and the Royal Party in a series of state coaches back to Buckingham Palace.

The occasion was the State Visit of Nelson Mandela, President of South Africa, in July 1996, just a few weeks after I had been elected the youngest Lord Mayor of Westminster in the city's history. We were in Horse Guards Parade for the start of the State Visit to welcome the President and his daughter.

As the most junior of the VIPs to receive the President, I arrived first and as I took my place at one end of the red-carpet-lined stage, I looked around and saw that Horse Guards Parade was full to the brim with members of the public watching from every vantage point. I already knew from having been driven in the mayoral limousine to the parade ground that the Mall was also at least ten-deep with throbbing crowds.

As the tension built, the other dignitaries who were to be received by The Queen started to arrive in full ceremonial dress. These were the most senior members of the British Establishment. The line-up was led by the Prime Minister (then John Major), the Foreign Secretary and the Home Secretary together with the Chief of the Defence Staff and the Heads of the Army, Navy and Air Force, all in their most illustrious uniforms full of medals and honours. Standing next to me was the Commissioner of the Metropolitan Police, Sir Paul Condon.

The last to arrive was the Lord-Lieutenant, Field Marshal Lord Bramall, again in his splendid military uniform, who waited in the middle of the platform to await the arrival of The Queen and the Duke of Edinburgh.

Then the formal part of the proceedings began, with the arrival of Her Majesty and the Duke. The Lord-Lieutenant received the Royal Party, then starting with the Prime Minister in descending order of importance, the Queen (wearing a yellow coat and matching pillar box hat) was introduced to the dignitaries. The final introduction was to myself as Lord Mayor.

After a few pleasantries about it being a special day, The Queen suggested that I must have been very busy since taking office. I replied that that was indeed the case. I said that I had undertaken over two hundred engagements in just two months. She smiled and turned away to face the parade ground and await the arrival of the President.

However, after a minute or so, Her Majesty turned back towards me and said 'Two hundred! – that's nearly as busy as Anne' before turning back to await the President's arrival. I had clearly given Her Majesty something to think about.

Moments later, the President duly arrived in his open state landau to be received by The Queen, who presented each of the dignitaries in turn. When the Queen eventually presented

me to the President, she explained that I was newly installed, yet had been a 'very busy Lord Mayor' in the few months that I had been in office.

After the President and the Duke had inspected the guards, the Royal Party and the President and his entourage were off in a series of open state carriages to the Palace accompanied by the Household Cavalry and the King's Troop in their black uniforms on horseback, pulling a series of gun carriages.

The State Banquet

That night I attended the State Banquet at Buckingham Palace. Dressed like one of the waiter-penguins from the film *Mary Poppins*, in white tie and tails, with my Lady Mayoress (my official consort and friend Carole Franco) wearing a glittering long evening dress and

a diamond tiara (we had borrowed from Asprey's for the occasion) sitting neatly on her newly coiffured hair, we were dropped off in the forecourt of the Palace by our chauffeur in the mayoral limousine. Greeted by a senior member of the Royal Household, we were led up the grand staircase through a series of imposing historic State Rooms before finally ending up in the Royal Gallery, where the pre-dinner reception was being held.

Joining the reception and drinking champagne from flutes with the royal

EⅡR

*The Lord Steward
has received Her Majesty's command to invite*

The Right Worshipful the Lord Mayor of Westminster
and the Lady Mayoress of Westminster

*to a State Banquet to be given by
The Queen and The Duke of Edinburgh
at Buckingham Palace in honour of
The President of the Republic of South Africa
on Tuesday, 9th July, 1996 at 8.00 p.m.*

*A reply is requested to:
The Master of the Household, Buckingham Palace, SW1A 1AA
Guests are asked to arrive between 7.20 p.m. and 7.40 p.m.*

*White Tie, Decorations
Full Ceremonial Evening Dress
for Serving Officers
or National Dress*

The Royal Command to attend the State Banquet.

monogram engraved on them, I looked around and realised that the other guests included the Prime Minister (John Major), several members of the Cabinet and the Leader of Her Majesty's Opposition (Tony Blair) as well as numerous distinguished and famous people as well as most members of the Royal Family. Our eyes marvelled at the beauty of the State Rooms of the Palace. High ceilings, gold leaf everywhere and some of the world's greatest paintings including Rubens' *The Assumption of the Virgin* and Frans Hals' *Portrait of a Man*. We stood there in awe of our surroundings.

Everyone seemed very friendly and several people approached us, introduced themselves and started conversations. One of these was the Director-General of the CBI, Adair Turner (now Lord Turner), who had been a friend at Cambridge and was not only a fellow member of my college Gonville & Caius, but was the first person I met when I joined the Cambridge University Conservative Association.

It was not long before we were summoned into dinner but before doing so, we had to pass into the Music Room where we were greeted by the official receiving line headed by The Queen and the President. Also in the receiving line were the Duke of Edinburgh and the President's daughter together with The Queen Mother.

On being formally presented to The Queen by the Master of the Household, I bowed and Carole curtseyed and after shaking hands with Her Majesty, she turned to the President and said 'You will recall the Lord Mayor of Westminster from this morning'. He responded by confirming that he did.

Remembering that receiving line reminds me of an amusing story about another State Visit, when my good friend the late Audrey Lewis was Lord Mayor in 2014. She was on her way to Horse Guards Parade to join the welcoming party on the arrival of the President of Singapore, when the official car got stuck in terrible traffic. An obstinate police officer refused to let her car go through the blockades.

Poor Audrey had to turn back and missed joining the receiving line. At the State Banquet that night (which she left for, very early), on passing down the said same receiving line, the Duke of Edinburgh, in a very loud voice, shouted – 'Oh! – You decided to turn up tonight then!!', much to the horror of our dear Lord Mayor. Audrey told me later that she did not know what to say or do but just curtsied and walked on.

After shaking hands with the other members of the receiving line, Carole and I walked through several further State Rooms, each of which were lined with the oldest Royal Body Guard in the world, founded in 1485 by King Henry VIII, the Queen's Body Guard of the Yeoman of the Guard. Each one was wearing their regal red tunic with purple facings, a white lace ruff around their neck and strips of gold lace ornaments on their tunic, red knee-breeches and red stockings with their flat hats adorned with white, blue and red rosettes and holding their ornamental spikes.

We eventually reached the ballroom, where there were two long tables running down each side of the room with a top table linking the two longer tables in front of the Royal Canopy. The room was surrounded by footmen in red uniforms standing behind the chairs where guests were to sit. A footman for every three guests.

We soon found our placings, which were on different spurs. As I stood in front of mine, I surveyed the room, initially looking up at the high ornate ceiling and then the spectacular tables laid out to perfection and covered in elaborate gold table decorations, numerous floral displays, gold cutlery and gold rimmed porcelain dinner plates with the royal monogram. There were enough glasses per guest to cover at least ten courses of different wines and beverages. My attention was then drawn to the balcony where the Band of the Scots Guards was playing a series of uplifting pieces of music.

I introduced myself to my neighbours as I was not wearing my chains of office, only the great badge of the City of Westminster (on a white ribbon) which had been gifted to the City by the Dean and Chapter of Westminster Abbey on the formation of the new City of Westminster in 1965.

Once all the guests were standing behind their chairs, The Queen accompanied by the President and followed by the senior members of the Royal Family, the prime minister and senior members of the President's entourage, processed into the ballroom to take their places.

The band then played the National Anthem after which The Queen sat down, as did all the guests. The Queen then stood up and I listened intensely as she gave a speech about the importance of the State Visit and about how much we all respected Nelson Mandela and how she had so enjoyed her own recent State Visit to South Africa. She then proposed a toast to the President. The President then rose and gave his response and finished this with a toast to The Queen.

I must add at this point that, although all the guests were in white tie and tails and magnificent long evening dresses with the ladies all wearing tiaras, Mandela was wearing one of his traditional long shirts in self-patterned black silk with white trimmings.

During the meal, Carole was busy chatting to her neighbour when one of the liveried footmen solemnly bent forward and discreetly whispered into her ear 'Madam, your necklace is about to fall into your soup!' Much to Carole's embarrassment, she touched her necklace and, yes, it had come loose and was slipping slowly down towards her soup. She quickly thanked the footman and fixed it back. A protocol disaster had been avoided.

After the banquet, we all moved into the State Rooms for post-dinner drinks and further conversations, before we felt it was time to take our leave. We wandered down to the Grand Entrance and

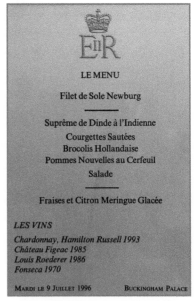

The Menu at the State Banquet for Nelson Mandela.

advised the doorkeeper who we were and he then made a call on an internal phone and within a few minutes the mayoral car arrived at the Grand Entrance and we returned home after one of the most magnificent evenings of my life.

Tree Planting

The next morning, we were up early as the President was an early riser. And I mean early! I was picked up by the mayoral chauffeur at 5.30 am to ensure I arrived at St James's Park where the President was to plant a tree at 6.30 am.

As we drove down the Mall, we were greeted by an amazing scene. Thousands of onlookers were lining the Mall at 6 am! We arrived at the chosen site to await the President's arrival, noting TV cameras were there in force as the tree planting was to be shown live on breakfast TV.

Mandela arrived wearing one of his colourful shirts and Carole and I were there to greet him. With hundreds watching, Mandela started shovelling the soil into the base of this newly planted tree. After several shovels, I politely whispered to the President 'You don't need to finish, Your Excellency, as there are a couple of guys over there (pointing to two large beefy gardeners standing to the side) who will finish it off'.

The President stopped. He turned to me, placed a hand on my shoulder and said 'Lord Mayor …. I was always taught, that when you start a job – you need to finish it!' I was rightly put in my place as he continued shovelling until the tree was fully planted.

With Nelson Mandela at the tree planting ceremony in St James's Park during the State Visit – July 1996.

Chapter 2

How It All Started

My political career started in my school's library. I spent my secondary school life at a boys' grammar school in the heart of Finchley, namely Christ's College. With its historic tower adorned with a crown-like pale green round roof, which could be seen from miles around, the school turned me from a mediocre pupil into one of its academic stars.

The year was 1974 and I was preparing for my O levels (now called GCSEs) when I was persuaded to give serious thought to which A levels I wanted to study. Knowing I excelled in Mathematics made that an easy first choice, but I had to find two more subjects if I was going to continue an academic career and study at least three subjects at A level. As my father was insistent that I become a professional and with my ability to master Maths, accountancy seemed the obvious career path and so an A level in Economics seemed the obvious second choice. But what of a third subject?

One day, I found myself in the school library browsing through some books, when I came across one written by the former deputy headmaster of the school, Dr Leslie Bather.

Christ's College, Finchley.

He was known at school as 'DB'. Intrigued that he had written a book, I sat in a corner of the library and opened the pages of his book, entitled *The British Constitution*.

At this stage in my life, I had no idea how the British Constitution worked, let alone what the House of Lords or indeed the Commons were. But as I sat and read all about electing members of Parliament, about the stages a Bill had to go through before being enacted into law, I was mesmerised. I took the book home and devoured it overnight. I was smitten. I wanted to learn more. I knew British Government would be my third A level.

After passing nine O levels, four with A grades, I returned to school to start my sixth form and commence my studies on how the British political system worked. The teacher who spurred on my interest was Mrs Millicent (Micky) Watkins and it was not long before she brought it alive for me and encouraged me to start reading more widely about the subject.

In 1975, the first volume of the controversial Crossman Diaries were published. Richard Crossman had been Minister of Housing and Local Government in the Wilson Government. The Diaries were published posthumously after the government tried (but failed) to block publication through the courts. What was so special about them was that they were the first published diaries of a cabinet minister, revealing in graphic detail what went on behind the scenes in Whitehall. They were dynamite and I read them and learnt more and more about the life of a politician, especially one in power. I was totally absorbed and they made me realise for the first time that politics was something I wanted to get involved in. I was hooked!

Chapter 3

My Family and Heritage

But let us go back a few steps and discover more about my family and where I came from.

My mother, Pamela (nee Lee), was beautiful with a lovely warm smile and dimples that I have inherited. Although born with jet black hair, because my father's eyes always turned to follow a blonde woman walking past, when I was quite young she dyed her hair and remained a blonde for the rest of her life. She inherited the family gene from her own mother which meant she always looked younger than she was. After she died, many of her friends would comment to me on how attractive she was and how her beauty stood out in a crowd.

I would often be out with my mother, when people assumed that she was my sister or girlfriend. On one holiday when I was a child, someone told my father that his three children were very well behaved. My sister Susan and I thought this hysterical. My mother was delighted, but my father was furious.

Married at the tender age of eighteen (this was common in the mid-1950s), she was only nineteen when she had me and twenty-one when my sister was born.

I adored her and remained close to her until her untimely death at the age of just fifty-eight from ovarian cancer. Once I returned to London after university, I would always ring

My parents – 1990.

her twice a day, at 8.45 in the morning and 5 at night. I would also join her and my father for Friday night dinner every week and once I was working in the West End, we would frequently meet up for lunch.

My father, Gerald, was eleven years older than my mother and during my childhood I saw very little of him as he worked a long six-day week and always returned home at the end of the day exhausted and so, after a cup of tea, he would have a snooze until dinner. Only Sundays were spent with him and then it was usually a day out as a family. We rarely spent time together, just father and son. But I understood and realised that we enjoyed a good standard of living due to his hard work.

Gerald was often tough on me. As a child, he would be the one who would punish me, when he returned from work, if I had been naughty during the day, occasionally using his belt to do so. He was also highly critical of me and rarely complimented me on my successes. However, I knew from their friends and our family, that behind my back he would go on and on about me and my achievements. He was clearly very proud of me but found it difficult to tell me directly.

I often wonder if my political drive later in life was my way of trying to make my father proud so that one day he would congratulate me directly. I think it took my election as Lord Mayor, when I was thirty-eight, for him to do so. But he did support me financially, not only at Cambridge but also after I first came back to London before I started earning sufficient income to keep myself.

But then everything changed. After my mother died, he became very dependent on me and we struck up a close relationship, and more importantly, a good friendship. We would spend a lot of time together in those few years before he died. In particular, he became my regular 'plus one' at all the exciting events I was invited to through my role as a councillor and he soon befriended many of my council colleagues. When he died, the Lord Mayor paid tribute to him at a plenary council meeting.

My only sibling was my younger sister, Susan. Although we grew up playing together a lot, we had very different personalities. Susan had many friends, was outgoing, vivacious and, in her teens, always going to parties, clubs and socialising. Studying was not on her shopping list. I, on the other hand, had few friends as a teenager and spent most of my time in my room studying hard.

My parents were forever putting pressure on me to work hard at school and do my homework but (in my view) rarely did so with Susan. They came from a generation where the son was brought up to become the breadwinner of his family while the daughter was expected to find a nice hard-

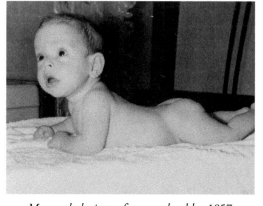

Me as a baby just a few months old – 1957.

My family in 1960.

working husband to take care of her. But once we were adults, although we had little in common, we were close and felt close and this was deeply cemented when she gave birth to Cassie and then Jessica, who I adored and would spend hours with.

But where were my roots? I am sixty per cent Polish. Five of my great grandparents were born in Poland. At the end of the 19th or beginning of the 20th century, they emigrated to England to escape the pogroms. In Poland as elsewhere in Eastern Europe at the time, there were violent government-authorised raids on Jews that often involved the destruction of their villages.

My Father's Family

My paternal grandfather Alf (his birth name was Abraham, but every one called him Alf) was the only one of my grandparents born abroad. He was born on 1st April 1903 in Yelisavetgrad (now known as Kropyvnytskyi), in the centre of Ukraine. In 1902, the city had been ravaged by famine caused by drought and poor farming methods. *The New York Times* wrote at the time that a reporter had observed 'general and acute destitution; death from starvation; widespread typus and little or no work to be found'. There were also several violent pogroms leading in 1905 to the killing of

My paternal grandfather Alf Pevovar.

many of the thousands of Jews who lived in the city and the plundering of the Jewish quarter.

Alf's parents were David and Raisa Pevovar and I have Alf's birth certificate in Ukrainian, duly framed on my wall at home. A Ukrainian-speaking friend recently translated this for me. Alf was brought to England in 1906, when he was just three years of age. How and why London, I do not know.

By the time I was interested and wanted to know more about my family history, it was too late and nobody was left to tell me. However, he had a number of siblings, two brothers and three sisters.

My sister Susan and I called my grandfather 'Pa Alf' and as children we adored him, especially when he showered us with toys every time we visited him. He died when I was only 13 and so I never got to know him as a person, as I had been too young before his death to build an adult relationship with him.

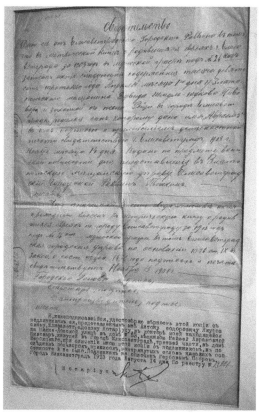

Alfred Pevovar's birth certificate 1st April 1903.

My paternal grandmother Jane (or Jenny as many knew her) was also one of six siblings – one brother and four sisters – all of whom were born in London. They had large families in those days. Their father Jo had been a kosher butcher in Poland and when he and his wife arrived for the first time in the UK, he was holding close to his chest his most important asset, his butcher's knives, all wrapped up in a cloth.

Appearing before the immigration officers on arrival, they asked him his name. He spoke no English, merely Yiddish. Not understanding the question and believing he was being asked 'what is in your bag', his response was 'Messer' which is knives in Yiddish (and German). The immigration officer wrote down on the official forms that his surname was Messer and hence the family were known as the Messers.

Once settled in the east end of London, Jo Messer opened a Jewish delicatessen and salt beef shop and, as his daughters (including my grandmother Jane) grew older, they would work in the restaurant after school serving the food and cleaning the tables. Jane also took an interest in the restaurant's kitchen as well as her dad's recipes and soon became a superb yiddisher cook. Jo died (I believe from complications arising from appendicitis) in 1936.

How my grandmother Jane and my grandfather Alf met and married, I do not know,

Jane Pevovar's nationality card.

but before the Second World War, they lived in a house in the east end of London two doors away from Jane's elder sister Becky Goldstein and her husband, Mottle, a coat manufacturer. Becky and Mottle had three children, Stanley, Frances and Rosemary. Because my grandparents were out at work all day, they left Becky to look after their two children, my father Gerald and his older sister Phyllis, with her own children making them supper in the evenings. Consequently, my father and Stanley became very close and until they got married, they were inseparable and spent time in the merchant navy together. Likewise, my father's sister Phyllis was very close to Frances and Rosemary.

During the War, Alf and Jane moved with Phyllis and my father to a flat on the lower ground floor of a mock Tudor-style mansion block in St John's Wood, Clifton Court, on the Edgware Road. As there were only two bedrooms, my aunt had to sleep on the couch in the living room.

My aunt Phyllis never married. From what I can ascertain, in her early twenties, she fell in love with a man who was known to be a bit of a 'villain'. What that meant, I have no idea, as it was never really discussed and any questions I asked were

My father as a boy working for his parents on their Walthamstow market stall.

Alf and Jenny Pevovar's wedding.

Clifton Court – Maida Vale.

always diverted to another subject. My grandparents were determined that she would not marry him and insisted she never saw him again. The story goes that she was so upset that she refused to date anyone else. And so, she never married or had another relationship and continued to live with her parents at Clifton Court. However, for me she became a third honorary grandmother who doted on me and my sister.

My grandfather Alf had a textiles and furnishings business based in a shop on Berwick Street in Soho, which I remember visiting as a small boy. This came in useful years later, when I was a cabinet member on Westminster Council with responsibilities for the famous Berwick Street Market. I had to deal with a lot of unrest among the street traders, after my predecessor had threatened to privatise the market. On taking on this new role, I immediately reassured them that

My father's sister Phyllis at 21.

My father with his mother and sister outside their flat in Clifton Court.

we would not do so and I would do what I could to reinvigorate the market, telling them of my grandfather's business in the street in the 1960s and my regular visits to see him there. This struck a chord and defused the crisis, as they all took a liking to me, telling me stories about life in the market in the 1960s.

Alf also had two market stalls in Walthamstow Market in north-east London which he ran on Thursdays, Fridays and Saturdays. On one stall, my grandfather sold dress materials, while the other sold furnishings. Phyllis worked for her father alone in the shops on Thursdays and Fridays, while Jane stayed at home except on Thursdays, Fridays and Saturdays when she accompanied Alf to the market.

They were wonderful grandparents and certainly spoilt me. During my early years, we would visit them for afternoon tea in Clifton Court every Sunday, when Alf would shower me with presents, including every new toy that had been released that week. He had a friend who owned a toy shop in nearby Church Street and I assume Alf was his biggest customer. Every autumn when all the annuals were published, he bought every single one for me. Not one a week, but all in one go. I was certainly the envy of all my friends.

Until her death in 1995, Jane was the grandparent that I was closest to. I adored her and, as a child, I loved spending time with her, either when she visited our family home or when my sister Susan and I went to stay with her in her St John's Wood flat. She would frequently lie on the bed with us, telling us stories that took us into the mysterious world of make-believe. She would cook delicious food for us including salmon fish cakes, gefilte fish balls and crispy raisin-filled biscuits, presumably based on her father's recipes.

In the late 1960s, when I was entering my teens, Alf was diagnosed with cancer. These were the early days of cancer care and, despite medical support, he passed away in July 1970.

This was the first time I had experienced death in my family and I remember being woken up one morning to be told the sad news. I sat there on the side of my bed, frozen in disbelief. The fact that Alf died just a few months before my 13th birthday and my bar mitzvah made things worse. My parents had been planning a lavish dinner dance at the Dorchester Hotel to celebrate, but because of my grandfather's death this was cancelled. I was devastated but even at a young age I understood and was more upset at losing my grandfather and the source of my growing toy collection.

Reading my bar mitzvah speech.

Instead of a lavish bar mitzvah at the Dorchester Hotel, my parents erected a large marquee that covered the entirety of the garden of our family house and after the Saturday morning service in our local synagogue (Kinloss in Henlys Corner, Finchley), we hosted a sit-down lunch for about one hundred guests but without music (as we were officially still in mourning). On the Sunday night, I was allowed to host a disco for my friends but with no adults present.

Following Alf's death, my father wound up Alf's businesses and Phyllis started working for him at his own wholesale textile business called Gee Dee Textiles based in Foley Street in East Marylebone.

As I have said, Phyllis was like a third grandmother to me. She continued to live with my grandmother Jane in Clifton Court for the rest of her life. With few friends, she

Dancing with my sister at my bar mitzvah October 1970.

lived a quiet life and apart from going to work at Gee Dee Textiles every day and visiting the hairdressers religiously every Saturday morning, she would stay at home doing housework as well as knitting and of course, looking after Jane. In about 1990, she was diagnosed with cancer and eventually succumbed to it in the spring of 1992.

After Phyllis died, Jane found it difficult living alone in in her ground floor flat in Clifton Court and things came to a head a year later when someone tried to break in through her bedroom window one night while she was in bed asleep. But gutsy Jane jumped out of bed and having opened the curtains to a startled burglar, screamed at him to go away. He soon ran off. But we did not like the idea of her being alone in that flat and so I took charge of moving her.

My parents were at this stage living nearby in Century Court, a 1960s block of flats built by the MCC (Marylebone Cricket Club) on land adjacent to Lord's, the home of British cricket. Through my parents, I had become the lawyer for the residents of the block who now owned the headlease, so I knew all about the block and knew most of the flat owners. The small one-bedroomed flat immediately adjacent to my parents had been occupied by an elderly gentleman who had become unwell and so had gone to live with his daughter. I had been in contact with her and so knew about this. I therefore approached her to see if she would rent the flat to my family, so we could move my grandmother into the flat, where she would be able to live independently but next door to my parents, who could keep a watching eye over her. We decorated the flat and Jane moved in and soon loved her new abode and the comfort of living adjacent to her son and daughter-in-law. She was then about 91 but over the next couple of years she sadly deteriorated and dementia took hold.

In the autumn of 1995, she fell out of bed and broke her hip. She was taken to St Mary's Hospital and after she recovered from the break, she was transferred to St Charles Hospital in Kensington which was a recuperation hospital for the elderly. However, while there she deteriorated further and eventually, at the age of 93, she passed away.

This was just a few weeks before I was selected to become the next Lord Mayor of Westminster in the following May, and so I was unable to tell her – something I regretted, as she would have been so proud.

Alf's family name was Pevovar. However, his birth certificate spells this as 'Pivovar'

My grandmother Jane with her daughter Phyllis in 1990.

which translates as 'beer maker'. He and his brother's family were the only Pevovars in the London phone book but I have subsequently discovered that it was a common name in the Ukraine and there are still a few in the United States and Canada.

At school, my father's friends teased him by calling him 'Pullover' and so shortly after his 19th birthday, he changed his name by deed poll to 'Davis'. You will note from the deed poll that it was actually sworn by his father Alf (or Abraham as was his birth name) as at that time, being under 21 years old, he was still a minor and could not do so himself.

The name Davis was chosen because his grandfather's name was David and Davis means 'Son of David' or so I was told. So, I was legally born a Davis, even though my father was not.

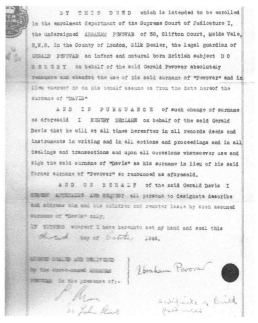

The deed poll changing my father's surname to 'Davis' in 1946.

My Maternal Grandfather's Family

My maternal grandfather, Arnold Lee, was born in England, the son of Joe and Jane Levy (they later changed their name to Lee). He was one of seven siblings, although one sister – Frieda – had died young, well before I was born. I am told she committed suicide – but why, I have no knowledge. The eldest, Cissie, was a half-sister, as Arnold's mother had a daughter from a previous marriage.

One of Arnold's sisters, Rose, married Bill Sonn, an American who had been posted to London as part of the United States Air Force during the war, and once it was over, she emigrated to New York and then, later in life moved to Florida.

Another sister, Dorothy married an English taxi driver (Alfred Burns). Alfred was not a successful businessman but Dorothy was and in addition was very ambitious, so she and Alfred, wanting a better life, soon followed Rose to New York

My maternal Grandfather, Arnold Lee.

with their young son Frank, where Dorothy (rather than Alfred) became a very successful and wealthy businesswoman.

The third sister was Edna who was married to Sam Mason. Edna also had entrepreneurial skills and set up a fashion business in central London. Sam and Edna never had kids but lived in the same block of flats as my grandparents Arnold and Anne and they were all very close.

The youngest sibling was Len who never seemed to work. I think my grandfather and Edna kept him. He always seemed very quiet, spoke very slowly, was forever glum and I thought, just very strange.

My grandfather's half-sister Cissie appears to have disappeared from his life as I never heard her mentioned. While undertaking research for this book, I was told that it is thought that she married a non-Jew and was accordingly ostracised by the family, as would have happened in those days.

Arnold's only nephew was Dorothy's son Frank who has only recently passed away. Before he died, he was living in retirement in Palo Alto in California with his only son Jeremy and Jeremy's wife, Liat, and their two children, Sammy and Mia. I kept in touch with both Frank and his late wife, Susan, visiting them regularly when they lived in New York. I continued to speak to Frank up until his death in early 2021 and continue to keep in touch with Jeremy and his family in Palo Alto.

Cousin Frank Burns and I on Fire Island, New York, 1980.

Frank and Jeremy undertook extensive research about our family and they discovered that my grandfather Arnold's family had originally emigrated from Germany.

The research further revealed that my grandfather's maternal grandfather was Mark Goldstein who had been born in 1845. He was married aged 28 in Whitechapel, London, to Emily, aged 30, who had been born in Stuttgart, Germany, in 1843.

Both the 1881 and 1891 census describe Mark's occupation as a hairdresser but we understand that subsequently he became a publican, owning the Three Crowns Public House at 1 Dunk Street (on the corner of Old Montague Street) in Mile End, Whitechapel. Dunk Street no longer exists but it ran north of Old Montague Street (which does still exist) towards Hanbury Street. This was not far north-east of what is now Aldgate East Tube Station.

Running behind the pub was an alley where the body of an Alice McKenzie was found in July 1889.

> At 12.50 am on the 17th July 1889 Police constable Walter Andrews found the body of local prostitute Alice McKenzie lying close to a lamp post on a pavement in Castle Alley. Her skirt had been pulled up and there was blood over her thigh and abdomen which, it transpired was coming from a zig-zag, albeit fairly superficial, that ran from just beneath her left breast to her navel.

The Three Crowns Public House.

One report of the murder quotes a police constable confirming that, just before the body was found, he recalls passing the Three Crowns Public House at 12.30 am and seeing the landlord close the pub. That must have been my great-great grandfather!

There was much speculation at the time that she was another victim of Jack the Ripper. Nowadays, experts do not believe she was a Ripper victim but this was not a view shared by a majority of those who lived in the area at the time.

Further research undertaken by Frank found that Mark Goldstein held one of the most senior positions in the British Freemasons and among some papers discovered by Frank, was a letter from the Private Secretary of the then Prince of Wales addressed to Mark, sent on behalf of the Prince, with reference to his work within the Freemasons.

My Maternal Grandmother's Family

My maternal grandmother, Anne, was born in December 1915 and died just short of her 102nd birthday in 2017. She was a remarkable woman and I was able to ask her a little about her family history before she died, but by the time I did, she was having trouble remembering very much.

Her parents were Solomon Schuveck, a tailor born in 1887 in Poland, and his wife Bertha (née Foule and known to the family as Buba but also referred to in some documents as Betty, and I presume that is what her friends called her). Betty was also born in Poland in about 1890.

They lived in a small village near Bedzin in southern Poland and until the Second World War it had a vibrant Jewish

My maternal grandmother Anne at 93 years of age in 2008.

31

community (about 51% of the population). For some reason unknown to me (but probably for a better life), they decided in about 1912 to emigrate to the United States, but the journey involved a stop off in Paris.

The intention was to then travel to London and subsequently to head north to Liverpool to catch a boat to New York. However, in Paris Betty fell pregnant and so they stayed a year until their son (Mark) was old enough to travel. Once they felt they could take the next step, they travelled to London and stayed with a relative in the East End, where in early 1915 Betty again fell pregnant with my grandmother who was born on 7th December that year.

Now with two children, they decided for some reason (probably for lack of money) to stay in London. Sadly, Solomon died not long afterwards (in Hackney in June 1930) and within a short period, Betty, now a single mother with two young children, married her brother-in-law who had also been widowed. He already had a son (Chaimi Maygar) and so Anne was brought up with two brothers (albeit one a step-brother).

My grandmother Anne was beautiful (something people who remembered her would frequently tell me when I introduced myself as her grandson). At school, she was very bright

Solomon Schuveck (my great grandfather), his wife Betty and their children Mark and Anne (my maternal grandmother).

and well behaved and won numerous prizes. I know this as she gave me several hardback books (including a dictionary) with inscriptions on the inside covers confirming they were awarded to her at school for various academic and behavioural achievements.

But Anne left school as soon as she could and found a job working in an office for a fashion house in central London. After a while, she was picked from all the girls in the office to model some of the sample clothes for a customer. She was so good at it that she was soon promoted to the role of the house model.

She never looked her age and was always stunningly attractive. Photos of her in her nineties would be seen by friends, who assumed she was in her fifties and my mother rather than my grandmother.

The fact that she looked much younger than her true age was inherited by my mother who in turn looked beautiful and decades younger than she was.

My maternal great-grandmother, Betty Schuveck, died on 28th June 1958, when I was just nine months old. However, I have several photos of her holding me in her arms. But I have no memory of her.

My maternal grandmother, Anne, at a young age.

After she died, my grandmother Anne had a row with her brother and step-brother. I am not exactly sure what the argument was about, but I believe it was something to do with Betty's will.

As a consequence, they never spoke again. I therefore grew up never having met my grandmother's two brothers let alone their families. If I was sitting next to one of them in a restaurant, I would never have known.

About five years before Anne died, she received a call from one of her brothers. I cannot recall which one. He explained that he was dying of cancer and wanted a reconciliation. Anne told me that she heard him out and then said 'no' and put the phone down. They never spoke again and a few months later we heard that he had passed away. It made the mystery murkier as to what the argument was all about, over fifty years earlier.

Anne with her own mother, Betty.

Marriage

Returning to my grandmother Anne's youth, her work required her to travel by bus to the showroom where she worked as a model. One day a young gentleman sat near her on the bus. She recognised him from previous journeys. But this time, as she walked past to disembark, he handed her a note with his name and telephone number. She ignored this but on the third time he repeated this, she called him and agreed to a date. This was Arnold and in 1935 they were married in a synagogue in Westminster and moved to a house in Willesden, where in 1936 Anne gave birth to a son Stanley (born on 29th February – so a leap year baby) and subsequently to my mother Pamela (or Pam as the family knew her) in 1938.

Arnold and Anne's wedding day photo.

When in September 1939, the war broke out, deeply concerned about the future, my grandfather Arnold immediately decided that he and his wider family had to leave London. So, in his brother-in-law Alfred Burn's taxi, Arnold, Anne, Dorothy and Alfred with their three children, drove to Northampton where they rented a couple of rooms in a bed and breakfast hotel.

But, after a few weeks, it was clear that the bombing of London was not going to happen immediately (it in fact took several months before it started) and so, bored with living in Northampton, they returned to London.

At the time, Arnold and Anne were living with their children in a house in Willesden. To protect them, Arnold built a bomb shelter in the garden but after using it only twice and finding it uncomfortable, wet and dirty, they refused to use it again and instead, decided to move home.

In 1942, they moved to a flat in Eyre Court, a mansion block on the Finchley Road in St John's Wood. Anne remained living in the block (albeit in three different flats at different times) until she died some seventy-five years later. The block is distinguished by the large grass lawn in front of the building and my mother and Stanley would play on that lawn during their youth. My sister and I would, in later years, also play there when visiting as young children.

However, with the arrival of the doodlebugs (the German V-1 flying bombs) in 1944, Arnold was again worried for his family and arranged for Anne and the two children to go to a hotel in Blackpool to live in safety, while he remained in London to keep on working. In Blackpool, my uncle Stanley told me, they delighted in living on fish and chips from the

My mother aged 5 with her brother Stanley aged 7 and my grandmother Anne 1943.

local chippy every night. But the one treat they enjoyed was an endless supply of ice cream. In London it was impossible to buy ice cream once the war had started. But, despite this, they were not happy there and after about a year they returned to London.

My grandfather Arnold, was originally a travelling salesman, selling ladies underwear door to door. During the war he had failed his tests to get called up to join the army due to his poor eyesight, so instead, had been sent to Bristol, to work in an aircraft factory as an inspector. However, this paid very poorly and with a family to keep, he went to greyhound race meetings, where he started making extra cash, by taking bets from his friends and acquaintances. This led to an interest in betting and after the war he decided to become a bookmaker.

Prior to 1964 and the liberalisation of the betting laws, anyone who wanted to place a bet on a horse or dog had to have an existing account with a bookmaker who had to operate from an office. High street bookmaking shops were illegal. The only place you could make a bet without an account was at the racecourse itself.

He was clearly successful in business and became quite a wealthy man and, although he could not drive, he had a Daimler (a very smart car at the time) with a chauffeur. They also had both a maid and a nanny to look after the children. The nanny was Ella, who lived with them for years and only left when the children grew out of requiring someone to look after them.

When the laws governing betting offices were liberalised in the mid-1960s, with betting shops opening on every high street, Arnold's business suffered. So he wound down the business and joined his sister Edna's business, Slick Wear, a wholesale fashion company.

Within a few years, he took over the business and found a successful and profitable niche, when he started to import evening dresses from Hong Kong for resale to the retail fashion industry. It was very fashionable in the mid-1960s and 1970s for ladies attending formal dinners and dances to wear full length dresses that clung to their bodies and were covered in sequins. The business operated from premises in Wardour Street in Soho and required him to frequently fly to Hong Kong to meet suppliers and manufacturers. This was often to my advantage, as he always returned with the latest technical gadget, as in those days before the days of Apple and Microsoft, the Far East led the world in electronic goods and not only were they cheaper than in the UK but they were also sold a year or two before they could be bought in London. One gift I remember well, at that time unknown in the UK, was an 'Eight-Track' stereo system, which produced amazing sounds when playing an eight-track cassette and was seen as state of the art before it was sidelined by music cassettes.

While I was at university in the late 1970s, early one Sunday morning, an IRA bomber set off an explosion in the doorway of the premises in Wardour Street, Soho, that my grandfather's business occupied. The building was owned by my grandfather and although he occupied the ground floor and basement, the upper parts were office suites that he rented out. As the bomb exploded early on a Sunday morning, no one was hurt but the whole building was very badly damaged. But once Arnold had got over the shock, the insurers agreed to pay for the total reconstruction of the building, allowing him to charge higher rents to his tenants for more modern office accommodation.

Sometime after the bomb, Arnold retired from business but continued to live off the income from letting out the property in Wardour Street. After my grandfather died in 1986, my grandmother continued to own the building, until she became too old and frail to manage it and it was eventually sold.

Once retired, my grandparents would fly to Miami to stay in a rented flat on Collins Avenue for three months during the winter, to spend time with Arnold's two sisters, Rose and Dorothy, who were living there.

Back in London, during the summer of 1985, Arnold collapsed in the street and once in hospital, they found he had suffered an aneurism. Their prompt action saved his life. However, while having various tests and X-rays, they discovered that he had advanced lung cancer (presumably because he was a heavy smoker). Barely a year later, around Easter 1986, he passed away. Just a few months later, his granddaughter (my sister, Susan) gave birth to her first child, a daughter Cassie (now herself a mother of two).

Arnold was an immaculate dresser, always wearing perfectly cut bespoke suits with an elegant overcoat in the winter. I believe I inherited his style, as I always made an effort to look smart and during my civic life, I would always wear bespoke double-breasted suits, a white shirt and an interesting silk tie. I had a fetish for silk ties and bought new ones whenever I was travelling. In fact, I recently counted my current collection and found more than two hundred hanging in my wardrobe.

After I came down from Cambridge and moved into my new shared flat in Paddington, I would (for the next five years) go to my grandparents for lunch every Sunday. Anne would make me a roast beef lunch with all the regular trimmings including Yorkshire pudding and wonderful tiny petit pois.

My grandparents would receive a weekly delivery of fresh fruit direct from the market and when I left to return home after lunch, I was always sent off with a large carrier bag full to the brim with fresh fruit, which I would share with my flat-mate Lawrence.

Although fond of my grandfather, I was scared of him. When I visited, he always made me sit still in an armchair opposite him and he would order me to tell him about what I had been studying at school that week. If I yawned or fiddled, I would be strictly told not to do so and to sit up straight. It was stricter than being at school. My grandmother, on the other hand, would always be warmer and once she was widowed, I became very close to her and would visit her regularly. I would phone her twice a day at 8.45 am and 5 pm and God forbid if I failed to do so, as I would get a telling off! I would also frequently take her to my sister's house for Friday night dinner and during my term as Lord Mayor of Westminster she would often attend events I hosted.

How My Parents Met

But I'm running ahead. So, let me go back to 1955, when on a Saturday night, my parents first met. In those days, the ice-skating rink in Queensway, Bayswater, was very popular, especially on a Saturday night. They were both queuing up to enter with their respective friends, when one of the friends introduced them to each other. My mother, however, was only sixteen at the time. But it was the start of a lifelong romance.

The ice rink is still there (albeit smaller) at the centre of the ward I would later represent on Westminster Council for over 30 years. Once selected as a candidate in my first election in 1982, I issued a press release stating 'Candidate returns to roots' emphasising that my parents had met in the area.

What my mother did not know at the time was that my father was eleven years older than her. They told me that she did not realise the age gap until after they were engaged, when she found his passport with his date of birth.

My maternal grandparents did not approve. Not only was Gerald much older (how much, they did not know), but they thought that Gerald's family were not of the same class as my maternal grandparents were and they believed my mother should marry someone from a more affluent family.

Despite this, Gerald and Pam continued to see each other and so they had to use my mother's best friend, Lesley Bennett, as a decoy. My mother persuaded her parents that she was going out for the evening with Lesley, when in reality she was going on a date with my father. Lesley would, however, still accompany them on their date, as the chaperone.

My father was part of a group of male friends around his own age that spent a lot of time together. These friends included his cousin Stanley Goldstein and his friends Cyril

Levan, Geoffrey Baskin, Harry Donn, Peter Wise, Martin Silver and Bernard Kutner. My father remained close friends with all these guys throughout his life.

Lesley Bennett tells me she recalls agreeing with my mother that one evening they would go to the Spaniards Inn Pub on Hampstead Heath hoping to bump into my father there. They started walking along Heath Street in Hampstead, when a sports car drove past and stopped. Inside were Stanley Goldstein and my father and another guy. The guys picked them up and they all drove off to the pub together.

A few months after my parents started dating, Anne and Arnold tried to bring the relationship to an end. They arranged for my mother to travel to New York to stay for six months with one of her aunts who had emigrated there. They were hoping that after this lengthy period they would each fall for someone else. Now, this was the mid-1950s, decades before easy travel let alone easy communication. No mobile phones or Facetime, let alone email. After just three weeks, my mother was terribly miserable as she was missing my father. She decided to cut short her stay and return to London.

When she got back, she ran straight around to the flat in Clifton Court where Gerald lived with his parents. She rang the doorbell, which was opened by my grandmother Jane. 'I have come to see Gerald' she cried. Jane paused and then told her that Gerald was 'away for the weekend in Brighton with his new girlfriend'.

Pamela was horrified, shocked and very upset. I do not know what happened next, but I am here as evidence that they were reconciled and in October 1956 they were married in the synagogue in Abbey Road with a lavish dinner dance in the Porchester Hall in Bayswater. It was in that same Hall, 25 years later, that I was elected a Westminster City councillor for the first time.

When my maternal grandparents finally agreed that Pamela could marry Gerald, they invited him for dinner. My father always told two stories of that fateful dinner. The first, was that while my father was cutting into the vegetables served with the main course, a slug walked out from behind the cabbage. He thought that was an omen! The second involved a heart-to-heart chat between my father and grandfather, when Arnold was supposed to have said to my father that 'whoever marries my daughter, will not have to do a day's work in their life'. My father would tell friends for years after that he was still waiting to retire!

My parents in 1958.

38

Left: My father and his sister, Phyllis.

Right: My mother and her brother, Stanley.

Below: My parents at their engagement party surrounded by my mother's extended family

Left: Anne and me in my mother's car.

Right: My father (centre bottom) in the Royal Air Force.

Chapter 4

My Childhood

On my father's side, I was one of the first grandchildren born to my grandparents and their numerous siblings. Accordingly, every Sunday during my early years, different brothers and sisters of my grandparents would come to our home with their spouses, for afternoon tea and to meet and play with me. This is probably where I got used to enjoying being the centre of attention. They rarely came without some gift for me – the latest toy or book.

One of my great uncles, Jack Carlton, who was married to my paternal grandmother Jane's sister Eva, brought unusual gifts. I recall him arriving with a box full of chicks. They were let loose and were soon running around our garden. My mother refused to keep them and insisted he took them with him, much to my regret as I was already planning how I would play with them. Another week, it was a rabbit but again this was sent packing by my mother.

An Arrival and Other Young Memories

However, in 1960, everything changed. One of my earliest memories was when aged about two and a half, my parents sat me down to ask me if I would like a brother or sister. I think I said yes. But in retrospect, I think it was not really my decision. And with a wave of a magic wand, the next thing I recall is my mother returning home with a little baby they introduced to me as my new sister, Susan. I recall holding her carefully and being delighted with my new toy.

The earliest memory I have, other than welcoming my sister to the family, was in 1963 (when I was six) and I was being taken by my mother to Woolworths in the Market Place, our nearest shopping street in Hampstead Garden Suburb, to buy the Beatles latest hit *She Loves You*. I recall that we were accompanied on this shopping expedition by my grandmother Anne. Anne used to visit us every Tuesday afternoon for lunch and to help put us to bed.

On her regular visits, Anne used to sing to me the song 'I am a Lady Policeman', written by Raymond Wallace and Susan

Meeting my new sister for the first time – July 1960.

Kelly and sung by Mal Waite with the chorus line 'I'm a lady policeman, ever so ladylike'.

In response, I used to say 'Annie Annie more'. Anne hated being called 'Annie', so she would wag her figure at me and say 'You dare' which only encouraged me to call her Annie again. So, Anne became known to me as 'Nana Dare'.

Susan and I continued to call her Nana Dare until my two cousins (my uncle Stanley's sons) were old enough to devise their own nickname for her. By this stage, Susan and I were in our early teens. For some reason, they started calling her 'Ga' for Grandma. Before long, we started calling her that too and the name stuck.

My first speech.

The Spot

I was born with a birth mark at the centre of my forehead. It was a round dark brown spot, quite small but very noticeable. It enabled my school friends to call me 'the boy with the spot on his head'. Worried that this could have a psychological effect on me as I grew up, when I was about four years old, I was taken by my parents to see the equivalent of a plastic surgeon. However, he was not concerned about this particular birth mark, which he said could be removed very easily, but he noticed another, much larger oval shaped birth mark that covered most of the top of my left foot. He said that he was concerned that when I grew older and started playing football (how little he knew me, as during my youth, I rarely played the great game), the birth mark could get septic and could lead to the need to amputate my foot. I was too young to really understand what he was saying, but on hearing that it was a very simple operation to remove it with an excellent prognosis, my parents decided that I should have both marks removed.

I was just five years old when I was admitted to Great Ormond Street Hospital and I have vivid memories of my time there. I recall my age because I remember that as I was over five, I did not need a cot but could be in a proper bed. That made me very proud.

When my mother left me that first night, I screamed the place down. I would not stop crying, calling for my Mum to return. She told me years later that she waited an hour in a neighbouring room for me to calm down before she went home, crying as she drove.

The complication with the procedure I was to undergo was that although the operation on my forehead was straightforward and the removal of the birth mark would quickly heal with just a stitch or two, the one on my foot was more challenging. The birth mark on my foot was quite large and the skin on one's foot does not regrow. I would require a skin graft from my inner (left) thigh. The consultant would remove a large area of skin from the upper inner thigh and the skin would (after some time) regrow and cover the wound. The removed skin would then be used to cover the area where the birth mark had been, held down by stiches while the new piece of skin bonded with the remaining area of skin.

The operation went well. I can still recall the smell of chloroform that was used to put me to sleep before I was taken down to be operated on and whenever I enter a hospital now the smell always reminds me of that day. A few hours later, I woke up to find my mother sitting next to my bed holding a koala bear soft toy. I loved it and 'Michael', as I named him, stayed with me until I went up to Cambridge, sleeping with me in my bed throughout my teens.

Because my foot and thigh needed time to heal, my entire left leg, right up to my groin, was covered in a plaster of Paris cast. I milked it and for the next two months made sure I was pampered at home by my family while I recovered and before the cast was removed.

Nearly sixty years later, I still have the scars on my foot and thigh. Most people do not notice but on the beach, when I show friends, they can see the shape of the former birth mark which covers the top of my entire foot as the texture of the skin from my thigh is different from the rest of my foot. Similarly, the texture on the scar on my thigh can be clearly seen, now measuring ten by five centimetres.

Left Alone

My parents would often go on holiday to the south of France without Susan and me and when they did, my grandmother Jane and my aunt Phyllis would come and stay to look after us. This was always a fun time, as we were given lots of treats.

As we got older, Susan and I would go and stay with Jane and Phyllis, where, as the oldest, I would sleep in Phyllis's bed with Susan sleeping next to me in a z-bed (a fold-away bed) and Phyllis was demoted to sleeping on the sofa (again).

We loved these sleepovers and the first morning always involved Jane taking Susan and I to Selfridges massive toy department or to Hamleys, the largest toy shop in Europe.

In those days, Selfridges' toy department covered half of an entire floor. In more

My paternal grandmother Jane with Susan and me.

recent years, Selfridges reduced the size of its toy department to a few shelves and only reinstated the larger department in 2019, when FAO Schwarz, the American toy shop took over the franchise for selling toys within the store. But in my childhood, the department was exciting and enchanting. Whether it was Hamleys or Selfridges, Susan and I were allowed to choose whatever we wanted as a gift from my grandparents. Susan always chose something small and cheap. On the other hand, I always chose the biggest toy I could find. I have not changed in all these years!

Chelsea FC

My mother's brother Stanley was a keen Chelsea fan and he would occasionally take me to Stamford Bridge to watch a game. But in the late 1960s, a new neighbour moved into the house opposite.

Bernard Davis (same surname but not a relative) was a mad Chelsea fan and went to Stamford Bridge every home game with his two sons; the youngest was only a year older than me. I became friends with Paul, who also went to my school. Bernard soon invited me to join them at Chelsea for every home game. So, my father bought me a season ticket and for the next few years, I became a regular at Chelsea's home games.

I was watching a game with the other Davis family one Saturday from our usual seat in the North Stand, when, after a goal was scored and we all stood up to cheer, the whole stand shook violently. The next day, it was headline news and it was only then that we realised how serious it had been and how it could have cost lives. The stand was never used again and within a few weeks, demolished and rebuilt. My fortnightly visits to watch Chelsea play ended in 1972. The last game I saw was at Wembley in March that year, when Chelsea lost the League Cup Final to Stoke 2 – 1.

But with my father's belief that the work ethic should be instilled in me as soon as I was old enough, he informed me at a family dinner a few weeks after that unfortunate Cup Final, that as I was now almost 15, it was time to get a Saturday job. So there would be no more Chelsea matches.

Ronnie Castle's and the Inside Leg Measurements

A few days later, my mother took me to see one of my father's friends, Ronnie Castle, who had just opened a menswear shop in Temple Fortune, one of the local shopping streets near to our home. Ronnie had been the manager of a menswear shop in east Marylebone, close to my father's business where my father had been a regular customer. Coincidentally, the owner of the shop had taught me to swim in the summer of 1966 (when I was nine), when we had stayed in the same hotel in Torremolinos in southern Spain for our summer holidays and he noticed that I was still swimming with rubber arm bands. My father could not swim and so had never taught me.

The reason my father could not swim and had an aversion to water was that, when he was a young boy aged about eight, he was sitting on the edge of the pier in Blackpool, hundreds of feet above the sea, when another kid pushed him over the side and he fell into the rough sea. Several men watching jumped in and rescued him but henceforth he had an aversion to being in water and swimming.

Returning to Temple Fortune, Ronnie agreed to employ me as a Saturday boy at £5 a day. I was resigned to having a Saturday job and thought that working in this shop was probably a good choice. I grew to love working there and my job entailed helping serve customers, measuring inside legs and making the tea. Ronnie Castle's was a traditional menswear shop, with the shop surrounded on two sides by glass counters with racks of shirts behind, while on the third side were rails of suits, jackets and trousers. The fourth side was an open window display.

In my school holidays, I would work full time in the shop and continued to work on Saturdays and school holidays, right up until I went to Cambridge University.

The Countryside

In the 1970s it was quite common for a businessman to be friendly with his bank manager. My father banked with Lloyds Bank on the Edgware Road and soon after the new manager, Fred Nagle, took over, my parents took Fred and his wife out for dinner. They soon became good friends and when it transpired that they had a beautiful cottage in the heart of the west Sussex countryside, near a village called Handcross, it was agreed that the whole family would go down one Sunday for afternoon tea. In the middle of a long country lane, we found this idyllic cottage in the midst of beautiful green fields and farmland. As soon as we arrived, we were introduced to Fred and Mildred's large dark Labrador called Bonnie, who my sister and I fell in love with.

It was decided between the adults that during the next school holidays, Susan and I would be sent down to stay for a week with Fred and Mildred (and of course, Bonnie). Spending the day in the countryside with my parents was one thing, but staying a full week alone, was something else. Susan and I did not want to go! We were petrified!

My parents were not prepared to accept any of our excuses. So, a few weeks later, Susan and I were dumped in the countryside and had to live with insects and weird noises in the night and even several mooing cows. We got used to it and actually quite enjoyed our time in Sussex but I do not think we actually became rural people.

The day I was sent to close a gate and was nearly bitten by a cow did make me wonder what I was up to. This was only made worse when I stood in some cow turd!

We were to return for several more holidays with Fred and Mildred, especially when my parents decided to go on a holiday without us. On one occasion, Mildred had this wonderful idea of buying us a tent, so we could live in it at the back of their long garden. This was intended to give us that 'outdoor experience'. I did not mind playing in it during the day but during the night we were supposed to sleep in it. After just a few strange noises and the sight of a spider, we both ran into the house and, despite pressure from Fred and Mildred to give it a little longer, we refused to return!

I even tried to learn to ride a horse but my bum did not like the idea and I refused to return for the second lesson. But on reflection, it was fun and a good lesson in rural life for a permanent urban guy.

Emily's Travels and Other Performances

Although Susan and I were never very close as children, as she was into girly things with her girlfriends and I was more of a loner, we nevertheless regularly played together. We would re-enact the Miss World competition with Susan and her friends walking down the catwalk, while I portrayed the Eric Morley role of compère and host. We would also replicate the Eurovision Song Contest but our pièce de résistance was our production of 'Emily's Travels'.

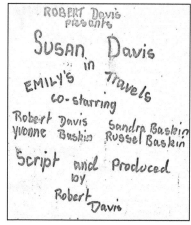

For this, we created our own scenery by painting backcloths on my parents' old white bedsheets. These were strung up from one side of my bedroom to the other. Props were found, a script produced and we even made programmes, which my grandfather Arnold photocopied on his office copier, for our audience of family members.

Friends were recruited for the smaller parts, which increased our audience, as their parents were invited to watch. Rehearsals took weeks and although it did not deserve an Olivier Award, it was my first attempt at theatre producing.

Family Holidays

Our first foreign holiday as a family was to a hotel in Milano Maritimo near Rimini in eastern Italy. We loved the holiday and the town the hotel was in and so returned again the following year, staying that second time in the more upmarket hotel, the Mare E Pineta. We returned year after year until the final time we spent a holiday there, in the summer of 1976.

I recall that holiday well. It was the last time I went on holiday with my parents as a family. I had planned not to join my parents and sister on this trip as I was looking forward to staying in London and entertaining my friend in my family house while they were away. But at the last minute, my parents persuaded me to join them.

The problem with this resort was that the only airport nearby was at Rimini but that was a military airport and only accepted commercial tourist flights during the night between midnight and six in the morning. So, having arrived at the hotel about five in the morning after an all-night flight, we were greeted by the night manager to be told that they did not have my father's booking. We were all tired, exhausted and looking forward to our two-week holiday. The manager said he could put us up for a week, but the following week was full. When morning arrived, my father was on the phone to his travel agent in London.

My sister, Susan, and I on holiday in Milano Maritimo.

They had accepted that it was their error and it was agreed that for the second week, we would transfer to Venice at their cost.

That was my first visit to that glorious city. It is very rare experience when you visit a new place and get that wow factor that makes your heart tingle and makes your eyes tearful. This has only happened to me twice. It never happened on subsequent visits.

We arrived in Venice by taxi and were dropped off at the station, where we transferred to a water taxi to take us to our hotel located adjacent to St Mark's Square.

As the taxi took us down the Grand Canal and under the Rialto Bridge, I saw around me one of the great wonders of the world.

Standing to attention along the Grand Canal like a military guard of honour were these large elegant pastel-coloured palaces, each grander than the next, a complete contrast to the drabness of the north-west London suburbs I knew. My heart certainly fluttered that afternoon. Despite returning several more times over the years, I have never felt like that first visit and arrival.

The only time that happened again was on my first visit to the city of New York. That was in 1980, just after leaving Cambridge for the last time, when I went to the United States on a four-week holiday. For my first week, I had arranged to stay with my mother's cousin Frank in his flat on the Upper East Side. But he was away the weekend I was arriving, so I agreed to stay in a hotel for the first night and move in with him the next day. I arrived in the city, late on the Sunday night, when it was already dark and took the taxi straight to the hotel in mid-town on 7th Avenue.

When I awoke the next morning, I had breakfast and then decided to take a walk outside. I stepped on to 7th Avenue and wow … my heart started to flutter again, as I looked around and saw that I was surrounded by immensely tall buildings racing to the sky. The thundering noise of traffic and horns as I watched thousands of people rushing along the pavements.

And along the carriageway, steam shooting out from the manhole covers like geezers spouting water in Iceland. It was overwhelming, buzzy and exciting. I had seen nothing like it. I have returned many, many times but again, it never felt like that first day.

Dorchester Gardens

When my parents got married, they moved into a semi-detached house they bought for £2,000 in a street called Dorchester Gardens. This lay within an estate of private houses built in the 1930s known as the Beaufort Park Estate and located between the North Circular Road and the Falloden Way as they met at Henlys Corner, just a mile south of Finchley Central. My family lived in this house for 26 years and it was the centre of my world for the first 19 years of my life.

My family home – 3 Dorchester Gardens, London NW11.

I moved out first. After I had spent four years at Cambridge University, on returning to London in 1980, I moved to a flat share in Paddington. My sister Susan subsequently moved out in September 1982, when she married her long-term boyfriend, Bradley Grundman. Soon after my parents were left alone in the house, they sold it and moved to a flat in Century Court, overlooking Lord's Cricket Ground where they remained for the rest of their lives.

Dorchester Gardens comprised about 13 detached and semi-detached houses built in the 1930s and each with a large rear garden. My parents became friendly with many of their neighbours and Susan and I befriended many of their children. I recall my aunt Phyllis making Batman and Robin costumes for us (I was Batman of course) and a superman outfit for one of our friends who lived in the street. The three of us would cycle around the block acting out scenes from the then popular Adam West's *Batman* TV series.

My primary school, Brooklands, was a ten-minute walk away and I would walk to school once I was old enough. When I moved on to my grammar school, this was a bit further away and would take about 20–25 minutes to walk. Initially, my Mum would drive me to school in the mornings and I would either walk or get the bus home in the evenings.

As I moved up through the school, I became friends with one of my neighbours and his dad would drive us to school every morning, until I passed my driving test during the first term of the lower sixth after which I would drive myself.

I had a great childhood. My parents were supportive. When I decided to go to university, my father very generously supported me financially. Although I received a local government (non-repayable) grant as was available in those days, he was very generous with my living allowance.

When I decided to do a fourth-year post-graduate course after my first degree at Cambridge, the local authority refused me a grant, so my Dad not only continued paying my living allowance but also paid for my expensive university fees. He also bought me my first three cars, until I started working for Freeman Box, who generously bought me my new cars instead, as part of my remuneration package.

Although they still went on their own holidays without us, my parents regularly took us on enjoyable holidays. Most bank holidays saw us staying at either the Royal Bath in Bournemouth or at the Grand Hotel in Eastbourne. Frequently, we would be accompanied by our grandparents too. I particularly loved staying at the Grand in Eastbourne, one of the grandest hotels on the south coast. Susan and I would spend hours with friends we made in the hotel's games room and we would love exploring the maze of the hotel's corridors.

In the late 1960s we would frequently enjoy family holidays in the south of France, when we stayed in a hotel in Villefranche-sur-Mer near Nice with two other families, the Levans and the Baskins. Two things stick in my mind about one of those holidays. The first was when one of my parents' friends (as a joke) unexpectedly pushed my mother into the swimming pool just after she had had her hair done. My mother was furious.

The second was my success in being awarded a silver and gold medal with accompanying certificates by the hotel's swimming instructor for swimming certain distances. Those framed certificates and medals stayed on my bedroom wall for years and I still have them.

Family Illnesses and Bereavements

I was at Cambridge when I got news that my mother was unwell and was being admitted into hospital. My commitments and lecture programme meant that I had to delay my return to London to see her for a couple of days, but as soon as I returned, I immediately went to visit her in her room at the Wellington Hospital in St John's Wood.

My father was with her and they broke the news that my mother had been diagnosed with ovarian cancer. I had to digest what I had just been told. I went on to the balcony of the hospital room and burst into tears. I could not believe that my mother was in danger from this cruel illness.

She survived that particular trauma and a further sixteen years. However, over the intervening years, she would have regular recurrences and each time she would recover, go into remission but relapse again.

My mother became a regular at the Princess Grace Hospital for chemotherapy sessions. In those days, one had to be admitted and stay in for a few days while having such treatment. In later years, I understand that most patients have chemo as day patients.

My mother collected elephants and one of her good friends, Diana Kutner, always arranged to send her an elephant sculpture whenever she was readmitted. On her death bed, my mother asked me to look after her elephants. So, when my father subsequently died, I took over responsibility for all 120 of them and they are now on display at home.

I have not added to them. All are still there and cause much grief to Maria, my cleaner, who has to regularly clean them.

I would often be woken in the early hours of the night by my father in great distress because my mother was in terrible pain. I would rush round and drive her to hospital again. It put a strain on both of them. My father found it very difficult. He ran his own business where his presence was vital and he found it hard balancing the needs of his business and looking after my mother.

Some of my mother's collection of elephants.

My father hated visiting hospitals and was always petrified he would catch something. He would never accept a cup of tea or even a glass of water while there. He also never took my mother a gift. She would frequently say that he could have at least bought her a bunch of flowers or even just a single rose. He would laugh it off. But after she died, we had a rose carved on each side of her gravestone, to commemorate the roses he never bought her. He would say that at least he had bought her two now.

A few weeks into my year as Lord Mayor, my mother was admitted again to the Princess Grace Hospital. At the time, the mayoral suite was temporarily close by in the Marylebone Council House on the Marylebone Road. The following day, my sister popped into the Council House to see me. She asked me to sit down and told me that while with my mother that morning, the doctor had taken my sister aside and told her that he thought that my mother would only live a few more months. The news was devastating. I could not believe it. I burst into tears again, as Susan did.

Over the following months, I tried to continue to enjoy my mayoral year while all along conscious of my mother's health. I would frequently visit her in hospital between attending

My mother and I in 1996 – just months before she passed away.

functions. The mayoral car would park up outside the hospital and I would jump out in full robes and chains and spend twenty minutes or so with her and then run off to another engagement. I became very popular among the nurses.

My mother's health would see good days and bad days and I am delighted that on a number of good days, she would accompany me as my Lady Mayoress or with Carole (my official Lady Mayoress) as an additional guest. This included a visit to a Norman Hartnell fashion show; to Harrods; and joining Carole and I in Trafalgar Square to meet Nelson Mandela.

On one particular occasion, Carole and I were in the official car being driven to a function, when I received a call on my mobile from my mother in great distress. She had fallen over and could not get up and my father was busy with a customer. We were ten minutes away and so we re-routed to my mother's flat and I rushed to her aid while Carole went to the function with apologies for my last-minute absence.

On a further occasion in early 1997, my mother was again admitted into hospital but this time, my father, Susan and I were summoned to the hospital late that night to be told that they did not expect her to survive the night. This was serious. We stayed with her all that night but by the morning she had rallied and was allowed home a couple of days later.

On the following Sunday, I was guest of honour at a Jewish Civic Service held in my honour at my own synagogue, the Marble Arch United Synagogue in Great Cumberland Place and hosted by my chaplain, Lionel Rosenfeld. I was delighted that my parents were able to attend, although my mother was at this stage in a wheelchair.

A fortnight later, at my mother's suggestion I hosted a Sunday afternoon tea party in the Mayoral Parlour at Westminster City Hall for all the nurses and doctors and support staff that had looked after her while in the Princess Grace Hospital.

My parents enjoying afternoon tea with the staff of the Princess Grace Hospital in the Lord Mayor's Reception Rooms – March 1997.

Macon Georgia

My mid-March, my mother seemed to be doing well, so I left London with Carole to travel to the United States on a civic mayoral trip. We flew to Atlanta, where we were picked up in one of those famous white stretch limousines and taken to the city of Macon, an hour's drive from the airport where we were to attend the Macon Cherry Blossom Festival.

Macon has more cherry blossom trees than any other city outside Japan and when they come into bloom each spring, they host an international festival.

I made many friends in Macon that spring and returned in a private capacity several more times including once with Simon, when we attended a weekend of engagement parties for one of our colleagues and friends, Duncan Sandys.

By coincidence, he was marrying a lovely lady called Mary Brown, whose family came from Macon. Another year, when the Lord Mayor of the day could not attend, together with my colleagues Alan Bradley and Jenny Bianco, we jointly represented Westminster at that year's Cherry Blossom Festival.

After visiting the Cherry Blossom Festival, we moved on to Washington DC where Simon's boss Margery Kraus, the chief executive of APCO, an international public affairs consultancy, introduced me to a variety of American politicians on Capitol Hill, including the Vice President Al Gore.

Attending the Cherry Blossom Festival in Macon Georgia USA in March 1997.

In Washington DC in March 1997 with Vice President Al Gore.

Return to London

After an amazing fourteen days in the States, I returned home to find my mother had deteriorated while I was away. Within a few days, she was admitted to the St John's and Elizabeth Hospice. We were with her almost continually during the day, throughout the following week and when I had official mayoral duties to perform, I would return to the hospice straight afterwards to sit with her.

It was Easter that weekend and, on the night of Easter Sunday, she started to deteriorate. On the Sunday night, we were told to go home and have a good night's sleep, as they did not believe anything would happen overnight but if things changed, they would call us.

In deep sleep, mainly from exhaustion, I was woken at 5 am by the phone ringing next to my bed. It was the hospice. They suggested that the family may wish to go there immediately. I phoned my father and Susan and within half an hour we were all sitting around the bed. At about 7.30 that morning, she passed away.

I then had the task of visiting my grandmother, Anne, my mother's mother, to tell her. That was not easy and we arranged for her GP to attend with me to give Anne support.

Further Tragedy Within the Family

Sadly, this terrible period in my life was repeated a decade later, when my sister became unwell and it was soon discovered that she too had ovarian cancer. She went through the same stages that my mother did, with numerous courses of chemotherapy and good days and bad days. With the advancement of medication, Susan did not have to stay overnight for her chemo sessions but would attend a clinic in Harley Street as a day patient. I would often visit her in my lunchtime to sit and chat, as my office was nearby. Longer stays in hospital were reserved for when she was quite unwell.

Then in the spring of 2010, she deteriorated and after a long stay in the new cancer wing of the London Clinic (which had since my Mum's death become the centre of excellence for cancer treatment in the West End), she was told by her doctors that there was little more they could do for her. The constant rounds of chemo were doing more damage to her body than the cancer itself. So, after much family discussion, Susan was moved to the North Finchley Hospice.

Susan knew that this was the end and I spent quite a lot of time sitting with her at the hospice together with her two daughters and my brother-in-law. On several occasions, she discussed with me her impending death and begged me to be strong. I had a close friend, Angela Hooper, who was a fellow councillor, who had also been through a terrible few years with cancer and constant chemotherapy. Sadly, Angela had passed away a few weeks earlier.

Susan knew Angela and was aware they were both going through chemo at the same time. One day at the hospice, during a moment of silence, Susan turned to me and asked me how Angela was. I could not bring myself to tell Susan that Angela had died. I lied and said she was fine and doing well.

Susan looked into my eyes and said 'please tell me the truth' and I burst into tears, confirming her fears that Angela had indeed died.

A few days later, Susan died early one morning (shortly before her 50th birthday) with her husband Bradley and daughters Cassie and Jessica at her side. I was on the way to the hospice about eight in the morning when I received the call that she had passed away before I could be there.

Coincidently, while in the hospice later that morning after Susan had passed away, I received a call from my American cousin Frank. I had assumed that he had heard the news and was calling me to give me condolences. But that was not the case. He did not know. What he had called me to say was that his wife (also called Susan but spelt Suzanne) had died that very same day.

The BCRA 1 Gene

My sister had discovered that the reason she inherited the same ovarian cancer as our mother and went through almost exactly the same stages of the illness was that they both had carried the BCRA 1 gene mutation. This is a defective gene that is inherited through families and can result in cancer.

The gene itself produces tumour suppressor proteins that help repair damaged DNA, but when mutated (as in my mother and sister's case), then the protein does not function properly and the DNA cannot be repaired properly and, as a result, cells are more likely to develop additional genetic alterations that can lead to cancer. In women, this is either breast cancer or ovarian cancer.

My grandmother Anne had had breast cancer in her sixties but had recovered from it. Research shows that children of a parent with the BCRA 1 gene have a 50% chance of passing it on to their children.

The BCRA 1 gene is highly prevalent in Ashkenazi Jews. This is because those Jews are descendants from families from Eastern Europe, who lived in small rural villages, where religious teachings obliged them to marry within their faith. However, in a small village, they had little choice but to marry their cousins, thereby causing mutation of their genes.

What both my mother and sister should have had was a hysterectomy. Sadly, in both cases, they only did so once the cancer had taken root.

Both my nieces (Susan's daughters) have been tested and both carry the BCRA 1 gene. Cassie (my eldest niece and born in 1986) therefore decided in her early thirties to have a double mastectomy. A big and brave decision by her, with reconstruction surgery which followed. But as she says, her chances of getting breast cancer (and possibly dying) were reduced from 50% to 1%. Bearing in mind what happened to her mother and grandmother, she had little choice. Now that she has had two healthy children, she has had a hysterectomy too.

My youngest niece, Jessica, has also had the test and she too carries the BCRA 1 gene. She has now had a mastectomy. As she remains single with high hopes of marrying and having kids, the question of a hysterectomy is not yet on the agenda.

Following certain blood tests showing a high PSA and with my family history, I was referred to the Royal Marsden Hospital and was diagnosed with carrying the BCRA 1 gene. In men, this can cause breast cancer (although much rarer than in women) but more likely, prostate cancer. So I am under watch from a leading prostate specialist. Although I have a raised PSA (the measurement for prostate cancer) it is not too high and quite stable and with MRI scans every two years, the consultant is quite happy to check me regularly. Like many cancers, early detection is important. Accordingly, in addition to the MRI scans, my PSA is tested quarterly and any jumps will require me to see the consultant again.

My Father's Last Days

While both my mother and sister died after lengthy illnesses, my father passed away too quickly. This was in 2000, when he was 73. He had been relatively healthy following my mother's death three years earlier.

He had, however, initially been very lonely following my mother's passing. He found basic living difficult. He was of the old school. He could not cook, let alone make a cup of tea.

My father trying on the mayoral chains.

Shortly after my mother's death, I visited my father to find him sitting in front of the washing machine, watching it rotate. I asked him why. He explained that he had never used one before and thought you had to watch it, while it worked.

He hated being alone and it was not long before he started a relationship with an old friend Lilah Vanger.

Lilah and my father had dated in the years before my father met my mother and both had gone on to marry other people and have children. However, Lilah's husband died quite young. Lilah was to suffer more grief, when at the same time as my mother was undergoing chemotherapy at the Princess Grace Hospital, her daughter Sharon was also doing so. My father and Lilah met up after all those years in the corridor of the hospital. Sadly, Sharon died a few months before my mother.

About a year after my mother's death, my father informed me one day that he and Lilah were now seeing each other and although he adored my mother and missed her terribly, he was lonely and saw Lilah as a companion more than anything. I was delighted, as I appreciated how lonely he was.

I was really pleased for him, when he started going to the theatre, going on interesting holidays and dining out regularly, giving him an exciting life again. This was important to me, particularly after he had retired from business just after my mother's death.

Susan did not take it well, and refused to speak to Lilah or be in the same room as her. But Susan was at that stage, leading a busy family life in the suburbs and looking after two young children. It was I who saw day after day how miserable, bored and lonely he was and how Lilah made him happy again.

About a year before his death, he and Lilah came to see me in my legal office to discuss Lilah making a new will. My father was a bit of a comic and enjoyed a good joke and mucking

My father and Lilah Vanger in 2000.

about. I was taking instructions from Lilah and we were discussing what would happen with her assets once she died; my father flopped back in his chair with his arms out wide, acting as if he had died. My instant reaction was that he was joking and playing at dying. But after a few seconds and looking at Lilah and again at my father, I realised he was not acting.

This was serious. I ran around my desk and on reaching him, realised he was unconscious. I immediately tried to wake him, but without success.

I yelled for my secretary to come in and when she did, I told her to call an ambulance. Within a few seconds, my father regained consciousness and told us he was fine, but I insisted he was seen by the paramedic, who arrived on a motorbike within a few minutes of our call to 999. He examined my father and insisted he be taken by ambulance to St Mary's Hospital in Paddington to undergo a full check-up.

My father had been seeing a heart specialist for various ailments including what his consultant had said was a leaky valve. I called him immediately and he arranged for my father to be transferred that evening to the Wellington Hospital.

The consultant arrived quite soon after he had been admitted and immediately took him down to surgery. A few hours later, my father returned with a pace-maker having been inserted adjacent to his heart, which had momentarily stopped in my office that afternoon. Within a few weeks, he returned to living a normal life.

Now that he was under the close supervision of his heart consultant, the doctor wanted my father to have an operation to repair his leaky heart valve. My father had a different idea. He believed he had had a leaky valve since his youth and that it was not affecting his health. But he agreed to consider it.

Months went past and my father started living his life again, going on holidays and enjoying life with Lilah. When I spent time with him, he was really happy. He would also frequently accompany me to council functions as my plus one and got friendly with a number of my colleagues, who all adored him.

During a telephone conversation with him during the evening of 18th July 2000, he told me that he had heard from his consultant that he wanted my father to consider having a new heart valve to replace the leaky one, sooner rather than later.

My father told me that he was scared and did not want to undergo such a major operation. I assured him that if he didn't want to have the procedure, he did not have to. I thought that over time he could be persuaded but it was no good upsetting him that evening.

Every morning at 8.45 I would ring my father for a chat. So, the morning after our discussion about his valve operation, I sat at my office desk and made my daily call but there was no reply. I tried a few minutes later but to no avail. I tried his mobile but he failed to answer. So, I called Lilah. She explained that she had spent the night at Century Court (where my father lived) but had returned home that morning to do some chores. He had been fine when she left. I called the resident porter in the block, who had a spare key. He promised to go up and see what he could find and ring me back. After a ten-minute anxious wait, I received the call. He simply said that I should get over to the flat straight away. Nothing more. But I knew.

When I got there, the porter was waiting outside the flat and told me that he was so sorry but that he had found my father dead on the kitchen floor while doing the ironing. He and another porter had moved my father to his bed. An ambulance had been called. On his kitchen table I found a letter from his synagogue letting my father know that that day was the 30th anniversary of his own father's death in 1970. That was spooky!

Because he died suddenly, a post mortem was required but within a couple of days, we were able to hold the funeral.

It took Susan and I about nine months before we could face clearing our parents' flat and then selling it. But we had little choice. It was the end of an era but I have kept many of my parents' possessions from their flat and even some from the family house in Dorchester Gardens, in my current flat as a memento of my parents and my youth.

My Dad and I.

Left: Me as a baby.

Right: My father and I meeting Father Christmas for the first time aged 2.

Below: Four generations – my maternal great-grandmother Betty; my grandmother Anne, and my mother Pamela with little me.

Left: Me as a cowboy.

Right: At Kerem House School dressing up for Purim.

Chapter 5
Cilla

Cilla Black was a household legend in the 1960s and a regular at number 1 in the pop charts. Discovered by Brian Epstein while performing at the Cavern Club in Liverpool and a childhood friend of the Beatles, she was one of only a handful of major British female pop stars at the time. When I reached the age when pop music became important to me and with my sister a mad fan of Peter Noone, the lead singer of the then popular Herman's Hermits, I felt that I had to find a pop star to idolise. My regular visits to buy a variety of music albums from shops such as Harrods had led me to buy several Cilla LPs as well as others by Cliff Richard, T Rex and Hot Chocolate to name a few. But my two favourites were Cilla and Cliff and as at that time, I had not given any consideration to my sexuality, I thought it more appropriate to follow a female star rather than a male one, so I decided that I would become a Cilla fan.

The problem is that when I decide to do something (even at the young age of eleven) I become obsessive. So, almost overnight, I became one of her biggest fans.

Not only did I ensure that I owned every album and single she had ever released, but I also bought not one but at least five copies of every magazine she appeared in. I then turned my bedroom into a Cilla Museum. Covering every inch of wall space with photos, newspaper and magazine cuttings, together with mementos and even a handwritten

My membership card for the Cilla Black Fan Club.

story of Cilla's life. When family visited at weekends, they were forced to tour the museum and hear my guided tour. This certainly gave me the early experience of curating exhibitions and events, that I would later in my life undertake on behalf of the Council.

Cilla was also the star of her own Saturday night prime time TV series *Cilla* broadcast live from the Shepherd's Bush BBC Theatre. I would regularly spend Saturday night setting up tape recording equipment, so I could tape the shows. Of course, in those days one could only use audio tapes on a cassette machine with the microphone held against the TV screen. Videos had not yet been invented.

I then discovered you could write to the BBC for tickets to attend the recording of the show in the Shepherd's Bush Theatre itself. So, on behalf of myself and every member of my family I could think of, I would apply for tickets for all her shows.

On attending my first one, I realised that if I got to the theatre about two hours before the official time to do so, I could queue up outside the theatre and be first in line, which would allow me to take a seat in the front row.

Often accompanied by my mother or sister or by a friend, I became a regular and would always wait outside the stage door after filming had ended to meet Cilla and be photographed with her.

Cilla was also one of the first TV show hosts who engaged with the audience and she would frequently go into the audience live on air to talk to someone, although I soon learnt that this was all carefully planned beforehand. Quite frequently I would find myself sitting next to the person interviewed and thereby appear on TV myself.

I was therefore pleasantly surprised when in the spring of 2020, ITV televised a retrospective about Cilla and her life after her son Robert had discovered lost photos, film and recordings when clearing out her house, following her untimely death in 2015. And twice in the programme, footage was shown of Cilla filming her *Cilla* TV series and talking to members of the audience and there was a young Robert Davis sitting in the front row next to the interviewee. What happy memories.

BBC's Cilla *recorded at the Shepherd's Bush Studio Theatre. I am sitting in the front row behind the gentleman being interviewed by Cilla.*

Eighteen months later, another TV programme about Cilla was aired on Channel Five and this time, I made a more prominent appearance sitting next my closest friend at that time, David Wiseman, with my sister sitting next to him.

My busy life as a Cilla fan also extended to travelling the country to see Cilla in her live shows at theatres around southern England. I particularly recall leaving school early

In the audience of the recording of a Cilla *show in about 1972 as shown in Channel Five's* Our Cilla: The One and Only.

one day to catch a train to Eastbourne with my best friend Douglas Bennett to see Cilla in her show at the Congress Theatre and then rushing back to the station after the show ended to enable us to get home that night, so we could be back at school the next morning.

Even more embarrassing, having discovered where Cilla lived in Denham, Buckinghamshire, together with a friend, I took a train one Sunday morning to Denham railway station and after spending about an hour finding and then walking to Cilla's house, we stood outside the front gates of the house for about four hours. I have no idea why and what I was expecting to happen.

With Cilla at the stage door of the BBC Theatre in Shepherds Bush after a recording of Cilla.

At about 4 pm in the afternoon, Cilla's Rolls Royce drove down the main road and swept past us into the driveway leading up to her house. I waved and took a picture of the rear of her car and it was all over. We returned home excited by having been there but disappointed at only seeing Cilla in her car for a few seconds.

Trying not to be too disappointed, my next task was to enter a competition held by the official Cilla Black Fan Club, of which I was a member. This required me to make as many words as possible from the letters used in 'Cilla Black'. After spending what appeared to be hours and days in the local library, I submitted my entry. The advertised prize was a special personal possession owned by Cilla.

Much to my surprise, my hard work paid off and I won first prize. It duly arrived by post a few days later. I opened the package and was rather disappointed when I found inside the packaging, a diamanté brooch. Nothing I could wear or use. But it took pride of place in my Cilla exhibition and in fact I still have it today, kept safely in a box at home.

My prize – a diamanté brooch.

On going up to Cambridge University, my interest in Cilla started to wane, although I have always had a soft spot for her to this day. When I was Lord Mayor and hosting regular black tie formal dinners in the Mayoral Parlour, I decided to invite Cilla and her husband Bobby Willis, as my guests, to one of the dinners. We knew she had a London flat near City Hall in Victoria and after tracking down her address, I sent her an invite. But as the date of the dinner got closer, we had still not received a response. We tried one more time and gave up. The dinner went ahead without Cilla.

A few weeks later, I was at a function as Lord Mayor when I started chatting to Christopher Biggins, who I had got to know after meeting him at several events as Lord

Mayor. Biggins (as he is known) is a well-known TV personality actor and comedian and appeared as Cilla's co-host in the first series of the TV programme *Surprise Surprise*. Knowing he was friendly with Cilla, I mentioned the invites I had sent her and the fact that I had received no responses. He immediately said: 'Leave it to me'. So I did.

Two days later the Lord Mayor's office received a call from Cilla herself, apologising for not responding to the invite, but explaining that she had been abroad and that she would love to join the Lord Mayor for a dinner. As we had a further dinner planned the following week, the office invited her and her husband and she was delighted to accept.

I was over the moon. When the day of the dinner arrived, one of my jobs was to prepare the seating plan. About forty guests were attending including my partner Simon, as well as three ambassadors. As protocol requires, I was required to seat the ambassadors in accordance with their seniority at the court of St James's. The strict pecking order for ambassadors is that they are given an order of seniority based on when they first arrived in Britain as ambassador and presented their credentials to The Queen. They take this very seriously, so if the American ambassador is seated nearer the host than an ambassador who had presented his credentials to The Queen earlier than the American ambassador had, this would upset the longer serving ambassador, who would be very put out and regard it as a slight on his country.

Now this was a once in a lifetime moment for me, with the opportunity to sit next to my childhood idol for dinner. I therefore placed Cilla next to me and Bobby (her husband) next to Simon. As soon as he saw this, my Private Secretary Kevin Taylor came rushing in to my office to emphasise that I could not do so, as I had to have the two more senior ambassadors each side of me. After a little row, I insisted Cilla sat next to me and that was it. Kevin eventually backed down.

The dinner was a great success and Cilla and I got on well. At the time, one of her sons was producing a play at the Victoria Palace Theatre near City Hall and we spoke about his project and my love of the theatre.

However, the time came for my after-dinner speech and rather bravely I explained to the assembled guests all about my fetish for Cilla and the story about inviting her to the dinner. In doing so, I accidentally said that 'I used to be a massive fan' implying that I was no longer one. Having realised the error I decided not to correct myself, in the hope that she had not noticed. If she had, she never mentioned anything and the evening ended well.

At the Lord Mayor's dinner with Cilla – 1997.

Cilla and I meeting up again a few years before she died at the unveiling of a plaque to commemorate her first manager, Brian Epstein, in Covent Garden.

Simon had got on well with Bobby and we both had photos taken with Cilla, which were duly framed and adorned our flat. I still have both photos on my mantelpieces in London and Mallorca.

I was devastated when I heard that she had died suddenly.

Chapter 6

The Enlightenment

I was lucky to get into grammar school. My parents were advised that it was unlikely I would and so rather than allow me to go to a secondary modern school (as they were then known) they started looking at private schools for my secondary education.

But surprisingly I received notification that I had been accepted to attend one of the best all boys state school in north London, Christ's College Finchley, a grammar school very close to the family home. It was due to become a comprehensive within a few years. However, shortly after I joined the school in the autumn of 1969, the Conservatives won the 1970 general election and the local MP for Finchley, one Margaret Thatcher, became Secretary of State for Education and within a few months took action to ensure that the school would remain a grammar school. It did eventually change to become a community school but not until after I had left.

My first few years were a disaster. I was not good at anything and so I became the class joker. This might have appealed to a few of my friends but I was forever getting into trouble with the prefects and the teaching staff. Staying behind after school for detention became a regular activity. I even remember been regularly sent out of class and being required to stare at a drawing pin on the corridor wall without averting my gaze for an hour!!

However, that all changed during the school holidays in the summer of 1972, a few months before I was due to start my two-year O level course (now known as GCSEs). I was supposedly doing holiday work, working for my father in his textile business in Fitzrovia, east Marylebone, but was bored out of my mind and so took a stroll around the Marylebone area. All I could think of was my lack of a future. However, as I was walking and thinking of how I could turn my life around, I suddenly saw the light. I do not know how or why it happened then, but I remember the moment so well. I resolved to return to school at the beginning of the new academic year and work really hard and in that way give myself a chance to succeed in life. I knew that if I did not change my life then, I may never have a second chance. And so it proved to be.

Phil Molloy

Not only did my new-found work ethic see me top of the class in the end-of-year exams in many subjects but I was also taken under the wing of one of the senior teachers, Philip Molloy. Mr Molloy was well known throughout the school and was head of mathematics but was also responsible for organising many of the big school events. This was helped by the fact that once I started working hard, I had a knack for Maths and soon started coming

Douglas Bennett (Head boy), myself (Deputy Head Boy) and Phil Molloy.

top in the weekly tests. I found Maths rather like a puzzle. Once you understood the code or the basic principle, whatever test would be placed before me, I could easily unlock the key and get the answer right.

When Mr Molloy set class tests, not only did I get it all right but I did so quickly and would frequently win the star prize for getting the answers right first. The prize was usually an empty used cigar box but it was the achievement that mattered rather than the gift. So, from coming bottom in everything I started becoming the class swot as well as the teacher's pet. It was not long before Mr Molloy started asking me to support him in organising various school events.

This included organising the box office for the school and house plays. Mr Molloy would prepare the tickets and look after the money but I would spend my lunchtimes sitting in one of the classrooms running the box office, with Mr Molloy popping in at the beginning and then at the end to take the cash. I then progressed to assisting him in keeping score at the annual school sports day and other similar events.

Prefects

As I took on more responsibilities my reputation as an organiser grew. I was therefore expecting to be chosen by the staff to be a prefect. The list of new prefects was supposed to be announced at a morning assembly, a few weeks into my first weeks in the lower sixth form. Like my friends, we were all surprised when we were told the announcement had been delayed.

Shortly after the assembly ended, Phil Molloy took me aside and explained that he had missed the staff meeting the previous week only to discover the following day that my name had not been on the agreed list of new prefects. He had been furious and so started a campaign to get the announcement delayed so he could persuade his fellow teachers to add my name. It clearly worked, as the next morning the list was read out by the headmaster at assembly and I was included. My first serious job!

The following year, another similar incident happened. Towards the end of July 1975, the staff were meeting to choose the Head Boy and Deputy Head Boy for the next academic year. Together with a number of my school friends, we were on an organised school trip to Stratford-upon-Avon to see a number of Shakespeare plays. We were accompanied by several teachers who had missed the meeting, but one had remained in London to participate and then travelled to Stratford to join us. Now, I had no expectation to be chosen for either role.

There were two other prefects (one a close friend) who were regarded as the favourites and we were just keen to find out which one would be Head Boy and which one Deputy Head Boy.

My prefect badges.
TOP *Junior prefect.*
BOTTOM *Senior prefect.*

When Mr Petrie – the teacher who had remained in London for the vote – arrived, we were all having a drink in a local pub after having seen a show at the Memorial Theatre. He explained that he was late getting to Stratford as there had been a tremendous row about who the staff were going to choose. The meeting went on for about three hours before a decision was made. But he told us he was sworn to secrecy about the actual decision. So we returned home a few days later none the wiser. We all assumed it had been a row about whether my friend Douglas Bennett was to be Head Boy and the other guy his deputy or vice versa.

The following Monday, I was asked to see the Headmaster Mr Ken James, who told me that the teaching staff had agreed that I would be Deputy Head Boy. I was shocked, but overjoyed, as I really was not expecting it, believing Douglas and the other guy were the only two in the running. I therefore concluded that the row had actually been about whether this other guy or me would be Deputy Head Boy.

But later that day, Phil Molloy explained that the row had actually been over whether Douglas (then one of my closest friends) or I would be Head Boy and that unfortunately (despite Phil's backing) I had lost out to Douglas. But I was just delighted to be deputy and, as Douglas was such a good friend, I knew we would be an excellent team.

O Levels

Turning the clock back to the summer of 1974, I was on holiday with my parents and sister at the Green Park Hotel in Bournemouth, when I rang home to ask my mother's cleaning lady to open the post that had arrived that day and read out my O level results. This would prove whether my decision to change the course of my life during that walk in the summer holidays of 1972 had been worth the hard work.

I was delighted to hear the news. In those days O level results were categorised with Grades A C and E as passes and F as a failure. I had achieved A in History, Pure Maths, Geography and Physics with a C for French and Additional Maths and an E for Art, English and English Literature. A total of nine O levels, the maximum my school allowed its pupils to take.

I knew I was weak at English (my spelling was terrible – these were the days before spellcheck). While I was satisfied with my E in Art, I was delighted with my C in French as I had been terrible at French and my parents had had to pay for me to have private tuition to help me through the exams, so getting a C rather than scraping through with an E was just fine. The teacher who gave me that tuition was Cynthia Shebbeare who, I discovered years later, was married to Sir Tom Shebbeare, the Chairman of the Prince's Trust (1988–2003) and Director of Charities to the Prince of Wales (2003–2011). As a Westminster councillor, I would frequently meet Cynthia and Tom at functions and we would reminisce about the time she taught me French.

The only result I was disappointed with was my C in Additional Maths. As I thought I was a hot-shot at Maths, this was disappointing and so with the agreement of Phil Molloy I retook Additional Maths the following autumn and got my deserved A grade.

My sixth form years were busy, working hard studying not only for my three A levels but also for the two S levels (special levels) which I decided to take at the same time, in Economics and Pure Maths. I also had my duties as a prefect and, in my final year, as Deputy Head Boy.

A section of the 1976 Christ's College school photo – I am third row up and fourth from the left (as Deputy Head Boy I am seated next to the first of the teaching staff).

My First Car and the Road to Cambridge

With a birthday in September, I was one of the oldest in my year and so on my 17th birthday in September 1974, my parents paid for driving lessons. It only took a few months and by early 1975 I had passed my driving test on my first attempt. My very generous father immediately took me out to buy me my own car. I chose a second-hand silver-grey Ford Escort and it became the love of my life. I was so proud of it and drove to school every day, as in those days there were no parking restrictions around the streets of Finchley. It was not long before I became very popular, and driving into town in the evenings with my friends became the norm. If it was not visiting the new concept of take-away that had just opened in the Haymarket called 'McDonalds', it was the newly opened ice cream emporium in the Finchley Road called 'Baskin Robbins'.

I also had a school friend who on reaching the age of eighteen became a member of the Playboy Club in Park Lane. Notorious for its bunny girls, the club was cheap to join and had a restaurant with a massive high-quality buffet. You could eat as much as you wanted for just £2 (about £20 today). We became regulars and before too long I too joined the club. We never gambled at the tables or at the slot machines, but none of the staff seemed to notice.

The car was a liberation and during the summer holidays between my lower sixth and upper sixth year, my friend David Glickman and I decided to drive around Britain. We plotted our route with great care. The intention was to drive north through East Anglia and then after a detour to visit Cambridge for the first time and visit the college I was hoping to apply to. We would then head for York and Scotland before returning through Liverpool, Wales and Bristol. We made it on the first night to Aldeburgh on the east coast of Suffolk and spent the next day in  Norwich, where we managed to obtain tickets to watch the recording of the then famous TV show *Sale of the Century* with Nicholas Parsons as the host.

The following morning, we set off for Cambridge. But disaster struck. Half-way there the car started making strange noises and shaking. We made it to Cambridge and on the outskirts of the city found a car repair shop. They gave one look at the car and said it was a big and expensive job and would take several days to resolve. However, they could undertake a (cheaper) temporary repair to get us back to London.

We had no choice but to abort our round-Britain trip and return to London. They made the necessary repairs overnight and David and I made our way in the meantime into Cambridge city centre. This was my first visit there and the first thing we did was to walk into and around Gonville & Caius College, the college I would shortly apply to join and where I would spend three very happy years as an undergraduate making many lifelong friends and influencing my life to a massive degree.

Walking around the Caius Courts, we followed the famous Caian 'academic route'. We first entered the College from Trinity Street through the Gate of Humility (where all newly arrived undergraduates pass through when they arrive for the first time) and entered Tree Court. This large court contained a path that led to the next gate. This path was lined on each side by newly planted smallish trees no taller than myself. What makes Tree Court unique is that a tree-lined court is unusual in Cambridge colleges. Trees had originally been planted in the court by John Caius while Master in the 16th century but the originals had not survived. The trees that lined my route that day are still there today but now taller than the buildings that surround them. They are huge!

At the end of the pathway, we walked through the Gate of Virtue, which undergraduates walk through during their studies. As we entered the neighbouring Caius Court, we saw the magnificent Gate of Honour – the symbol of Gonville & Caius College, adorned with six magnificent sundials which had only recently (in the mid 1970s) been installed. They were new replicas of ones that had been installed when the Gate was first built by Dr Caius (physician to Queen Elizabeth I and one of the founders of the College) but had been lost some time in the college's history.

It is through the Gate of Honour that the college's undergraduates progress to the adjacent Senate House to receive their degrees – a route I would take in the summer of 1979 to receive my BA and then three years later, to be awarded my honorary MA.

I was smitten. The architecture, the cosiness of the courts and the historic market town that surrounded the colleges, was a world new to me. I returned to London at 20 mph, in my injured car, determined that I would not only apply to Caius but would do whatever I could to get in.

The Gate of Honour in Gonville & Caius College, Cambridge.

Once home, my father decided that buying me a brand-new car would be more economical than repairing the second-hand Ford Escort. Within a few weeks, a brand-new Datsun Cherry the colour of English mustard with a black vinyl roof was delivered to me and became my transporter for a number of years including the four years I spent in Cambridge.

My Datsun Cherry with my friend Mark Galloway.

Why Cambridge?

What made me think of applying to Cambridge? By the time I had to think about university, I was doing well academically and coming top in my class in every exam. But my parents had not been to university and made no attempt to suggest or persuade me to do so. If anything, my parents had indicated that they would prefer if I did not go to university. This was the mid 1970s and student riots and left-wing student sit-ins were common. Cambridge had been the subject of the Garden House Riots. My parents thought that if I went to university, I would return as a long-haired lefty. In reality, I returned as a short-haired righty!

To be truthful, I did not originally even consider Oxbridge as an option. But one of my responsibilities as a prefect was to be a careers librarian. We had a specialist careers library where Duncan Rodgers, a history teacher gave advice on careers at lunchtimes and I and my fellow careers librarian would, on a rota basis, assist and help file and sort out careers advice literature. I would frequently sit in on careers interviews between Duncan Rodgers and a fellow pupil seeking advice.

On one particular occasion, I overheard Duncan advising his interviewee to apply to Cambridge University for a degree in Engineering and in doing so he talked about Cambridge and why both Cambridge and Oxford were different from all the other universities. I was intrigued and so started researching both. I was hooked and decided that that was what I wanted to do.

My further enquiries revealed that with my Maths expertise and following my father's advice, I should become a professional; a career as a chartered accountant seemed the option for me. With this in mind, it was Cambridge that was offering the better course for me. While it did not teach accountancy per se, its Economics degree course was very mathematically based and so seemed appropriate for me with my interest and success in Maths.

I sought an interview with our headmaster who was in charge of Oxbridge admissions, as the school had various connections with several of the Oxbridge colleges. One could not apply to Cambridge or Oxford universities themselves but to one of their separately independent colleges. Ken James, our headmaster, suggested that with my interest in Economics and because of his connection with certain colleges, I 'should apply to Queens, Trinity or Gonville and Caius'. Not knowing any of the colleges, I made a decision on the names of the colleges he mentioned and I suggested that I apply to Caius first, with Gonville as my second choice. I was rather embarrassed when he explained that Gonville & Caius was the name of one college and not two separate ones.

Mr James explained that the school had sent many pupils to Caius (as it is commonly known) and that his connections with the admissions tutor would be helpful. My mind was made up.

Most Cambridge applicants applied post A level results, when they were aware how well they had done and then took an entrance exam in the late autumn of the year following A levels. This required the applicant to stay on at school after everyone else in his class had left and undertake a further term of Oxbridge Entrance Exam studies. It was then usual for the pupil to spend the rest of the academic year, before going to university the following autumn, either working or travelling. While this was standard for public schools, who often set up specific provision for the extra term, my school had no such facility to support me in doing so. The only choice I had was to apply before receiving my A level results. That required an interview at the college followed by the college (if they wanted me) offering me a place subject to my attaining specific grades at A and S level.

My Application to Cambridge

The application made and with a reference from my headmaster, I was called for interview to read Economics at Caius in early December 1975. I recall my drive to Cambridge. I had decided not to stay overnight in college, as I had been offered. I was too shy. (Well, I was in those days!) I parked the car in a public car park and walked to the college.

The porters directed me to the interviewer's rooms in Caius Court, where I was told to wait outside in the court until I was called. This Elizabethan court was beautiful with the ornate Gate of Honour on one side. Looking around as I waited made me determined to do well.

Added on to the college by Dr Caius, the second founder of the college (the college had originally been founded as Gonville Hall in 1348 by Edmund Gonville but re-founded by Caius in 1557), Caius Court was unique in design. As Doctor to Queen Elizabeth I, Caius had the idea to create a three-sided court (whereas all the other colleges had four-sided courts) 'lest the air from being confined within a narrow space should become foul.'

In essence, Caius had discovered that many illnesses prevalent at the time, were caused by the foul air that was not able to circulate around the college courts and it was his view that if no buildings were erected on the fourth side, the air would circulate better and reduce sickness. He believed this so strongly that he changed the Ordnances of the College prohibiting the fourth side to be built upon after his death. That fourth side remains unbuilt upon today, save for a six-foot brick wall and the magnificent Gate of Honour.

The wait outside the interviewer's rooms seemed to go on for ever. After a while I was joined by another applicant, Julian Treasure. He had been public school educated and had sat the entrance exam. We chatted a bit and as I realised how bright he was and how we came from so very different backgrounds. I became very nervous and pessimistic about my chances. Eventually I was asked to enter the interviewer's rooms.

The Director of Economics was sitting in his 16th century rooms in a wheelchair. He beckoned me to sit down in an armchair facing him. I looked around to see this quaint college room full of book-lined bookshelves; a desk full of papers and books and a suite of comfortable couches and armchairs. This was the Cambridge dream.

Gonville & Caius College stands behind the Senate House as viewed from King's Parade

He introduced himself as the College's Director of Economics and started asking me about myself and my interests. I explained to him about my interest in politics and how I was keen to get involved with the Cambridge University Conservative Association (CUCA) and the Union Society (the famous debating society with its own historic debating chamber and club premises). We engaged in a chat about politics before he turned to Economics. The one question I recall him asking me was about the difference between micro economics and macro economics and how this could be reconciled by some companies having a larger turnover than some nation states. I do remember blustering through my answer. After about an hour, the interview was over and I said goodbye and left with instructions to ask Julian Treasure to come in.

I returned home excited about going up to Cambridge but nervous as to whether I had convinced the interviewer I was good enough, particularly after I had met one of my competitors.

It took about two weeks before a letter arrived at home and it was nerve-wracking opening it. The news was amazing. I had been accepted subject to my attaining two A grades and a B grade at A level and a grade 2 in an S level. I also had to pass an exam in 'Use of English' which all Oxbridge entrants in those days had to take and pass.

I knew the A and S level grades were attainable but worried about passing the Use of English exam. This would require me taking extra lessons in a subject I was not very good at. At O level I had only attained E grades for English and English Literature. It did worry me that having got so far, having passed the interview and having obtained the necessary grades, I would fail to get into Cambridge because of my inability to pass Use of English.

But the school was extremely helpful and provided me with special tuition with an aged Mr Tallis and within a few months I had passed my Use of English exam.

The next step was to continue to work hard and get the three A levels I was anticipating and hopefully, as I was taking two S levels (Economics and Maths), I should get a grade 2 in one of them.

A Levels

The summer of 1976, when I was due to take my A and S level exams, has gone down in history as one of the hottest on record. A lengthy heatwave made studying and revising very difficult. To make matters worse, I suffered from severe hay fever as a teenager. That summer I had to have a cortisone injection to reduce the effects of the bad hay fever season. All went well until the night before my British Government exam. I had expected to do really well, as my love of politics and the constitution meant I was heading for an A grade. But my hay fever combined with the hottest night in years meant that I found it difficult to revise or sleep and the exam itself was taken in a room more like a sauna than an exam room.

Later that summer I arrived at my school to find out my exam results and to see whether I had attained high enough grades to go to Cambridge. I found the headmaster and he handed me the sealed envelope. I walked to a quiet corner and opened it.

I had achieved an A in Economics, an A in Maths but only a B in British Government. As far as my S levels were concerned, I had attained a grade 1 in Economics and a grade 2 in Maths. I had achieved the necessary grades to go to Caius the following October. But I was nevertheless upset in only gaining a B in British Government. So, I asked the headmaster if I could challenge the grade and seek a remarking of my papers. He persuaded me not to be silly, as I had achieved sufficient grades to go to Cambridge, whereas many of my fellow pupils had failed to get into their chosen universities and appeals for them were more important. I accepted that he was right and returned home to tell my family and start the celebrations.

In fact, only three of us in the school had managed to get into Oxbridge. My friend Nick Collins had got into Worcester College, Oxford, and I would frequently travel to Oxford while I was in Cambridge to visit him and other friends. Paul Simon was the other fellow pupil who had won a place at Caius College too. We would remain friends throughout our Cambridge days and lived in the same house in both our first and second years. After Cambridge we both became lawyers with Paul specialising in immigration law. While practising myself, if asked by clients for advice and help in obtaining visas and obtaining British citizenship, I would refer them to Paul as my own firm were not experts in this field. In fact, Paul helped Carole Franco obtain the necessary legal documentation to come to London to be my Lady Mayoress.

My School Reports

I recently discovered all my school reports from my kindergarten school right up to my final term at my grammar school before going off to university. They certainly track how I changed over the years from someone who was shy, an introvert and an average student to someone who was repeatedly top of the class in all my subjects with a great prospect for going to university. Here are some of those comments:

Kerem House Kindergarten – aged 3

'It took quite some time for Robert to settle in. He is a shy little boy and does not take quickly to new friends.'

Kerem House Kindergarten – aged 4

'Robert has really blossomed this term and seems to have overcome a deal of his shyness. He seems more confident when playing with the other children and is much more talkative in the classroom.'

So, you can see that I started shy but became more confident from attending school for the first time and playing with other kids.

Brooklands Primary School – aged 9

'His work is often handicapped by lack of confidence, which he must learn to overcome.'

Well, I certainly overcame that 'lack of confidence', becoming in some people's views, over-confident in the later stages of my political career!

Christ's College Finchley – aged 14

'Should stop complaining and get on with some serious work.'

I have no idea what that was about!

Christ's College Finchley – aged 15

I was given a double 'A' for Maths with the comment from my Maths teacher Phil Molloy of 'An excellent result – he seems keen to do well.'

Christ's College Finchley – aged 16 – O Level Year

PHYSICS Double A 'Excellent work'

HISTORY 'He does excellent work'

GEOGRAPHY 'Excellent – his approach to work is keen and industrious'

MATHS An 'A' grade and 96% in exam and 1st in class – 'Excellent results'

Christ's College Finchley – aged 18 – Upper Sixth (prior to taking A Levels)

BRITISH GOVERNMENT 'Excellent work. A tireless contributor to discussion and a great help in keeping us up-to-date with developments in government. He came top in the exam and deserves to get the A he hopes for in his A Level'

ECONOMICS 'He deserves success in view of his mature and hard-working attitude to the subject.'

PURE MATHS 'An excellent mark (88%) to take him to first position again.'

As Aristotle once said: 'give me a boy until he is seven and I will show you the man!'

My school report from Christ's College Finchley – aged 18 – (prior to taking A Levels).

Cambridge Days

I loved my days at Cambridge. Not only was it my first experience of living independently, but it would open a whole new life for me. With my sheltered family life in north-west London added to my innate shyness and lack of close friends, I was a very unworldly young man, that day in October 1976, when my parents and sister drove me up to Caius for my first day of term. I was nervous and apprehensive. But I was really proud to be joining this historic university and starting a new journey in my life and one that I hoped would lead to great successes in later life. And I was not wrong!

Armed with a kettle and a suitcase of clothes, I arrived to find that the room I had been allocated was in an old converted house on the other side of the Backs (the famous lawns and fields that ran along the western side of the River Cam and on the opposite side to all the historic famous Cambridge colleges). Sitting adjacent to the relatively (then) newly built Harvey Court in West Road, I set to making my room habitable. I said goodbye to my parents and sister and decided to walk over to the other side of the Backs and find the main college buildings and meet my fellow freshers (new boys – it was then an all-male college).

The Backs at Cambridge.

Unbeknown to me, on the journey back to London, my mother and sister cried their hearts out worrying if I would cope. I amazed myself by not only coping but blossoming. I soon learnt that unless I bought my own milk no one else would and if I didn't pick up my dirty underwear from the floor and wash it, no one was going to do so for me. I did enjoy the benefits of a 'bedder', the lady the college arranged to clean my room and those of my neighbours every weekday but her responsibilities were limited.

I soon realised that my single three-amp round-pinned plug socket (yes – that's all I had in the room) was so powerless that it would take over forty minutes to boil a kettle. And inadequate heating meant I had to buy a little electric fan heater to keep me warm. But this was against the rules, so every morning after waking up, I would hide the heater at the back of my cupboard so my bedder would not find it and report me.

My fire escape was a trap door in the floor of my room with a rope to allow me to slide down to the corridor below. But I could not complain as mine was the largest room on my landing. It had character and, armed with several posters, including one of Margaret Thatcher, I made it my home.

It did not take me long before I was joining several societies including the famous Cambridge Union (the debating society) and CUCA (the Conservatives Association).

ABOVE *Tree Court in Gonville & Caius College, Cambridge. The guy on the left with the white sleeves is me. Those sapling trees are now taller than the surrounding college buildings.*

RIGHT *Tree Court now.*

BELOW *Speaking at the Cambridge Union – 1978..*

I auditioned for Footlights (the famous acting club) but never got the return call and then even tried rowing. I was useless. I kept getting a crab (when the oar gets stuck in the water) and when I concentrated on ensuring I didn't get any more crabs, I was totally out of sync with the rest of the eight-man crew. I did not give up but after the first 5 am practice in freezing foggy weather, I decided I had had enough and I would never make the college crew let alone row in the annual Oxford v Cambridge Boat Race. So that ended that attempt at a Cambridge Blue. But I had ticked that box. An all-night motor rally was just another attempt at trying everything at least once.

Although at school I had come top in every subject I studied, I soon realised that at Cambridge nearly everyone around me was academically brighter and certainly more worldly and widely read. But I learnt. I was soon making lots of friends, not only in my own college but from other colleges throughout the university. It did not take too long before I was introduced to the Gilbert and Sullivan operettas, which I immediately fell in love with. A friend opened a new world to me, in the appreciation of modern art. I was soon understanding the difference between Cubism and Impressionism and visiting galleries whenever I could – something I had never considered in my school days.

My first year was spent studying Economics. In the summer before arriving in Cambridge, I was sent a reading list. I took it to one of my teachers from school who suggested that if I only read one book it should be one about economic history written by the renowned Phyllis Deane. So that is what I did. To my delight, within the first week of arriving at Cambridge, I was told that I would be supervised by Phyllis Deane herself. I had never met anyone famous before (apart from Cilla) and I was excited. I would be joined at my weekly supervisions by a fellow Economist Angela Wilson, who was an undergraduate at Newnham College, where Miss Deane held her supervisions. Angela and I became good friends.

Phyllis Deane.

My fellow Caius economists were immensely jealous, as I was the only one being supervised by her, and more importantly, it gave me an instant entrée into Newnham College, a women-only college, which most of my hot-blooded friends were keen to explore.

After gaining a 2:1 in Economics at the end of my first year, I spent the summer vacation thinking about my future. I had chosen Economics because my father had instilled in me the importance of becoming a professional and with my excellence at Mathematics at school, accountancy appeared to be the obvious career choice. Economics was the clear preference for a degree at Cambridge, but I was not really enjoying it. But by coincidence, that summer I was watching a TV dramatisation of a court case and was really impressed by the oratory of the barrister presenting his case. It gave me food for thought. Maybe becoming a lawyer would be a more interesting career.

My mother's brother Stanley was a solicitor, so I sought his advice. After a lengthy discussion with him, I decided that becoming a lawyer was probably my vocation. But what type of lawyer? Stanley was a solicitor and he took time to explain to me all about life in a law firm. He also had a close friend who was a barrister and so he arranged for me to meet him and learn more about practising at the Bar (as it is known). But the one element that struck me and made my decision for me, was the fact that a barrister works for himself with no support (other than a clerk to arrange his diary and ensure he is paid). While of course he may be aided by a 'pupil' (jargon for a trainee barrister), if the barrister is not working there is no one earning money on his behalf. On the other hand, a partner in a law firm could employ many assistant solicitors as well as share the work load with his fellow partners and so his income would be a share of the firm's profits and not just what he personally had earned. This became a reality, when a few weeks later, Stanley became ill and had to spend a few weeks in hospital and yet his partners and staff continued the practice in his absence, while an infirm barrister would have no income if he is incapacitated. With a long-term hope that maybe one day I would need time off from work to expand my political career, I thought this was important. My decision was made. I was going to become a solicitor.

I returned to Cambridge and asked my College Tutor if I could change to Law. However, the law course was over-subscribed and I was informed that this would therefore not be acceptable. I therefore decided that I needed an academic change and after further discussions I was allowed to study SPS (Social and Political Science) instead.

I was the last person to live in Room A2 in St Michael's Court at Caius.

In those days, Caius did not approve of such a modern subject and so I was sent to Emmanuel College where I was supervised by two brilliant academics, one of whom was Gerard Evans who taught me about the political systems of countries around the world. We would have weekly one-to-one supervisions that went on for hours, discussing politics, current affairs and the political constitutions of countries such as the Soviet Union and the United States.

One evening, Gerard invited me to join him at High Table for dinner in his college. I arrived at the Porters Lodge. There was no one there to assist or direct me. Eventually a gentleman walked in and went over to a pile of papers, ignoring me. I shouted at him that I had been waiting for ages and could he please urgently call Dr Evans to tell him I was here, as I did not want to keep him waiting. The gentleman in question came forward and apologised and did as I commanded.

Dr Gerard Evans in 1996.

After a drink in Gerard's rooms, I accompanied him to Hall for dinner and sat down next to him. After a few minutes, the porter I had earlier reprimanded arrived and took his seat on the other side of me. I was shocked. He then introduced himself as Professor David Williams, a well-known law academic. We did laugh and became friends.

A few years later, he was knighted and became vice chancellor of the University and on his retirement, I gave a dinner in his honour during my term as Lord Mayor of Westminster, in the mayoral suite. In his speech at that dinner, he made reference to my thinking he was a college porter.

But what about my legal career. By coincidence, a school friend was undertaking his undergraduate degree at another university but was applying to undertake a post-graduate degree at Wolfson College, Cambridge.

I accompanied that friend on a tour of Wolfson, a college I had never been to before. It was a relatively new college only founded about ten years earlier as University College but renamed Wolfson after the Wolfson family had bestowed a large endowment on the college. It was one of a handful of post-graduate only colleges. The only undergraduates were mature students.

Professor Sir David Williams.

During the walk around and chat with several members of the college we met, I learnt that they were introducing a new course the following year which enabled anyone with a non-law degree to undertake a single year's course during which the graduate would study all the six principal legal subjects (criminal law, tort, equity, contract, constitution and land law), necessary to satisfy the Law Society, so enabling a non-law degree to be converted into a law degree, thereby allowing the graduate to become a solicitor.

Accordingly, I would be able to complete my degree in SPS and then transfer colleges, allowing me to study each of these six core subjects and meet the Law Society's requirements enabling me to go to the College of Law in London, to train to be a solicitor. I immediately applied and after a series of interviews was accepted.

Me in my rooms at St Michael's Court, Caius

The irony was that my friend who introduced me to Wolfson failed to be accepted. I became their first student who had undertaken their first degree at another Cambridge college and transferred, as all the other post-graduate students had come from other universities.

There were two main benefits of moving college. The first was that I would live in college rooms on site, whereas if I had chosen to undertake this year at Caius, I would have had to live in lodgings far out of town. Secondly, I was a new boy again and invited to all the parties for those newly arrived and so able to meet new friends, whereas at Caius I would have just been a fourth-year student. Moreover, most of the staff at Caius had not realised I had left and so I would frequently visit Caius to see my friends and dine in Hall. I did pay though.

One of the friends I met at Wolfson was Carole Franco. We sat next to each other in Hall one night and over dinner, we just hit it off. We became good friends and after I left Cambridge, I flew to the United States for a month's holiday, spending half the time with Carole exploring the north-eastern states. This was the first of several vacations together and after she returned to the US, we kept in touch as friends. Years later, when I was looking for someone to choose as my Lady Mayoress, she was my first choice.

Carole Franco and I in her family home in Connecticut, 1980.

My official graduation photograph, 1979.

My Sexual Awakening

Until I arrived in Cambridge, I had not seriously considered sex or my sexuality. I had dated a few girls, but nothing happened or developed. I thought it was my shyness and inexperience rather than anything else. I did rather fancy other handsome men I saw but was equally impressed by an attractive woman. I put down any feelings I had for other men as a phase in my life that I thought would be short lived. I learnt that many young men experimented with their sexuality during their teenage years but ended up finding a wife and getting married. That was what I assumed would happen with me. But those feelings did not seem to dissipate.

That all changed at Cambridge. I was having a late-night drink with a friend, when after a bit too much to drink, he confessed that he fancied me and invited me to get to know him more intimately. That was my first time! I had lost my virginity! Rather late, but better than not at all. Although that was the only time with that particular friend, we remained friends and he went on to marry (twice) and have several children.

Then a few months later, again after a bit too much to drink, I was dancing at a party in one of the college rooms, when one of my good friends made it clear to me that he would like to take our friendship to the next stage. Nothing happened that night but the next day we met up and a long-term secret relationship started and he became my first lover. We continued seeing each other for a few years after I left Cambridge but we eventually moved on with our lives. I still keep in touch but, forty years on, just as friends. I never had a further serious relationship until I met Simon, but in the intervening years I had to accept that I was gay and this 'phase' in my life was permanent. But in those days, being gay was nothing to shout about, let alone tell your parents. I am upset that when I did eventually 'come out', my parents had passed away and I never had the opportunity to tell them. How I wished I had! But of course, times have changed.

Chapter 7

Cambridge Conservatives

Studying British Government for my A levels got me really fired up about politics. So, in late 1974, the logical step forward was to get involved with my local Conservative Party. Why the Conservatives, I am often asked? The answer was simple. I just related to the ideology of the Conservative Party in seeking to support the private sector while supporting those in need. Encouraging the work ethic and its rewards while allowing for great freedoms from authoritarian restrictions were just some of the reasons that came to mind in the mid-1970s. One of course has to put this in perspective with the background of the Heath and Wilson governments at the time.

I contacted the Finchley Conservative Association whose member of Parliament was an opposition front bencher called Margaret Thatcher. The agent suggested I joined the Young Conservatives who met monthly at the Association headquarters in North Finchley. So, I went to a few meetings. Only about a dozen young Tories attended and they were really boring and with no one making an effort to befriend me and with my own shyness at that stage not helping. I stopped going.

Meeting My MP
At about the same time, intrigued to learn more about how Parliament worked, I was keen to visit the House of Commons for the first time. On advice from my British Government teacher, Mrs Watkins, I wrote to Mrs Thatcher as the local MP and asked if she could arrange for me and my close friend Douglas Bennett to be given a tour of the Palace of Westminster. Within a few days I received a reply from Mrs Thatcher's office inviting Douglas and I to the House to be given a tour.

At the time, Margaret Thatcher was the Shadow Financial Secretary to the Treasury and although she kept us waiting in Central Lobby, we were quite happy to take in the magnificence of Pugin's spectacular gothic designs. She eventually arrived dressed in one of her smart two-piece suits, pearls, her notorious black shiny bag hanging from one of her arms and wearing a large rimless hat, of the type she famously wore in her early days as Leader of the Party. Leading from the front, walking at a pace, she gave us a fascinating guided tour of the Palace of Westminster, not only explaining the history of the place but also how the Commons operated. When the tour finished, she led us down to the Strangers' Cafeteria and bought us afternoon tea and several tinfoil-wrapped chocolate biscuits.

We had a biscuit each over a most enlightening conversation during which Douglas and I fired numerous questions at her about how Parliament worked. However, sitting all

*Dressed in my robes as a Westminster councillor with Margaret
Thatcher at the ceremony which bestowed on her the Freedom
of the City of Westminster in 1991.*

by itself at the centre of the table, was one chocolate biscuit left uneaten. All of a sudden, Margaret stopped talking and turned to us, offering it to both of us in turn. Politely, we both declined. So, she took it and placed it in her famous handbag, saying, 'I will take this one home for Mark'. We could not help but smile.

Leader of the Party

Just a few months later in February 1975, Margaret Thatcher stood against Ted Heath for the leadership of the Conservative Party. Margaret had won the first round resulting in Ted Heath standing down from the race and allowing William Whitelaw and others to enter the race. The Friday before the second round, Margaret Thatcher, as our local MP, agreed to continue to honour her earlier commitment to address our sixth form. I was deputed by the headmaster to meet our distinguished guest at the car that was bringing her and escort her to the headmaster's office. This I did, but she was no longer just our local MP but the favourite to become the Leader of Her Majesty's Loyal Opposition. Accordingly, the entire national press and numerous TV cameras were there. On the following Monday, when discussing her leadership bid, all the TV news-shows showed Margaret arriving at my school with me greeting her and then walking alongside her. My first encounter with that 'five minutes of fame'.

Arriving at Cambridge

My first opportunity to get really involved in politics came at Cambridge University. Within a few days of 'going up' I received an invitation to attend a Cambridge University Conservative Association (CUCA) 'Squash' in my college. A Squash was the Cambridge name for a reception held in Freshers Week (the first week of the Michaelmas term in October) to entice the newly arrived undergraduates to join a society.

CUCA, like many of the larger societies, held a separate Squash in each college. This was my opportunity to get involved with the Conservative Party and pursue my political interests. I turned up dead on time to find I was the first one to arrive. I was met by the chairman of CUCA, Adair Turner. Adair went on to become (inter alia) President of the Cambridge Union, Director General of the CBI, Chairman of the Financial Services Authority and ennobled as Lord Turner of Ecchinswell.

I introduced myself and told Adair that I wanted to be an MP. Well, it was my secret ambition at that time in my life. That showed up my naivety immediately, not realising that everyone else going to the CUCA Squashes were budding MPs. But I was the only one to be so open about it and so I got the nickname of 'Robert 'I want to be an MP' Davis'. Agh! A bad start to my political career.

Not long after I joined, CUCA were advertising a trip to the Soviet Union over the 1977 Easter holidays. This would include visits to both Leningrad (now St Petersburg) and Moscow. My parents kindly agreed to fund the trip and about twenty of us departed by Aeroflot for three days in Moscow and then a further three days in Leningrad. We were split into pairs to share hotel bedrooms and I was teamed up with someone who had gone down (left Cambridge) the previous year, Stephen Freeland, who as a friend of the chairman was allowed to join us. Stephen and I got on very well and became friends for many years after. At the time he was an Edinburgh councillor and when I saw this title on his baggage label, I was very impressed.

Making Lunch

At the end of the Lent (spring) Term, I had been elected to the CUCA committee, albeit in last place of those elected. I was therefore not surprised when the incoming chairman, Chris Whalley asked me to take charge of lunches. My first political appointment was as CUCA lunches secretary.

CUCA's main activities comprised twice weekly lunchtime speaker meetings. Members would meet in the Union Society headquarters behind the Round Church after lectures ended at about 1pm. A buffet lunch would be served for half an hour before the speaker (usually a Conservative MP visiting from London) was introduced by the chairman, who then gave a speech for about 45 minutes, with questions afterwards. My job was to buy and lay out the buffet lunch and collect the money in payment.

During my first term, these lunches consisted of French bread with chunks of cheddar cheese and a variety of pâtés. So that's what I thought was the norm.

When I mentioned my new responsibilities to

The Cambridge Union Society buildings.

Stephen over a drink one night in our Moscow Hotel bar, he told me that when he first joined the CUCA committee, he had also had the great honour of being lunches secretary and that he had impressed his fellow members when he served smoked salmon and cream cheese in addition to the cheese and pâté.

That gave me a brilliant idea to do likewise and to generally uplift the quality and variety of the food offered. However, when I went back to Cambridge, I was told that the chairman had appointed an assistant lunches secretary. This initially annoyed me. Why could I not do this job myself? I was then introduced to Christine Smart. Christine was not actually a formal member of CUCA as she was not at the university but a local (townie) living with her parents in a house next to Wolfson College.

When I realised she was not really competition in my ambitions to move up the CUCA hierarchy, I found her to be a lovely sweet person and she became a good friend and a great help. She went on to marry one of my closest friends at Cambridge, Mark Bishop (now His Honour Mr Mark Bishop, the Resident Judge of Luton Crown Court) and at one of her parties in her home, she introduced me to Lawrence Mallinson, who became my flat-mate/landlord, when I moved back to London. It was Lawrence who subsequently introduced me to his mother, a Westminster councillor, who in turn persuaded me to become a councillor in Westminster. It's like that butterfly again. Meeting Christine led to my becoming a councillor and then meeting Simon!

With Christine's help, we served a superb buffet including smoked salmon, cream cheese and really nice fresh bread and all at the same cost. Overnight, I became very popular and at the next CUCA elections, at the end of the summer term, I came second on the list of committee members entitling me to one of the top jobs. My first year in political life had been a great success.

Up CUCA's Greasy Pole

After the summer vacation, I returned to Cambridge early in late September to help Andrew Mitchell, the new chairman of CUCA, organise the recruitment campaign and Squashes for the upcoming freshers. Andrew went on to become an MP and not only a cabinet minister under David Cameron but also his Chief Whip.

The previous term, I had managed to persuade the university Proctors that I needed special permission to keep a car in Cambridge (most undergraduates were banned from keeping a car) on the basis that I could collect the guest speakers for the speaker meetings, from the station. I became very popular as one of the few undergraduates with my own car.

The campaign to recruit new members to join CUCA after the new academic year started was very successful and we had signed up more than a thousand new members – a record. A few weeks after I got back, Andrew asked me if I would drive him to Blackpool for the day, to enable him to speak at the annual Conservative Party Conference. I duly did and, because Andrew's father was a leading MP himself, Andrew was given a speaking slot that afternoon.

On standing before the massed gathering of Tory faithful, Andrew announced that he and a colleague had arrived 'hot foot from Cambridge where we have recruited a record one thousand new members at the start of the new academic year' and received a rapturous applause.

That was to be the first of numerous visits to the annual Conservative Party Conference, including one in 1990 when I too spoke from the podium, calling on the then Conservative government to transfer the responsibilities of parking enforcement from the police (who regarded it as low priority) to local councils (who would take it more seriously). At that time, I was chairman of the council's Traffic Committee and keen to see effective parking controls in central London where, until then, parking was a free for all with little or no enforcement. The government accepted this demand and a few years later enacted a law to do exactly what I requested. You can therefore blame me for the heavy-handedness of parking enforcement in London and elsewhere.

Back to my Cambridge days, after coming second to top in the CUCA elections after the success of my smoked salmon lunches, I was appointed Social Secretary. One of my main responsibilities was to organise the annual CUCA dance. This was a social highlight of the Michaelmas (autumn) term and held at the Graduates Centre (The 'Grad Pad'). I had to arrange the venue, the music and the food and drink and make sure it made a profit. I even designed the posters and flyers that were distributed around the university.

The poster I designed and drew advertising the CUCA Freshers' Dance.

Another successful job saw me promoted the next term to editor of the CUCA weekly newsletter.

The Cambridge Tory Reform Group

In the meantime, I had also started getting involved with another Conservative Cambridge society, the Cambridge Tory Reform Group ('TRG'). This group had been set up in Cambridge in the 1960s by an undergraduate as PEST (Pressure for Economic and Social Toryism) and soon became a national group with branches around the country as well as in Westminster. Just before I came on the scene, PEST had joined together with three other groups to form the Tory Reform Group. Cambridge's branch was, however, the most active and the playground for future national leaders of the Group.

Then one day the chairman suggested I take over from him as chairman. The Group had a rather low profile and hosted a series of mediocre speaker meetings with only a handful of people attending. My ambitions were to become chairman of CUCA, but that would take me over a year to achieve.

I accepted the offer and was elected chairman of Cambridge TRG unopposed (no one wanted the job) at the end of my first year, so would be chairman during the Lent (spring) and Easter (summer) terms of my second year (1977/1978). TRG only elected a chairman twice a year, while CUCA did so each term (three times a year).

Over the Christmas holiday period, between being elected in early December to term starting in mid-January, I spent the time writing to members of Parliament inviting them to Cambridge as speakers at each of our speaker meetings. I was excited when the positive responses started falling through my letter box at home in Finchley and I was able to put together a very exciting schedule of meetings.

All of those who accepted were well-known Conservative politicians of the time and included MPs from all wings of the party including Peter Bottomley (still an MP and at the date of writing, Father of the House), Teddy Taylor, Sir Ian Gilmour, Nicholas Fairbairn QC, William Van Straubenzee and Leon Brittan QC.

I also persuaded the famous Cambridge economist (and friend of Maynard Keynes) Professor Lord Kaldor to speak, as well as the BBC's favourite psephologist and BBC political pundit and inventor of the 'swingometer', Robert McKenzie.

By coincidence, CUCA had elected a lovely friend called Rosemary Chubb as its chairman. But, although very popular with the CUCA committee and membership, she was not very political or a great organiser. Her programme of speakers was extremely

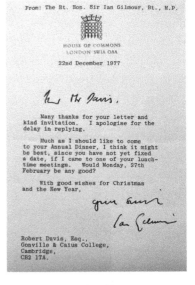

RIGHT *Letter from Sir Ian Gilmour agreeing to speak at a TRG lunchtime meeting.*

BELOW *The TRG programme for my chairmanship – 1978.*

boring, with most of her guests unheard-of MPs.

Using my skills learnt in my first term as a committee member of CUCA, I ensured the lunches we offered members attending the meetings were first rate (well, for undergraduate tastes) and within a month, my TRG meetings were standing room only and packed while the number attending the CUCA meetings dwindled to a handful of loyalist and aspirant committee members. My reputation as an organiser and someone who can turn an organisation around was boosted and the lessons learnt helped me to do a similar turn-around job when I took over as chairman of the London Mayors' Association twenty years later.

The Cambridge TRG stall at the 1978 Freshers Fair with my friend Mark Bishop behind the table waiting for potential members.

The Annual Dinner

One of the highlights of my term as chairman was the TRG annual dinner. I decided to host this in my own college (Caius) and hired the Senior Combination Room, a very traditional wood-panelled dining room in the medieval part of the college. The college had a great reputation for the quality of its food on such occasions and they did not disappoint.

My guest speaker was to be Lynda Chalker, a well-known MP whose future husband (Clive Landa) was to shortly become chairman of national TRG and was a friend. In fact, I attended the wedding party that followed their family-only registry office marriage ceremony.

But two days prior to the dinner, Lynda left a message at the Porters Lodge requesting I call her. In those days, no one had mobile phones, so I had to queue for the one communal phone box in the college. When I got through, sounding very rough, Lynda told me she had the flu and could in no way attend the dinner as my guest of honour and speaker. She was terribly sorry, but could not get out of bed. I was devastated. This was to be my big night.

I returned to my rooms and sat and gave thought as to who I could invite and who would accept at such late notice. As I did so, I noticed a book on my shelf. I had become a fan of the novelist Tom Sharpe. More recently known for his Wilt series of novels, he had made his name writing the humorous book *Porterhouse Blue* about life in a fictional Cambridge college revolving around the hapless head porter Skullion. I had also enjoyed reading his very amusing books including *Blott on the Landscape* and I knew that he lived in Cambridge.

I had found my speaker. If his speeches were as funny as his books, he would be a hit. But how to persuade him at short notice to attend and speak and, more importantly, how do I find him to ask? But it did not take me long to find his number through the help of my own college porters and their collection of telephone directories.

I rang and was surprised that he answered himself. I briefly explained my predicament. He immediately invited me over for coffee to discuss my request and for him to find out more about TRG and the dinner.

An hour later, I arrived at his front door and knocked. After a short while, he opened it slowly, peering out to check me up down and once approving of me, invited me in.

I explained my predicament and after a long chat about myself and of course, his books, he agreed to join us. I left with a signed copy of his latest book.

Tom Sharpe speaking at the TRG annual dinner with me sitting to his left.

Two days later, after a four-course dinner comprising Avocado Vinaigrette, Filet de Sole Meuniere, Boeuf en daube with courgettes and pommes croquettes, and finishing with Vacherin aux fraises, Tom Sharpe brilliantly and amusingly entertained the guests.

Everyone who attended (including Cambridge's MP Robert Rhodes James) agreed that his speech was much more enjoyable than a political one. Another great success.

The National Stage

My success did not go unnoticed and I was soon invited to London to have dinner with the national chairman of TRG, Gerry Wade. A former chairman of the National Young Conservatives and a senior executive at IBM, Gerry and I got on very well and he told me how impressed he was with what I had achieved with Cambridge TRG. We met up on several subsequent occasions and he would often invite me as his guest to join him at the opera. After I retired as chairman of Cambridge TRG, Gerry asked me to become the Assistant National Secretary of TRG to Keith Brown, a former vice chairman of the National Young Conservatives and a Chelmsford city councillor. I was honoured and delighted and agreed that I would come down to London about once a fortnight for meetings and to do any necessary work at the TRG offices in Poland Street.

A couple of years later, both Gerry and Keith decided to retire and Clive Landa (who subsequently married government minister Lynda Chalker, now Baroness Chalker) became chairman and invited me to become the National Secretary of TRG. This was my first serious political appointment and I took my appointment very seriously.

I was responsible for all the administration, for organising meetings, seminars and conferences and for all publications and distributions to members. These were the days before the internet, so distributions to members of our regular newsletter and adverts for events, were all sent through the post. I was supported by a full-time administrative secretary, but I was responsible for her workload. It was a great responsibility and I was just twenty years old! I would regularly drive to London for a few days and spend time in the office.

Through my work in TRG, I met many members who were either leading members of Parliament or would subsequently be elected as MPs, with many of them later serving in government. It was a great training ground and I learnt so much about politics and the political system.

In 1981, I was selected to stand for Westminster Council in the elections the following year and so I decided not to seek re-election as National Secretary of TRG at the AGM that year.

The Battle for the Top Job

Returning to Cambridge, with my standing in the Cambridge political sect improving, at the end of my second year the opportunity arose for me to try for the chairmanship of the Cambridge University Conservative Association. This was, by tradition, a four-stage project. Members usually first fought over being Registrar. Once elected and having served a term, they would progress unopposed to Secretary and then a term later, elected unanimously for the role of vice chairman. Again, the vice chairman was usually unopposed for chairman in the fourth term. Of course, if an officer had not performed well or had upset colleagues he could be opposed and that frequently happened.

It was of course a prestigious post to hold as many chairmen of CUCA had gone on, not only to become MPs but Cabinet Ministers, Ministers and Opposition Front Bench Spokesmen. Few had been Prime Minister – that was an Oxford tradition – but the Conservative parliamentary front bench at the time were predominately from Cambridge, even though the Leader of the Conservative Party (we were initially in opposition until the 1979 election) Margaret Thatcher was an Oxford girl.

At the end of the Lent (spring term) of 1978, I put my name forward for the position of Registrar. But where CUCA politics differed from many other undergraduate Conservative groups, including the Oxford equivalent, was the Association rules that prohibited canvassing in elections for CUCA officers and committee. I was therefore very careful not to persuade any of my many friends to vote for me.

Election day came and friends returned from weekends at home to vote for me. Polling was high. There were three candidates to be Registrar. One of the candidates was not deemed a threat. He was very sweet but with little political nous or ambition. The other candidate was my main threat. He was a member of the right wing of the Conservative

Party while I had been chairman of the more moderate Tory Reform Group. He was, however, clever and politically astute. So, while he was a threat, all I could do was smile and be nice to my friends and colleagues.

When the polling closed, each of the candidates was entitled to attend the count with a friend. I chose not to attend myself but to ask one of my friends to do so on my behalf. Both the other candidates insisted on attending.

What I understand from my representative was that on the first count, my main opposition won by just a handful of votes but without the required absolute majority. I had come a close second but as the voting had been based on preferences, the third candidate's second preference votes were distributed and this resulted in both my main competitor and I having exactly the same number of votes. A dead heat. At the request of the other main candidate, a second count was undertaken and again the voting was the same. No change.

I was informed that my main opponent then started making a fuss as did his companion and insisted on a further third recount. As soon as the rumpus calmed down, someone in the room left to go to the toilet. After he returned, they re-counted a third time. On the third recount, my main competitor beat me by one single vote. A vote (in my favour) appeared to have gone missing. A fourth count was demanded by my representative but again the other candidate won by one vote.

My opponent was declared the winner. However, my representative was convinced that after the second count and during the arguments that ensued, someone had stolen one of my voting slips.

I was really upset. Soon many of the other senior members of CUCA had heard this story and my friends persuaded me to refer the matter to the Hon Treasurer of CUCA, an academic, and to demand a 'Requisition' which formed part of the CUCA rules and required the Hon Treasurer to hold an enquiry and chair a Tribunal to investigate and make a determination on a complaint. As this became more widely known, several members approached me with evidence of one of the other candidates canvassing for votes prior to the election in breach of the rules.

A Tribunal hearing was heard by a small committee of academics, chaired by the Treasurer, the Reverend James Owen, the Vicar of Little St Mary's Church and held in a room in the Union Society's building. I presented my case as did the candidate accused of breaching the rules and then awaited the decision.

A few days later, numerous members of CUCA gathered at the Union Society to hear the Treasurer read out the Tribunal's decision. The tension mounted as we awaited the judgment.

The Tribunal had determined that the other main candidate had cheated and would be disqualified. I felt vindicated. But to my surprise, they decided that in their view it was appropriate to appoint the third candidate who came a poor third, as the new Registrar. I was dumbfounded. My friends rallied round but the decision had been made. So, I resolved to move on and spend my third year doing something other than politics and retire from active work within CUCA.

Me on the right appearing as the hapless son in Habeas Corpus.

To move on, the following term, instead of being Registrar of CUCA, I was asked by my friend Stephen Galloway to appear in the play he was directing in Pembroke College, *Habeas Corpus*, a comedy by Alan Bennett. My interests turned to the world of theatre.

Rab Butler

I was recently reminded of my meeting with the President of CUCA. This was an honorary role held by an eminent member of the university. During my time at Cambridge, our President was Lord (Rab) Butler, the Master of Trinity College.

Those Conservatives with a long memory will recall that Rab was famous as the 'best Prime Minister we never had'. He was also known for his view that politics 'was the art of the possible' – a leading MP who held all the top offices of State including Chancellor of the Exchequer, Foreign Secretary, Home Secretary and Deputy Prime Minister. But both in 1957, and again in 1963, although expected to succeed as Prime Minister, he was overlooked and failed to be chosen by Her Majesty The Queen (who in those days chose the Leader of the Conservative Party on the recommendation of the outgoing Leader).

Disappointed once too often (I was beginning to know how he felt), he became Master of Trinity College in Cambridge and subsequently President of CUCA.

So, as a keen political historian, I was really impressed when I had the opportunity to meet him on several occasions including attending regular drinks parties in his Master's Lodge for CUCA committee members. Then on one occasion, we decided to have a CUCA committee group photo and asked Rab to join us. This was taken in the centre of Trinity

Great Court in front of the central fountain. After the formal photo, Rab left us and we had a very amusing photo taken too.

Much to my surprise, over 35 years later, a book was published to celebrate Cambridge University's 800th Anniversary and there in the middle of the book was the funny version of that photo in Trinity Great Court, by which time two of the committee members had served in the Cabinet: Andrew Mitchell and (Sir) David Lidington; and a third is now Lord (Adair) Turner of Ecchinswell.

We were quite an Alumni.

The formal and more relaxed CUCA committee photographs.

Chapter 8

My Oscar

In one of my first press releases as a candidate in the 1982 local elections, the headline read 'Candidate wins Oscar'.

The story, however, goes back to the end of my second year of Cambridge when in early 1978, my friend Stephen Ball told me at a Union Society debate that one of his good friends from school (Windsor Grammar) was not only coming up to Cambridge the following academic term but was going to my college, Caius. So quite early in the following Michaelmas term, I was introduced to Stephen's friend. Mark Galloway was to become my closest friend, not only during those final two years at Cambridge but remains so until this day. He was my best man at my wedding (my civil partnership ceremony to Simon) and I was best man at his marriage to Marian.

The Galloway Twins

What I soon discovered was that Mark had a twin brother, Stephen. They were not identical and, with Mark's beard, many would not even know they were brothers. They were not close either. Stephen was studying at Pembroke College. I cannot recall whether Mark or Stephen Ball introduced me to Stephen Galloway, but Stephen and I also became friends. I soon discovered that apart from Stephen Ball, I was the only person who was friends with both of them. As Mark and Stephen rarely socialised together, when I visited them in the holidays at their parents' home in Ascot, I would have to spend half my time exclusively with Mark and half my time exclusively with Stephen, so as to not upset either one.

So, as our friendship developed, so did Stephen's ambitions to become a leading film director in Hollywood. As part of his Hollywood ambitions, Stephen arranged an interview with David Puttnam the famous film producer and they got on really well. By coincidence, David Puttnam was at the time working on his next project, a film called *Chariots of Fire* about two athletes attempting to win gold medals at the 1924 Olympics. One of these runners was a Caian, Harold Abrahams, a superb runner who, as a Jew, suffered widespread prejudice, particularly from the university authorities. He overcame such pressures to win the 100-metre gold medal while his competitor Eric Liddle overcame a different sort of prejudice, for being a devout Christian and for his refusal to run against Abrahams in the 100-metre final on a Sunday – the Christian Sabbath. Eric too eventually won a gold medal in the 400-metre final which was held on a Thursday.

Location Location Location

Puttnam contacted Stephen a few months after the interview and asked him to help his location manager find suitable sites in Cambridge to film. Knowing I had become a bit of an amateur expert on Cambridge history and the geography of the place, Stephen enlisted me to assist.

I invited both Stephen and the location manager for dinner at Formal Hall (where undergraduates are required to wear gowns) in my college and after dinner, gave the location manager a tour of the college, where Harold Abrahams had been an undergraduate. He then invited me to join him the following day for a tour of the rest of Cambridge, looking for suitable locations.

As filming got closer to starting, Puttnam asked Stephen to help him and his team recruit undergraduates to be extras in the filming of the Cambridge scenes. Stephen added my name to the list. When I told my parents I could be an extra in a film being shot in Cambridge, they were concerned I was not concentrating on my studying, as I had my finals coming up. But I ignored their pleas to work harder, as this was a unique opportunity I could not miss.

A number of my friends and I were recruited and I was sent to the Union Society a day before filming started, where the film crew had set up their headquarters. First, I was given a free haircut. Hair in the 1920s was worn short, so off came my locks. Next was wardrobe, where I was put into a pair of baggy flannel trousers, a white shirt and a white cricket sweater with a Cambridge Blue stripe below the V-necked collar and then embellished with a navy scarf. I looked the part. An undergraduate straight out of the 1920s.

Filming Starts

The first day of filming took place on the Sunday morning in King's Parade (the main street running through the centre of Cambridge with the majestic King's College Chapel sitting on the west side). This was also the first day of filming for the whole film.

Waiting to be given my role for the first shoot, with my costume on and wearing (at the director's request) my college gown, I was eventually handed a three-wheeled bicycle and given my starting point half way down King's Parade, right outside the main entrance to King's College. The main camera on its rigging crane was at the northern end of King's Parade just outside Caius College and the scene was to film the arrival of Harold Abrahams in his taxi, at his new college, Caius.

As we waited for what seemed like hours for the camera to roll, tourists were allowed to wander down the street and chat to us. The extras in our costumes, with many like myself on historic bikes, became very popular to these excited tourists, who all sought photos with us. I could have made a small fortune if I had had the nerve to charge for each photograph.

One tourist, not realising we were making a film, said to me, in a deep American accent, that she thought we Cambridge students were very elegant in our uniforms, believing that is what we wore every day in quaint old England.

On my bike, filming Chariots of Fire.

After the director (Hugh Hudson) called action, I had to pedal towards the camera and then out of shot as Harold Abraham's taxi drove past. The whole scene took no longer than ninety seconds to film, despite having been waiting on set for over five hours. My first lesson in film making. The second lesson was that we had to re-take the shot no less than five further times before the director was happy.

As soon as that shot was in the can, the crew moved to the front of Trinity Hall college, which was to be the substitute for the Porters' Lodge of Caius. They had to use Trinity Hall because the Master and Fellows of Caius had (I only then discovered) refused filming in its college. This was because, having read the script, they did not like the way the Master of Caius at the time was being portrayed by Lindsay Anderson (the well-known film director and actor who had directed the iconic film *If*) as antisemitic. The film makers had unsuccessfully tried to persuade Caius that Lindsay's character was just symbolising the anti-Semitism in Cambridge at the time, which was very real and had affected Harold Abraham's attempts to succeed in athletics. But to no avail, and so Trinity Hall it was.

I was lucky, because only a few of the extras were asked to remain for the next stage of filming and that included me on my bike. This scene showed the taxi actually arriving outside the college and Harold (played by Ben Cross) stepping out of the beautiful 1920s style taxi with his luggage and walking in to the college for the first time. All I had to do was cycle past him on my bike when told to do so. Simple – and this part of the filming only took a couple of hours. Filming ended for the day after just a few takes.

I was a film star! Well, almost. That really happened the following day when filming moved to the Senate House, one of the grandest buildings in Cambridge and one of the few buildings that is actually part of Cambridge University itself and not an independent college. The Senate House is one massive hall which is principally used for the annual degree ceremony.

The Societies' Fayre

For the day's filming, the Senate House had been converted into the Societies' Fayre. At the beginning of each academic year, with thousands of new undergraduates arriving at the university for the first time, the Societies' Fayre is an opportunity for the numerous Cambridge societies from the college rugby clubs, to Footlights (the acting society), to scientific societies and drinking societies, to attract members to join. In my first term, this was held in a boring council community hall but for the 1920s, the film makers sought a more appropriate set.

I was assigned a position by the Athletics Club stall where one of the professional actors played the chairman of the club and I and another guy were potential new members. The director explained to us that he was going to film the entire five-minute shoot in one go with no breaks. The camera would sweep through the room as the main characters, Harold Abrahams and his friend Henry Stallard (played by Daniel Gerroll), walked around the stalls enquiring about different societies. After singing a tune with the Gilbert and Sullivan Society (one of the main themes in the film is Abraham's love of G and S), Harold peels off and the camera follows his friend to the athletics stall where he signs up as a member. He then also moves on, while the camera focuses on the actor playing the Athletics Club chairman, who turns to me and says 'what do you do?'. I replied off the cuff 'cross country' and then he asked me 'what distance?'. Not expecting to have to use my initiative, I said 100 metres. The director then shouted 'cut'. 100 metres for cross country!! I had failed my big test.

I was lucky, however, because for a reason not associated with my error, a re-take was required. This time the professional actor turned to me and said, 'and what do you do?'. Again, I responded 'cross country' but learning from our cock-up earlier, he then followed up by asking 'what's your name' and this time, the true professional I was becoming, replied 'Davis' and the director shouted cut. He then shouted 'that's a wrap'.

The next day we were due to do more filming but when we turned up at wardrobe, we were told that further filming in Cambridge had been cancelled as the university authorities were fed up with the chaos caused by filming in the city.

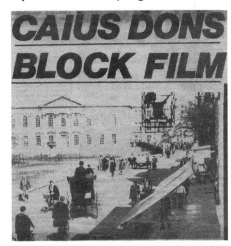

The front page of Stop Press, *the weekly student newspaper.*

Eton

A few days later, we received notification that filming would resume in Eton College in Windsor which would pretend to be Cambridge and that coaches would collect us early the next morning outside King's College and we would be taken down to Eton for a day of filming and returned later that evening.

When we arrived in Windsor, instead of driving to Eton we were taken to Bray Studios about seven miles away. There we were ushered into make-up and then wardrobe where I was given a tail coat and white tie. After all the fifty or so extras from Cambridge were ready, we were taken by coach to the famous school of kings and prime ministers and ushered into the Great Hall of Eton College, where it was laid out for a formal dinner with candelabra and silver covering the white table cloths of the c-shaped table. I was given one of the seats at the table a few places from Lindsay Anderson, playing the Master of Caius. While we waited for ages (as usual) for filming to start, I approached Lindsay Anderson and told him I was a fan of his famous film *If* which ends with a pupil shooting his fellow pupils and all the staff. He was delighted to talk about the film and his other work.

After the Matriculation dinner was filmed, we had to wait for over an hour in the courtyard of the college while they redressed the set and we were returned to film an amateur performance of *The Mikado* by the Cambridge University Gilbert and Sullivan Society. I was to be a member of the audience sitting behind Harold Abrahams as he watched the actress playing Yum Yum (the leading lady), who he falls in love with and subsequently woos. After a couple of takes, we had finished filming and were returned to Cambridge.

A few weeks later, we were asked to return to Eton College for filming of the famous race around the court. This is where Harold is challenged to run around the massive court at Trinity, within the toll of the noon chimes. This was a Trinity tradition and the real Abrahams did succeed in the challenge. Although originally run in Trinity College, Eton College was the substitute for filming. However, the date of filming was set for when I was to be abroad on holiday during the Easter vacation and so I had to decline. My short-lived film career was at an end.

However, I was paid £10 a day for my efforts, which in 1980 was a large amount for a poor student. And do not forget the free haircut I got prior to filming!

The Film's Premiere

A year later, Stephen and I were invited to the film's premiere in the Odeon Leicester Square. It was my first film premiere (although as a Westminster councillor I was to attend many later in my life).

I was excited as the film started and I saw myself cycling like mad, along King's Parade as Harold's taxi meandered down the street. Well, you could not miss me, because I was riding the only three-wheeled bike, even though my face was indistinguishable. Again, as Harold's taxi drops him off outside the College, there I am again on my tricycle, whisking past. But ten minutes later, as Harold and his friend arrives at the Societies' Fayre, I started getting excited.

My big moment was about to arrive and to ensure that everyone watching the film, knew it was me, there was my response to the question 'what is your name?', when I replied 'Davis'.

As the shot follows Harold and his friend around the stalls and the camera pans on to the athletics stall, there I am taking up half the screen standing next to Harold's friend Stallard. After Stallard agrees to join the Athletics Club, the guy from the club turns to me and pointing at me, says 'and what do you do?'. But instead of showing me saying 'cross country' and then exclaiming that my name was Davis, the film cuts to the next scene. My speaking part was on the cutting room floor!!

But on reflection, I do appear for at least thirty seconds covering at least half the screen. When the film was released on VHS, the machines were so primitive that if you paused on my bit, the frozen picture was blurred. But as soon as digital DVDs arrived, I could be frozen and seen in all my glory. Many friends would ring me to say they had watched the film and had seen me.

Later that year, the film won four Oscars including Best Film and Best Original Screenplay. Hence my claim in my press release as the new candidate fighting the Bayswater ward in the 1982 local elections, that I had won an Oscar. Although the small print did make it clear I was merely an extra in the film, it was exciting enough to make page ten of the local papers. And this was before 'spin' had entered our dictionary.

In 2012, London celebrated hosting the Olympics and my friend Councillor Angela Harvey was Lord Mayor. Knowing of my part in *Chariots of Fire*, she decided to host an Olympic Sunday lunch party in her and her husband David's flat in Westminster. After lunch, my hosts and I with the other guests (all fellow councillors) gathered round her large TV and watched the film. Each time I appeared, we froze the DVD and I pointed myself out. Of course, as soon as they saw the Societies' Fayre scene, they all recognised me straightaway, despite it having been filmed over thirty years earlier.

The Group Photo

At the end of filming the Societies' Fayre scene, in the Senate House, all the extras were invited to be photographed in a group photo including all the professional actors filming in the Cambridge scenes and with the full crew, including David Puttnam as producer and Hugh Hudson, the director. We were subsequently given the photo and I immediately had it framed and hung it in my college rooms.

I have kept that framed photograph with me for the rest of my life. When I moved to Freeman Box with my own office, it took pride of place on my wall and then when I retired from Freeman Box, it appeared on the wall of my City Hall office. It is now on the wall of my TV room at home in London.

Looking at it now, some forty years later, many of the extras standing with me have gone on to achieve great things in their lives. Of course, I can only comment on those I knew and have kept in contact with. Included in the photograph is Stephen Fry (then a fellow undergraduate – but sadly not a friend of mine); Andrew Noble (at the time of writing, British Ambassador to Romania and still a good friend); Derek Pringle (who went on to play cricket for England); Sir Bernard Jenkin, the famous MP, and at least one High Court Judge.

Part of the photograph of the actors, crew and undergraduates filming scenes for Chariots of Fire *in Cambridge in 1979 – can you spot me? Answer at the end of the chapter.*

Some thirty-five years after the photo was taken, I was at a dinner at the residence of the Canadian High Commissioner in Grosvenor Square and sitting next to Ann, the wife of the TV presenter Peter Snow.

In conversation, I told her about my *Chariots of Fire* experience and the photo and that I knew several of my fellow extras and what they had achieved in their lives but emphasised that all these years later, it would be fascinating to research what had happened to the other fifty or sixty, to see what they had achieved. She called me the following morning to tell me she had told my story to her son, the TV historian, presenter and producer Dan Snow. Dan had loved the story and wanted to carry out the research and work with me on making a TV programme about the photo. A copy of the photo was sent to him but alas, I never heard again. Presumably, more exciting projects took up his time. But it would make a good TV programme one day.

In the Olympic year of 2012, a theatrical version of *Chariots of Fire* was produced on the West End stage in one of Cameron Mackintosh's theatres and I was delighted to be invited to attend the opening night. During the interval at the VIP drinks reception, I was standing near the director of the film, Hugh Hudson, and so went up to him and explained that I was Deputy Leader of Westminster Council but that in my youth I had appeared as an extra in the film of *Chariots of Fire*. He was interested in meeting me and we chatted for a while about the making of the film.

The Lady Puttnam

One of the last functions I attended as Lord Mayor in 1997 was the BAFTA film awards in the Royal Albert Hall. In those days, the event took place over a formal black-tie dinner. As Lord Mayor, I sat at the top table with Her Royal Highness the Princess Royal a few seats along from me. Sitting on one side of me was the actress Julie Christie, while on the other side was David Puttnam's wife Patty. Patty and I got on very well, especially when I relayed to her my *Chariots of Fire* story, which she loved. Towards the end of the evening, I explained that I was days away from retiring as Lord Mayor and was very upset about this. She then asked me what I was going to do after I had stood down as Lord Mayor. I had a stock answer for this question, as during those last few weeks in office, I often got asked that same question. I responded with a deadpan face by saying 'I am going to cry!'

A week later, I retired as Lord Mayor and the next day flew with Simon to Florida for a well-earned three-week holiday. On my return to London, I found on my desk at my law firm, a gift waiting to be opened. It was beautifully wrapped. I quickly tore the paper off and found a box. I opened it and inside was a solitary linen handkerchief with a message 'for when you cry' signed Patty Puttnam. I was humbled and impressed. A lovely gesture.

Answer to the Chariots of Fire *group photo question: I am in the third row up, second in from the right.*

Chapter 9

Freeman Box

I spent thirty-two years of my life as a solicitor with Freeman Box, a firm based in Marylebone, central London.

My Articles

When I was looking for articles (the historic name for a training contract), I went for interviews with a number of large firms in the City of London and was therefore delighted when I was accepted by a famous firm called Markbys. Their claim to fame was that they are mentioned in Oscar Wilde's *The Importance of Being Ernest*, when Lady Bracknell refers to her solicitors 'Markby, Markby and Markby'. I was to undertake a two-year training contract spending six months in each of their four main departments namely, litigation, property, company and insolvency.

Although I was employed by Markbys, a few months before I joined in the September of 1981, Markbys merged with another similar-sized firm called Cameron Kemm Norden and became Cameron Markby. However, throughout my two years there, they remained in essence two firms, with red files for Cameron Kemm Norden clients and blue for Markby clients. In retrospect, I think they failed the test of how to successfully merge two firms.

I was articled to one of the senior partners, David Allibone. It was a Law Society requirement that one had to be articled to a particular partner, who would be responsible for your training throughout the two-year period, even if you were not working for him directly. But I rarely saw him. He took no interest in me, my training or my career.

My Training

For my two years of training, I worked in four different departments for six months each. I started in the litigation department and then progressed through the company department, the property department and ended up in the insolvency department which was a small niche part of the firm, but highly recognised in the field. Its senior partner, Peter Totty, had written one of the most important books on the subject and I sat in an office with his senior assistant.

During my six months in the company department, I shared an office with a solicitor called Carole Blackshaw. We became friends and Carole often took me with her to meetings. At one stage, she was conducting an enquiry before the Civil Aviation Authority about an airline licence for her clients, TradeWinds, who were a commercial airline company that transported cargo and part of the Lonrho empire. Lonrho was at that time one of the major companies operating in the UK with a wide diversity of operational subsidiaries. We were their main lawyers.

Years later, when I was Lord Mayor and attended my first function in the City of London at Guildhall, Carole came running up to me and asked me if I remembered her. Of course I did. I soon learnt that her close friend, Gavyn Arthur (later Sir Gavyn), was an Alderman in the City and on the ladder to becoming Lord Mayor. I soon became friends with Gavyn and friends again with Carole and after a few further years, Gavyn did indeed become Lord Mayor of London with Carole as his Lady Mayoress. They kindly invited me to many functions and dinners in the City during their term of office. Some years later, Gavyn sadly died suddenly. I have remained friends with Carole.

Qualification and a professional move

I was not enjoying my time at Cameron Markbys. The firm was large, highly competitive and unfriendly. So, during my last six months and just before I was due to qualify as a solicitor, I started applying for jobs elsewhere. I started a round of interviews but was getting nowhere. By this stage, I had been elected to Westminster City Council and on leaving a heavy interview session with one of the large city firms, I rushed off to Westminster City Hall to attend a meeting. I ended up arriving early and so went for a coffee in the Members' Room where I found my friend and fellow councillor Peter Hartley.

Over a cup of coffee, he asked me how my day had been and I replied that it had been tough, particularly the interview I had just completed. He then told me that his own solicitors were looking for a new assistant solicitor and he asked me if I wanted him to contact them, to put my name forward for the job. I thought that there would be nothing to lose in doing so.

There and then, Peter phoned his solicitor and told him about me in a most flattering manner. The solicitor explained to Peter that having considered and interviewed about thirty candidates, they were now re-interviewing a shortlist of four candidates for the job. But as I was a friend of Peter's, they would be happy to meet me and have a chat.

A week later, I arrived at Freeman Box's offices (then) in Welbeck Street and waited in the reception for about thirty minutes, to see one of the partners, Trevor Box. While reading the glossy magazines in reception, I was interrupted by the arrival of the two partners of the firm, Trevor and Jeremy Freeman.

They introduced themselves and suggested that we conduct the interview in their club in Green Street, Mayfair. Every single interview up to then had been in some dark and gloomy boardroom but now I was being entertained to champagne in a swanky London club. This, I thought, was impressive.

The interview seemed to go well. Very relaxed, a lot of laughing and joke telling (mainly by Trevor) and I departed feeling quite happy but conscious of their having reminded me that they had already shortlisted four candidates and this interview was just a favour to Peter, their client. But I did think we had clicked. We were all Jewish from north-west

London and had much in common socially. But I was conscious that this was not an interview for a new friend but for a new solicitor. I was warned they may take a few weeks to make a decision.

A month passed and I was going on holiday to the United States to stay with a friend and his wife in the suburbs of Washington DC. I advised Trevor that I was going to be away and gave him the phone number for my friend (this was before mobile phones).

My holiday was great fun. One morning I was having a lie in. My host had gone to work and his wife had gone out shopping. She was returning at lunchtime to take me out on a trip. The phone rang. I answered it and there was Trevor, crystal clear on the other end. He said that they had given careful thought to all the candidates and had decided to invite me to join the firm as an assistant solicitor. Wow! I was not expecting that. I had to think quickly. I decided that I needed to play the tough guy and so I said that I need to think about it. I explained that I was returning home in two days and would call him once I was back in London. He understood and agreed. Well, it took me all of two seconds to decide that I would accept, but I did wait until my return to phone Trevor, when I confirmed that I would be delighted to join them in September.

I am not sure who got the best deal, but I joined Freeman Box that September in 1983 and stayed thirty-two years, until I retired in May 2015, although I remain a consultant to the firm to this day.

My New Career

When I first joined Freeman Box, they were just two years into their partnership. They had both been partners in a larger firm but decided to break away and set up by themselves. They took a lease of the second floor of a Victorian building at 54 Welbeck Street on the Howard de Walden Estate in Marylebone which comprised just two large rooms, a central corridor and a walk-in cupboard.

Trevor occupied the office facing onto the street while Jeremy's office looked into a central lightwell. The single secretary worked from a narrow desk in the corridor while the office junior sat in the cupboard. I kid you not!

Despite these cramped conditions, business was thriving and hence the need to take on an assistant. To find room for me and to cater for the expanding practice, just before I arrived, they took on a lease of the third floor. Trevor moved into a newly decorated office at the rear of the new floor and I occupied his old office. The other large room on the new floor became a general office with desks for up to four secretaries and an office junior together with a new photocopying machine.

They had recently bought their first computer, a Wang machine which had a screen with a dark background and bright green text. It was amazing and definitely a novelty. We could type a whole lease on it, save it and amend it. We could even copy a document and amend the parties and terms and use this for other clients. Now this all seems pretty basic, but in those days, it was revolutionary because until then, all we used were simple typewriters

Working at my desk at 54 Welbeck Street – 1984.

and every document had to be typed from scratch and any amendment amended by using Tippex – white paint. Those were the days!

The intention was that I was to work for both Jeremy and Trevor. Trevor was a litigator while Jeremy a conveyancer (property transactions). But there was a big difference between them, particularly in the way they worked. Trevor was not good at delegating. He would frequently ask me to carry out specific projects or send me to Court to file a document or appear before a Master (a form of judge) about a procedural issue, but not run my own case. Jeremy on the other hand, just dumped a file on me and expected me to get on with the matter by myself. And for the first time, I learnt how to be a good conveyancer.

Within a few years, my workload for Trevor just dissolved away, while on the other hand the workload for conveyancing just spiralled and began occupying not only a full working day, but my evenings, my early mornings and even my weekends. Hence, I became a property specialist.

Promotion

The practice was doing well and we wanted to expand, so about a year later, we moved a few doors along into two floors at 42 Welbeck Street.

In the summer of 1985, after two years of hard work, frequently working in the office on Sundays, Jeremy and Trevor invited me in to Trevor's office and invited me to become a partner. I was delighted and this time, I did not repeat my 'play hard to get' attitude, but accepted immediately and ran off to phone my parents to tell them. My father was particularly proud. We signed the new partnership deed on my twenty-eighth birthday on 27th September 1985.

A couple of years later, the workload that Jeremy and I were carrying became so heavy that we both employed assistants. Chris Mills started working for Jeremy and on the same day, a young lawyer called Howard Granville started work for me at a desk in the corner of my large office. Chris subsequently left to join another firm, but Howard worked his way up to become a partner himself and continues to be a partner to this day.

In 1989, we expanded again and moved around the corner to 8 Bentinck Street. This was a major step in the success of the firm. We were to occupy the whole building with our own reception and our own boardroom. I was provided with an extremely large office on the second floor facing the street. Jeremy and Trevor took me with them to see one of our clients, who sold office furniture. They chose very modern office furniture for their new offices and for the boardroom. But I did not want a modern office. I wanted something much more traditional, so they allowed me to invite Neville Johnson, the bespoke office furniture company, to design a large wrap around dark mahogany wooden desk with drawers, glass-fronted cupboards and a very large main desk top. I occupied that office with that splendidly impressive desk for twenty-six years. I covered the walls with photos of myself undertaking mayoral and civic engagements and meeting a variety of famous people from The Queen and Prince Charles to Cilla Black and Sir John Gielgud. Most clients could not concentrate on what I was saying to them, as I watched their eyes studying all the photos around the room.

Chris Povey

After my mother died in 1997, I had persuaded my father to retire and I helped him to wind down his business. That was pretty straightforward apart from one major issue. My father had employed a young Chris Povey aged fifteen as an assistant in his business twenty-seven years earlier. Over the years, Chris was promoted and stayed with the business through thick and thin and became an unofficial member of our family. The one thing that concerned my father was his fear of having to tell Chris that after twenty-seven years he would have to be made redundant. But I had an idea!

At Freeman Box, we always employed young school leavers to run our general office, photocopying, making coffee for clients, doing the post and ordering stationery. I thought Chris would be perfect in the role and, being older, would stay a few years at least and would give continuity as the youngsters never lasted more than a few months at a time. I spoke to my partners and they agreed with my idea and suggested I invite Chris in for an interview.

I also thought it sensible if I explained the position to Chris, as I did not think my father could cope, as he found the whole thing too stressful. I called Chris into my father's office and explained that my father was going to retire and close down the business and that Chris would be made redundant with the appropriate redundancy payment. But I explained that I would like to invite him to join Freeman Box subject to an interview. Chris was very upset. I don't think he had seen this coming. He was also nervous about working for a firm of solicitors but after thinking about it, he agreed to meet my partners. Well, the story has a happy ending, as in the summer of 1998 Chris joined Freeman Box and some twenty-three years later, he is still working there and we often said that without his running the general office, the firm could not survive. So, a win-win for everyone.

My Work

Several of my clients operated restaurants and bars. So, it was not long before I started advising them on licensing issues as well as their property matters. When clients bought a restaurant, I would not only undertake the conveyancing but also made the necessary licensing application before the local magistrate's court in order to obtain for them the licence required to sell alcohol.

One of my clients owned a chain of Chinese restaurants in the West End. They were buying a new restaurant in Holborn and I accompanied them to the local magistrates court. This was an application for a transfer of the justices' licence held by the vendors to my clients. The court wanted to be reassured that my clients understood the law of licensing. So, before the hearing, I had briefed them by insisting they read a document I had prepared on the law affecting licenced restaurants. They had promised me that they had read it. I was conscious that one of them spoke very poor English and I was not convinced he had taken in all that I had taught him. His wife on the other hand spoke perfect English and had clearly undertaken her homework. Conscious of this, I addressed the court and explained about my briefing and that my clients understood the law. Usually, my reassurances were sufficient and the application quickly granted. This time, the chairman of the Bench chose to ask a question to one of my clients. It could be either of them. But the chairman turned to the wife and asked her about the permitted hours in a restaurant. My client, in perfect English, answered the question correctly. Satisfied, the magistrate immediately said 'granted' and the case was over. I was relieved. Had the chairman asked that simple question to the husband, he would have had no idea what was being asked of him, let alone what the answer was. Luck was on my side that day.

Over the years, using my contacts and friendships I developed through my public life, I attracted a number of very special high-profile clients to Freeman Box, from members of both Houses of Parliament to leading household business names. I even acted for a very famous (albeit retired) footballer.

Retirement

When Simon died in 2011, I threw myself into working all hours at the council and in my legal work. Seven-day weeks, working fifteen hours a day were the norm. I would have early morning council meetings, getting to the office for 8.30 am and then have further a council meeting with officers or a stakeholder over lunch. At 5 pm I would rush off to City Hall for meetings until about 8 pm, when I returned home, had a ready-meal for supper and then did three or four hours of drafting a complicated legal document in the peace and quiet of my flat, before going to bed and then starting all over again the next morning.

But within a few years, I was getting bored and frustrated with the law. Instead of being hungry for more work, I felt pressurised by any new work that came in. I knew that these were not good signs. On the other hand, I was really enjoying the council and with ever-increasing responsibilities, I wanted to spend more time at City Hall while I had the opportunity to do so.

After a long chat with my partners, we decided that I would henceforth work a four-day week at Freeman Box and on Thursdays I would spend the day at City Hall in back-to-back meetings. This started well and I looked forward to Thursdays every week. But in reality, I still did five days of work at Freeman Box but over four days. Those four days saw me looking after my client's work late into the night and doing more work at weekends as well as on Thursday evenings. By late 2014, I made a decision and I convened a partners' meetings and told my partners I was going to retire from the partnership by Christmas. They were not happy. They liked me being part of the team and relied heavily on me not only as a fellow partner but also for bringing in lots of work and for carrying a heavy workload.

But after some detailed negotiations, I agreed with Jeremy and Trevor that I would retire at the end of April the following year. I would prepare notes on all my files and pass on all my work to my property colleagues.

On 30th April 2015, I emptied my office and left the building for the last time as a partner. They very kindly agreed for me to continue my association with the firm, by making me a consultant with my name on the notepaper, but this was limited to my advising on various issues on an infrequent basis.

I was honoured that they respected how much I had put into and added to the business over thirty-two years with the firm. I am still invited to firm events and have kept in contact with my former partners as friends. Whenever I am in Marylebone, I pop into the office to say hello and have a chat as well as use the facilities!

Chapter 10

Westminster Calls

Why did I become a councillor? A good question for someone like me, who did not even know what a councillor did.

Having taken an academic interest in politics at school, pursuing a political education at Cambridge and having spent several summer holidays working for members of Parliament in the House of Commons, I thought my political ambitions were in becoming an MP.

But that changed in 1981.

But first, let me go back a year to my last term at Cambridge. I was invited to a summer party by Christine Smart (of assistant lunches secretary fame) and not knowing many people there, I started to talk to a handsome tall fellow undergraduate from Jesus College called Lawrence Mallinson. We got on really well and spent most of the evening huddled in a corner just chatting. We became firm friends and I subsequently bumped into Lawrence at a Cambridge May Week party, when we started to talk about what we were going to do when we left Cambridge.

I explained that I was due to start at the College of Law in Lancaster Gate in the September of 1980, in order to take my Law Society Finals – the next stage in my attempt to become a solicitor.

65 St Michael's Street, Paddington.

Lawrence was to start his training to become a chartered accountant with KPMG, one of the largest accountancy firms. He told me that he had just purchased a house in Paddington and was in the process of doing it up. The house was divided into two flats and he had inherited a sitting tenant in the top two floors – Sammy Graham and his wife and young daughter. He was converting the ground floor and basement into a self-contained maisonette and, once the works were complete, he would be moving in and would then be looking for a flat-mate to share the costs of running the flat.

Having loved the independence of living by myself in Cambridge, I dreaded the idea of returning home to live with my parents again. While I loved visiting my parents for a few days during the holidays and at weekends, I could not see myself living at home again.

I jumped in quickly and said that I would love to be his tenant and share his new flat at 65 St Michael's Street in Paddington, yards from the Edgware Road and Praed Street.

A rent was agreed and the location was perfect, just a five-minute walk from the College of Law. As soon as I returned to London, I joined Lawrence at the weekends and evenings, decorating the flat and within a few weeks the flat was ready to move into.

College started and I enjoyed my new life, having fun in central London while attending the College of Law in Lancaster Gate every afternoon for lectures.

Then something happened that changed my life.

Lawrence's parents, Anne and Terrence Mallinson, came for dinner. Over the dinner conversation, Anne asked me what my interests where. I said that although I was training to be a solicitor, I loved politics and explained that I had worked for a couple of MPs.

Anne told me that for the past eight years she had been a Conservative councillor on Westminster City Council and that with local elections approaching in May 1982, I should consider standing to become a councillor.

I was a bit taken back and explained that I did not really know what being a councillor involved. So, Anne tried to explain and suggested I attend a meeting of the council to get a flavour of what was involved.

My First Westminster Council Meeting

So, two weeks later, I was Anne's guest at a full meeting of Westminster Council in the 1960s refurbished council chamber, situated within the 1920s Marylebone Town Hall, now known as The Council House. I sat in the public gallery and watched my first council meeting. I was hooked.

In those days, the councillors would leave the meeting on a rota basis to have dinner in the adjoining reception room. Councillors were allowed to bring their guests to the dinner.

Dinner was a help-yourself buffet. So Anne and I piled our plates high with food and found somewhere next to each other on a long table, to sit, talk and eat our meal.

As I was mid-mouthful, a petite elderly woman appeared next to me and at the top of her voice, aimed directly at me, shouted 'You're sitting in my seat!'. The room stopped and everyone stared at me, as this lady stood and just glared at me. I was highly embarrassed until Anne suggested we both move to another table, which we duly did. That was my first encounter with the formidable and now late Councillor Pamela Batty, who would go on to become a dear friend, even though we frequently rowed about council policy.

As an aside, it was amusing watching my first council meeting. In those days the councillors ate their supper during the meeting. They would disappear to eat and then return to the debate. It was the Chief Whip's job to ensure that there were at least always ten Conservative councillors in the chamber at all times, so that if a vote by hands was called and lost, then so long as ten councillors stood up, a recorded vote would be required and a bell rung (like in the Division Lobbies of the House of Commons) requiring all members to return to the chamber to vote in a roll call.

The Chief Whip at the time was a lovely eighty-five-year-old called Wing Commander Bill Kearney who I believe spent most of the meetings fast asleep. As I sat there watching the meeting, the Labour councillors noticed that there were only about seven Conservative councillors in the chamber, as the rest were in the reception room stuffing their faces with food and drink.

The Labour councillors quickly moved a motion to increase the housing budget by four million pounds. On a vote by hands called by the Lord Mayor, the motion was passed and so the Conservatives present all stood but there were fewer than ten of them and so the original vote stood and no recorded vote could be held. The leadership were furious.

An extraordinary council meeting was called ten days later when the original motion was reversed, costing thousands of pounds to hold and poor old Bill Kearney was sacked as Chief Whip. From then on, the Council supper took place at 6 pm before the start of the meeting, with no food served after the meeting started.

Pondering my Future

A few days later, I went back to my parents for Friday night dinner and stayed over in my old bedroom until the Sunday night. Lying in the bath the following night, I started to think about becoming a councillor. I rather liked the idea of being called 'Councillor Davis'.

The following week, I called Anne and said I would love to become a councillor. She was delighted and put me in touch with the Conservative Party chairman in the constituency where I lived, then called Paddington. He turned out to be a neighbour and quite famous. Ian Harvey had been a government Foreign Office minister in the Macmillan government but had to resign in 1958 when he was found one night in Hyde Park having sex with a guards officer from the Household Cavalry, when sex between men was illegal.

Ian took a liking to me and decided to help me. Of course, as I was just a year out of Cambridge, I thought I was God's gift to mankind and expected to be offered the safest seat on the council. Alas, I was mistaken.

I lived in the Hyde Park ward and there was a vacancy there, so I thought that as a local resident I would be a shoo-in. But this was 1981 and the relatively new Prime Minister, Margaret Thatcher, was highly unpopular and the Conservatives trailed in the opinion polls. The last local elections had been won by the Conservatives, as they had taken place during the bad days of the Callaghan government with Margaret Thatcher very popular. Fearing the worst, several newly elected councillors who had won seats in 1978 with slim majorities thought they would lose and so were seeking to move to safer seats such as Hyde Park ward. I soon realised after talking to several members of the ward committee, that I had little chance of being selected for Hyde Park in competition with these experienced councillors.

I decided not to put my name forward and instead I joined the selection committee as a member living in the ward. My hunch was correct and several councillors were vying for the seat and eventually Pamela Batty, who had earlier berated me, but was a hard-working councillor and who had won the marginal neighbouring Bayswater seat four years earlier, was the successful candidate.

I therefore turned my attention to the Hamilton Terrace ward in St John's Wood and was granted an interview. Within a few weeks, I appeared before the selection committee chaired by a formidable lady, and a wide range of difficult questions were put to me. Alas I was called later that evening to be advised that I had not been selected and that one of the other Bayswater councillors had been chosen instead, bearing in mind his considerable local government experience. His name was Francis Maude (now Lord Maude of Horsham) who subsequently became not only an MP but chairman of the Conservative Party and then a successful cabinet minister in the Cameron government. No wonder he beat me to the selection.

At this stage, there were no more safe seats seeking a new candidate, so I had an idea.

Barnet

My parents were at this stage still living in the family house in Hampstead Garden Suburb in the London Borough of Barnet. I therefore decided to pretend that I was still living with them (although in reality I only went back at weekends) and applied to become a councillor in Barnet. The ward where my parents lived was looking for a candidate and I applied. The initial interview involved two elderly ladies interrogating me at my parents' home, presumably to see if I was genuine. Having passed that test, I was asked to the formal interview but was subsequently told that I had failed again. Not deterred, I was advised to apply for the nomination in the neighbouring Golders Green ward.

I applied and was interviewed in a grand house just off Golders Green Road. In the waiting room (the house owner's TV room) I met one of the other candidates being interviewed, a nice, rotund gentleman called Melvin Cohen. I had only a few hours to wait to receive the call telling me I had failed again. In retrospect, this was a blessing, as I would have ended up a Barnet councillor rather than having the successful career I did as a councillor in Westminster.

Melvin was the chosen one and has had a successful career on Barnet Council where he is heading for his 40th year on the council and has served as Mayor of Barnet and chairman of its planning committee. As chairman of the London Mayors' Association, I got to know Melvin and we became friends and we would often joke about who was the real winner that evening.

Back to Westminster

Turning my attention back to Westminster, I put myself forward for selection in the Labour-held ward of Little Venice. Traditionally a Conservative seat, we had lost it to Labour in 1978 and, while we were hoping to win it back, this was not certain. But again, I was unsuccessful and they chose, Robin Walker, who, although he did win the seat he retired at the following election after only one term.

The next seat up for selection was Bayswater ward. This had been won by the Conservatives in 1978 but with the unpopular Thatcher government affecting the polls, it was widely believed that the seat would be lost to Labour. Two of the sitting councillors had found safer seats and the third had decided to retire. So, I decided to have a go, thinking that a marginal seat was better than nothing as I had clearly failed to obtain a safe seat in either Barnet or Westminster.

I was pleasantly surprised to be chosen with two other new colleagues, Neil Heywood, whose wife I knew through my involvement in the Tory Reform Group, and Simon Mabey, who had just been married and had stood unsuccessfully four years earlier in another ward. We formed a great team and were determined to fight a good and energetic campaign to regain the ward.

We started the campaign in late 1981 with canvassing sessions three times a week and on Saturday mornings with a street stall outside the supermarket (now a Waitrose) on the corner of Porchester Road and Bishop's Bridge Road. It was tough going. Thatcher was two years into office as Prime Minister and introducing many hard-hitting policies and so widely hated. Door after door was slammed in our face with the electorate telling me where to go. It was an uphill struggle and I was getting very depressed.

Canvassing one day in the large council estate on the southern boundary of my ward – the listed Hallfield Estate designed by Berthold Lubetkin (architect of the world-

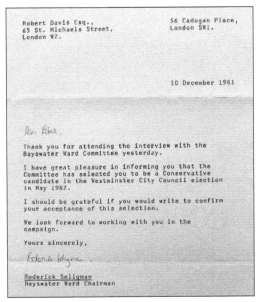

ABOVE *The letter confirming my selection as the Conservative candidate for the Bayswater ward in the 1978 local elections.*

RIGHT *Canvassing in 1982 with the local MP, (now Sir) John Wheeler.*

The Hallfield Estate, Bayswater.

renowned Grade 1 listed penguin pool at London Zoo) and Denys Lasdun (architect of the National Theatre) – I learnt from an elderly lady I had canvassed that the residents' association on the estate held a weekly bingo session on Tuesday nights in the estate's community hall.

I went to the next one and introduced myself to the organiser, one of the elderly residents on the estate. I was introduced to the participants who numbered about thirty residents. The organiser suggested I call the numbers out as I withdrew the numbered balls from the machine.

I was a great success and for the next six months I called the numbers at the Hallfield bingo sessions every Tuesday, and in doing so, made lots of friends among the participants and more importantly a lot of fans and supporters who ensured that they, their family and friends loyally voted for me in the forthcoming election.

Over the months of calling numbers – from 'Legs Eleven' to '21 – Key of the Door' – I helped many of the members with their personal problems, from legal advice to helping them get a new kitchen sink from the

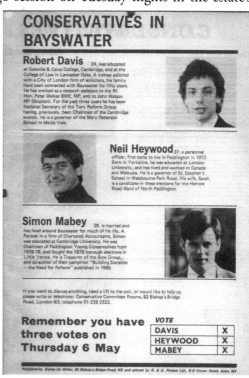

My first election address – April 1982.

council and getting their daughter a new council flat to helping them complete complicated forms.

Many years later, while canvassing Hallfield I was invited into a flat by a resident who remembered me and my bingo calling and was keen to show me a framed photo of myself on her mantelpiece. She said she had never forgotten my kindness all those years ago and had continued to watch my progress over the years. I must admit to shedding a small tear as I left.

There were also the reports from fellow councillors and canvassers who visited Hallfield over the subsequent years that many residents spoke highly of me and my contribution to the community.

As I described earlier, what changed my life started 8,000 miles away when President Galtieri of Argentina decided to invade the British Falkland Islands.

Up until then, despite my hard work on the Hallfield Estate, canvassing was depressing with household after household having a go at us, criticising Mrs Thatcher and her government. Then news arrived of the Argentinian invasion of these British Islands that most people had never heard of, let alone knew where they were.

Senior members of the Westminster Conservative Party sent us all an edict that we were to stop canvassing, as it was assumed the bad canvassing experience would be made much worse with voters blaming Thatcher for what was happening.

A few days later, Thatcher announced that she was sending a Task Force of warships to regain the Islands for the UK and we were allowed to re-commence canvassing. And what a surprise. As you knocked on doors, the residents came out to kiss me and talk of how amazing Margaret Thatcher was, in sending the troops to the South Atlantic. From the wicked witch from Finchley to the fairy godmother in a matter of days. And by the end of April, the British troops had re-taken the Island of South Georgia and by the time of the local election on Thursday 6th May 1982, the war was in full gear and the tide had turned in favour of the British. Despite the loss of HMS *Sheffield* and the British sinking of the Argentinian light cruiser the *General Belgrano*, support for the Prime Minister remained high.

The emergence at the same time of the new Social Democratic Party (the SDP) as a serious political contender, who had hard-working candidates standing against me and my two colleagues, meant we were still pretty nervous as election day arrived.

Many friends joined me to 'knock–up' – the art of reminding those voters who we had recorded over the previous six months as agreeing to vote Conservative, to actually go out and vote.

The Count

The count was to take place the following day at the Porchester Hall in Bayswater, so I went home exhausted after the polling stations closed at 9 pm that night (the law was only changed some years later requiring polling stations to remain open until 10 pm).

I tried to stay awake, to watch the results from the other London borough elections coming in and, while they looked encouraging, we had no idea what would happen in my marginal ward.

The next morning was my mother's birthday and I invited her to join me at the count. I hoped this would be a good omen and, moreover, the count was taking place in the Porchester Hall, where my parents had had their formal dinner after their wedding, some twenty-five years earlier.

It was a nerve-racking few hours but when the results were announced, we had won the election with all three Conservatives getting elected with an amazing majority of about 300. And what was most rewarding, was that I came top of the poll, beating my two colleagues. I put this down to my bingo calling!

The die was cast. I was elected a councillor and later learnt I was the youngest member of the council and one of only three Conservative councillors under the age of thirty. What I did not know that day was that I was to spend nearly thirty-seven years as a Westminster councillor and retire as the longest-serving councillor in the council's history.

Chapter 11

My Life as a Public Servant

First Step – A Leadership Election

Within twenty-four hours of being elected to Westminster Council for the first time, I found myself at the centre of a leadership fight.

The Leader of the Council at the time of the election was David Cobbold, the senior partner of a large firm of solicitors. But it was quite clear that he was part of an old guard that had been running the council for years. Both David and most of his chairman's group (this was well before cabinet-style local government when the council was run not by a cabinet but by a series of committees) were in my eyes, as a twenty-four-year-old, very old. In reality they were middle aged, although several were certainly in their seventies or eighties. The one exception was Shirley Porter, the Tesco heiress.

Shirley was the younger of the two daughters of Tesco's founder Jack Cohen. When she was old enough to take on responsibilities in the family business, it was not then acceptable for a woman to do so. Instead, her elder sister's husband and Leslie – Shirley's husband – were taken into the business. After Jack retired, Shirley's brother-in-law took the helm of the business but that did not last. Leslie soon took over and was an extremely successful chairman and took the business to new heights.

Shirley concentrated on her golf and once she had become Ladies Captain of her golf club, she looked for something else to keep her busy. It was not long before she was elected a Westminster City councillor for the Hyde Park ward where she lived and within a short time, she became chairman of the council's Highways Committee.

At the time, the Highways Committee was responsible for keeping the streets clean. This was never a high priority and dirty streets were the norm. Well, that was until Shirley took up the chairmanship. Within months, keeping the streets clean became the council's top priority and Westminster became well known for its clean streets. With bright green uniforms for all the sweepers (when they had previously worn undistinguished clothes and went unnoticed) they were now high profile with all the street rubbish bins and the sweeper's push carts painted in a similar bright green livery.

This was also the time when Ken Livingstone was running the Greater London Council (the GLC) and being accused of extravagant expenditure. In response, Shirley had created a campaign called WARS (Westminster Against Reckless Spending) with a by-line of 'I love London – but it's over-rated' and plastered the council's buildings with WARS posters and banners and at council meetings she and colleagues wore WARS T-shirts. So, her reputation for action was in complete contrast to the current leadership who were laid back and left the council to be run by the officers.

With a new intake of councillors, Shirley decided to go for the leadership and challenge the then Leader, David Cobbold.

Having just been elected, I knew very few fellow councillors personally but the exception was Peter Hartley, who had been elected four years earlier. He was first to call me after the election and sought to convince me to vote for Shirley Porter.

I had only met Shirley once before, just after I had been selected for the Bayswater seat. It was at a memorial service and I plucked up courage to introduce myself. I explained who I was and she abruptly asked me why I wanted to become a councillor. I explained that I liked helping people. She huffed and said that 'that was not a sufficient reason' and turned and walked off! My first encounter with the great Shirley Porter!

Back to the leadership election and Peter arranged for me to meet Shirley for breakfast at her penthouse in Chelwood Court on the Hyde Park Estate.

David Cobbold never once made any attempt to speak to me. I was too junior and a new boy. This summed up everything about his leadership.

There was also to be an election for Deputy Leader (a post I subsequently held for a record ten years). The incumbent, Sir Jonah Walker-Smith, whose late father had been a member of Parliament and a baronet, was being challenged by David Weeks, who worked for G-Plan, the furniture company. David did invite me for a drink with him at a Victoria pub.

When the vote came, I voted for both Shirley and David, the two who had made an effort to speak to me. But I was also impressed by Shirley's vision for the future and her record of achievements as Highways chairman.

At my first meeting of the Conservative Group on the Council, the leadership elections were held and David Cobbold retained the leadership by two votes. That said everything. David Weeks lost the deputy leadership too.

Learning the Ropes

Within a few days of my election, I was called to see the Chief Whip and told not to open my mouth at meetings for at least a year, not to expect to be promoted to a vice-chairmanship of a committee for eight years or a chairmanship for twelve years. The secret, I was advised, was to behave, be quiet, listen and learn.

In the meantime, Shirley was asked by the Leader to chair a small informal group of councillors to look at how the council could modernise. I quickly volunteered to be a member of this Policy Review Sub-Committee, as did the other youngish councillors who had supported Shirley and what she was trying to achieve.

Shirley was also given a new chairmanship, that of the General Purpose Committee, which had responsibility for a variety of miscellaneous departments. While most of the new councillors sought membership of the Highways Committee, as this had been the most high-profile committee under Shirley's chairmanship, I had recognised that the profile was down to Shirley and not the committee and so I sought membership of the General Purposes Committee and this brought me within sight of Shirley, who in turn took me under her wing.

As one of the new boys, I was expected to sit on a second committee and without much choice I was given membership of the Personnel Committee. With responsibility for human resource issues (as this area of the council's work is now known) it comprised a chairman (the elder statesman Tony Prendergast – married to a member of the Marks and Spencer family) and included myself, another Conservative and a lone Labour councillor. I sat next to the Labour councillor – one Diane Abbott.

The Personnel Committee also had co-opted to it a local representative from the trades union that covered City Hall, namely NALGO (the National Association of Local Government Officers), now Unison. Its representative, who attended the committee and could speak but not vote, was one Jeremy Corbyn, more recently Leader of Her Majesty's Opposition.

Without trying to spread too much gossip, after the meetings ended, I could not help but see Diana and Jeremy walking off together down Victoria Street.

One thing I will always remember from those first few weeks as a councillor was my attempt to meet the Chief Executive of the council, David Witty. Wanting to push myself forward in those early days, I wrote to the Chief Executive who I had yet to meet, to ask if I could arrange a meeting to get to know him. A week later, I received a reply from his secretary, to the effect that 'the Chief Executive did not meet new councillors'.

This said everything about the regime I found myself a part of and before Shirley's eventual success at taking over the leadership of the Council. Years later, when I was Chief Whip, I made sure that the Chief Executive had a one-to-one with new councillors immediately after their first election.

I was one of a number of keen newly elected councillors put on Shirley's new Policy Review Sub-Committee. This was David Cobbold's sop to her. He had been taken aback by her challenge to his leadership and was clearly aware that her strong support came from those who had been newly elected. He therefore allowed her to harness their keenness by putting them on this committee, which she saw as a 'blue sky' think tank to consider new policies which she would introduce when she sought the leadership again. David Cobbold had hinted to her, after his narrow success, that he would likely stand down the following year, allowing her a free run at the leadership.

The committee met within weeks of my being elected for the first time. I was raring to go and to start making decisions. I soon realised that a new backbench councillor had little power or responsibility. After a lengthy discussion about what was wrong in the council, we were all given departments to research into and see if we could come up with some ideas for improvement. I was allocated the libraries.

The Libraries Review

Now, when I get set a task, I do it thoroughly. I immediately contacted the City Librarian Melvyn Barnes. Melvyn was highly recognised as one of the country's leading librarians, having served as president of the Library Association and president of the International Association of Metropolitan City Libraries. Several years later, he left Westminster to be City Librarian at the City of London.

Melvyn was a little suspicious but he was keen to help and introduced me to his four deputies. We agreed a programme whereby I would be escorted over a period of two months around all our libraries and central offices, to learn how our Library service ran. It was, I must accept, recognised as the best local government library service in the country but I was determined to see if I could improve it.

My libraries report.

I should also mention that Westminster was the first local authority in London to establish a public library. This started as the private library of the Westminster Literary, Scientific and Mechanics' Institution founded in 1837 in Great Smith Street, but when it ran out of money and was forced to close, the Vestries of St Margaret and St John (the predecessors of the council) acquired the premises and its books and reopened it as a public library on 10th March 1857. It is now the famous Indian restaurant 'The Cinnamon Club'.

I used the tours of the libraries to speak to members of staff at all levels and to engage with library users. I soon discovered numerous anomalies which I felt required addressing.

I still have a copy of my report. The Introduction says: 'I have spent since Christmas 1982 working on this report, visiting numerous library departments and talking to the people involved in the day-to-day running of the service.' I went on to explain that 'I have sought ways in which the service can be improved within existing resources, as well as a means of reducing inefficiency and of cutting waste and duplication, while ensuring that the Library Service as such retains its fundamental responsibilities towards the community of today and tomorrow.'

My report made numerous suggestions. These included a new logo for the libraries (shown on the front cover of the report), which was fun and easily distinguishable as representing a library.

I also suggested a new slogan:

> *'I thought Reading was a town in Berkshire*
> *until I discovered Westminster City Libraries'*

Sadly, neither were adopted due to officer resistance.

I also suggested we started selling books as well as loaning them, that we sell off old books and tapes and other material no longer being used (as they now do), that we convert the library windows into display units which could be rented out for promotions thereby producing income, that we rent out wall space in the libraries for advertisements, that we vary opening hours to suit the demands of the users, so extending opening into the early evenings for residential parts of the City while reducing evening openings in business areas.

There were about one hundred recommendations in total plus specific recommendations for each library, such as bringing in to public access use, space in basements and in upper parts of the library buildings, which were used for storage rather than for extending the book collection.

A more controversial suggestion, which never saw the light of day, was to sell advertising space on the front of all the books.

But the one proposal that set the cat among the pigeons was my proposal to amalgamate or close specific libraries. The north-west of Westminster had two libraries near each other in predominantly residential areas, one in Sutherland Avenue and the other at the top end of the Harrow Road. Both were relatively small and the Maida Vale one (a converted church) was held on a lease, costing us money in annual rent. We owned the freehold of most of our libraries. At the same time, the council owned a large high-profile building at 313 Harrow Road (half-way between both the libraries), which was underused. I suggested that the two libraries be merged into one newly refurbished one on this new site. This did not go down well! However outdated the existing buildings were, the users liked them where they were.

Despite some of my suggestions being more controversial than I thought, the report was extremely well received not only by the library staff themselves but also by my own colleagues, who realised for the first time what a hard-working and capable councillor I was.

Leadership Re-run

A few months after the report was circulated to staff and colleagues, the annual leadership election was due to take place. This time, David Cobbold had decided to stand down and his deputy, Sir Jonah Walker-Smith, put his name forward as Leader, on the 'let's not change anything' ticket against Shirley's 'I want to change everything we do' ticket. David Weeks stood again as Deputy Leader and came out supporting Sir Jonah while Angela Killick stood under Shirley's umbrella for the deputy leadership.

The result was a win by just one vote for Shirley with David winning the deputy leadership. Shirley soon swept out the old guard of elderly councillors who made up David Cobbold's Chairman's Group and brought into all the principal jobs young maverick councillors like Peter Hartley, Alan Bradley and Patricia Kirwan (who had just lost her seat on the Greater London Council but had been elected to Westminster with me in 1982). I was promoted and given the chairmanship of the Leisure Sub-Committee and made vice-chairman of the Environment Committee under the chairmanship of Peter Hartley, a good friend of mine. Don't forget these were the pre-Blair days when councils were based on committees and cabinet-style government had not yet been introduced.

I was delighted and honoured. I had risen to the ranks of a chairmanship, albeit a sub-committee, within a year of my election to the council. And this was only eleven months after I had been given that lecture that I should not expect to receive a vice-chairmanship for eight years.

Furthermore, Shirley asked me to become the equivalent of her PPS. A parliamentary private secretary or 'PPS' is a parliamentary term whereby younger members of parliament are made PPSs by a government minister, which involves a lot of bag-carrying for the minister but also includes attending meetings with the minister, briefing colleagues on behalf of the minister and being the minister's eyes and ears. It's a great training ground for future promotion. My new responsibilities included attending Chairman's Group (comprising all the major committee chairmen – not me as I only chaired a sub-committee) where all the major decisions were taken. It was great experience, as I was able to watch the leadership running the council from close quarters. I certainly learnt a lot from Shirley and other senior colleagues, which I put to good use when I eventually reached the ranks of a senior councillor.

The Little Portland Street Library

Now I was in charge of the Library Service as chairman of the Leisure Sub-Committee, I set about trying to implement the recommendations of my libraries report. There were so many that we had to phase them over a number of years. One of the important ones that I wanted to include in the first batch of decisions was to close the library in Little Portland Street, in east Marylebone. The reason was based on the fact that this library was small and not only leasehold (so we were paying a large rent for these central London premises) but it was not well used, situated in a predominantly business area. Over subsequent years, the residential population in this part of east Marylebone has increased substantially, but this was not the case in 1984.

Portland St. library axed

THE Little Portland Street Library in the heart of Marylebone has been given the axe by Westminster councillors.

The council's environment committee voted last week to close the library after it heard a deputation from the Save Our Library Campaign.

The decision still has to be formally rubber stamped by the full council meeting on December 5.

It has angered local residents who were campaigning against closure.

Ms. Rosie Slater, a campaign organiser, said of the vote: "We haven't given up yet. We're actually quite angry and resentful about the whole thing.

"We feel the amount of money being saved — £120,000 next year — is absolute peanuts in terms of Westminster's overall spending."

East Marylebone was a deprived area and the library was about the only service the council provided.

She thought that local businesses which paid a lot of rates deserved something directly back for their money.

Local people — especially the elderly — would not be able to get to the nearest alternative libraries, such as the one at Marylebone Road.

Councillor Robert Davies, the environment committee vice-chairman, told it that there were plans to expand the 'house-bound' service so people would still be able to get books.

The decision was taken and the library was to close early the following year. Everything was going to plan and then a month before the proposed date of closure a number of library users took over the library and announced to the press they had occupied it and would not leave until the council reversed its decision and agreed to keep it open.

When the sit-in continued beyond the first week, the police were brought in, but this just made things worse. The sit-in lasted about a month before a court order was obtained requiring the protesters to leave. By this time, the closure date had passed and the library never opened again. I was in the dog house for closing the library and for the resultant bad press. Shirley was not a happy bunny!

The Porchester Hall

One success I achieved as chairman of the Leisure Sub-Committee was to prevent the closure of the Porchester Hall and Baths in my ward of Bayswater.

The Porchester Centre (as it is now known – I changed the name during the process I am about to describe) is a massive leisure complex comprising two swimming pools, an extensive gym, Turkish baths, and two halls for hire for events from dinners and dances to conferences and exams. It also houses the principal library in north-Westminster.

The Porchester Centre in Bayswater.

However, when I took over as chairman in 1983, the place was run down. The second pool was being used for storage. Most of the library occupied a separate building around the corner and there was no gym. The area now used as a gym was an old boiler room. Here was a lot of redundant space too. The first floor of the pool side of the building comprised a large number of 'slipper' baths. Yes, these were baths to bathe in, each within a separate cubicle.

In 1982, there were hundreds of flats in the area with no bathroom or bath and so to wash yourself you would come to the public baths to take a bath. Hence the name the 'Porchester Hall and Baths'. Although there were many who used these baths, the council was upgrading its own properties by incorporating bathrooms with baths and encouraging the private sector to do so too, through improvement grants. The need for these slipper baths became redundant. Moreover, there were no proper changing facilities for those wishing to swim in the large pool. Instead, there were small single wooden cubicles surrounding the edge of the pool to change in.

The Porchester Pool and Baths had originally been built in 1925. Four years later, the large hall and library building also containing the Turkish baths were added. This replaced the original baths and washhouse erected in 1874 on a nearby site adjacent to the Whiteleys department store.

There was a lot of concern during my election campaign in 1982 as to the future of the place and its state of neglect. George Walker, a well-known retired boxer, was (through his company Brent Walker) a successful property developer and had converted the old Hendon Greyhound track into the Brent Cross Shopping Centre with its business partner Hammerson Estates. He also ran several leisure businesses. The rumours were that he had his eye on the Porchester Hall for redevelopment and the council were talking to him about selling the site to him.

On becoming a councillor, I soon realised that as a backbencher there was not much to do. Yes, I was on two committees but they only met once every six weeks, while full plenary council and group meetings were monthly but in between there were few meetings to occupy my talent and willingness to work hard.

So, shortly after being introduced to Eddie Pow, the Director of Halls and Baths, I told him of my concern about the future of the Porchester Hall and asked if I could be shown round the entire centre. He willingly accommodated me and introduced me to everyone who worked there. I left full of ideas for turning the centre around. On my own initiative and with full support from Eddie, I started writing a report on how I would propose we altered the centre to improve it, bringing it into the 20th century and making it more viable, thereby shelving any ideas of selling it off. To the locals, it was the centre of their community and the pool, the library, the Turkish baths and the halls were used by many who would have nowhere else to go if the place was closed down.

I also had a personal connection with the Porchester Hall. My parents hosted their wedding dinner and ball there. In the 1950s it was a very fashionable venue for weddings and in particular for Jewish ones, catered by Schaverien, a famous Jewish catering company.

But some twenty-five years later, I was a newly elected councillor, trying to save the Porchester Hall single-handed.

I spent months working on my ideas, drafting a report and discussing this all with Eddie. Eddie and I became great friends as a result and I would frequently be invited around to his home for dinner on the pretext of discussing the report.

I really liked Eddie and his wife, Ivy, and I would enjoy their company and hearing Eddie's stories about life in Westminster since the 1950s. Eddie was originally a swimming instructor, who taught himself how to become a pool technician. He worked

My parents on their wedding day on the steps of the Porchester Hall in 1956.

his way up the hierarchy, ending up not only as head of the council's Halls and Baths Department, but as a well-respected president of his professional body.

After a few months' research, I published my report. This included provisions for creating proper communal changing rooms for the pools and bringing back into use the smaller pool for teaching. I suggested decorating the walls of the large pool, once free of the changing cubicles, with a mural of scenes from the local area. I suggested selling off the library building in Westbourne Gardens and moving the library into the basement of the centre under the Great Hall. I also proposed reducing the size of the slipper baths as usage had fallen, and using the part vacated as a gym.

My Porchester report – 1983.

But how to pay for it? I realised that I could not just propose thousands of pounds of expenditure for carrying out the refurbishment required without a business case for doing so.

The Porchester Hall was not the only public hall for private hire that the council operated. We also owned a large complex of public halls in a building in Victoria. This was the famous Caxton Hall, which had been used by the Registrars Department and many a famous person was married there in its heyday.

Caxton Hall was a Grade II listed building and not only held many celebrity and high-profile weddings, but also many famous political meetings, rallies and a series of artistic events. Originally built in 1883 as the local town hall (before the creation of Westminster Council in 1900), it ceased being the central offices for the council when in 1900 the newly created council moved into offices in Charing Cross Road. During the Second World War, Winston Churchill used the building to give a series of major speeches. It was also used frequently by the suffragette movement.

But marriages were now conducted at the Council House in Marylebone Road. Caxton Hall was attractive but business was bad. It had about thirty different rooms for hire but with little investment over the years, it had limited electronic equipment and so found it impossible to compete with all the five-star hotels around Westminster which would offer far superior services to support the hiring of the venue itself. Despite the history associated with the building, I suggested we sold off the building for development and invest the receipts in refurbishing Porchester and this would include one large hall for major events for those who still wished to hire a hall.

The officers turned my report into a committee report and my committee approved it. Within months, Caxton Hall held a final farewell party and, the following month, work started on refurbishing the Porchester Hall and Baths.

*Unveiling the plaque to commemorate the 60th anniversary of
the opening of the Porchester Baths in 1925 with the grandson
of the councillor who had opened it.*

The Paddington library moved its entire collection into the main building, the smaller building in nearby Westbourne Gardens was sold and the Porchester Centre (as it was renamed) subsequently opened to a fanfare.

In 1985, to celebrate the completion of the works and the 60th anniversary of the centre first opening, I hosted a party at the Porchester and unveiled a plaque commemorating the occasion. This was to be the first of many plaques bearing my name and is one that is still in position some thirty-five years later. Well, it was the last time I checked!

A few years later, to celebrate Eddie Pow's years of service to the council and in particular to Porchester, just before his retirement, I officially renamed the small pool 'the Eddie Pow Pool'. Eddie was delighted and honoured. We kept in touch after his retirement and I would often visit him and Ivy in their retirement home in Stokenchurch. However, after only a few years of retirement, he sadly passed away. I attended his funeral. I subsequently lost touch with Ivy.

Lancaster Gate

The 1986 election was looming. I was concerned that I held a marginal seat and without the Falklands effect, I might lose my hard-earned seat. I had been working hard as a councillor, not only at City Hall but in the ward, but I knew that however much hard work I put in, I might still lose because of the national swing, which four years after the Falklands war may have been against the Conservative Party.

My fellow ward councillor, Simon Mabey, had already jumped ship and had been selected for the Belgravia ward and my third colleague, Neil Heywood, had announced he would not stand again. I was the last man standing.

However, I had my eye on the neighbouring ward, Lancaster Gate, which was deemed a safe seat. One of the councillors was retiring, so I knew there was a vacancy. Planning ahead, about nine months before the selection was to commence, I started befriending the elderly members of the Lancaster Gate Conservative ward committee.

For most people, Bayswater is an area between Hyde Park to the south and the flyover (M40) to the north, with the Kensington and Chelsea border to the west and Paddington Station, the border to the east. But in council terms, the area was at that time divided with a horizontal east-west division through the middle (running down Westbourne Grove and Bishop's Bridge Road), with Bayswater the marginal seat to the north, and Lancaster Gate the safe seat to the south.

As chairman of the Leisure Committee, I hosted a number of events for the council in the area, including celebrating the 60th anniversary of the opening of the Porchester Hall. I took the opportunity to invite the members of the Lancaster Gate ward committee to these events. I also attended all the Lancaster Gate parties too and started to befriend its committee members and ensure that they were impressed by how hard I worked, both locally and back at City Hall.

When I told the Agent and the Association chairman of my intentions, they were not happy. I therefore made a risky and brave decision. I wrote to the Bayswater ward chairman to advise him that I was not going to stand again for Bayswater and that he should find three new candidates, not just two. It was a big risk. I was turning down the opportunity for standing again in Bayswater and yet there was no guarantee that I would be selected for neighbouring Lancaster Gate or in any other ward. I had already been told that the Conservative Association for the southern part of the Council's area (there were two Conservative parliamentary seats and consequently, two Conservative Associations in the area covered by Westminster Council), would not look favourably at me seeking to get selected there as Simon Mabey's selection for Belgravia in the south of the borough had caused a storm.

With no other vacancies at the time, all the chips were on my selection in Lancaster Gate. Bayswater swiftly selected three candidates to fight the 1986 elections, which meant 'no turning back' either for Margaret Thatcher or me. However, a few weeks later, I was shortlisted for Lancaster Gate – but then horrified to discover that I was up against Sandy Sandford.

Sandy had been a councillor on Westminster Council in the 1950s and 1960s and was famous for introducing parking meters in the UK for the first time, as chairman of the Highways Committee in the early 1960s. We take them for granted now, but in the 1960s no one had been asked to pay to park on the street, let alone know how to use a meter.

Selection

Sandy Sandford had retired from Westminster to become a councillor on the Greater London Council, where he had risen to become one of the most senior councillors. But with the abolition of the GLC on the horizons, he was looking for political office elsewhere. Although he had an amazing record of public service, he was by this time in his mid-eighties.

Despite the tough competition, my hard work and schmoozing the committee members paid off and I was selected to fight the safe seat of Lancaster Gate with existing councillors Peter Hartley and Patricia Kirwan as my colleagues. The election went well for us in the ward and I was returned as the councillor for Lancaster Gate, where I would remain a councillor for another thirty-two and a half years, breaking all records as the longest-serving councillor in the council's history.

Election Problems

However, elsewhere in Westminster the Conservatives did not do well and nearly lost control of the council. They were saved by just seventy or so votes in Cavendish ward (east Marylebone). Had the councillors there not won, the council would have seen the Labour Party take control, as the majority slipped to 32–28 (although one of the Opposition councillors was Lois Peltz, who sat for the West End ward as an independent resident).

Shirley was furious. She could not believe she had come so close to losing control of the council and vowed to ensure that this would never happen again, at least under her watch.

I mentioned Lois Peltz. Lois and her colleague Brigadier Viner had surprisingly won the two seats in West End ward in 1978. West End ward included Mayfair and the thought of the Conservatives losing this seat was not even on the agenda.

But there was a very good reason. The ward also included Soho and by the early 1980s, the council had lost control of the spiralling sex industry there. There were hundreds of sex shops, sex-related clubs and venues mainly controlled by the Maltese mafia. Many were rip offs rather than sex establishments. Guys on a business trip to London or away with the lads for a few days, would be looking for fun. These of course were the days before the internet and so Soho was the main place to find that fun.

'Near Beer' bars would entice these men into the premises with photos of beautiful almost naked women displayed outside and promises of fun inside. But once in the establishment, you were taken to your seat in a dark basement and told that it was compulsory to buy a drink. You were then advised that they only sold champagne and that this came by the bottle. After £100 was paid for a bottle (cash up front of course) the champagne was produced comprising nothing more than sparkling water as the premises had no alcohol licence. A girl would then arrive. She would frequently be much less attractive than on the photos outside and she would demand her own (expensive) drink which was charged to the customer. After some flirting, she would make an excuse and leave without anything happening. The customer would get annoyed only to be confronted by two large bouncers and led to the exit and told not to make a fuss or else! Too frightened and embarrassed to complain to the authorities, the Near Beer bar owner had got away with it again. You would think the customers would cotton on, but they didn't and millions were made. Of course, no taxes or VAT were paid to the authorities.

Shop after shop were sex-related and the area soon became the centre for vice, prostitution and drugs, as well as the handling of stolen goods. The council was then run by a number of elderly men in grey suits who had no idea, let alone cared, about what was going on and despite claiming they were doing what they could, they did very little. The local residents' association, fed up with the way Soho had deteriorated, decided to put up two candidates (it was at that stage a two-member ward) to fight the local election. Lois and Viner stood as independent residents against the sex industry and on a ticket demanding the law was changed to control the industry. Surprise surprise, they won by about sixty votes and the council had to take note.

As a result, contact was made with the Home Secretary and within a few years legislation was brought in to give councils the powers to licence sex establishments (there were no laws before then). The council worked with Customs and Excise and teams of officers from the Excise Office swarmed all over Soho searching for VAT records. Within months, most of the businesses had closed save for a handful who sought legitimacy by applying for a licence from the council and paying a hefty annual fee.

Viner retired from the council in 1982 and Lois's running mate as the residents' candidate at the election that year was a local headmaster. But he was not well known enough to succeed against the Conservative candidate, David Avery, who was also at the time the high-profile GLC member for Westminster and a long-term resident of Soho. Both Peltz and Avery won, leaving only one Independent on the council. Lois won again in 1986 before being defeated in the 1990 elections.

Lois and Viner were the only two councillors elected to Westminster Council since its creation in 1900 who were not either a Conservative nor a member of the Labour Party. The council has never had elected a Liberal or Liberal Democrat councillor. Occasionally, a councillor has resigned their party whip and served as an independent but then lost or retired in the following election. This is very rare in local government.

Changes at City Hall

Following the 1986 election, Shirley immediately reshuffled her team. Still annoyed about the way I had handled the closure of the Portland Street library, she removed me from my chairmanship of the Leisure Sub-Committee and my vice-chairmanship of the parent committee and made me one of two Deputy Chief Whips. Basically, a non-job without any executive responsibilities. My only responsibility was to arrange the appointment of councillors and members of the community to a variety of outside bodies, where we had nomination rights. This included (in those days) governors of schools, places on the boards of housing associations and a variety of other societies and organisations who sought a member of the council on their boards.

It sounds an important job and powerful but in reality, it is far from it. The top jobs were not in my domain, as the Leader or Chief Whip took responsibility for those nominations and those left to me to fill were usually the ones that no one wanted. I was devastated. I thought my meritocratic rise through the council was at an end.

But I decided to redeem myself and play the loyal team member. I played the next year low key. As fate had it, this was probably the best thing that could have happened to me.

Exclusion

As I was only a Deputy Chief Whip, I was now excluded from Chairman's Group, the then equivalent of cabinet. Therefore, when Shirley took the members of Chairman's Group to Cambridge for a long weekend to discuss strategy and how to address the close shave that nearly cost us control of the council, I was upset at being excluded. But it turned out to be one of the best things that happened to me.

This was because, over that fateful weekend, the chairmen decided to create a new policy of 'Building Stable Communities' which would lead to the biggest scandal in local government and the suicide of one councillor and the surcharging and ruin of several others. But having been demoted and also excluded from that Cambridge weekend, I managed to avoid the heat and came out the other end (eventually) almost unscathed other than by reference to my friendship to Shirley. It shows that, one day, it can seem like you are at the end of your career, but with time, what initially seemed disastrous, turns out to be for the good.

ABOVE *David Weeks, Shirley Porter, Elizabeth Flach and me, visiting a street market – 1985.*

RIGHT *Me in Queensway within the Lancaster Gate ward sitting on a 'Cleaner City' sponsored litter bin – 1984.*

Chapter 12

Scandals at City Hall

Following the fiasco with the 1986 local elections, the years leading up to the following elections in 1990 saw the Labour Party in Westminster smelling blood. It was not long before they started an aggressive and high-profile campaign criticising everything the council had done and was doing.

Shirley Porter was not one to sit back and do nothing. She responded with her own campaign, claiming that 'an unprecedented campaign to wreck Westminster City Council has been launched by left wing extremists'. She argued that 'council meetings have been systematically broken up; a succession of strikes orchestrated; council facilities wantonly abused; officers intimidated and visitors to the public gallery [of council and committee meetings] assaulted'. She went on to say that

> crucial to this campaign has been a succession of smears, innuendo, out of context quotations and an expensive public relations campaign run by leading members of the Labour Party. Its aim has been to render the City Council unworkable and to discredit the majority Conservative Party group.

In a series of statements and documents she released, Shirley emphasised that 'Westminster City Council had a proud record of providing efficient, cost effective frontline services to local residents'. She went on to state that

> of course, we ruffle feathers. We are trying to improve local government for the better. Instead of living in ivory towers, we want to reverse the pecking order – customers come first in Westminster – the resident is always right!

As a General leading her troops into battle, she claimed that 'we have seen the damage caused by Labour elsewhere in London. They will not succeed in Westminster!'

The fight was on.

Building Stable Communities
Building Stable Communities (or BSC as it was known) was the new strategy devised at the Cambridge away weekend after the 1986 election (which had excluded me following my demotion). Its principal intention was to increase the number of council flats that would be sold to key workers (such as nurses, doctors, teachers, community workers). These were people important to the Westminster community and yet squeezed out by the high cost of

owning properties in the private sector while earning too much for public housing and so needing support to continue to live in Westminster.

The policies developed that weekend under the BSC banner also extended to a variety of other areas of the council's work, with a view to improving the council's reputation and winning back the support of its residents and, in doing so, ensuring that we never came close again to losing control of the council.

On 8th July 1987, the Housing Committee met and decided to extend the council's sale of council flats programme by an additional 9,360 properties, which was expected to generate approximately 500 sales per annum. This was an increase from an average of 20 a year.

Sale of the Cemeteries

Meanwhile, a crisis blew up over a decision taken a few years earlier. Peter Hartley (my fellow Lancaster Gate ward councillor) had agreed in April 1986 to the sale of the council's three cemeteries. None of them were in Westminster because of the shortage of space in the city. They had been acquired many years beforehand. Westminster's three cemeteries were in Mill Hill, Hanwell (in Ealing) and east Finchley.

By coincidence, the east Finchley cemetery was very close to my childhood home in Hampstead Garden Suburb and could be clearly seen from the playground of my primary school (Brooklands). I have memories of my childhood, playing in the school playground at lunchtime and looking across to the cemetery and watching funerals take place. Adjacent to the cemetery was a crematorium and from school we could often see the smoke from the tall chimney making patterns across the sky.

At the time that Shirley became Leader in 1983, the council had a large architects department, a large property department and a large legal department. Shirley and her fellow leadership team took the view (supported by majority of the Conservative group) that these departments needed to be slimmed down and private sector firms brought in, to carry out much of the work then being undertaken in-house. Architecture was a good example. Why have a large team of in-house architects when you can tender for a private sector firm of architects to design a building at a lower net cost?

The officers were totally opposed to the slimming down of the council administration and this led to numerous strikes and other political action. But Shirley was determined to see this through and, in time, the council did start to outsource much of this work. But, as a number of the senior officers were unhappy, they discreetly did what they could to be uncooperative. Accordingly, when specific projects were given to an external firm, the senior officers decided not to monitor the work or act as a filter before members were advised.

The Head of Property Services, annoyed with the politicians massively reducing the size of his department and not personally supporting the sale of the cemeteries, delegated full responsibility for handling the whole matter to a very junior and newly recruited officer. The eventual District Auditor's report into the sale concluded that 'too much responsibility, including that of carrying out most of the negotiations with the purchaser, rested with a comparatively junior officer'.

What happened was that the 'junior officer' was well out of his depth negotiating with a very commercial property dealer. The District Auditor's report went as far as saying that the officer leading these negotiations was 'outmanoeuvred by him [the purchaser] at every turn' and that 'members should have been better served by their officers'.

The three cemeteries owned by the council comprised not only the burial grounds themselves, which were nearly all full with little room for new burials, but a propagation centre (providing freshly grown flowers and plants for the city's gardens), various houses for residential staff and caretakers as well as some undeveloped peripheral land, ripe (it was thought) for residential house building.

In 1987, the cost of maintaining the cemeteries in immaculate condition was in excess of £400,000 a year. After advertising for offers, the Director of Property Services (through his junior officer) recommended to members the sale to a company who both the officer and the members believed was a Jewish cemetery operator, at a price of £65,000 (but excluding the propagation centre, which would be sold separately to a nursery operator for £120,000). This price assumed that the purchaser would be burdened with the cost of paying for the high-quality upkeep of the cemeteries with little ability to raise income because of the small number of vacant plots.

With regard to the vacant peripheral land, if planning permission were ever obtained for development (and this was by no means certain, as it was designated open land or cemetery use only), the council would receive an overage (proportion of any profits made on any such development). Furthermore, with regard to the various staff houses, if these were sold, then the council would receive thirty per cent of the sale price.

After contracts were exchanged, problems started to arise. Firstly, all the staff in the houses indicated that they would refuse to vacate, claiming legal rights to security of tenure which could only be tested in lengthy court proceedings.

In addition, the junior officer unilaterally agreed (after exchange and without member approval) to split the sale, so that the vacant development land would be transferred to one company, the cemeteries themselves would be transferred to a different company, the house at Hanwell to a different party and the residential property in Mill Hill to yet another company. It also became apparent that none of the purchasers were 'Jewish cemetery operators' or any sort of cemetery operator.

As completion approached, the staff living in the various houses within the cemeteries were continuing to refuse to leave without a court order (which would take months if not years to obtain) and so in order to ensure no delay in completion being effected, the junior Council officer agreed that the originally agreed sale price of £65,000 would be reduced to £1.00 to take into account that vacant possession of the houses could not be given and the fact that the cost to the purchaser of subsequently obtaining possession was estimated to exceed the contract price.

After completion of the sale, it subsequently became apparent that the original company purchasing the cemetery land had 'turned' the sale, immediately selling it on to a Scandinavian property company (which, it later became apparent, had never even seen the properties) for £1,250,000, on the basis that the Scandinavian property company thought that they could redevelop the entire cemetery and build an estate of private houses on it.

Meanwhile, under pressure from the politicians to use external solicitors rather than the in-house team of lawyers, the external solicitor that had been instructed to represent the council in negotiating the sale, while experienced in ecclesiastic law, had little experience in acting for a local authority and in particular in drafting deeds of transfer of burial grounds. Accordingly, the deed of transfer to the purchaser of the cemetery failed to include a reference to Section 33 of the Local Government (Miscellaneous Provisions) Act 1982.

As any lawyer or someone with some legal knowledge knows, a transfer of property that includes a restrictive covenant (a covenant not to do something, like not placing cattle on the land being sold) and who retains adjacent land would benefit from that restrictive covenant and can enforce the covenant, not only against the purchaser but also against any subsequent owner of the land.

However, if a deed of transfer of land incorporates a positive covenant (like an obligation to make a payment, or as in the case of the sale of the cemeteries, a covenant to maintain the cemeteries in good condition) then this covenant is only enforceable against the first purchaser, that is the party who executed the deed of transfer as purchaser. The covenant cannot be enforced against subsequent owners of the land.

So, as happened with the cemeteries, if the direct purchaser sold the land on to a third party subject to a positive covenant such as maintaining the condition of the cemetery, then the original seller cannot enforce the covenant against subsequent owners. It can still enforce against the original purchaser, but this would be of little use, if the first purchaser was no longer in existence (or had no assets to enforce against).

However, as anyone experienced in local government law would have known, if the original deed of transfer from the local authority includes a reference to Section 33, then the local authority has legal powers to enforce such positive covenants (the covenant to maintain the cemeteries in good condition) against whoever owns the land. This only applies to local authorities and only if Section 33 is specifically referred to in the deed of transfer.

Completion was effected and the cemeteries remained open for families to visit their departed relatives. Life went on as usual for a few years. Then, when the Scandinavian owners realised that there was no chance that they would get permission for developing their land nor recover the money that they had paid for the property, they stopped maintaining the cemeteries. Within months, the cemeteries became overgrown with waist-high weeds and with damage and destruction throughout the cemeteries including vandalised headstones.

As soon as the state of the cemeteries started to deteriorate, the council found itself unable to enforce the covenants to maintain the cemeteries to a good standard against the eventual owner because of the failure of the deed of transfer to explicitly refer to Section 33.

The widows of three men buried in the cemeteries, who would regularly visit their late husbands' graves, became acquainted with each other and soon started discussing the poor state and condition of the graves as well as the cemetery generally. It did not take long for them to start a campaign, to bring this to the council's attention.

The council initially ignored the problem, claiming the cemeteries were no longer their responsibility. But then the three widows started attending council meetings and sitting in the front row shouting out at the top of their voices about their concerns at the state of the cemeteries. At one stage, their shouting and screaming from the public gallery of the council chamber resulted in Shirley deciding to erect a soundproof glass wall separating the public watching council meetings from the councillors and officers. But after that caused a stir, Shirley backed down.

Egged on by the Labour councillors, the three widows got the local papers interested in the story. And not before long, the national media were onto the story. Front page photos of grieving widows, overgrown graves and sad stories kept the issue in the headlines. The council had to act.

The first thing that happened was my ward colleague and friend Peter Hartley, chairman of the Environment Committee and the councillor who pushed through the sale of the cemeteries, resigned in February 1988. The resultant by-election changed my life, as the candidate chosen to replace Peter and fight the by-election was Simon Milton, who later became my life partner and husband and who was knighted for his leadership of Westminster Council before becoming Deputy Mayor of London.

Over the ensuing years, attempts by the owners of the cemeteries to obtain planning permission were constantly thwarted. After years of embarrassment for the council and constant lobbying by the Labour group, by the media and by the families of those buried in the cemeteries, in June 1992, the council and the cemetery owners agreed for a transfer back to the council of all the cemeteries (less the vacant land and houses) for £4,250,000 and the council immediately reinstated the quality of the upkeep of the cemeteries. They remain in Westminster's ownership today.

Leadership Challenge

With the cemeteries issue still rumbling and BSC becoming more and more controversial, Shirley's leadership was now starting to be criticised by her own colleagues, leading to a number of them regularly rebelling. One in particular decided to stand against her in the annual leadership election. Both the Leader and Deputy Leader are always subject to re-election every April and when the Conservative group are happy with the leadership, the incumbents are re-elected unopposed. In April 1989, Patricia Kirwan, one of my fellow councillors in the Lancaster Gate ward, decided to stand against Shirley for Leader. Backed by some of the older councillors and those not happy with Shirley's style or her policies, the campaign got really heated, especially as both candidates were adept at getting lots of national TV and media coverage.

It was a close shave, but Shirley won by a handful of votes and immediately sacked Patricia from her position as chairman of the Housing Committee. Patricia was furious and announced her intention to cause mischief for Shirley from the backbenches. And this she did, in bucketloads, using her ability to get TV coverage as a former leading member of the Greater London Council (as the incumbent she had been defeated for the Paddington seat on the GLC by Ken Livingstone).

It was therefore not surprising when we subsequently heard that Patricia was talking to the BBC's *Panorama* programme about making a documentary about Building Stable Communities, despite the fact that she had been at the heart of the evolution of the policy.

Then at 9 pm on a Monday night (peak TV time) in July 1989, the BBC's *Panorama* programme broadcast a documentary that claimed to expose what Westminster was doing under its BSC policy. Many of the allegations were in my view exaggerated and just not true, or true but taken out of context. I do not want to go into the details of the allegations and facts in this book, as there have been at least two books written about the details of the allegations and resultant investigations for anyone interested. I would, however, suggest that the two main books were written from the viewpoint of those making the allegations against Shirley and the council and were not unbiased.

We will have to wait until publication of Shirley's own autobiography for her side of the story, which she has promised her family will only be published after her death.

Another By-election in Lancaster Gate

Patricia Kirwan and Tony Prendergast (a long serving councillor who had never been a fan of Shirley) both appeared in the programme criticising Shirley and the policy. Shortly after *Panorama* was broadcast, Kirwan resigned from the Council, causing another by-election in my ward.

Simon and I sprang into action to find an appropriate candidate to run in Kirwan's place and we wanted to ensure that that person was someone we could both work with.

Our agent advised us that he had someone in mind and that we should meet her. On the Sunday after Kirwan's resignation, Simon and I went to meet Olga Polizzi in her beautiful mews home near Hyde Park. The eldest daughter of Lord (Charles) Forte, the famous hotelier and brother of Rocco Forte, she is married to William Shawcross (the official biographer of Her Majesty the late Queen Mother) and mother (through her first marriage) of Alex Polizzi, the TV *Hotel Inspector* and broadcaster. Her son-in-law is the well-known restaurateur and TV food judge Oliver Peyton, who is married to Olga's other daughter.

After a cup of coffee in her conservatory and small talk introducing ourselves, with William occasionally joining us to say hello and help serve the coffee, we gave her the third degree, asking her a number of questions about her life, her commitment and her availability. She came up trumps and we agreed to back her for the candidature and within weeks she was elected with 63% of the vote.

The Enquiry

A few months before the by-election, a number of Labour councillors and their supporters made an official objection to the District Auditor about BSC, under the Local Government Act 1982. The District Auditor was an accountant appointed to audit the council's accounts and investigate unlawful expenditures of monies. John Magill, a partner in Touche Ross, the then District Auditor for Westminster, who had also undertaken the investigation into the sale of the cemeteries, started work on this investigation and report.

In January 1994, after months of work, Magill called an early morning press conference. Standing before a large group of press and TV cameras and adjacent to a report that, with its background papers, stood six feet tall on the table next to him, he announced that he had come to an 'initial view' that the decision of the Housing Committee on 8th July 1987 to adopt the council's new housing policy was 'unlawful, unauthorised and to the detriment of local taxpayers.'

He went on to state that he was 'minded to apply to the High Court for a declaration that the items of account identified [spent on pursuing the policy] are contrary to law' and that he would ask the Court for an order requiring six councillors (or former councillors) and four officers to repay to the council the expenditure unlawfully incurred of over £30 million. That amounted to over £3 million each, but as the debt would be 'joint and several', if the order was made then the council could seek repayment of the whole amount from any one of them and/or recover different amounts from each of them found liable. [Note, these would be civil proceedings and any monies held to be due would be owed as a civil debt. They would not be criminal proceedings.]

However, despite the pomp and ceremony in the way he sensationally gave his press conference, he did state that these were only his preliminary findings and that he invited those accused to submit their arguments in defence, which he would consider before then publishing his final decision.

Michael Dutt

Within a few days of his press conference, news was received that Michael Dutt, one of the councillors accused, had committed suicide by shooting himself in his flat. We were numb. Whatever had happened, it did not warrant this, the loss of the life of an intelligent, affable and successful professional with his future ahead of him.

Michael had been elected to the council at the 1986 election and, within a short period, found himself a committee chairman. To spread the limited chairmanships around her colleagues, Shirley frequently appointed joint chairmen of committees and so in 1987, he was appointed joint chairman of the Housing Committee with Judith Warner and together they led implementation of the BSC policies and the sale of council flats in particular.

Michael was also a doctor practising in St Albans Hospital. It later became apparent that he had been accused by a patient of some sort of malpractice and an enquiry into what he had allegedly done was ongoing. His colleagues have assumed that having realised he was going to have to defend himself on another front, it was clearly too much for someone who (from our understanding) had few friends. It was reported that when his body was found, it was surrounded by the District Auditors report and numerous background papers. He was only 43.

A friend claimed in *The Independent* newspaper (on 28th January 1994), that

Michael Dutt and the other people accused, have been pilloried in the media by the publication of the District Auditors report but they have not been allowed to release ... documents they believed would prove their innocence. He publicly denied the charges against him, but he would have been ruined by the costs of defending himself. If you drive a man to despair in this way, something like this is bound to happen.

The sad irony was that after the remaining accused councillors and officers submitted their case to the District Auditor, in his final findings published in 1996, he dropped this case against a number of the accused including both Michael and Judith. The only six he ended up accusing were Shirley (as Leader); David Weeks (Deputy Leader); Peter Hartley (the subsequent chairman of Housing); Bill Phillips (the Chief Executive); and two officers in the Housing Department.

The Legal Challenge

The matter was then referred to the Divisional Court and in 1997 the judges found Shirley and David liable to repay the costs incurred and lost by the council in pursuing the BSC policies but dismissed the case against Peter Hartley and the officers.

Shirley and David appealed that determination to the Court of Appeal where the judges, by a verdict of 2-1 determined the case in favour of Shirley and David, exonerating them from all the allegations.

I would point out that the principal allegation made was that the councillors and officers knew what they were doing was unlawful. One of Shirley's main arguments was that at every stage of the various processes, she sought legal advice to ensure that everything was lawful. This involved one of the country's leading Queen's Counsel, Jeremy Sullivan QC (subsequently a Court of Appeal Judge), who advised her and the council that to adopt the policies in question was perfectly lawful and where they were not, he advised as to what action was required to make them lawful.

In following leading Counsel's advice, how could a lay politician know that he (or she) was doing something illegal? Surely, Shirley argued, you had to know what you were doing was unlawful whereas she was assured it was lawful. Well, two Court of Appeal judges agreed with her! Everyone was delighted.

Not satisfied with this result and under pressure from Labour councillors and agitators, Magill appealed to the House of Lords, then the highest court in the UK.

The case reached the Lords in 2001 where the decision was reversed, with the peers finding Shirley and David liable for a surcharge of over £40 million, including interest and costs.

Many eminent lawyers I spoke to at the time said that the speeches (the name for judgments in the House of Lords) were very political and that a different composition of law lords may well have supported the views of the two Court of Appeal judges. But a final decision had been made.

I accept that I have only given you a summarised version of the facts, when the District Auditor's report ran to thousands of pages. I also accept that the facts I have described are principally as seen from my point of view. Yes, biased maybe, but this is my autobiography, not a book trying to set out all the facts and so I have relied heavily on what I understood, thought and believed during these difficult times.

My Mention

The one thing that I have failed to mention is that included in the District Auditor's Provisional Findings is a page about me. During my year on the backbenches as Deputy Chief Whip, I had been keen to impress Shirley as to my abilities and hard work and so be offered an executive job in her next reshuffle. I therefore undertook a number of projects for Shirley including writing a report on the priorities for our enforcement teams. The resultant report 'Review of the Environmental Protection Group' was considered by a private meeting of the Chairman's group in December 1987.

In the report (which was in my view prepared from a political basis for consideration by my political colleagues at a private political group meeting), I suggested that the council prioritise its enforcement work in the 'targeted' or more marginal wards. For example, I suggested that we were investing a large proportion of planning enforcement costs in enforcing against short-term lettings in blocks like Park West in the Edgware Road (in a safe ward) and that to be more political, we should shift these resources to more marginal wards. My naïve suggestions were given short shrift at the time and never taken further.

My report was a private paper circulated at a private meeting of councillors only, but it later became apparent that one of my colleagues had given my paper to the District Auditor.

Reference to me and my report was included in the District Auditor's original Provisional Report, just to prove that this targeting of certain 'marginal' wards was known to a wide range of councillors, not just the members of the Chairman's group. But he then makes no other reference to me throughout the report or during the following proceedings. This was presumably because there was clear evidence that my ideas and proposals were dismissed by my colleagues as not lawful and the evidence would also have shown that this policy was never acted upon.

The District Auditors Final Report was published by him at the beginning of May 1996 and no reference was made to me at all in that report.

Finding the Money

By the time the House of Lords made its decision and the council subsequently sought (on instructions from the District Auditor) to recover £40 million, Shirley declared that her assets were worth no more than a few hundred thousand pounds. David Weeks was never someone of great means and the council knew that it would not be cost effective to recover the monies from him.

But they took the view that Shirley had assets worth more than the £40 million. This was because Shirley was the daughter of Jack Cohen, who had founded Tesco and not only had her husband, Sir Leslie Porter, been chairman of Tesco, but it was believed that Shirley was a large individual shareholder in Tesco with what was thought were homes in London, California and Israel. The council concluded that she must have transferred all her assets to family members and to offshore hidden trusts.

After months if not years of trying to trace her wealth, they decided to apply to the Court for a worldwide injunction, freezing not only all her worldly assets but those of her entire family. This wide-ranging injunction was rare and everyone was surprised that the Court agreed to grant it.

Her son John was a successful businessman in his own right and when he found his assets frozen, he and other members of the family put pressure on Shirley to sort this out, once and for all. Therefore, at the beginning of 2004 (some seventeen years after the BSC policy was initiated), Shirley decided to act and to enter into negotiations with the council to find a compromise acceptable to Shirley, the council and the District Auditor.

By this time, Simon was Leader of the Council but he felt that he should not lead the negotiations or make the eventual decision because his long-term friendship with Shirley would be a conflict of interest. Simon therefore delegated the negotiations and approval to his then Deputy Leader Kit Malthouse (subsequently a cabinet minister in the Boris Johnson government).

As Shirley did not want to return to the UK, Kit flew with senior officers to a city in Europe to conduct a series of meetings. The outcome, which was approved by all the parties, was that Shirley would pay £12.3 million in full and final settlement. This brought this whole horrible affair to an end, despite Ken Livingstone (then Mayor of London) attempting (without success) to persuade the (Labour) Attorney General to prosecute Shirley for perjury.

My Thoughts

People frequently ask me what I thought of Shirley and the whole saga I have just described. I was a great fan and admirer of Shirley. She could be tough and abrasive to some, but once you got to know her, you soon realised she had a very soft, kind centre and a great sense of humour. She was my mentor and I will never forget the kindness she showered on me, the education she gave me to become an effective local politician as well as the opportunities she opened up for me at such a relatively young age. In particular, I admired the way she broke the mould in local government, sweeping out the 'ancien regime' and bringing in the young and the talented. She bulldozed through bureaucracy and traditional ways of working and introduced a series of more customer friendly initiatives from 'one stop services' to the high-profile street cleaning service. Using her experience of Tesco, the resident became the customer and the officers their servants. This was revolutionary at the time resulting in much resistance from the officers and the old guard, many of whom did what they could to disrupt her mission to modernise local government. What she introduced (to much criticism and opposition) all those years ago is now commonplace.

Her successes in improving the city and improving the Conservative vote as a result, brought jealousy from her political opponents. Furthermore, what she did in the City of Westminster very much reflected what was happening nationally with Margaret Thatcher and her crusade to modernise national government and recognise the importance of individuals over the state. Building Stable Communities was nothing more than Shirley's version of Thatcher's 'Right to Buy', bringing home ownership to everyone.

You also had to put what was happening in the City of Westminster in context with what was happening nationally. Labour councils up and down the country from Liverpool (with Derek Hatton) to Lambeth (with Ted Knight) were bringing the Labour Party into disrepute, particularly in managing local government. So, the Labour Party needed to bring down a high-profile Conservative council to balance their own negative publicity. Who better to attack than Shirley Porter in Thatcher's favourite borough? It was therefore not surprising that in the early 1990s, with Tony Blair's government-in-waiting and their politically motived journalist friends keen to criticise Conservative administrations, this whole issue was pushed to the top of the news agenda.

Working closely with Shirley over many years, I know exactly how she worked. She was an ideas and strategy person who left the details to others around her to develop and implement. As with all her policy initiatives, she expected her officers to do the hard work of bringing such ideas to fruition and in doing so, check that what they were doing was lawful. That is why in respect to the 'Building Stable Communities' policy, she ensured that officers obtained the advice of a leading barrister to confirm that the proposals were lawful and when he indicated some parts were not, she relied on the barrister's advice on what was required to be done to ensure its implementation was lawful. She demanded and expected that anything implemented passed the lawfulness test. As a layman, she had to rely on such advice. Indeed, that is what the Court of Appeal agreed (by a majority I accept). Accordingly, I cannot to this day understand how the House of Lords (in what I believe was a political decision) came to the conclusion that Shirley knew that what she was doing was unlawful, when two Court of Appeal judges accepted that she did not.

Shirley and I continue to keep in touch and I will continue to have fond memories of our time together at Westminster. As someone who was around at the time, watching at close quarters, it is my considered view that the city is a better place as a result of Shirley's leadership.

Chapter 13

Amusement Arcades

Shortly after becoming a councillor in 1982, I was made a member of the Council's General Purposes Committee which had responsibility for licensing, under the chairmanship of Shirley Porter.

One day Shirley called me to ask me to stand in for her at a meeting she was due to attend with a number of Wandsworth councillors about the issue of amusement arcades. So, after supper at home, I drove to Wandsworth for the meeting, with very little knowledge about the issue. But I did not want to own up about my lack of knowledge, as I was trying to impress Shirley.

The meeting took place in a large suburban house owned by Wandsworth councillor Lois Lees. I was introduced by my host to two of her fellow councillors, Ravi Govinda (subsequently to become Leader of Wandsworth Council) and Peter Bingle. Like myself, all three had recently been elected for the first time.

After a few drinks in Lois's sitting room, chatting and getting to know each other, she invited us in to her dining room for dinner! What? I had eaten well before I left, expecting this to be a chat over a drink. Being polite and keen to impress, I ate a second heavy meal! Not for the last time, I must admit. Years later as Lord Mayor, on a couple of occasions, I would attend an event and be invited unexpectedly to have lunch, only to leave for the next engagement where I was again offered lunch and of course, being the constant diplomat, I always ate the second lunch so as not to offend my host.

Returning to the dinner that night in Wandsworth, my new friends explained about the numerous problems associated with amusement arcades and the fruit machines they housed. There were no (or very limited) legal powers for local councils to restrict or control them and they were consequently opening in high streets throughout London. There were in particular no restrictions on children being allowed to enter these arcades and play on the fruit machines. Children and adults alike would frequently become addicted and this in turn led to other anti-social problems, from turning to theft to feed their addiction to children congregating around the arcades and causing mayhem as well as children playing truant from school to hang out in the arcades. Some children even resorted to stealing money from their parents to feed their addiction.

The Wandsworth councillors wanted to work with Westminster, as the other leading Conservative London council, to campaign for a change in the law to give councils more powers to restrict their proliferation and to add controls on where they could open (not near schools) and how they operated (such as prohibiting children under 16 from entering these premises or at least playing on the machines).

I agreed that it would be sensible to pursue such a campaign but I explained that I needed to get approval from my chairman Shirley Porter. So, the following day I went to see Shirley about the issue and she was keen to support them. Shirley offered to host a follow-up meeting which was held a few weeks later, when we were joined by Westminster Council's City Solicitor, Terry Neville who was also legal adviser to the London Boroughs Association (which represented all the London boroughs) and who had been involved with Shirley in successfully campaigning to change the law on the licensing of sex shops with Terry drafting the consequent legislation.

A campaign strategy was approved, with a further meeting to be held a month later. But the day before the subsequent meeting, Shirley called me to say she could not attend the next meeting and could I chair it for her. I did so and we collectively decided to create the Amusement Arcade Action Group and to invite councillors from Kensington and Chelsea to join us (they were the other leading Conservative London council at the time). Shirley never attended another meeting, always making excuses and so after about six months she suggested I remain as chairman which I did for fourteen years.

AAAG (as the Amusement Arcade Action Group became known) soon decided that we needed to employ a firm of lobbyists (as they were then known, although they are now called public affairs consultants). On a recommendation, we chose Richard Faulkner (now Lord Faulkner of Worcester) and his firm. To pay them, we wrote to all the London boroughs, reminding them of the problems associated with this issue and asking them to support us by becoming members of AAAG and paying an annual fee which would go towards paying the consultants fees. This was successful and we were off. We soon attracted member local authorities from around the country and at one stage had eighty councils as members.

In 1985, Terry left Westminster and became the senior in-house solicitor for the John Lewis Partnership. But he soon missed the cut and thrust of the political world, so in 1986 sought election to Enfield Council (where he lived) and after a successful campaign, became a councillor. His vast local government experience meant he soon rose to hold senior positions and in doing so, continued to be a member of the AAAG committee, bringing in Enfield Council as a paying member.

We started working with doctors and psychiatric consultants about the dangers of gambling and, in particular, youth gambling. With Richard's support, we soon found that our issue was something that the national media thought worthy of reporting and I started doing a number of TV interviews on the subject, for national and local news programmes like Nationwide and London Tonight.

I gave interviews to the national newspapers and several columnists wrote about the issue, frequently quoting me. One such columnist was Glenys Roberts who wrote a regular column in the *Daily Mail*. We got on very well and coincidently years later, Glenys became a Westminster councillor for the West End ward and we became colleagues.

Working with various gambling addiction support organisations, we organised a series of conferences on the issue, inviting MPs to address us together with academics and doctors. I also wrote regular newsletters, which we distributed to our members, to supporters and to other interested parties. These not only updated everyone on what we were doing but also kept our campaign alive.

I took a personal interest in the law of amusement arcades and the ability of local councils to control them. While Terry Neville was still Westminster Council's solicitor and legal adviser to AAAG and with Shirley Porter's support, Terry and I started writing new policies for amusement arcades applying to open in Westminster.

We were pushing at the boundaries of the law but based these rules on those introduced for licensing sex shops (which had been introduced a few years earlier). I took the view that we should restrict the number of arcades in given areas; we should ask the applicants to agree to voluntarily ban youngsters under 16 and ensure that they did not open near schools, churches and other similar establishments. If an applicant refused to accept these rules, we would argue that the council was being fair and reasonable in refusing to grant the application. We would then defend any attempt to challenge that decision at appeal. Although we lost several appeals against our refusals, we did on occasions convince an understanding judge to support our view. We were surprised how many judges did. The industry started getting worried. It was not long before they invited us to a series of meetings.

BACTA was the trade organisation representing the arcades and they started from an aggressive stance, arguing that the arcades were harmless. They were led in these negotiations by their chairman, Sonia Meaden (mother of Deborah Meaden, star of BBC TV's *Dragons' Den*), whose company ran a chain of arcades around the country. Initially we got nowhere.

At about the same time, we drafted simple legislation (with help from Terry Neville) and I spent hours writing a detailed case for a change in legislation, quoting a substantial amount of research undertaken by academics and medical specialists who were supportive of our case.

We managed to arrange a meeting with the Minister of State at the Home Office, the Department responsible for amusement arcade licensing, Douglas Hurd (subsequently Home Secretary and now a peer). I believe we made a good case. We argued that we were non-political and had support from councils controlled by all the principal parties. Douglas Hurd was very polite (as he always was) and agreed to go away and think about it and consult with his civil servants. But despite being patient and chasing on numerous occasions, we heard nothing further. By the time we managed to get a second meeting, the minister responsible had changed and we had to start all over again. Alas, we never did get the law changed.

With all this campaigning and research, after several years I had become an expert on amusement arcades and in particular on the law controlling them. As such, I was frequently contacted by both officers and members of local authorities around the country for advice.

Fed up with repeating the same advice, time and time again, I decided to write a book on the subject. After months of writing and getting Terry to proofread it and check the legal aspects, it was ready for printing.

A friend of mine designed the book and in early 1989, I arranged for several hundred copies to be printed. My mother was a housewife, looking for something to do from home. I produced an advert inviting councils to buy copies. I knew from my own legal experience that legal textbooks sell for a lot of money and I also knew that if a council wanted to buy a book as specialised as this, then the cost was not an issue.

The advert invited councils to buy six copies for £70. My mother, sitting at her dining room table, stuffed hundreds of envelopes and wrote out the address for the Legal Department and Licensing Department of every council in the country and posted the adverts over a period of a few weeks.

My book on the law of amusement arcades.

The response was amazing. The order forms were sent to my mother and on receipt, she bundled seven books into an envelope and posted them off. Cheques were paid into my account and it did not take too long for the costs of printing and distribution to be covered and I started making a profit for my endeavours.

With our campaign continuing to gain support and a lot of media coverage, BACTA, concerned that we might persuade the government to introduce restrictive legislation and because of the continuing adverse media coverage, decided unilaterally to introduce a new voluntary code in all their members' premises. This included a prohibition on entry for anyone under 16 years of age. We felt this was a success and a major step forward.

In 1996, with my election as Lord Mayor of Westminster imminent, I retired as chairman and passed the baton on to Terry, who continued to chair the group for several years before it was wound up. Sadly, legislation was never introduced but the industry did stick to their voluntary code and my book of advice on how to use the existing law (as evidenced by what we did in Westminster) allowed many councils to restrict many arcades from opening or only opening after agreeing to voluntary conditions.

Chapter 14

The Westminster Initiative

In 1990, I was invited by the Leader, Shirley Porter, to become chairman of the Council's Environment Committee and in doing so, I took responsibility for a new environmental project. Shirley has always been keen on environmental issues, years before it became fashionable. The idea was that I would chair a weekly meeting comprising officers from around the council, led by Dr Leith Penny, one of the council's senior officers.

The entire programme was called the 'Westminster Initiative' and under this umbrella we introduced a number of exciting new environmental programmes that at the time (early 1990s) were revolutionary. We were in many cases, the first council in Britain undertaking these green programmes.

It was to be a partnership and so we described the Westminster Initiative as 'an environmental partnership between the council, residents, voluntary organisations and businesses working together to protect and improve the environment in the heart of London.'

One of the backbones of the Initiative was a scheme that I devised and which we called 'the Citizens Task Force'. We created Citizen Task Forces in a number of areas, such as in Bayswater, St John's Wood and Marylebone. We recruited about twenty or thirty local residents to join and invited them to attend the quarterly meetings held in a local venue. We would divide the evening into three sessions, with guest speakers or officers addressing members for two half-hour slots and then finishing with a question-and-answer session.

The members of the Citizen Task Forces were asked to be the council's 'eyes and ears', monitoring the state of the environment where they lived. The Council could not be everywhere and so by recruiting local residents who cared about their area, they could report to us such issues as broken pavements, street lighting that did not work, pot holes and rubbish being dumped.

I designed a report card which on one side had

A leaflet describing the Westminster Initiative.

145

room for the complainant's name and address (these were the days before emails) and a list of issues such as 'broken street light' or 'pot hole'. The complainant had to tick the relevant box against the relevant issue. A further box required details of the problem to be written out. The reverse of the postcard-sized report card was the address of the relevant council department and a franked stamp allowing the card to be posted free of charge. The council then guaranteed to advise the complainant of what action had or would be taken within three days of receipt.

Members of the Task Force loved the report cards but problems arose when eighty per cent of the report cards being received every week were from one individual. Once I had ceased being in charge (I was promoted to chairman of the Planning Committee in 1992) my successor wound the scheme down, even though it worked really well. Years later a similar scheme was re-introduced but using the internet to report issues.

We introduced a 'Greening the City' programme by planting a series of flower displays around the city, particularly in high-profile areas. I had this vision of a 'ribbon' of bright red flowers all the way along the central reserve of Park Lane. This would be very impressive as one drove up or down Park Lane. Until then, the central reserve had just been grass.

The cost of a continuous ribbon was too expensive, so our gardeners planted a series of oval flower beds paced every hundred yards, in which they planted a large number of red geraniums. They looked magnificent. But as always, there was someone who complained.

The red geranium planting in Park Lane.

A well-known local resident wrote to the Leader complaining that these geraniums were too 'municipal' and made Westminster look like Milton Keynes. I was summoned to appear before the Leader and challenged over this. But I managed to argue my case and they were allowed to remain. They subsequently won an award and have remained until today. Every time I drive up Park Lane and see them, I give myself a pat on the back.

The roundabout under the flyover, where the Harrow Road meets Bishop's Bridge in Paddington with Little Venice to the north, had at its centre an area covered in bushes, which had become a dumping ground for rubbish. Under this greening project, we reclaimed the area and cut back the bushes. At the south-western side, facing Bishop's Bridge, I wanted to construct a floral clock. I had been to Switzerland on numerous occasions and had been impressed by their many floral clocks. I mentioned it to my Swiss friend Albert Kunz, who was the director of the Swiss Tourist Office.

My experience of floral clocks was that they frequently broke down. I mentioned this to Albert. He assured me that Swiss clockmakers were the best in the world and that he would guarantee that a Swiss clock would never break down unless vandalised. Despite officer reservations, I insisted we went ahead to create a floral clock. I also insisted that they use Albert to source a Swiss watchmaker to supply the clock mechanism. But the officers explained that under the council's procurement rules we had to undertake a full tender, but that they knew I wanted to go with the Swiss company recommended by Albert to ensure quality.

However, a different set of officers made the decision as to which tender to accept and they went for a British company, much to Albert's and my disappointment.

The floral clock and display were actually quite beautiful and after a grand unveiling, they were much commented upon. However, a few months later the clock started breaking down. I am afraid I had no choice but to tell officers 'I told you so'. After a few years, despite the locals loving it and once I had moved on to another council job, the officers removed the broken clock, leaving just a static floral display.

We also introduced a number of hanging baskets in streets throughout the city. We even persuaded 10 Downing Street to allow us to hang some in Downing Street and Norma Major (the Prime Minister's wife) joined me in a photo call outside the famous black door.

Street cleaning was always high on the agenda at Westminster since Shirley Porter's Cleaning-Up initiative in the early 1980s. But as part of the Westminster Initiative, we introduced a number of new cleansing machines. This included the 'Elephant Vac' which had a funnel like an elephant's trunk that came off the back of a small motor vehicle and was used to suck up leaves in the autumn. Fido, was a similar machine (similar to one I had seen on a civic visit to Paris) that hoovered up dog mess.

Norma Major unveils the hanging baskets in Downing Street.

I was conscious that dog mess was a big issue for residents and, while we encouraged residents walking their dogs to remove the mess themselves, in those days, they rarely did. So, one day, sitting in the bath, I had an idea that we should affix on lamp posts throughout the city condom machines but dispensing little bags for removing dog mess instead of contraceptives. We would charge a nominal amount to stop children removing them for no justifiable reason.

We approached a company which made the machines that dispensed condoms and they agreed to adapt them for our use. It worked and to launch the first one, we arranged for the newly appointed junior minister in the Department of the Environment, Lord Strathclyde, to join me for a photo call for the press and media. (Lord Strathclyde subsequently became Leader of the House of Lords and a cabinet minister under David Cameron.)

Breakfast TV wanted to do a live interview after the main photo call for the press and we were both keen to do so. As we went live, the interviewer asked the minister how the machine

Lord Strathclyde launching the 'pooper scooper' dispensing machine in St John's Wood.

worked and as the minister put in a coin to show how the plastic pooper scooping bag was dispensed, the owner of the house immediately behind the machine (which had been installed overnight on a lamp post) came rushing out of his house and, oblivious to the TV camera live-streaming the footage to the whole of London (it was live on BBC London News), screamed 'get that fxxxing machine away from my property!'

A very embarrassed minister tried to calm the man down, explaining what it was. But the resident did not care what it was, he wanted it moved away from outside his house. The interviewer soon returned the broadcast to the studio, explaining that this new initiative was clearly controversial. Once the filming stopped, we agreed to move the machine somewhere else to the relief of this resident. However, the machines proved successful and were rolled out around the residential parts of the city, but alas one of my successors had them removed when they became too expensive to maintain and people became more responsible, carrying their own bags with them.

These were the early days of recycling, but under the auspices of the Westminster Initiative, we made recycling a key element of the programme.

To support residents recycling, we designed an on-street mini recycling centre to be placed around the city. Comprising a series of large black bins, allowing different coloured glass to be separately collected, they also included paper recycling bins and separate bins for clothes.

The bins were surrounded by an attractively designed metal structure with a canopy above the bins and with concise signage. They were successful and can still be seen around the city, although in one street the bins have gone but the metal structure remains. These were the first on-street recycling centres in the country.

An on-street mini recycling centre.

We also designed a series of attractive and amusing posters encouraging residents to recycle more. These were erected on large hoardings around Westminster. A press campaign was launched and I have fond memories of one photo shoot in particular. To promote a new mini recycling centre in St John's Wood, we wanted an older resident to be photographed placing paper in the recycling bin with me.

There was no better resident to accompany me than my own 92-year-old grandmother Jane. I have on my wall at home the framed front page of the *Paddington Mercury* (the main local newspaper at the time) with Jane and myself placing piles of paper for recycling into the big black bin. Sadly, Jane died shortly afterwards, so it is a lovely memory for me.

By the time of the creation of the Westminster Initiative, Shirley had already set up the Considerate Builders Scheme. This brought together developers and construction firms working throughout Westminster, with a view to persuading them to be more responsible contractors, by limiting noise and disturbance and keeping their sites and the surrounding streets clean and tidy, as well as adopting more environmentally friendly practices. The scheme grew and grew and is now run nationally by a large independent and self-funded secretariat supported by the construction industry. You can still walk past building sites all around the country and see their logo on the site hoardings.

My grandmother Jane and I launch the recycling initiative.

We decided to follow the success of this scheme by establishing the Considerate Hoteliers Scheme, by bringing together all the general managers of the main five-star hotels and encouraging them to run their hotels with environmental concerns at their forefront, with more recycling, the greening of their hotels with enhanced plants and flowers and the provision of more bins around the hotels. Fifty hotels joined and although it is accepted that this is something all hotels now consider as part of their daily life, in the early 1990s this was not only a new initiative but one that the main hotels were keen to support. I would chair the monthly meeting of the committee until it became large enough to become self-sufficient.

As this was so successful, I decided to extend the scheme to restaurants by setting up a separate Considerate Restaurants Scheme on a similar basis to the hotel one. I persuaded Earl Bradford, who owned Porters, a restaurant in Covent Garden, to chair it. It too was extremely successful as restaurateurs seemed keen to be greener.

Another issue we now take for granted was clean air, but in the early 1990s no one really cared about this. As part of the Westminster Initiative, the council set up 'Exhaust Watch', which enabled residents to report

Lord Bradford and I launching the 'Considerate Restaurateurs Scheme'.

vehicles with smoky exhausts using pre-paid postcards (like the report cards use by the Citizens Task Force) and every few weeks council officers, with the support of the police, would conduct road blocks to test car exhausts.

Noise was a further environmental issue that became a major part of the Westminster Initiative. We set up a dedicated Noise Team, the first in local government, with a team of officers that would guarantee to respond within an hour of a complaint being registered. I insisted that this was available 24-hours a day, seven days a week and not just during office hours. Again, for many years, we were the only authority which provided a 24-hour service. The service investigated noise from parties, unruly neighbours, barking dogs, alarms going off for ages, noisy machinery as well as from road works and building sites. It is a service that continued until 2018 and one I am very proud to have established.

Under the banner of the Westminster Initiative, we also addressed graffiti and flyposting. I took the view that unless you removed it immediately, those responsible will continue flyposting and spraying graffiti on buildings and hoardings. Many a city in Europe is scarred by both and yet their local authorities just leave it, without any attempt to remove it. Before I took on the responsibility, the officers took the view that when graffiti or flyposting was found, we had to take action to require the landowner to remove it. This would take weeks and sometimes the offending graffiti and flyposting were never removed or just replaced. I emphasised that we had to take action immediately at our own cost. Without such investment, we would never get on top of the issue.

I set up a Flyposting SWAT Team which would remove the offending flyposting or paint over the graffiti within an hour of being called out. A team back in City Hall would then prosecute any company found to be behind the flyposting. It actually worked, and the city found itself without any graffiti or flyposting while the team was in operation.

There was a lot of flyposting on traffic light control boxes or telephone exchange boxes. These are the waist-high boxes found at road junctions containing either the control systems for traffic lights or the connection points for telephone lines. We worked with both the traffic light authority and British Telecom in designing new external covers for these boxes that incorporated uneven surfaces which made flyposting difficult. We also developed a paint that prevented the glue drying so that the posters would just fall off.

The noise initiative poster.

I was very proud of the Westminster Initiative and all that we achieved. I continued to be responsible for it after Shirley was replaced as Leader by David Weeks. I received a lot of recognition for what we were doing, especially in respect of the environmental initiatives (bearing in mind that we were the first local authority to take these issues seriously) and our awareness of such matters as air quality. I found myself in great demand, speaking at conferences around the country. The Conservative Party nationally had set up the Tory Green Initiative and I would be regularly asked to speak at their meetings.

As a result of my work on this project, David Weeks, the Leader of the Council, subsequently promoted me to chairman of the council's Planning and Transportation Committee, one of the most important jobs on the council. I was on the rise.

Chapter 15
The Day that Changed My Life

Following the controversy that resulted from the council selling its three cemeteries, my fellow ward councillor Peter Hartley, as chairman of the council committee responsible, resigned on a Friday afternoon in February 1988.

A by-election in my ward – Lancaster Gate – was therefore required. There were three councillors representing Lancaster Gate, myself, Peter Hartley and Patricia Kirwan. It was regarded as a safe seat and so I knew there would be lots of interest from hopeful councillors wanting to seek election notwithstanding the controversy that would surround the by-election as a result of the sale of the cemeteries.

I went to work as usual the following Monday and the morning saw me engrossed in my legal caseload. Then at about 11 am my phone rang. I reached over to answer it. My receptionist was on the other end telling me that a Simon Milton was on the phone and that he wanted to speak to me. Not knowing who he was, I asked the receptionist to ask him what he wanted. She called back after a moment and advised me that he was a friend of Melinda Libby (a friend of mine from my days at Cambridge University). I took the call.

Simon introduced himself as someone interested in standing in the by-election and requested a meeting so that I could brief him about the ward for his pending interview to be the Conservative candidate.

My first reaction was that this would be the first of many similar calls but with a busy workload at the office and every evening full of council meetings, I was reluctant to give him much time. I hesitated and explained that I was very busy and would have to check my diary.

He then said that he owned a restaurant in Bond Street and asked whether I would like to join him there for lunch one day. I responded immediately and without any hesitation. I said I was free that day and could be over at one o'clock!

I walked over to Bond Street which was no more than a five-minute walk away. As I entered the door of this brasserie called Milton's, I was received with a smile by Simon. He was gorgeous. My heart missed a few beats as I faced this extremely handsome man.

From that moment my life changed!

Although I was smitten from the moment we first

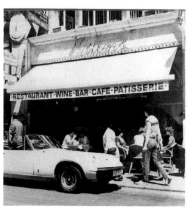

Milton's restaurant in Bond Street.

met, it took Simon a couple of weeks to reciprocate the feeling. However, we saw a lot of each other in the ensuing days, becoming closer and closer. Just three weeks after we met, I was invited to join Simon's family for the annual Passover dinner at his father's house. This was starting to become serious.

Within six weeks he was elected a councillor in the City of Westminster with a good majority, despite the cemeteries controversy hogging the headlines and within eight weeks we were living together as a couple and, apart from stays in hospital and the odd business trips alone, we never spent a night apart until his untimely death in April 2011.

I am often asked what was the spark I saw in Simon. Firstly, he was, in my eyes, intensely handsome and after just a few minutes of conversation over that first lunch together, I realised we also had much in common. Not only did we both have a fascination for politics but we both came from similar north-west London Jewish families and during our earlier lives we had had similar experiences from going to the same hotels on family holidays to attending the same college at Cambridge (although four years apart) and having several mutual friends.

Until I met Simon, I had had no serious relationship since my Cambridge boyfriend and I had gone our separate ways, several years earlier. But we just fitted together like a good jigsaw.

Simon's official photograph for his 1988 by-election, showing him as he looked when I first met him.

Chapter 16

Realising My Ambition

and in doing so breaking a record

After several years on the council, I had one ambition that I wanted to achieve and time was not on my side. Ever since I became a councillor, I had wanted to become Lord Mayor as I watched colleagues undertake their duties in the role. As someone who loved history, combined with pomp and ceremony as well as revelling in meeting new and interesting people, I thought I would make the perfect Lord Mayor.

In 1994, some twelve years after first being elected to the council, I invited Miles Young, the then Leader of the Council, for drinks at my home with Simon and told him that I had decided that I wanted to be Lord Mayor the following year. The only person who was entitled to it before me was my colleague, Alan Bradley, also a major committee chairman and with four more years on the council than me. But my understanding was that he was happy being a chairman and did not want to do the job yet. Miles was happy with my suggestion and said that if Alan did not want it, he would support me.

The reason I wanted to be Lord Mayor then was because my mother's cancer was getting worse and she was almost constantly on rounds of chemotherapy and I wanted her to be able to enjoy and be part of my mayoral year before it was too late.

I was the only candidate and things were going well until two days before the meeting to decide. I was having supper with other councillors, as is usual, just prior to a full meeting of the council, when I overhead two colleagues discussing the fact that Alan had decided to put his name forward. I was dumbstruck. I was really worried that if I had to wait a year, my mother would not be well enough or still be around to see me and be a part of the special year. I wanted her to be proud.

I had heard correctly and as soon as Alan had said he wanted to be Lord Mayor, he was selected having been a councillor longer than me and having served as a committee chairman for longer too. The decision was actually taken by the Party Advisory Committee, set up by the Conservative group and consisting of senior councillors and former Lord Mayors and with the single task of choosing a candidate to be Lord Mayor subject to a vote at the Annual Council Meeting. With a large majority, the Conservative candidate always won.

The chairman of the committee was my good friend and fellow councillor, Cyril Nemeth, who was also doctor to both Simon and me. Cyril assured me that if I wanted the mayoralty next year, he would help me. So, when Melvyn Caplan became Leader a few months later, although he asked me to continue as chairman of the Planning and Transportation Committee, I asked him if the following year he would support me to be Lord Mayor. He agreed.

The Party Advisory Committee only met once a year and that was always in November. But conscious of Alan Bradley's last-minute change of mind the previous year, Cyril and I contrived to bring the decision-making meeting forward to get it resolved before someone else joined the race. We agreed that Cyril would call the meeting for the end of September and I suggested 27th September, my 38th birthday. I hoped it would be a lucky day for me.

As the day got closer, I became more confident that I would be chosen and so arranged that after the meeting, I would meet my parents and sister with her husband Bradley for dinner at a restaurant in Victoria to celebrate my birthday and I invited Cyril and his wife Lucille to join us. Of course, Simon would be there too. My family had no idea what I was hoping to do or what the meeting was about.

Second time lucky. I was waiting for the committee decision in a neighbouring committee room. It was not long before the white smoke was seen across Westminster. Cyril entered the room, shook my hand and told me that I had unanimously been selected as the Conservative Party candidate to be the 32nd Lord Mayor of Westminster.

We then went to join the others at the restaurant. When everyone had arrived, I asked for silence. I think they thought I was going to say something about my birthday. I told them that they were looking at the next Lord Mayor of Westminster, one of the most important civic positions in the country.

After congratulating me, my mother expressed how upset she was that I had not told her earlier, particularly when she found out that I had been aware of the pending decision for a while. But once I explained that I wanted it to be a surprise, they were keen to know what was involved and would I meet The Queen.

Carole Franco

One of the first decisions I had to make was the choice of Lady Mayoress. I had already made my decision a year earlier when I thought I was going to be chosen instead of Alan Bradley. As soon as the idea of being Lord Mayor crept into my mind, I knew the decision as to who to invite to be my Lady Mayoress would be important.

Usually, a married Lord Mayor would invite their spouse or partner to be Lady Mayoress (or where the Lord Mayor is a woman, her Consort). If they are single, they are entitled to invite a friend or a family member to undertake the role of accompanying the Lord Mayor to most functions and co-hosting events in the Mayoral Parlour in City Hall. Some more recent Lord Mayors have chosen not to appoint a Lady Mayoress or Consort but just ask a number of family members and/or family to join them at different events

Simon had made it clear that he did not want to undertake the role. He hated the pomp and ceremony associated with the job and disliked attending dinners night after night. In addition, our relationship was still firmly in the closet. Simon had also been selected to stand for Parliament in the upcoming general election in the Leicester East constituency. Standing against my Cambridge friend, the incumbent MP Keith Vaz, Simon knew he had no chance of winning but wanted to prove he was a worthy and a hard-working candidate who deserved to be selected in a subsequent election, for a safe seat. He was therefore intending to spend most of his spare time in Leicester, knocking on doors and kissing babies.

Carole Franco and I had met in Cambridge. My fourth post-graduate year (1980–81) was spent as a member of Wolfson College, whose members came from a wide range of countries.

At a formal dinner in the College Hall one night, I happened to sit next to Carole and over dinner we just clicked and became firm friends. After leaving Cambridge in the summer of 1980, I flew to Connecticut to stay with Carole and her family and together we toured much of the north-eastern states. A couple of years later, Carole joined me on a ten-day holiday around Italy and, like most Americans, we managed to visit a different city every day. It was exhausting but we saw a lot of the country.

Carole and I at Cambridge – 1980.

We kept in regular contact and frequently visited each other and so I knew instantly that she would make the perfect Lady Mayoress. She was interested in people, she had an extensive knowledge and interest in both international affairs and politics and was just a lovely friendly person. Moreover, unlike most Lady Mayoresses with an independent life to continue to enjoy, Carole would come over and give one hundred per cent of her time to the role. I knew she would go down well. And I was right.

Just before my selection as Lord Mayor designate, Carole happened to be in London. I invited her for afternoon tea at the Dorchester Hotel, her favourite venue for what she always saw as the perfect English pastime of taking afternoon tea, scones, crustless sandwiches and all.

Over a cucumber sandwich, I told her that I was expecting to become Lord Mayor and then dropped the bombshell. Would she fly over to London and become my Lady Mayoress? She was stunned and immediately accepted, once she had digested the question.

A week before I became Lord Mayor, Carole flew to London, having given up her job, to join me for the exciting year ahead.

But where would she live? She could not live with me, as I was living (in secret) with Simon. Even Carole did not know. The mayoralty came with a flat in City Hall for the use of the Lord Mayor. But it would not be available to me during my year in office as it and the mayoral suite were due to be refurbished and so we would be required to vacate the top floors of Westminster City Hall. I insisted that we were provided with a flat somewhere for Carole to live in, as all previous Lord Mayors had been provided with a flat and it was not fair that when it was really needed, the council had determined that it had to be refurbished.

Eventually, after support from several former Lord Mayors, we were offered a staff flat above the council's waste disposal facility in Mayfair. It had been traditional for all senior officers of the council to be provided with free living accommodation above many of the council's operational facilities such as swimming pools, libraries and refuse centres. The flats were small and basic and the one chosen for Carole was directly above the Mayfair refuse depot where every morning at 5 am thousands of glass bottles that had been collected from the night time hospitality trade, were emptied into a crushing machine, waking up everyone living close by.

The Lady Mayoress's flat on the top floor above the Farm Street cleansing depot.

But it would be home for Carole and within easy walking distance of most of central Westminster, which would be useful when we were not being driven on formal occasions in the mayoral car.

A week before we were due to take up office, the Labour Party decided to make mischief! They issued a press release stating that they did not want an American Lady Mayoress and suggested that she return home instead of taking up the role. They also complained that she was going to be housed in an 'expensive Mayfair penthouse' at council taxpayers' expense.

£13,000 bill as new American mayoress gets flat in Mayfair

The Evening Standard *covers Carole's flat.*

What they did not mention was that all Lord Mayors were provided with a flat and this one was about a fifth of the size of the City Hall one and was above a noisy cleansing depot. Not exactly what everyone who read the press release realised.

The press loved this story! One national newspaper even sent a journalist to New York to track Carole down. They found her and doorstepped her at a dinner she was attending in New York City, days before flying to London and started questioning her about the flat and why she had been chosen. She was mortified and phoned me in tears.

The day of the mayor-making ceremony saw the London TV news programmes seeking to cover the story and so we were interviewed outside the Council

House (where the ceremony was going to be held) about why I had chosen an American. Being the experienced politician that I am, I told them what a wonderful Lady Mayoress she would be. The journalist then turned to Carole and started asking her detailed questions about the council's housing policies. Poor Carole did not know what hit her, but she politely explained that as Lady Mayoress she was outside the political ring and could not comment. Phew … we got away with it.

The pieces ran as headlines on both *London Tonight* on ITV and BBC London. How many newly installed Lord Mayors made headline TV news!!

Chaplain

It is also traditional for the Lord Mayor to appoint a chaplain for spiritual advice and to accompany the mayoral party to a variety of important religious services and events. Being Jewish I wanted to appoint a Rabbi. I was not a member of a synagogue so there was no one obvious to appoint. However, I did have a synagogue within my ward, so I approached the Rabbi of the beautiful Moorish-style St Petersburg Place Synagogue. We sat down in his office and talked about the role and I invited him to accept the chaplaincy. He said he would be delighted to but on one condition. He would not attend a service in a church or a mosque. I explained that that was a major issue as he would certainly be expected to attend several very important services at Westminster Abbey including my own Civic Service as well as attend several services in other churches and mosques. But he was adamant and so I had to suggest politely that it might be better if I looked elsewhere. He agreed and wished me well.

So back to the drawing board. I mentioned my search to my friend Richard Loftus who suggested I meet Lionel Rosenfeld from his synagogue in Great Cumberland Place, Marble Arch. We met for a coffee and it turned out that Lionel's father had been the Rabbi at Finchley's synagogue, who had bar mitzvah'd me twenty-six years earlier. We also got on very well and so there was no need to look elsewhere and he agreed to become my chaplain and to attend services at the Abbey and elsewhere.

My Election as Lord Mayor

On 15th May 1996, with all my family and numerous friends present in the Council House in Marylebone, the council held its Annual Council Meeting and the first item of business was the election of a new Lord Mayor for the City of Westminster.

Simon gave a speech nominating me for the highest office in the city with Cyril Nemeth seconding my nomination. The Labour councillors usually abstained from the vote but this time a number of them spoke opposing my election. This was because the election was taking place just a few weeks after the publication of the final District Auditor's report into the 'Homes for Votes' Scandal (as the enquiry into the 'Building Stable Communities' policy became known) and my friendship with Shirley Porter was of course an excuse to oppose my nomination.

As mayor-making is supposed to be a joyous occasion, the incoming Lord Mayor is allowed to invite about eighty personal guests comprising family, friends and colleagues. Many distinguished guests also attend such as the Dean of Westminster and the head of Westminster's police service.

I had all my family, my close friends, my colleagues from my law firm present, only for them to hear from the speeches of Labour councillors, that I was a 'crook' and 'corrupt' and unfit to hold the office of Lord Mayor, purely because of my association with Shirley. I took it in my stride, as a politician having sat through so many acrimonious council meetings for over ten years and also having lived through the whole unfortunate episode of the District Auditor's investigations.

Despite this nasty opposition from the Labour councillors, I was duly elected at 38 years of age, the youngest ever, the Right Worshipful the Lord Mayor of the City of Westminster.

After having been vested with my blue and gold robes and my chains and badge of office, I accepted office as Lord Mayor and the separate office of Deputy High Steward of Westminster Abbey.

I then entertained all my guests and the councillors (including those who had minutes earlier insulted me) to a buffet reception in the wood-panelled adjoining Reception Rooms.

I think my family and friends who had been watching from the public gallery were

My acceptance speech after having been elected Lord Mayor of Westminster with Bill Roots, Chief Executive, on the left and my chaplain Lionel Rosenfeld on the right.

My family with Carole and I immediately after my election as Lord Mayor – May 1996.

BACK ROW (L TO R)
Brother-in-law Bradley; my sister Susan; Bradley's mother Marie; Bradley's father Arnold;
my mother's brother Stanley and his wife Caroline.

FRONT ROW (L TO R)
My father; Carole; me; my mother and my grandmother Anne
with my nieces Cassie and Jessica kneeling at the front.

taken aback at the abuse thrown at me, when they had anticipated attending a coronation rather than a public hanging and so it took much of my energy at the reception to assure them that I was not bothered as this was all part of the 'rough and tumble' of party politics.

The next few weeks were like a whirlwind, with hundreds of engagements, receptions, visits, dinners, foreign visits and in particular, my Civic Service in Westminster Abbey attended by over six hundred of my friends, colleagues and family, and ending with a luncheon party in the gardens of the Abbey.

I was now part of the establishment and the first Citizen of Westminster, outranked only by The Queen and members of the Royal Family. There began the most exciting and fantastic year of my life.

Arriving in full civic state at Westminster Abbey at the commencement
of my Civic Service – July 1996.

With the Dean of Westminster and Carole, speaking at the post service
reception and lunch in the gardens of the Abbey.

Chapter 17

State Visits

On average, twice a year, Her Majesty The Queen (on the recommendation of the Foreign Office) entertains a foreign Head of State to the United Kingdom. Seventy per cent of these state visits are held in London, with the Head of State staying at Buckingham Palace, while the remainder are held in Windsor Castle. Each State Visit follows almost identical programmes to ensure no favouritism is given to any one country. When held in London, the Lord Mayor of Westminster plays an integral role.

I am frequently asked about the best thing I did as Lord Mayor and I always respond by referring to the State Visit of Nelson Mandela in July 1996.

To put the visit in context, Mandela was President of South Africa and was at the height of his popularity. The Queen together with the Duke of Edinburgh had been to South Africa on her own State Visit in March 1995 and this had been a great success with Her Majesty and the President getting on well. In a report by the then British High Commissioner to South Africa, Anthony Reeve, to Douglas Hurd, the Foreign Secretary, dated 5th April 1995, the High Commissioner emphasised the success of that visit and how the visit has 'set the seal on South Africa's return to the international fold'.

There was much hope for the return State Visit and a great deal of interest from the press. What no one expected was the amazing interest taken by the general public.

I have described at the beginning of this book various aspects of this state visit, including the President's arrival on Horse Guards Parade, the State Banquet at Buckingham Palace and the early morning planting of a tree in St James's Park, but there were many other fascinating, unique and amusing aspects of this state visit, in which I played a key part.

The Address of Welcome
Following the arrival of the President at Horse Guards Parade and the formalities of the State Lunch, Mandela followed the tradition, set for all state visits, by going to Westminster Abbey to place a wreath on the Tomb of the Unknown Soldier. Following this, it was standard procedure that the Head of State would travel to St James's Palace to receive a formal Address of Welcome from the Lord Mayor and ten councillors from Westminster City Council.

This was to be one of the most important parts of the State Visit for me, as I had to read President Mandela an Address of Welcome. I was very keen that I said something profound and important. However, protocol dictated that this Address was written by the Foreign Office, so as to ensure that the right things were said in line with government policy and the government's strategy behind the State Visit. When the first draft of the Address arrived for my approval a few weeks before the President's visit, I decided I would amend it, to add something personal.

As one of my good friends from university, Andrew Noble, was First Secretary in the British High Commission in South Africa, I faxed him (these were the days before email) a copy of the Foreign Office's draft and asked what he thought of it and for suggestions to improve it before I added my own amendments. Two days later he replied by stating that it was perfect without any need for amendment, as he had drafted it!! Oops.

While The Queen was enjoying lunch with the President after the formal arrival on Horse Guards Parade, I and ten of my colleagues, who had been selected by ballot to join me in giving the Address of Welcome, donned our robes, jabots and white gloves and rehearsed (several times) the formalities required of us when we arrived at St James's Palace.

After a cup of tea and biscuits, we headed to the fleet of limousines that would transport us to the Palace. They were led by WE1, the mayoral car (a Daimler limousine with tied-back curtains on all its windows and a flag on the bonnet and named after its personalised number plate, WE 1), we were accompanied by a number of police officers on motorbikes to give us a police escort. People going about their daily business all stopped and watched as the fleet of cars, led by five of the police outriders, drove down the wrong side of the street and through red lights, direct to St James's Palace. We all agreed that this was indeed the way to travel through central London.

On arriving in Friary Court at the side of St James's Palace, we formed in to our pre-rehearsed column of two councillors side by side, led by me as Lord Mayor and accompanied by the Chief Executive of the council. We processed through the Armouries Room covered in military armoury, through the Tapestry Room where a new monarch is proclaimed sovereign by the Accession Council and into the two ceremonial rooms leading to the Throne Room. However, at this stage the huge doors leading into the Throne Room were closed, awaiting the arrival of the President and his entourage. We had time to undergo a further rehearsal before waiting a few minutes for the President's arrival, which gave us

WE1, the mayoral car during my year in office.

some time to marvel at the lavish room we were waiting in, with several historic paintings of past monarchs hanging on the wall, looking down on us.

We were then told that the presidential cavalcade was arriving direct from Westminster Abbey and so we formed up into our pre-rehearsed positions and the room fell silent.

After a couple of minutes passed (although it seemed like half an hour), the double doors in front of us opened and I led my colleagues into the Throne Room. Standing directly in front of Her Majesty's throne (one of several in each of her Palaces) which itself sat below a majestic canopy of red velvet adorned with the Royal Coat of Arms, was President Nelson Mandela and, by his side, his daughter, with both of them surrounded by about thirty members of his entourage (including his own government's ministers) and members of Her Majesty's Household deputed to accompany the President during his state visit.

What struck me and my colleagues was that despite all the entourage being very formally dressed, as would be expected on such an important state occasion, the President was wearing one of his trademark brightly coloured open-necked shirts flowing over his trousers. Very informal!

As we entered the Throne Room, those behind me fanned out, as rehearsed, into two rows facing the President and bowed. We took two steps forward and bowed again.

I alone then made two further steps forward and bowed. I then addressed the President by welcoming him on behalf of the City Council and its citizens to Westminster and

Reading the Address of Welcome to His Excellency the President of South Africa Nelson Mandela, with his daughter on the left and his entourage behind in the Throne Room of St. James's Palace – July 1996.

reading from my speech inscribed on vellum (a form of parchment made of animal skin) to give the formal Address of Welcome drafted by my friend Andrew Noble.

Once I had finished, the President then read his response from a scroll and when he finished, he handed me the parchment on which his speech had been inscribed enclosed in a silver tube and in exchange, I gave him my Address of Welcome. I then bowed and said: 'May it please your Excellency, if I may present my delegation'. He nodded and in turn I enunciated the names of each of my colleagues as they processed one by one in front of the President. They in turn bowed or curtsied and shook his hands and then left the room. As my colleague Councillor Nick Markham, then one of our youngest councillors, in his early twenties and looking even younger, shook his hand, the President at the top of his voice, said 'You cannot be a councillor in such a great city – you're too young – you should be at school'. At first there was a stunned silence and then laughter sprung out from everyone including the President's entourage.

After the last councillor shook his hand, I moved in front of the President, bowed, shook his hand and left the Throne Room. The audience was at an end. Relieved it had all gone well, we processed back to the awaiting cars and once back in City Hall, we celebrated with champagne and canapés in the Mayoral Parlour.

The 'Thank You' Lunch

The Thursday of the State Visit gave the President an opportunity to say thank you to his hosts by hosting a luncheon at the Dorchester Hotel. The Queen and most senior members of the Royal Family, as well as most of the government, were to be present as it was such a high-profile state visit. As a result, Park Lane was closed off for security reasons but Carole and I, in WE1, had been granted permission to go through the barriers to be dropped off at the front entrance of the Hotel.

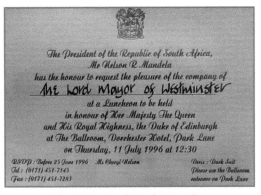

The invitation from the President.

However, as we approached the entrance to the ballroom (a hundred yards further north than the main entrance) the car was signalled to stop and as we did, the car doors were opened by hotel staff and so we got out, but believed rather embarrassingly that we were in the wrong place, as our instructions had firmly said we should alight the car at the main hotel front entrance with all the other guests.

But we were swiftly ushered into a private room and handed glasses of champagne. There were only about sixteen to twenty people in the room. This was clearly not the main pre-lunch reception. Our immediate reaction was that there has been an error and we were in the wrong function. Another luncheon in error? Then as we looked around the room, we soon realised where we were. Almost everyone in the room were members of the Royal Family. Clearly, this was the VVVIP reception.

We stood for a few moments, with our mouths open wide, until someone approached us to break the ice, by saying hello. It was John Major, the Prime Minister. He made small talk to make us feel at home before presenting us to the Duke of York and Princess Alexandra. Mandela himself then came over to welcome us, before we were ushered into the main dining room, where a further two hundred guests were waiting.

1.	Dep Min Gill Marcus
2.	Duke of York
3.	Mr C Landa
4.	Dame Kiri Te Kanawa
5.	Mrs V Ramgoolam
6.	Rt Hon Dr N Ramgoolam
7.	HE Dr L M Singhvi
8.	Lady Mayoress
9.	The Lord Mayor of Westminster
10.	Mrs S Singhvi

The table plan at the Mandela lunch in the Dorchester Hotel.

We found our table directly in front of the top table. Sitting with us were the Duke of York, Dame Kiri Te Kanawa and Dame Shirley Bassey. It was quite an awe-inspiring luncheon.

Walkabout Trafalgar Square

The Friday of the State Visit required me to be at Trafalgar Square to welcome the President before he undertook a walkabout through the Square prior to giving an address from the South African High Commission on the east side of the Square. This was also going to be broadcast live on TV.

My mother was having a period of remission from the side effects of her ovarian cancer treatment. She indicated that she would love to attend the morning's activities. I therefore made a request to the Comptroller of the Lord Chamberlain's Office at Buckingham Palace, Sir Malcolm Ross (who we had got to know quite well), to seek consent for my mother to join Carole and I on this part of the state visit. Sir Malcolm said she could, provided that she kept out of the way. My mother was delighted to join us and I drilled into her the importance of blending into the background and not taking centre stage.

We arrived at the southern end of Trafalgar Square, where we were met by Virginia Bottomley (now Baroness Bottomley), then Secretary of State for Culture, Media and Sport and the minister in charge of Trafalgar Square.

We were shortly joined by Prince Andrew, the Duke of York, who was to represent Her Majesty in the Square. After my mother was briefly presented to the Duke, she was ushered to the inside of the barriers that had separated us from the massive crowds that had filled the Square that morning, keeping clear the central area of the Square, to allow Mandela to walk through.

Mandela was coming from a walkabout in Brixton and arrived in the Square in one of Her Majesty's state limousines. The Duke was the first to greet him as he stepped out of the car. As the First Citizen in Westminster, I took precedence over the Secretary of State and so I was the first person the Duke introduced to the President.

The Duke extended his arm to present me and said 'This is the Lord Mayor of Westminster, Your Excellency!'

Mandela shook my hand and as he did so, he turned to the Duke and said 'I know who he is ... but I bet he has forgotten who I am!'

After being presented to the Secretary of State and Carole, I led Mandela towards the cheering crowds and the TV cameras behind the barriers. As I did so, I saw out of the corner of my eyes, my mother shifting quickly to the left as otherwise she would be the first person Mandela would have met as he approached the barriers. Clearly under instructions from me and the Palace, she was desperately trying to keep out of the limelight.

Mandela saw this and turned to me and said 'Who is she?' I explained that she was my mother. On hearing this, he immediately went up to her, shook her hands and said how pleased he was to meet the Lord Mayor's mother. He then moved on to talk to members of the public behind the barriers.

This amazing moment (my mother was to pass away just a few months later) was very special to me and was broadcast live on TV so all my mother's friends and relatives were able to watch it.

SKY TV News showing my mother shaking hands with Nelson Mandela – July 1996.

While Mandela was greeting members of the public, who were clambering over each other to shake his hands, I noticed that he would grab the outstretched hand with both of his own hands. As he did so, without letting go for a few seconds, he would look into their eyes (many politicians rarely do this) and would say to them in his quiet, soothing voice 'I am so honoured to meet you'. They would recoil in astonishment, that this iconic figure was honoured to meet them. They would insist it was in reality their honour. Humbling and a wonderful scene to watch.

I learnt from watching Mandela greet his fans. From then on, whenever meeting someone new, I would follow Mandela's approach and hold the person's hand with both of my own and looking directly into their eyes, say 'how honoured I am to meet you'. They would melt and become fans for life!

After walking through the Square, packed with so many people that some were hanging from street lights and standing on

Mandela waving to the crowds in Trafalgar Square at the end of the state visit.

the famous statues, the President eventually arrived at the South African High Commission where, accompanied by me, the Duke, the Secretary of State and the South African High Commissioner, Mandela unveiled a Jubilee Walkway Panel on the pavement outside the High Commission. He then entered the High Commission and re-appeared a few minutes later on the High Commission's balcony overlooking the Square, from where he addressed the thousands gathered all over Trafalgar Square.

Towards the end of his speech, he widened his outstretched hands and said 'I love you all and only wish I could gather you all up and place you in my pockets and take you home to South Africa with me!' The audience melted in admiration.

As he left the building and entered his Royal limousine for the return visit to Buckingham Palace, I bade farewell as it was the last time I would see him on this state visit. And what a success it had been.

Oxford

A couple of months after Mandela had returned to South Africa, I was surprised and delighted when I received an invitation from the South African High Commissioner to attend a lecture being given by President Mandela in Oxford. Not only had the President requested I attend as his personal guest but I was also invited to attend an after-lecture dinner for just twenty guests, many of whom were the heads of various Oxford colleges. While of course I was sitting at the other end of the table to the President, it was still a great honour to be invited and more particularly to be remembered by him.

The President of Israel

My second State Visit during my tenure as Lord Mayor was equally special to me, as it was the visit of the President of Israel, Ezer Weizman (President from May 1993 to July 2000). Weizman had been a commander of the Israeli Air Force and Minister of Defence before being elected twice as President.

As a Jew, this was important to me and I was eager to participate with leading members of British Jewry in a number of the events.

STATE VISIT

THE PRESIDENT OF
THE STATE OF ISRAEL
AND
MRS. REUMA WEIZMAN

February, 1997

Ceremonial

The ceremonial booklet published for all participants of a State Visit by the Palace.

Raoul Wallenberg

Some months before I assumed the role of Lord Mayor, I had as chairman of the council's Planning and Transportation Committee, got to know Sir Sigmund Sternberg, a renowned philanthropist and inter-faith campaigner. Siggy (as he was known) was keen to erect a statue of Raoul Wallenberg in Westminster and together with David Amess, the MP for

Basildon at the time, he came to see me to ask me to help them obtain the necessary consents for doing so.

When I first met them, I had not heard of Wallenberg. What they told me about him turned me instantly into a major supporter of their campaign to erect the statue.

Raoul Wallenberg is said to be one of the heroes of the 20th century by personally saving the lives of tens of thousands of Hungarian Jews during the Second World War. He was born in 1912, into a renowned Swedish family of bankers, politicians and diplomats. He graduated from the University of Michigan as an architect but then returned to Sweden to become a businessman. This required him to travel widely and led to him becoming involved with the Central European Trading Company which resulted in him making frequent visits to Budapest, the capital of Hungary.

In March 1944, Hitler invaded Hungary and it was not long before the new political leadership handed over 450,000 Hungarian Jews to the Nazis, most of whom subsequently perished. The 200,000 remaining Jews in Budapest were rightfully concerned.

The Swedish Embassy was keen to protect the Jews and so started issuing them with Swedish passports which would help them leave the country. But the task was overwhelming and so the Swedish government, in consultation with the World Jewish Congress, decided to appoint Raoul Wallenberg (who had some knowledge of Budapest from his business trips) to lead a mission to rescue the Jews of Budapest.

Wallenberg's first action on arriving in Budapest with a diplomatic passport, was to issue 'protective passports' called Schutzpasses. These were blue with yellow corners, symbolising the Swedish state.

From a limited permitted run of 1,000 Shutzpasses, Wallenberg persuaded the Hungarian authorities to raise the quota to 4,500, although it is believed the true number he issued was more like 15,000.

Wallenberg ran his operation from the Swedish Embassy and had help from over three hundred volunteers. The work he led also involved establishing over thirty-two safe houses under the protection of the Swedish Embassy. Through Wallenberg's tireless work, it is said that over 100,000 Hungarian Jews were saved from the Nazi gas chambers and from the post-war Soviet control of Budapest.

After the war ended, he was called to a meeting at the Soviet military headquarters in eastern Hungary. He was never seen again. It is believed that the Soviets arrested him and took him to a Moscow prison. Why, it is not known, although the Soviet leaders were suspicious that he was an American spy. It is believed (but has never been proved) that he subsequently died in the infamous Lubjanka prison in July 1947.

At the time of the unveiling of the statue in 1997, his family believed that as there was no evidence of his death, he could still be alive, held somewhere in a Russian prison. That's why the Wallenberg family insisted that the statue should be called a 'monument' and not a 'memorial'.

Siggy's ability to deliver on projects he was passionate about led to the statue being granted all the necessary permissions to be erected outside the synagogue in Great

Cumberland Place, near Marble Arch. The synagogue is situated in a crescent owned by the Portman Estate. In front of the synagogue was a semi-circular piazza at the centre of which the statue would be positioned.

The sculptor was well known to me. The renowned and highly respected Philip Jackson and I had worked together on the small statue of Mozart aged eight years old that was unveiled by Princess Margaret in Belgravia in September 1994 during my tenure as chairman of the council's Planning and Transportation Committee.

Siggy Sternberg had managed to call upon his amazing contacts to arrange for The Queen to unveil the Wallenberg statue in the presence of the President of Israel, as part of the state visit. I was invited as Lord Mayor to attend the ceremony and, as First Citizen, to receive The Queen and the President and the other distinguished guests on their arrival.

I arrived at Marble Arch early to ensure I was in my place for the arrivals to start. It was a windy February morning and I was in full civic state. That is, I was wearing the blue and gold robes that dated back to 1900, which incorporated a long-integrated train together with my jabot, white gloves and the chains and badge of office.

Among the VIPs I had to receive was the Secretary General of the United Nations, Kofi Annan (who was married to Raoul Wallenberg's maternal half-niece), Princess Margaretha of Sweden, the King of Sweden's eldest sister (representing Sweden) and the Chief Rabbi Jonathan Sacks. A number of Holocaust survivors also attended, as did many leading members of the Jewish community in London.

Precisely on time, the Royal car arrived containing The Queen and the President of Israel. At the moment that The Queen stepped out of the car to be received by me, a gust of wind took hold and, as the photo of this shows (see below), The Queen raised her arm towards me with her black gloved hand stretched out to shake mine, when my robes were caught in the wind and flew out behind me.

Her Majesty being greeted by the Lord Mayor on her arrival to unveil
the monument to Raoul Wallenberg – February 1997.

ABOVE *Her Majesty, the Lord Mayor and the President of Israel outside the Western Marble Arch Synagogue at the unveiling of the Wallenberg Monument during the State Visit – February 1997.*

RIGHT *The Queen inspects the Wallenberg Monument.*

After The Queen and the President were introduced to each of the VIP guests, The Queen accompanied by the President unveiled the monument. I accompanied The Queen as we wandered around the monument to view it from all angles and I mentioned how I had been briefed that no one knew if he was still alive. 'Oh no!' she declared to me. 'He died some years back'. Clearly convinced that that was the case and clearly having done her homework before attending, who was I to argue with the Monarch?

After the ceremony was over, we moved towards the front door of the synagogue. Underneath the synagogue there is a large banqueting suite which was then known as the King David Suite (although now it is the ballroom for the adjacent Montcalm Hotel) and this was to be the venue of the post-ceremony reception.

My sister's wedding reception had been held there fifteen years earlier and so it had a special meaning to me. Several years later when the ballroom reopened after a refurbishment by the Montcalm Hotel, I was honoured to be asked to open it and there is now a brass plaque adjacent to the new entrance to the ballroom that says that I opened it.

Before the Royal Party entered the synagogue, the Chief Rabbi recited a blessing, which he explained is the one given when in the presence of a monarch.

Then something very special happened, which meant a lot to me as a Jewish Lord Mayor. Accompanied by the President of Israel, some of the other dignitaries and myself as Lord Mayor, Her Majesty The Queen entered through the doors of the synagogue. This was the very first time that The Queen (or in fact any British monarch) had ever entered a synagogue in Britain. A very moving moment for me.

Chapter 18

Mayoral Stories

Can't Stand the Heat

The call came into the Lord Mayor's Office requesting a meeting about a TV programme called *Men Cooking*. A few days later, I received a visit from a TV producer and learnt that they were making a new series about famous men cooking and talking about their lives. They wanted me to participate. I asked why me? I was not famous. But they assured me that being Lord Mayor was famous enough and they would be keen to film me in my chains and badge of office.

Modestly conceding that maybe I was famous enough, I explained that I could not cook. I had never been taught to do so. As a young man in the 1960s and 70s, men were not expected to cook or learn to do so. My father and I were kept in the living room, while my mother and sister prepared our nightly evening meal. Besides, my mother was not a great cook. She could and did cook basic and simple meals but nothing interesting – she and my father never liked sauces or unusual dishes.

I recall taking my parents to a fabulous restaurant in a pretty village just outside Cambridge when I was studying there. It was a pub called the Tickell Arms run by an eccentric publican. The front door of the pub had a large sign on it stating that 'long-haired lefties are prohibited from entering'. Inside he played Wagner non-stop and the menu was unusual but always delicious. My parents gave one look at the menu and announced that they did not like anything on it and, when they ordered the simplest thing they could find, they left most of it uneaten. I was mortified.

Thinking on my feet, I suggested to the producer that it would be fun if I made a ready-meal dinner and joked about doing so. He did not think this was funny. I then remembered that as a student, I used to make steak and mushroom pie. I therefore suggested that was what I would make. He seemed happy enough and a date and time for filming was arranged.

A few weeks later, early one Saturday morning, the film crew arrived at my flat in Little Venice. There were about ten of them and it was difficult for them all to squeeze into my kitchen. As they set up the two cameras and lighting, Anna Maria Ashe arrived. In the 1990s Anna Maria was a famous newscaster, fronting the daily *London Tonight* local news broadcast every evening after the main ITV News.

Anna Maria was going to be the presenter. When she and the crew were ready, they started by filming sections of my flat and my numerous memorabilia. The one thing I am not is a minimalist. My entire flat is covered in photos of my exciting life as a councillor

*Anna Maria Ashe watching me (trying to)
cook in my kitchen.*

The crew filming in my kitchen.

with every surface full of memorabilia, gifts and mementos. There was a lot to film. Having put on my morning suit, chains and badge of office, I was then filmed in different positions around the flat before being interviewed about my life and the role of Lord Mayor.

After a break while the crew set up the cameras in the kitchen, the cooking began. As I prepared the steak, Anna Maria asked me a series of questions while helping me by chopping the onions. She then enquired as to what seasoning I was going to use. Naively, it had never occurred to me to add seasoning and I had to think quickly on my feet as I responded by reaching for the salt and pepper.

I then turned to the pastry. I admit that I cheated a bit, as I had purchased some ready-made pastry that merely had to be rolled out. But to stop it sticking to the tabletop while rolling out the pastry, I covered the counter with flour. But my sprinkling of flour saw more of it on my floor than on the counter, much to the amusement of Anna Maria and her crew.

I then decided to make the Council coat of arms from pastry, to sit proudly on top of the pie's crust. This impressed Anna Maria. With the pie now ready, I put it in the oven to cook. We then took a break and the crew decided to rearrange my kitchen, turning it into a dining room. After the pie was cooked, I took it out and put it aside with the potatoes I had also baked. But it took some time, for the crew to be ready for the next part of the filming.

With the crew ready to start again, the table was laid with a mixed salad in a large bowl (which one of the crew had prepared

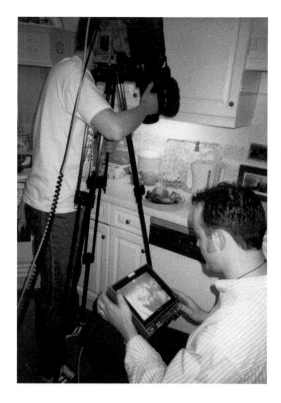

The film crew photographing my steak and mushroom pie with baked potato and salad.

during the break from filming). I cut into the pie, which was now cold and placed a piece on each of the two plates left out and added a baked potato to each. I then served Anna Maria, who was by now sitting at the table. I joined her and she started asking me more questions as we ate and the camera rolled. Being a bit of a performer, I ate the stone-cold food as if it was piping hot. Anna Maria, however, just moved the food around her plate and if you watch the programme carefully, you will see that she never actually takes a bite. A true professional!

We finished about 7 pm that night after eleven hours of filming. I was exhausted. A few months later, the series, now renamed *Can't Stand the Heat*, was shown on the Carlton Food Channel at three in the afternoon. I was sent a video of my programme. I sat there watching it and gasped when towards the end, Anna Maria told those watching that if they wanted to make steak and mushroom pie Lord Mayor's style, then the recipe was on the screen. I had this vision of elderly ladies around the country taking notes and trying to replicate my meal.

About a year later, a friend of mine called to say he had been unable to sleep the previous night and so turned on the telly at 3 am, only to discover me cooking! I understand from others that the programme would be regularly repeated at some unearthly hour during the night on some satellite channel, for several years.

For those who know me, the idea of me cooking on a TV cooking programme is not something that they would ever have envisaged.

Mayoral Chains

Mayoral protocol dictates that when a mayor is in a Royal Palace including Buckingham Palace, Hampton Court and St James's Palace, the mayor must not wear their chains of office. As the Palace of Westminster (the Commons and Lords) is also a Royal Palace, this applies there too. Wearing the chains in another borough is similarly not allowed as it is the prerogative of the local mayor to wear them. However, with the consent of the host mayor, chains can be worn on certain occasions.

Embassies are deemed (in protocol terms) to be the sovereign soil of that country and so again, chains are prohibited. However, the Ambassador's residence is not deemed sovereign soil and so chains are allowed. A subtle distinction.

When I chaired the London Mayors' Association, a number of mayors were to attend a viewing in the Queen's Gallery attached to Buckingham Palace and I sought permission from The Queen's Private Secretary for the incumbent mayors attending to wear their chains of office (the Lord Mayor of Westminster had given consent). However, the Palace refused this request.

When chains cannot be worn, the mayor wears the badge of office on a ribbon. For some reason, which I never discovered, although the mayor is deemed non-political, the colour of the ribbon denotes their political party. One or two London boroughs, however, use a black ribbon (as non-political) but most use a ribbon of their political colouring.

The New Zealand High Commission

During my tenure as Lord Mayor of Westminster, I was invited by the New Zealand High Commissioner to a reception at his High Commission situated on the top floors of New Zealand House, a 1960s office tower block with amazing views across London and situated in Haymarket not far from Trafalgar Square.

New Zealand House.

As the function was in a High Commission, I wore my morning coat, striped trousers and black waistcoat, with the mayoral badge on a blue ribbon. As Carole (my Lady Mayoress) and I were leaving the reception, we walked down the grand staircase towards the lobby, when Carole whispered in my ear that she needed to use the 'ladies' before we left. I left her to go off to 'powder her nose' as one says, while I waited patiently at the bottom of the stairs.

As I stood there, an elderly and frail man came down the stairs and almost tripped on one of the final steps. Being the gentleman that I am, I went over to help him and taking his arm led him safely down the last step.

As I did so, he placed a fifty pence coin into my hand and said 'thank you young man', before walking off. I think he thought I was a footman or the concierge. I did not have the heart to tell him that he had just tipped the Lord Mayor.

You don't know who you might meet in the loo

LOOSE found himself at the theatre the other night, in Regent's Park under the stars and clouds watching a production of *The Tempest*.

Looking out across the audience (mainly huddling under blankets and drinking mulled wine as the heavens decided to mimic the play) his eye alighted on a most unusual sight.

For there, just a few rows ahead, were the gold chains of office — glinting in the strobe lights. Yes — the Lord Mayor (of Westminster), Cllr Robert Davis, was out on the town with his entourage of hangers-on.

■ **Cllr Robert Davis, Westminster's mayor**

Throne

But what, thought Loose, was he doing slumming it with the proles? No special throne for him, just a bog-standard plastic-covered, hard-backed chair.

But wait — there's more... during the unsightly rush to the toilets at the interval who should Loose spy once again but the Lord Mayor, er, doing what everyone else does in the toilet.

But without wishing to come across as a voyeur, Loose did notice something rather unusual about the Mayoral habits which he hopes will not become a standard setter among the good citizens of the borough.

OK, the final bell rang and it wouldn't look good for a top dignitary to come in late but surely, in the interests of hygiene, even a Lord Mayor should wash his hands after going?

Open Air Theatre – 'to loos or not to loos'

A few months later, I was invited as Lord Mayor (in morning coat, chains and badge) to attend a performance at the Open Air Theatre in Regent's Park. I was enjoying a drink in the bar with my hosts and colleagues when the bell went announcing the start of the second half in a couple of minutes. Wanting to be comfortable during the second half, I discreetly disappeared to the gentlemen's toilet. As I was finishing, the bell went again announcing the start of the second half within seconds, so not wishing to arrive late in full mayoral outfit, I rushed out of the gentlemen's and managed to get back to my seat in time.

Much to my embarrassment, it appears that a journalist from a newspaper was present in the gentlemen's while I was there and noticed that in rushing back to my seat, I failed to wash my hands. The following day in a gossip column of one of the national papers, an article appeared about how the Lord Mayor of Westminster had failed to wash his hands after using the toilet at the Open Air Theatre! I was mortified!

I learnt my lesson, and to this day, I always – without fail – wash my hands after using the toilet. But conscious of this story, I regularly notice how so few men do wash their hands after using the toilet!

Princess Anne and My Watch

Simon and I were great fans of Walt Disney World and I proudly wore an expensive Mickey Mouse watch Simon bought me on one of our holidays there, even when performing as Lord Mayor.

On one mayoral engagement, dressed in morning suit with full insignia, as I was chatting to Princess Anne, I glanced at my Mickey Mouse watch to check on the time. As I did so, I noticed Her Royal Highnesses expression as it changed to absolute horror at seeing a Lord Mayor wearing such a watch. I never wore it again!

Greeting Princess Anne as Lord Mayor.

Chapter 19
New Leaders and Consequential Changes

Post Porter

In early 1991, Shirley Porter decided to stand down as Leader of the Council after more than seven years in the job, in order to become Lord Mayor. Her Deputy Leader, David Weeks, was recognised by most colleagues as her obvious successor, as he was seen as competent and experienced. However, one of my newly elected colleagues Bill Griffiths, decided to challenge him on the premise that the council needed a complete break from the old guard. In my years of experience as a councillor, I have noticed that a few newly elected councillors would, after just a year or two on the council, seek to challenge the establishment or were so personally ambitious that they thought they could be Leader, with little experience. Usually, they never got far and after attempts at a challenge, most would disappear after a few years on the council. Bill fell into that category and of course he picked up a few votes from friends, other new colleagues and by those with grudges against David for whatever reason.

As David was standing for the leadership, a vacancy arose for Deputy Leader. Simon decided to run, even though he had only been a councillor for two years. He probably fell into the category described earlier. But this time, his talents were recognised by his colleagues and his lack of experience and his modesty trumped any concern about him being yet another usurper. In his two years as a councillor, Simon had impressed everyone by his ability, hard work, kind and gentle nature and his amazing oratory. But one of our colleagues, Marie Louise Rossi, daughter of Hugh Rossi, MP for Hornsey, thought otherwise and decided to stand against Simon, believing she would walk it.

When the results were announced, as expected, David won with a big majority and so did Simon. Marie Louise was furious and walked out of the group meeting immediately after the announcement was made. She didn't speak to Simon for about a year. She subsequently retired from the council and, as a pro-European, joined the Liberal Democratic Party and stood unsuccessfully for both the council and for Parliament (in the Cities of London and Westminster seat). Sadly, she died a few years later, from ovarian cancer, at a very young age of 58.

Simon was very successful as Deputy Leader and chairman of the council's Finance Committee. I was chairman of the Environment Committee for the first year of David's leadership and then promoted by David to chairman of the Planning and Transportation Committee.

Clive Milton

Simon's father, Clive Milton, had been born in Germany but in 1939, just before the Second World War started, when things were getting tough, especially for Jews, his parents took the difficult and brave decision to send the teenage Clive and his sister Dagmar to London as part of the 'Kindertransport' to stay in Maida Vale with cousins they had never met. Clive and his sister got on the train for London and never saw their parents or older brother again – they lost their lives in one of the concentration camps. Many years later, when Simon and I visited Yad Vashem in Israel, we found their names recorded there in commemoration.

Clive Milton.

Clive and his sister were sent to Essendine Primary School in Maida Vale, where coincidentally some fifty years later Simon became chairman of the Governors. Once old enough to work, Clive found employment working on a farm in Wiltshire. To earn extra cash, he would spend his evenings working in the local pub. But on attaining the age of eighteen he found himself called up for National Service

By 1951, having completed his National Service he found work in a series of hotels. However, wanting to learn more about the business, he volunteered to work free of charge in a continental coffee shop (then very fashionable) in Maddox Street, Mayfair.

It was not long before, with financial support from his cousin, he decided to open a patisserie shop with its own bakery at the rear, in Cricklewood, North London, called 'Sharatons' (an amalgamation of Milton and his cousin's name). The business soon grew and eventually they became a famous name on the high streets of London with about twenty shops and a large standalone bakery on the Cricklewood Trading Estate.

Clive's intention was that Simon would be groomed to take over the business and so, when Simon graduated from Cambridge in 1983, Clive was supportive of his attending Cornell University in upstate New York. Cornell is globally recognised as the best hospitality school in the world.

Simon loved his time in Cornell and as he approached the end, he started looking for a traineeship in one of New York's great hotels. Worried that Simon would not return to the UK for many years (if at all), Clive enticed him back to London, by buying him a restaurant in Bond Street which they called 'Milton's', which he asked Simon to run.

*Simon wearing his toque – the chef's hat – in the kitchen of Hotel Ezra
in the University of Cornell.*

That way, Simon could learn the trade and eventually take over the running of the whole business from Clive.

Simon's Career Move

I met Simon for the first time when he was running Milton's. However, once Simon had become a Westminster councillor, he started thinking of a career in politics instead of staying in the bakery business. With Simon elected to Westminster and spending more time at the council, it was decided to sell the Bond Street restaurant (although continue the Sharatons chain) with Simon working from head office.

After a couple of years, Simon told his father that he wanted to go into politics full time and join a firm of public affairs consultants. Instead of challenging Simon and thinking of the long-term interest of the business, Clive was very supportive. It was not long before Simon found a job working for Roger Rosewell, who ran a small consultancy from offices in Baker Street. Simon loved the work and with Roger's support, he started looking to join a large consultancy firm to widen his experience.

Simon applied to join one of the top public affairs consultancies at the time, Ian Greer Associates, based in Victoria. However, the initial interview did not go well and Simon left despondent. He just felt he did not perform as well as he could have done.

As soon as he got home, he contacted them to ask for a second interview, explaining that he felt he could do much better. Ian Greer told him that he was off to Blackpool for the Conservative Party Conference, but if Simon was also going to be there, they could meet for a drink. Simon and I were indeed attending, so one afternoon, we went to Ian's hotel and while I waited in the reception, Simon met Ian in his suite. Simon returned to say it had gone well and within a few months Simon started work at the firm.

APCO

Simon did well working for Ian Greer, not only making lifelong friends but also learning the business. Then in 1994, Simon received a call from a woman based in Washington DC called Margery Kraus. Margery had set up a public affairs consultancy in the US capital with the backing of Grey, the large global advertising agency. The business had grown so rapidly that she now wanted to open an office overseas and had decided that London would be the first choice. She was looking for someone to set up the new London office and a client of Ian Greer Associates had recommended Simon.

Margery Kraus of APCO.

After some negotiations, Simon accepted and so left Ian Greer and setup APCO London with just an office and two colleagues that Margery had recruited from other agencies, namely Rosemary Grogan and Nick De Luca. Simon was made managing director and took charge. He soon recruited two former colleagues from Ian Greer Associates, John Fraser and Angie Bray (Angie later becoming a GLA member and then MP for Ealing Central and Acton).

But setting up a new business from scratch was not easy and so, two years after being elected as Deputy Leader, Simon decided to stand down. He wanted to stay on as a councillor but needed a few years on the backbenches while he grew the business.

Miles Young and Melvyn Caplan

Not wanting to leave the Leader (Miles Young, who later became worldwide chief executive of Ogilvy and Mather, the global advertising agency, and subsequently Warden, the equivalent of Master, of New College, Oxford) without a good replacement in the wings, Simon persuaded Melvyn Caplan to stand as Deputy Leader. At the necessary by-election for Deputy Leader, Melvyn won without any opposition.

Miles and I worked well together. I was then chairman of the Council's Planning and Transportation Committee and one of Miles's senior team. He confided in me and also regularly sought advice from Simon, even after he had retired to the backbenches. However, within a few months of Simon standing down, Miles called me into his office one Monday evening. He dropped a bombshell. He was resigning as Leader the following morning to take up a new job in Hong Kong. I was not only shocked but upset. We got on really well and I found him an inspirational Leader.

There was really no choice for Leader. Melvyn put in his name and no one else had the ability, inclination or support to stand. Melvyn became Leader without a contest. He did, however, ask me to remain as chairman of the Planning and Transportation Committee, although not long after, I was chosen to be the next Lord Mayor of Westminster and so stood down from the chairmanship.

Melvyn's leadership of the council was different from that of his predecessors. The impression he gave was that he did not feel that the council should look externally and work with other London local authorities nor with a number of London-wide bodies that had been established after the demise of the GLC (at a time before the new GLA had been created). He and the small hand-picked team around him also tended to work in isolation from the rest of the group. This was a time before emails, social media or the everyday use of computers, let alone smartphones.

The only time members of the Conservative Group on the council heard from the leadership was at the monthly group meetings. Even the notices for the next group meeting would arrive on a typewritten sheet of paper through the post with nothing other than the simple agenda on it. At the group meetings themselves, Melvyn as Leader would chair the discussion and, in doing so, prevented awkward questions being asked or critics from speaking.

The cleanliness of the city was declining, cuts were being made to frontline services and the council's reputation was being dented. In addition, there was the fallout over the publication of the District Auditor's report on Building Stable Communities and the attempt to surcharge Shirley Porter (by this stage no longer a councillor) and a number of other serving councillors.

In late 1999, after four and half years, many members of the group started complaining to each other about the way the council was being run and its inward-looking leadership.

Ian Wilder to the Rescue

There was no one who wanted to challenge Melvyn nor anyone able enough to do so and win the vote of a majority of the group in any leadership election. The Leader is subject to election by the group every year at the group's AGM in April but in most years the election for Leader and Deputy Leader is uncontested.

Ian Wilder.

Ian Wilder was a maverick. A successful accountant who had at one time been the Welsh singer Shirley Bassey's manager. He had built up his own chartered accountancy firm, called Wilder Coe, with over a hundred staff and offices in Marylebone. As joint senior partner with Robert Coe, the firm had coincidently been Simon's father's accountants.

Bored with just being the senior partner in his firm, Ian decided to get involved with the Conservative Party, becoming chairman of Baker Street ward. His first taste of playing politics was when he got annoyed about the heavy-handedness of the council's traffic wardens. When the councillors in his own ward failed to do anything about his concerns (mainly because they were backbenchers and had little say in the major decision-making process), he started a campaign to get the council to change its policy. He cleverly contacted all the other ward chairmen and persuaded them of his case and he then got the ward chairman to pressurise their own ward councillors, threatening them with possible deselection, if they did not support and fight for the change.

At the next group meeting, all the backbenchers were demanding a change in policy, claiming they would not be reselected if the policy was not changed. Under this sort of pressure, the Leadership capitulated and Ian won his first political fight with little blood on the carpet. It did not take long for Ian to get himself selected as the Conservative Party candidate at the next election for Baker Street ward from his position as chairman of the ward committee.

As senior partner in his practice, Ian's word was an order. The first problem he therefore encountered as a new councillor was to understand that local government and the public sector worked in a very different way to the private sector and that, as a councillor, he could not order everyone around as he did at his accountancy practice.

Newly elected, Ian was placed on the council's Information Technology Committee. In local government, the procurement process is enmeshed in complicated procedures and tendering processes including ensuring any tender satisfied the European Union's requirements (including OJEU).

After nearly two years of a fully compliant tendering process, the officers had brought to Ian's new committee a proposal to award a major multimillion pound contract for a new IT system for approval. But neither the officers nor the committee chairman, knew anything about this new councillor, Ian Wilder.

After hearing the officers' presentation, Ian advised the committee that he had a client (of Wilder Coe) that supplied IT and that his client would provide the IT system that had been tendered, at a 10% discount on the lowest price agreed through the lengthy tendering system. Despite the officers advising the committee that this was not in accordance with the OJEU procedure and unlawful, and despite pleas by the chairman that they had to follow the statutory procedure for such a large contract, Ian moved an amendment to the officers' recommendation, proposing that the council enters into a contract with Ian's client and not the successful tenderer. A vote was taken and the committee, made up of a majority of newly elected councillors, supported Ian's amendment and his proposal was adopted. There was a gasp and following mutterings between the chairman and the chief officer present, the meeting was then abruptly adjourned by the chairman.

The next morning, the Leadership read Ian and his new colleagues the riot act and a few days later the committee met again, the earlier decision was reversed without dissent and the successful legal tenderer was awarded the contract. Ian had made his arrival on the council an unforgettable one.

But Ian's real legacy was reserved for the late-night entertainment industry. Ian soon discovered that the council had been granting numerous licences allowing entertainment venues and vertical drinking venues (where patrons drink alcohol standing rather than sitting) to open throughout the night.

Ian started trawling the West End between midnight and 5 am, not only at weekends but during the week, discovering that the nature of the West End changed as it got later. He was horrified by what he found. Armed with a video camera (these were the days before mobile phones with high-quality cameras incorporated) and his motorbike, he videoed what he saw and would show the footage to several of his colleagues, including Simon and me.

Because most of us were tucked up in bed by midnight, we had no idea what was happening. The huge number of people on the narrow streets of Soho made it impossible for people to walk without pushing past others and squeezing through. Most were drunk and many were shouting, singing and some were being held upright, unable to stand up by themselves. Research subsequently undertaken revealed more people in a handful of Soho streets than found leaving a Chelsea football match. Added to this was the thumping loud music emanating from all the licensed establishments and the filth left on the ground.

Even with a twenty-four-hour cleansing service operating in Soho, the street sweepers could not cope and one could not even see the carriageway and pavement to clean because of the volume of revellers. With the Tube (then) ending before 1 am, many of the revellers were unable to get home until the trains started running again early in the morning, so would fall asleep on the kerbside or in doorways. One particular video filmed by Ian showed a couple, completely naked in a doorway, having full sex, while watched by about a dozen onlookers.

Because of the lawlessness and lack of police presence, some establishments took it on themselves to employ their own security or bouncers. In one video, taken by Ian outside a takeaway in Soho at about 3.30 am, we saw a handful of drunken guys shouting and screaming at the bouncers on duty outside. The bouncers go inside and return, holding large wooden batons. The video then shows the bouncers hitting the drunken guys. Within seconds, several of the drunken guys are on the ground with blood pouring from their heads.

We were all shocked. The council leadership did not know how to respond. When Ian's campaign was initially ignored by the council hierarchy, he gave the video to BBC London who showed it as part of their London News programme.

Unperturbed by resistance to change from the leadership, Ian just kept on going, filming night after night and then taking colleagues around the West End with him during the early hours of the morning.

Some of us were extremely worried about the risk Ian was taking. The owners of many of the establishments encouraging this behaviour were aware of his campaign and we were worried that they might wish to silence him, to preserve the millions they were earning from the relaxed attitude taken by the police and the council.

Whenever Ian tried to raise the issue at the monthly group meetings, he was prevented from doing so. Frustrated that the council were not really addressing the issue, he tried to persuade Simon to stand against Melvyn at the forthcoming annual leadership election.

Having resigned as Deputy Leader to create APCO UK, Simon had subsequently been required to undergo a bone marrow transplant to try and address his leukaemia (CLL). I describe what Simon went through during this period later in this book, but after a horrible year, during which Simon became very ill, he did return to moderately good health.

Because he had taken a year off from APCO to deal with his health issues, he had stepped down as managing director and was now chairman. His colleague, Nick De Luca, had taken on the responsibility of managing director, taking the pressure off Simon.

In theory, Simon now had more time to take on the leadership. But Simon, being very honourable, did not want to challenge Melvyn, who he had always liked and respected. He repeatedly turned Ian down when he kept trying to pressurise Simon to stand.

Getting nowhere with Simon, Ian decided to stand himself. While I and many other councillors admired Ian's persistence and hard work in addressing the problems of the West End and despite liking him very much as a friend and colleague, we did not see him as capable of being leader of the most important council in the country.

Despite our reservations, Ian launched his campaign by hosting a series of suppers in local Italian or Chinese restaurants to which he invited backbench councillors and colleagues he knew to be sympathetic to the need for a change in the leadership of the council. I was a backbencher at this time (late 1999 – early 2000), having resigned as chairman of the Housing Operational Sub-Committee in May 1999. Simon did not want to attend and be seen as disloyal to Melvyn. I would therefore attend and report back to Simon on what was said.

With the election a month away, Ian started contacting colleagues to see if they would vote for him. He was astounded by the response. His figures revealed that he would walk an election between himself and Melvyn. But he did not really want the job. He just wanted to act as a stalking horse to show others and Simon in particular, that they could beat Melvyn and see a change in the leadership of the council.

One Sunday, Simon and Ian had breakfast together. I was not allowed to join them, despite my protests! But a few hours later, Simon returned to advise me that he had been persuaded by Ian that he should stand and would win. But he needed to do his homework first, so started his own ring around. His conclusion was that he could and would do it. He called Ian, who was delighted and immediately agreed to withdraw from the race.

Simon, being a gentleman, wanted to tell Melvyn of his intentions, face to face. He therefore called Melvyn and invited him for a coffee at Raoul's, our favourite coffee shop near both our flat and Melvyn's house. They met up a few hours later. I waited at home on tenterhooks.

When he returned, he explained that he had told Melvyn of his intention and that having talked to colleagues, he felt he would win and win with a large majority and that in respect to Melvyn, he had suggested that Melvyn announce his retirement as Leader and withdraw his name for re-election at the forthcoming group AGM.

Melvyn responded by stating that he intended to stand as his own soundings had shown that he would be re-elected comfortably and that Ian's followers were a small minority. Simon begged to differ and with Simon not liking confrontation, they agreed to respect each other's views. The meeting ended and Simon returned home.

Simon sat in his usual chair at home and read the Sunday papers. After just half an hour, the phone rang. Simon answered it. It was Melvyn. He explained that he had thought about their chat and had decided to stand down as Leader of the Council at the AGM and that Simon would have his full support from the backbenches.

Two weeks later, at the group AGM, Simon was elected leader of Westminster City Council unopposed to great acclaim by the group members present. Simon's and my life were to change for ever.

Leadership

As soon as Simon had been formally elected, he announced to the group that I was to be his Chief Whip and that other cabinet positions would be announced in due course. That sent a message to our colleagues that Simon and I were now in charge.

The following morning at 8 am, Simon and I met in his new office with Peter Rogers, the recently appointed Chief Executive. The council under Melvyn's leadership had been criticised for failing to keep the city clean and, just a few years after taking over responsibility for education from the Inner London Education Authority (ILEA), for a poor-quality school system. Accordingly, Simon's first instruction that morning was that he wanted to designate one million pounds from reserves for additional cleaning services and a further million for schools. This was well received not only by our colleagues but by the press and local residents' groups.

One of the first things I did in my new job was to improve the communications within the Conservative Group by circulating a weekly written newsletter which I called the 'Whip'. It was sent every Friday night by email. It gave news of everything going on in the council and I required each cabinet member to provide a weekly report on what they had been up to in the previous week and were intending to do the following week. It was a great success and continues today with most Conservative councillors believing it has always been circulated, not realising that it was one of my early initiatives in my new role.

Simon also asked me to take on a role in the cabinet as cabinet member for customer services. One of Simon's new initiatives was to put customer services at the top of the agenda and, under my leadership, we would set up a dedicated department to improve the customer experience throughout the council. Vic Baylis, the Director of Housing, was recruited to become the new Director of Customer Services while Terry Cotton, one of the senior directors in social services, became the deputy director.

The priority initiative was the setting up of a council-wide call centre which would be outsourced. At the time, anyone trying to contact the council would have over a hundred different numbers to ring and finding out which was the correct one could be like looking for a rabbit in a forest. Even when you did find the correct number, you would often ring it to hear it ring and ring without anyone answering. Very frustrating for the public. The concept we were to develop would involve one public number for all enquiries and for a call to be answered within a few seconds. The operator would be fully trained to answer any question over the full range of the council's services.

If the operator had to transfer the call to an individual officer, they would ensure the call was followed up. In either case, the operator would follow up the call with an email or subsequent call to ensure the matter had been satisfactorily dealt with. Well, that was the idea.

After a long and complicated procurement process, we awarded the contract to a company called Vertex, who became our partner in the project. They set up a state-of-the-art customer service centre in a building behind Buckingham Palace and after extensive training and a pep talk from me, we went live. It went extremely well and as one of the first councils in the country to introduce such an extensive service of this nature, we were soon inundated by requests for tours of the centre. When councillors from other councils were involved, I would attend to host the tour. As part of our deal with Vertex, if these tours resulted in Vertex providing a similar service to another council, then Westminster would share in the profits.

After a couple of years, because of the cost of central London premises plus the fact that in central London we had a high turnover of trained staff, it was decided to move the call centre to Dingwall in Scotland (near Inverness) where the overheads were substantially cheaper and the call centre was the major employer in the town, ensuring low staff turnover. I made a visit and was impressed. All went well with the transfer until I phoned on one of several test calls (I would regularly make calls anonymously) and when referring to an issue in Paddington, the operator asked where Paddington was! Like in a North Korean call centre, she was sent for retraining within hours!!

Simon introduced a number of new impressive initiatives throughout the council from establishing a Housing Commission with external experts to improve our housing provision, to a new system for dealing with crime and addressing problem families.

Within four years, Simon had turned the council around into the most respected council in the country, winning the Local Government Chronicle's highly prized Council of the Year Award in 2004 and being recognised as the best independently assessed performing council in the country for several years in a row. Simon could do nothing wrong. He was highly respected throughout the local government world, frequently being asked to visit other councils as part of a team of peer group reviewers. It was not long before he was asked to get involved in the Local Government Association (LGA), the national organisation representing all the councils and councillors in England and Wales.

The national government recognises the LGA as the main body it negotiates with and consults on all local government issues.

And Simon being Simon, it was not long before he was elected chairman of the LGA and recognised for his leadership of Westminster Council and how he turned it around, by being awarded a knighthood.

As a postscript to this chapter, I must pay due respect to Melvyn following Simon's bloodless coup. Despite Simon being constantly praised for turning the council around and by third party endorsements of how Simon's leadership had turned a failing council into the best in the country, Melvyn remained quiet and loyal to Simon on the backbenches. Not once did I hear him criticising Simon or his leadership nor complaining about how outsiders were interpreting Simon's running of the council. When required, Melvyn supported Simon and sought no position of responsibility. Simon respected this.

When Simon stood down as Leader eight years later to become Deputy Mayor of London, Colin Barrow as the new Leader appointed Melvyn to succeed me as Chief Whip, on my election as a Deputy Leader. He continued in that role under Philippa Roe's leadership but, on becoming Leader in late 2017, Nickie Aiken returned Melvyn to the backbenches. Again, he behaved perfectly and on Rachael Robathan becoming Leader in early 2020, Melvyn was appointed Deputy Leader. Several former colleagues of mine call him 'Mr Boomerang' as he keeps coming back.

Sir Simon Milton following his
investiture as a Knights Bachelor.

Chapter 20

Managing the City

The Fall in Paris

When David Weeks was Leader of the Council, he was very keen to take senior councillors on foreign trips. One of these was a trip of about ten councillors to meet our counterparts in Paris and to learn from them about their services. The visit coincided with the French Referendum about the European Union and so we were taken to a number of polling stations to watch the local residents vote.

We were also interested in seeing how the Paris Authority dealt with the street homeless, but on being taken around the streets late at night, we found almost no one sleeping rough. However, the following day we met some local politicians and when we told them that we were impressed by the fact that Paris had few street homeless, they quickly told us that the local authority had forcibly moved the street homeless from the area we would be visiting in order for us to believe that they did not have a problem, when the reverse was the case. It was suggested we returned another time, without prior warning.

On another day, we were taken to see their cleansing service in operation. At Place de la Concorde, we were shown their notorious 'Pooper Scooper'. This was a liveried council employee on a motorcycle who had attached to his bike a trunk-like hoover. He would drive around the city of Paris, and whenever he saw any dog poop, he would stop and hoover it up.

The machine also dispensed a perfumed cleaning material to ensure that the pavement was appropriately cleaned. We loved it and after numerous demonstrations, we agreed we would order one for Westminster.

David Weeks and Miles Young being shown a pooper scooper machine.

A few years earlier, when I was vice chairman of the Planning and Transportation Committee, I accompanied David Weeks, then my boss as Deputy Leader and chairman of that committee, on a visit to Paris to see street furniture. We were interested in purchasing modern and better designed street furniture, like lamp posts, bollards, phone booths, advertisement hoarding and public automatic toilets from a firm called J C Decaux. Their factory and headquarters were situated on the outskirts of the city in massive grounds. The HQ itself was clearly once a grand house but within the grounds the owning family had built state-of-the-art offices and a massive factory.

Decaux were the main supplier to most of the French local government authorities but wanted to expand in the UK. They knew that the key to that was getting a foothold in Westminster, the most high-profile area in the country.

I flew out on the Sunday night and stayed at my own expense at a hotel near the Champs Élysées. A car picked me up the next morning and I met up with David and our colleague Miles Young at the Decaux HQ. David and Miles had flown in early that morning.

After coffee in their boardroom and introductions, the chairman and chief executive Jean-Claude Decaux and his son Jean-François, showed us around their garden which was lined with examples of different pieces of street furniture, from advertising hoardings to automatic toilets and bus shelters.

David Weeks and Jean-Claude Decaux viewing street advert structures in Decaux's Paris headquarters.

I had taken my camera with me. I was a keen amateur photographer and loved taking photos on all my trips. So, when we came across a newly designed bus shelter with an integrated phone box, David and I were impressed. I suggested that I took a photo of David pretending to use the phone. He did as I suggested and posed with phone in hand. However, I could not get David and the whole bus shelter in the shot, so I took a couple of steps back.

What I did not realise, was that I was standing in front of an ornamental pool with a central fountain. However, for maintenance reasons, the fountain had been turned off and the pool emptied. As I stepped backwards, I fell six feet into the bottom of the pool.

Luckily, it was made of plastic so was not too hard to land on. But the next thing I knew, I was lying flat on my back with the Decaux family, Miles and David looking over the side of the pool at me. Within seconds, a whole army of staff were surrounding me. I could not move. I was conscious but my back ached. I was told not to move and that an ambulance would be on its way.

I was rushed by ambulance to the local hospital where no one seemed to speak English (or admit to it) and of course I only spoke pidgin French. After examining me, they managed to explain to me that there was no serious damage and I was merely badly bruised and that the bruises would clear up within a few days although I might ache for a while. They also reassured me that I had no concussion and so was free to leave. A taxi was arranged to return me to the Decaux HQ, where I joined David, Miles and our hosts half way through lunch. As I explained to them, on my arrival, the only real damage was to my ego. My camera lens was the only real casualty as it now had a major dent. But I would continue to use it for years and whenever I saw the dent, it reminded me of my great fall.

Oxford Street Furniture

As a result of our visit to Paris, David, Miles and I were keen to contract Decaux to design a new style of street furniture for Oxford Street. The Decaux family agreed to come up with some unique designs and so they invited the renowned architect Norman Foster to prepare some ideas and, a few months later, Jean-François came to London to show us the Foster proposals. David and I loved them, but our Director of Planning hated them and came up with numerous technical and legal reasons why we could not accept them. As David and I wanted some new original designs for our proposed revamping of our prime retail street, the Director agreed to find a London-based architect to come up with some alternatives. Of course, the Decaux family were disappointed, as they were very proud of the designs.

The irony was that the designs which came from the Director's favoured architects, were bland and did little to add to the quality of the streetscape in Oxford Street. But we reluctantly agreed to accept these (in my view) second-rate designs in order to deliver the project. The results are still in place today.

However, having spent a vast amount of money in instructing Norman Foster, the Decaux family wanted to find some use for their new designs. After negotiations, they sold the designs to the Council of Paris and the Foster street furniture, and in particular his spectacular new lighting columns, now adorn the Champs-Élysées itself. And to our embarrassment, the Council of Paris won numerous awards for their new street furniture while we won none.

Marble Arch

When Colin Barrow became Leader of the Council in 2008 (after Simon resigned to take on the role of Deputy Mayor of London), he asked me to take the lead on refurbishing the Marble Arch island. The Arch was originally designed in 1827 by John Nash, as the state entrance gates to Buckingham Palace. It stood in the same position as now occupied by the subsequently constructed East Wing of the Palace, which incorporates the famous balcony on which The Queen and Royal Family appear on special occasions. In 1851, to enable the architect Decimus Burton to create the East Wing, the Arch was moved to the north-east corner of Hyde Park. In the 1960s, when the northbound carriageway of Park Lane was created out of the park, the Arch found itself in the centre of a new traffic island.

By the turn of the Millennium, the Marble Arch island had become run down, with overgrown vegetation, the fountain no longer working and the landscape barren. It is quite a prominent site, as vehicles heading north up Park Lane, or from the west down the Bayswater Road or travelling south down the Edgware Road, cannot miss the Arch or the islands (there are two separate islands divided by a road used as a bus stand). The state of the islands left a poor impression on the thousands of people who travelled past them every day.

I decided we had to be radical and using some of the ideas I had adopted under the Westminster Initiative, I proposed that we surround the islands with large flowerbeds full of red geraniums to continue the carpet of red running through the centre of Park Lane. I argued that these flower beds had to be at a 45-degree angle, so that drivers could not help but see the beds.

The officers were resistant, coming up with a variety of arguments as to why they did not like my ideas. But I persevered and those raised flower beds are still there today. One of the officer's objections was that the budget amounted to about 40% of their total budget for flower beds. But the Leader supported me, arguing that they had to meet the cost from their existing budgets, whatever proportion of the budget it cost. The pavements were also given a deep clean.

Martin Low, our Director of Transportation and Highways, managed to persuade Thames Water to sponsor the repair of the three fountains and to introduce a coloured lighting scheme. Those fountains continue to work today, with different colours displayed each night.

While I was working on this project, my friend and colleague Christabel Flight (Councillor the Lady Flight) forwarded to me an email from an artist and sculptor called Nic Fiddian-Green. Nic was famous for sculpting large-scale horses' heads and he was looking to loan the City of Westminster one of his heads for six months and asking if there was anywhere in Westminster that he could put it.

I immediately contacted him and asked if we could put it on the main Marble Arch island. So, one night, Colin and I turned up at about midnight to watch a massive crane place the thirty-foot tall horse's head in place. The response was amazing. Everyone loved it and saw it as a new London landmark.

When the six-month loan period was due to expire, Nic contacted us to say that he needed to remove the sculpture, as it had been sold but would we allow him to make another almost identical one (albeit taller) and donate it to us on a permanent basis. We were delighted and within a month or two the sculptures were swapped and no one noticed, even though they are not identical. I am sure Nic sold many replicas and other horse head sculptures on the back of this landmark. It remains in situ today.

Nic Fiddian-Green's Horse's Head.

Activities around Marble Arch

Over the years, Westminster became the centre for many Romani people (or 'Romas' – nomadic Indo-Aryan itinerant people from central Europe) coming from Romania to beg and steal on the streets of London. After a month or two of lucrative work, they return home to their villages and families with enough money to live on for several months. Many of them are part of organised gangs which bring the Romas over to London and, while offering protection, take a slice of their rich pickings. Under the then EU rules, there was little the authorities could do, as they enjoyed free right of entry and, believe it or not, living in camps on the street is not illegal. All we could do was constantly move them on. Of course, the police arrested them for begging or in some cases stealing, but our prisons are too full to cater for these miscreants, so they would just be returned to the streets.

I have heard many stories of tourists giving these beggars tens if not hundreds of pounds, believing them to be genuinely in need or homeless. Yes, they did sleep rough when in London, but most (so the police advised us) had homes to return to in Romania.

Marble Arch was a prime target for them, because of its proximity to the Middle Eastern community which dominates the Edgware Road. Charitable giving is a strong cultural tradition in the Middle Eastern world and so many of the Arabs congregating in the area would give not insubstantial amounts to the beggars.

Sitting on the pavement, pretending not to speak English or walking around carrying sleeping babies, who we found were rarely their own – borrowed for the day and drugged to keep them asleep (as mothers with babies attracted higher donations) – the Romas would flood the West End at certain times of the year. The residents would constantly complain to us and we were often powerless to do much. Occasionally, social services would be brought in, if the children were being maltreated, but if they did get involved, the child and minder disappeared quite quickly.

Because of its island nature and open space near the Middle Eastern part of town, the grass lawn of the Marble Arch island was where the Romas would set up their village of tents on to live in during their few months in the UK 'working'. The fresh water from the fountain added to the facilities they benefitted from as well as the proximity of public toilets intended for use by tourists.

Not only did the tented village cause many social issues, such as litter, graffiti and the use of the area as an outside toilet, but the sight of the tents as one drove around Marble Arch, a main artery as one entered or left the West End, was damaging to the reputation of the city. So, after constant pressure from residents and the media to take action, we would regularly turn up with police support, accompanied by social workers, officers from the immigration service and representatives of other statutory bodies to move them on. But they just went elsewhere and within a few days would return to Marble Arch. Each 'raid' would cost the council tens of thousands of pounds. A solution had to be found that minimised the cost to the council taxpayer.

I came up with the idea of putting some attraction on the Marble Arch island, run by a commercial company, who would charge for the use of the attraction. The operator would pay us a rent and a share of any profit made but take all the commercial risk. As part of the contract, we would insist that the company running the attraction employed security guards around the Island, 24 hours day. We knew the presence of visitors to the attraction all day and the security overnight would deter the Romas from camping there. And we were right.

One year we arranged for a Ferris wheel to be erected over the summer, in which members of the public, for a fee, could ride in a capsule on an observation wheel, to see the views over the West End. I spent an afternoon, while the wheel was being erected, taping a commentary about the history of Westminster from the viewpoint of what they could see, such as stories about the Tyburn Gallows a few yards to the north, where hundreds of thousands were hanged until the last hanging in November 1783.

The Ferris wheel at Marble Arch.

I used to drive past and look up at the wheel turning and imagine these tourists in their pods listening to me, Robert Davis, giving a lecture on London's history. Who would have thought it? But it worked and that summer the Romas lived elsewhere.

One of the successes of West End Live (which I created and I describe later) was the Spiegeltent erected in Leicester Square. This is a large travelling tent constructed in wood and canvas and decorated internally with mirrors and stained glass and intended as an entertainment venue.

In early 2017, I was approached by the company that operated West End Live for us, Underbelly, with a proposal to erect a Spiegeltent in Embankment Gardens on the Thames's north bank adjacent to Charing Cross station and to use it as a temporary theatre.

I loved the idea, and we started making plans. However, what we did not anticipate was the uproar from all the local residents. Many people are probably unaware that hundreds of residents live around the Adelphi and the Victorian streets south of the Strand. Attempts were made to persuade the residents that the temporary theatre would not disturb them, but this failed, as they argued that this was just one of a number of events in the gardens and would not be the last unless they made a stand. The ward councillors were brought in by the residents who supported their concerns. Two of the councillors were good friends and councillors whose views I respected and so I reluctantly agreed that it could not go ahead.

A couple of days after we made the decision, I was giving Louise Hyams, one of the local councillors who had lobbied me, a lift home in my car from a meeting at City Hall. The subject of the theatre came up and Louise explained that she loved the idea of the theatre, but our proposed site was the problem, not the idea. She begged me to find another site where there would be little or no objections from local residents.

At this stage in our conversation, I was driving around Marble Arch, when Louise shouted, 'why not put your Spiegeltent in Marble Arch?' And as she said that, I looked across at the large lawn adjacent to the Arch and agreed that it would make a perfect setting. Moreover, a theatre on this site would bring a 24-hour presence to the Marble Arch island and help (at no cost to the Council) to deter the Roma community from setting up camp again on the island that summer.

So, the following morning, I called the officer working with me on the project, and told him what happened. Within a few weeks, the producers and the council agreed that this would be perfect and plans were commenced to open in the summer of 2017.

However, despite us believing that it would be easier to obtain the necessary consents for a temporary theatre at Marble Arch, without many objections, we found that this was not the case. A small number of residents did object, but the reality was that they all lived quite far away and could in no way be affected by the theatre. One strong objector lived about two miles away!

The one objector I was concerned about was a fellow councillor who did not represent the area around Marble Arch but lived nearby. I invited my colleague to a meeting in my office in City Hall and we discussed her objection. She was concerned that she would be kept up at night by the noise coming from the theatre and that her front garden would be used as a public toilet by drunks leaving the theatre after the show. I had to explain that theatre goers do not get drunk nor do they pee in front gardens. That just was not characteristic of theatre goers. Secondly, the show would finish at about 10 pm and the site would be cleared within half an hour, so there would be no fear of noise or disturbance late at night.

Marble Arch is a listed structure and Hyde Park protected, so I was conscious that a permanent structure would not be acceptable to the statutory authorities such as the Royal Parks Agency and Historic England. I suggested that we would only allow the theatre to operate for a limited period of eight months and I gave an assurance that after that time, we would clear the site. This certainly reassured my colleague living nearby.

In the meantime, Underbelly decided they wanted to put on *Five Guys Named Moe* the musical revue based on a piece written by Louis Jordan and reconceived by Clarke Peters. Cameron Mackintosh owned the rights and Underbelly agreed with Cameron to jointly produce it and Clarke Peters was persuaded to direct. I was honoured that in the programme, I was listed as one of the co-producers.

The show opened to tremendous reviews and was for the first six months a sell-out. I made sure that all the residents who had objected were invited to the first night and they all loved it. Several of them apologised for objecting.

A few weeks later, my colleague living nearby told me she loved the show and had seen it several times and she had had not been affected by any disturbance whatsoever and would love it to stay there for a much longer period.

The temporary theatre in Marble Arch.

Green Plaques

I cannot claim to have invented the Green Plaque, but for about twenty-five years I was in charge and responsible for not only expanding the scheme but for initiating and unveiling over a hundred of them.

Since 1866, the traditional blue plaques have been the responsibility of English Heritage and recognise famous people who once lived in the property on which the plaque is erected. However, they only erect about ten a year throughout the country.

In 1991, one of my colleagues decided that Westminster needed its own scheme as there were so many buildings with famous histories. People enjoy passing by a building and learning about its history.

The procedure was that we would usually receive nominations from the public and then I would determine whether to approve them. We required the nominator to pay the cost (originally about £400 but over the years this increased to cover all our expenses). The sponsor would also be recognised at the bottom of the plaque.

Names we commemorated (and I jointly unveiled with a family member of the deceased) included Vera Brittain (author and mother of parliamentarian Shirley Williams), Charles Babbage (inventor of the computer), Sir Edward Elgar, Sir Arthur Conan Doyle (author of the Sherlock Holmes series), Oscar Wilde, Anna Neagle and Herbert Wilcox (a joint plaque for the actress and the director, which I unveiled with the Princess Royal), Mary Seacole (Jamaican nurse in the Crimean War), TS Eliot (who wrote the poems on which the musical *Cats* was based) and Lionel Logue (speech therapist to King George VI, whose story is told in the Oscar-winning film *The King's Speech*).

I started to commemorate events associated with buildings as well as people and these included the headquarters of the Norwegian Government in Exile (during the Second World War); the 2i's Club (the café in Soho where British rock and roll was born – I unveiled this one with Cliff Richard); the site of the founding of the Liberal Party (unveiled with Nick Clegg, then Deputy Prime Minister) and the 100th anniversary of the opening of the Ivy restaurant. Susan Hampshire, the actress, accompanied me in unveiling the plaque outside the Savoy Hotel to recognise that it

With the late Shirley Williams unveiling a Green Plaque to her mother, the novelist Vera Brittain.

was the first public building in the country to be lit by electric lighting.

On the Queen's Diamond Jubilee, I came up with an idea for the 100th plaque, by unveiling (with the Lord-Lieutenant) a special green plaque on the site of the house where The Queen was born in Bruton Street, Mayfair.

Another fun one was the unveiling of a plaque to King George Tupou V of Tonga who had lived in Cleveland Square, in my ward. One of my residents, who I knew well, had suggested the plaque because the late King, while a student in London, had stayed with him. My resident was from

Sir John Gielgud and I unveil a Green Plaque for Oscar Wilde at the Haymarket Theatre.

Tonga and was also a good friend of the current King, who came to London to unveil the plaque. The Duke of Gloucester, a friend of both Kings attended and I unveiled the plaque (in my red robes and chains as Deputy Lord Mayor*) with the King. After the ceremony,

The King of Tonga and I (doubling up as Deputy Lord Mayor that afternoon) unveiling a Green Plaque in Cleveland Square, Lancaster Gate.

a full traditional English afternoon tea was served in a large marquee in the Cleveland Square gardens. I sat with the King on one side and the Duke on the other. A Royal sandwich filling!

A special one for me was the Green Plaque for Francis Crick, the Nobel Laureate who discovered the structure of DNA. Crick had been a researcher at Caius, my college at Cambridge, and a number of fellows from my college together with the Master of the College were coming to London for the ceremony in St George's Square in Pimlico.

I decided to arrange a luncheon in the Lord Mayor's Reception Rooms for the Caians, with the then Lord Mayor as host and attended by Simon (who had also been at Caius) and me. After lunch we were all driven to the site for the plaque unveiling.

---

* In 1991 to save costs, the council decided to abolish the full-time role of Deputy Lord Mayor and instead when the Lord Mayor was unable to attend a function, a former Lord Mayor still serving on the council would attend the event as Lord Mayor Locum Tenens. However, most people did not understand what a 'Lord Mayor Locum Tenens' was so we used the title Deputy Lord Mayor instead. We would take on this role on a weekly rota basis.

City of Sculpture

In 2010, Simon and I spent a long weekend in the beautiful Swiss town of Vevey on the banks of Lake Geneva. While walking around the town, we were impressed with the large number of pieces of public art that were placed on nearly every street corner and even, in one case, poking out of the Lake.

On my return to London, I called together a number of my senior officers and told them that I wanted to create a Festival of Sculpture that would place works of art all over the city and that they should remain in situ through the forthcoming Olympics. They liked the idea and, within months, we started placing large pieces of art on the streets of Westminster.

We approached several of the famous Galleries in Mayfair and asked them to loan us artworks. They would be responsible for delivering the piece, insuring and lighting it but we would not charge them rent and it would be good promotion for their artist and the gallery. Winners all round as the residents and visitors to Westminster would enjoy the pieces.

We soon realised that the best sites were in and around Park Lane because of the amount of traffic that used Park Lane each day. Of course, the horse's head was already a welcome addition to the Marble Arch island but we found an additional position adjacent to the fountains. Other locations included the middle of the central reservation of Park Lane opposite the Dorchester Hotel and on the roundabout just north of Hyde Park Corner. The idea was that each piece would be in position for six months to a year and so would allow for a regular turnover.

Mauro Perucchetti's Jelly Baby Family *at Marble Arch.*

Artists whose works were exhibited included Dale Chihuly (who works in colourful blown glass), Lorenzo Quinn (son of the famous actor Anthony Quinn), David Breuer-Weil and Dashi Namdakov.

Dashi Namdakov's Genghis Khan *at Marble Arch.*

The one that got me into trouble was Dashi Namdakov's massive 16-foot bronze statue of the Mongolian warrior, Genghis Khan. The leader of the Labour group on the council accused me of endorsing Khan's massacre of millions of his civilian population. Although regarded as a tyrannical and brutal leader, he created the largest contiguous empire in history, was seen as a masterful military leader and is credited for creating the world's first bureaucracy. In any event, he died over 850 years ago and is now one of the most famous characters in history. The papers had a field day but Genghis stayed in position for about a year.

The next problem came from a statue in Cavendish Square just off Oxford Street. At the centre of the Square lies a plinth with nothing on it. It had been vacant for years and no one at City Hall knew why.

When I was approached by a Korean artist from Hong Kong, Meekyoung Shin, who wanted to replicate the statue that had originally stood on the plinth, I was interested.

However, she explained that the equestrian statue would be constructed in soap (called *Written in soap – a plinth project*) and over a period of three or four months, would dissolve from the rain and this would make a statement about pollution in central London as passers-by would see a melting figure. I thought that, as it would only be in position for a handful of months, it would be fun.

I am afraid my Scottish history is rather lacking as my interest in history at school had concentrated on the Tudors and Stuarts. When I enquired as to who the statue would be, it meant nothing to me when I was advised that it would be the Duke of Cumberland,

Written in soap – a plinth project *in Cavendish Square.*

third and youngest son of King George II. It was only a few weeks after it was erected that the furore erupted in the Scottish press. I was headline news north of the border. It was soon explained to me that while the Duke was famous for his success at the Battle of Culloden, he was known as 'Butcher Cumberland' for his defeat of Bonnie Prince Charles and the Jacobites as well as the slaying of thousands of Scots.

Culloden is renowned as the bloodiest battle between the English and the Scots, and with the massacre of the Scots, it is a sore point between the two countries. Any celebration of the Duke is seen by the Scots as provocation! Accordingly, my giving of the necessary consent for the return of the Duke to the Square, albeit made in soap, really riled the Scots. It turned out that the original statue erected in 1770 had been removed in 1868 to appease the Scots and that is why the plinth had remained vacant ever since. Why none of my officers explained this to me, I do not know. I got the blame and one paper in Scotland almost claimed that I would be the cause of the next Scottish-English war!

To make things worse, the soap failed to melt and it took eighteen months to do so, leaving the full statue in full view throughout this period.

Bushra Fakhoury

One day, my colleague, councillor Susie Burbridge, asked me to allow one of her friends to exhibit a piece somewhere in Westminster. I said I would have to see what her work was like. I was accordingly shown a booklet showing the artist's work. I really liked a particular one. *Dunamis* depicts a naked man holding up a massive elephant by his trunk. So, it was agreed that a large version would be made to stand on the roundabout just north of Hyde Park Corner, opposite the Hilton Park Lane.

The sculptor was Bushra Fakhoury and the first time I met her was when I attended its unveiling one Saturday lunchtime. The piece was massive and anyone driving up or down Park Lane could not fail to miss

Dunamis *by Bushra Fakhoury in Park Lane.*

it. The statue was extremely popular and as a result stood in Park Lane for about three years.

After the success of *Dunamis*, I asked Bushra if she had another large piece that we could place in Marble Arch. The issue with the Marble Arch position is that the sculpture has to be big to be seen and few sculptors had artwork that large. Bushra invited me to her studio, which was full of small maquettes of all her work. The one I loved was *Danse Gwenedour – Celebration of Life*. This is based on a traditional dance from a village in France and depicts four male dancers holding hands in a circle with three of them with their legs in the air. Bushra told me that she could make one seven metres high; within months, it was seen by everyone driving around Marble Arch.

Bushra and me unveiling Danse Gwenedour *at Marble Arch.*

Marble Arch Tower

Over at Marble Arch, I was talking to Mike Hussey and his property development company, Almacantar, about his proposals for the total redevelopment of Marble Arch Tower and the famous Odeon Cinema at the junction of Edgware Road and Oxford Street, by the famous Tyburn Stone, which marks the place where thousands were hanged from 1196 until 1869.

Mike had appointed the architect Rafael Viñoly to design the replacement buildings. I thought that this was one of the most important sites in Westminster, as it was the gateway to the West End from the north and west and the building could be seen head on, driving from the south up Park Lane. I therefore wanted a fantastic statement building so that people would go 'wow' when they drove or walked past.

What I was shown was in my view a pleasant but bland design that would in no way stand as a gateway. My attempts to persuade both Mike and Viñoly to change the design and up their game fell on deaf ears.

I had a suggestion. What if we regarded the Viñoly building as the plain canvas backdrop and cover it with a massive piece of art? Mike asked me to explain my idea. I took a sheet of paper and drew the outline of the proposed office building and, bearing in mind that the site was directly opposite Hyde Park, I drew on the front of the building a massive tree wrapping its branches around the building. Mike and his colleague Kathrin liked the idea and agreed to go away and develop it.

A few months later, I was invited to their office and was shown their revised proposals. They had commissioned the glass sculptor Dale Chihuly to design the tree I had proposed. This would be a real coup, as Chihuly was so well respected and seen as an iconic artist. It would become a major London landmark. The sculpture would be made of glass leaves and coloured glass flowers hanging off the branches, running right across the front of the building as far as the roof. My Director of Planning and I loved it. They were given the green light.

A few weeks later I was invited to another meeting, when I was told that Chihuly's estimate of the cost of constructing the art work would be excessive. In addition, it was unlikely that the building would take the weight of the glass and the health and safety guys were concerned about what would happen if a piece of the glass fell off and crashed to the ground. It was not a practical starter!

It was back to the drawing board. A few weeks later, I was called to a further meeting where I was shown several designs by two different artists. One I really liked because it reflected my original idea more than the other. It too involved a tree, but would be much lighter with the flowers made of a very light resin. Furthermore, the cost was acceptable to Almacantar. The young artist who had designed it was Lee Simmons. I was very impressed by the way he explained his design and how he sold his proposal to me.

Lee is an artist who specialises in street level sculptures as well as artwork that adorns buildings. After obtaining a degree at Sheffield Hallam University, he obtained a Master's

Lee Simmons's door in Wimpole Street – Grandioso.

degree at the Royal College of Art. His first professional assignment was from the Howard de Walden Estate, which invited him to design a front door for a new hospital they were constructing at 77 Wimpole Street.

The resultant door, called *Grandioso*, is just stunning and led to more work coming his way not only from De Walden but other major developers throughout central London.

Lee and I had a number of meetings as the design for Marble Arch was developed. A year later, we were approaching the centenary of the start of the First World War, when my colleague Rachael Robathan (subsequently Leader of the Council but then a fellow cabinet member and the council's 'Armed Forces Champion') asked to see me for help in the commemorations the council were planning. It appeared that the officers and staff who had worked for the original (pre-1965) Westminster Council and had lost their lives during the Great War, had been commemorated by a large plaque in the original City Hall in Charing Cross Road but, after the move to Victoria Street in 1965, it had been lost. Rachael sought my help in raising funds to have a replacement plaque made for the current City Hall.

However, I suggested that instead of just a simple plaque with an inscribed 'Roll of Honour', we should create something special to commemorate their lives and the centenary. I suggested we ask Lee to design something and, if we liked it, I would seek sponsorship to cover the cost from private companies.

When some weeks later Lee produced his proposal, we were all taken aback by his idea. We loved it. It was perfect. It would stand adjacent to the entrance to City Hall in a pedestrianised side street off Victoria Street and would consist of eighty-two Carrara marble shards of varying heights, each shard representing a council officer who had fought and died during the conflict. Their names would be inscribed around the base.

We gave Lee the go ahead and I then set about raising sufficient sponsorship to pay for it and obtaining consent from Land Securities, the property company that owned the freehold to City Hall and the adjacent land on which the memorial would sit. Neither were easy and I had to use all my charm and a bit of arm wrestling to raise enough money to cover all the costs and to persuade not only Land Securities but all the statutory authorities to approve the proposals. In December 2016, the Lord Mayor of Westminster together with Rachael, myself and other councillors attended a formal unveiling ceremony during which the Dean of Westminster conducted a brief service, using the prayers and words

The Dean of Westminster blessing the new war memorial outside
Westminster City Hall with me in robes.

from the original service in 1921, when the Roll of Honour was unveiled by the then Mayor and Dean.

A few years later, Lee was staying in Mallorca and we were due to meet up over lunch when I received a last-minute invitation to lunch the same day from Andrew Lloyd Webber and his wife Madeleine. Andrew and Madeleine have a holiday home, not far from mine on the island. I explained that I was due to meet a friend from London that day and so had to decline, but they immediately told me that they would be delighted if he joined us.

Over lunch, I explained a little about what Lee did and then left him to amplify, while I showed them photographs of his work. They were very impressed and suggested that when they return to London, they would like to consider asking Lee to design a new stage door for the London Palladium, which they owned. In October 2018, the resultant *Wall of Fame* was unveiled by Des O'Connor, Sir Tommy Steele, Jimmy Tarbuck and Sir Cliff Richard. I had the honour of being invited and was thanked by everyone for introducing Lee to the Lloyd Webbers.

The London Palladium's Wall of Fame
by Lee Simmons.

The wall itself comprises of a number of stainless-steel square frames, each depicting a famous star who had appeared at the Palladium including Cilla Black, Ronnie Barker, Judy Garland, Bruce Forsyth and Bob Hope. There are a number of blank ones for future additions. Each frame is cut in to hundreds of tiny holes using a digital process so the larger the hole the darker that part of the picture. Quite a unique process.

Returning to Lee's tree design that I had approved for the Marble Arch building, I was hoping that this would have been one of my greatest achievements as a councillor. But alas, this was not to happen, as later on during the development process, without me on the council to insist on the tree, it was dropped from the project and replaced with a standalone piece by Lee at ground level. Although Lee's replacement piece is stunning, I think the loss of the massive tree was a great loss to London and Westminster. C'est la vie!

The Royal Opera House

In the mid 1990s as chairman of the Council's Planning and Transportation committee, I led negotiations with the Royal Opera House on their renovations and extensions which included incorporating the old Floral Hall into the complex, the creation of new wings in Russell Street and James Street, including a new fly tower. This involved me attending weekly breakfast meetings in a hotel in Marylebone (near my office) with Sir Jeremy Isaacs, then General Director of the Royal Opera House, Sir Jeremy Dixon, the renowned architect, and Bill Stewart, one of my planning officers. When the plans were ready for approval they appeared before the main Planning Committee which I chaired.

However, during the planning process one of my colleagues, trying to show off his green credentials, insisted the Opera House make its new roof greener! Accordingly, a few weeks later, Sir Jeremy Dixon sent me a drawing of how this could be achieved showing a meadow on the roof with sheep grazing. I framed the signed drawing and it now hangs on the wall of my flat in London.

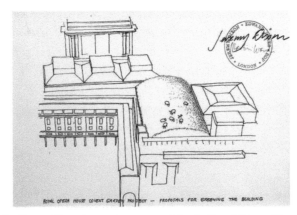

Sir Jeremy Dixon's greening proposal for the Royal Opera House.

Chapter 21

My Marriage

In the spring of 2007, Simon and I had lived together for almost twenty years but we had been very discreet about our relationship. In the 1980s and 1990s, we genuinely believed that our political careers would have suffered if we had been openly gay in the Conservative Party. This was the time of Section 28 (the Thatcher government's banning of the teaching of homosexuality in schools) and the controversy surrounding it. Attitudes were very different from today. I frequently said that if you admitted to being gay in the Conservative Party in those early days, you had no chance of getting anywhere. However, nowadays I jokingly argue that if you are not openly gay in the Conservative Party, then your chances of promotion are limited!

We did not even tell our families that Simon and I were in a relationship. I very much regret not having told my parents and by the time I came out, they had both passed away. Why did I not tell them? I really do not know. I think I was just frightened as to how they would react. But once I had come out, my sister told me that they had guessed, as Simon and I were always together. My parents would always invite Simon to join me at family events. Similarly, I was always invited to join Simon at his family's dinners and other functions including his mother's marriage to Ronald Gross in 1990.

In 2007, Simon was about to become chairman of the Local Government Association (the LGA), the national body representing all councillors and councils in England and Wales and the body which the national government negotiated with and consulted with on local government issues.

As leader of Westminster City Council, Simon had become involved with the LGA and soon became chairman of its Improvement Board. Through leading this committee, he worked closely with John Prescott, then Deputy Prime Minister and Secretary of State for Local Government, who had recommended Simon for his knighthood.

Simon had also impressed his colleagues, so when Lord Bruce-Lockhart retired after his statutory three-year term, his colleagues urged him to stand as chairman. The respect that they had for Simon led to him winning a massive victory.

However, when he decided to stand for the chairmanship, he told me over dinner one night in our flat that he thought we should be open about our relationship, as he did not want to succeed to the chairmanship of the LGA with the high profile that it brought, without being open and honest, as the press would have a field day if we continued to keep it a secret. *Private Eye* had already repeatedly referred to Simon Milton and his 'very close friend' Robert Davis and he thought this would continue if we were not more open. He suggested that we get married.

No bended knee or ring but a matter-of-fact proposal!

This was not long after the law had changed allowing same sex civil partnerships. Sadly, we were never able to 'marry' as same sex marriages (as opposed to civil partnerships) were not made lawful until after Simon died.

I was more cautious, and concerned at the reaction from friends, family and colleagues. So I suggested that we hold a low-key ceremony with just the close family in attendance. Simon disagreed and, as always, he was right. He suggested a full-blown wedding with all our close friends in attendance.

I came up with the idea of getting married (as we called it despite it only being a civil partnership) at the Ritz Hotel. I knew the sons of one of the owners, as well as the general manager of the Hotel, who would help us organise it and hopefully agree an affordable deal. With that agreed, Simon and I arranged to meet Stephen Boxall, the general manager, and the plans started to flow. A date was set and it was agreed that we would hold the ceremony itself in the garden of the Hotel with seventy of our close friends and family (as that is all it held) and this would be followed by 'Afternoon Tea at the Ritz' in the beautiful state rooms of the adjoining William Kent House with an additional two hundred guests joining us for tea and the speeches.

With everything set, invitations were printed and on a Monday morning in May 2007 they were posted to our guests. For most of our guests, this was our 'outing' because until then, they had no idea that we were a couple.

One of our friends, we do not know which one, but I have a hunch that I know who it is, decided to pass a copy of the invitation to the *Evening Standard*, the widely read London daily evening newspaper.

On the Wednesday afternoon, I was walking down Bond Street when I noticed one of the *Evening Standard* billboards propping up a stand containing a pile of the papers. In large letters I read 'Westminster Chief to wed gay lover'. With my heart thumping I ran over to the paperman and bought a copy.

My heart stopped thumping and actually stopped for a second as I read the headline covering half the front page of the paper and two large photos, one of me (in my mayoral chains of office) and another of Simon giving a speech.

The front page of the Evening Standard *– 23rd May 2007.*

This was the outing of outings!

Now everyone in London knew, not just our close friends and family. As well as a short piece on what was left of the front page, the paper included a double page spread containing more photos of Simon and me and an extensive article about us. However, despite the lurid headlines, the article was very positive and spoke highly of both Simon and me and our decision to go public.

Now we were all over the press, with several other national papers following up on the story in the ensuing days. Several gossip columns started speculating on who would be invited, including the *Daily Mail* suggesting that David Cameron, the Leader of the Opposition, would be there as he had attended Simon's party to celebrate his knighthood.

On Sunday 17th June 2007 the day arrived and in glorious sunshine and in front of our close friends and family, Alison Cathcart, the Superintendent Registrar, presided over our civil partnership in front of a wall of stunning flowers. The most important part of the ceremony, the signing of the register, had to lawfully be conducted in a building and not outside. So, at this juncture in the ceremony, Simon and I together with our two witnesses, our sisters Susan and Lisa, left our guests and with Alison, moved inside to the Marie Antoinette Suite where we all signed the register. While we disappeared for fifteen minutes, the guests were entertained by the children of the Sylvia Young Theatre School singing a variety of songs.

When we returned, with Alison's blessing she left us and as she did, Rabbi Mark Winer, the Rabbi from Simon's synagogue in Upper Berkeley Street, walked in and took over the service. He then presided over a full Jewish marriage ceremony. He later confessed that this

Simon and I being married by Rabbi Mark Winer in the garden of the Ritz Hotel – 17th June 2007.

Raine, Countess of Spencer, with my grandmother Anne and me at my wedding reception.

was the first all-male wedding he had conducted but he told us he was proud to do so, as he had so much respect for us. The ceremony even included both Simon and I smashing the traditional glass under our feet. Although our civic partnership was not a marriage, our Jewish service was a proper marriage service!

As Simon and I exchanged wine glasses to drink from each other's glass, as is traditional, Simon started to cry. I looked into his eyes and had to control myself from doing likewise.

Once the service was over, we joined all the other guests arriving for tea including my friend Raine, the Countess of Spencer, who got on well with my 92-year-old grandmother.

Simon and I received over seven hundred letters and messages from friends and acquaintances congratulating us and telling us how brave we were. One has to put this in context, as we were among the first same sex couples with both of us having high profiles within the Conservative Party, openly and publicly getting hitched.

Several letters mentioned sons or relatives who were still in the closet and how difficult they and their families found it and that our openness and the positivity that resulted was a clear message that everyone should be open and honest to themselves and to their friends and family and that only love will come from that.

I have frequently been asked to speak to groups and sometimes individuals about our coming out story. I liken the experience of being outed on all the *Evening Standard* billboards to a baby being thrown in the deep end of a swimming pool and being expected to swim to the side, having never been in a pool before. You sink or swim and instinct kicks in and makes you swim. One day we had been secretive and discreet about our relationship

Celebrating our wedding with tea at the Ritz.

with just a few close friends knowing and even our close family kept in the dark. The next week the whole world knew – well, the whole of London at least. If someone had told me that that was the way we would be outed, I would have probably declined Simon's proposal. But am I pleased I did go ahead and once I had got over the initial shock of my private life being plastered over the front page of the largest selling evening newspaper in the country, it was liberating and I could, for the first time in my life, be honest and be myself.

Chapter 22

My Love of Theatre

My interest in the theatre started at a young age. I think it was being taken to a pantomime at the London Palladium that first gave me the goosebumps and that got me intrigued by the world of theatre. At first it was seeing Cilla Black as Aladdin at the Palladium, but I was also taken every Christmas to the annual pantomime at the Golders Green Hippodrome and, after it closed, to the former Odeon in Temple Fortune.

My Pollock's Toy Theatre

When I was about ten or eleven, my parents bought me a Pollock's Toy Theatre. Toy theatres were very popular in Victorian times and comprised a cardboard proscenium arch toy theatre, about fifteen inches high and operated by moving cut-out characters on long wires from each side of the stage. With a fly tower above the stage and with simple lighting, plays could be performed. Half the fun was creating the backdrops and props. Originally these were purchased from Pollock's toy shop but subsequently I started making my own from cutting out photos in glossy magazines.

A Pollock's Toy Theatre.

Benjamin Pollock had inherited a Hoxton-based printing business from his father-in-law and soon moved the business to Monmouth Street in Covent Garden selling toy theatres and paper backcloths and sets (known as sheets) in addition to cardboard cut-out characters. These were sold for a penny for black and white (allowing the owners to colour them in themselves) or tuppence for coloured versions.

The shop (albeit on a different site) still exists in Covent Garden and more recently was owned by Peter Baldwin, who played Derek Wilton in *Coronation Street* for many years. Knowing my interest in Pollock's toy theatres, the owners of Covent Garden, Capital & Counties, arranged for me to meet Peter and we became friends. Peter even arranged an evening in my honour, when he performed a show for me and other invited guests using his own Pollock toy theatre. It was a special evening.

Once I had grown bored with my Pollock toy theatre, I decided to think big. I was about 15 years of age when I built my own toy theatre, twice the size of the traditional Pollock version. Made from wood and hardboard and with my basic knowledge of electrical circuits learnt during my study of physics for O level, I built my own circuit of stage lighting, operated from large battery boxes. I adapted the Pollock cut-out characters and used my initiative to create a variety of different backcloths and sets. The miniature furniture from my sister's dolls house became very useful.

It was a weekly tradition that all my grandparents would visit us at our family home on a Sunday afternoon for tea. My Mum always made the same tea. Bridge rolls covered either in smoked salmon and a small slice of cucumber, cream cheese with a sprinkle of paprika or smoked herring. I hated the herring but would stuff myself with the others. This would always be followed by beautiful fresh pastries from a local patisserie called Sharatons, with all of us unaware that it was owned by my future husband's family.

After tea, I would insist that the family all sat in rows of dining room chairs to watch my latest play performed on my toy theatre. However, most weekends, the afternoon would end with me walking off in a huff, halfway through the performance as my family would not stop talking among themselves about some family gossip instead of concentrating on watching the performance.

School Plays

At school, my interest in the theatre led me to volunteer to appear in the house play competition. Held every November, each of my school's houses put on a forty-five-minute performance in competition with each other to win the prized trophy.

When I was in the fourth form (aged 15), I auditioned for the East House play, Chekhov's *The Cherry Orchard*. I passed my audition and found myself with a very minor walk-on part with just a handful of words. But I loved it and was very proud of being part of the camaraderie among the acting and producing team. The following year I auditioned again and this time got the larger part of Snug the Joiner (and consequently the lion) in the Mechanicals scene from Shakespeare's *A Midsummer Night's Dream*. That required me to roar. And roar I did on cue! We won first prize.

With some confidence, I offered to produce and direct the house play the following year together with my then best friend David Wiseman. I went up to Southampton Row in Covent Garden, to a shop called Samuel French, which specialised in selling sets of play scripts. After a couple of hours of browsing through their stock I got excited about a play I found called *The Ghost of Jerry Bundler*, a 19th century ghost story written by WW Jacobs. I cast myself in one of the lead roles and cast a number of my friends in other roles and held auditions among the younger pupils for the other parts. One successful candidate was Michael Prescott who went on to become one of the main investigative and political journalists for *The Sunday Times*.

Feeling even more confident, going into my final year at school, I decided to produce and direct *Macbeth* as the East House entry in the annual house play competition. Knowing that it was too long to perform in full, I decided to take the famous murder scene and rewrite it to ensure it ran for the required forty-five minutes. We were allowed to bring in girls from other schools to play Lady Macbeth and other female parts and I dressed the cast in remodelled old velvet curtains. We were successful again and won first prize. I was getting the hang of this acting lark and so when the school play, directed by the head of English, Mr Dudley, was auditioning, I volunteered.

My audition for Shakespeare's *Much Ado about Nothing* went well and I was cast as Don Pedro, one of the main parts. But rehearsals did not go well and after the third day, the Director decided he wanted someone else to play Don Pedro and asked me to play the friar who marries Hero and Claudio instead. It was then that I started to think that acting was not necessarily my future. I accepted that acting was not one of my strong points despite enjoying the limelight.

Cambridge

On arriving in Cambridge, I decided to try again by auditioning for Footlights, the seedbed for many famous actors and comedians such as John Cleese, Eric Idle, Peter Cook, Clive James and Jonathan Miller. I was told after the audition that I would hear if I had been successful. I never heard again! When I later discovered that my contemporaries that had auditioned that day included Emma Thompson, Stephen Fry and Hugh Laurie, I was not surprised.

But I had one more go. Early on in my third year, my friend Stephen Galloway, was intending to direct an Alan Bennett comedy called *Habeas Corpus*. He invited me to take on the role of Dennis Wicksteed, the main character's idiot son. [Some said – perfect casting!]

Appearing in Alan Bennett's Habeas Corpus *at Pembroke College, Cambridge 1979.*

When we started rehearsing, a problem soon materialised. The script required me to sing. But I had always been unable to sing. I was tone deaf. At school, I was one of only five pupils in my year (of ninety pupils) who was not allowed to be in the choir because I was so bad.

When Stephen realised that I was hopeless and had no idea how to use my voice, he sent me to a music teacher who spent three hour-long sessions trying to teach me to sing. But even he gave up, saying I was just tone deaf. Stephen therefore rewrote the script, removing the singing. The one lesson I did learn from this episode was that I was definitely not destined for the stage. I would have to enjoy the theatre from the auditorium.

With my theatrical ambitions being brought to an end, I turned to my interest in politics. They do say that all politicians are failed actors. We all do the same thing … perform.

The West End Stage

Jumping ahead twenty years, my partner Simon was now Leader of Westminster Council and I was his Chief Whip, when one day we both read an article in the *Evening Standard* in which theatre producer Sir Cameron Mackintosh criticised Westminster Council for its lack of support for West End theatres. Simon immediately wrote to Cameron inviting him to a meeting. He accepted and Simon asked me as a theatre fan to join them. As always, Simon had thought carefully about the meeting and informed Cameron and Nick Allott, the managing director of Cameron's company, who had accompanied him to the meeting, that he would be investing hundreds of thousands of pounds into improving the West End and in particular the areas outside the theatres and this would include creating a special identity for theatreland with designated 'Theatreland' signage on all street nameplates in the area. Cameron was impressed and invited Simon and me on a tour of some of his theatres to see the works he was undertaking to improve them. Cameron also began inviting us to the first nights (called 'press nights') of his new shows.

I had actually met Nick Allott a few years earlier. As Lord Mayor of Westminster, I was frequently invited by Patrick Deuchar, the chief executive of the Royal Albert Hall, to see shows at the Hall. Patrick would often host a dinner in his private suite after the show. On one such occasion, I sat next to Nick and we became friends.

Andrew Lloyd Webber

I had always been a fan of the work of (Lord) Andrew Lloyd Webber. Therefore, when he wrote to me about his proposal to create a yellow brick road from Oxford Circus tube station to the front door of the London Palladium, to promote his new production of *The Wizard of Oz*, I suggested we meet to discuss his proposal.

We met at Andrew's office and despite my accompanying officers' concerns, I agreed that Andrew's team could lay the yellow brick road provided that the surface was not slippery. As it happens, for a whole variety of reasons, Andrew subsequently decided not to install it. But after the formal meeting ended, I went up to Andrew and started chatting about the state of West End theatre and his latest projects.

Andrew Lloyd Webber and me at my 60th birthday party at Annabel's.

When I got home that evening, I sent Andrew an email suggesting we meet up for lunch to chat further. He replied, inviting me to lunch at the Ivy Club opposite his office.

When we met, we found that we had a common interest in not only the theatre but in architecture. Andrew was extremely enthusiastic about architecture as well as gothic churches. We became friends and when he learnt that I had a holiday home in Mallorca, not far from his own holiday home in Deia in the Tramuntana mountains, about forty minutes' drive from my flat, he invited me to join him and his family for dinner when we were both next in Mallorca.

Andrew lives up a steep and windy narrow lane behind the village of Deia and my first visit to dinner was just the two of us, because his wife Madeleine had returned early to London on business. Our chat was fascinating and our friendship was cemented and thereafter we frequently met up for lunch or dinner when were both on the Island.

At my 60th birthday party, which I held in Annabel's, the Mayfair night club, Andrew very kindly gave the main speech wishing me a happy birthday.

Nica Burns

Most of the West End theatres are owned by just four companies: Delfont Mackintosh (Cameron Mackintosh); LW Theatres (Andrew Lloyd Webber); the Ambassador Theatre Group (founded by Sir Howard Panter and his wife Dame Rosemary Squire); and Nimax Theatres owned by Nica Burns and her American-based business partner Max Weitzenhoffer.

I first met Nica when the Crown Estate were redeveloping their Quadrant 3 site just behind Piccadilly Circus, formerly the home of the Regent Palace Hotel. The proposals (after lengthy negotiations) were acceptable and heading to my planning committee for a decision. Out of the blue, I received a letter from Nica demanding to see me before the application was considered by my committee. I agreed to meet her and what appeared to be a whirlwind entered my office and, without stopping for a formal introduction and before she could sit herself in a seat opposite me and my officers, she started haranguing me about how the development was going to affect her neighbouring theatres, the Apollo and the Lyric in Shaftesbury Avenue. She did not stop for at least ten minutes before I could even say hello and introduce myself and my team.

Her main beef was her concern that the noise from the building works would be heard and would interfere with matinees at her theatres, which frequently showed serious plays requiring quiet.

I understood the issue but suggested that this would only be a problem during matinees as noisy works were unlikely to be happening at night and it was probably just one afternoon a week as most theatres only did two matinees a week, one of which was on Saturdays when there would be no construction work.

I explained to Nica that I knew the senior management team at the Crown Estate and would see if I could persuade them to agree a condition that would prevent them undertaking noisy work during Nica's matinees, so long as she gave them notice of the

Nica Burns speaking at the party given in my honour by the property industry on my retirement as chairman of Planning on Westminster Council, held at the Royal Academy in April 2017.

times and days. She was delighted and I changed the subject to discuss my love of theatre and the state of West End theatre.

After the meeting, I immediately phoned David Shaw, the Crown Estate executive in charge of the development and he agreed to include such a condition. I had made a new fan in Nica and we became firm friends.

Sir Howard Panter and Dame Rosemary Squire

To complete the 'Gang of Four', the other main theatre owner is Ambassador Theatre Group (ATG), which owns more theatres throughout the country than any other company. What differentiates them from Cameron, Andrew and Nica is that they also own theatres outside the West End. The company was originally set up by Howard Panter (now Sir Howard) and his wife Rosemary Squire (now Dame Rosemary); however, they subsequently sold their interests in ATG and have set up a group of companies under the Trafalgar Entertainment banner and now own the Trafalgar Theatre in Whitehall.

Simon and I got to know Rosemary during her tenure as President of the Society of London Theatres (SOLT), the organisation representing the owners of the West End theatres as well as the producers of the shows. Originally, Simon got to know her better than I did and would frequently sit next to her as Leader of the Council at SOLT events and particularly at the Olivier Award dinners. She very kindly added Simon to her press night guest list and so Simon and I (as his plus one) would frequently attend. Very kindly, after Simon died, she added my name to the guest list and allowed me to continue to attend press nights.

At one such press night, Rosemary mentioned that she was going to Mallorca for her summer holiday and when I told her about my flat and the fact that I would be there at the same time, she invited me to join her and her husband for lunch in Deia, where they were staying. At lunch that summer I got to know Howard, who I had previously met but never really talked to and found we got on really well. It became a regular date and every summer, when they went to Deia for their holidays, I would join them for lunch.

The Astoria Theatre, my greatest legacy: the first new West End theatre in fifty years
The Astoria at the northern end of Charing Cross Road was known in recent times as the venue for G-A-Y, the popular gay nightclub. The building had originally been a pickle factory and then in the 1930s it turned into a dance hall where my grandmother Anne told me she and my grandfather would frequently attend dances. The building also spent time as a cinema before becoming a theatre. Changing use frequently, it finally became a live music venue and the home for G-A-Y.

However, in order to construct the new Crossrail (to be known as the Elizabeth Line) that would connect Paddington in the west to Liverpool Street in the east through an underground tunnel running under the length of Oxford Street, the site was compulsorily purchased to create the new Tottenham Court Road Crossrail station.

One day, the senior Directors of Derwent London, the property company which owned the site, came to see me to discuss their proposals.

The Astoria Theatre in 2004.

Once Crossrail had completed constructing the station underground, the surface would be returned to Derwent and they proposed to construct a large office building on the site. Once the plans were explained to me, I asked where the theatre was. They started huffing and puffing. I explained that a theatre had stood on this site for nearly a hundred years and that theatres were protected and so we would expect the site to include a theatre, although we accepted that it would be smaller than the original. It could be argued that I was on weak ground as the building had actually only been used as a theatre for a proportion of its history and was a music venue or dance hall for much longer. However, I took into account the public outcry and campaign for the Astoria and the right thing to do was to ensure that the new development included a theatre. I convinced the chairman, John Burns, that his legacy to London should not be a collection of office buildings but also the first newly built theatre in the West End for nearly fifty years

A few months later, they returned to see me with their architect, the well-respected Simon Allford of Allford Hall Monaghan Morris, to show me an amended proposal which now incorporated a one-hundred-seat theatre. We were getting there! I explained that from my knowledge of the theatre world, one hundred seats would not be commercial and that they needed to include at least three hundred seats to make it a viable venture. Reluctantly, they went back to the drawing board.

A third meeting was arranged and I was pleased to see that they had incorporated a much larger theatre which satisfied my requirements to make it commercial. I then asked them who would operate it. They looked at each other and it was clear that they had not given it any thought. One of the directors answered by suggesting they would find some community theatre to do so. I explained that there was little money available to subsidise such a theatre and they needed to find a commercial partner to satisfy me and ensure that it would operate successfully. John Burns responded by admitting that they did not know any theatre people who they could approach. I said that I did and I would talk to a few of my theatre friends and back to them.

I immediately called Cameron Mackintosh and told him about the project. He set his architects onto the case but a few weeks later he called me to a meeting to explain that it was too small a project for the type of work he wanted to produce so he would have to decline.

I then approached Nica Burns. She loved the idea. Nica produced, and her theatres housed, many plays (as opposed to Cameron's large-scale musicals) and so this new small theatre would fit nicely into her style of theatre production and management. I arranged a meeting to introduce Nica to John Burns and one of his senior directors, Paul Williams.

It was a marriage made in heaven and now (as I write this) Derwent are building a six-hundred-seat standalone theatre with back of house, a rehearsal room, restaurants and bars, facing onto its own piazza. The theatre will be flexible, allowing it to be formatted for productions in the round (with seating in the round on all four sides – the first in the West End) and with various other combinations of layout including the traditional proscenium arch.

A computer-generated image of the new theatre.

*At the reception given in my honour at the Royal Academy in March 2017, Nica Burns gave
a lovely speech about me and showed a slide depicting a mock-up of her new theatre with
'Westminster – the musical' playing and starring one Robert Davis.*

Whenever I met John Burns, the chairman of Derwent, he always joked that I had cost his company millions in the additional money they have pumped into the project but he did so with a smile as he always ended by stating that he was very proud of what they were creating. The directors of Derwent had clearly taken on board my suggestion that this should be their legacy project.

People often ask me what my greatest legacy was as a senior Westminster councillor for over thirty-six years and I always say that this project is certainly top of my list.

When it opens in 2022, I will sit there at the first night and know that if I had not pushed Derwent into including a theatre in this office development, the first new theatre in the West End in decades would not be there for the world of entertainment to enjoy.

The Other Palace

The other new London theatre I can claim credit for is the aptly named 'The Other Palace' sitting, as it does, adjacent to Buckingham Palace in Victoria. The theatre sits on the site of the old Westminster Theatre which was owned by 'Moral Rearmament', an international moral and spiritual movement created by an American minister in 1938, concerned that the answer to the rise of Hitler was not going to be resolved by the world powers rearming themselves. When not in use by the movement, the building would be rented out for theatrical productions and eventually converted into an arts centre. However, in June 2002 the building was almost completely destroyed by fire.

A developer subsequently acquired what was left of the site and sought planning permission to build a block of flats. However, mindful of the council's policy to protect theatres, it included a three-hundred-seat theatre in the basement.

About two years after that consent was granted, the developer came to see me at City

Hall to explain that his development was just not commercially viable if it had to include a theatre and requesting that he be allowed to drop that requirement. He would, however, be happy to pay a sum of £100,000 for improvements to other theatres in Westminster. I explained that it was just not acceptable. I emphasised that it was essential to provide a theatre to replace the lost one, although I had accepted it could be smaller at just three hundred seats, but £100,000 would not go very far towards the improvement of another theatre and quite soon such a donation would be long forgotten. I refused his request.

The old Westminster Theatre, Victoria.

After much haggling, I indicated that one way forward would be for the council to agree another storey on the building to increase the number of flats which would help the developer's viability. I wanted to ensure that a theatre reopened on this site and I did not think another floor would be an issue. The developer went away happy.

A year later he returned and again emphasising that the development with a theatre included was still unviable, asked if he could have consent for yet another floor. After extensive negotiations, we agreed to the further floor but we told him that would be the final extension and we would not consider any further such applications and would continue to insist on a new fully fitted out theatre being included. But like a boomerang, he returned a third time, just a few months later, continuing to argue that the development was still not viable and if we insisted on the theatre remaining, then he would have little choice but to put his company into liquidation and we would end up with nothing. But knowing my planning law better than he did, I stood my ground, explaining that if his company went into liquidation, a subsequent owner buying the site from the liquidator would be bound to include a theatre. Because a purchaser would have bought the site for a relatively cheap sum, they would be able to afford to fund the development with a theatre. He left the meeting despondent but within months, I learnt that he had started construction on the new block of flats and, importantly, with a theatre included as originally agreed.

The new theatre with the flats above.

I am advised that once the project got going, the developer fell in love with the theatre and from his own funds paid for the installation of a magnificent Carrera marble staircase that connects the theatre lobby to the first-floor restaurant. The theatre eventually opened to great fanfare and I was kindly asked by the theatre operator to say a few words at the opening ceremony.

The Carrera staircase.

After a number of successful seasons, the theatre operator sold the lease of the theatre to Andrew Lloyd Webber as a home for new musicals. Andrew subsequently contacted me to advise me that he was proposing to change the theatre's name and, knowing of my involvement with the creation of the theatre, wanted me to know that he had visited The Queen to seek her permission to call the theatre The Other Palace. He assured me she had consented (or at least not objected) and hoped that I would not object, particularly as my department at the council had the power to refuse the name change. Knowing The Queen had been consulted and not objected, how could we?

Chapter 23

West End Live

West End Live is a theatrical phenomenon. It is an annual theatrical event that takes place over a weekend in late June each year. Starting in Leicester Square in 2005, it now takes place annually in Trafalgar Square.

Fair in the Square

The full story goes back six years earlier to the autumn of 1999 when I was sitting on the backbenches of the council. Simon was recovering from his bone marrow transplant and I had decided to retire from my chairmanship of the council's Housing Operational committee. I wasn't enjoying the housing portfolio as I was frustrated by how little impact I could have as chairman. Most of the decisions were taken by others and every time I suggested improvements to the housing stock, I was told it would require lengthy consultations and votes by residents.

Then one day, I received a call from the Leader of the Council, Councillor Melvyn Caplan, inviting me to take charge of the council's plans to celebrate the Millennium. Events were being organised throughout the country and the government was supporting several national events. Melvyn had employed an officer to coordinate the council's own events. She was a young graduate called Julia Corkey.

Julia had already organised a public meeting at the Westminster Council House in Marylebone Road which was to take place the following evening, so when I made telephone contact with her following my appointment, it was agreed we would meet for the first time at the public meeting and would then continue our discussion afterwards.

I turned up the following evening and was met at the top of the grand stairs by a beaming Julia and shown to a seat in the front row. There were about a hundred invited community leaders and we sat and heard Julia and leading councillors talk about the community events the council would be organising over the following year. This included a big community fair in Paddington Recreation Ground in Maida Vale. This was the Council's largest park, set in the north of the city in a predominantly residential area.

I was surprised at the lack of ambition for the proposed events. Having attended several community events in Paddington Recreation Ground (Pad Rec), I knew that they only attracted a few hundred people and mainly those living locally. I strongly believed that as the capital of the capital, we should be doing something grander and something more central. At first, Julia was very resistant but I said I would only continue to lead the project if we did something spectacular.

I suggested we moved the location of the central feature of our celebrations to Berkeley Square in Mayfair, which was not only big enough but was also quiet at the weekend, as it was mainly surrounded by offices and very few retail shops. My vision was a form of Expo with a range of marquees containing exhibitions of what made Westminster special.

The result was 'Fair in the Square' which took place on 22nd and 23rd July 2000. At the south end of the square, we put up a stage, and a mix of professional entertainers and voluntary groups entertained the visitors who sat on the grass or on a number of deckchairs we had placed in front of the stage so that they could watch the performances.

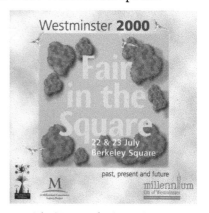

A number of large marquees were erected around the north and east sides of the Square. One was called Our Living City and included models of various buildings that had been granted planning permission, all centred around a very large model of the whole of Westminster made of wood by the model makers Pipers.

The 'Fair in the Square' poster.

The 'Pipers model of London.

Entertainment from participants of the Notting Hill Carnival.

Another pavilion was Our Living Culture and included exhibitions from (inter alia) the National Portrait Gallery, English National Ballet, the Royal Academy of Arts, the Palace of Westminster and London theatres. Madame Tussauds loaned us life-size wax statues of Queen Victoria and Winston Churchill which added to the glamour of the event. These were all organisations that participated through my personal connections.

The third pavilion was Our Living Community in which we allowed several local community groups to set up a stall and advertise what they do. Around the square, on the closed-off streets, were parked a variety of classic cars and unusual vehicles like an early London Bus and a fleet of Rolls Royces lent by neighbouring Jack Barclay.

The cost of putting on the weekend event was funded from sponsorship from a wide range of companies that operated in Westminster, each of whom I had visited on a one-to-one basis, meeting their chairman or chief executive, to persuade them to support us.

A few weeks before the weekend itself, the leadership of Westminster Council changed and my partner Simon became Leader of the Council and I was made Chief Whip and a cabinet member whose responsibilities included special events. This helped me ensure the full backing of the council in organising the event.

Three days before Fair in the Square was due to open, my father died unexpectedly. It was a major blow. My colleagues and staff, however, rallied round and finalised the preparations without me.

The funeral was held the following day and, as is traditional in Jewish culture, my sister and I sat shiva for several nights. However, we could not sit shiva on a Saturday, being the Sabbath, so I was free to attend the opening of Fair in the Square and to stay all day. On the Sunday, I attended during the morning but left after lunch to go to my sister's house where we resumed sitting shiva.

Fair in the Square was a great success. So, eighteen months later we decided to celebrate The Queen's Golden Jubilee by hosting Fair in the Square part two or, as we called it, Fayre in the Square. This time the theme was Westminster and its connection with royalty and again it took place in Berkeley Square, on 22nd and 23rd June 2002.

The contents of the marquees included Westminster Abbey displaying the copes worn at the Coronation and exhibitions from the police, fire brigade and ambulance service of their equipment from the 1950s. As Cadbury had their London HQ in Berkeley Square, I persuaded them to take over half of one of the marquees with a display of chocolate including a kitchen where staff from Cadbury showed visitors how to make chocolate bars and allowed them to do so as well.

I also arranged through a friend at the BBC for their newsroom to set up a BBC News studio with a TV camera. Visitors were invited to sit at the newsreader's desk and, after the theme music and opening credits for the 6 O'clock News, they would read the news of the day from an autocue. The resultant video (then a VHS) was given to the visitor to take home with them.

Again, we persuaded Madame Tussauds to loan us a number of their wax models including a splendid one of Queen Elizabeth I.

I invited Prince Edward and the Countess of Wessex to open the Fayre at a special Friday night party. The Lord Mayor showed the Earl around the exhibition, while I escorted the Countess around each of the exhibits and introduced her to the participants.

The Earl of Wessex opens Fayre in the Square.

The West End at War

A year later, one of the officers at the council who had been involved on the periphery with Fayre in the Square, suggested to me that it would be a good idea for the council to commemorate the 60th anniversary of D-Day (6th June 1944) and call it The West End at War, showcasing life in Westminster during the war. I though it an excellent idea and brought back together the Fayre in the Square team to help organise it. However, I did not believe that we would be able to raise the money to put on another large event, so I thought Berkeley Square too large. I decided to host it in the smaller Leicester Square, which like Berkeley Square, was controlled by the council and so no third-party consents would be needed.

The event was another great success and fitted perfectly in Leicester Square. We received substantially more visitors to the event in Leicester Square (which is right in the heart of Westminster) than we did in Berkeley Square, which at the weekend is a much quieter area and further away from the busy centre. Moreover, the north terrace of Leicester Square has one of the highest footfalls in the UK. Clearly Leicester Square was the perfect site for such an event.

The West End at War included a series of marquees displaying wartime exhibits such as a Kindertransport stand where children were given labels with the names of those who had been on the original Kindertransport.

A tribute version of *Dad's Army* actors recreated the famous TV platoon, marching through the square and acting out scenes from the famous show. Marguerite Patten, the wartime celebrity chef, gave cooking demonstrations using her renowned wartime recipes. On the main stage at the southern end of the square, a variety of entertainers performed, from an Andrews Sisters tribute group to a swing band with dancers doing many famous wartime dances, including the jitterbug, with all the audience joining in. It was fun.

Supporting the West End

In early 2005, concerns were raised about the impending opening of the new massive shopping centre in Shepherd's Bush known as Westfield and the impact this would have on businesses in the West End. This was particularly of concern because of the large supply of car parking at Westfield, while parking in central London was difficult and expensive.

At this time, I was a member of the board of the New West End Company, the largest Business Improvement District (BID) in the country which covers Oxford Street, Regent's Street and Bond Street. Its membership comprises all the major retailers and landlords in these streets. At several meetings we addressed the threat of the new retail utopia that was to attract away many of those who would otherwise visit the West End. In order to encourage people to continue to visit the West End, I suggested an expo-style exhibition profiling what the West End had to offer. Our selling point was that the West End did not only have the best retail shops and department stores in the country but thousands of restaurants, cafes, pubs and bars as well as numerous cinemas, many playing first-run films. In addition, there are the West End theatres, the two opera houses and the most famous museums and art galleries in the world. Nowhere in the UK (including at Westfield) could you find all these together in one area.

I thought we should invite all the companies and institutions that made up the West End to participate and set up stalls and exhibits of what they had to offer, in a series of marquees. Following the success of the West End at War, Leicester Square seemed the obvious venue and was seen by many to be the epicentre of the West End. The marquees would surround the inside of the railings around the square and we would erect a large stage on the southern end of the square (as we had in the West End at War) for live entertainment.

I needed to raise sponsorship for the event, as the Council would only contribute a certain amount, so I approached all my business contacts including Land Securities, the Crown Estate and Veolia (the Council's cleansing operators) and managed to raise the monies required. Many West End institutions agreed to participate including the National Portrait Gallery, the Wallace Collection, the National Gallery, the Museum of London, the English National Opera and the Science Museum. Chinatown also participated and we had a number of famous film cars including Chitty Chitty Bang Bang, representing the fact that Leicester Square was the centre of the film industry and home to many large first-run cinemas.

As far as the West End theatre was concerned, I had an idea from a visit that Simon and I made to New York a few years earlier. While walking around the streets near Times Square on a Sunday morning, we were intrigued by the fact that all the streets were closed to traffic and thousands of people appeared to be watching some entertainment.

We moved closer to the small stage, made up of just a small platform, to discover a handful of singers in jeans and t-shirts singing songs from famous musicals. It was a free event that lasted a couple of hours and, on investigation, we discovered it was an annual event called Broadway on Broadway and the singers were each stars of the musicals performing on Broadway at the time.

The programme front cover for the first West End Live in 2005.

I decided we would replicate this to represent the theatres' contribution to the West End. I contacted my friend Nick Allott, the chief executive of Cameron Mackintosh's company. At that time, he was the only person in the theatre world I knew. I begged him to participate with extracts from some of his shows. He agreed and on the main stage we showcased twenty-minute extracts from *Mary Poppins* and *Mamma Mia!*, which were both playing in his theatres at that time. In addition, he persuaded a friend to send us

Me with the cast of Mamma Mia.

the understudies from Chicago. They all performed in full costumes and with original props on both the Saturday and Sunday and the rest of the time we filled in with other musical entertainment such as the English Baroque choir, the Woody Herman Orchestra from Ronnie Scott's and performances from several schools. On the Sunday morning, Christopher Biggins narrated an orchestral performance of Prokofiev's *Peter and the Wolf.*

On the Friday night we launched the weekend with a private summer party in the square for invited guests. And because the event was about showcasing the West End, we called it West End Live.

It was another success and the square was crowded all day but it soon became clear that the visitors were mainly watching the shows on the stage. The following week we were contacted by the producers of *Mamma Mia!* to tell us that their sales had rocketed over the weekend and continued to do so during the following week. They wanted to know if we were going to do it again.

Therefore, on 17th and 18th June the following year (2006), we returned for a second year with the same sponsors and, because of word of mouth in the theatre world, with seven musicals including *Guys and Dolls, The Producers, Blue Man Group, Footloose* and *The Lion King.* And for the first time, the main cast of *Chicago* performed instead of their understudies.

The Sylvia Young Theatre School joined the line-up (through my friendship with Sylvia) and soon became regulars, performing in every subsequent West End Live. I even recruited my primary school friend Marvin Berglas, the famous magician (of Marvin's Magic fame).

By year three we had ten musicals performing and a growing number of exhibits. Duncan James of Blue, then playing the lead role in *Chicago,* opened the weekend for us, at what would become the traditional Friday night alfresco opening party.

The cast of Priscilla Queen of the Desert *with me backstage at West End Live.*

In 2008 we had twenty musicals including for the first time, the *Jersey Boys*, who would become regulars and one of the favourites year after year. That year also saw several big movies promoting up-and-coming film premieres in the square with exhibits and photo opportunities with characters such as Kung Fu Panda. Even Disney joined in. In 2009 we also hosted a Harry Potter exhibition to promote the opening of *Harry Potter and the Half Blood Prince* with costumes from the film.

West End Live had gradually transformed from a showcase for the West End generally to a showcase for West End musicals with a side show around the square which continued to promote the other cultural institutions of central London.

Simon and I would stay in the Hampshire Hotel on the square for the weekend, so I could be on site the whole time. One year, I woke up on the Saturday morning at 5 am to go to the toilet and peeped out of the window. To my amazement there was a long queue of people waiting to be allowed into Leicester Square for the event to start some six hours later. The queue ran around the square and along Coventry Street towards Piccadilly Circus. I was stunned. It was a free event and people were admitted on a first come first served basis, so once the word got around how much fun West End Live was, particularly for fans of musicals, everyone wanted to be there.

We tried including some non-musicals such as an extract from *A Midsummer Night's Dream*, that was performing at the Regent's Park Open Air Theatre, where I was a director. But it became clear that it did not quite work.

2010 was a special year for four reasons. Firstly, my partner Simon (now Deputy Mayor of London) arranged for Boris Johnson as Mayor to open the event. Secondly, it was to be the last in Leicester Square. This was because I was also leading a project to carry out a major upgrade and refurbishment of Leicester Square as a public space. The works were to take eighteen months, which meant we had to spend one year in a temporary location while the works were carried out before we could return two years later.

The third reason, was the arrival of Julian Bird as the new chief executive of the Society of London Theatres (SOLT). His predecessor had taken no interest in West End Live and had never attended. But Julian attended the 2010 event and was introduced to me by Nica Burns, who at that time was President of SOLT. Julian was bowled over by West End Live and offered to partner us the following year on the basis that he would use his influence with theatre producers to get even more shows to participate.

The fourth and final reason was that this was to be the last one attended by my partner Simon, who as Leader of the Council had ensured I had the full support of the council to organise the event each year, as he was to die before the 2011 West End Live.

During the autumn of 2010, I sought the advice of Nica Burns, Nick Allott and Julian Bird on where we should move for the year away from Leicester Square. I wanted to move to Berkeley Square which was controlled by Westminster Council and which I knew worked as an event space from the two Fairs in the Square, although I accepted that it was a bit out of the way. The others all wanted us to use Trafalgar Square, but I was concerned it was too big and very noisy, as it was a traffic roundabout. Added to this was the fact that the council had no jurisdiction over Trafalgar Square (apart from the north terrace) as it is under the control of the Greater London Authority and I did not want to be controlled in any way by the GLA or the Mayor of London. However, I had to concede as I was outnumbered by the experts and took on board the benefits of this new location. They were right and I had been wrong. Trafalgar Square was a tremendous success. The noise from the traffic could not be heard and we could fill the square with three or four times more people than in Leicester Square. In fact, as the years progressed, the queues every morning to get in, got longer and longer, hours before we opened the doors.

We never did go back to Leicester Square. And with Julian's help and support we would regularly have appearing over the weekend, every single musical performing in the West End at the time. We would also receive pleas from the producers of shows opening later in the year, begging to be included to plug their shows.

I soon persuaded Andrew Lloyd Webber to add *Phantom of the Opera* to the repertoire and eventually Cameron Mackintosh agreed to add *Les Misérables*. These two shows together with *Miss Saigon* became hot favourites for the crowds, especially when

Being interviewed by the 'Katie Cam' – Katy Federman at West End Live in Trafalgar Square.

they added a number of props to their performance such as the gondoliers and candelabras from *Phantom*. Another highlight was when Elphaba, the wicked witch from *Wicked* sang *Defying Gravity* from the roof of Canada House on the west side of the square.

Having a sword through my neck at West End Live.

One year, I tried to persuade Marvin Berglas to cut me in half on stage as part of his magic show. He explained that he would not do this but invited a fellow magician to do so. However, once I started my discussion with Marvin's colleague, it became clear that I was too large for the prop used in that illusion. So instead, the illusionist stuck a long sword through my neck. It went down very well and for a couple of weeks afterwards, every time I drank water, it would spurt out the side of my neck!!

Another time, we were honoured when Plácido Domingo conducted the choir of the Royal Opera House on our stage. Chatting to him back stage, I said it was sad that he was not singing. He said that if I had asked him to sing, he would have been delighted to do so, but he needed a bit of notice. I was heartbroken that we had not been bold enough to have asked, when we heard he would be attending. Sadly, in future years he was never in London on West End Live weekends.

If I had thought the queues in Leicester Square were massive and started very early in the mornings, the queues for Trafalgar Square were even longer. The doors would not open until 10.45 am but by 5 am earlier that morning the queues would already wind all the way back up to Piccadilly Circus. People arriving during the day would have to wait about two hours to get in to the square.

With Plácido Domingo at West End Live.

Me in my Boss's chair and t-shirt in the VIP enclosure in Leicester Square.

Awards and Personal Performances

In 2009, Simon and I attended the Visit London Awards held (ironically) at the

Westfield Shopping Centre where I was delighted to be called on stage to receive the award for Best Musical Event of the year.

In about 2015 I decided that I wanted to film a series of face-to camera interludes for broadcasting during the show. These would be shown between acts and right at the beginning and end of each day. From the stage of a West End theatre, I would film a number of speeches to camera about West End Live. But in 2017, I took this one stage further when the producers of *The Play that Goes Wrong*, wrote a storyline for me to star in.

At the time they were running two shows in the West End, one at the Duchess Theatre just off the Aldwych (*The Play that Goes Wrong*) and the other (*The Comedy About a Bank Robbery*) at the Criterion in Piccadilly Circus. In the film, I arrive at the theatre to interview the cast about West End Live but accidently turn up at the wrong theatre and after banging at the closed front door of the Criterion, I realise that it is the wrong theatre, so I am seen dashing over to the Duchess Theatre.

Cut to the cast on the set of *The Play that Goes Wrong*, who are pacing up and down on stage complaining that I have not arrived on time to interview them. They get a message that I have gone to the wrong theatre and so carry on relaxing on set. Cut to my rushing (out of breath) into the correct theatre. On stage they are told I am on the way and then I arrive and walk on to the stage introducing myself pompously. And as I do so, the entire set collapses around me, leaving me standing in what was a window of the set. Cut … to a close-up of me standing there covered in dust saying 'Welcome to West End Live'.

I mentioned earlier that I was a failed actor turned politician. Now I was a politician turned failed actor!

The Boss at West End Live in Trafalgar Square.

Chapter 24

Switzerland and the Glockenspiel

In 1984, as chairman of the council's Leisure Committee, I noticed how Leicester Square, one of our most high-profile garden squares, was falling into disrepair and how the area had become rather sleezy. The roadway around the square was open to traffic and parked cars blocked the view of the gardens themselves.

Leicester Square

Responsibility for Leicester Square rested with my committee and, as chairman, I decided that action was required. I thought of other major beautiful city centre squares throughout Europe such as the piazza in front of the Duomo in Milan. Why not clear the square of its railings and the lawn, remove the traffic and create a large open piazza? So, I asked my officers to prepare drawings.

A few months later, I hosted a public meeting in one of the hotels near the square to show the local residents (although there are not many) and local businesses, our ideas and various alternative designs.

Leicester Square with traffic and parking around the gardens – 1960s.

Those attending the meeting were unanimously opposed to my ideas. My first political setback. They hated it and reminded me of the history of the square and the importance in Britain of garden squares. London in particular, is unique in having so many garden squares, while Europe is known for its open piazzas. It was the general view that we should protect that heritage and not seek to emulate the European cities where their traditions and, more importantly, weather is so different from that in the UK.

As I was leaving the meeting, feeling very despondent, a gentleman approached me and introduced himself. He was Albert Kunz, the director of the Swiss Tourist Office based in the Swiss Centre, in the north-west corner of the square. He wanted to emphasise that a piazza was not what Leicester Square needed. Yes, he pleaded, more care and attention and the removal of the traffic, but not clearance of the railings and greenery. I got the message. After his lecture, he invited me to meet him for a coffee one day and so we exchanged phone numbers and a few weeks later we met up.

Albert Kunz.

At the meeting, Albert told me how he had created the Swiss Centre in the early 1960s. He had conceived the idea and after having sold the concept of a building full of Swiss businesses that would promote Switzerland to his superiors back in Zurich, he went about raising the money from the Swiss Banking Corporation and Swiss Air to acquire the land and build the Centre.

However, his new dream was to construct a Glockenspiel clock on the exterior of the Swiss Centre. A traditional Swiss Glockenspiel clock is a very ornate clock that plays music when set to do so, with various wooden characters moving to the music. The proposal was for this Glockenspiel to comprise twenty-three separate bells, each paired and engraved with the name of a Westminster Council ward and a Swiss canton. At the centre of the piece was a large clock supported on either side by wood-carved women in Swiss national costumes holding a baton and, on the hour, they would twist around and strike one of the largest bells. A wooden cockerel would crow on the hour and a globe would show if we were in darkness or sunlight.

Below the clock and bells was a blank wooden wall, but on the hour, the plain backcloth turned around and revealed a Swiss mountainous landscape. In front of this landscape a parade of wooden carved cows led by wooden Swiss herdsmen in traditional costumes and a cheese maker stirring his caldron meandered around the front of the Glockenspiel. In fact, the wooden cheese stirrer was modelled on a young Albert Kunz, but clearly recognisable as him. His memorial.

I loved the idea and supported Albert through the planning process. In those days, I was not on the council's Planning Committee and was mortified when some older colleagues, who sat to hear the application for planning permission, refused the application, saying it was too like Disneyland. Albert was terribly upset and I was extremely embarrassed. But I advised Albert to make some alterations and a couple of months later he resubmitted the application. In the meantime, I did some lobbying of my colleagues and the application was granted on the second attempt.

The Casting of the Bells

A few weeks later, over dinner to celebrate, I suggested to Albert that it would be a good idea for the Swiss to invite the then Lord Mayor of Westminster, Roger Bramble, to visit Switzerland to watch the bells being cast in the foundry in Aarau, just outside Zurich. Albert loved the idea but insisted I came too. Well, how could I say no?

In June 1985, I joined the Lord Mayor and his Lady Mayoress, Cathryn, the Countess Cawdor, together with the Lord Mayor's macebearer (Ernie), on the first (of what would become a regular) civic visit to Switzerland. We flew to Geneva Airport and were taken by minibus to Montreux where we stayed the night at the Montreux Palace. It was my visit to Switzerland. I recall waking the following morning and opening my bedroom window after drawing the heavy curtains, to see one of the most beautiful sights I had ever seen – the snow-capped Alps across the skyline, with a blue sky behind and in the foreground the beauty of Lake Geneva reflecting the mountains in the shimmering water.

After a couple of days of meeting local mayors in Montreux and other neighbouring towns, we reached Aarau, where in robes and jabot, with the Lord Mayor wearing his badge and chains and the macebearer carrying the Westminster mace, we watched as several of the bells that would adorn the Glockenspiel in Leicester Square were cast. As the molten bronze was poured into the casts, I stood there feeling very proud.

In Aarau at the casting of the bells for the Glockenspiel.

The Blessing of the Bells

When the bells arrived in London to be attached to the exterior of the Swiss Centre, Albert organised a blessing ceremony. One of the largest bells was placed on the back of a carriage led by two horses and after leaving City Hall in Victoria Street, with the Lord Mayor and Lady Mayoress on board and Albert, me and a number of other invited guests following behind on foot, the horse and carriage made its way to the Great West door of Westminster Abbey, where the Dean of Westminster blessed the bell. He then joined the growing crowd following the carriage, as we moved on to Westminster Methodist Central Hall opposite the Abbey, where the Superintendent Minister again blessed the bell.

Outside Westminster Abbey for the dean's blessing of the bells.

Finally, we moved en masse to Westminster Cathedral, the principal Catholic church in the country, where the Administrator (the most senior clergyman reporting to the Archbishop and responsible for day-to-day life in the Cathedral) also blessed the bell, before we all returned to the Lord Mayor's Parlour for a drinks reception.

A month later, the Glockenspiel was unveiled in all its glory and on the hour between 3 pm and 7 pm, the Glockenspiel

The original Glockenspiel on the Swiss Centre, Leicester Square.

would come to life and hundreds of people passing would stand and watch the performance.

The civic visit to Switzerland was a great success, particularly for the Swiss in the way that it cemented the special Anglo-Swiss relationship. The Glockenspiel was a great promotion for Switzerland and the Swiss saw it as a permanent advertisement for travel to their beautiful country.

Further Visits

A couple of years later, Albert suggested we organise a second trip. I introduced him to the incoming Lord Mayor, Elizabeth Flach, and her barrister husband Robert and they jumped at the chance of a civic visit. Albert again insisted I travelled with them. This time we visited Geneva, Luzern, Lugano and Zurich, where in robes and chains, we processed down the historic streets of each city and met the local mayor.

During the visit to Lugano, we were taken to the art gallery owned by Baron Thyssen, then housing some magnificent paintings, including the famous Holbein portrait of King Henry VIII. As we were being escorted around the gallery by the principal administrator, word came to us that the Baron was in residence in his house next door and having heard that the Lord Mayor was touring his gallery, invited her and her party into his home for coffee. We were delighted to accept and were overwhelmed by the stunning house and in particular the art work exhibited in his private rooms. We were even taken into his bedroom, where the paintings on the wall would take pride of place in any national art gallery in the UK. It was a very special experience. Years later, the Baron transferred his entire collection to a specially built gallery in Madrid after the British Government turned it down.

Over the years that followed, Albert Kunz and his successors as the British director of Switzerland Tourism (the new name for the Swiss National Tourist Office) would invite the incumbent Lord Mayor and I to visit Switzerland for further civic visits. This would take place every two or three years and as the visits become more successful, in the sense that the Swiss were delighted to receive us and many local mayors would compete to host us, other councillors were invited to join the delegation.

When my good friend Angela Hooper was Lord Mayor, together with Angela's sister Gloria (Baroness Hooper) we flew to Geneva, where we were entertained by the Mayor, Michel Rossetti, a communist whose charm and flattery ensured that he and Angela got on very well.

In Geneva as Lord Mayor with the Mayor of Geneva Jacqueline Burnand.

At the dinner hosted by the Mayor of Geneva, in a beautiful chateau on the lake, I sat next to the councillor who would take over as mayor of Geneva a couple of years later, Jacqueline Burnand. We got on very well and so when I became Lord Mayor in 1996 and found out that Jacqueline was now Mayor of Geneva, I arranged a further visit to Geneva with Angela in tow. That trip further cemented the relationship between Westminster and Geneva and so I invited Jacqueline to visit Westminster, which she did a few months later and we appropriately entertained her in City Hall with a black-tie dinner. She also accompanied Carole and me on a number of civic visits.

My Year as Lord Mayor

When I became Lord Mayor in 1996, Albert Kunz insisted on organising a very special civic trip including a full week's programme of visits (rather than the usual three or four days) with the opportunity for us to stay an extra few days at the end to relax.

Angela Hooper joined us on the trip and we were accompanied by Albert Kunz, now retired from his lengthy tenure as director of Switzerland Tourism in London. We were also joined by Urs Eberhard, the vice president of Switzerland Tourism, who had arranged the visit. Urs and I had been friends for many years, having met years earlier when Urs had succeeded Albert Kunz as director of Switzerland Tourism in London. He had since been promoted to the number two position at headquarters in Zurich.

We flew out to Zurich on a Sunday night in mid-August 1996, where we stayed the first night. The following morning, after meeting the Mayor of Zurich, we were entertained for lunch by my friend Michel Favre, the chief executive of the then second largest newspaper group in Switzerland, Tages-Anzeiger, before travelling to Winterthur to meet the mayor and visit the spectacular art gallery Reinhart-Gemaeldegalerie.

The rest of the week included a visit to Davos, known around the world for hosting the annual World Economic Forum but equally famous for all its buildings being made of pine wood both internally as well as externally. The smell from the pine was overwhelming.

We met the Mayor of Davos, who entertained us for dinner. In those days, the mayoral budget included a sum for gifts and I used this sum to have a number of letter openers made, which incorporated a pewter handle comprising a small statuette of myself in my mayoral robes and chains of office. The Mayor of Davos was a recipient of one of these 'little me' letter openers!

The next morning we left Davos on the Glacier Express to Fluelen where we picked up a steamship which took us across Lake Lucerne, past the William Tell monument to the town of Vitznau, where we stayed the night at the beautiful Park Hotel. After dinner with the Mayor, Angela, Carole and I went midnight swimming in the hotel's heated pool.

The 'little me' letter opener.

The following day we dashed to the local station to catch the historic wooden steam train that had been entirely reserved for our party, to climb the 5,748-feet-high Mount Rigi. Half way up, we stopped for half an hour, so that we could visit Urs Eberhardt's parents, who lived in a Swiss chalet on the Rigi. After enjoying morning coffee with them, we continued in the steam train with me donning the traditional uniform of a Swiss steam train driver, to the top of the mountain.

Dressed in the traditional driver's uniform, steering the Mount Rigi Train.

But luck was not with us. Having spent the whole journey being told about the spectacular views from the summit, by the time we reached it, we were in thick cloud and we could not see beyond our noses! Literally! We had to be guided a few steps as we could not see where we were going. We were ushered into a café, where we had more refreshments before descending by train, down the other side of the mountain.

At the bottom, in Arth-Goldau, we were met by representatives from the local council with two massive Swiss flags being waved by two very strong flag bearers in traditional Swiss costumes. We were led to the town centre where we found a gentleman with a huge Swiss alpine horn (at least twenty feet long) playing traditional Swiss tunes. I was asked to have a go for the photographers that had joined us.

Blowing an alpine horn.

We were then entertained in a beautiful Swiss restaurant to the most amazing Chateaubriand (one of my favourites). After lunch, the mayor presented me with a round wooden cheese block on a wooden sledge with a working clock on the cheese, engraved with details of my visit. I loved that clock and it has remained ever since on the wall of my kitchen at home in London. Even after I recently modernised my kitchen, the only thing from the old kitchen to go back into the new kitchen was this Swiss clock. Underneath the clock hangs a framed photo of me in the restaurant in jabot and chains being presented with the clock and every day, while enjoying my breakfast, I look up to check the time and I remember this wonderful day in Switzerland.

Our final stop was in the Ticino (the southern Italian part of Switzerland) where we were staying in Ascona, sitting majestically on Lake Maggiore. The hotel was called the Albergo Giardino and everything in the hotel, including the hotel itself, was pink. Not only were all the soft furnishings from blinds to sofas and carpets to linen pink but the hotel cars and mini bus sitting in the driveway outside, were also pink. The owner of the hotel was there to greet us on our arrival, wearing a dark pink jacket and light pink trousers.

The Hotel Albergo Giardino in Ascona, Switzerland.

We were joined that night for dinner in the hotel by the Mayor of Ascona, Aldo Rampazzi, and his wife Miriam. We got on with them extremely well and the following day he took time off from the office to accompany us on a walk around his town and the lakeside.

On the third day, we were taken by the owner of the hotel, in his pink mini bus, to visit the 721-feet-high dam in the Verzasca Valley which was made famous in the James Bond film *GoldenEye*, when Pierce Brosnan jumped off it in the opening scene.

Rest day in Ascona with the Mayor of Ascona outside his town hall.

That night the formal part of the visit ended and all our escorts returned to Zurich and Angela returned to London. But Carole and I stayed a further three days to enjoy the sunshine. On the Sunday, the mayor and his wife Miriam offered to entertain us and show us around his town hall. We met at his home where we had coffee and we were shown Miriam's collection of miniature elephants. I found this fascinating as my mother also collected elephants (and following her death, I still have all 120 of them on display in my flat). After visiting the town hall, Aldo and Miriam took us by boat to the island of Brissago for lunch. It was a wonderful end to a special week in Switzerland.

Aldo, Miriam and I kept in touch for many years afterwards (including having lunch together on another visit I made to Ascona some years later), and when their son visited London, I met up with him and took him for dinner.

Further Visits

Over the following twenty years, several more civic visits to Switzerland were arranged by Albert and Urs covering most of Switzerland and I was honoured to have been included in each of them.

When Michael and Stephanie Brahams were Lord and Lady Mayoress the trip included a visit to meet the Mayor of Grächen in the Valais. It had been arranged that our luggage would travel separately and we were told that our cases would be waiting for us in our hotel rooms on arrival. After the six-hour journey from the previous town on the east of the country, we all went to our rooms to relax and change for dinner. But with dinner approaching, my suitcase was yet to arrive. We had travelled in casual clothes and we were expected to change into more formal attire for dinner with our hosts. As the time approached, I started to panic and called the host from Switzerland Tourism accompanying us. She assured me that my suitcase would be with me shortly as everyone else had theirs. But as the time to leave for dinner arrived, still no case or clothes to change into! Not even a shaver or toothbrush to freshen up with! So, one more call to our host and it was suggested I joined them for dinner in casual attire and everyone would understand. I did so and was assured that they were tracing where my case had got to. It did not turn up for two days, during which I had to wear the same casual clothes and to buy a shaver and toothbrush from a local shop. I cannot tell you how relieved I was when the suitcase eventually arrived!

When Louise Hyams was Lord Mayor, we stayed in Gstaad. We were accompanied by her (then) partner Alex Langsam, Angela Hooper and her sister Gloria, Alex Nicoll, Steve the macebearer as well as Simon. The highlight of this trip was our early morning hot air balloon trip, high over the Alps and then slowly gliding through the valleys. It was one of the most exciting things I have ever done. I often fondly recall the sensation of gliding through the silent air among the clouds and looking down to see the mountains and valley beneath us. Just mesmerising and peaceful.

Our guide, me, Louise, Simon, Gloria, Steve and Alex at Château-d'Oex with our hot air balloon.

Heidi

A year before the Louise Hyams trip, I had celebrated my 50th birthday and Urs Eberhard, the vice president of Switzerland Tourism, gave a lunch party in my honour in a private room at Mossimans, the Swiss club in Belgravia. After lunch, Urs and his Swiss colleagues surprised me by presenting me with a very special birthday present … a cow named Heidi! I was grateful that he did not produce Heidi herself. Instead, he presented me with a photograph of Heidi and a certificate confirming that she had been sponsored by Switzerland Tourism in my name. In addition, I was presented with a full-size cow's bell engraved with the fact that it had been presented to me on my 50th birthday. I was also assured that once a year, I would be sent a full roundel of cheese made from Heidi's milk.

While in Switzerland with Louise as Lord Mayor and her entourage, the Switzerland Tourism representative insisted we make a detour to visit Heidi. The only issue was that because it was summer, she and her herd were grazing high up a Swiss mountain. But that did not deter our hosts.

After over an hour driving up this winding mountain road with a trailer behind full of our luggage and with all the other members of the delegation complaining about why it was necessary to waste time making a detour to see 'Robert's cow', we soon drove into low-lying cloud. We eventually arrived outside a shepherd's wooden barn in thick fog.

The rest of the delegation were rewarded with wine and cheese, while I was taken over to meet Heidi. Now, I am not the best with animals and to be honest, was petrified of getting too close. But my hosts insisted that I at least feed Heidi with an apple for the official photographer who had accompanied us.

As I was being photographed, posing with this apple and nervous that Heidi might choose to eat my hand rather than the apple, I did not notice Heidi's friend and neighbour standing behind me.

Heidi and I get to know each other.

Unbeknown to me, it appears that Heidi's neighbour had a bad stomach. As I was posing for the photographs, I noticed Heidi's neighbour's tail rise and then without any notice, she covered me (from head to foot) in watery cow's dung. A cow with diarrhoea was not something I had been warned about! After recovering from the shock, I looked down and realised I was covered in it. Not only had my face turned a pale brown but my Aquascutum raincoat was equally covered in wet cow dung. Even my shoes did not avoid the explosion. I quickly used my handkerchief to clear my face and the first thing I saw was all my colleagues on the ground rolling about in absolute hysterics. They all agreed that it had been well worth the long trek up the mountain to see me covered in shit.

I must say that I never received the promised cheese, but after seeing how massive it would have been, I was relieved as it was twice as large as my fridge.

The Lady Flight Trip

In 2015, Christabel Flight became Lord Mayor, with her husband Lord Flight (Howard) as her Consort. Urs Eberhardt, egged on by Albert Kunz, was keen to invite her on a civic visit, as I had told them how wonderful and vivacious she was. This time they suggested she bring with her four colleagues plus me. Christabel chose Nickie Aiken, Rachael Robathan, Steve Summers and Daniel Astaire, two of whom (Nickie and Rachael) subsequently became Leaders of the Council. Lots of fun was had on our tour through central Switzerland with us ending up in Zermatt.

On one day, we went for a long walk through the mountains ending up in a remote restaurant where we stopped for lunch. But several of us (Howard, Steve and I) said we were too exhausted to make the long walk back to the station to catch the train to the hotel and so were offered a taxi. We jumped at this offer but the egg was on our face when the so-called taxi turned up to collect us. It was an open-back lorry. The seats were just a reconstituted wooden crate on the back, fully open to the freezing air. To say it did not have shock absorbers would be an understatement but we did laugh and we got back in one piece.

Staying overnight in one hotel we were enjoying the benefits of the hotel spa, after a long and tiring day meeting civic dignitaries. There we were, relaxing in the main pool when Christabel suggested we joined Howard in the steam room. We all got out (wearing our swimming attire) and as a group wandered over to the steam room and entered it together.

Steve Summers, Howard Flight and me in our Swiss mountain taxi.

There in the middle of the steam room was Howard standing facing the door, stark naked. Christabel let out a scream, shouting 'Howard!' He just remained there unabashed saying 'It's nothing they haven't seen before!'. Christabel quickly found a towel and ran up to him, covering him up.

The final trip was just a year later, when my good friend Steve Summers became Lord Mayor. This time we took with us Louise

Me, Nickie Aiken, Christabel and Howard Flight, Steve Batt (Macebearer), our guide, Rachel Robathan, Daniel Astaire and Steve Summers.

Hyams and Tim Mitchell as well as John Walker, the Director of Planning. Albert wanted John to accompany us, to thank him for the help he had given him in ensuring that the new Glockenspiel in Swiss Court, Leicester Square, was properly maintained by the owners of the Swiss Centre. John had insisted they complied with their obligation to do so, as required by the conditions in their planning consent to rebuild the Swiss Centre.

Tim Mitchell, me, Steve Summers and Louise Hyams on top of the Hoher Kasten mountain in the eastern part of Switzerland.

Swiss Celebrations

In the meantime, we need to go back in time to a few years after the Glockenspiel was unveiled. Albert wanted to celebrate the 800th anniversary of the creation of the Swiss Confederation by installing another Swiss folly in Leicester Square. His idea was to construct a Swiss cantonal tree, which was shaped like a flat-tree, but from the branches hung the crests of each of the Swiss cantons. This got all the necessary consents with little problem and it was also decided by the council (at my suggestion) that the area outside the Swiss Centre, although officially part of Leicester Square, would be renamed Swiss Court.

Despite this little part of London being recognised as an honorary Swiss canton, problems lay ahead.

A Diplomatic Incident

In the mid-1990s, the Swiss Banking Corporation decided that they wanted to sell their majority shareholding in the Swiss Centre, despite Albert Kunz's best endeavours to persuade them not to do so. By this stage, Albert was retired and living in Switzerland but continued to have a lifelong love of his Glockenspiel.

The Swiss Banking Corporation eventually sold their interest to British Land, a well-known property company, which then proceeded to persuade the Swiss National Tourist Office and Swiss Air to sell them their interests too. Albert went into battle but failed and British Land, with a 100% ownership of the building sold it on to a developer called McAleer and Rushe. They in turn sought planning permission to knock down the Swiss Centre and replace it with a new building.

It became clear to me that McAleer and Rushe had no intention of retaining the Glockenspiel and so I set about persuading my colleagues and the planning officers that we must preserve the Glockenspiel in some form and make the eventual owners of the new building to be built on the site of the Swiss Centre, pay for its maintenance.

After extensive negotiations, McAleer and Rushe agreed to pay for the construction of a new large arch at the entrance to Leicester Square stretching the full width of Swiss Court, with the Glockenspiel erected along the top of it. Planning permission was granted with the obligation to create the arch and Glockenspiel before the building was finished.

In the meantime, the council was working on the major redevelopment of Leicester Square itself. Simon (as Leader) had come up with a new vision for the square, which would retain the idea of a garden square but introduce modern style railings which would incorporate seating around the square and create at the centre a water fountain for kids to play in. By this time, however, Simon had resigned as Leader to become Deputy Mayor of London and Colin Barrow was now Leader. Colin gave me the job of leading the refurbishment of the square, which was programmed to start within a few months. The only issue was the cost and who was going to pay for it.

Colin was insisting that while Westminster would pay the bulk of the multimillion-pound costs, he wanted the local landowners to contribute about a third of the cost. There are four large property owners around the square and they in turn advised Colin that they would be happy to pay their contribution but only if the Glockenspiel was never returned to the square!

I was shocked and could not understand why they hated it so much. They in turn argued that with a modern design for the square, the large traditional gate on which the Glockenspiel would be positioned, did not fit in with the new ethos. Colin told me that he would rather have their financial contribution than the Glockenspiel and if it was one or the other then the Glockenspiel had to go.

I had to think fast. I was at that time friendly with the Swiss Ambassador. With Albert's blessing, I rang the Ambassador and we plotted. Within 24 hours, Colin received a call from the Ambassador's office asking him to attend an urgent meeting with the Ambassador. I soon got a call from Colin, to tell me he had been summoned to appear before the Ambassador and assumed it was about the Glockenspiel. He asked me to attend with him, as I knew more about the issue than either he or anyone else at the council. I was glad to do so and we met up outside the Embassy in Bryanston Square, Marylebone.

I briefed him and we then rang the bell of the imposing front door. We were soon ushered into the Ambassador's office. We sat down and the Ambassador began a passionate tirade about the Glockenspiel being one of the most important icons of the centuries-old close relationship between Switzerland and the UK and emphasising that its removal would be an affront to

that relationship and cause an Anglo-Swiss diplomatic row. He left us with the impression that World War Three could start over a Glockenspiel in Leicester Square.

Colin responded by saying that he heard what the Ambassador was saying and would discuss it further back at City Hall. We made our farewells and left. We walked down the street in silence and then suddenly Colin stopped and turned to me and said 'OK, you win. You can have your [...] Glockenspiel'. He agreed to persuade the landowners to accept the Glockenspiel, while he asked me to go back to the Swiss and McAleer and Rushe to redesign the Glockenspiel so that it was smaller and standing alone in the centre of Swiss Court. The deal was done.

Within a few weeks, a new design was agreed. This was circular and held up on a single post. A year later, the new Glockenspiel was unveiled and blessed in another grand ceremony in Swiss Court which included a

The unveiling of the new standalone Glockenspiel in Swiss Court, Leicester Square.

number of traditional Swiss dancers and musicians flown over to the UK to perform.

Swiss Court, the Cantonal Tree and the new Glockenspiel still entertain the millions of visitors to Leicester Square each year in this very Swiss corner of London.

Sadly, after my departure from the Council, the special relationship between the City of Westminster and Switzerland has dissolved and the Glockenspiel remains the sole physical reminder of those special days.

I am delighted that my contribution to this relationship and to the creation of the original Glockenspiel (and the survival of its newer version) is commemorated by a plaque on the Glockenspiel which mentions my involvement.

With two of the Swiss men being restored before being affixed to the new Glockenspiel.

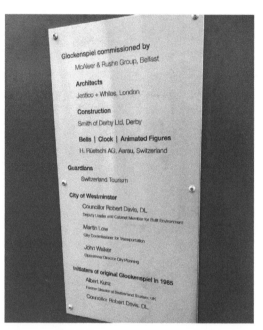

The Plaque on the Glockenspiel.

Albert Kunz with the sculpture from the Glockenspiel based on him.

Two of the cows from the Glockenspiel being restored before being returned to their position on the new Glockenspiel.

Chapter 25

The London Mayors' Association

The London Mayors' Association (LMA) represents the thirty-one mayors and two Lord Mayors of the thirty-three London boroughs as well as former mayors and Lord Mayors. The LMA was created in early 1901 by His Grace, the Duke of Norfolk KG, who had in the previous September been elected the first Mayor of Westminster, following the creation of Westminster City Council under the Local Government Act of 1899.

On 4th December 1900, His Grace hosted a meeting of all the mayors of the Metropolitan Boroughs (the inner London boroughs), the object being 'to discuss matters of ceremonial procedure with a view to uniformity being adopted by all the mayors of the Metropolitan Boroughs'.

Early the following year, the Metropolitan Mayors' and Ex-Mayors' Association (as the London Mayors' Association was originally known) was formed with the purpose of 'promoting discussion of general matters affecting the Metropolis' and to enable mayors and former mayors to meet on a social basis.

In 1950, all the mayors and former mayors of the other boroughs of Greater London were invited to become members and the name was changed to the 'London Mayors' Association'. With the reorganisation of local government in London in 1965, the mayors and former mayors of all thirty-three boroughs were entitled to join as were the Lord Mayors and former Lord Mayors of the City of London and of the City of Westminster.

From its inception, the Mayor of Westminster (from 1966 the Lord Mayor of Westminster) was automatically the chairman of the LMA. However, the person who actually ran the LMA on a day-to-day basis was the chairman of the Executive Committee. The President was usually a former executive chairman.

My Initial Involvement as Lord Mayor

As Lord Mayor of Westminster and ex officio chairman of the LMA, I was invited in July 1996 to chair the Annual General Meeting, which was held (as it usually was) at Westminster City Hall. I had never met the other members before and so as chairman I made an effort to introduce myself to the other twenty or so members attending, several of whom were mayors of the other boroughs. I thought nothing of the LMA again for a few weeks, as I was busy attending functions during the height of the summer season. Then one day, a flyer was received in the office inviting me to join the LMA on a civic visit to Brussels. Keen to be supportive of the LMA as its new chairman, I agreed to join the tour.

In late October that year, I boarded the Eurostar taking us to Brussels and, with Carole at my side, we took our seats among the other members. We were seated with another couple, Ronnie and Rosemarie Barden. I knew Ronnie as he had previously served as Leader of Redbridge before becoming Mayor of Redbridge in the municipal year prior to my own mayoral year.

We had both served on the Parking Committee for London, which was charged with coordinating parking enforcement among all the London boroughs. Ronnie had been chairman of the committee but following the local elections in 1994, the Conservative had lost control of Redbridge Council and Ronnie lost his leadership of the council. I had replaced him as leader of the Conservatives on the Parking Committee but in opposition, as Labour had won most of the London boroughs during that election and so took political control of the committee. We spent the train journey catching up.

Sitting in seats next to ours were Munroe and Suzette Palmer. Suzette had previously served as Mayor of Barnet, where I had grown up and gone to school. Both were serving Barnet councillors. I was impressed. When I was at Christ's College, my grammar school, and first taking an interest in politics, Munroe had stood for Parliament as the Liberal candidate, standing against Margaret Thatcher, our local MP. In addition, his sons were at school with me. So, I knew who he was and was honoured to meet him. We went on to become firm friends and a few years later Munroe was elevated to membership of the House of Lords as Lord Palmer of Childs Hill. Despite his busy life as a Liberal peer, he continued to join LMA trips with Suzette.

Brussels

While Carole and I enjoyed the weekend getting to know the other attendees, visiting the Mayor of Brussels and enjoying an interesting trip to the site of the Battle of Waterloo, the trip itself was an organisational disaster. The organiser was former Hammersmith and Fulham mayor (four times in fact), Bill Smith, who was by that stage in his eighties. We had paid a basic fixed fee but were expected to pick up our own hotel costs direct with the hotel reception desk. The hotel was a two-star, very basic hotel. Modern but with tiny rooms. I knocked my head just getting out of bed.

The London Mayors' Association civic visit to Brussels – meeting the Mayor of Brussels.

No arrangements were made for lunch or dinner. We were on our own. Now, as Lord Mayor, members flocked around me and several suggested that Carole and I join them for dinner. A gang of us would go for meals together. But it became clear that several members were excluded and were seen eating by themselves, not necessarily by choice.

We had to pay for our own food and I recall one evening having dinner in a local Flemish restaurant where I suggested that the ten of us sitting together split the cost equally. But one member exploded, saying that her meal was a few euros cheaper than the others and demanding she only be charged for what she ate and that she was not prepared to share the cost equally. In addition, every time we went to a museum, we each had to find the cash to pay for our own entry. If we had a guide, Bill would undertake a whip round to give the guide a tip. It had to be done better!

Action Required

On my return to London, and having made many friends among the members, Carole and I started attending more of the events.

As chairman, I was also entitled to attend Executive Committee meetings. My predecessors had not done so for years. But I started joining the meetings and contributing to the discussions. Should we charge £3 or £4 for an event was just an example of the exciting discussions we had.

The black-tie annual dinner was held in the Wandsworth Council Town Hall. I was to be the main speaker. When I arrived, I walked into the hall and my heart sank. What I thought would be one of the highlights of my year was to become the opposite. The room was laid out with several rows of trestle tables covered with a paper tablecloth covering just sections of each table. At the centre of the tables were water jugs and cheap Tesco bottles of wine. The cutlery was laid on one side of the main plate. A hard white roll sat on the tablecloth and for each lady a red rose. The only nice touch. The Dorchester Hotel it was not. Forgive me, but I was not being a snob. I just thought that the annual dinner of the London Mayors' Association should be a special occasion, one notch above normal civic dinners. I was clearly mistaken.

Once a member, you stayed a member for life so there are usually several hundred members at any one time plus all the incumbent thirty-three mayors of the London boroughs. But when I attended events, no more than a dozen members would attend and I soon discovered that several attendees were not members but merely friends of the chairman, filling up otherwise empty spaces.

I persevered, becoming an active member of the Association during the year following my retirement as Lord Mayor, mainly to keep in touch with the mayors of the other boroughs who I had got to know during my mayoral term of office. But the activities I participated in were embarrassingly poor quality and badly attended.

It also became apparent that most of the active members were from just five of the thirty-three boroughs and mainly Conservatives. Moreover, most attendees of events were white, clearly not representative of diverse London nor reflecting the cosmopolitan members of London's councils.

Things Had to Change.

A few months after I retired from being Lord Mayor, I had lunch with Ronnie Barden and it appeared that we had both come to the same conclusion – that the LMA needed to change.

During my year as Lord Mayor, I had come to realise just how much value the mayoralty brought to civic life. Not only did it give non-political leadership to a council but it enabled the mayor to act as the council's ambassador at a series of events throughout the borough and in London generally. I was also conscious of the delight and pride it brought to those who the mayor came into contact with, whether a company, institution or just individuals who shook the mayor's hand. I was, however, conscious that in many councils, the political leadership wanted to downgrade the mayor's role and in particular, reduce the cost of servicing the mayoralty. These views were often held by councillors who did not really understand the impact the mayoralty had on residents, businesses and local charities, nor how much joy the mayor's involvement in an event meant to the host or guests.

The LMA was therefore in the unique position of being able to increase awareness of the important role that mayors play and impress on councillors the need to properly support the mayor, the mayor's office and the mayor's support staff, in particular through the proper funding of the mayoralty.

Having thoroughly enjoyed my year as Lord Mayor, I also wanted to continue the friendships that I had developed with colleagues who had served as London mayors in the same year, as well as with other members of the LMA who I had met, all of whom had shared a very special experience. It was only when talking to fellow mayors and former mayors that the person could really understand stories of life as mayor. Having experienced a year as mayor, I also wanted to pass on advice to newly installed mayors on the do's and don'ts of being mayor. The LMA was clearly the right vehicle to do so.

We were a unique club with very restricted membership and I saw the opportunities of turning this rundown association into something that would not only strengthen those bonds between mayors and former mayors (and of course their consorts) but also highlight how important the mayoralty was in civic life.

The more I thought about it, the more I became convinced in my own mind that I could turn the LMA around and highlight the importance of the civic mayor in London life.

We therefore agreed that at the next AGM I would stand as executive chairman and Ronnie as vice-chairman. Ronnie, as the longer-serving member of the committee was deputed to tell the executive chairman of our plans. But I think she guessed what was happening, as she told him that she was delighted since she was intending to retire and would be happy to become President. So, an easy solution.

At the AGM, I was duly elected executive chairman and things did begin to change. The first thing I did was to draft a newsletter. Until then, the only notification the members received were typed details of forthcoming events. We had to do better, so I designed and wrote a four-page newsletter on a computer! The newsletter heralded my arrival as chairman and, as they say, from acorns oak trees grow.

Within a year, my amateurish newsletter became a glossy A4 sized magazine with a house style and full of photographs (taken by me) of all the events we had organised. To promote the Association, I sent copies to everyone I knew. This brought the work of the LMA to many who had not even known of our existence, let alone what we did. It also persuaded people to take us seriously and helped me persuade them to host events for us.

I found a cartoonist who I persuaded to draw a number of amusing cartoons depicting mayors at work. These were brilliantly received.

One cartoon, for example, showed a mayor (in full robes and chain) at a council meeting exclaiming 'Councillor Parkinson, you have one minute to speak on local government reform – without hesitation, deviation or repetition'.

An example of the LMA newsletter.

I used my wide connections from my lengthy time on Westminster Council and my friendships developed during my mayoral year to arrange visits to a wide range of fascinating and interesting places. Private tours of the Tower of London, a day at Ascot races with a private lunch in one of the VIP suites, a visit to the Cabinet War Rooms with my colleague and friend Duncan Sandys, Sir Winston Churchill's great grandson. These became very

"He's had eleven events today..."

A cartoon from the LMA magazine.

popular and I would arrange about ten such visits every year, trying hard to find more fascinating and interesting ones than previous visits. Rather than having to fill spaces with friends, we had to create waiting lists for cancellations and even turn members down.

A further idea I had was to order a variety of gifts with the LMA coat of arms on, to sell to members. These ranged from cufflinks, brooches, ties, scarves, umbrellas, postcards, mugs, salt and pepper sets, display plates and lightweight briefcases. These all sold quickly.

Foreign Trips Mayoral Style

Although the foreign trips had been disastrously organised, I was determined to continue this annual pilgrimage to European capital cities to meet the mayor and sight-see. Shortly after becoming chairman, I approached my friend Urs Eberhard, deputy chief executive of Switzerland Tourism. Together we prepared an amazing programme for a four-day visit to Switzerland. We would stay at the grandest hotel in Berne, the capital, and would take day trips to Geneva and to Biel.

I was determined not to make the same mistakes as my predecessor, so the first thing I organised was for all the meals to be pre-arranged for everyone, with the costs included in the price of the trip. In fact, all the costs would be included – entry to museums, travel between the cities, the hotel and flights. The only costs an attendee would be required to pay would be for souvenirs or the occasional coffee when we had free time. The total cost was much more than in previous years, but it was all inclusive and the hotel and restaurants were all five star. It was a risk. Would members be prepared to pay a substantially higher upfront cost but accept the quality would be better and no further cost would be incurred. Twenty-two members did join us that year and it was a great success. We had meetings with the mayors of Berne, Geneva and Biel and drinks with the British Ambassador as well as tours of all the major sights.

As the years went by, the foreign trips became even more interesting, exciting and professional. I single-handedly organised trips to Amsterdam (and the Hague), Warsaw (and Krakow with a visit to Auschwitz and the salt mines) and Oslo (and Bergen). Each visit would follow a similar pattern with me arranging a visit to meet the mayor of the capital city on the Friday; a visit to another town within an hour's drive on the Saturday where we would also meet the local mayor and, at some stage over the four days (Thursday to Sunday), we would be received and entertained by the British Ambassador in the Ambassador's Residence. The success of the trips soon got round and within a few years we were taking over sixty members on each of these trips.

The trip to Amsterdam was memorable from the tour we all made one night around the red-light district, when we lost the mayor of an inner London borough. I won't mention which one! He was later seen returning to the hotel rather sheepishly with a large package in a brown paper bag.

I organised almost everything myself. I found a travel agent to arrange the hotel and travel and they helped me to find a local agent to provide us with guides. I drafted and sent to all our members an advert inviting them to join us. I would invite myself to a meeting with the Ambassador of the nation we were visiting and persuade them to host a reception at their Embassy. These ambassadorial receptions always went down well and made our members really excited about the pending visit.

Bob Bone Steps in to Help

In 2001, after discussions with Bob Bone, who ran the New Year's Day London Parade, and with Bob's assistance, I took about fifty LMA members to Edinburgh over the Easter weekend. This was because Bob was organising a parade of American bands in Edinburgh on the Easter Monday. I asked Bob to help me with the organisation of our visit. The trip went extremely well and we were entertained by the Lord Provost of Edinburgh at a Burns Night dinner with the traditional piping-in of the haggis. We also visited the Castle and Holyrood Palace and undertook a private tour of HMY Britannia, now a museum in a dry dock in Leith, which ended with a private reception on the main deck.

Bob's involvement in organising the trip was extremely helpful. This was a time when I was also a busy solicitor as well as a cabinet member at Westminster Council, so any help in reducing the burden on me was very welcome. When it came to thinking about the following year's trip to Madrid, I asked Bob to arrange everything for me. Although Bob's business was organising the annual New Year's Day Parade through the streets of Westminster as well as a number of other similar (albeit smaller) parades around Europe, he was in essence a professional tour operator in organising tens of thousands of Americans to travel to London and other European cities and in doing so, organised everything from hotels to flights and travel arrangements as well as visits to all the sights. So, helping us organise these trips was just an extension of what he was doing anyway.

In Madrid we were due to meet the Mayor. However, two days before we flew out, terrorists set off a number of bombs at the Atocha railway station in the heart of Madrid, killing nearly 200 and injuring 2,000. Initially, I thought the visit would have to be cancelled but the Spanish were keen to receive us, as they wanted to make a statement about life continuing as normal.

On the Friday morning, we were due at Madrid City Hall at 11 am. We had planned a couple of brief speeches by the Mayor of Madrid and myself with a few gifts being exchanged.

On the coach to the City Hall, I received a call from the mayor's head of protocol to advise me that the mayor had invited the national and local press to attend our

With the Mayor of Madrid.

Paying our respects at the site of the Atocha railway station bombings.

meeting as they wanted to emphasise that as their first official guests after the terrible incident, life was returning to normal and it was ok to visit Madrid. But I had only prepared a few basic words. So, in the ten minutes before we arrived, I had to write an appropriate speech that would be broadcast around the country. Pretty daunting!

On arrival, we were faced with over a hundred journalists, numerous TV crews and many photographers. It was a very moving experience and I hope I spoke well. Later in the day, we paid our own respects at the site of the bombing.

The United States and Further Afield

The following year, with Bob's support we took over more than seventy members to Washington DC and to Richmond, Virginia, in the United States. Bob arranged for us to tour the White House and I organised a briefing (through a diplomat friend) with the State Department. Simon's boss Margery Kraus, chief executive of APCO, arranged for us to visit the Capitol, where she hosted a drinks party for about fifty senators and congressmen. In Virginia, we met one of the state's senators (who had been a former Mayor of Richmond) as well as the Governor in his residence.

Subsequent LMA trips included visits to Lisbon, Vienna, Paris, Malta, Berlin, Switzerland (again), Budapest, Florence, Pisa and Siena. The final trip I organised before retiring was to Seville, Cordoba and Jerez.

Presenting the Mayor of Washington DC with a gift from the London Mayors' Association.

As the years progressed, Bob took over more and more of the organisation of the trips, leaving me little to do other than approve his suggestions.

The trips became so popular, the price rises did not deter members and we started having to cap the numbers joining us as the groups became too large to effectively manage. With a cap of over seventy, we had to start a waiting list for cancellations.

The Diplomatic Dinner

One of the initiatives I started was an annual Diplomatic Dinner. As Lord Mayor, I attended numerous National Day receptions hosted by the Ambassadors accredited to the Court of St James's and by doing so, I got to know many of them. In fact, some remain friends to this day. But in turn, I was conscious that most of the other mayors of the London boroughs rarely met an Ambassador (and in this respect I include High Commissioners).

I therefore decided to host a black-tie dinner in the Lord Mayor of Westminster's reception rooms in City Hall. Jenny Bianco had been a councillor at Westminster for about eighteen years and in 1993 served as Lord Mayor. By profession, she ran a business that provided catering for private companies and for community and political events. Not only was she a good cook but she also brought her own regular team of helpers and waitresses. More importantly, her prices were very reasonable, and far cheaper than most professional catering companies. I asked Jenny to help and she swung into action, preparing a first-class three-course plated dinner with wines, all for a very acceptable price, to allow me to charge the guests an amount that they could all afford, whether Mayor of Kensington and Chelsea or Mayor of Barking and Dagenham.

The idea was that I would invite ten Ambassadors (or High Commissioners) each of whom would sit on a different round table. I also arranged for at least one incumbent mayor to sit on each table to host the Ambassador. The dinner sold out and proved a great success.

However, before the first dinner, I had to turn away at least fifty members, as I had no space to accommodate them. Accordingly, the following year, I organised two separate dinners, a couple of weeks apart and invited different Ambassadors to each one. Members and mayors could attend either but not both. Again, these were so popular that we still had to create a waiting list and disappoint many members. We continued to host these annual diplomatic dinners for several years and they became one of the highlights of the year.

Me with Robert Holmes Tuttle the American Ambassador – 2008.

The Civic Service

The annual Civic Service had been established long before I came on the scene. This was an evensong service held in Westminster Abbey on a Sunday afternoon each October hosted by the dean, at which all the mayors of the London boroughs attended in civic state (in robes and chains and preceded by their liveried macebearer carrying their ceremonial mace). All the mayors (the 'Chain Gang') process through Dean's Yard and the Sanctuary into the Abbey through the Great West Door. It is a pretty amazing sight.

The Mayoral procession at the LMA Civic Service – 2011.

Prior to my becoming chairman, after the service concluded, the congregation were invited to the Great Hall of the neighbouring Westminster School and served a cup of tea. But on taking over responsibility for organising the service with the Protocol Office of the Abbey, I invited Jenny to do the catering and asked her to serve wine and food including sandwiches and cakes.

I was keen to ensure that the service was well attended, unlike in previous years, when the congregation merely comprised members of the public who happened to be visiting and a handful of LMA members. I therefore invited all councillors throughout the entire thirty-three London boroughs.

I also invited a number of Ambassadors and distinguished Londoners such as Sir Sigmund Sternberg, the respected philanthropist (who always attended in his bright green papal knighthood uniform), Raine, Countess Spencer (stepmother to Princess Diana, who I had become friendly with during my own mayoral year) as well as many others including those who had hosted LMA events in the past. While the Lord-Lieutenant had always attended, I also invited all his Deputy Lieutenants to do so as well. The Abbey would be packed and the reception well attended.

Wider Recognition
In an attempt to make the LMA better known in London society, I persuaded the Tate Galleries to allow me to host a drinks reception in Tate Britain to which I invited several hundred guests, many of whom I did not know but thought might attend and learn

more about us. Those who attended included leading politicians from both Houses of Parliament, eminent judges, Garter King of Arms and the directors of many of London's famous attractions. Again, it was very successful with over a hundred attending to learn more about the LMA.

Following in the Footsteps of Dick Whittington

During my mayoral year, I was invited together with the other London borough mayors to join the LMA annual walk, following in the footsteps of Dick Whittington, the 14th-century Lord Mayor of London. It was traditional to congregate in the restaurant of the Whittington NHS Hospital in Highgate and to walk (downhill) through the streets of Islington until we came to the City of London and then finish the walk at Mansion House, where the Lord Mayor of London entertained us to a buffet lunch and a ceremony in which the mayors all received a certificate confirming their participation. A number of mayors would use the walk to raise money for their mayoral charity.

It was also customary for the mayors to start the walk in robes and chains and, after a hundred yards, we would be photographed around the famous monument of a stone cat (Dick Whittington's reputed cat) on the spot where Dick Whittington was believed to have heard the bells of London calling him to return to London and become Lord Mayor.

The start of the London Mayors' annual walk from the Whittington Hospital with me at the centre representing the Lord Mayor of Westminster as Deputy Lord Mayor.

I was informed that mayors would then disrobe and continue the walk in whatever they were wearing underneath, whether a three-piece suit or jeans and a t-shirt. But in my year as Lord Mayor, I insisted we kept the robes and chains on throughout the walk, not only to keep us warm (the robes are very thick and heavy) but also to make a statement about what we were doing. My fellow mayors loved the idea. Ever since then, the mayors have continued to wear robes and chains on every subsequent walk.

While I enjoyed the walk, I did feel that the route very boring, as we just passed through a series of residential streets and along the busy Holloway Road. When we reached the City of London, being a Sunday, it was deserted as we walked alongside a series of nondescript office buildings.

When I became executive chairman, I was delighted that Graham Holland (former Mayor of Bexley) who had been organising the walk since 1993, agreed to continue to do so. But I suggested that we changed the route to make it more interesting. I therefore arranged for the mayors to congregate in the Tower of London for coffee and then walk along the north bank of the Thames ending up at Westminster City Hall in Victoria, where the Lord Mayor of Westminster hosted a buffet lunch.

However, several of my fellow members were not happy with the new route and, although it was more interesting, they preferred the historic route. The Mayor of Islington got upset too, as the traditional route mainly passed through her borough. I therefore had to concede and we reverted to the old route the following year.

New Mayors

By 2005, I was conscious that newly elected mayors received little advice from their own council and colleagues so I started a 'New Mayors Induction Day'. This was an away day held in Westminster City Hall a month after the mayors came into office. I brought together a number of my colleagues on the Executive Committee and gave each one responsibility for lecturing on a different aspect of being mayor.

I also decided to host an evening reception for all the new mayors, just after they came in to office in the spring of each year. This would allow them to get to know each other. The reception would be jointly hosted by me and the Lord Mayor of Westminster and I would give the main speech about the LMA and what we did with a view to recruiting new members. The evening would be sponsored by Bob Bone, who would use it to tell the new Mayors all about the New Year's Day Parade.

Protocol

In 1905, the committee of the London Mayors' Association published a book on the protocol of the London mayoralty. This set out the rules and protocols for mayors in London acting in their official capacity and in particular the relationship between them – that is the order of precedence when more than one mayor was present at the same time. In their own borough, a mayor takes precedence over everyone except the Monarch (or other members of the Royal Family or the Lord-Lieutenant of Greater London, when representing the Monarch). But what happens when there are several mayors at an event together? An updated edition was published following the major reorganisation of the London boroughs in 1965 and further updates produced in 1970 and 1974 and then again in 1988 after the abolition of the Greater London Council.

As chairman of the LMA, I was constantly being asked to give advice on mayoral protocol to mayors and their officers. One of the sources of such advice was the LMA booklet but I was conscious it was years out of date. I wanted to update it, but every time I started, the considerable work involved meant that with my busy life, it never got past the first ten pages.

I mentioned this to my friend, common councilman Edward Lord, a member of the City of London Corporation, who offered to have a go at rewriting it on the basis that he would ask his friend, barrister and City of London Alderman Simon Walsh JP, to assist him. They then set about redrafting it, while I started some research. The major change since the last version was the creation of the Greater London Authority and a directly elected executive Mayor of London. So, the question that arose is who took precedence at an event in a borough, where the local mayor was present at the same time as the Mayor of London.

The Mayor of London was very different from the civic mayors of the London boroughs, who the LMA represented. We had taken the view that the Mayor of London was an executive position and not a civic mayor. The civic role of representing the Greater London Authority was frequently delegated to a deputy mayor or to the chairman of the Greater London Assembly.

In the late 1990s, as chairman of the LMA, I had led a campaign to persuade the Blair government, which was creating the Greater London Authority and the position of Mayor of London, that to save confusion as to the difference between the traditional civic mayors we represented and the proposed executive Mayor of London, that the name of the Mayor of London be changed to 'Governor of London', in that London was very much like an American state. The title 'Governor' in the US ensured no confusion between that role and that of the city and borough mayors within that State.

But this was not acceptable to the Blair government, which was basing its idea of a new style mayor of the capital on the powerful Mayor of New York, who after 9-11 was seen as a great civic leader. My campaign argued that the name would confuse the public as well as foreign political leaders as to the difference between the civic Lord Mayor of London (who was just like all the other civic mayors, as Mayor of the City of London Corporation) and the new (executive) Mayor of London. But this was ignored.

Returning to the updating of the protocol book, there was the view that I and my LMA colleagues held that, as first citizen, a mayor took precedence in their own borough over everyone except royalty, and that included an executive Mayor of London.

But when I asked the Home Office (which is the government department responsible for mayors and civic precedence), they made it clear that the Mayor of London took precedence in any of the London boroughs, notwithstanding that the mayor of that borough was present. I wrote to both the Comptroller of the Lord Chamberlain's Department at Buckingham Palace and to the Lord-Lieutenant seeking their support for my view. But both deferred to the Home Office (which I can understand). The argument put forward was that 'while the Mayor of London was not a civic head in the traditional sense, the office of Mayor of London is intended to provide leadership to the Capital and accordingly should be accorded due precedence'.

In reality, issues did not arise under the first three Mayors of London as they all held little regard for protocol and were very happy to defer on the ground to the precedence of the local mayor and would take a back seat unless of course it was a Mayor of London event.

With Edward and Simon's suggested amendments and the result of my research and enquiries, I proceeded to finalise a draft of the booklet for publication. I sent final copies to both the Comptroller of the Lord Chamberlain's Department and to the Lord-Lieutenant asking for their approval, and in both cases this was received. Hundreds of copies were printed for sale to members and all the mayors. That same version is still being used and sold to new mayors now.

The Annual Dinner

One of the reasons I became chairman was to upgrade the annual dinner. Accordingly, the first thing I did after becoming chairman was to find a new venue and better caterers. One of our committee members, Doreen Weatherhead, a councillor on Kensington and Chelsea Council, suggested we move the location to the Great Hall within the Kensington Town Hall complex. Their in-house caterers came with a good reputation. The only problem was that I felt the décor of the room very bland. It was just brickwork. To get round this, I employed a form of theatrical set designers to dress the room.

I also hired a band from the Household Cavalry to entertain the guests during dinner, which they did in full military uniform. Wine was poured by the waiters, not left on the table for guests to help themselves and I introduced entertainment after dinner. I also found sponsors for the additional cost involved.

Again, a great success and in the following years, I hired different military bands, surrounded the room with different set designs and added a variety of entertainment. I would also invite someone famous to be our guest of honour to give an after-dinner speech. I also persuaded the Lord Mayor of London, his Lady Mayoress and the two Sheriffs and their ladies to attend.

Speakers over the years included the Metropolitan Police Commissioner, the Attorney General, the Lord Chamberlain, Andrew Neil (the broadcaster and former newspaper editor), the Dean of Westminster, LBC's Nick Ferrari and the Lord Lieutenant.

In 2001, we celebrated the centenary of the founding of the LMA and so I decided to invite royalty to attend that year. Using my contacts at the Palace, HRH Princess Alexandra agreed to be our guest of honour. The Company of Pikemen and Musketeers (the ceremonial unit of the Honourable Artillery Company) provided a guard of honour and nearly two hundred members filled the Great Hall. As I mentioned earlier, the LMA had been founded by the first Mayor of Westminster, the 15th Duke of Norfolk. I borrowed a painting of the Duke in his mayoral robes from the Westminster Council House, to hang behind the top table.

The Princess was gracious and seemed to enjoy the evening. She also brought with her, as her Lady in Waiting, the niece of the then Duke of Norfolk and so a descendant of our founder.

HRH Princess Alexandra arrives at the 100th annual dinner of the LMA and is greeted by me, as chairman, and the Mayor of Kensington and Chelsea.

By Royal Appointment

I decided that despite this special dinner to celebrate our centenary, I would go one better. As Lord Mayor, I had become friendly with the Comptroller of the Lord Chamberlain's Office, one of the principal officers of the Royal Household, in charge of all Royal protocol, Sir Malcom Ross. I wrote to him suggesting that Her Majesty might like to attend a reception I proposed we hosted in her honour at St James's Palace to celebrate this important anniversary. I knew that one could hire St James's Palace for receptions and other events, so long as a member of the Royal Family were present. After months of waiting, I eventually received a response from Her Majesty's assistant private secretary, advising me that Her Majesty's diary was too busy and therefore she had to decline our invitation.

But not deterred, I invited Sir Malcolm to lunch and a few weeks later, he joined me at the Mirabelle in Mayfair for an enjoyable meal (at my expense). It was worth it, as towards the end of the meal, I explained a little about the LMA and our centenary and having told him about the rejection, sought his advice as to how to secure Her Majesty's attendance. He understood the message and asked me to leave the issue with him.

About a month later, I received a call from Her Majesty's assistant private secretary to advise me that Her Majesty and the Duke of Edinburgh would be delighted to attend a Centenary Reception at St James's Palace, on a date in December 2001.

Helen Watson (our secretary) and I immediately started work on organising the event which included several meetings at St James's Palace and a walk through. We had to arrange caterers, invite our members and work out not only who was to be presented but who should be presented to The Queen and who to the Duke. We knew that if members were told before the reception that they would be presented to the Duke and not The Queen, they would be upset and complain. So, we advised everyone that those being presented would be placed in groups of five (as this is what the Palace requested) on each side of the room and that we would not know which side The Queen would go down until she actually walked into the room. This was a white lie, as we knew she would walk down the right-hand side with the Duke on the other side.

As the reception was being held in a Palace, officially The Queen was hosting the event, not us. As such, it was protocol at the Palace that I and the Lord Mayor of Westminster would not greet the Royal couple on the driveway outside the Sovereign's Entrance to the Palace, as would normally be the case, but inside, in the entrance lobby. Another protocol lesson learnt!

The Royal car arrived and the Royal couple entered the lobby to be greeted by the Superintendent of the Palace. As soon as she walked in, clearly audible to the Lord Mayor and I who were waiting to greet her, she asked the Superintendent why a particular table had been moved since her last visit and suggested it be returned. She clearly noticed such matters, despite owning numerous Palaces, each with hundreds of rooms.

The receiving line consisted of the Lord Mayor of Westminster (as our President), me as chairman, and Helen Watson, our secretary. I then escorted Her Majesty up the stairs to the first State Room, the Council Chamber, with the Lord Mayor escorting the Duke.

In the Council Chamber, I presented each of the members of the Executive Committee to Her Majesty, while the Lord Mayor did likewise with the Duke. There was then a brief pause before we moved on to meet all the other guests waiting behind the closed doors that led into the principal State Rooms.

As we waited, I stood chatting with both Her Majesty and the Duke. The Duke started asking me all about the mayoral badges that we were all wearing. The incumbent mayors

With Her Majesty in St James's Palace.

were not wearing their chains, merely their mayoral badges on ribbons as one of the most important protocols of the mayoralty is that mayors cannot wear chains in a Royal Palace. We explained that the past mayoral badges were presented to the mayor of each borough on their retirement and reflected the coat of arms of that borough. He then inspected the badges of several committee members.

Presenting members of the LMA to Her Majesty at St James's Palace.

The doors then opened and we entered the first of the three principal State Rooms, the Throne Room, where the first set of members were waiting in their groups of five, with others who were not being presented, milling about behind them. I took the right-hand side of the room with Her Majesty while the Lord Mayor (as planned) took the other side with the Duke.

These State Rooms are magnificent, hung with deep red silk wallpaper, gilt framed portraits of royalty going back centuries, and gold leafed surrounds around the gigantic double doors at each end of the room. The first room being the Throne Room was distinguished from the others by the presence of a magnificent golden throne beneath a crimson red canopy.

The Duke of Edinburgh examines the mayoral badge of Beryl Jeffery, the former Mayor of Wandsworth, while Her Majesty watches with interest.

The protocol used during all Royal receptions is that the host (me in this case and the Lord Mayor with the Duke) presents (note – one is presented to royalty, not introduced) the leader of each group, who then in turn presents the other four members standing with him or her. Her Majesty is an expert in saying a few words to everyone and then moving on. As she got to the last person in the line-up, she would turn to me and I would lead her on to the leader of the next group. As we approached the grand doors separating this room from the next, the doors would open and we would pass through, with the same arrangements in the next room. At the end of the third room there was a podium, where I was to address Her Majesty, the Duke and everyone attending.

It was so well organised you would think that nothing could go wrong. But of course, it did. One member, not happy to be on the Duke's side of the room, ran to the other side of the room after having been presented to the Duke. He then positioned himself at the end

*Addressing Her Majesty and the guests present at the end of the Centenary
Reception in St James's Palace – December 2001.*

of a group of five about to be presented to The Queen. I realised what had happened, but
could do nothing but admire his audacity.

One of the members who was presented to The Queen was my Westminster colleague,
John Bull, who had been Lord Mayor of Westminster sixteen years earlier. John owned
several racehorses and so had something in common with Her Majesty. He reminded her
of his interest and that he had served as Lord Mayor all those years before. She immediately
recalled him and referred by name to a couple of the horses he owned. What a remarkable
memory! John was delighted.

One of our non-member guests was Peter Moore, the London Town Crier, who
frequently supported our events in his bright red cape, feathered hat and large bell. After
my speech and the presentation of a specially created LMA centenary plate to Her Majesty,
I started to escort the Royal couple as they took their leave. As we left the room, we passed
Peter, so I presented him. He explained to The Queen and the Duke that earlier that day
he had had his bell stolen after thirty years in the role. The Queen thought this hilarious
repeating to the Duke 'The Town Crier has lost his bell!' and turning back to Peter, didn't
stop asking him a series of questions about its loss, as he accompanied me and the Royals
to their car. An amusing end to a wonderful and historic afternoon.

New Venues for the Annual Dinner

Returning to the Annual Dinners, after a few years at Kensington's Town Hall, I decided
that it was time to find a new venue. I thought a West End Hotel would be appropriate.
At this time, I was a regular attender of the London Rotary Club's weekly lunch held at

the Radisson Portman Hotel in Portman Square. Through my attendance I got to know the banqueting manager and so asked him to do us a special deal to bring the LMA annual dinner to their banqueting suite. The room was large and suitably decorated to save the necessity of my incurring costs in decorating it.

The Children of the Sylvia Young Theatre School entertain the guests at the LMA Annual Dinner – February 2005.

I decided that with the large room, we could have an expanded cabaret. A few years earlier, I had befriended Sylvia Young, the proprietor of the famous Sylvia Young Theatre School in Marylebone. Sylvia kindly provided the cabaret with a twenty-minute show of about forty dancing and singing pupils from her school. The guests loved it. The children were very professional, amusing and just great fun.

A few years later, at another Annual Dinner at the Portman Hotel, we had just finished the dinner and were enjoying a comfort break before the speeches, when the toastmaster, Peter Moore (the Town Crier who had lost his bell) whispered into my ear that my presence was urgently required outside in the hotel lobby. I was in the middle of an interesting conversation with my neighbour but sensed the urgency in Peter's request. I stood up and went to see what the fuss was about.

The Lord Mayor of Westminster that year was known to enjoy her drink. As President she was not only hosting the evening but was also due to give the first of the speeches that night. As I entered the lobby, there was the Lord Mayor in her robes and chains spreadeagled on the floor, having collapsed, surrounded by a number of colleagues trying to revive her. We managed to lift her upright but she waved us all away saying she was fine. She brushed herself down and staggered back in to the main room.

Having all returned to our seats, the Toastmaster tugged at my jacket and whispered in my ear, saying that we could not possibly call her to give the first speech as she was, as he exclaimed, 'plastered!'. I responded by saying that things would look equally bad if she was not called, as the menu cards made it clear that she was to give the first speech. Furthermore, she was sitting at her place on the top table fiddling with her written speech. I insisted he call her to speak. After a few minutes, the Toastmaster banged his gavel and introduced the Lord Mayor.

My heart was thumping as the Lord Mayor rose slowly. She looked around the room in silence. She stopped, looked ahead and said in a very slow monotone voice: 'You think I am going to give a long and boring speech......well I am not!' And as she said that, she tore up the pre-written speech (written by her private secretary) and threw the hundreds of pieces in the air like confetti and then promptly fell back into her seat looking down at the floor.

The Toastmaster immediately called the guest speaker to give his speech, which he did without any reference to what had just happened.

On the following Monday, the gossip column of the *Daily Mail* relayed this story. One of the guests must have leaked it to them. The Lord Mayor's private secretary had provided a statement on behalf of the Lord Mayor, quoted by the paper, saying that her behaviour had been caused by some medication she had been taking, which had disagreed with her!

In 2008, after about five years at the Portman Hotel, it was again time to change the venue as numbers would start to decline as members got bored with the same venue year after year. I therefore approached my friend Michael Gray, the chief executive of the Hyatt Hotel chain in the UK. I had first met Michael when he was general manager of the Hyatt Carlton Towers Hotel in Knightsbridge. After the Hyatt Group sold their interest in the Carlton Towers to the Jumeirah Hotel chain, they subsequently acquired the Churchill Hotel in Portman Square and turned it into a Hyatt Hotel and Michael became their general manager. Michael was delighted to host us and so we moved there for our annual dinners for the next few years.

I wanted Boris Johnson, then the Mayor of London, to be the guest speaker at our 2009 annual dinner. Simon was at this stage Boris's Deputy Mayor and Chief of Staff and I therefore asked him to arrange this, as Simon was ultimately in charge of Boris's diary.

Simon said he would arrange it, but he insisted I wrote in officially and so I did. But to my horror, a few weeks later, I received a formal response from some junior member of the Mayor's team, advising me that the Mayor was very busy and could not attend. I knew that Boris rarely attended events at the weekend (our annual dinners were always on a Saturday night) but Simon thought addressing the London Mayors' Association was important, not just because of our personal connection. As soon as I received the rejection letter, I called Simon and told him how let down I felt. Simon was equally horrified and said he would come back to me.

Twenty minutes later, he called me back to explain that his research had discovered that because Boris received over eight hundred invitations a week, they were all initially passed to a small team of very junior officers who filtered them. Ones that look important were sent to Simon's team in the Mayor's office while the majority were sent a standard rejection letter in the form I was sent. Simon explained that mine had slipped through but that he had just spoken to Boris and Boris would definitely attend with his wife, Marina. We were delighted and it did not take too long before we were sold out.

On the evening itself, Simon had to pull out of attending the dinner as he was ill in bed with a heavy cold. Boris was due to arrive at 7.15 pm and I was to receive him with Michael Gray outside the main entrance to the hotel. The timings for the evening were tight as we had a lot to get through and we did not want to finish too long after 11 pm when many guests would require public transport to get home. The intention was that guests would arrive at 7 pm with dinner starting at 7.45. Boris would arrive at 7.15 pm and meet guests in the pre-dinner reception in the hotel's library. At 7.30 there was no sign of Boris.

I was starting to panic. I knew he was coming from his country home in Thame but was assured by Simon that Boris had intended to leave early and go to his London home in Islington to change into black tie first.

I phoned Simon, who was watching TV in bed. He in turn phoned Boris. Within minutes I received a call on my mobile from Boris to apologise, promising he was five minutes away. Twenty minutes later, he and Marina arrived in their rather small and battered car. By this time, it was past 8 pm. Guests had been already herded into the dining room and so I escorted Boris and Marina straight into dinner.

The Mayor of London (centre) with the Lord Mayor of London (left) and the Lord Mayor of Westminster (right) at the 2009 LMA annual dinner.

As we entered the ballroom, the entire audience rose to their feet and cheered. One must remember that Boris was a Conservative mayor and a large number of my members were Labour or Liberal members. But they did not see him as a party-political politician, just as Boris – their Mayor of London.

It took another fifteen minutes to get Boris and Marina to the top table, because as we walked past the tables, all the mayors and former mayors and principally Labour ones, sought to shake his hand and take selfie photos with him. Boris is brilliant working a room like that and was happy to pose for photos, sign autographs and chat. I failed to move him on quickly and so it was not until 8.30 that we could start the formalities, some forty-five minutes late. But it was a great evening, enjoyed by everyone who attended especially after they all were amused by Boris's after-dinner speech, for which he had clearly researched the history of the mayoralty.

By 2012, it was time to move the dinner venue again, this time to the Corinthia Hotel just off Whitehall and the new venue hit all the right notes with our members, with the food, wine and ambience being superb. Again, the annual dinners sold out. We had come a long way from that first annual dinner I attended in Wandsworth Town Hall all those years earlier.

Constitutional Change

The constitution of the Association had historically provided for the Lord Mayor of Westminster to be its chairman and for the Association to be run by the chairman of the Executive Committee and with a distinguished member (usually the recently retired executive chairman) to be president. I thought this absurd and confusing. In addition, a number of the rules of the Association were outdated, last having been reviewed properly in 1901. Once I was established as executive chairman, I rewrote our constitution and the amendments included changing the status of the senior officers. My proposals, which were adopted, provided that at the AGM, the members would elect a chairman to chair the Association as well as all the meetings of the Executive Committee, while the incumbent Lord Mayor of Westminster would take on the role of president. Eminent senior members including former chairmen would be made vice presidents.

When I became chairman of the LMA, I inherited the incumbent secretary, Freda Barter. Freda had not been a mayor or mayoress but a constituency agent in the Wandsworth Conservative Association headquarters. I worked with her for the first two years but as she did not have a computer, merely an old-fashioned typewriter, I ended up taking over much of the administration myself, using the office infrastructure provided at my law firm. This was not sustainable.

One of the annual events the LMA organised was the Rifle Shoot. This inter-borough shooting competition was held at the Ham and Petersham Rifle and Pistol Club and had taken place every year since 1912. On taking over as chairman, I had sought to cancel this event, as I thought supporting anything to do with firearms was inappropriate, in the current climate of crime and disorder. But my Executive Committee members disagreed and thought it was a historic event and should continue. I invited a member of the committee to run it for the LMA, as I was not prepared to do so myself. Major Gerry Harsant, a former Mayor of Harrow, accepted the job, but as he could not type, he needed support. Freda agreed to support him with the administration of the event.

But after a couple of years Freda decided to retire from the LMA. I invited a former assistant private secretary to the Lord Mayor of Westminster to take over as secretary of the LMA. But she did not want to run the Rifle Shoot as well.

Diana Whittington, a committee member and Mayor of Wandsworth at the same time that I was Lord Mayor, offered to take on running the administration of the Rifle Shoot. But a year later, she advised me that it was too much work and wanted to step aside. However, she suggested that we ask a friend of hers to take over. Helen Watson had worked with Diana at the Red Cross. I met Helen and she agreed to give it a go for a trial year. She had had no involvement in the mayoralty until then. But not only did she enjoy helping but she got very involved and when the interim secretary for the LMA told me the work was too much and wanted to stand down, I persuaded Helen to become the LMA secretary.

Helen Watson, secretary of the LMA during most of my chairmanship.

Helen's enthusiasm and terrific capabilities in organisation soon saw her take over much of the running of the LMA and the big events in particular. She was very much a details person, ensuring that everything for an event was written down and clearly and carefully planned.

She was so efficient in helping me run the LMA from her kitchen table that when out shopping or playing bowls (as she loved doing) and therefore unable to answer the phone, a caller (when eventually making contact) would complain that they had tried earlier to call but no one in the office had answered. They had assumed that because of the efficiency in the organisation of LMA events, the LMA was supported by an office full of secretaries and staff. She had to explain that it was just Helen and her kitchen table.

Helen continued as secretary until I announced my retirement as chairman in the summer of 2016, as she wanted to retire at the same time as me. We made her an honorary member of the LMA and she subsequently moved to Preston to live close to her family. We were a great team and while we occasionally argued, we nevertheless remained friends.

Retirement

In early 2016, after nearly eighteen years as chairman, I was beginning to consider retiring. I had been proud of what I had achieved in creating an active and well-respected association with a superb reputation not only within civic government in London but with many of the other agencies that serve London. I had been honoured to have been made a Deputy Lieutenant (DL) by Lord Imbert when he was Lord-Lieutenant, in recognition of my work as chairman of the LMA. But I was also working extremely hard at Westminster as Deputy Leader, undertaking that role full time and so taking on more and more responsibilities. In addition, I had retired from Freeman Box, so no longer had the support of the general office there.

I also felt that I had exhausted myself in trying to improve everything we did. It was difficult to continuously find even more exciting places to visit and speakers to address us each year. And the work never stopped. As we finished organising one event, we had to start the next day organising the next one. I thought that I had done all I could and it was time to pass the baton on to someone else. But to whom?

I was taught as a young aspiring politician that a successful chairman of an organisation was one that not only turned that association around, making it very successful, but one that found someone excellent to succeed them. I gave great thought to my successor.

One of my goals as chairman was to involve all the political parties and to be fully inclusive. Bearing in mind that the LMA that I took over was one where most of the active members were from just a few Conservative councils and nearly all were white Conservatives, I had made it my goal as chairman to be fully inclusive, to ensure that all races, religions, genders and political parties were represented. I also made a big effort to ensure that active members came from all the thirty-three London boroughs, including the City of London, which had never been involved before. I was therefore very proud when

I achieved all these ambitious goals and even saw a number of past lord mayors of the City of London regularly attend events and even join us on the foreign civic trips.

My successor had to continue this and had to personally engage with all the members and get to know all of the active members by name – and their families too. I then thought of someone who in 2000 had been an excellent Conservative Mayor of Lambeth and was the Representative DL for Merton and had been awarded an OBE for her services to local government. Clare Whelan was well respected and I knew that she was capable of running the LMA and would follow my lead in making the Association fully inclusive. I invited her to a breakfast meeting and told her of my plans and my request that she take over.

She had been involved with the LMA during her mayoral year and for a few years after that, but had not attended events for years. But I just knew she was the right person to take over from me and, over a series of breakfasts, persuaded her to accept. I then had to break the news to my colleagues on the Executive Committee. The problem was that most of them had never heard of her and were concerned about passing the chairmanship to an unknown. I persuaded them to rely on my judgement that had served me well over eighteen years as chairman. They agreed and she was duly elected chairman unopposed, in July 2016 and was a great success.

I eventually stood down as Chairman at the 2016 AGM and I was honoured and delighted when I was told that the members had clubbed together to present me a parting gift of a number of beautiful heavy crystal wine glasses, which I now use in my flat in Mallorca.

I was sorry to leave the LMA, but after eighteen years I felt the timing was right. But as is clear from everything I have written here, I am very proud of what I did to make the London Mayors' Association the respected organisation it is today.

At the February 2016 annual dinner, announcing my retirement as
chairman of the London Mayors' Association after eighteen years.

Chapter 26

Timewasting Tales and Other Stories

There are a lot of eclectic stories from my time as a councillor, whether as a backbencher, a cabinet member, chairman of the London Mayors' Association, Lord Mayor, Deputy Leader or as chairman of a wide range of committees. Here are a few of those stories.

The Timewaster Letter

One of the many roles I undertook as chairman of the London Mayors' Association (the LMA), was editor, writer and official photographer for the twice-yearly newsletter. Despite asking my members on a regular basis to contribute articles, they rarely did so, leaving me to write most of the articles myself.

I was therefore delighted to receive a letter in January 2004 from a Robin Cooper claiming to be interested in civic affairs and claiming to have run a catering company that supplied 'sundry items' to his local mayor. He explained that he had become fascinated with the 'glorious tradition of the mayors most important civic item – the mace'.

He then went on to tell me that he had spent some time designing some new style maces and wished to show me the designs. I responded by return, enclosing a copy of the latest edition of the newsletter and suggesting a meeting. He responded immediately, explaining that he could not meet as he was recovering 'from a rather nasty accident' he had suffered 'while visiting a local glue plant'. He then enclosed a number of drawings of some very weird ceremonial maces.

Maces were originally instruments of war. A type of club that uses a heavy head to deliver powerful strikes. Used during medieval times, they became more ornate because warriors who did not wear military uniforms to distinguish whose side they were fighting on decorated their mace with the arms of their leader.

Over the years, the mace became the symbol of authority and in particular the authority of the sovereign. Each mayor has a mace to show his or her authority within their borough as does the Speaker of the House of Commons and the Lord Speaker (of the House of Lords).

If a mayor of a borough is in the presence of the sovereign, then because the sovereign is present, there is no need to show the authority of the mayor, so the mace (when carried by the macebearer) is carried upside down and, when placed on a table or stand, is covered with a black cloth.

The principal mace used by the City of Westminster has a long history. It is reputed to be the mace used by the Speaker of the House of Commons at the time of Oliver Cromwell.

There is a famous scene in British history when Oliver Cromwell, fed up with Parliament decides to suspend it and enters the chamber of the House of Commons seeking to arrest two MPs and, in doing so, points his finger at the mace, the symbol of the then deceased King sitting before the Speaker and orders that 'that bauble' be taken away and melted down.

It is believed that the person responsible for doing so could not bring himself to carry out this instruction with regard to such a beautiful piece of silver gilt and so hid the mace in the sanctuary of neighbouring Westminster Abbey. When Westminster Council was subsequently created in 1900 and took over civic administration in the City of Westminster from the Abbey, the civic insignia held by the Abbey were handed over to the newly incorporated council and this included the mace. There is no evidence as to whether it is the same mace but it has been carbon dated to the correct period in history and is identical to the mace depicted in all the paintings of that historic moment. We will never know.

Returning to Mr Cooper, you will appreciate that as I was also fascinated by the civic mace and in need of content for the LMA Magazine, I wrote back asking if I could have his permission to publish his designs in the next edition of the LMA newsletter.

He was delighted and responded positively. So, in the spring 2004 edition of the newsletter, the Cooper maces appeared as a large article on the back page. I thought nothing more of these maces for a couple of years.

Steve Batt, the Lord Mayor of Westminster's Macebearer carrying the Westminster mace.

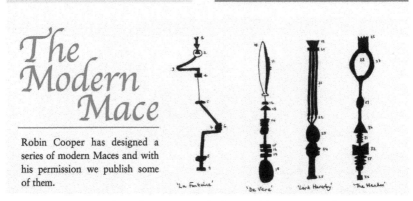

An extract from the spring 2004 edition of the LMA newsletter.

I was just finishing my sandwich lunch sitting at my desk at my law office one day in 2006 when one of my business partners came into my office holding a book called *The Timewaster Letters*. He had seen it in a local bookshop and purchased the book to read over lunch. In reading it through, he came across a whole chapter reproducing my series of correspondence with Mr Cooper and a copy of the maces as they appeared in the LMA newsletter.

It appears that Robin Cooper was a prankster and I had fallen for his prank. To be honest, on rereading the correspondence I should have realised something was up when his excuse for not meeting up with me was because he was 'stuck at home' recovering from an accident in a glue factory.

The book contained a series of exchanges of spoof correspondence with the chairman or chief executive of numerous organisations and associations. This included letters to and from the secretary of the British Egg Society and the chairmen of the United Kingdom Spoon Collectors Club and the National Association of Fish Friers. He even wrote to the Archbishop of Canterbury asking for advice on how to set up his own religion and to the managing director of IKEA in Sweden enclosing his designs for a new self-assembled bed-come-shelf-unit with instructions that appear to be impossible to understand. Clearly, I was not alone! At least I was polite!

'Cooper's letters are absurd, pointless, and very, very funny.'
RICKY GERVAIS, *The Office*

'This is the funniest book I have ever read.'
MATT LUCAS, *Little Britain*

Robin Cooper's
The Timewaster Letters.

The Mortuary Turkeys

Within a year of being elected to the council I was promoted to vice chairman of the General Purposes Committee which included responsibility for environmental health and trading standards as well the council's mortuary in Horseferry Road.

The mortuary had just been extended with a large new section full of freezers for bodies. I was asked to formally open the extension. This was the first time I had been asked to do anything like this and I was extremely proud. At the ceremony, I met for the first time, Dr Paul Knapman, the Westminster Coroner, who went on to become a friend and a fellow Deputy Lieutenant.

A few weeks later, my chairman was abroad when an issue blew up just before Christmas and I had to take responsibility and front all the TV and press enquiries. And did it make the headlines! It appears that one of the mortuary assistants had decided to make some money on the side and had set up a black-market sale of Christmas turkeys. No one would have cared until he decided to store the turkeys in the freezers reserved for the recently departed. Not just in the empty ones but sharing freezer containers with the bodies.

Well, at least the turkeys were well refrigerated, even if they might have smelt a little strange!

Robbie Williams

During my term as Lord Mayor, Robbie Williams flamboyantly left the successful boy band Take That and a few weeks later moved into a flat a couple of doors along from my own flat in Randolph Avenue, Little Venice.

As soon as his fans found out, they would spend hours outside the flat waiting for him to appear or arrive back home. When I would return from a mayoral function, wearing my morning suit and chains of office in the official mayoral car, a beautiful Daimler limousine with a large crest on the roof and a flag flying from the bonnet, the fans all assumed that I was Robbie returning to his flat. So as the car swept around the corner driven by the mayoral chauffeur, all the kids (mainly girls in their mid-teens) would scream and run towards the car, peering in and following it back to my flat.

The mayoral limousine outside my flat.

The chauffeur and macebearer would get out and open the rear doors to let me out, only for the girls to realise that I was not Robbie Williams and sigh with regret and slowly return to their original positions outside Robbie's flat, disappointed it was only me!

The Great North Museum

Would you believe it, but I am an exhibit in a museum?

I received a phone call one day from Ed Vaizey, then an MP (but now Lord Vaizey). Ed was a friend of Simon's and was Minister for the Arts and we had worked together on a number of issues.

He told me that as Minister he was in Newcastle opening the new Great North Museum and was on a tour of the exhibits. He then asked me if I knew that there was a life-size photo of me in one of the galleries. I was shocked. I had no idea.

It appears that one of the galleries included an exhibition about power and costumes, arguing that in British society, people with power tended (historically) to wear clothes and insignia to show off that power. To illustrate this, they had chosen to show how mayors dressed in robes and chains to show their importance as first citizens, by exhibiting a life-size photograph of me in mayoral robes and chains.

Why they chose me, I have no idea. I was never told nor asked for my permission.

My initial reaction was that he had made a mistake and the photo was another mayor looking like me. I called my friend and fellow councillor Steve Summers, whose parents live in North Shields near to the Museum. I told him the story and he immediately sent his parents off to investigate. The following day Megan and Don emailed me a photo and, yes, it was me. Subsequently, several friends have seen it and let me know.

The only issue, had they asked me, was that in the photo I am not wearing the blue and gold robes of the Lord Mayor of Westminster but the red robes I wore as a past Lord Mayor albeit with chains, as it was taken during the London Mayors' Association annual Whittington Walk, when I was acting (in the absence that year of the Lord Mayor) as Lord Mayor Locum Tenens (Deputy Lord Mayor). But who cares? I am a museum exhibit!

Me as an artefact in the Great North Museum.

Suits You

While chairman of Planning, a planning consultant wanted to meet me to discuss a project but I had to decline, explaining that I was going to be staying in my flat in Mallorca for a couple of months over the summer and so was not around. While I indicated that I would be happy to chat over the phone, a face-to-face meeting would be difficult.

The consultant told me that he too would be in Mallorca over the summer, staying with his in-laws and would be delighted to meet up there, over a coffee. A date and time was therefore set for us to meet at my favourite café in the local port (Puerto Portals).

In London, when undertaking my duties as a councillor, whether at meetings in City Hall or elsewhere when attending functions and events, I always dressed smartly. In this respect, I took after my maternal grandfather Arnold Lee, who was always immaculately dressed. I had my own preferred look, which I always maintained. My suits were bespoke, made by my tailor Matthew Norton. I had discovered Matthew just before I became Lord Mayor. As a male Lord Mayor, the uniform at the time was that, except for evening dress, one always wore a morning suit, that is black tails with striped trousers and a black waistcoat. Never a lounge suit. That distinguished you as a Lord Mayor, while mayors wore lounge suits.

Having been selected as Lord Mayor, I spent two separate afternoons visiting all the bespoke tailors in Jermyn Street and Savile Row, trying to find one who could make me two suits and a dinner suit at a reasonable price. I was shocked to discover that they wanted nothing less than four or five thousand pounds per suit (1996 prices) without the cloth. That was extra.

At the time I was Lord Mayor, I was given a small budget for clothes, but just one suit would have eaten into the entire amount. So desperate and upset at my discovery,

I mentioned my dilemma to my father. By coincidence, he had just seen an article in the *Daily Mail* about a bespoke tailor with very reasonable prices.

I made contact and Matthew turned up at my office to discuss how he could help. He offered me a fantastic deal and for the price of one suit from Savile Row, Matthew produced two morning suits with two styles of waistcoats (one thick for the winter and one without a back for the summer). On his advice, one of the morning suits was made of a very thin material and so could be worn in the hottest of summers. Many of my successors have ignored my advice about ordering a second suit made of very thin material and found themselves melting in the heat of the summer.

In one of my Matthew Norton suits with tie pin and badge, together with a member of the military.

On retiring from the mayoralty and returning to work at my law firm, I decided to ask Matthew to make me a couple of suits. I have always admired a high cut double-breasted suit with three buttons rather than the usual two, with double vents to the back. The resulting suits were smart and frequently commented on and so over the next twenty years, while practising law and pursuing my political career, I always wore a double-breasted Matthew Norton suit.

Ties were my weakness. My suits were always dark and my shirts white. But I believed that the tie had to be colourful in order to stand out among an otherwise dull colour scheme. My favourite shopping experience was looking for unusual ties. A recent count revealed more than 250 ties in my wardrobe!

When I was leading a new public realm scheme for the Strand, I met and got to know Giles Shepherd, the then general manager of the Savoy Hotel (and subsequently general manager of the Ritz Hotel). What struck me about this dapper man was the fact that he always wore a pearl tie pin which was placed in his tie just a few inches below the knot and which slightly pushed up the lower part of the tie. I thought this most elegant and so, after a search, I found a beautiful tie pin in a shop in Paris and began wearing a tie pin in exactly the same way that Giles did. This became my trade mark and when wearing a suit and tie, I always wore a tie pin and soon began collecting these as well as ties.

One of my council friends recently told me that he and a number of my colleagues had believed that when I was Chief Whip, my tie pin contained a microphone, so I could record all my conversations with colleagues for future use! I am afraid it was not true. Maybe I missed something there!

I also started collecting beautiful and unusual cuff links and have built up a collection of over a hundred, some very expensive while others are special in other ways. I also designed a Westminster Council cufflink depicting the council coat of arms and persuaded the officer at Westminster in charge of members services to order a number to sell to councillors and officers.

Westminster cuff links.

I always wore a pin brooch in my suit collar depicting the council crest. My colleague and friend Elizabeth Flach when Lord Mayor in 1988, initiated the idea by designing a badge depicting the shield alone. She gave me one and for several years I was the only councillor to wear it at all times. But at the same time that I was designing the cufflinks comprising the full council coat of arms, I used a similar design for a pin brooch. These were advertised to my colleagues and I encouraged them all to wear them. Many did. I wore mine whenever I wore my suit or a jacket. That is, until the day I resigned from the Council. I have never worn it since.

But I have been distracted from the story I was starting to tell. The planning consultant having arrived in Mallorca and staying with his in-laws, started preparing for the meeting with me over coffee at Cappuccino in Puerto Portals. It then dawned on him that I was always well dressed and that he had never seen me without my double-breasted suit, tie and tiepin. Realising he had nothing smart to wear to meet me, he rushed with his wife to El Corte Inglés, the famous Spanish department store, where he bought a suit, smart dress shirt and new tie.

Arriving at the Cappuccino to meet me, he stood horrified as I sat waiting for him, dressed in shorts and a polo shirt. I greeted him and was surprised to see how he was dressed, but thought that that was what he wore on holiday and so said nothing.

We had our chat over coffee and said our goodbyes. It wasn't until several years later, when chatting to a mutual friend, that the full story of his dash to the shops was revealed and his surprise at seeing me so casually dressed.

Although I dressed smartly when working, I always dressed for the occasion and in Mallorca I always dressed casually.

Even at home, when arriving back after a day of meetings, I would immediately undress and put on a tracksuit bottom and t-shirt to roam about my flat. This was unlike one elderly councillor colleague who, whenever I made an unplanned visit to his home, whether at the weekend or evening, I would always find him watching TV in his suit (jacket done up) and still wearing his tie. I was not that bad!

Elephants, Eggs and Dreams

In 2001, London became the home of a herd of hundreds of cows as part of what was called Cow Parade. This was organised by an American charitable organisation that held these Cow Parades around the world. The idea was that the company created three moulds of cows in different positions (one sitting) in a bland white colour and then invited famous artists and celebrities to design a piece of artwork to cover the cow's body. The completed cows would then be placed around the city hosting the Parade and the public were encouraged to walk around the city looking for them.

After the ninety-day event, the cows would be sold at auction and the monies raised given to a chosen charity. Some of the designs would go for up to £50,000 each. The person employed by Cow Parade to liaise with Westminster Council was the person who had been previously employed by the council to assist in running the Fair in the Square in 2000.

One day, she called me to arrange a meeting to seek the council's consent to install about fifty of these cows around Westminster with more planned for the City of London and Camden. At this stage, Cow Parade had only been undertaken in one American city and so London would be the second city to host it.

I liked the idea but was concerned at the precedent that would be set. After discussion with some senior colleagues, we decided to give the project the green light and, later that year, the cows invaded London. And what a success they were. Everyone loved them, children in particular. Miniature cows with designs from the favourite larger ones were sold in souvenir shops as well as in all the West End's major department stores.

In 2010 Mark Shand came to see me with the idea of a similar event but this time with elephants. I was interested. Mark was the brother of the Duchess of Cornwall and was passionate about protecting the elephants of Asia. His enthusiasm was contagious and, bearing in mind the success of Cow Parade, I readily agreed to an Elephant Parade.

After all the necessary consent had been granted and the elephants started to be designed by a collection of Royals, celebrities and artists, Mark phoned me to see whether I would like to design one of the elephants. I accepted immediately.

But what design should I suggest? In practical terms, this involved me coming up with a rough idea and a basic sketch and then a designated artist would work up the final design. After some thoughts, there was only one choice… a mayoral elephant. An elephant in red robes with ermine trim and wearing the chains of office. I even gave it a name. Ella May which when said, sounded like LMA – London Mayors' Association.

Ella May took her place on the streets of Westminster. The end of the allotted time for the elephants to remain on our streets coincided with West End Live. Therefore, a few days before West End Live that year, fifty of the elephants were placed, one behind the other, in a real parade leading from Leicester Square to Piccadilly Circus for five days including the two days of West End Live. Another great success.

At the subsequent auction, one of my friends was successful in purchasing Ella May and phoned me to say he wanted me to have it as a gift. I was delighted and suggested to

Simon that we place Ella May on our balcony at home. Simon just said one word in response: 'No!' A home therefore had to be found. I called Annie Walker, the chief executive of the Regent's Street Association and she willingly agreed to adopt it and place it in Regent's Street on the corner with Princes Street. There Ella May stood amusing passers-by and being the focus of photographs for tourists lining up to take selfies with her. However, after a few years, Annie thought Ella May needed new pastures and persuaded our mutual friend Margaret Newman, the chief executive of the St Christopher's Place Management Team to take over responsibility for Ella May. With bags packed, Ella May moved to Barrett Street, opposite Selfridges side entrance, a collection of restaurants and outdoor diners.

Me with Ella May.

Sadly, a few years later, Ella May was damaged by a hooligan who stabbed her, so she had to be taken to the elephant hospital to be repaired before being returned to enjoy the attention of Marylebone. Since my retirement from the council and Margaret's own retirement, Ella May has vanished and I have no idea where she now lives. But she had a good life for over ten years on the streets of Westminster.

A couple of years later, Mark Shand wanted to repeat the fundraising campaign for the protection of the Asian elephant but, not wanting a direct repetition of the successful Elephant Parade, decided to organise an Egg Parade at Easter, with hundreds of five-foot-high decorated Easter eggs around the streets of Westminster and other central London boroughs. Again, we agreed and he allowed me to design a mayoral egg which we called 'His Eggcellency'. Again, my friend bought the egg for me at the auction that followed and,

His Eggcellency.

because it was a more moderate size, we placed it on display in the Lord Mayor's Reception Rooms in City Hall.

The public loved the eggs too and this encouraged the producers of the upcoming live action film of Michael Bond's Paddington to suggest a similar idea with hundreds of Paddington Bears placed around central London with a trail for children to follow, from one to the next. While we appreciated that its prime object was to promote the film, we agreed that people would love them, with the proceeds from the subsequent sale of bears going to various charities.

Yet again, the organisers asked me to design one and, not surprisingly, I chose a mayoral theme and the Mayor of Paddington was born.

The Mayor of Paddington and I.

Before the reorganisation of London councils in 1965, there had been a Paddington Council with a Mayor of Paddington and the council still have the chains and badge of the Mayor of Paddington. Photos were taken and a fibreglass Paddington was created wearing a copy of the original chain and badge worn by the Mayors of Paddington Borough Council. Standing in his red duffle coat, looking rather like the red mayoral robes, he waves his hat – made to look like a mayoral tricorn – and holds his famous suitcase in the other hand.

He stood outside the side entrance to Paddington Station so commuters could say hello every day as they caught a train. After the event ended, the film's producers kindly gave me the original. I gave him to the council and he was positioned in the front window of City Hall facing Victoria Street, where he still lives, admired by passers-by as well as officers, members and visitors to City Hall.

As a result of the success of the Paddington Bears, the PR company behind it approached me in early 2016 for consent for yet another series of painted statues around Westminster. This time they were promoting a film made by Disney called *The BFG* (The Big Friendly Giant), based on Roald Dahl's iconic children's book. I had not read the book (although I subsequently attended the film's premiere as Disney's guest) but I was told that it was based on a giant who stole people's dreams and captured those dreams in a jar.

The proposal was for a number of Dream Jars to be placed around the city. Each jar was about a metre high and would contain a 3D model depicting a famous person's dream. Yet again, I was asked to design my own Dream Jar.

So, what was my dream? It could only be one thing. Something that combined my love of the mayoralty with my love of Walt Disney World. My Dream was to be 'Mayor of Disney World'. Because of copyright issues with Disney, they had to change its formal name to 'Mayor of Dreamland'.

The Dream Jar (identical for all the two hundred created), contained a large mystical fairyland style castle floating in a sea of white clouds. In front of the castle was a 20-cm miniature little me in full mayoral robes and chains. For this, I had to attend a specialist photographic studio in Clerkenwell, where I entered a special room wearing my past Lord

Mayor's red robes (which are the same robes worn by mayors – not Lord Mayors) and the mayoral chains (borrowed from City Hall). The room was surrounded on all sides by about one hundred cameras, which each took a number of photos of me from all angles. This was then used to make a coloured plastic 3D copy of me.

My Dream Jar was placed in Victoria where it lived for about three months. When the event ended, the PR company very kindly gave me my Dream Jar and it was duly delivered to my office in City Hall, where it lived for a few weeks. I then had it couriered to my flat in Mallorca, where it sits proudly on my terrace, although slightly faded by the intense heat of the Spanish sun.

Little me.

Robert's Dream Jar – me as the Mayor of Dreamland.

Boris's Housekeeper

Busy at work one day, I received a call from Simon who was then the Mayor of London's Chief of Staff. Boris had just remembered that his long-serving housekeeper was attending a ceremony at the Westminster Council House that afternoon to receive her British citizenship from the Lord Mayor of Westminster. Marina (his then wife) had given him orders to join the rest of the family at the ceremony, so he asked Simon to cancel his afternoon meetings. Simon told Boris that he would ask me to arrange for Boris and his family to be looked after at the ceremony and for the staff conducting the ceremony to be warned of his attendance. Simon called me for help.

I said I could go one step further. I knew that the Lord Mayor was not actually attending the ceremony that day but was being represented by one of my colleagues, another former Lord Mayor as Lord Mayor Locum Tenens (Deputy Lord Mayor). I phoned her and asked if she would mind standing down and allowing me to attend as Lord Mayor Locum Tenens instead. She was delighted as she was so busy. I then called the Lord Mayor's macebearer and told him what was happening and that he should bring champagne glasses as I would be bringing bottles of champagne. I also phoned the registrars to warn them too.

The Superintendent Registrar (Alison Cathcart – who had married Simon and I)

Boris, Simon and I in our flat.

received Boris and his family and showed them to their seats and after the formal ceremony with about fifty new citizens (including Boris's housekeeper) receiving their citizenship certificates from me in my red robes and chains of office, the Johnson family with their housekeeper were brought to the Lord Mayor's retiring room where I was waiting (still in my robes and chains) to greet them and to open the champagne and celebrate.

I know Boris was very grateful as he wrote to me afterwards to thank me for my kindness to him and his family that day.

The Church Street By-Election

Church Street Ward was one of the safest Labour seats in Westminster and comprised about ninety per cent social housing and had never elected a Conservative councillor. In 2007, the population included a large number of Bangladeshi residents. This ward was also one of the most deprived wards in the country with a large number of people on benefits. But Simon as Leader did not want to ignore the area, despite most of his predecessors having written it off.

Simon started meeting leading members of the community and helping them with a range of issues and when he found out that the local community met at their community centre regularly on a Sunday, he started attending at least once a month. I would often get annoyed that our Sundays together would be ruined by his disappearing all afternoon to speak at a Bangladeshi event in Church Street.

The Conservative vote was so poor in the area that there was not even a Conservative Party committee operating there. Simon was impressed by one of the leading members of the community, Mehfuz Ahmed, and persuaded him to set up a Conservative ward committee and start campaigning for the party. This went well and the Tory message started getting through on the estates in the area.

Then in the spring of 2008, the very nice and respected Labour councillor for the area, Tony Mothersdale, sadly died, causing a by-election. Simon immediately swung into action setting up a coordinating committee room in the ward and persuading Mehfuz to stand. He also gave instructions to every other ward in Westminster to send helpers to saturate the ward with canvassers for the whole of the three-week election campaign.

The Labour Party, on the other hand, arrogantly thinking that because it was safe seat, they could just run a similar campaign to previous years. Despite the Conservative candidate being a leading member of the Bangladeshi community, the Labour Party selected Dave Rowntree, a white pop star. He was the drummer of the famous boy band, Blur.

At the count, the Labour Party seemed relaxed and were surprised when so many Conservatives turned up to hear the results being read out. But when the results were announced, you could see the blood drain from their faces as Mehfuz won with a large majority. 935 votes against Rowntree's 652 votes. It was a fantastic reflection on Simon and his leadership not only of the council but of the city.

Sadly, at the next local council elections when every ward was being contested, with the Labour Party selecting another Bangladeshi candidate, they won the seat back. But it showed what we could do if we set our minds to it.

Canvassing

Canvassing for votes can lead to some amusing encounters. Residents opening the door naked or in their underwear is quite common. Being abused and shouted at is an even more frequent occurrence. An amusing incident that I recall happened when I was canvassing in Kensington Garden Square in my ward. I rang the bell and a lady answered it. She was wearing a short see-through nightdress.

I told her that I was canvassing for the Conservative Party and seeking her support. She paused and then said that she was definitely voting Conservative as she was a small businesswoman. She then whispered in my ear that she was 'a prostitute!' She paused walked away and then returned and said 'but I am an upmarket one. I work in W1 – not here in W2!'

All I could think of saying in response was 'oh!' and thanked her and left.

Canvassing in the 2018 Elections.

Christmas Lights

One of the highlights of the municipal year, was the turning-on ceremonies for the Christmas lights in Oxford Street and Regent Street. Both were high-profile events televised live on the evening news as was the turning-on of the Christmas Tree lights in Trafalgar Square.

I would always be invited to all three ceremonies. In Oxford Street and in Regent Street, the lights would always be turned on by a celebrity or two and in more recent years the turning-on of the lights themselves would be accompanied by performances by a pop star promoting their latest single. I was usually invited backstage at these events and introduced to and photographed with the celebrities.

For several years running, the turning-on of the Oxford Street lights and occasionally the Regent Street Lights coincided with other big pre-Christmas events and so the Lord Mayor would not be able to attend. I managed to ensure that on each occasion, I was the duty Deputy Lord Mayor and I would attend in red robes and the chains of office and give a speech from the stage. I would then find myself standing next to or behind the celebrity turning on the lights that year.

Backstage at a Regent Street lighting ceremony the members of the current pop group were on their way to perform and turn on the lights. Their management were represented by some young know-it-all. I was attending as Deputy Lord Mayor in the red robes and

Addressing the crowds as Deputy Lord Mayor prior to the turning-on
of the Oxford Street Christmas Lights.

Backstage at the turning-on of the Regent's Street Christmas lights with my nieces
Jessica (on left) and Cassie (far right) and Cassie's husband Daniel.

chains of office and accompanied by my nieces Cassie and Jessica and Cassie's husband Daniel.

We were quite sternly ordered that when the group arrived, we were not to look at them, and in particular, not look into their eyes and must divert our eyes away and look elsewhere!! We tried to observe the absurd rules, but as soon as this world-famous group arrived, they came straight up to us and sought photos with me in my robes and chains. A good example of where the management of these 'stars' are more precious about their clients then their clients themselves.

Backstage at the turning-on of the Oxford Street lights one year, the very famous female pop star arrived in her large chauffeur driven car with blacked out windows and parked up right behind the temporary stage. The whole purpose of inviting a star to turn on the lights is for the publicity it brings to the event and the street. As well as actually turning on the lights, the star is required to meet and greet a few selected children

My turn to turn on the Oxford Street
Christmas Lights.

as well as a few VIPs (like myself and fellow councillors) and the organisers and their families and also undertake a series of TV and radio interviews.

But on this occasion, we had already been told that the star was refusing to do any interviews, which really upset the organisers. To make matters worse, when she arrived in her car, with a number of children waiting backstage to meet their idol, she refused to leave the car and meet anyone. After about thirty minutes of her hiding away, she was called to the stage and, surrounded by four beefy bodyguards she rushed on stage, ignoring the children on her way. She gave her brief speech, turned on the lights and then turned around and marched straight to the car, again ignoring everyone backstage before the car zoomed off. Appalling behaviour.

One year, Oxford Street decided that they could not afford a full-blown ceremony nor a celebrity to turn on the lights and they kindly invited me to do so. In front of about a hundred people instead of the usual thousands, I pressed the famous large red button and turned on the Oxford Street lights.

Another year, when the star pressed the lever on stage in Regent Street, the lights did not go on. The street remained in total darkness! After much embarrassment and in-filling by the celebrity star, the lights eventually just lit up. It turned out that a vandal had deliberately cut one of the main wires. From then on, in both Oxford Street and Regent Street, they now employ an army of individuals to turn on each set of lights separately from the mains on cue. This has prevented any further sabotage.

In the early years of my involvement, the lights would be sponsored but as part of the agreement the council reached with the Street Associations, the amount of advertising was limited to just ten per cent of the decoration.

In 1998, Regent Street decided to be clever and having obtained the sponsorship of the fizzy orange drink, Tango, they complied with the council's rules by limiting the word 'Tango' to ten per cent of the decoration but then the entire decoration and all the lights along the street were lit in a bright gaudy orange. The street certainly got 'tango'd' that year and the council spent weeks defending the huge amount of criticism levelled at the Street Association and the council for making the country's smartest street so tacky.

Regent Street being Tango'd.

Eventually, the Crown Estate, which own the freehold to the whole of Regent Street, decided to take over responsibility for the Christmas lights from the Street Association and agreed to pay the costs without the need for advertising and sponsorship.

Eros

On New Year's Eve, revellers in central London tend to get carried away and so the council takes action in early December to protect certain structures. One in particular is Eros, the statue dedicated to the Greek god of love, standing in the centre of Piccadilly Circus. This would historically be surrounded by plain hoardings to protect the statue from revellers climbing up it and hanging from Eros's bow and, as has frequently happened, snapping the bow or, in some cases, Eros's arm too.

My team and I decided one year to add a number of advertising panels around the hoarding to cheer it up and enable us to earn some income in doing so. The adverts would be Christmassy and include some public awareness adverts. Above the hoardings we hung lights and decorations to enhance the Christmas feel. This worked well and so in a subsequent year we decided to go one stage further.

The idea was to position a large transparent ball on top of the hoardings to replicate a glass snowflake shaker. In our childhood, many of us have been given a glass sphere with an object inside and if one shakes the ball, snow appears in the sphere and falls gently. We sought to replicate this. In our case, the sphere was to be made of transparent plastic and inside the base of the sphere we installed a number of blowing machines. Small pieces of shredded paper were used to replicate snow and when the machines were turned on, you could see Eros inside surrounded by falling snow.

But we failed to take into account the British weather. One evening, a strong gust of wind raced down Piccadilly and as it hit Piccadilly Circus, it picked up the plastic sphere containing all the snow and blew the Christmas ball half way down Coventry Street, almost reaching Leicester Square, before it was stopped.

Another lesson learnt, resulting in future years seeing the top of the hoardings replaced with large metal Christmas boxes, carefully secured to the hoarding and wrapped to look like Christmas presents. Boring but safe.

The Eros Snowflake sphere.

The Norwegian Christmas Tree

When the Norwegian King fled Norway following the German invasion in 1940, he escaped to London where, in a large mansion flat in Knightsbridge, he and members of his government set up a 'government in exile'. After the war and the King's return, to thank the British and London in particular, the King sent a large Christmas tree from the forest outside Oslo to London for erection in the centre of Trafalgar Square. Dressed in the traditional Norwegian style, with vertical rows of simple white lights, the tree continues to be donated to London every year.

The lighting up ceremony for the 1996 Trafalgar Square Christmas tree.

Meeting the Mayor of Warsaw at the 400th anniversary of Warsaw as the capital of Poland – July 1996.

Carole and I presenting the Mayor of Oslo with a gift in Oslo's City Hall – November 1996.

During my term as Lord Mayor, I was invited to attend a conference of mayors from around the world in Warsaw to celebrate that city's 400th anniversary as the nation's capital city. At dinner one night, I sat next to the Mayor of Oslo, Per Ditlev-Simonsen. I mentioned the Norwegian Christmas tree and Per told me that the forthcoming Christmas would see Norwegians give us the 50th tree.

I then said that as it was such a special year, it would be lovely if I could fly to Oslo to help him cut it down. He liked the idea. Once back in London, arrangements were made and in early December, Carole and I flew to Oslo. We were greeted by the British Ambassador's chauffeur and taken straight to the Ambassador's residence where the Ambassador and his wife were waiting to receive us. After dinner we all went to bed as the following day was going to be a long one.

The next morning, we awoke to thick snow, which had fallen overnight, and were taken to the Oslo City Hall, the venue for the ceremony of the annual Nobel Peace Prize. We met the Mayor in his office and, after an exchange of gifts, we were given a tour of City Hall. It was then time to leave for the cutting-down ceremony. In the mayoral car, Carole and I with the Mayor and his wife, drove to a forest just outside Oslo.

By a log fire with the Mayor of Oslo in the forest for the tree-cutting ceremony.

With Tim Vincent the then Blue Peter *presenter.*

In the forest, we were met by a log fire surrounded by a choir of schoolchildren. As it was the 50th tree, Tim Vincent, one of the presenters of the famous children's television programme *Blue Peter* was there, filming the cutting-down ceremony for a piece for *Blue Peter*. Tim interviewed me and the Mayor, after which the Mayor and I jointly started cutting down the chosen tree (each of us holding a different end of the massive saw) while being filmed and photographed by a number of photographers and Norwegian TV companies as well as the *Blue Peter* crew.

We were only allowed to cut two-thirds of the trunk as it was too dangerous to cut it completely. As we moved with everyone else to a safe distance, the professionals came in to finish off the job and arrange the tree's transportation via ferry to London.

The Mayor of Oslo and I cut down the 1996 Trafalgar Square Christmas tree.

After the ceremony, Tim Vincent made my day. He presented me with a treasured *Blue Peter* badge. It was one of my childhood ambitions to win a *Blue Peter* badge and now I had one. This was heaven.

A week after we returned to London, it was time for the lighting-up ceremony itself. Because it was the 50th tree, we received notice that Her Majesty the Queen of Norway, Queen Sonja, would fly to London to press the button. I was invited to host a pre-ceremony reception in my parlour at Westminster City Hall. I also learnt that it was Royal protocol that when a foreign Royal was invited to undertake a ceremony in the UK, a member of the British Royal Family would accompany them. On this occasion we were told that Prince Andrew, the Duke of York, would join us at City Hall and at the lighting-up ceremony itself.

Again, protocol dictated that Prince Andrew would arrive first, which he did. I was in the street outside City Hall with Carole to receive him. We all then waited together for the arrival of the Queen.

The Prince greeted her first (with a kiss and bow) and presented me and then Carole. We then escorted Queen Sonja up to the 18th floor and into the reception where we were met by the Mayor of Oslo and his wife. During the reception, I presented a number of other guests to the Queen. When the time came, we all retuned to our cars and with a full police motorbike escort, drove to Trafalgar Square for the ceremony itself.

Outside City Hall, Prince Andrew escorts the Queen of Norway accompanied by Carole and me.

With Prince Andrew and the Queen of Norway on the podium.

I hosted the ceremony and from the podium in front of the tree, I welcomed the guests. We were then serenaded by a choir of Norwegian singers and eventually to a square full of Norwegians and Londoners and, live on both ITV and BBC news, the Queen of Norway turned on the lights on the 50th Norwegian Christmas Tree.

After the ceremony, I escorted the Queen around the Square for her to meet and greet the Norwegians who had come to watch. We then returned to our cars and were driven to the Norwegian Ambassador's residence for drinks.

I kept up my friendship with Per, the Mayor of Oslo, for several years and a couple of years later, I was invited by the King and Queen to join them at a Norwegian Concert in the Royal Albert Hall.

When I accepted, I assumed that we would be sitting in the main body of the Hall or in a box near to the Royal Box. But to my surprise, on arrival I was escorted to the Royal Retiring Room, to be met not only by my friend Per, the Mayor of Oslo, and his wife, but by the King and Queen themselves. The Queen remembered me and told the King about the Trafalgar Square ceremony.

I was surprised as more guests arrived to join us in the Royal Retiring Room. Next came the exiled King and Queen of Greece followed by the Queen of Spain (the King of Greece's sister) and finally by Princess Anne, who curtseyed to the King and Queen of Norway, as they clearly outranked her. She also curtseyed to the other Monarchs present. It was fascinating watching all these senior Royals engaging with each other and the protocol involved, each knowing their exact pecking order.

When the concert was about to start, we all entered the Royal Box and I was sitting at the rear with some of the other non-Royal guests. It was quite an evening.

My visit to Oslo to help cut down the tree was such a great success that Per invited my successor to do so the following year. It has now become a tradition and each and every year since, the Lord Mayor of Westminster travels to Oslo to cut the tree down and stays at the British Ambassador's residence. But I was the only one to receive the Norwegian Queen in London.

*I escort the Queen of Norway to the podium in Trafalgar
Square to light the 50th Norwegian Christmas tree.*

Chapter 27

Fascinating People

Over the many years I have spent in public life, I have met a wide range of interesting people. I could write a whole book about them but here are few of my stories.

Robert De Niro

Robert De Niro owns a fashionable hotel in Tribeca in the heart of New York City. The Greenwich is a one-of-a-kind boutique hotel with an award-winning restaurant. He wanted to open an identical hotel in London and, after searching for a while, he found a site in the heart of Covent Garden and began negotiations with CapCo, the property company which owned the site as well as most of the central Covent Garden area.

With his plans for this special hotel advancing, he wanted to present his ideas to me as chairman of the council's principal planning committee. Accordingly, I received a call from Sarah Jane Curtis, a senior director at CapCo, telling me that Robert de Niro was coming to London and would like to meet me to explain his concept for this new hotel.

I explained to Sarah Jane that I was due to fly to the United States on a speaking tour with the London Parade organisers, to recruit schools to participate in the following years New Year's Day Parade on the day he was arriving in London and so had to decline. Sarah Jane asked whether I could go a few days earlier to New York and meet Robert De Niro there instead.

The Greenwich Hotel, New York.

The tour was going to start in Miami, but after a conversation with Bob Bone, the director of the London Parade, he agreed that he would send me via New York, a few days earlier and that he would then arrange a connecting flight to Miami on the day I had originally intended to fly out. However, in New York I would have to fund my own hotel cost. I did not mind, as I would use the opportunity to catch up with Carole Franco, my Lady Mayoress, and so was happy to spend a few days there at my own expense.

I booked a Hilton hotel on Sixth Avenue and flew out on the Thursday. However, my flight was delayed and then on arrival at JFK, the lines for immigration were horrendous and it took me over two hours to get through. By the time I had collected my bags, the driver waiting for me warned me that the rush hour traffic was worse than usual and he would not be able to get me to my hotel to offload my baggage, shower and change before taking me to the Greenwich Hotel to meet Robert De Niro on time.

So, we headed direct to the Greenwich Hotel with all my baggage. Sarah Jane and Andy Hicks from CapCo met me there and I was introduced to Robert's business partner and the man who ran his hotel group day to day, Ira Drukier. They stored my luggage while I was taken to the bar for a welcome drink.

I was told that Robert and his son were on the way and that Robert had told Ira that he was very nervous to meet me. Robert De Niro nervous to meet Robert Davis! I was shocked and embarrassed. I was the one nervous to meet one of the greatest film stars of his generation and someone recognised the world over. Well, as they say, 'that's show business'!

After about half an hour, Robert and his son Raphael arrived. We were introduced and after some small talk he offered to show me around the hotel. Escorted by this great film star, the two of us walked around the hotel, leaving all the others enjoying their drinks in the bar.

He explained that all the paintings on the walls had been painted by his late father Robert De Niro Senior, a renowned abstract expressionist painter in his own right. As we walked from room to room, he pointed to different pieces of the eclectic furniture and explained how he had seen each piece while making a different film and had decided to buy it for the hotel or he had seen it in a shop while on location. Each piece told a story about his work and life. It was fascinating to hear him reminisce about his life reflected through the hotel's furniture.

Finally, he showed me the penthouse suite and we sat on the terrace of the suite chatting like close friends. It was quite surreal. He told me of his love of London and his frequent visits there and how much opening his own hotel in London based on the Greenwich was such an exciting prospect for him. I plucked up courage to ask him for a photo of the two of us, which he agreed to.

The new hotel would be called the Wellington, named after Wellington Street on which it was to be situated. The works would involve the demolition of the existing buildings on the island site, apart from a listed building in one corner. The hotel would be designed as an almost replica of the Greenwich Hotel in New York.

With Robert De Niro on the roof terrace of the Greenwich Hotel.

After about an hour, we joined the others. Robert had to go to another dinner but his son and Ira hosted a dinner for us in the hotel garden. When dinner was over, I reminded them that I needed to get a taxi to check into my hotel in Mid-Town and take my luggage which they were storing. Ira and Raphael, however, insisted I stayed the night in one of their suites and check into my own hotel the following morning. How could I resist and, in any event, I was exhausted, after a day of travelling and then this amazing evening.

However, the story does not have a happy ending, as the subsequent negotiations between Robert De Niro and CapCo did not go well. After a few months of discussions and hard bargaining, the negotiations broke down on the question of cost and financial contributions and the parties walked away and the plans for the new De Niro Hotel in Covent Garden were shelved. I believe that was a great shame, as the hotel would have become one of the most high-profile celebrity hangouts in London.

Mayor to Mayor

About a year after Boris Johnson was first elected Mayor of London, arrangements were made for him to visit his counterpart, the Mayor of New York, Michael Bloomberg.

Simon was due to accompany him as Boris's senior Deputy Mayor and Chief of Staff for the series of meetings on the Monday to Wednesday. Simon decided to fly out on the previous Friday afternoon and asked if I would like to accompany him. Simon's air fare and hotel costs were being paid for by the Mayor's Office but he said that if I paid for my own flight, we could of course (as his civil partner) share the hotel room and we could spend the weekend together. I could then go sightseeing, shopping and see members of my family who lived in the city, while he was in meetings with Boris.

On the Saturday night, as Simon and I were enjoying pre-dinner drinks in our hotel bar, Boris made an appearance, having just arrived from London. After a drink with us and a catch up between Simon and Boris, we invited Boris to join us for dinner at a nearby restaurant. But having just arrived, he declined as he said he needed to catch up on various work-related matters and wanted an early night.

The next day, we all met up with Boris at the Fifth Avenue Disney Store to undertake a promotional event for the media. As a Disney fan, I was in my element in being allowed to roam around their largest store before the store was open to the public.

On the Monday, Simon attended a conference on city management and invited me to go with him and to sit in on the first discussion but suggested that I left after an hour, so I could do some shopping before meeting my New York cousins for lunch.

My mother's first cousin Frank lived in New York and had done so since childhood. He was married with a son, and when I first left Cambridge in the summer of 1980, I went on my first visit to the United States and spent much of that visit staying with Frank and his wife, Suzanne, in their apartment on 64th and First Avenue in New York City.

Whenever I returned as a poor student or trainee solicitor, I would stay with them and when I was able to afford a decent hotel, I nevertheless visited them or joined them for dinner in a restaurant. This was to be a poignant visit. We met in a restaurant on a lake in Central Park and had a lovely lunch, after which they proudly showed me a bench they had sponsored in the park, which had been engraved with words to the effect that they both enjoyed spending many hours together in Central Park. It was to be the last time I saw Suzanne, as she died a few years later.

My mother's cousin Frank with his wife, Suzanne, and me in Central Park.

When I got back to the hotel that afternoon, Simon advised me that I had been invited to join him and Boris at a dinner being given that night by the Mayor of New York at his personal home in the Upper West Side. I was excited!

The three of us arrived on time and were met at the front door of this magnificent brownstone house by Bloomberg himself. We were ushered up the staircase to the principal reception rooms where the other guests were already assembled, waiting to greet us.

I have attended a number of high-profile dinners in my life including ones in Buckingham Palace and many in my capacity as Lord Mayor, but this was an A list 'to die for'. We were introduced to Tina Brown and Harold Evans as well as Rupert Murdoch and his then wife Wendi and at the dinner I sat between Oscar De La Renta, the famous fashion designer, and the guy who was running the Bloomberg companies while Michael was busy as Mayor of New York.

During dinner Bloomberg stood up in his immaculate three-piece suit and preppy tie to welcome Boris to his city and Boris then replied. Boris stood there responding to Bloomberg and in his usual style had the guests present roaring with laughter. With his blond mop of hair sticking out in every direction as if it had not been combed for days and with his white shirt hanging out of his trousers and clearly visible between the opening in his jacket, the Bloomberg CEO sitting next to me, whispered in my ear in a deep American drawl, 'Is that really your Mayor – really?!!!'. I confirmed that indeed it was! And again, he emphasised 'Really?!!'.

After dinner, Bloomberg took Boris, Simon and I on a tour of the house including a visit to see his bedroom on the top floor and in particular to see some of his magnificent paintings – many by painters whose work would normally only be seen in a national art gallery.

That was one dinner I would never forget and of course as I write this, the principal guest that night is now Prime Minister of the UK and the host recently attempted (unsuccessfully) a run for office as President of the United States.

Gemma Levine

Gemma is a famous photographer best known for her portraiture of famous people including politicians, sportsmen, actors, writers, dancers and business figures. Each decade she would publish a hardback book of photos of the icons of that decade.

We first met in 1997, sitting next to each other at the dinner at Spencer House given by the President of Israel, Ezer Weizman, for The Queen as part of his State Visit to the UK. I was attending as Lord Mayor and although Gemma and I had never met before, we got on like a house on fire. She took a particular interest in my chains and badge of office and begged me to allow her to photograph me wearing them.

Accordingly, a few weeks later, in full civic state (blue and gold robes, jabot, chains and badge with cuff-frills and white gloves), I went to her then studio in Wimpole Street and over a series of shots, cemented our friendship.

Simon and I would be invited to all Gemma's book launches and when in the late 2000s, she was invited to publish a book on a year in the life of Mayfair, she asked to photograph Simon and me (Simon was still then Leader of the Council) for inclusion in the book. We met Gemma at the southern end of Berkeley Square and she took a number

Gemma Levine's photo of me – 1997.

of photos of us standing next to the statue of the Fountain Nymph by Alexander Munro and inscribed in 1867 in memory of the 3rd Marquis of Lansdowne.

Subsequently, knowing of the good work of the Sir Simon Milton Foundation (which friends and I established after Simon's death), Gemma approached me with a suggestion. The idea was that she would take a series of photos of a year in the life of Westminster as well as a number of photos reflecting Simon's connection to the city. The book would then be published as a coffee table style book, which the Foundation could sell to raise money for its work. I loved the idea, as did my colleagues at the council and Foundation.

Gemma introduced us to her publisher, Naim Attallah of Quartet Books. However, after further discussions, Gemma stood back from the project and Naim introduced us to Alice Rosenbaum, a photographer he had worked with before, to take on the challenge.

The resultant book called *The City of Westminster – A celebration of people and place*s with a foreword by Simon Jenkins, the well-known journalist, columnist and former editor of the *Evening Standard*, sold extremely well and made the Foundation a nice profit.

I am very proud of the book and I know many who bought copies enjoyed it too. But it was all down to Gemma, who had come up with the idea and who had put us in touch with Naim.

Simon and I in Berkeley Square taken by Gemma Levine and included in her book Mayfair.

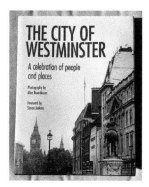

The Sir Simon Milton Foundation's book The City of Westminster – A celebration of people and places.

Joanna Lumley

Simon was deputy mayor when one of Boris's advisers suggested the idea of a living bridge over the Thames. Boris loved the idea, which would have created a Rialto Bridge style of structure with shops along each side of the bridge. Simon thought it a stupid idea and persuaded Boris to drop it.

A few years later, colleagues representing Pimlico wards close to the Thames started getting excited by a unilateral proposal by Wandsworth Council to build a footbridge linking the new developments at Battersea Power Station to Pimlico, landing on the river bank in front of Dolphin Square, described by Pevsner as the largest private residential block of flats in Europe.

Wandsworth wanted their new development to have easy access to Westminster and the Tube but Westminster residents did not want their peace and quiet disturbed. The council therefore started to campaign against the bridge.

Bumping into Boris at an event, he started lobbying me about supporting his new bridge. I assumed he was going on about the Battersea bridge and I tried to defend the council's stance. But after a few minutes of crossed lines, I realised that he was talking about a new proposed Garden Bridge that would cross the Thames upstream between an area adjacent to the National Theatre and the Temple to the north. Not knowing too much (at that stage) about his Garden Bridge, I tried to get him to support our objection to the Battersea bridge in exchange for our support for his Garden Bridge. But before I could get any sort of binding deal agreed, he wandered off to meet someone else.

A few weeks later, I was invited by the famous designer Thomas Heatherwick to his studio to discuss his designs for the Garden Bridge. I had met Thomas before, through Simon. They had worked together on designing Boris's new Routemaster bus and the London Olympics Cauldron.

I attended with my Director of Planning, John Walker and the other person present was the actress Joanna Lumley, who had conceived the idea for the bridge. Just being in Thomas's studio was spellbinding, as it was full of prototypes for his numerous projects and designs.

In the meeting, Joanna was compelling, enthusiastic and a superb salesperson, glowing about the concept of the Garden Bridge, which she claimed would become one of the wonders of the western world. They showed me plans and photos of the High Line in New York which was based on a similar concept. I was bowled over and loved the idea in principle.

Joanna and I kept in touch by email and I plucked up enough courage to invite her to be my guest of honour at the AGM of the London Mayors' Association, which I was hosting at the London Film Museum in Covent Garden a few weeks later. She readily accepted and gave a fascinating and amusing speech. But what really impressed me was the way she worked the room during the reception after the formalities, making an attempt to speak to everyone, frequently sitting down next to an infirm or elderly member. They adored her.

With Joanna Lumley.

We had previously agreed that, after the AGM reception, I would take her as my guest to dine at the neighbouring Delaunay restaurant, owned by my friend Jeremy King.

By coincidence, Carole (my Lady Mayoress) was in London and joined us for dinner. Carole had no idea who she was, and I was amused by Carole's interest in what Joanna had achieved in her life.

Sadly, the wonderful Garden Bridge project failed. I had chaired the Planning Committee that approved the Bridge from the Westminster side of things, subject to some tough conditions to ensure that it was viable and that the council would never have to pick up future costs or liabilities. But the bridge got caught up in the petty party politics of the changeover of London Mayor from Boris to Sadiq Khan and the project was aborted. In my view, that was a great mistake as the bridge would have been one of the great wonders of London and used and enjoyed by millions. The Battersea bridge meanwhile still lies in limbo, on the drawing board.

Banksy

I must first own up to never having met Banksy. Has anyone? But the problems arising from Mr Banksy's work did cross my desk.

While I do like some of his work, I am strongly of the view that they should be seen somewhere lawful, in a gallery, on someone's wall or in an exhibition. But not on public property – without permission. Many see me as a killjoy. But I need to defend my view!

One of the many things I am proud of is that Westminster has very little or almost no graffiti. Visit any other city around the world and you will travel from street to street and see walls and buildings covered in graffiti. Some of it may be seen as artistic, but most is not and this defacing of the public realm brings down a city and, from the research I have undertaken, encourages other crimes.

In Westminster, we had a zero tolerance to graffiti and as soon as any was seen, a team of the council's staff were off to remove it. I even set up a dedicated team to do so, with a branded vehicle, so residents and visitors alike would see that we meant business. The graffiti artists themselves soon learnt to display their work elsewhere. It really does work and even areas that were otherwise in need of some more civic care and attention were graffiti free.

It is my view that Banksy, when working in the public realm without consent, is just another graffiti artist. While I respect and like his artwork, the way he goes about it just encourages other graffiti artists. What right do I (or anyone else) have to say that Banksy's work is acceptable and should remain in place while other graffiti is not?

I strongly believed that if we did not stop Banksy displaying his work in the public realm, without all the necessary consents, how can we take enforcement action against all the other people who want to paint or exhibit what they believe to be art (but may not be seen as such by others), wherever it was displayed on our walls or on our street furniture? It would in my view lead to a downward spiral.

Therefore, when Banksy painted a large painting on the side of a tall flank wall in east Marylebone, I ordered it to be whitewashed over. Similarly, when other work by him appeared, we demanded that the property owner remove it or face prosecution or we whitewashed it ourselves. One or two land owners did remove the smaller paintings and sold them for a nice profit, but we had to be seen to be serious about the guerrilla activity that this endorsed. Why should anyone need to apply for consent to do anything unless we made it clear that we were in charge and regulated the streetscape of central London?

Princess Michael of Kent

One of the roles of the Lord Mayor is to raise money for charity. Each Lord Mayor chooses their own charity or charities. I agreed with Carole, my Lady Mayoress, that we would choose a charity each. Carole had an interest in the brain and so her friend Professor Sir Colin Blakemore introduced her to SANE (Schizophrenia: A National Emergency), a mental health charity with a helpline based in Westminster. I chose Fight for Life, a charity recommended by my mother's oncologist, which was raising money for a dedicated room in the then Middlesex Hospital in Marylebone, for children under eleven years of age undergoing radiotherapy.

The first big event we organised to raise money for our chosen charities, was a black-tie dinner at the Wallace Collection, an amazing gallery with an outstanding collection of paintings, sculptures, furniture and armour. I was a good friend of its Director, (now Dame) Rosalind Savill, and she agreed to allow us the full run of the House with pre-dinner drinks in the ground floor galleries and the dinner itself in the Great Gallery on the first floor, enabling us to sit between Frans Hals's *The Laughing Cavalier*, several Rembrandts, Rubens and a couple of Van Dycks.

But what we needed to sell the tickets was a special guest of honour. Pat Withers, one of the assistant secretaries in the Lord Mayor's office suggested Princess Michael of Kent. Pat knew the Princess's private secretary, as they had worked together years beforehand.

A few phone calls later, we had bagged our Royal guest and all the protocol surrounding such an event started from recces by the Palace to police checks and sniffer dogs.

Carole and I, in our best finery and wearing our most elaborate insignia, greeted Her Royal Highness at the main door of the

Escorting Her Royal Highness the Princess Michael of Kent up the grand staircase of the Wallace Collection.

Wallace Collection and after introducing her to many of the guests during the reception, I escorted her up to dinner and sat on her left at the top table. We got on extremely well.

The Princess could not stop telling me throughout dinner how young she thought I looked. I know I look young. It is inherited.

My grandmother Anne never looked her age. In her sixties, she looked like she was forty and when in her nineties she looked like she was in her late sixties. Similarly, my mother never looked her age.

When in my youth, we were on family holidays (my parents, my sister Susan and I), people would frequently say to my father that he had three well-behaved children. This really annoyed him but my mother loved the compliment.

A newly elected young-looking councillor with a member of the Council's cleansing team.

When I first became a councillor, aged 24, I actually looked 14 and this caused several issues. When an officer came to my flat in Paddington for a meeting, I answered the door and the officer immediately said 'I have come to see your father!' I explained that my father did not live there. He immediately followed up by saying that he had come to meet 'Councillor Davis'. I had to explain that I was indeed Councillor Davis!

In the early 1980s, City Hall had little or no security. Anyone could walk in and wander through its corridors. In the evenings, however, I was frequently stopped and asked who I was and whether I was authorised to be in the building. Many were taken aback to be told that this young-looking man was indeed a councillor.

Eventually, after being stopped so frequently, the Chief Executive's office arranged for me to have a security pass made for me to flash. Nowadays, of course, you cannot move five yards in City Hall (or any building) without using your security card.

I had a similar problem when, as Lord Mayor, I attended the first National Day reception hosted by the newly arrived Ambassador for Georgia, a country which had only recently become an independent sovereign state. The Ambassador, Teimuraz Mamatsashvili and his wife, Irina, were very proud that they were the very first Ambassadors from Georgia and were delighted that their reception was going to be honoured by the presence of the Lord Mayor of Westminster.

Wearing my morning coat decked out in my chains and badge of office, I arrived at the hotel hosting the reception with Carole at my side. We were ushered up to the front of the receiving line and greeted by the Ambassador and his wife.

I noticed that the Ambassador was not smiling when we shook hands. But thinking nothing of it, we went off to meet other guests leaving them to greet others. I did notice the Ambassador talking to the Marshal of the Diplomatic Corps, the Queen's representative in charge of the Diplomats accredited to the Court of St James. They both seemed to be looking at Carole and me.

About twenty minutes later, with the receiving line over, the Ambassador and his wife came rushing up to us. They explained that this was a very important day, not only for them, but for their country, bearing in mind that the British Government had only recently recognised the country. But as a new country, he had assumed, when seeing me arrive, looking so young, that I was just a young deputy mayor sent to represent the Lord Mayor, on the basis that the real Lord Mayor had thought that Georgia and this reception were not important enough for the Lord Mayor's presence.

With the Ambassador for Georgia and his wife at their first National Day reception.

However, the Marshal of the Diplomatic Corps had corrected this. He was now elated that we were the genuine article.

A few weeks later, they invited me to officially open their new Embassy by cutting a ribbon stretched across their front door. Teimuraz and Irina became close friends to both of us and, several years later, Carole went to visit them in Georgia. They remain good friends today.

I relate this story about the Georgians and my family's looks to emphasise that as a young man, I looked several years younger than my true age. So, returning to the Princess Michael story, as Carole and I were escorting her back to her car at the end of the evening, she turned to the assembled guests who had created a passageway for her to walk through and, pointing

Addressing guests at our Wallace Collection charity dinner with Princess Michael and Dame Ros Savill listening intently and Ivor Spencer our toastmaster behind.

to me, said in a loud voice to be heard by everyone, 'He is my Toy Boy Lord Mayor!'.

I met the Princess again on several more occasions as Lord Mayor and she would tell everyone around us that I was her favourite 'Toy Boy Lord Mayor'.

I laugh now about the fact that I look younger than I am, but as a young ambitious councillor, looking like I was still at school was not good for the ego let alone for getting taken seriously. In those early years, I am sure my slow rate of political progress was because everyone else believed that I was still a kid.

Now that I am much older, but looking at least ten years younger than my true age (if I may say so myself), it gives me much joy.

A few months after the Wallace Collection dinner, Carole and I attended another black-tie dinner, this time at the Banqueting House in Whitehall. This is one of the most historic and beautiful buildings in the country, with its Rubens ceiling and Royal throne sitting below a crimson velvet canopy. It was also the place of execution of King Charles I. The guest of honour that night was Princess Michael of Kent and protocol saw me sitting next to her again.

After reminding all the other guests at her table that I was her 'Toy Boy Lord Mayor', over dinner she confided in me that she slept in a separate bedroom from her husband, the Prince Michael of Kent. Her explanation, not that I asked for one, was that she spent much of her time writing historic novels and during the night she would suddenly wake up with an idea for the book and, in order not to forget the idea in the morning, she turns on the lights and writes the idea down. Separate bedrooms were to prevent her waking up her husband. She did assure me that (not that I asked) for more intimate nights she would share his bed. I did not respond other than saying 'How interesting'. All the rules of protocol I had learnt did not cover this aspect of a Royal engagement!

When Carole decided that, as Lady Mayoress, she wanted to organise a Viennese Ball at the Savoy Hotel with an orchestra and several dancers flying in from Vienna, we had no reluctance in inviting Princess Michael to again be our guest of honour. She accepted straight away.

The problem this time was that I was expected to open the dancing by partnering the Princess. The one thing I cannot do is dance. Especially a Viennese waltz. Despite practising, I was awful and my nerves were starting to get to me. At the last minute, I decided I could not go through with it and so asked the Austrian Ambassador's husband to partner the Princess, while I danced with Carole to jointly start off the dancing that night.

It went well and when I saw what an elegant dancer the Princess was, I was relieved it all went off perfectly, raising substantial funds for our two charities.

Dancing with Carole at our Viennese Ball in the Savoy Hotel.

The Rt Hon. The Lord Walker of Worcester MBE PC and my Commons Days

Peter Walker was the member of Parliament for Worcester from 1961 to 1992 after which he was ennobled. During the Heath government of 1970–1974, Peter was one of Ted Heath's closest confidantes in the Cabinet as Secretary of State for the Environment (1970–1972) and Secretary of State for Trade and Industry (1972–1974). However, when Margaret Thatcher won the leadership of the Party, she sacked Peter from her Shadow Cabinet.

Peter Luff (now Sir Peter) and I were good friends at Cambridge. We met in 1977, when we both joined the Cambridge University Conservative Association trip to Moscow and Leningrad (subsequently renamed St Petersburg).

After graduating, Peter Luff went to work for Peter Walker and became his principal aide. Knowing of my involvement in the Tory Reform Group (which Peter Walker had jointly founded and of which I was the then chairman of the Cambridge University branch) as well as of my interest in politics generally, Peter Luff invited me to join their office during my four-month summer vacation, as a researcher.

I had always wanted to work in Parliament and to walk those famous corridors. I was over the moon and accepted immediately. I was to share a large office in the 'Norman Shaw North' building which had in a previous life been 'New Scotland Yard' until the police moved to a building in Victoria Street and it was converted into offices for MPs. I had a desk opposite Peter Luff. My main role was to be a bit of a dogsbody, photocopying, preparing briefs, researching facts and running errands. I occasionally accompanied both Peters down to the constituency in Worcester. I would also attend meetings in Peter Walker's house nearby in Cowley Street and deliver documents to his friends and colleagues.

I remember being asked to deliver a document to Dennis Stevenson, then chairman of the Peterlee New Town Development Corporation (and later a peer and chairman of HBOS Bank). I was petrified. After being greeted by a member of his staff, I was ushered through to his office where he sat in an armchair. I waited, standing there silent while he read the contents of the document I had delivered. He returned the document to me signed and sent me on my way. Years later, he became friendly with my partner Simon and so when I was looking for an independent member of the council's Standards Committee, Simon suggested I ask Dennis (then Lord Stevenson of Coddenham and chairman of the House of Lords Appointments Commission).

I invited Dennis to lunch to get to know him and, if I thought it appropriate, invite him to join the Standards Committee. We got on extremely well and he accepted my invitation and became a valuable member of the committee. I did mention during that first lunch my experience many years earlier of appearing before him with papers from Peter Walker and he thought it quite funny.

I had a similar experience with John Selwyn Gummer (now Lord Deben) a former Secretary of State. As a young councillor, I joined Shirley Porter (then Leader of Westminster Council) at a meeting with John who was the Secretary of State for Local Government, in his office in Whitehall. Again, I was in awe. I was nervous – I had never been in the office of a Secretary of State before – and felt very much out of place. I said nothing, just sitting there nodding when Shirley spoke and staring at John when he spoke as if he was a great guru who we were seeking advice from.

I therefore found it amusing that, many years later, when I was Deputy Leader of the Council and Cabinet Member for Planning, John, now retired from the Commons but a member of the Lords and a political consultant, often came to see me in my office in City Hall. Sitting in front of my desk, I used to joke with him that I thought it funny how roles occasionally get reversed.

I worked for Peter Walker over the summer holidays, at Christmas and during the Easter holidays over a two-year period. But in May 1979, Margaret Thatcher, on becoming Prime Minister brought Peter back into the fold, by appointing him to her Cabinet as Secretary of State for Agriculture, Fisheries and Food. With all the civil servants he needed, I was no longer any use and so I started looking for a new holiday job in politics.

At this time (late 1970s and early 1980s), MPs did not receive an allowance to pay for research staff, so to do this type of work you either had to do it for free or find a wealthy MP who could afford to pay you nothing more than pocket money. Peter Walker had made his millions in the city, particularly with the infamous firm Slater Walker, and so could afford to pay for Peter Luff and me. But finding another MP who could afford to employ me would not be easy.

At this time I was still active within the Tory Reform Group and at one of their dinners, I sat next to a newly elected MP called John Watson. John's family owned Waddington Games, the company making Monopoly, the world-famous board game. His brother Victor ran the business and John worked there part time. Knowing he could afford a research assistant, I brokered the subject and he agreed to take me on during my holidays from Cambridge. When I left Cambridge and started studying for my legal professional exams at the College of Law in Lancaster Gate, I continued to work with John on several afternoons and evenings during the week. At the beginning of the year-long law course, other than attending three hours of lectures in the morning, I had little other work to do. But as it got closer to exams, I had to stop working with John to concentrate on passing my Law Finals.

I adored working in the Commons, both for Peter Walker and John Watson. I loved the atmosphere in particular. Every day you met or passed in the corridor some famous politician. I recall regularly meeting and chatting to Tony Benn in the photocopying room. I also got to know Frank Dobson, the Labour Cabinet Minister, whose office was opposite mine.

I occupied a large office on the fourth floor of the Norman Shaw (North) Building, which was shared with about fifteen other research assistants, some on a part-time basis and others full time. The full-time ones tended to be those working for wealthy MPs or whose boss was on the front bench when their salary was paid by the Party.

Several of these fellow researchers (many of whom I became good friends with) went on to become MPs and Cabinet Ministers themselves or well known in other fields. Peter Luff, who got me the job working for Peter Walker, became MP for Worcester and then Mid Worcestershire as well as Minister of State for Defence. David Willetts (now Lord Willetts) worked for the Shadow Secretary of State for Health and went on to become MP for Havant and then Minister of State for Universities and subsequently Paymaster General. Michael Brown, who worked for a Conservative MP, became the MP for Brigg and Scunthorpe and after a short spell in Parliament, a leading political columnist.

Tony Travers supported a backbench Labour MP and although he never made it in to Parliament, he became the country's leading expert on local government (particularly in London) and local government finance as a Professor at the LSE and he is regularly interviewed on the subject on TV. When I moved to Westminster Council, Tony and my paths crossed numerous times when he advised the council on several occasions.

Tony wrote a book celebrating the 50th anniversary of London government (following its reorganisation in 1965) and I was touched when he made reference to me and my contribution to Westminster.

Sir Peter Bottomley MP

One MP I met and became friendly with while working in the Commons was Peter (now Sir Peter) Bottomley (and currently Father of the House). I originally met him in the photocopying room of the Norman Shaw North Building. In those days, photocopiers were massive and only one was available on each floor of the Norman Shaw Building and which we had to queue up to use it. I met many political friends in those long waits.

When I subsequently became chairman of the Cambridge University branch of the Tory Reform Group, Peter agreed to travel to Cambridge to speak to my members. Years later, when Peter was Minister for Transport and I was chairman of the council's Traffic and Works Committee, we met up again when we jointly launched a 'Don't drink and drive at Christmas' poster campaign with posters plastered over hundreds of London black cabs.

However, returning to my Cambridge days, in my final undergraduate year (1978–79), I was required as part of my degree, to write a dissertation. I chose to write mine on the subject of the Conservative Trade Unionists (the CTU).

It was very topical at the time. This was because, after four years of a Labour government, with the power of the trade unions at its height (after Ted Heath had lost an election over the issue), the question was, 'could the Conservative Party ever win power again without the support of members of the trade union movement?'

To address this, the Conservative Party had established a Conservative Trade Union group with a base at Central Office. I saw my dissertation as an attempt to explain why only with the support of the trade unions could the Conservatives win the next election. I argued that the Conservative Party had to work closely with the unions and their members and in doing so could win their support.

I was given full access to the Conservative Party officials running the organisation as well

Sir Peter Bottomley and I launch the Christmas 'Don't Drink and Drive' campaign with posters on the side of black cabs.

as its members and when I completed the work, my dissertation was awarded a First Class by Cambridge University's examiners.

The Director of the CTU wanted to publish my work as a book, which they would sell and distribute to their members. I therefore worked closely with his team and a firm of printers. A designer gave us several front covers to approve and everything was set for printing. Margaret Thatcher even wrote a foreword for the pamphlet, although I am sure it was actually penned by an aide.

The approved front and back cover of my book on Conservative Trade Unionists.

By the time my book was ready to publish, the 1979 election had been won by Margaret Thatcher and she was safely ensconced in No 10 Downing Street.

Then one day I received a call asking me to attend a meeting with Peter (Lord) Thorneycroft, the then chairman of the Conservative Party, at Conservative Central Office in Smith Square. I was surprised to receive this command and assumed I would be meeting one of his staff. I had no idea why!

I arrived in my best suit and waited in the outside office and was eventually ushered in. There, sitting behind his desk was the bulky figure of the Chairman of the Conservative Party and member of Margaret Thatcher's Cabinet. No one else. Just the Chairman and young Robert Davis, just graduated from Cambridge.

He told me that my book, which the Party was about to publish, had been brought to his attention by someone in Central Office and that he was not happy with its contents. He made it clear that he did not agree with my conclusions as the Conservative Party had won the election without the support of the trade union movement and so he did not want this book published by the Party – or at all. He then said he needed to discuss the issue with the Prime Minister. He asked me to wait while his car took him to No 10 to discuss it. I waited. I sat there thinking that the Prime Minister was being asked her thoughts on me and my work! It was surreal.

He returned an hour later. He was joined this time by the Treasurer of the Party, Lord McAlpine. Thorneycroft explained that the PM had agreed with his assessment and that they did not want the book published at all and that they would pay me £500 (a lot of money for a poor student in 1979) to buy the copyright and compensate me. I had five minutes to choose whether to accept. He made it clear that if I did not, I would have to consider my future in the Conservative Party. That was the killer! I had no choice if I wanted to have a political future. I accepted. A cheque was written out there and then by the Treasurer and handed to me together with a letter to sign relinquishing all my rights in the work. I signed and took the cheque. I walked outside alone, wondering whether I had done the right thing or whether I should have said no and published it myself and risked the repercussions.

I immediately rang Peter Bottomley, who was also then Honorary President of the CTU, and told him what had just happened. He was furious. He wrote a long letter of complaint to Thorneycroft, which he had hand delivered to Central Office, saying that it was no way to treat a young, up-and-coming member of the Party. He never received a reply! However, on 12th March 1980, an article appeared in the *Daily Telegraph* describing this fiasco. My first appearance in a national newspaper.

The Rt Hon. Ted Heath MP

In the autumn of 1978, rumours abounded that the Prime Minister James Callaghan was about to go on TV and announce a surprise general election. Peter Luff had recommended me to Ted Heath's office, which were looking for an aide to accompany Heath on his tour of the country during the election campaign. I went to Heath's office and after an interview by his Chief of Staff, I was offered the job, subject to the calling of the election.

Two days later, Callaghan went on TV to make an announcement. I watched it live in the TV room in Norman Shaw North with about twenty MPs. Many had already packed their belongings and had started to move out of their offices.

But in that memorable television broadcast, Callaghan surprised everyone by saying that he would not call an election until the following year and in the meantime would continue at No 10. This turned out to be a big mistake, because the next few months saw the disastrous Winter of Discontent, which resulted in Margaret Thatcher easily defeating Callaghan at the election the following May and taking the premiership.

After the Callaghan speech, Heath's office asked me to come on board when the election was eventually called the following spring. However, when it did, it was called for the same week as my final university exams and so I had to turn down the invitation and concentrate on getting my degree.

Dame Hilda Bracket

As Lord Mayor and Lady Mayoress, Carole and I were invited to the first night of the London Film Festival in Leicester Square, which involved attending the premiere of the latest new high-profile film followed by a black-tie dinner at the (then) Café Royal.

At the dinner, Carole was seated opposite me on a round twelve-seat table. We both got on well with our neighbours, who we had not met before. However, after the dessert was served, the people seated each side of me decided to leave, claiming they needed an early night for work the next morning. Left sitting in my chains and badge of office with no one to talk to, I moved around the table to an empty seat two chairs from Carole. She introduced me to the gentleman sitting between us, a Mr Patrick Fyffe. Carole explained that they had got on so well that they had not stopped chatting all evening. I then asked Patrick what he did for a living. Patrick told me that he was an actor, so I asked him what he had been in that I would have seen, either on the large or small screen or in the theatre.

Patrick explained that he was a female impersonator and that he played the role of Dame Hilda Brackett in the famous TV and radio comedy musical series *Hinge and Bracket* about two spinsters living a genteel English life in the fictional village of Stackton Tressel in Suffolk. I was a great fan and told Patrick so. Carole, coming from the States, had no idea what we were talking about or who Hinge and Bracket were. But after a further hour chatting, we agreed we would meet up again and a few weeks later we invited Patrick to join us at a mayoral dinner we hosted in the Mayoral Parlour.

Dame Hilda Bracket.

A few weeks later, Patrick invited us to see him and his stage partner George Logan (Dr Evadne Hinge) in pantomime in Basingstoke. After the performance, we joined Patrick for dinner. We remained in contact for a while but after the mayoral year ended, we lost contact and in 2002 I sadly learnt of Patrick's death from cancer.

Michael Xavier

Michael is a well-known and highly respected musical actor and has starred in a number of West End and Broadway shows. He has also appeared in several TV dramas. We first met when he was performing in the dual role of Cinderella's Prince and the Big Bad Wolf in Stephen Sondheim's *Into the Woods* at the Open Air Theatre in Regent's Park, where I was Chairman of the Board. He later starred as Captain Georg Von Trapp in my favourite production at the Open Air Theatre, *The Sound of Music*. We would regularly meet up for lunch and I subsequently invited him, on several occasions, to be one of the compères at West End Live.

In the summer of 2015, I was having lunch with Andrew and Madeleine Lloyd Webber in their Mallorcan home, when Andrew told me that he was working on his new production of *Sunset Boulevard* at the London Coliseum. However, he explained that he was struggling to find the right actor to play the male lead of Joe Gillis.

I immediately suggested Michael. Andrew knew of him and said it was a good idea and he would think about it. When I got home from lunch, I texted Michael and told him that I might have got him a new job. He responded by promising me lunch if it worked.

A few months later, Michael texted me again, to tell me that thanks to my intervention, he had just been cast by Andrew as Joe Gillis and thanked me for my involvement. I was therefore delighted when I received an invite to the First/Press Night.

Michael shared the spotlight in the show with Glenn Close, the award-winning American actress, and through the show they became firm friends, so when Glenn was subsequently contracted to star in the Broadway transfer, it was reputed that she told the producers she would only do it if Michael played opposite her again. Michael went off to New York for over a year, not only playing in *Sunset* but subsequently starring in the *Prince of Broadway* on Broadway. I was proud to have played a small part in Michael's success. And to complete the story, yes, he did take me out for a celebratory lunch.

With Michael Xavier the co-star of Sunset Boulevard at the first night party.

Chapter 28

More Westminster Stories

Many funny and amusing incidents happened and occasionally sad events occurred, during my many years in public life and here are a few more of them.

The Avis Hotel

Avis, the car rental firm, occupied a large building in Mayfair, on the south side of Oxford Street adjacent to Brown Hart Gardens. It was a white art deco building and on its flat roof, in gigantic lettering was the word 'AVIS'. For commercial reasons they vacated the site and it reverted to their landlord, the Grosvenor Estate. The Estate decided to convert it into a hotel with a destination restaurant and teamed up with Jeremy King and Chris Corbin of the Wolseley restaurant.

As planning chairman, I worked closely with them in negotiating and approving their plans and overcoming numerous issues. They commissioned the famous sculptor Sir Antony Gormley to design a feature for the front of the building. The result was a gigantic cuboid robotic seated man made of steel boxes sitting on the left-hand side of the hotel's exterior. Inside is a bedroom that has no windows or lights and so when you sleep in it you do so in pitch darkness. Gormley recommends doing so naked, so (he claims) you experience going back to your mother's womb!

I was told by numerous people working on the project that the development team used to call the seated man 'Bob' – after me!

When the application came before the committee I was chairing, we unanimously approved the officer's recommendations to grant it subject to a number of conditions proposed by the officers. But, as I announced the decision, I explained to the packed audience, full of the professional team working on the project as well as representatives of the Grosvenor Estate, that I wanted to add one further condition of my own. Their heads moved forward in unison, to hear what this condition would be.

I told the assembled crowd that the additional condition would require that the letter 'D' be added to the name on the roof. At first there was silence in the

The Beaumont Hotel with 'Bob' sitting on the left.

room and I could see everyone looking at each other, as if I was mad, as they had no idea what I was talking about. But after a moment, the penny dropped and they realised that it was a joke. The 'D' added to the name on the roof would have changed the word from 'AVIS' to 'DAVIS'. The room erupted into laughter.

Solemnity or Bust

In July 2005, I was in a meeting of the trustees of the Savoy Educational Trust in the bowels of the Savoy Hotel. My mobile phone was on but getting intermittent signal and during a dull part of the meeting I discreetly managed to check the BBC News.

On driving to the meeting, I had heard on the car radio that there had been an incident on the Tube but at that stage they knew little more. But when I saw the BBC News on my phone, it was clear that this was more than another incident. Four separate terrorist bombs had gone off killing many and maiming hundreds in separate locations, one on a bus and three on the Tube, one being at Edgware Road station in Westminster. It was carnage.

Simon (then Leader of the Council) was in Harrogate at the Local Government Association annual conference. I immediately left the room to call him. But I could not get a connection. The already poor reception was exacerbated by the whole mobile phone network collapsing from the strain of millions of people trying to phone friends and relatives to check up on them. I was worried that he would be concerned about me. I knew he was out of London and presumably safe. It occurred to me that as I was rarely out of the office (I was then still working every weekday at my law firm), if Simon or my family tried to call me and I was not in the office and not answering my mobile phone, they would all be worried.

I eventually got a message to my family that I was all right and then managed to speak to Simon. Simon told me that he would try and head home immediately, if he could catch a lift from someone. He asked me to go to City Hall to take political charge of our civil response until he returned.

I left the trustees meeting and drove through empty streets to Westminster City Hall, where I joined the Chief Executive, Peter Rogers (now Sir Peter) with his senior management team. My job was to politically approve all that he and the team were doing. However, they had everything under control, as they had been rehearsing for a major incident in the city for years.

One of the priorities we had to address was what to do with the children still in our schools. All public transport in London had been stopped, as the authorities did not know if there were any more bombs or attacks coming. How would the children get home and how would we unite them with their parents? There was also the question of how we would get everyone who worked in Westminster home without any public transport. Would we need to book hundreds of hotel bedrooms or use our leisure centres for them to sleep in?

While the emergency services are the frontline in such an attack, the council follow through in a second stage, looking after those affected and cleaning up the mess. Someone has to wash away the blood.

Simon arrived home late that night and took control the next day. One of the actions he took that next morning was to establish a family centre in the sports hall in our Queen Mother's Sports Centre in Victoria. Hundreds of people were arriving in London wandering the streets looking for missing family members who had not been in contact. Many feared the worst. We provided a centre for them to wait in for news, to receive counselling and to give details, so we could keep them in touch and help the authorities identify bodies and those in hospital.

Once the centre was established and operating with numerous members of our staff in attendance, many of whom were experts in counselling, the Secretary of State, Tessa Jowell, came to visit. I accompanied Simon and her on a tour of the centre. She was impressed and the work of the centre was crucial to address the bewilderment, grief and concern of so many. The Secretary of State later told us that this centre would become a blueprint for future incidents of this nature.

The country's anguish and grief was immense and Simon, recognising that what was needed was some formal acknowledgement of the grief, arranged that on the following day he would host a small remembrance service in Victoria Embankment Gardens adjacent to Charing Cross Station.

He invited the Mayor of London, Ken Livingstone, the Lord-Lieutenant, our MPs as well as the Lord Mayor of Westminster. The intention being that each dignitary would place a wreath on a memorial stone. The national media would be present and BBC news would broadcast it live.

The Lord Mayor of Westminster had separated from his wife and so on each mayoral engagement invited a different young lady he was trying to impress, to join him as his consort for the event.

I appreciate that this was not a planned engagement and that the very young lady he had invited to spend the day with him was not experienced in civic affairs, but someone should have tipped her off about the tone of the event. She had never been on a mayoral engagement before let alone a civic one and so turned up in the mayoral car with the Lord Mayor, as the last ones to arrive (as is protocol when the Lord Mayor attends functions as the First Citizen). The Lord Mayor stepped out of the car first and was followed by his new friend. Everyone attending was in black and otherwise appropriately dressed for a memorial service at a time when the country was in mourning. With the media and TV cameras zooming in on the mayoral party, everyone held their breath when they saw the Lord Mayor's new consort in a bright floral dress with a very low-cut cleavage. Added to this, was the length of her dress, which made the miniskirts of the 1960s look long. Of course, everyone continued as if nothing was awry. But once the formalities were over, the gossiping started.

A few years later, a number of my senior colleagues and I attended a full day's training on how to give political leadership in a crisis such as a terrorist attack. I am afraid that, although I was given a certificate for attending, the lecturer did tell me that as a result of my actions in the role-play scenario we enacted, I had managed to lead a bus load of schoolchildren to their deaths. I was grateful that it was only a training session.

King Henry IV

On 20th March 2013, Westminster Abbey commemorated the 600th anniversary of the death of King Henry IV in the Jerusalem Chamber, a large antechamber within the Abbey, in which Westminster councillors would meet and robe before civic services. It is also used by the Dean and Chapter for meetings and formal dinners.

The fascinating story of King Henry's death, one which I frequently used to tell new councillors when attending a service in the Abbey for the first time, is that the King's reign was marked by serious health issues and so his wish to endure a pilgrimage to Jerusalem was never realised. However, Henry had been told early on in his reign that he would one day die in Jerusalem. Shakespeare in his play repeats this prophecy.

Henry was praying in the Abbey on 20th March 1413, when he collapsed and was immediately taken to lie before the fire in the adjoining chamber. Shakespeare portrays the scene in his play, describing how he awoke and asked where he was. One of the clergy responded 'Jerusalem, Sir' and Henry is supposed to have smiled and died there and then. Shakespeare then goes on to suggest that his son, Prince Hal, who is at the dead King's side, takes off his crown and places it on his own head and crowns himself King Henry V. The chamber was henceforth renamed the Jerusalem Chamber, a name it has retained ever since.

There are two busts placed on plinths in the Jerusalem Chamber, one of the young King Henry V and the other of the elderly King Henry IV.

Exactly six hundred years after King Henry's death, the Dean of Westminster, John Hall, hosted a black-tie dinner in the Jerusalem Chamber to commemorate that important day in the Abbey's and country's history.

I was honoured and delighted that the dean invited me to join him and a further twenty-three guests to the dinner. Once the meal had been consumed, we were entertained by the renowned actor Simon Russell Beale (a college contemporary of mine at Cambridge) and a colleague of his from the Royal Shakespeare Company, who re-enacted King Henry's death scene from Shakespeare's play. It was very moving and I was so delighted to be present at this historic occasion.

The bust of Henry IV in the Jerusalem Chamber.

Over the Rainbow

Westminster has a planning policy that prohibits the flying of flags outside buildings, other than at roof level. This is to prevent many of the retail streets from being covered with advertising banners masquerading as flags. A few exceptions are allowed and Bond Street has been designated as a street where they are allowed. In every case, planning and, if necessary, listed building consent is required and exceptional cases can be made for non-designated streets.

During Simon's leadership of the Council, a flag problem blew up. It appeared that many of the shops, restaurants, bars and clubs in Soho had, over the years, erected flag poles outside their premises to fly the LGBT rainbow flag. A resident had complained and so a relatively junior member of the planning team, visited all the offending premises telling them that they need to apply for planning permission but that under current policies, they would likely be refused.

Within a few days, the entire national press was running stories saying that Westminster was homophobic and trying to close down the gay bars and clubs of Soho. Of course, this was furthest from the truth, particular when Simon and I were ourselves gay.

Flags flying in Soho.

Simon received a call from Ken Livingstone, the Mayor of London. He was incandescent with rage accusing Westminster of being homophobic and demanding Simon sort out the embarrassing mess.

Simon explained our policy and that the officer in question was only doing his job but assured Ken that he would see what he could do to resolve the issue as he was supportive of the flags remaining in Soho.

Simon turned to me as Cabinet Member for Planning to resolve the issue. I spoke to one of the senior planning officers who was aware of the issue. It was agreed that the officers would invite the offending premises to make an application for retrospective consent. When the subsequent applications went before the planning committee, they would be considered for an exception to the policy.

All went according to plan and within a few weeks I was advised that the initial six applications received would be considered at a forthcoming planning committee meeting.

I checked the rota to see which councillor would be chairing the meeting. I then arranged to see that councillor, who happened to be a good friend of mine. I explained to him that this had become a political issue and the council had to be seen to be supportive of the LGBT community and that a permitted exception should be made on this occasion. The councillor assured me that he understood the message and that Simon and I should not worry.

At the planning committee meeting, the chairman opened the debate by immediately condemning the flags as a breach of the council's policy and making it clear that in his view, there were no grounds for making an exception to the council's policy and proposing that all the applications be refused. The other majority party committee members, believing he was adopting the official group line, voted with him to refuse all the applications.

When Simon heard, he was apoplectic. Simon rarely raised his voice or lost his temper. This was an exception. Not only did he believe that this councillor had breached the faith that we had in him to deliver the result we wanted, but it meant that Simon had to face Ken Livingstone to explain why his promise to sort it out had resulted in the opposite happening.

The further issue, which became evident a few days later, was the bad press that resulted and claims that the council and Simon in particular were homophobic.

However, I found a solution. As Cabinet Member for Planning, I had the power to change the council's planning policies, which would include changing the policy on flags and providing for the LGBT rainbow flags in Soho to be a formal exception. It would clearly take longer to resolve as the change in any council planning policy required extensive consultation, but this appeared to be the only solution.

We advised the applicants what we were doing and asked them to orchestrate a campaign to support the changes and, within a few months, I was able to formally sign off the change in policy. The original applicants and other establishments were all asked to reapply under the new policy and within a further few weeks, planning consent and listed building consents were granted by a different planning committee and the issue was resolved – not that Simon or I got any credit as the damage had been done.

The one casualty was our friendship with the councillor who had chaired that original planning committee meeting. We made it quite clear to him as Leader and Chief Whip, that we were not happy, particularly as he had assured me that he would sort it out. Had he told me of his concern, we could have addressed it before the matter was before the committee. We removed him as a rota chairman of the planning committee and made it clear that he was now a persona non grata.

I am pleased to say that the story has a happy ending, as after about eighteen months, we agreed to put the past behind us and all three of us became friends again and although he later retired from the council, I continue to see him and keep in touch with him to this day. The rainbow flags are never mentioned.

The Leicester Square Funfair

In the mid-1980s while I was in charge of Leicester Square, one of my officers introduced me to William and Emily Wilson, the proprietors of Bob Wilson's Funfairs (Bob was William's late father). They had provided the funfair for a big event in Hyde Park and it was suggested to me that they could operate a funfair in Leicester Square for the Christmas season. We liked the idea as it would bring some Christmas sparkle into the West End in the days when the only Christmas decorations were in Oxford Street and Regent Street and there was no funfair in Hyde Park.

It was a great success and the Wilsons would return year after year. The incumbent Lord Mayor was always invited to formally open the fair about a month before Christmas. A number of councillors would be invited to the ceremony and to ride the dodgems and the carousel as well as play a number of the games. All the councillors and the Lord Mayor in particular, would win amazing prizes at the side shows including extremely large stuffed toy animals, which would be donated as gifts for future mayoral charity events.

A number of local residents opposed the funfair, claiming it was downgrading the Square. However, the council thought it did the opposite, as it attracted families and more particularly, because of the presence of the Wilsons' security, the anti-social issues around the Square disappeared for the duration of the fair.

Enjoying the funfair in Leicester Square as Lord Mayor accompanied by Carole.

One year, we persuaded the Wilsons to add a typical Scandinavian Christmas market and a small stage with seasonal entertainment to enhance the family side of the event. They also added Father Christmas in his grotto for the children to visit.

However, as the years progressed the number of local residents and businesses that opposed the funfair increased. Once the Heart of London Business Improvement District (representing the landowners and retailers in the area) was established, they wanted to undertake their own activities in the Square over the Christmas period and so put more pressure on the council to replace the funfair with something else. Under pressure, particularly from the local councillors and a number of officers, the Heart of London were given the opportunity to come up with an alternative idea to replace the fair. But year after year they failed and the fair continued.

Then matters came to a head one year, when the Wilsons moved the agreed position of some of the rides and, to make them fit, allegedly cut off a number of branches from several of the historic trees in the Square. To be fair to the Wilsons, they argued that officers from the council had given them approval to do so, but it turned out that the junior officers in question had no authority to give such consent and senior officers were on the warpath. These senior officers were determined to stop the fair returning and, supported by some of the local councillors, using this tree-cutting incident as an excuse, decided that they did not want the fair to return and so officers were charged with finding a replacement Christmas event for the Square.

I remained the Wilsons' sole supporter among both councillors and officers and was ordered to back down in my opposition to a change. Forced into a corner, I had to accept defeat. Instead, an extensive and attractive Scandinavian Christmas market replaced the fair and in one corner the new contractor installed a Spiegeltent (a round wooden and canvas tent, decorated with historic stained mirrors around the interior, seating and a stage, rather like a big top) and over the six-week period a series of burlesque-style shows were put on with tickets sold to the public for several performances a day.

Audrey Lewis

I first met Audrey when she was chairman of the Marylebone Association, the residents' society for the area. I turned up at the Association's AGM one year and was the first to arrive, save for Audrey herself. I took my seat and waited. Audrey came up to me and introduced herself. Immediately she realised I was a senior Westminster councillor, she asked me to move to the top table.

We soon became friends and it was not long before I persuaded her to stand for the council. She was not only elected but within a short period she became a fellow cabinet member responsible for licensing. Over time, she became the country's leading expert on licensing and would travel the country talking to other councils and councillors about the subject.

In the autumn of 2013, I persuaded her to put her name forward to be Lord Mayor. She was reluctant to do so at first, because she was enjoying her licensing responsibilities

Addressing the London Mayors' Association annual Civic Service reception with Audrey Lewis as Lord Mayor standing next to me.

which she knew she would have to stand aside from if she accepted my offer. I was chairmen of the Party Advisory committee, which chose the Lord Mayor each year and it was my job to interview all the potential candidates and suggest a name or two for the committee to consider and approve.

Without any real challenger, she was selected and in May 2014 became our new Lord Mayor. After a few weeks in the job, she took me aside to thank me for pushing her into doing it, as she was absolutely loving the role.

Then in the autumn, we had both been invited with other councillors to a colleague's 40th birthday party at the Ritz Hotel. It was a Saturday night and although Audrey was Lord Mayor, she was attending in her private capacity and so had arrived by taxi, rather than with the mayoral car. As we did not know many of the guests, Audrey, my friend and colleague Steve Summers and I, sat around a small round table in one corner of the room. A special cocktail was on offer that night and Audrey and Steve were knocking them back.

Audrey had clearly drunk too much and realised this. But Steve kept insisting she had another. Each time she tried to resist but gave in to Steve's persistence. At about 11.30 we decided to leave. Audrey could hardly stand up.

I helped her up, but after a few steps I had to hold her upright with my arm. Now Audrey was short in stature and a little overweight. It was quite an effort to keep her straight and walk her through the main corridor running through the Ritz, without attracting too much attention. As we got to the front door, I asked her how she was getting home. At this stage, I did not know how she had got there. She said she would get a taxi. But I insisted that I drive her home. Once outside her block of flats, I helped her out of the car, albeit with great difficulty. She insisted she could get to her second floor flat unaided but I ignored her and helped her to the front door of her flat. I left her entering her flat, assured she could at least get to bed herself.

The following morning, all the councillors were attending an important service in Westminster Abbey. Steve and I, wearing our robes and civic insignia, processed through the Abbey with our colleagues and took our seats in the Quire. Steve was seated directly opposite me in the South Quire, while I was seated (as Deputy Leader of the council) in the North Quire next to the seat to be occupied by the Lord Mayor.

Audrey Lewis as Lord Mayor with myself as Deputy Leader sitting next to her in the Choir stalls of Westminster Abbey during the service.

We all stood as the Lord Mayor arrived in full civic state. That is, she was wearing the heavy blue damask robes covered in gold braid, her jabot, mayoral hat and her heavy chains and badge of office. She was preceded by her macebearer carrying the historic Westminster mace.

The eyes of nearly two thousand members of the congregation were watching her process up the Nave and through the Quire. As she passed between Steve and I, she collapsed on to her front, her arms spreadeagled. Several Abbey stewards ran to her aid. Two of them tried to lift her up, but she was so heavy, especially wearing the weighty robes and chains, that they struggled to get her up. Eventually they did and other than denting her ego, she was fine and unhurt. She resumed her position and was led to her seat. At this, I pointed to Steve and mouthed 'it's all your fault!'.

About three weeks after Audrey stepped down as Lord Mayor, having told me that it was the best year in her life, she went on the missing list. She failed to turn up to a meeting with one of our colleagues. That colleague called me because she had not only not turned up but was not answering his calls to her.

I was in Mallorca and felt helpless. I suggested he go to her block of flats and ask the resident porter for assistance. Keeping me regularly informed by phone of what he was doing, he and another friend got to the block and with the porter's help, he accessed her flat. They found Audrey but sadly she had passed away the previous night all alone. It was devastating for us as we all adored her.

Twenty Questions

In 2017, I was invited to be interviewed on a radio programme called *Twenty Questions*. This was similar to *Desert Island Discs* and I was asked twenty questions about my life and had to choose five pieces of music that meant something special to me, that would be played between the questions and my answers.

The five pieces I chose were: 'She Loves You', the Beatles single released in 1964 and the first record I bought (albeit with my Mum's help), 'Step inside love', the Cilla Black single that she would start her Saturday night TV shows with and which I would regularly attend, 'I have a song to sing, O' from Gilbert and Sullivan's *The Yeoman of the Guard*, which was my favourite song from my undergraduate days when I was a great Gilbert and Sullivan fan, the 'Toreador Song' from Bizet's *Carmen*, one of my favourite operatic pieces and finally to end the programme, Pharrell Williams's 'Happy', because whenever I hear it, I just feel happy!

I was also asked to choose the book I would take to a desert island. I explained that I adored Agatha Christie mysteries as one had to use one's little grey cells and even then she always surprised you. And if I had to choose one, it would be *The Murder of Roger Ackroyd*. This was of course the book that made her famous and voted by the British Crime Writers' Association in 2013 as the best crime novel ever. Its innovative twist ending made it a masterpiece.

The Scottish Sun

The *Scottish Sun* is the Scottish version of the *Sun* daily newspaper. On 24th August 2017 they published an article covering an entire page of the paper, headlined 'Twit of the Week'. Below the headlines were the photos of three councillors awarded the title 'Twit of the week' and the middle one was a large photo of me.

The article claimed 'Coming soon to Channel 5: Britain's lamest-brained councillor'. The piece then goes on to lampoon various tweets made by councillors. The article refers in particular to a tweet made by 'Forth and Endrick Ward Councillor Robert Davies', who it claimed 'was busy spending his taxpayer-funded time posting a photo of black people waiting to board a plane and adding a caption about them putting spears in the overhead lockers and wanting to eat the cabin crew'.

I was shocked. Of course, while it was my photo, the Councillor Robert Davies referred to was clearly not me. The name was spelt differently and I was clearly not the councillor for Forth and Endrick, Sterling, in central Scotland, four hundred miles north of Westminster and I certainly did not send the offending tweet.

I was horrified that these awful racist comments were being attributed to me through my photograph appearing, even though on reading the article, it was clear that it related to another Robert Davies (spelt with an 'e') who was a councillor in Scotland.

It was easy to guess what happened. The author of the article had, either himself or by instructing a colleague, searched the internet for a photograph of the Scottish Councillor Robert Davies but probably dropped the e in the alternative spelling of my surname and using an image search engine found numerous photos of me, as the higher profile Councillor Robert Davis and used one of them without checking it was a photo of the correct councillor.

I was extremely worried that someone seeing the headlines and my photo would, without careful consideration of the article, believe I was a racist. I had to do something. My then business partner, Trevor Box, wrote a solicitor's letter to the *Scottish Sun* claiming that I had been defamed and demanding damages and a correction published in the paper.

After lengthy negotiations between Trevor and the paper's solicitor, with the *Scottish Sun* arguing that while I am well known in London, I am relatively unknown in Scotland and so my reputation could not have suffered substantial harm, they accepted that they had made an error. In recognition of their error, they agreed that they would print an apology, pay the sum of £2,000 to my nominated charity (the Sir Simon Milton Foundation) as well as pay my legal costs. I accepted.

On 12th January 2018, the *Scottish Sun* published an apology which read:

> In Bill Leckie's column of August 24, 2017, relating to Councillor Robert Davies of the Forth and Endrick ward, in error we published a picture of Councillor Robert Davis MBE DL Deputy Leader of Westminster City Council. We apologise to Councillor Robert Davis for our error and the embarrassment it has caused him.

Although the Sir Simon Milton Foundation benefitted this time, it reminded me of a separate defamation case which Simon pursued. *Private Eye* had libelled Simon and he had been so annoyed that he instructed the well-known defamation firm of solicitors Carter Ruck, to take appropriate action against *Private Eye*, ending up with an apology and the payment of compensation to Simon. We went on a fantastic Christmas holiday to Dubai on the damages Simon received.

The Young Planner

The planning team at City Hall would regularly take on students from local Westminster schools for a week's work-experience. I was due to host a meeting in my City Hall office with a developer to discuss a new planning application and as usual I was to be accompanied by several planning officers. The lead officer dealing with the application contacted me a few days beforehand to seek my approval to bring one of these students to the meeting to observe how a leading member engages with developers. I was happy to allow the young fifteen-year-old to join us.

Shortly before the meeting was due to start, the officers joined me in my office to brief me on the outstanding issues to be discussed. They were joined by the student. I introduced myself and explained to him how the process worked and my role.

The applicant then joined the meeting with his professional team. They made their presentation which included proposals for a relatively tall building. Once they had finished, I explained to them that their proposal was far too high and needed to be brought down in size by a number of floors. The applicant appeared to accept that, presumably having made an attempt to persuade me otherwise, realistically knew that what I was telling them was in accordance with the Council's policies.

But as I completed my speech, the work-experience student raised his voice and asked me whether he could say something. Not sure how to respond, I said that of course he could. He then leant towards the applicant and said in an authoritative voice, that he thought they should be bold and make the building much higher with an additional five or six stories and not reduce the size.

I looked at my officers who were going bright red and were staring at me open mouthed and speechless. I then turned to the applicant and his team who were all smiling. The silence was broken when the applicant asked if that was the Council's official view! I had to let them down and explain who the young student was and that my view was the most important in the room for the application to proceed with a positive recommendation to committee. They looked dejected and I quickly closed the meeting. As I was saying my good byes to the applicants, the officers quickly ushered the new young planner out of the office. I presume that young confident man is now a leading planner working for a council somewhere. We can certainly claim credit for confidence building.

The Paddington Pole

I had never been to or visited the Shard and although I had heard of Irvine Sellar, I had never met him. That is until I sat next to him at a property industry luncheon in Guildhall in the City of London. He sat down after me and I introduced myself. I proudly told him that in my teenage years I used to buy my flared trousers from his shop in Carnaby Street. Mates by Irvine Sellar was a well-known trendy clothes shop that catered for the 'young discerning man' and in the early 1970s famous for its flared jeans. It was during this period that I was first allowed to go shopping in the West End by myself with pocket money I received from both my parents and grandparents. Irvine found this story amusing and he assured me he had moved on to bigger projects.

I thought nothing more of Irvine until I received a request to meet him. With my open-door policy, I was happy to do so and met him with one of his senior colleagues and my Director of Planning, John Walker. He explained that having completed the construction of the Shard, which he had conceived as an idea and painstakingly pursued through numerous planning and other hurdles, he was now turning his attention and time to creating a similar landmark building to the west of London and that he had started negotiations with Network Rail and Transport for London about a new development adjacent to Paddington Station.

To put this in context, the area in Paddington around the main line station had become very run down and the immediate approach to the station itself is very uninviting. It consists of a dingy concrete slope bordered on each side by high brick walls. No great welcome for people arriving from the west of England or from abroad via the Heathrow Express. Praed Street itself is full of low-quality shops, takeaways and tourist shops. The site Sellars was interested in was formerly part of the local Post Office sorting office which was now on the market. The site was also above the Bakerloo Line station at Paddington, whose access was through a steep set of steps off Praed Street itself.

Irvine was in negotiations to buy the Post Office site with the intention of carrying out a major redevelopment within its boundaries. This would also provide a new large attractive piazza to replace the sloping entrance to the mainline station as well as series of subterranean floors linking the main line station with the underground station and providing easily accessible entrances to the street and including an underground shopping arcade. This would be very similar to the redevelopment he masterminded at London Bridge adjacent to the Shard.

By coincidence, both sites were next to major London hospitals, St Mary's Hospital in Paddington and Guy's Hospital next to the Shard. Irvine emphasised how the whole area around the Shard had been re-energised and improved and argued that he could do the same in Paddington.

However, the cost of the public realm works required to create the new piazza together with the creation of a new large void under the site, to enable Transport for London to construct a new station for the Bakerloo Line, would need to be paid from the development and so he proposed another tall building to mirror the Shard and in the same way that the Shard is now seen as the marker for that part of London, so he argued that a tall building in Paddington would put the area on the map.

Our initial response was positive as we too wanted to see the regeneration of the Paddington area but we told Irvine that we needed to see details of what he wanted to build and in particular to have more information regarding its height. He told us that he intended instructing the world-renowned Italian architect Renzo Piano (who had designed the Shard) and would bring Renzo to meet us when his proposals were more advanced. As we were saying our goodbyes, Irvine asked me if I had been to the Shard. I had to say that I had not. Irvine immediately invited John Walker and I to do so.

A few weeks later, we all met up at 6.30 pm one night and Irvine and his team gave us a full tour of the Shard including the offices, the hotel and restaurants, in addition to showing us a couple of the residential flats. While I thought they were all beautifully designed and fitted out, nothing could compete with the amazing views. We were also shown around the wider area, the shopping arcade and the new access that Irvine had created into London Bridge station. All very impressive.

I was very excited at the prospect of seeing Paddington regenerated very much in the way that Victoria and King's Cross had been and was looking forward to meeting Renzo Piano. When the day came, we met about 7 pm on a Friday night after Renzo had flown to London for the weekend. He brought with him a model of Paddington Station with its famous roof comprising four glass spans each curved in design. He then took off two of the spans and stood them on end which together formed a column. He then placed this column in the middle of a separate model of a large piazza next to the Station. This was his idea for a 'Paddington Pole' to stand as the other book end to the Shard.

John and I looked at each other, as we knew immediately this would be controversial. But we understood Irvine's arguments about the need not

The proposed Paddington Pole.

only to make a statement but to fund the public realm and the place shaping required to turn the area around and to provide a first-class transport interchange. We also saw the advantages of an iconic building in the north of Westminster with an amazing rooftop restaurant and viewing platform.

We told Irvine that he needed to take the local residents with him and in particular the local councillors. On our recommendation, he employed a firm of public affairs specialists with this particularly in mind.

A few months later, an application was made and the local councillors and residents were duly briefed and explained the advantages of their proposals. But Irvine and his team made one big mistake. They had only consulted the councillors and residents living immediately around the site, forgetting the impact the development would have over a much wider area. We were therefore all surprised when hundreds of objections started to pour in from Maida Vale a couple of miles to the north, from St John's Wood, Marylebone and from Bayswater, all of which would have had their views affected by the Paddington Pole. Most did not like it and were clearly furious with the proposals and the audacity of the applicants. It was not long before they started complaining to their ward councillors and I found myself besieged by annoyed colleagues. This came to a head at a Saturday seminar of the Conservative members of the council (convened to discuss other issues), when it became clear that most of my colleagues were against the tower.

Philippa Roe, the Leader of the Council, had been supportive of my views and was backing me, but straight after the group seminar ended, we met up in her office and I had to accept that we could not support the Pole, as this would just be too controversial. Philippa offered to meet Irvine with me, to tell him to back off on the Pole proposal. A few days later, Irvine came to City Hall and we broke the news to him. I was surprised how well he took it, but I think he had read the newspaper headlines and had heard the chatter and knew that this was on the cards. I urged him to redesign the building but to ensure that he retained the large piazza. However, I emphasised the need to ensure that the building height could not be seen from further away than the local area.

A couple of months later, Renzo and Irvine returned to my office where John Walker and I were shown the latest proposal. The proposed new building was now a perfect cube but raised off the ground, thereby retaining much of the size of the piazza and ensuring that the height of the new proposal was only seen in a few long views and would no longer dominate the skyline. I thought that this was the perfect way forward, as it would bring the regeneration required and yet would not disfigure the views of nearly half of Westminster. I genuinely thought that this would be widely accepted as a sensible solution. How wrong I was.

While the new building seemed to placate my own colleagues, a number of vocal residents were still on the warpath. This time, however, a new objector appeared. The senior executives of St Mary's Hospital, which lay next door, came to see me. They explained that they were concerned about the road that gave access to the hospital and was used by ambulances when taking emergencies to A&E. Irvine needed to reroute this road as the existing road went right through the proposed new piazza and to leave the road in place would negate the advantages of the new open space. There was an alternative existing route, but the hospital claimed it took a little longer for the ambulance to reach the hospital. In response, Irvine proposed to move the existing road by creating, at his own expense, a new road on the other side of his cube, but even though this seemed a good compromise, this was not acceptable to the hospital.

The proposed Paddington Cube.

The hospital formally opposed the application, claiming lives could be lost by any different route for the ambulances. They then launched a public campaign and of course the public took their side, fearing the worst at the hospital. A number of colleagues started to support the hospital, blind to the argument that the Irvine compromise route was deemed acceptable to the traffic engineers who had undertaken technical tests. The engineers argued that this new route would be perfectly acceptable and not endanger lives. The heat was on.

About this time, I gave an interview to a property magazine about my work as Cabinet Member of Planning and during that interview, I expressed my view that the regeneration of Paddington would be a good thing and that the Cube would be one way of achieving this. I then said that while the previous proposal had been nicknamed the Paddington Pole, I joked that the new design could be nicknamed the 'Paddington Ice Cube' as it would make the area 'cool'. I was trying to be humorous but the objectors jumped on this, claiming that I had prejudged the application before considering it at committee. I had not at all! But even if I had hinted at a view I held, I was perfectly entitled in law to do so.

There had been case law and changes in legislation brought in by Eric Pickles as Secretary of State that had said that councillors on planning committees could make positive or negative comments about an application before they sat to hear the application, so long as they went in to the meeting with an open mind, listened to all the arguments and were prepared to change their views. I was very much in that frame of mind and felt confident I had done nothing wrong. I was supported by the council's legal team.

When the application came before the committee I chaired, John Walker devised a compromise to the hospital access issue, which addressed the hospital's concerns and was acceptable to Irvine and accordingly the application was granted. As I write, the development is now under way. I am excited to see how the whole area will be upgraded and turned into a 'cool place' to live, work, transit and visit.

I had got to know Irvine quite well through our numerous meetings and really liked him. He would regularly phone me on my mobile asking me how the application was going and each time I told him I did not know, as it was still with the officers. He was a cheeky guy but knew how to undertake a major development like this and the Shard.

In February 2017, I was on my way back from a weekend in my flat in Mallorca when as I was about to board the flight, my mobile phone rang. The message said 'Irvine Sellar calling'. I didn't want to take the call as in doing so, I thought I might lose my place at the beginning of the queue getting on the plane. I always like being first on board, so that I can get my small suitcase in the locker above my seat. But, not wanting to be rude, I answered, with the intention of explaining to Irvine that I was boarding the plane and that I would call him back when I got to London. But to my surprise, it was not Irvine's voice on the phone. It was his son James. I said hello and explained where I was. He apologised, but responded by telling me that he wanted me to know that his father had died that previous evening and he wanted me to hear this from him rather than from the press. I was devastated. I gave him my condolences and said I would call when I got back to London.

Irvine was a visionary who will be forever remembered every time we look up at the Shard or (when it is completed) the Cube and the new public piazza at Paddington. I attended his shiva (when prayers are said at the home of the deceased) a few days later, to pay my respects to his family.

Brick by Brick

The Carlton Tavern was a pub in Maida Vale at the entrance to the Paddington Recreation Ground. Built in 1920 for the Charrington Brewery, it replaced a pub destroyed by a German bomb during the Gotha Raids of 1918. It was then the only building in the area to survive the Blitz during the Second World War and was renowned for its well-preserved interiors.

In about 2014, it was bought by a developer who applied for planning permission to knock it down and build a block of flats on the site above a much smaller pub. The application came before my planning committee. There were few objections and none about the reduction in size of the pub.

It was recommended for approval but I hated the design of the proposed new building, which was quite out of keeping with the area and was (in my view) of very poor quality. My committee, on my lead, therefore refused the application suggesting they submit a revised application based on a design more akin to the original building.

A local resident aggrieved at the potential loss of the building, lobbied Historic England to list the original 1920s pub. Historic England, following its procedures, wrote to both Westminster Council and the owners of the Tavern advising them that after careful consideration, they were minded to list the building Grade II and giving the council and the owners a limited period in which to make comments or object to the listing.

A few days later, on Easter Monday 2015, the manager was told to close the pub for a few days for an 'inventory'. But when she returned two days later, she found that before

Historic England could formally list the pub, the building had been demolished.

Within a matter of days, hundreds of local residents were campaigning for the pub to be rebuilt and it was not long before the national press and the London TV news programmes were carrying pieces about its demolition.

This was followed a few days later by a full council meeting and a demonstration of about forty local residents outside the Council House shouting at councillors and officers arriving for the meeting, demanding we do something.

As the Cabinet Member for Planning, it was down to me to answer any questions raised during the question time session that each council meeting starts with. One of my colleagues representing the Maida Vale ward, stood up at the beginning of questions and asked me what I was doing about the demolition.

The Carlton Tavern public house, Maida Vale.

The demolition of the pub.

I had to think on my feet and I told colleagues that 'Westminster is home to the West End – not the wild west' and went on to promise councillors that I would take all appropriate action to make the developers rebuild the pub 'brick by brick'.

The press loved my 'brick by brick' quote and it was repeated in all the national newspapers and continued to be quoted for years afterwards. I am pleased to report that the owners rebuilt the pub 'brick by brick' and in the spring of 2021 it reopened as a public house – which looks identical to the original.

LBC

Through my friendship with Ashley Tabor the founder and Executive President of Global Radio which owns LBC, Capital Radio, Heart FM, Classic FM and a variety of other independent radio stations, I was invited to appear regularly as a guest newspaper reviewer on Nick Ferrari's morning *Breakfast Show*.

While I loved doing the show, there was a downside. This is because it involved me staying awake the night before until midnight to watch Sky News go through the following morning's papers, to see what the big stories were and what the panel of experts thought about them. Then, after just three hours' sleep, I would be woken up at 3 am by a courier delivering all the morning papers.

I would sit up in bed and try and read them all, picking out three or four major stories being covered by all the papers and think of a slant I could add to those stories. I then had to find about another three or four less prominent stories with some interest to the listeners and then, finally, I particularly enjoyed finding a funny story which I could personalise or make an amusing point about. It is not easy doing all this with little sleep beforehand, making notes, cutting out the article and thinking about the angle I would use, all in the early hours.

Added to that I would then have to get up, wash, shave, shower and dress before driving to the studios in Leicester Square by 6 am. I would be the only poor soul sitting in reception before I was invited by the producer to join him at his desk. I would be offered a tea and at 6.30 I would be joined by Steve Allen after he came off doing the early morning show. Over the years we got to know each other and I found him very amusing and we would have a great laugh chatting until Nick Ferrari arrived.

I had also got to know Nick well, not only through Ashley and our mutual friends Gerald and Gail Ronson but from a London Mayors' Association annual dinner which I had organised and, as chairman, had hosted Nick as our guest speaker. He had also taken a keen interest in what was happening on Westminster Council.

Nick would arrive, have a coffee and re-read the papers he had been reading in the back of his chauffeur-driven car. We would chat briefly as he psyched himself up to go on air. We would then both go through to the studio, ready to go live at 7 am.

With Nick Ferrari at the LMA annual dinner – 2011.

After the news headlines, Nick would go into the first story and an interview and at about 7.10 am, he would introduce me and invite me to comment on the papers that morning. I would talk about three pieces I had chosen and he would then engage me in a discussion about them and my views. We would do this for about five minutes and then he would return to another interview or story but then return to me about twenty minutes later when I would talk about three or four other stories. This would be repeated a third time as we approached 8 am, when I would include the funny story that I had chosen. Nick always treated me well and with respect and I think he enjoyed our conversations, not only live over the radio but privately during the adverts and when the news and weather was read from another studio.

When I had finished and been thanked, I would leave the studio and go off to the office, feeling quite high. I would subsequently be sent the tapes and I learnt from listening back to them how to improve my style. The first time I did the show, I spoke too quickly and tried to squeeze in too much, so I learnt to take it more slowly and to accept I would not need to go through all the pieces I had chosen.

Sadly, towards the end of my political career at Westminster, LBC decided to cut out the daily newspaper review by an invited celebrity guest and so my radio broadcasting career came to an abrupt end.

Hotels

During my time at Westminster, I became quite involved with the hotel industry. Not only have I acquired an understanding and knowledge about the world of hospitality from my twenty years as a trustee of the Savoy Educational Trust (discussed in more detail later in this book) but I have been intimately involved in the planning process for a number of new five-star hotels being built in Westminster.

I was very supportive of the growth in the number of hotels. However, some of my former colleagues on the council have attempted to tighten up the council's planning policies making it more difficult to build new ones. I think this is regressive, as I believe hotels are important for the economy, not only in bringing in visitors who spend money in Westminster but more importantly, in employing thousands of people in numerous jobs, from chambermaids to kitchen hands to receptionists and waiters. At the time of my departure from the council, I had persuaded several hotels to take on otherwise difficult-to-employ residents of Westminster, many from our ethnic communities and council estates.

I am therefore proud of the new hotels I have nurtured. These include the Peninsula Hotel at Hyde Park Corner, the Raffles Hotel in the Old War Office in Whitehall, the new Waldorf Astoria Hotel in Admiralty Arch, the new hotel in what was the American Embassy in Grosvenor Square, the Beaumont in Mayfair, the Mandarin Oriental in Hanover Square, the Corinthia in Whitehall, to name just a few.

The new Londoner Hotel in Leicester Square is deeper than it is high. Simon led the revitalisation of Leicester Square when he was Leader of the Council and I like to think I continued the good work by approving the Londoner. I am proud to have ceremoniously dug the last piece of earth, when they reached the bottom of the deepest excavation in Europe. As I dug out that last slither of mud, I did fear that I would find myself in Australia!

A CGI of the new Raffles Hotel in the Old War Office (OWO) in Whitehall.

But approving all these hotel developments was not a piece of cake, as I put each and every one of the hoteliers through the mangle and pushed and squeezed them to ensure we got the best deal for Westminster.

With the Londoner, when the hotel operators came to see me with their original plans, I sent them away with a long list of issues and problems including my insistence that they substantially reduce the height of the proposed new building, which would have peered over Nelson's Column and the National Gallery in views from Whitehall. The director responsible for the project later told me that he left my office and, in the lift down, burst into tears. But we worked together with my officers and after numerous meetings and redesigns, we found a solution and the hotel is now open and one of the finest in London, in a fantastic location.

The Londoner Hotel nearing completion.

The Parking Fiasco and a Catalogue of Leaders

During Colin Barrow's leadership of the council, the perennial issue arose about finance … the need to balance our budget with the Conservative group's resolute view that we should not increase the council tax. My colleagues were determined to retain our reputation as the best council in the country, which came from the fact that we had the second lowest council tax (at that time – second only to Wandsworth which always deliberately beat us by a small margin) and yet were renowned for the high-quality services we delivered.

When officers warned us about a ten-million-pound hole in our budget, the Cabinet got worried. One of the suggestions made to help, came from a newly promoted member of the Cabinet. This proposed extending our parking controls in the West End, so that they operated through the evenings and at weekends. They currently ended at 6.30 in the evenings (except on resident parking bays) and there were no controls on Sundays. The existing rules supported the hospitality and entertainment industry centred around the West End and enabled those from the suburbs and outside Westminster to drive in to the West End and park on the streets to visit restaurants, bars, clubs, theatres and cinemas without incurring huge parking charges. However, my colleagues liked the idea of extending parking controls, because of the revenue it would bring in to fill the financial hole. However, we were not legally allowed to change our parking policies just for financial gain, so certain officers came up with some spurious excuse for the extension of controls being needed to help the environment.

When this went public, the whole West End business world was aghast and started a campaign to prevent the policy being implemented, citing the damage it would do to business and in particular, to the evening and Sunday economy. The Mayfair restaurants, for example, would be severely affected by a reduction in the number of available parking spaces around in the evenings. Single yellow lines which previously allowed parking after 6.30 in the evenings (Monday to Saturdays) would instead continue in force all night! For the retail trade, Sundays was their busiest time and with no controls at all on a Sunday, the free parking brought thousands to the West End when they could easily be attracted away to the major shopping centres around London with onsite parking.

At the first meeting this was raised, I opposed the proposals because of the serious effect I believed such a policy would have on West End businesses from restaurants to theatres. But I was outvoted. I was conscious that as I was directly elected as Deputy Leader, I had the freedom to vote as I thought right, while all my other colleagues around the cabinet table were appointed by the Leader and so wanted to support whatever view he was pursuing.

Several months went by with all the retailers, restaurateurs and theatre owners campaigning for a reversal of the policy before it was to be implemented, but my colleagues were determined to proceed.

Colin Barrow and I after we won the leadership and deputy leadership in May 2008.

Then everything changed when the *Evening Standard* newspaper was alerted to the story and within days it became front page news. The editor was on a mission. Photographers started following Colin Barrow and his wife around town and in particular photographing them while parking Colin's Maserati.

Despite this, the Cabinet continued to support the project, arguing that we should not be bullied by the media. I continued to argue against, suggesting we should be humble and back down saying that we had learnt from the consultation.

Then the stakes were increased in the autumn of 2011, when a Mayfair property agent led a consortium of West End businesses in applying to the High Court for an injunction to stop the implementation of the new policy. The High Court heard the application to squash the council's policy at the end of the year, when the judge dismissed ten of the twelve grounds for judicial review but stated that two warranted a full hearing and, pending a court date, imposed an injunction preventing the new policy being implemented until the Court had made its final decision.

I had just returned from Christmas in my flat in Mallorca when I was called to attend an emergency meeting of the informal cabinet (in private with only senior officers attending) to discuss the injunction. After a lengthy discussion, it was decided that we had little choice but to delay implementation of the policy and having accepted the injunction, we resolved to postpone the implementation of the policy until after the London Olympics that summer. This would give us breathing space and to some extent save face.

Then a couple of weeks later, following continuing press attacks on us and Colin in particular, the members of the Cabinet met again in private and at the beginning of the meeting Colin raised the subject. He said he had been giving a lot of thought to the issue but would be interested in everyone's views. As Deputy Leader I was sitting on his left. He turned to me first. I made it quite clear that I had been opposed to this policy from the beginning and that the injunction was a good reason to reverse our policy without too much backlash. We obeyed the rule of law and if the courts were unhappy, then we should accept that and move on to other important matters.

He then sought the views of all the other cabinet members sitting around the table. One by one, they all said that we had to stick to our guns and support the policy and not be browbeaten by litigators and the media. Again, I was in a minority of one on this issue. Or so I thought! After hearing from everyone, Colin then said that he had yet to tell everyone his view. He then proceeded to explain that having given much thought to the policy, the onslaught against it, the media coverage and the effect it was having on him and his wife personally, he agreed with Robert (me!) that we should concede and reverse the policy forthwith.

Everyone was initially shocked but then one by one, each member (apart from one) said that they agreed with Colin and would support this about-turn! Wow. In two minutes, their views had all swung around 180 degrees! I learnt that day the real power of patronage!

Despite the lone dissenter, it was agreed that we would keep the decision absolutely confidential and put our views to the group meeting the following week for endorsement before announcing it the following day. It was felt that our colleagues deserved to be consulted first.

That Sunday, Colin was asked to go on the *Politics Show* on BBC TV and be interviewed live about the parking issue. But the day before the show was to air, I received a call from Colin. He told me that he had given further thought to everything and after pressure from his wife, Anna, he had decided to resign as Leader and as a councillor. Of course, this would be kept secret until the group meeting but he was going to tell the other cabinet members that day. I was surprised and told him he would be missed.

On the Sunday, Colin went on BBC TV, forced to support the council's official stance of pursuing the new parking policy after the Olympics were over, knowing full well that we intended to reverse the decision and more so, that he was about to resign. I must give credit where it is due. I think he was brave to do so and even braver to reverse the decision and resign. I really liked Colin and enjoyed working with him as his Deputy Leader and we have remained friends.

A footnote to the parking fiasco. A few months after Colin's resignation, the cabinet was advised that a mistake had been made and we were not in fact facing a ten-million-pound hole in our budget and that our financial position was very strong. We had just been through this debacle and had lost a good leader over nothing.

A New Leader is Required

An hour after Colin's call on that Saturday, I received a call from my good friend Ed Argar, a fellow cabinet member. He was stuck in a French ski resort on a skiing weekend with friends but wanted me to know he was putting his name in the ring. I said I would support him but, as Deputy Leader, I would have to formally stay neutral as I would have to be loyal to whoever was elected the new Leader.

The other leading candidate was Philippa Roe, who had been a very competent Cabinet Member for Housing. She was highly intelligent and a lovely person. A heated but professional campaign ensued and when the votes were eventually cast Philippa won by just three.

Although Ed and his campaign manager, my friend Steve Summers, were devastated, I must say that Philippa turned out to be a fantastic leader and someone who I got on really well with. We became a great team and she trusted me to get on with my roles without any interference. We also became good friends.

Then, after several successful years as Leader, with my supporting her as Deputy Leader, I was in Mallorca for the summer when Philippa rang. She said she wanted to tell me something in absolute confidence. She explained that she had received a call from David Cameron who had just resigned as Prime Minister following the Brexit Referendum and that he had proposed that she become a member of the House of Lords in his Resignation Honours List.

I was delighted for her but concerned about the future for Westminster. I did not want her to resign as Leader as I thought we were a great team. She explained that she hoped to continue doing both jobs as the House of Lords was so close to City Hall and she could pop back and forth quite easily. I explained that when Simon was Leader and chairman of the Local Government Association, he would pop back and forth from their offices in Smith Square.

In September, the list of new peers was announced and plans were made for Philippa to be introduced as a member of the Lords as Baroness Couttie of Down in the County of Kent. When the day came, she kindly invited me and a couple of colleagues from City Hall to watch the ceremony from the balcony of the House of Lords and to join her and her family for lunch afterwards. It was a truly magnificent occasion with Philippa in her deep red robes trimmed in white ermine.

After a few months as a working peer, Philippa realised she could not continue with both roles and remain a good mother and wife, and so in the late autumn she decided to stand down as Leader of Westminster Council.

While Philippa made it to the House of Lords, her rival for the leadership several years earlier, Ed Argar, soon realised his ambition. After losing to Philippa, he turned his focus to the House of Commons and soon got selected for the safe Conservative seat of Charnwood and in the 2015 election won a parliamentary seat for the first time. Not before too long, he started a meritocratic rise up the ministerial ladder being appointed Parliamentary Under Secretary of State in the Department of Justice in June 2018 and then in September 2019 promoted to Minister of State in the Department of Health (number 2 in the Department) and becoming a regular on the TV news during the Covid-19 pandemic.

A Further Leadership Election

The race to succeed Philippa as Leader started straightaway with my friend Nickie Aiken coming into my office to seek my support. Again, I told her that I was happy to support her privately but I emphasised that as Deputy Leader I had to keep out of the race, so that I could work with whoever was successful. I also saw Rachael Robathan in my office and we discussed her intention to stand. But after a few weeks of campaigning, Rachael decided to withdraw from the race and, on our return to City Hall after the Christmas and New Year holidays, Nickie was crowned Leader with no other candidate standing against her.

Three years later, Nickie resigned as Leader after being elected as the MP for the Cities of London and Westminster in December 2019. Just a month later, Rachael stood again and this time won the leadership election against Tim Mitchell (who had been Chief Whip towards the end of my time as Deputy Leader).

Nickie Aiken (Leader) and me (Deputy Leader) in Westminster Abbey before the annual Civic Service.

Royal Advisor

In 2012, one of my neighbours called me on behalf of her friend, the renowned photographer Hugo Rittson-Thomas. It appeared that he was producing a book depicting how the British emphasise the power of leading members of the Establishment by wearing elaborate clothing.

On my friend's suggestion, Hugo wanted to photograph me in the mayoral robes wearing the chains and badge of office. While I was delighted to do so, I had to explain that I was no longer Lord Mayor, so could not wear the blue and gold mayoral robes but as one of the Lord Mayor Locum Tenens (Deputy Lord Mayors), I could wear a red robe similar to that worn by other mayors together with the chains and badge of the Deputy Lord Mayor. I also explained, that it would only be right to invite the Lord Mayor (then Angela Harvey) to join me at the photo shoot on the basis that she could wear the blue ceremonial robes of the Lord Mayor of Westminster. They loved the idea.

A few weeks later, Angela and I went off to Hugo's studios and, wearing our respective robes and chains of office, we were photographed in front of two full-length mirrors at right angles to each other, so in one photo-shoot you could see our front, back and two sides. We heard nothing further for several years and forgot about the photo shoot.

But then in August 2015 I was staying in my flat in Mallorca when I started getting messages asking if I had seen the *Sunday Times* magazine that day! I had not until someone sent me photographs.

The magazine was dedicated to a series of full-page colour photographs of what it described as 'The Queen, her family and some of her closest aides'.

The magazine then included a series of full-page photos of The Queen, Prince William in military uniform, the Duchess of Cornwall in official state dress, the Queen's Bargemaster, the Earl Marshal, Black Rod, Garter Principal King of Arms and Robert Davis, past Lord Mayor of Westminster! I was constantly teased for being described as one of Her Majesty's 'closest aides' but I was indeed very proud.

ABOVE *The lead photograph in the* Sunday Times Magazine, *as portrayed by Hugo Rittson Thomas.*

BELOW *One of Her Majesty's 'closest aides'. . .*

Chapter 29

The Americans and
Tale of the Crispy Duck

The American Embassy was situated in Grosvenor Square in central Mayfair (although it subsequently moved south of the river). Constructed in 1960 it occupied the entire west side of the Square, on land leased from the Duke of Westminster, at a peppercorn rent. A few years ago, the Americans sought to buy the freehold reversion from the Duke. However, it is said that the Duke's response was that they would only transfer the freehold reversion to the United States, if in return the Americans returned the Duke's ancestral land confiscated by the US Government after the American Revolution, namely the City of Miami. Nothing happened!

On 11th September 2001, four separate, but coordinated, devasting terrorist attacks changed the world we knew forever. Security became a central part of our day-to-day life. While the United Kingdom had sadly experienced Irish terrorism for years, the rest of the western world and the United States in particular, had been immune from the devastation of continuous attacks on civilians by international terrorists, particularly on their own soil. The fallout from 9/11, as that day became known, was an upgrading of all security in all the United States embassies around the world.

The American Ambassador in London in 2001 was William Stamps Farish III, a personal friend of The Queen, through their shared love of horses. The Queen would frequently lend her mares to Farish to enable his stallions to breed.

Farish's immediate reaction was to tighten security around the embassy in Grosvenor Square. Local residents, wound up by the Ambassador, started demanding that we close the whole of western Mayfair to traffic. This was just a non-starter. The chaos it would have brought to the area would have been unacceptable politically and commercially. The residents' concern was that because of the tightened security around the immediate perimeter of the Embassy, the potential terrorist bomber in his lorry, being prevented from blowing up the Embassy itself, would instead blow up the neighbouring residential properties.

But Simon and I had been briefed by the 10 Downing Street Security Unit, which emphasised to us that terrorists in the days after 9/11 were after a photo of an iconic building being destroyed, that would hit the front page of every newspaper around the world. The damage to a residential house in Mayfair would not make the headlines they sought and so the risks of an attack were very low. We therefore felt we had a strong case to refute the pressure.

I was then called in by the Ambassador to receive a rebuke for my refusal to agree to the closure of western Mayfair. I was adamant that the council would just not do it. I was happy to work with the Embassy in enhancing the security around the Embassy but I would not agree to the closure of the entirety of Mayfair between Oxford Street, Bond Street, Park Lane and Piccadilly. The Ambassador accused me of being 'arrogant' and ended the meeting without a handshake or goodbye. I had clearly upset him!

A few weeks later, a white Russian countess, Anca Vidaeff, who lived across from the Embassy's side entrance went on a three-day hunger strike claiming to the press 'my life is in danger'. She told one reporter interviewing her that 'only Robert Davis could save her life by closing off Mayfair'. I declined to respond and a few days later after extensive press coverage she resumed eating and I was off the hook.

Then something happened that could only happen in Mayfair. The residents clubbed together and raised over £15,000 to place a double page advertisement in *The Times* complaining about my unwillingness to close off Mayfair. Their big mistake was that the double page spread contained no artwork or photographs and was just two entire pages of small text. Most people just did not have the interest or time to read it.

We decided to calm the situation by holding a public meeting in the local Mayfair Library. Simon chaired it and the room was packed with residents crammed into every corner of the room and halfway down the stairwell outside. We were joined by the local police chief and our chief executive. It was a hostile meeting, as we were accused of putting the residents' lives at risk. But the police chief did an excellent job of trying to reassure them as did Simon.

After the meeting ended, one of the residents present, who had asked me an awkward question, introduced himself as Sir George Iacobescu. I knew who he was straightaway. As chief executive of Canary Wharf, he was a well-known and highly recognised leader of the property industry. He said he wanted to congratulate Simon and I for having the strength to attend such a meeting and put ourselves up for scrutiny. He explained that he did not agree with our response, but respected us for attending and trying to find a way forward. George and I kept in touch afterwards and over time, became good friends, regularly dining together.

A few months later, Farish retired as US Ambassador and his successor Robert Tuttle asked to see me. He was a totally different character and on first meeting, could not have been more kind and friendly. He told me that he had been briefed about his predecessor's spat with me but that he wanted to take a different approach and work with me in finding a solution.

Robert Tuttle and I, together with our staff, designed a new scheme for the western end of Grosvenor Square, which would be funded by the Americans. We gave the green light and work soon started on implementing the scheme. This included rising bollards in the middle of the carriageway on the north and south sides of the Embassy to close off those roads when the risk was high. We also agreed to the permanent closure of the road in front of the Embassy as well as the enclosing (by a new set of ornate railings) of Culross Street and Blackburne's Mews at the rear of the building.

Installed to a high quality, the new public realm was safe and secure but fitted in well with the surrounding area. It was a great success and satisfied the Ambassador and the Embassy as well as many residents, such as Sir George.

There were a few residents who were still annoyed, believing we should have done more. One resident went even further, by continuing to complain about me in the local press and in residents' meetings.

When the works were complete, the Ambassador invited me to officially open the scheme. It was a grand ceremony, taking place on the new piazza outside the front of the Embassy, at which both the Ambassador and I spoke. We then jointly unveiled a plaque which was inscribed with both the Ambassador's and my name as the persons responsible for the scheme. The Ambassador also presented me with a framed certificate which read:

Department of State – United States of America

Certificate of Appreciation

Presented to
Councillor Robert Davis
Deputy Leader of Westminster City Council

For his sustained support for the project to enhance the security and beautify the
perimeter of the Embassy of the United States of America in London

Robert H. Tuttle
Ambassador of the United States of America

This certificate now hangs proudly in my TV room at home in London. When Robert Tuttle left London, following Obama's election as President (Robert was a Bush nomination), Martin Low (the Director of Transportation) and I gave him a Westminster street name sign with his name on, as a memento of his time in London. We still keep in touch and he sends me a Christmas card every year.

His Excellency Robert Tuttle with Martin Low and me in the Embassy.

Meanwhile, I was continuing to undertake my public duties as a councillor at the same time as I was practising as a solicitor. One of my specialities as a lawyer was alcohol licensing. Before 2003, licensing was the responsibility of the local magistrates' courts and when acting for clients in buying or opening new restaurants, bars or clubs, as well as doing the conveyancing I would also do all the necessary legal work associated with transferring an existing licence to sell alcohol or applying for a new licence. Most of the work was administrative requiring lots of paperwork, preparation of notices and letters and serving them on a variety of consultees.

With an application for a new licence, there was an onus on the applicant to persuade the magistrates of the need for a new licence and to prove the premises had been sufficiently designed and completed in accordance with the court's requirements (for example, the way the doors were positioned in the toilets). In such cases, I would instruct counsel to appear on behalf of my client at the court hearing itself. But when the application was just for a transfer of the existing licence to my client, the application before the magistrates was quite straightforward and I would appear in court myself and make the necessary representations to the bench of magistrates.

However, in 2003 the law changed with the enactment of the Licensing Act 2003. This had a major impact on my practice. The responsibility for licensing was transferred from the courts to the local council (apart from appeals on decisions made initially by the council) and so my personal involvement in licensing applications before the council had to change.

I would not be able to appear before the council's Licensing Committee to represent my clients, as the members of the Licensing Committee were my friends, foes and/or colleagues. But I believed it would be acceptable to continue to act on my client's behalf in respect of such applications on two conditions. The first, was that I would not appear before the Licensing Committee but would always instruct a barrister to do so on my behalf, and that all correspondence with the council would not show my reference on the letters but those of one of my colleagues in the firm, so the recipient would not know of my involvement. This way, the council (both officers and members) would not know I was involved and so would not be influenced in any way.

In 2006, I was instructed by a Chinese restaurant in Chinatown called Crispy Duck to apply on their behalf for consent to extend their licence to incorporate the second and third floors of their premises. I thought I could accept those instructions as long as I met the conditions I had set myself and in that way no one at the council would know I was involved.

The owner of Crispy Duck, an elderly Chinese gentleman, had been running his very reputable Chinese restaurant for many years with no issues or complaints. I therefore assumed it would be a straightforward application and go through quite smoothly. What I had not properly considered was the fact that the local residents society were at war over the expansion of restaurants in Soho and Chinatown and so opposed this application, even though (in my view) the impact of two additional small floors in this small old Victorian building with an additional fifty covers (twenty-five on each floor) would have little or no effect on the local area, let alone on the residents of Soho. But they had a blanket policy of opposing all applications for new or extended licences and, as a result, the application was deemed appropriate by the officers to be determined by the Licensing Committee and not as a delegated decision by officers.

Although I had instructed my secretary to ensure that my reference did not to appear on the letters to the council with regard to this application, I failed to notice one letter where she had forgotten and this included at the top of the letter, my reference 'RD'.

I had briefed counsel to appear at the hearing on behalf of my client and so the committee would not know of my involvement. When the papers were compiled by the officers, to distribute to the members of the committee in order to be read before the committee meeting, the officers included as an attachment, the one letter that had the RD reference at the top. Most people would not have even noticed it, as it was very discreet. But the Labour councillor on the committee did notice and guessed what the reference RD meant.

This is where the Crispy Duck and the American Embassy get entwined. It appears that one of the residents living near the Embassy, who was extremely annoyed by my actions or, more correctly, lack of actions in Mayfair, was determined to get one over me.

Somehow, the totally unrelated application for an extra two floors for a Chinese restaurant in Chinatown two miles away caught the attention of this resident as did the one letter in a pile of dozens of documents relating to this transaction with my RD reference on. I can only assume that a Labour Party councillor had brought it to the attention of the resident, because this resident (with no links to Chinatown or Chinese restaurants) decided to report me to the Standards Board for England, claiming I had breached the council's code of conduct for having a conflict of interest.

The Standards Board for England was a centralised independent body created in 2000 by the Blair government to take national responsibility for ethical standards in local government and for dealing with complaints made about councillors. Anyone wanting to make a complaint about a councillor had to do so directly to the Board. Bizarrely their procedural code on receiving a complaint was to investigate the complaint before they advised the councillor complained about of the reference to the Board or of the allegations. In fact, their rules went further in that they were required to deny that they were investigating a reference to them until they had satisfied themselves that they were justified in pursuing a case.

A few weeks later, when I opened my copy of the latest edition of *Private Eye*, there in the Rotten Boroughs column was an article about me! It stated that a conflict of interest had arisen when I acted for the owner of Crispy Duck in applying for a licence for these extra two floors and that consequently, a complaint had been referred to the Standards Board of England. This was the first I knew of this. I was shocked.

I immediately called the Westminster Council's Director of Law to ask him what he knew. He explained that if he did know, he could not discuss it with me or confirm that an investigation had been started. He advised me to contact the Standards Board directly, which I did. They too explained that even though I was the person complained about, they could not confirm or deny that a complaint had been made or that an investigation had been commenced. If they were to investigate, I would hear in good time. I referred them to the article in *Private Eye* and emphasised the absurdity of *Private Eye* knowing and making it public, but no one at the council or the Standards Board could confirm this with me – the person complained about. They simply did not care and were extremely unhelpful.

Eventually, after a few weeks, I received a letter from the Standards Board confirming the complaint and consequential investigation. It confirmed that the complainer was the aforementioned lady living near to the American embassy, over two miles away from Crispy Duck. How two extra floors in this relatively small and harmless Chinese restaurant (where little alcohol is served) could upset or offend the lady living near to the embassy, was surprising. I had no doubt that it related to my refusal to close off all of western Mayfair to vehicles.

I decided to represent myself, as I was confident that I had done nothing wrong. In fact, the irony was that when the application was considered by the council's Licensing Committee, it was refused on the basis of the blanket objections by the residents. So, there was no way I could have been guilty of influencing anyone with this outcome.

Within a few weeks, two officers from the Standards Board came to City Hall to interview me. I told them very much what I set out here. They thanked me, after asking a few questions and said I would hear in due course.

A few months later, I received a letter from the Standards Board advising me that their investigation was now complete and they had come to the conclusion that I had done nothing wrong and had not breached the code of conduct for councillors. That was the end of the matter.

I immediately sent a copy of the judgment to *Private Eye*, who had regularly been making amusing jibes about me and Crispy Duck, asking them to refrain from doing so again.

However, in their special New Year edition, a few months later, as they do each year, they devoted two pages to their Rotten Boroughs annual awards. There was me, winning the Crispy Duck Award of the Year. It was my first award as a councillor ... something to be proud of? Well, you have to look on the bright side of life.

In 2012, for reasons nothing to do with crispy ducks, the Standards Board was abolished by the Cameron government.

Chapter 30

My Times at the Palace

My first visit to Buckingham Palace was as Lord Mayor of Westminster for the State Visit of Nelson Mandela, which I have described earlier. However, I had the honour of returning not only as Lord Mayor for the Diplomatic Reception in November 1996, but also on a number of other occasions after my retirement as Lord Mayor, some formal and others informal.

The Diplomatic Reception

The Diplomatic Reception is held in November each year and is a white tie and tails event with tiaras for the ladies. All Ambassadors and High Commissioners accredited to the Court of St James's (High Commissioners represent the countries which are members of the Commonwealth) are invited and are able to bring with them not only their spouses but a number of their more junior diplomats. To entertain the diplomats, the entire Royal Family attend as do many members of the government and senior members of Parliament. The Lord Mayors of London and Westminster attend with the top brass from the Army, the Royal Navy and the Air Force together with senior civil servants and British Foreign Office staff.

The format has changed over the years, but in my year as Lord Mayor, the evening did not start until 9.30, on the basis that you ate before you arrived. Guests assembled in one of several State rooms, with the Ambassadors and High Commissioners on one side of the room with their staff behind them and the other guests on the opposite side of the room. The gigantic double doors at each end of the rooms were closed.

The Ambassadors/High Commissioners would stand in order of precedence. In Britain, the order of precedence is based on the date the Ambassador/High Commissioner presented their credentials to The Queen. For example, the Kuwaiti Ambassador, His Excellency Khaled Al-Duwaisan GCVO, who is the longest-serving Ambassador having presented his credentials in 1993 (and is still in place in 2022) would take precedence over the Ambassador from the United States, because of his longer tenure and not the importance or size of the country he represents.

Carole (my Lady Mayoress) and I were in the middle room and a hush swept through the room as we expected the arrival of The Queen. The large double doors at one end of the room, decorated in gold leaf, were pulled open by two liveried footmen, to reveal The Queen being led by the Marshal of the Diplomatic Corps, Vice-Admiral Sir James Weatherall KCVO KBE, holding his wand of office. A former captain of HMS *Ark Royal* (the aircraft carrier), he and his wife Jean became good friends of mine. The role of the Marshal of the Diplomatic Corps (a senior position within the Royal Household) is to be The Queen's link with the diplomatic community based in St James's Palace.

The Queen then proceeded down the side fronted by the Ambassadors and chatted with each one after having been formally presented by the Marshal. The Ambassador in turn is allowed to present two of his staff. Her Majesty times it perfectly, ensuring she meets everyone she is required to in the entire room within her allotted time.

She was followed by the Duke of Edinburgh and other members of the Royal Family at a distance who are led by senior Foreign Office staff, each taking their time to chat with the diplomats. We, the non-diplomatic side of the room, merely watch and take in the occasion.

When the last Royal entered the room, the doors through which they entered were closed. Those in the previous room could then mingle, drink and enjoy the canapés that start to be circulated. Likewise, when all the Royals had moved in to the next room, the doors were closed and we were able to relax and enjoy the party.

Carole on route to the Palace.

The Queen and the Duke, having met all the Ambassadors and High Commissioners, then retire to their private quarters and that's when the party really started. The main ballroom of the Palace (usually used for State Banquets and Investitures) was converted into a disco. Not wanting to miss out on one of the most glamourous evenings of my life, Carole and I spent the rest of the evening dancing to a live band until they finally stopped at 1 am and we had little choice but to leave.

At the end of the evening, the Palace organised the departure of hundreds of VIP guests all leaving together, like clockwork. Before we arrived, we had been sent a little leaving card with our details on. As we congregated with our coats at the Grand Entrance, we passed these cards to the footmen and they notified our chauffeurs that we were ready to leave. We were asked to wait in the main lobby, which we did and where we chatted to the other guests. Every so often the tannoy system would announce a guest's name and as they did, their chauffeur-driven car arrived at the entrance to pick them up. We did not have to wait long before the announcement said 'car for the Lord Mayor of Westminster' and there outside was WE1, the mayoral car.

I was extremely lucky, because most Lord Mayors only attend the Diplomatic Reception once. That's why we danced until we were almost thrown out. But several years later in November 2005, the Diplomatic Reception clashed with the then Lord Mayor's visit to Oslo to cut down the Trafalgar Square Christmas Tree. By simple luck, I happened to be the rota Lord Mayor Locum Tenens on duty that day and so it fell on me to attend and represent the Lord Mayor. Carole flew over from Connecticut for the evening and we both loved re-living this special occasion.

This time the format had changed and we were expected to arrive much earlier at about 7.30 pm to enjoy a stand-up supper in the ballroom comprising numerous bowls of food that were offered by footmen in their regal red and gold uniforms. The disco, on the other hand, had been moved to the Supper Ballroom and again we danced until they turned the lights off, suggesting it was time to leave.

The Queen's Jubilees

In 2002, the Queen celebrated her Golden Jubilee with a large concert in the gardens of Buckingham Palace. Simon was by this stage Leader of Westminster Council and as such was invited to the concert. I was of course his plus one and when the day arrived we were surprised to be escorted in a different direction from the other members of the public who had applied to attend via a ballot. The next thing we knew, we were shown in to one of the great State Rooms on the ground floor of the Palace with large French windows looking out onto the vast gardens. The concert itself was to take place in the gardens, with a massive temporary stage erected facing the Palace at the other side of the extensive lawn.

Outside the Palace with my Royal picnic basket.

As they entered the gardens, the public were each handed picnic baskets which contained a selection of picnic-style food and invited to sit anywhere on the lawn to eat their supper. Simon and I, on the other hand, were with the VIPs and we were soon joined by a number of minor Royals. We were encouraged by the liveried footmen to enjoy a supper from the buffet on display. We took some food and went to a corner of the room to balance our plates and drinks, where we found ourselves talking to Ingrid Seward, the editor of *Majesty Magazine*.

After a while, we were escorted into the gardens to watch the concert itself, only to discover that we were sitting in the raised Royal Box, behind the rows of deck chairs the public were occupying. We were not only sitting in full view of the TV cameras focused on the Royal Box, but three rows immediately behind Her Majesty's own seat.

However, The Queen did not attend the first half of the concert, although you would not have known from the TV coverage. I assume pop concerts were not her thing! We enjoyed performances by Paul McCartney, Queen (the band), Elton John, Shirley Bassey and Cliff Richard with appearances from Dame Edna Everage and Tony Bennett. The highlight was when Brian May, the guitarist from Queen, performed a solo from the roof of the Palace. After the interval we were joined by The Queen and the Duke of Edinburgh for the rest of the concert.

Ten years later, for the Diamond Jubilee, Her Majesty hosted another concert organised by Gary Barlow, but this time the concert took place in front of the Palace in the Mall, with the stage positioned in front of the Queen Victoria monument.

However, by 2012, Simon had passed away and so I presumed that I would not be invited again. But, to my delight, Philippa Roe, the Leader of the Council at the time, who had been invited, could not take her husband as he was abroad on business, so she kindly invited me to be her plus one instead. This time, when we arrived at the Palace, we were shown to the Music Room (the large bow-windowed state room facing the gardens on the first floor) where a reception was being held for the VIP guests and minor Royals, such as Beatrice and Eugenie, Zara and Peter Phillips as well as Princess Anne and the Earl and Countess of Wessex. The Prime Minister and a number of Cabinet members were also present.

After about an hour of drinking and mingling, we were asked to leave in order to take our seats in the VIP box. As we left the Music Room, we were handed beautiful picnic baskets full of picnic-style food for our supper, which we proceeded to eat in the VIP seating in the Mall, opposite the stage. I still have my picnic basket.

Sir David Walker

In 2008, at a luncheon party in City Hall hosted by the Lord Mayor, I sat next to the Master of the Household, Air Marshal Sir David Walker KCVO OBE (although then only Vice-Air Marshal and yet to be knighted).

The Master of the Household is one of the principal officers of Her Majesty's Household and is rather like a hotel general manager. He is responsible for the running of the Royal Household in all the Palaces, from the maintenance of the buildings to the administration of the kitchens and all the domestic duties such as housekeeping. All receptions held in any of the Palaces including the famous garden parties also fall under his responsibility.

David and I got on extremely well and agreed to meet up again for a one-to-one lunch. A few months later, David joined me at the Wallace Collection restaurant for lunch and this soon became a regular date, with us either lunching in some restaurant in Marylebone or my joining David at the Goring Hotel near the Palace.

One day, David asked me if I wanted to join him for lunch in the Palace. I jumped at the invitation. The senior members of the Household, including the Private Secretaries for each member of the Royal Family, the Equerries and the Ladies in Waiting are entitled to enjoy lunch in the Marble Hall (on the ground floor of the Palace adjacent to the Bow Room). They may also invite guests.

When I arrived, I was taken to David's private office where I was introduced to his secretary and we chatted before he took me to Her Majesty's Equerry's Room where we joined a number of the other members of the Household lunching that day, for pre-lunch drinks. I was introduced to them all and we chatted over a gin and tonic served by the Queen's Equerry, before we were all ushered into lunch.

The Marble Room overlooks the magnificent lawn at the rear of the Palace, accessed through a pair of French windows. The table sat majestically at the centre of the room, with about twenty places set. It appears that the Master of the Household (my host David), as the most senior courtier present, sat at the head of the table and I was placed to his right. On my other side was one of Her Majesty's Ladies in Waiting, Lady Diana Farnham, who I knew quite well. She is a close friend of Roger Bramble, a former Lord Mayor of Westminster and a fellow councillor for many years. Roger is very involved with the London New Year's Day Parade and attended the event each year and he always brought Diana as his guest. I therefore got to know her through watching the Parade together. She had just returned from accompanying Her Majesty on an official visit. It is her responsibility to accompany The Queen and take responsibility for holding any flowers or gifts handed to Her Majesty. After the event, she will write on behalf of The Queen to the hosts to thank them.

Although there were two footmen present, we were required to help ourselves from a small buffet laid out on a table on one side of the room. David led me to the buffet, but conscious I had to be on my best behaviour, I uncharacteristically only took a small portion of the food on offer. No starters, just a choice of main courses from a cooked meal to a vegetarian and salad option. A choice of desserts was also offered. Coffee was, however, served by the footmen at the table and they kindly provided me with my preferred green tea. However, I nearly made a fool of myself, when I leant across to this beautiful silver pot and was about to help myself to some sugar to add to my green tea, when a footman leant over my right-hand shoulder and whispered into my ear 'you should wish to know, Sir, that that is the salt'. He then presented me with a separate silver bowl containing the sugar! I was relieved The Queen was not present!

Works to the Palace

After lunch had finished, as I was rising to leave, I was approached by one of the other members of the Household, Roy Brown, the Deputy Director of Property at the Palace. He told me that he knew who I was and of my interest in planning and historic buildings. He explained that the Palace was carrying out major renovations to the external fabric of the eastern part of the central courtyard after a piece of marble had fallen off and just missed the Princess Royal's car, as she was driven through one of the arches.

He invited me on a future tour of the Palace and in particular to see the works being undertaken. I could hardly refuse and so, a few weeks later, I turned up again at the Privy Purse Door and Roy joined me. He gave me a full tour of the Palace, not only through the State Rooms, which I had seen during my visits as Lord Mayor and on visits when the Palace was open to the public, but to other parts that I had never seen before, including the east wing which houses the large central room with the French windows which open onto the famous balcony. I was also shown the guest rooms that are used overnight for guests such as Ladies in Waiting on duty for a few days, assistant equerries and other guests.

I was also shown the Belgian Suite, occupied by a visiting Head of State during a State Visit, the Chinese Suite and the Royals' private corridor, although we avoided Her Majesty's private quarters (quite understandably). I was then taken into the basement and shown along the corridor full of offices occupied by various members of the Royal Household.

Finally, as we walked through the ballroom where State Banquets and Investitures are held, we noticed in one of the corners water pouring through. We immediately went over to inspect and, after assessing the problems, Roy called a colleague and within a few minutes a handful of staff had joined us to take control of the problem. I later read in the papers that the leak had revealed major repair issues with the roof of the ballroom.

Satisfied that his colleagues were on top of the leak, Roy took me to put on some safety gear and we accessed the scaffolding in the central courtyard and examined at eye level the work that was being carried out to repair and clean the intricate ornate stone carvings that adorned the east wing. It was a privilege. Several experts carrying out the work were there to explain the process and the history of the sculptures.

After the tour, Roy took me as his guest to the Household lunch in the Marble Hall, where I experienced a similar lunch to the one a few weeks earlier. About a year later, David Walker invited me again and I enjoyed a third Household lunch, meeting different members of the Household.

Receptions and Garden Parties

As Master, David would host a series of private receptions in the Palace and on several occasions he invited me as one of his guests. I recall joining him at a preview of an exhibition in the Queen's Gallery and on another occasion to a drinks party in the room which leads on to the famous balcony. I was allowed to bring a guest to the latter and so I invited my friend and colleague Steve Summers.

Steve had never been inside the Palace and was in awe of the place. Towards the end of the reception, David offered to take us and a number of the other guests on a tour of the State Rooms. Although I had seen them before, for Steve, it was like entering heaven.

Among the highlights of the year are the three garden parties hosted by The Queen. They are an amazing experience and I have been to about seven. I have taken my parents, my mother-in-law, Ruth, and my sister.

To do it properly, you need to queue in the Mall from about 2 pm so that you can get in quite soon after the doors are opened at 3 pm. There are various entrances for guests to access the gardens, but I always recommend entering through the Palace itself as you experience the grandeur of arriving at the Grand Entrance and walking through the Palace into the Bow Room and out into the garden.

The Queen arrives with other members of the Royal Family at 4 pm, so you have an hour to explore the gardens. Most guests rush to the tea tents and stuff their plates with dainty sandwiches (including cucumber ones), scones covered in jam and cream, as well as miniature cakes and either lemonade or English tea. My advice, however, is don't waste your time queuing up as you arrive and then not finding a table to sit at, but take a walk around the magnificent gardens. They are the largest private gardens in London.

At 4 pm precisely, The Queen and the Royal Family arrive on the terrace in front of the Bow Room and everyone stands still while the National Anthem is played by one of the two military bands on duty that day. By this time, the royal ushers have divided the crowds into several lanes and each member of the Royal Family is escorted down a separate lane, meeting guests who have been singled out to be presented. This is the time to have tea. Everyone is so keen to watch the Royals that all the tables are empty and the queues for tea disappear. I appreciate that those who have never seen a Royal before are keen to do so, but as I had met them on numerous occasions, I was ensured a good table to watch from afar, enjoying at least two rounds of afternoon teas.

At 5 pm precisely, The Queen, who is an expert at timekeeping without anyone noticing, arrives at the Royal Tea Tent. This large marquee at the lakeside of the lawn is guarded by several members of the Yeoman of the Guard in their splendid and colourful historic uniforms. The oldest British military corps still in existence, it was created by King Henry VII in 1485. They are The Queen's official bodyguards.

In the Royal Tea Tent, by very special invitation are about twenty distinguished guests. They include the Prime Minister and/or other members (or former members) of the Cabinet, the leaders of the other major political parties and a couple of the more senior Ambassadors and High Commissioners. In addition, there are some distinguished members of the establishment such as the Archbishop of Canterbury, the Lord Chief Justice and the

One of Her Majesty's Garden Parties at Buckingham Palace.

Speaker. The Lord Mayor of Westminster is also included and so in 1996, Carole (my Lady Mayoress) and I were invited into the Royal Tea Tent.

As Lord Mayor, I had used my position to arrange with the Palace for my parents to attend the garden party with us. However, their invite did not extend to joining us in the Royal Tea Tent. I therefore found my parents two seats facing the tea tent, so they could watch us hobnobbing with the Royals. As the clock struck five, The Queen escorted by the Lord Chamberlain entered the tea tent followed by the other members of the Royal Family attending that day (not all of them do). What surprised me, as I stood in the tent making small talk with other guests, but with one eye on Her Majesty, was that The Queen and the other Royals head immediately to one end of the tea tent where a section has been roped off. There, Her Majesty and the other Royals enjoy a cup of tea chatting to each other, totally ignoring the other distinguished guests in the Royal Tea Tent.

Maybe she knows them all and so doesn't need to meet them. Maybe she is entitled to a break after shaking hands with hundreds of her guests and making small talk for an hour and so deserves a cup of tea with no pressure, but I was rather disappointed.

After twenty minutes, she made her way towards the other guests and we were presented by the Lord Chamberlain. But after a brief chat to each of us, she was off.

The next secret (if you're not too tired) is to linger and tour the gardens again before you're thrown out by the staff. A very special day.

In 2010, just after the election that saw David Cameron become Prime Minister, Simon was invited to the Buckingham Palace garden party and as Deputy Mayor of London, he was invited to join the Royal Tea Tent. I joined him as his husband (we had had our civil partnership three years earlier). So, for my second time, I found myself enjoying afternoon tea with other VIPs and the Royal Family.

While The Queen was enjoying her own tea chatting to the Duke of Kent, Simon and I were talking to Eric Pickles and his wife. Eric had just been appointed Secretary of State for Local Government. Then before we realised what was happening, Her Majesty appeared before us. The Lord Chamberlain, escorting her, presented us. Here we had the Monarch, chatting to two of the most important people in local government, the Secretary of State and the Deputy Mayor of London and the subject of our discussion? The weather that day. After no more than two minutes, she was off.

Afterwards, I could not help thinking that many people would have been enthralled at having a chat with these two eminent experts in local government and, with a new government in place, would be keen to discuss what the future held for so many of the services that make everyday life work, and yet all Her Majesty wanted to know was their views about the weather!

A few years later, David Walker announced his retirement and over a farewell lunch at the Goring Hotel, he invited me to attend a forthcoming garden party. I of course accepted and took my friend Steve Summers as my guest. This was his first garden party (although a few years later he would attend as Lord Mayor and join the Royal Tea Tent).

When the tickets arrived, we were delighted to find that we would be invited into the Diplomatic Tea Tent. This was the private tea tent adjacent to the Royal Tea Tent and hosted the Ambassadors and High Commissioners attending but not the handful invited into the Royal Tea Tent. Other guests in the Diplomatic Tea Tent were current and former government ministers and other distinguished guests.

The Royal Warrant Holders Association

In 2012 as part of the celebrations for the Queen's Diamond Jubilee, the Royal Warrant Holders Association was allowed to hold a trade fair in the gardens of the Palace. The Royal Warrant Holders are those companies that have supplied goods or services to The Queen, HRH the Duke of Edinburgh and to HRH the Prince of Wales for at least five years and are awarded a Royal Warrant as a mark of recognition of their services to the Royal Family. David Walker sought my support and input into their plans about a year ahead of the event. I joined him at the Palace for a meeting with him and his colleagues to discuss logistics and the necessary consents he would need. When the event opened, he very kindly invited me to join him and his guests at the opening party. After a tour of the fair, I joined David and his other guests in one of the marquees for a splendid dinner.

The Privileged Bodies

The Privileged Bodies are the twenty-seven most important bodies in the United Kingdom which have been given the rare privilege of being entitled to address the Monarch and to receive a reply. These Privileged Bodies include The General Synod of the Church of England, the Universities of Oxford, Cambridge, London, St Andrews, Glasgow, Edinburgh and Aberdeen, the General Assembly of the Church of Scotland, the Board of Deputies of British Jews, the Deans and Chapters of Westminster Abbey, St Paul's Cathedral and St George's Chapel (Windsor Castle) as well as the Roman Catholic Church and the Governor and Company of the Bank of England. The Privileged Bodies also include the Greater London Authority and the councils of the Cities of Westminster, London and Edinburgh and the County of Berkshire and the town of Windsor (each having a Royal connection).

In years past, the privilege was a valuable way of getting your message to the Monarch, when the Monarch had real power and before Parliament became supreme. Nowadays, it is largely symbolic and ceremonial. I am not aware that any of the privileged bodies have in modern times sought a private audience. But on very special Royal occasions, the Privileged Bodies are invited to the Palace to give separate addresses to Her Majesty. Previous occasions were the Accession (in 1952) and Her Majesty's Silver and Golden Jubilees.

In March 2012, during Her Majesty's Diamond Jubilee, a Privileged Bodies ceremony was held in the presence of The Queen and the Duke of Edinburgh. Each Privileged Body is allowed to take about twelve members including the head of their delegation. As cabinet member for the mayoralty and protocol issues, I decided that the Westminster Council delegation would be led by our Lord Mayor (who would also be required to read our address to Her Majesty) and include the Leader, the Deputy Leader (of course – as that was me), the Chief Executive and eight other councillors chosen by a ballot and including one member of the minority group.

We assembled at City Hall in the Lord Mayor's Reception Rooms and left in a fleet of cars to the Palace, in our robes, jabots and white gloves. The Lord Mayor was wearing the blue and gold robes and her chains of office. Special permission had been granted for the mayors to wear their chains as this is usually prohibited in a Royal Palace.

We arrived through the Grand Entrance and made our way to the ballroom to take our designated seats. All the other Privileged Bodies also took their seats wearing their robes or other ceremonial dress. It was quite a sight.

After Her Majesty and the Duke arrived and took their places on modest thrones on the dais, the heads of the delegations of each of the Privileged Bodies took it in turn to walk up to the dais and, after bowing, they read their individualised Addresses, congratulating Her Majesty on her Diamond Jubilee.

Several of the Privileged Bodies had as their ceremonial head the Duke of Edinburgh. Accordingly, as every fourth or fifth delegation was called, the Duke stood up from his throne next to Her Majesty and manoeuvred himself in front of The Queen and then read the address on behalf of the relevant Privileged Body. He did this about five times, much to the amusement of those assembled.

Susie Burbridge, our Lord Mayor gave the address on behalf of the Council in which she said:

> We are proud that on this memorable occasion for gratitude and rejoicing, the City of Westminster, accorded city status by your Majesty, and which great city encompasses Buckingham and St James's Palaces, where you and many members of your family reside;

Susie Burbridge, Lord Mayor of Westminster, hands the City of Westminster's Loyal Address on vellum to Her Majesty.

Westminster Palace, the seat of your Government; Marlborough House, the headquarters of the Commonwealth; and the homes of so many of the Royal institutions of which your Majesty is patron, will be the setting where families and friends from all parts of the Nation will gather to show their loyalty love and support to their Beloved Sovereign.

She concluded:

It is with thankful hearts and in the sure knowledge that Your Majesty will always work for the happiness and prosperity of your peoples, that we most earnestly pray Your Majesty may long be spared to continue Your beneficent reign over the devoted people of your City, Nation and Commonwealth.

The parchment on vellum on which the address had been handwritten was signed by the Lord Mayor against the Great Seal of the City of Westminster.

After the formal ceremony, all the guests moved to the Great Gallery where a reception was held and we were joined by Her Majesty and other members of the Royal Family. As my friend and colleague Louise Hyams and I were chatting, who should appear but Her Majesty accompanied by my friend Sir David Walker, Master of the Household. We were presented and Louise told Her Majesty how much she was looking forward to the Diamond Jubilee celebrations, some three months away. The Queen said that she thought that most people were not interested in the forthcoming celebrations but Louise insisted that by the time of the major celebrations that summer, everyone would be excited to celebrate with Her Majesty. The Queen said she hoped Louise was right.

She then told us that she was concerned about climbing the steep and numerous steps of St Paul's Cathedral for the special service that would be held over the Jubilee weekend as her knees were not good anymore at climbing steep steps. We assured her she would be fine. A few weeks later, I read in the paper that St Paul's had added a set of railings on the steps, presumably to assist Her Majesty. On the day itself, I watched it on TV and noticed that she used the rail to assist.

Farewell Reception
As I have mentioned, I was friends with Sir David Walker, the Master of the Household, and so when he retired in 2013 from the Mastership, he kindly invited me to his leaving party in the Great Gallery of Buckingham Palace. The Queen joined us and was clearly in a relaxed mood and mixed among the guests, who included most members of the Royal Family.

Alas, with David's retirement, my invitations to the Palace dried up.

Chapter 31

Plaques Galore

I have many legacies and achievements reflecting my life as a councillor, many of them highlighted in this book, but the ones that will outlive me and my memory will be the numerous plaques with my name on positioned all over the city. Here are details of some of them.

Oxford Street

My favourite one has sadly gone. It was in the early 1990s that I led the regeneration of Oxford Street. Earlier, I described my visit to the Decaux headquarters in Paris to look at street furniture and the difference of opinion I had with our then Director of Planning and Transportation, Syd Sporle, as to whether to use the Norman Foster designs for new street furniture. The end result was a widening of the pavements and the introduction of new lamp posts and seating (but not designed by Foster).

When the works on the first section outside Selfridges were completed in late 1993, we decided on an early morning press launch and photo call. To attract the national press, we enrolled the *Carry On* and *EastEnders* actress and local Marylebone resident, Barbara Windsor, to formally open the completed street with me as chairman of the council's Planning and Transportation Committee.

Barbara Windsor and I unveil the first stage of the Oxford Street public realm refurbishment in November 1993.

In front of the assembled press and photographers including the London regional TV crews, I opened the new scheme by cutting the ribbon around a gigantic Christmas gift wrapped box sitting right outside the main entrance to Selfridges. And as I did, the box opened up to reveal Barbara Windsor (the press up until then had no idea she was coming) standing there!

We then unveiled a large plaque in the pavement right under the large Selfridges canopy, announcing the unveiling of this stage of the streetworks by me, 'Councillor Robert Davis, Chairman of the Planning and Transportation Committee'. I was very proud of this bronze plaque and many friends shopping in Oxford Street would let me know that they had seen it. Not even Gordon Selfridge had a plaque outside his world-famous store.

In about 2014, my friend Joe Trotter (the former Mayor of Islington) phoned me in an agitated state to tell me that on a shopping expedition to Oxford Street he had noticed that my plaque was gone. I was at work in my legal office which was five minutes away, so I went to inspect and yes, there was just a gap where the plaque had been.

THE SECOND PHASE OF THE
OXFORD STREET
IMPROVEMENT PROJECT
WAS UNVEILED ON THE
29th NOVEMBER 1993 BY
COUNCILLOR ROBERT DAVIS
CHAIRMAN OF THE
PLANNING AND TRANSPORTATION
COMMITTEE
WESTMINSTER CITY COUNCIL

My Oxford Street plaque.

I immediately reported this to Martin Low, the brilliant Director of Transportation, who immediately alerted the Metropolitan Commissioner of Police's private office. Although both Martin and I knew the Commissioner, when Martin told me what he had done, I did say that I thought that was probably over the top. Martin then went further and obtained the Selfridges CCTV footage and one of his staff was instructed to find out what had happened. He discovered that at 4 am one morning, a van had driven down Oxford Street, stopped outside Selfridges' main entrance and two gentlemen wearing balaclavas got out and dug up the plaque and threw it on the back of their lorry and drove off. Martin told me it had been stolen for its metal value and was probably now melted down and the bronze sold on.

Martin, however, ordered a replacement to be made and it was not too long before the new plaque was in place and no one would have known it was a duplicate. Alas, in 2017, it was stolen again, but by this time Martin Low had retired and his successor was not keen on incurring the expense of a new one and it was merely replaced by a new pavement slab. My association with Selfridges was at an end!

Returning to the early 1990s, when the second stage of the Oxford Street works was completed, instead of recruiting an attractive actress to open it with me, I was accompanied by the then Secretary of State for Local Government, John Selwyn Gummer (now Lord Deben) and a plaque with both our names on was unveiled on a traffic light junction box

The Seymour Place plaque.

outside the front door of the Marble Arch branch of Marks and Spencer. Sadly, years later the junction box disappeared together with my plaque.

Seymour Place

When I worked with the Portman Estate on the new streetscape scheme for the southern end of Seymour Place in Marylebone, at the opening of the completed street, Gareth Clutton (the then Chief Executive of the Estate) and I unveiled another plaque with my name on. Sadly, Gareth died in office a few months later. A great loss as he was such a nice man and doing such great things with the area.

Lancaster Gate

In Lancaster Gate itself, the war memorial that dominates the square had been badly damaged in one of the storms that had hit London and thanks to the endeavours of local residents' association chairman, John Zamit, the memorial was restored.

To commemorate this, and as part of the new public realm works that surrounded the newly refurbished memorial, was a piece of art work engraved in the new pavement that includes the names of the then three Lancaster Gate Ward Councillors namely: Simon, Susie Burbridge and me.

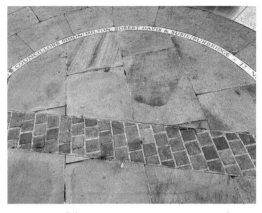

Part of the Lancaster Gate war memorial.

Penguins

In May 2011, I was invited by the Director General of London Zoo to formally open the new penguin pool (known as 'Penguin Beach'), having a few years earlier given planning permission for it. This replaced the Grade 1 listed Lubetkin pool opened in 1934 but nowadays deemed inappropriate to house penguins.

Penguin Beach is great fun and the glass walls on one side allow you to see the penguins swimming under the water.

I am proud that there is a plaque by the keepers' hut that states that I opened it. Many friends visiting with their families have sent me photos of their children with the plaque.

Penguin Beach at London Zoo.

Blandford Street

I had been involved with the planning process to knock down an old electricity depot in Blandford Street, Marylebone, and replace it with a block of flats comprising both private flats and social housing. As part of the planning consent, the developer was required to add an art installation on the exterior of the building. They chose artist Ron Haselden to design it and in March 2008, I was asked to unveil the resultant lighting scheme that reflected the Tyburn River that used to run through Marylebone.

The Blandford Street plaque.

This was commemorated with a plaque adjacent to the entrance to the flats explaining that I had unveiled the new art work.

The Brighter Subway and Loo Initiatives

One of my ideas as part of the Westminster Initiative (discussed earlier in this book), was the Brighter Subway Initiative, where I brightened up our grim looking underpasses with bright lighting, murals and freshly painted walls and new flooring. The first one was at Cockspur Street where the underpass leads to Charing Cross Underground Station. The walls are now adorned with large murals of the history of the area and near the entrance into the station itself, I unveiled a plaque which confirms that I opened this new Brighter Subway as part of my 'Brighter Subway Initiative'.

The drawing of 'RD NW1'.

A second refurbished underpass at Hyde Park Corner also had a similar plaque with my name on but, several years later, that underpass was filled in as part of a road widening scheme around Hyde Park Corner and my plaque buried like Tutankhamun for archaeologists to find in hundreds of years' time.

A similar scheme to my Brighter Subway Initiative was my Brighter Loo Initiative which brightened up our public conveniences. The walls would be adorned with murals of the area and, when I opened the refurbished toilets in Marylebone Road (opposite Madame Tussauds), the artist revealed that one of the murals he had painted was of a car with the number plate 'RD NW1', the toilet being in the postcode NW1 and the RD of course being my initials.

The artist presented me with a framed drawing which hangs on my wall at home.

Jubilee Walkway Trust

Through my chairmanship of the council's Planning and Transportation Committee in the mid-1990s, I met and became friendly with the famous Royal biographer Hugo Vickers, then the chairman of the Civic Society. As well as writing some absorbing biographies, he also chaired the Jubilee Walkway Trust which commemorated the Queen's Golden Jubilee with a series of large plaques situated near famous views. Each one depicts an engraving of the view from the plaque with descriptions of all the buildings and statues that can be seen, allowing visitors to understand more about the views they are looking at.

The Trafalgar Square Jubilee Walkway Trust plaque.

Hugo would ask famous people associated with London as well as members of the Royal Family to unveil them. They were so successful that he continued them well after the Jubilee ended. During my mayoral year, I had attended the unveiling by Nelson Mandela of a plaque on the east side of Trafalgar Square and a few years later one by The Queen outside Westminster Abbey. It was therefore a great honour when Hugo invited me to unveil a new one on the south side of Trafalgar Square under the nose of the other Nelson (Lord Nelson) looking down Whitehall to Parliament and Big Ben. If you are ever there, you can see the plaque with my name clearly marked confirming my role in its unveiling.

The Hippodrome

The Hippodrome is a beautiful Frank Matcham Theatre in Charing Cross Road. Matcham was a renowned architect who specialised in theatres and many West End theatres were designed by him. The Hippodrome was originally built in 1900, to house a circus style of show with elephants and other large animals entering the arena from a slide running down from the top of the dress circle.

It soon became a music hall venue and then in the early 1960s 'the Talk of the Town', a dinner show and cabaret that was

The London Hippodrome.

televised live on a Saturday night. Many famous artists appeared there including Judy Garland, Sammy Davis Jr, Diana Ross and the Supremes to name a few.

In 1983, shortly after I became a councillor, Peter Stringfellow turned it into a nightclub and I was one of several councillors invited to the first night party. But after he closed it in 2005, when the police objected to his licence, it was used for various purposes until Simon Thomas and his father, Jimmy, bought it in 2009. They had visions of turning it in to a first-class casino and, in doing so, restoring the Matcham Theatre to its early 20th century grandeur.

They spent millions of pounds on the décor ensuring that the alterations necessary to turn it into a casino were all reversible, so that one day, if the casino ever vacated the site, it could easily be converted back into a live theatre. He also turned the stage itself into a cabaret room known as the Matcham Theatre where he originally put on daily cabaret style performances. However, in 2018 he reconfigured the theatre and introduced a permanent show, a raunchy all-male dance review called 'Magic Mike' based on the film of the same name.

I first met Simon in late 2011, while he was carrying out the conversion works. He was having problems with the planning officers on a number of relatively minor issues but he was getting nowhere so he had asked to see me. I helped him through the issues and I was impressed with what he was trying to achieve. I was given a tour of the building on several occasions and then delighted when he asked me to co-open the casino when everything was complete and he wanted a grand launch. It then transpired that my co-opener was to be the Mayor of London, Boris Johnson (our current Prime Minister).

Simon was insistent that we would jointly open the casino. But of course, with all the national press there and after a few photographs with Simon, Boris and me, the photographers asked Simon and I to move aside so they could take a photo of Boris alone. I know my place and knew that the photos in all the papers the next day would be of just Boris.

One photograph was taken around a roulette table and after I was asked to move aside yet again, one of the photographers shouted to Boris to place all the chips that had been placed in front of him on the number ten! Boris refused.

Boris and I unveil the plaque with Simon Thomas behind us.

But I was rewarded, as after the photo call, Simon asked us both to unveil a plaque at the entrance of the venue and on that plaque, it clearly states that the casino was opened in July 2012 by 'Boris Johnson, Mayor of London, and Councillor Robert Davis, Deputy Leader of Westminster Council'. The plaque is still there and whenever I visit, Simon always assures me that it is regularly polished.

Simon Thomas has been a been a great supporter of the Sir Simon Milton Foundation, allowing us to host fundraising events in his theatre and a few years ago accepted our offer to become a trustee.

356

Chapter 32

Mallorca

Anyone who knows me knows how special Mallorca is to me.

Childhood Visits

I started going to Mallorca during my childhood for family holidays. We always stayed in the same hotel, the Melia Victoria, on the sea front in Palma. It was the best hotel on the island in those days.

This was the early 1970s and one year, very proud of the long knee-length sleeveless jacket that my mother had bought for me, I wore it with pride one evening for dinner in the hotel. Men wearing long sleeveless jackets down to their knees was very fashionable at that time. But someone my father knew was also staying in the hotel and remarked to my parents later that evening that he thought their two daughters were very well behaved. My sister thought this immensely funny and I do not think she let me forget it for many years. I certainly never wore that jacket again!

Jackets in Mallorca seem to be very much part of my story. A few years later, my parents bought me a mock-leather jacket from a trendy menswear shop in Notting Hall Gate. Now that I think about it, it was probably quite cheap and definitely not real leather or anything close to it, but it did look trendy and I was very proud of it. I would not take it off. I insisted I wore it to travel to Palma for our two weeks away and, once settled in the hotel, despite the very hot weather, with everyone just wearing a thin t-shirt, I insisted on wearing a long-sleeved shirt with my faux leather jacket. My parents thought I was mad. Again, this episode would stay with me for many years with stories frequently told of Robert and his leather jacket.

After several years of return visits, my family started trying other places including Marbella and Milano Marittima in eastern Italy. Eventually, I stopped holidaying with my parents and my next visit to Mallorca was not until the early 1990s when I was in my thirties.

Visiting with Simon

Simon and I decided to go to Mallorca for our Easter holidays and to stay inland at the 5-star Son Vida Hotel. But the trip was disastrous. First, we both forgot to take our driving licences, so our attempts to hire a car failed. As the hotel was several miles from Palma and even further from the coast, we found ourselves marooned at the hotel as taxis into town were expensive and we were both still living on a budget. Then there was the weather. It poured most days and when it was not raining, it was cold and cloudy. Thinking we were headed for the sun, we only took summer clothes, t-shirts, shorts and swimwear. We had brought nothing warm and the only relatively warm clothes had to be worn every day.

We did not visit again until my mayoral year. Simon's mother, Ruth, and her husband, Ronald, had owned a flat in the south of France, half way between Antibes and Juan-Les-Pins but had sold it to spend their holidays travelling around Europe on their boat. But after a transient period visiting the hot spots of the Med, they had paid a visit to Mallorca, loved it and decided to leave the boat there and to visit regularly while living on the boat.

Holidays with Ronald and Ruth

Then in 1996, Ruth and Ronald decided to buy a flat just outside Palma, the capital of Mallorca. Simon and I spent the following Christmas staying with them in their new flat. I needed a break from my extremely busy life as Lord Mayor as did Simon. We were picked up by Ruth at the airport and driven back to see the flat for the first time. It was stunning. Directly overlooking the sea, we could hear the lapping of the sea against the rocks from our bedroom window. A large veranda allowed us to sunbathe privately and below us was a beautiful pool for swimming.

Ruth told us that we were going to spend Christmas Day with some friends of theirs. She said I would not know them but they were friends from London who she had bumped into at the airport and who had invited us all over for Christmas lunch. She assured me that I would like them. I was a little unsure, as I was concerned that I would feel uncomfortable with people I did not know.

As usual when visiting someone I had never met before, I was a little nervous as we walked into their lobby and rang the bell. After a pregnant pause and hearing footsteps,

Ronald, Ruth, Simon and me in Mallorca.

358

the door opened and standing there, apron on and a bottle of wine in one hand, was my mother's best friend, Diana Kutner. What a surprise. It turned out that Ruth knew the connection and thought it would be a nice surprise for me if she did not tell me beforehand. We had a great lunch and afterwards I phoned my Mum back in London to tell her and she spoke to everyone by phone.

We loved Ruth and Ronald's flat and Mallorca too and would return three or four times a year. Bank Holidays, Christmas (six years running at one stage) and for long weekends at other times, we made it our unofficial second home. Simon loved it too, particularly because his mother spoilt him. She would fill the fridge with goodies from ice cream cakes to special desserts. The bonbon dishes around the living room would be filled with all kinds of sweets. Ronald always told us how much he enjoyed our stays, because Ruth bought in food he was normally forbidden to eat.

Meanwhile, returning to Mallorca, with Ronald fully retired, Ruth and Ronald virtually moved there full time, eventually taking up formal residency. They sold their central London flat and bought a smaller flat in Stanmore near to Luton Airport for regular visits to see family. Simon and I continued to visit and in doing so, started to explore the island. Before my father died, he would often join us with his friend Lilah, although they would stay at nearby hotels.

Simon's Health

Going back to 1990, Simon was not feeling well one day and so went to see his doctor who suggested a series of blood tests. The cause of Simon's illness that day was not serious but the blood tests revealed Simon had too many white blood cells and this was an indication that he had leukaemia. To be precise, he was diagnosed with Chronic Lymphocytic Leukaemia otherwise known as CLL.

This was a shock to Simon and me, but the doctor assured Simon that as he had no current symptoms, he need not worry too much at that time but would be put on certain mild medication to keep it under control.

A few years later the consultant he was under explained that now would be a good time for Simon to have a bone marrow transplant to give him a chance of a longer life. Having the transplant at a time when Simon was perfectly healthy was the best course, rather than wait until he became ill and was too unwell to undertake the treatment without great risks. Bravely, Simon decided in the summer of 1998, to step down from being chief executive of his company APCO UK and take a sabbatical in order to undergo the transplant.

The procedure itself involved a course of chemotherapy followed by two weeks of intensive radiation with the purpose of killing Simon's bone marrow. Without bone marrow, Simon lost all immunity and became neutropenic. As soon as he finished the radiation, he was admitted into University College Hospital in central London where he was placed in semi-isolation. When Simon's mother, sister and I visited, we had to wear full protective clothing and masks. The extensive chemo and radiation resulted in every external soft tissue on Simon's body becoming subject to sores and, because he had lost his appetite, he soon lost a lot of weight as well as most of his hair.

In the meanwhile, his sister was a good match and so offered to be his donor. The procedure to remove some of Lisa's bone marrow was probably more painful for her than for Simon with the transplanting of the bone marrow into Simon, which was just like a normal blood transfusion.

It took Simon over six months to recover his health but, before he did, he suffered a few setbacks. On one occasion, he caught pneumonia and had to spend several days in intensive care with the result that it scarred his lungs, which his consultant told him meant that he had the lungs of an eighty-year-old despite him being in his late thirties.

But he did return to relatively full health and a normal life. However, he never recovered full immunity. At least once a year he would catch a cold but, unlike anyone else, he would find it difficult to shrug it off and after a week of trying to do so, would end up in hospital in need of intravenous antibiotics. After a further week in hospital he would recover and return to work and his political career. He did, however, find it difficult running or walking upstairs due to the poor state of his lungs. Despite this, it was after his transplant that he went on to become Leader of Westminster Council, knighted for his services to local government, elected chairman of the Local Government Association and appointed senior Deputy Mayor and Chief of Staff to the Mayor of London, Boris Johnson.

Simon Has an Idea

In January 2011, some thirteen years after his transplant, Simon started struggling more than usual with his breathing. The winter weather was very bad that year resulting in some very cold mornings. Simon would be out of breath just walking from our front door to his car parked nearby. This concerned us and so he arranged an appointment with his specialist.

The consultant checked Simon out and told us he was concerned about Simon's lungs. Of course, Simon knew they had been damaged following the effect of radiation prior to the transplant and the damage from the pneumonia he suffered, but we had assumed that his lungs had not got worse. The consultant indicated that he feared they had and so decided that he would continue to keep an eye on Simon and review the situation in a few weeks after further tests.

Simon had noticed that in warmer weather his breathing improved. So, a few days later, Simon told me that he wanted us to buy a flat in Mallorca, so that when it got very cold in London and his breathing started to deteriorate, we could fly there and work remotely.

My initial reaction was negative. I told him that I did not want to own my own flat with all the responsibilities that went with that. More particularly, I did not want to make my own bed nor make my own breakfast! When on holiday, I enjoyed being pampered in a five-star hotel. But if Simon wanted to fly to Mallorca and search for a flat, I would not stop him.

Ruth was in heaven, thinking Simon would soon be living near to her. She and Ronald did not wait twenty-four hours before rushing off to estate agents to find the perfect flat or two.

With six or seven to see, they suggested we fly out as soon as possible before any of those flats they had found were sold. Simon was free the following weekend, but I had to host a London Mayors' Association event. We agreed that he would fly out alone and view the properties with Ruth and Ronald. He took my camera with him to take photos and videos of the properties he liked. The problem was that he was useless with cameras and I had to spend some time teaching him how to use it.

Bendinat

To take the story further, we have to go back about two years. Ruth and Ronald had sold their original flat in Mallorca and were looking for a new one. They were living in a beautiful flat in Port d'Andratx on the west coast of the island thirty minutes from Palma. Ronald had spent a lot of time and money renovating the flat to a high standard. It was situated half way up a tall hill, with a large wraparound terrace with stunning views of the port, and Simon and I loved this flat. But Ruth missed the proximity to Palma and all her local shops and friends. Ronald wanted to test the market and so put the property up for sale and found a buyer almost immediately at the asking price. They accepted the offer and were now looking for somewhere to move to.

They were recommended a development in Bendinat. This was on a hill behind the resort of Illetas, just west of Palma. They were shown one of the penthouse flats with a large roof terrace. It too had amazing views and seemed perfect, although needing quite a lot of money spent on it to bring it up to standard. They enquired about the price. It was well over their budget, so they made an offer. This was refused by the vendor, the daughter of the couple who had owned it. She was acting as their executor, as both had recently died. She was adamant that she would not accept anything less than the asking price.

Disappointed, Ronald and Ruth heard that another flat in the development was on the market. The development comprised three blocks surrounding a communal swimming pool with amazing views across the Bay of Palma.

The original flat was in Block Three (which comprised twelve flats). Blocks One and Two had eight flats in each. The flat they were now shown was on the second floor of Block Two and they loved it. And before long they were moving in.

Moving back to Simon's trip to find a flat for us, the day before Simon was arriving, Ruth heard from Jose-Louis, the caretaker of her development, that the original penthouse they had seen a couple of years earlier was still on the market. It seems that after two years the vendor had not been able to find a buyer at the price she had originally sought and had been let down by three buyers, who had all commenced legal negotiations but then pulled out before exchanging contracts. She was now pretty keen to sell and was prepared to lower the price for a quick sale. So, this was added to the itinerary.

Simon returned to London very excited. He had found the flat of his dreams. It turned out to be the flat in Ruth's development and the one that Ruth had wanted to buy two years earlier. Nothing else he saw in our price range came anywhere near it.

The flat needed to be decorated, a new kitchen installed and numerous other changes made. Ronald was now experienced in refurbishing flats, as he had successfully renovated the flat in Port d'Andratx and more recently their current flat in the same Bendinat development as the flat Simon had chosen. He was happy to mastermind the refurbishment works required and supervise them, find the builders and search on our behalf for furniture. The flat comprised a master bedroom and en suite bathroom with a floor-to-ceiling window leading on to the balcony.

In addition, there were two other bedrooms and a main bathroom to serve the other bedrooms. There was also a guest toilet in the main hall and a large living room with floor-to-ceiling plate glass windows along one wall facing onto a generously sized balcony looking out to sea. A small kitchen had two doors, one into the living room and one into the hall. Off the kitchen was a utility room for a washing machine and separate tumble dryer.

From the balcony, one looked down a valley with trees on both sides and beneath us in the distance, the Bay of Palma. On the other side of the Bay and the vast expanse of blue sea was the resort of Arenal and the east of the island.

On one side of the balcony was a metal spiral staircase leading to a private sun terrace that covered the whole of the roof of the flat. This was in poor condition with broken floor tiles and littered with a number of satellite dishes serving this and several other flats. But it had great potential.

I watched the videos Simon had taken and studied numerous photos of the flat as well as those of the other flats he had seen and I agreed that the Bendinat flat looked the most promising. I started to think that maybe Simon was right (as he nearly always was) and so I said I would love to see it for myself. We arranged to travel to Mallorca a week later to visit the flat together.

Although not in a wonderful state of repair, I fell in love with it the moment I saw it and knew this was for us. I had already started to think that owning our own flat in Mallorca would be lovely and seeing both the flat itself and the amazing views were deal makers.

Simon took control of the negotiations. We knew the vendor was now desperate to sell, having had the flat on the market unsuccessfully for over two years and having been let down by several buyers, so we made a low offer. She asked for twenty-four hours to think about it and then came back the following day to say that she would accept our offer but only on the condition that we exchanged within seven days. We agreed but said that we needed a two-month delay for completion so that we could raise the capital needed. We were going to pay cash using money from the sale of Simon's flat in London, when he moved in with me on our marriage and from my own savings. Our savings had been invested in the stock market and we needed the time to arrange the sale of sufficient investments to fund the purchase. She agreed to this and we instructed local lawyers recommended by Ronald.

The view from the apartment in Bendinat across the Bay of Palma.

We achieved the deadline for exchange and Ronald was subsequently instructed to employ builders so that we could start work as soon as completion had taken place.

Simon was not known for taking responsibility for household matters. He usually left that to me. I would arrange builders, decorators and repairs to our London flat. I would arrange the cleaning, the washing and even the shopping. But on this project, Simon was excited and took control. He started liaising with Ronald and Ruth about furniture, about the colour schemes as well as all the other changes proposed to the flat. Of course, he consulted me before any decision was taken but he took the lead and coordinated everything. In fact, his colleague Ann Sindall (Boris's private personal assistant, whose desk was situated one side of the Mayor's office door with Simon's desk on the other side – the gate keepers) later told me that all Simon talked about was the Mallorcan flat and how he spent every spare moment on the phone or internet making plans. She had never seen him so excited about a project before.

Completion: The End and the Beginning

At the end of March, I took the London Mayors' Association on our annual civic foreign trip, this time to Malta. I left early on the Thursday morning and said goodbye to Simon, who was still half asleep. He was fine. It appears that on the Friday, Simon was due to be interviewed for the BBC's *Politics Show*. Although broadcast on the Sunday morning, it was recorded on the Friday afternoon at Broadcasting House in Portland Place.

Simon drove there and managed to park nearby on a meter. But he subsequently told me that he really struggled walking just a few yards to the studio. He was totally out of breath, even though it was all flat with no steps or gradient. He knew something was wrong. Later that day he started feeling worse and in fact over the weekend put himself to bed. I arrived back on the Sunday night and despite calling him several times over the weekend, Simon never told me how unwell he was feeling.

When I woke up on Monday morning, Simon had developed flu-like symptoms and was feeling terrible. In addition, his breathing had got more difficult even when he wasn't walking. Simon told me he wanted to be admitted to hospital and so I arranged for our doctor Cyril Nemeth to arrange his admittance into the London Clinic. I drove him there and once settled in his room, he was attended not only by the in-house doctors but also by the various specialists who had been looking after him since his bone marrow transplant.

His chest consultant was worried about the breathing and suggested that he go on oxygen. He was already on intravenous antibiotics to address the flu, but this was more serious. The consultant advised that Simon should remain on oxygen even after he returned home. Arrangements were therefore made for oxygen canisters to be delivered to the flat with the necessary pipework. Simon also arranged for oxygen canisters to be delivered to City Hall so that he could use them there too, when he returned to work.

By the following weekend, the flu symptoms had gone and Simon was able to return home but wearing the oxygen mask all the time. He was given a small canister for travelling but would be connected to the large canister when at home (or in the office).

Ruth had returned to London to help me look after Simon. But we had a problem. Completion of the purchase of the Mallorcan flat was due the following Thursday. Under Spanish law, the purchasers have to attend (in person) a completion meeting where the money is handed over and various documents executed before a Notary Public. The necessary cash had been released and sent to our Spanish lawyer but there was no way Simon could travel to Mallorca to attend in person and I did not want to leave him.

We were advised to appoint Ruth to act on behalf of both us under a power of attorney. The Spanish lawyer sent us the necessary documents by email but the power of attorney had to be executed before a British Notary Public. Unfortunately, there are very few of them in London. But the brother-in-law of a friend of mine was one. As Simon was not fit enough to leave the flat, I had to persuade the Notary to come to our flat. He was happy to do so, the documents were executed and Ruth returned to Mallorca for 48 hours to attend the completion meeting on our behalf.

While she was in Mallorca attending the completion meeting, Simon started to deteriorate. Ruth was due back on the Friday morning, but during the previous night Simon was taken quite ill. It appeared to me like a minor heart attack but I was no doctor. Our doctor Cyril arrived early the next morning and arranged for Simon to be readmitted to the London Clinic immediately. The ambulance service could not guarantee picking him up for some time, so Cyril arranged for a private ambulance. Simon went off in the ambulance and I followed in my car.

Within minutes of our arrival at the hospital, Simon was whisked off to his room with me following with a suitcase of clothes and other things that Simon would want, including a number of Sudoku books, which he was hooked on.

Ruth got back from Mallorca having completed the purchase of the flat and joined me at the hospital.

A number of doctors came to see him and expressed concern. He had indeed suffered a minor heart attack earlier that morning. However, we left him that Friday night, resting and appearing stable.

Simon in his chair in our London home doing his Sudoku.

The next morning, Ruth and I arrived quite early but it appears that overnight Simon had deteriorated. At about lunchtime, the nurse told us they were transferring him to the Intensive Care Unit as this would enable him to receive better care around the clock. We were assured that this was just to support him and nothing sinister. I accepted this. But as he left the room, the nurse took off his wedding ring and gave it to me for safe keeping, explaining that it was best if he didn't wear jewellery in the IC unit. I immediately thought this was a bad omen.

During the day, Simon's breathing got worse and so they decided to put him on a ventilator. But to do so, they had to sedate him. While we were waiting for them to set this up, Boris arrived and sat with us, chatting to Simon for about half an hour before we were all asked to leave to enable the machine to be fitted. Ruth and I returned and sat with him until late that night, when it was suggested that we go home to sleep and return the next morning.

At this stage, I was still confident that while Simon was certainly unwell, he would eventually recover. He had been ill so many times since his transplant and yet always recovered and went on to achieve great success.

Simon's leadership of Westminster Council, his knighthood, his election as chairman of the Local Government Association and his appointment as Chief of Staff to the Mayor of London and senior Deputy Mayor of London all happened after his transplant and after numerous hospitalisations. Why would this time be any different?

On the Sunday, Ruth and Simon's sister Lisa sat with me by his bedside all day and evening. He was more stable but heavily sedated and so not able to talk to us. Whether he could hear us, I will never know. We talked to him but got no response. We asked the nurses if we should sit with him all night but they insisted we return home to have a good night's sleep but if anything changed, they would ring me. We reluctantly went home.

I could not sleep despite being very tired. But eventually I must have fallen asleep, as I was woken suddenly at 3.30 am by the phone ringing. I answered it. It was the news I feared. Simon had had a second heart attack and I was advised to get to the hospital as soon as I could. I phoned Ruth and woke her up to tell her. I got to the hospital in about twenty minutes and Ruth and Lisa arrived shortly after. After Ronald parked the car, he joined us.

Simon was surrounded by nurses and doctors including the lead consultant. They were extremely concerned but despite a further heart attack just before we arrived, he had stabilised and by the morning was lying asleep, in remission. The consultant took me aside and explained that they were doing what they could but Simon had now developed pneumonia and despite pumping into him numerous drugs, he was not responding and in fact his body was not coping at all well. He told me to prepare for the worst.

Until then, I never really thought he would die. I just had this instinctive feeling that he would recover and life would return to normal as it had done on so many previous occasions. How wrong I was.

We stayed with him all day. During the late afternoon, I received a call that Boris was on his way. I had been updating Boris regularly by phone as to what was happening. Boris arrived at about 6 pm and I met him at reception and, accompanied by two beefy bodyguards the hospital thought necessary, we walked along the corridors to the IC unit and Boris sat down with Ruth, Lisa and me.

Boris started telling us funny stories and while we laughed, Simon appeared to give us a slight smile, or so we thought. Boris and Simon had been disagreeing over the potential sacking of a particular senior adviser to the Mayor. Simon thought the adviser useless and wanted Boris to sack him. Boris hated sacking his staff and so had been sitting on the decision. Boris at one stage turned to Simon and told a sleeping Simon that if he woke up and got better, on his return to City Hall, Boris would immediately sack the adviser. He kept saying 'I promise, I promise'.

Boris, Ruth, Lisa and I sat there as the minutes passed. Simon was clearly slipping away and the nurses were surrounding him, monitoring him continually with the senior doctor on duty-giving orders. It was Monday 11th April 2011 and at 7.45 pm Simon passed away.

Boris, Lisa, Ruth and I all hugged each other and we all wept a few tears. They moved into the adjoining family room leaving me alone with Simon for a few minutes. Just the two of us, alone together for the last time. My whole world, my whole life, had just disintegrated. I was devastated. I thought I was in a dream and I would wake up and life would be normal again.

Boris stayed with us for a further half hour, comforting us all and repeatedly telling us how he adored Simon and how he did not know how he would cope without Simon at his side.

The News

News of Simon's death dominated the local news on all the TV channels the following morning and he was talked about on LBC throughout the day. The national papers all covered the story with several columnists saying really lovely things about Simon.

All the major papers published lengthy obituaries. Simon's closest friend, Dean Godson (now Lord Godson), who had been at St Paul's and Caius with Simon had been the lead obituaries writer for *The Telegraph*.

He told me that it was important that he wrote the authorised obituary (with help from me as someone who knew Simon well) for *The Telegraph* and published it immediately, as all the other papers would use the first one to appear in print as a reference. Dean wrote an amazing piece that contained statements that were subsequently repeated by many other publications over the months that followed.

The Funeral

The funeral was to take place on the Wednesday. I arranged for a double plot at the cemetery in Edgwarebury Lane in Edgware. I wanted to be buried beside him. Our colleague and friend, Alan Bradley, was a member of our Synagogue's burial committee and arranged for the grave to be in the front row of the cemetery, visible to everyone visiting. We could not have asked for a more prominent position for our final resting place.

Over four hundred people attended the funeral. Those attending included not only Boris and his entire City Hall team, but Sir Cameron Mackintosh, the chairman of the national Conservative Party, the Secretary of State for Local Government, numerous members of both Parliaments, the Lord Mayor of Westminster, the Mayor of Barnet (where the cemetery was situated), Sir Stuart Lipton, Gerald and Gail Ronson and many more friends, relatives and colleagues. There were even press photographers at the gates of the cemetery taking photos but showing respect by not entering the cemetery itself.

In the Jewish religion, when someone dies, the immediate relatives being the parents, siblings, spouse and children 'sit shiva'. This is the way that Jews mourn the departed. The immediate family sit on special low chairs (loaned by the synagogue) in a close relative's home and relatives and friends visit during the day and particularly between 7.30 pm and 9 pm to pay their respects. At 8 pm prayers are said, led by a rabbi.

I hosted the shiva in my flat and while religious Jews tend to sit shiva for seven days, many less religious people, like my family and me, sit for just two or three days. Although I only sat shiva for my parents and my sister for three days each, I decided to sit shiva for Simon for the full seven days, as I could not bear the idea of being alone in the flat and wanted to be surrounded by friends and relatives for as long as possible. And it worked. The flat was crammed each day and evening with people coming to pay their respects and to comfort me, Ruth and Lisa.

For me, it was like living in a nightmare. I could not quite believe Simon would not just walk back into the flat or, in TV series *Dallas*-style, walk out of the shower. I felt I was walking around in a cloud and it was only the friends and family who spent most of the days in that first week comforting me who enabled me to cope. I lost my appetite and just felt numb. Anyone who has lost their life partner will know exactly how I felt.

Mallorca or Not?

During the shiva, Ronald took me aside and reminded me that the builders were due to start work on the flat in Mallorca the following Monday. He told me that he assumed that I would want to sell the flat now that circumstances had changed and so, with my say-so, he would cancel the builders. I immediately said that was not the case. I wanted to keep it. Everything good in my life had evaporated overnight and I needed something positive to look forward to.

But that night, lying awake in bed, while confident that I had made the right decision, I was worried about whether I could afford it. We had been two adults with two incomes and one flat. Now, I was one adult with one income with two flats. Mortgages were not an issue. I had paid off the mortgage on my London flat from my inheritance when my father died and Simon and I had bought Mallorca without the need for a mortgage with investments we owned (and sold). I took a positive view and told myself I would manage. It was the second best decision I took (that is, after agreeing to marry Simon).

Moving In

Over the next few weeks, I liaised with Ronald on finishing the building works and choosing furniture, fixtures and fittings and then in late April, I flew to Mallorca immediately after watching the Royal Wedding (William and Kate's) on TV, to stay with Ronald and Ruth to inspect the works. While there, we used the opportunity to go shopping for items such as beds, pillow cases and pictures for the walls.

By the late May Bank Holiday, the flat was ready to move into and so I flew to Mallorca for a ten-day holiday. I stayed the first two nights with Ronald and Ruth while I finalised everything in the flat, cleaning it and getting it ready to move into. Then on the third night, I stayed in the flat for the first time. It was an amazing experience and yet tinged with the sadness, as I should have been sharing that first night with Simon.

A couple of days later, I collected my two friends Steve Summers and Louise Hyams from the airport and they became my first guests, staying with me for a week.

Regular Visits

I fell in love with Mallorca and for the next few years, I would go as often as I could, including two weeks at the beginning of August and a week over the August Bank holiday weekend. As soon as I retired from my legal practice in 2015, I started going more regularly and for longer periods as I could do much of my council work from Mallorca. Once I had stood down as Deputy Leader, I started spending even more time there and by 2019 I was spending just under six months a year there, going back and forth regularly and spending ten weeks there from early July to mid-September and then, a month at Christmas. Brexit has now changed that and has limited the time I can spend in Mallorca. But I will make the most of the days I am allowed.

Friends

I have made many friends in Mallorca, several of whom are local Spanish residents on the island. This includes Javier Moreno Quintero, who I met through another friend in the summer of 2014. Javi works for the Council of Mallorca as a sign language interpreter and we always spend time together when I am in Mallorca. He has got to know many of my friends and he has been to stay with me in London about three or four times.

Many friends have holiday homes on the island and I always arrange to meet them when we are there at the same time. They include my former colleague from Westminster Michael Brahams and his wife Stephanie who live very close by in Illetas, Jonathan and Nadine Horne (friends of my late sister) who have a flat in Santa Ponca, John and June Chichester who have a beautiful

Javi and I in London.

home in the mountains just outside Soller, Lisa Ronson and her husband Paul Althasen who have a stunning modern house in Deia, Bob Bone (the Director of the London Parade)

Laura Stadler, Jess Conrad and his wife and me.

and his wife Geri who have a home in Port d'Andratx, and Neil and Gill Dunford with their flat with stunning views directly over the ocean, in nearby San Agustí.

One evening, Ruth and Ronald invited me to join them at a restaurant in Port d'Andratx with some of their friends. I was seated next to a lady called Laura Stadler. Laura was quite well known on the island as she wrote a fortnightly column in the daily English newspaper, *Majorca Daily Bulletin*. We did not stop talking all night and Laura and her husband Michael have since become good friends of mine.

Over several dinners in her beautiful apartment overlooking Puerto Portals, Laura has in turn introduced me to many of her own friends including the famous pop

369

and film star of the 1960s Jess Conrad and the iconic rock star Suzi Quatro.

I have a couple of American friends, Robin and Robyn Engel from Wisconsin. A few years ago, I was chatting to them in London and the subject of the conversation turned to Mallorca.

They told me that they were going to Mallorca later that year. I asked them why they would travel all the way from Wisconsin to Europe and of all the places in Europe, choose to stay in Mallorca rather than on the mainland. They told me they

With Susi Quatro in Mallorca.

were fans of a series of books about life on the island written by a local British resident, Anna Nicholas. They asked me whether I knew her and could arrange a meeting as they were such great fans of hers. I told them that I had heard of her because she wrote a weekly column in the *Majorca Daily Bulletin*, but I did not know her personally.

Then about a year later, I was chatting via email to Michael Gray, the former Chief Executive of the Hyatt Hotel Group in the UK. At the end of my email, I signed off 'Robert in sunny Mallorca' as I frequently do. Michael responded, advising me that he was having

In my favourite café Cappuccino in Mallorca reading the Majorca Daily Bulletin *with a photo of the editor and me on the front page.*

lunch that day with Anna Nicholas, a friend of his who lived in Mallorca and wrote books about the island. I responded, saying I knew of her. He told me that he would tell her all about me and suggest she contact me so we could meet up in Mallorca.

Within weeks, Anna and I not only met up for lunch but became friends and I now regularly see her and her husband Alan when I am on the Island.

Once I got to know Anna, I told her about her American fans and she agreed to meet them on their next visit. This she did and the Engels were delighted.

Reflections

Mallorca is now part of me and I love spending half my life there and when I am there, I think of Simon and our life together, even though he never actually lived with me there.

Chapter 33

Remembering Simon

We were honoured when the Dean of Westminster Dr John Hall attended Simon's shiva to pay his respects. In conversation with Ruth and me, John suggested that we hold a memorial service for Simon in Westminster Abbey. We were rather taken aback as we had never thought of that as an option. In particular, Simon was Jewish and the Abbey was a Christian place of worship. Ruth and I looked at each other and I turned to John and thanked him for the honour and asked if we could give it some thought, but in theory we loved the idea. John emphasised that he was conscious of Simon's religion and he would ensure that the service reflected this. He also added that it was a rare honour for someone's life to be remembered by a service in the Abbey itself. Most politicians including former members of the government and members of both Houses of Parliament had their memorial service in the neighbouring smaller sister church of St Margaret's, Westminster. The only two other people whose lives had been remembered by memorial services in the Abbey that year were Dame Joan Sutherland (the world-famous soprano) and the former Lord Chief Justice, Lord Bingham of Cornhill.

After some family discussions, we decided to accept John Hall's offer, despite the issue that a 'nice Jewish boy' would have his life celebrated in a Christian church, albeit the country's most important one, the scene of coronations and Royal marriages and funerals. It was such a great honour and a tribute to Simon that we had to accept. However, John reassured us that we could involve a rabbi of our choice in putting together the service.

We agreed a date, Monday 31st October 2011, which would give us enough time to organise the event. We needed to fill the Abbey with two thousand guests and so Lisa, Ruth and I started drafting an invitation list. We chose a Monday lunchtime for the service, as this was usually a quiet day and so there would not be much competition and by holding it at noon, those attending could take a long lunch break from work and would not need to take off the afternoon or morning to attend.

The Abbey were extremely helpful and over the summer, Ruth, Lisa and I attended a planning meeting with the dean, the minor canon responsible for the service and various other heads of departments including those from the Protocol and Press departments. Lisa wanted to seek support and advice from the rabbi of their childhood synagogue. He had retired, so Lisa spoke to his son, also a rabbi, and Rabbi Stephen Katz agreed to attend the planning meeting at the Abbey to make suggestions and advise the family.

With a long guest list prepared, we arranged printed invitations and Lisa and I spent every night for a whole week stuffing addressed envelopes with the invitation and sticking on hundreds of stamps. The Abbey placed an official notice in the Court Circular of both *The Times* and *The Telegraph*, inviting anyone who wanted to attend to apply through the Abbey.

As soon as the applications for tickets started arriving, we knew we would get a full house. Most of those applying were distinguished members of British society and that truly reflected the respect that Simon was held in.

Our minds then turned to organising a reception for after the service. We had to offer people a drink and a light lunch. Many would be coming from far and wide, with several relatives and friends coming from Mallorca, from the United States and from other parts of the UK. We needed to find a venue close to the Abbey without costing a fortune.

Through Boris, Simon knew the owner of the venue at the top of Millbank Tower, Justin Etzin of 'Altitude'. Simon was going to be fifty years old on 2nd October 2011 and had been planning a large birthday party. He had made contact with Justin and they had arranged for the party to be held at the top of Millbank Tower, half a mile along the river from the Abbey, in one of Altitude's function rooms. Of course, I had called Justin to cancel the birthday party after Simon's death.

But why not use that same venue. Not only was it close to the Abbey but it would also be poignant in being a sort of party celebrating his life rather than his half century. Justin was happy to change the date and time on similar terms but the room that Simon had booked for his party was already in use that day, so he offered to allow us to use another function suite he operated on the first floor. To be honest, it made no difference, as most guests would be interested in meeting and chatting with each other and not looking out of the windows at the magnificent views of the city from the top of Millbank Tower.

The acceptances and applications for tickets just flowed in and by the date of the service, we knew we would fill the Abbey. We then had to do a seating plan. This would be difficult! Just like a 2,000-piece jigsaw. How do you ensure you do not upset too many of the most important people in the country, from the Deputy Speaker, Cabinet Ministers, Ambassadors and a whole chain gang of London Mayors? Many senior members of Her Majesty's Opposition and Shadow Cabinet had indicated a wish to attend, which showed the cross-party respect that people held for Simon.

There was also the entire membership of Westminster Council with officers from most departments, the membership of the Mayor of

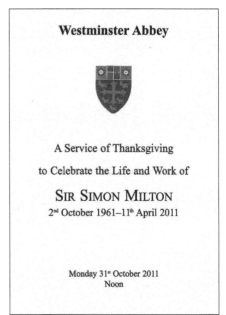

Westminster Abbey

A Service of Thanksgiving

to Celebrate the Life and Work of

SIR SIMON MILTON

2nd October 1961–11th April 2011

Monday 31st October 2011
Noon

The Order of Service for the Westminster Abbey memorial service.

London's team, the members and officers of the Greater London Authority on top of the members and staff of the Local Government Association, where Simon had been Chairman.

At the time, I was chairman of the London Mayors' Association, so in addition to most of the London Mayors, over a hundred members wishing to pay their respect to me wanted to attend too. On top of this were our close friends, our families and Ruth's friends from Mallorca (many of whom had flown over specially). In addition, we had to find good seats for Simon's school and university friends and his colleagues from APCO, where he had been chief executive and chairman for many years.

At one stage, David Cameron, the Prime Minister had indicated his wish to attend. But it subsequently became apparent that he would be abroad attending a World Leaders Summit that weekend and his plane back to Heathrow together with the journey from the airport by car to the Abbey (even with outriders) would not get him to the Abbey in time to attend. He wrote a beautiful letter which we included in the official Order of Service.

I think it important enough to quote it in full:

From the Prime Minister Rt Hon. David Cameron – 31st October 2011

In politics there are the talkers, and there are the doers – those who actually roll up their sleeves, and work to make a difference. Simon Milton certainly fell into the latter camp – an extraordinarily talented leader of local government in London: a pioneering leader of Westminster City Council; and, in recent years, a tower of strength to the Mayor of London and his administration at City Hall, as Deputy Mayor and Chief of Staff. He was in public life and public service for all the right reasons and still had a huge amount to give and a great future ahead of him.

Simon was also a much-loved and much-admired member of the Conservative family, and a familiar presence at Party Conferences and Party gatherings. In all the years I knew him he was always kind, reliable, trustworthy and incredibly hard-working. We have lost one of our most committed and loyal champions in Simon, and he is greatly missed.

Simon left an outstanding legacy in London for which he will be long remembered. A gentle and modest man, he earned the respect and admiration from politicians of all political colours and from the communities he served so diligently.

While my thoughts and prayers remain with Robert and Simon's family and friends, on their terrible loss, I hope that today will also be a time for everyone to celebrate and honour Simon: a great public servant, a true Conservative, and – for me – someone I was lucky enough to call a colleague and a good friend.

David Cameron

The service was very special and I made ecclesiastic history by being the first person in the one-thousand-year history of Westminster Abbey to say kaddish from the High Altar of the Abbey. Kaddish is traditionally said by the immediate male members of the family of the deceased as a mourner's prayer.

I recognise that this is a book about my life, but to know me, you will need to appreciate that Simon is part of me and part of my life. I therefore do not apologise for setting out here the full texts of the eulogies said at the service by myself, by Simon's sister Lisa and finally by Boris (then Mayor of London and of course subsequently Prime Minister).

MY EULOGY
at Simon's Memorial Service in Westminster Abbey

Simon was my life. He was my inspiration. My being. We were a team. We were one. And I miss him terribly.

Simon and I met in early 1988, when a by-election was called in my ward. He rang me asking to meet, to discuss his standing for the vacancy. I told him I was very busy. But when he told me he would entertain me for lunch in his restaurant in Bond Street, I said I was free – that day.

We met and the rest, as they say, is history. Within four weeks he was a councillor and within six weeks we were living together.

And what a career Simon had. From academic success at St Paul's to the political double in Cambridge as chairman of the Conservatives and President of the Union Society and then two years at Cornell in the States learning amongst other things to be a culinary expert, which he was.

Returning to London to help run the family patisserie business, turned out not to be the future for Simon. With parental backing, Simon soon established a highly successful career in public affairs, creating and running one of the most successful public affairs companies in the UK before full-time politics enticed him away.

It was not long before he started winning plaudits for running Westminster Council and achieving recognition for his vision and policies.

I have been overwhelmed in the last few months by the wonderful comments of so many people who Simon influenced as Leader, particularly from those in communities that were not used to a Tory politician listening to them, let alone helping to improve their lives.

As well as from staff who just felt inspired by his leadership. His vision for Westminster, from 'Civic Renewal' to 'One City', were breathtaking in their audacity and in the way they broke the mould of local government. On launching One City, Simon said, and I quote 'We need to be united in something more than residing in the same city. It is about finding ways to tie people together, to integrate people, and to give them the means to a better life. It's about creating better opportunities and also, greater choice'. Words that still echo six years on.

Recognised as a leader of not just Westminster but of local government in general, it was not surprising that he was knighted by a Labour government and was soon not only chairman of the Local Government Association but also voted by his peers as the most respected councillor in local government two years running.

But at Boris's side, he came into his own, and as Boris has said, his influence across London will be his legacy.

During our 23 years together, I had only one real rival for his affection – his Sudoku – although in the last year that had moved on to Killer Sudoku. A night relaxing with his

*Me giving one of the eulogies at Simon's memorial Service
wearing the same tie I wore at our wedding.*

Sudoku was Simon's idea of heaven. I am sure that is what he is doing now as he half gazes down on us today.

Simon and I were, however, the perfect couple. We complemented each other. He gave the speeches and I made all the decisions. He ran Westminster and then London, I did the shopping and cleaning. He was the quiet one, whilst I did all the talking.

Our civil partnership, however groundbreaking it was for two men with high profiles, it was no flash in the pan, but a genuine and lifelong commitment, albeit cut short – much too early.

We were not just life partners, but soul mates. We endured the good times together as well as the difficult times. We were there for each other, supporting and encouraging each other emotionally, personally and politically. We accepted each other's shortcomings and relied on the other's strengths.

We often said to each other, when times were tough, and in politics, in work and in our private lives, that was quite frequent, that if everything went pear shaped, at least we had each other.

Sadly, that is no longer the case, and I ache each and every day without him; to phone (as we did fifteen times a day), to seek his counsel, to holiday together and to just be together watching TV or reading our council papers.

I was always amazed by Simon's determination through all his regular bouts of ill health. However, I never once lost hope or felt pessimistic.

Even in those dark days when he went through his bone marrow transplant, I just knew deep down that he would pull through. That's why the end was such a shock.

How I miss him. How his family miss him. How Boris and his team miss him. How London misses him.

There will, however, only ever be one Simon Milton.

Lisa Milton's tribute to Sir Simon Milton
at his memorial service at Westminster Abbey

On my 10th birthday my brother punched me so hard, he made me cry. I phoned my mother at work: 'He hit me. He hit me and it's my birthday'. She made him give me all his sweets and that's what I call a result.

Simon hitting me was not a regular event, obviously, although I'm pleased to report that the giving of sweets was. Actually, any violence was in the opposite direction, I'm afraid. Look closely at the photographs. That's not a birthmark on Simon's face, it's a knife wound. Not a bad shot for a five-year-old if I say so myself.

When we were children, Simon was the calm, studious, sweet-natured one and I was the shankalooly. Roughly translated that means 'hooligan'. Not much changed over the years. But whatever I did or said, and I do like a good rant from time to time, he never judged or criticised me, not even so much as a tut tut, he just smiled and loved me anyway. All he ever did was love me.

One of my favourite memories is of the time Simon took me to the cricket at Lord's. Surely a 15-year-old boy wants to go to the cricket with his friends but no, he took his annoying little sister. It was boiling hot; no wickets fell and I got a numb bum but Simon bought me the biggest ice cream you've ever seen in your life.

And so, the pattern was set. Simon took me to his friends' parties at Cambridge, he took me to Cornell for a week, he took me to Wimbledon, he took me out to dinner, he took me, with Robert of course, to the theatre and the opera and do you know what? If he had taken me to a rubbish dump, I would have loved it because no matter where we went, I only ever felt one thing: 'Look everyone, that's my big brother and he's taken me out with him.'

Simon was one of those people who knew everything about everything. If he wasn't such a bubbelah it would have been quite irritating. Whatever you asked him he knew the answer and if he didn't know the answer then he sounded like he knew the answer. Should've been a politician. He always answered my questions with patience, humour and love. And there were a lot of questions. 'What exactly is Crossrail anyway?'; 'Why can't I phone my local police station anymore?'; 'How do you cook a veal chop'. He was never too busy, never too important to help and advise me on anything and everything. He even tried to help me with my love life once. One of his rare failures. Even the great Sir Simon Milton can't help you when you've a penchant for nutters.

To me, Simon meant laughter and love. I've never met anyone with such a capacity for affection. He couldn't sit at a dinner table without grabbing my or my mother's hand and kissing it, stroking our cheek or, in my case, sticking his finger in my ear while pretending to study the menu. I called him by his Hebrew name, Herschel, and he called me his Little Moo. He used to phone me up, from the office I might add, and just make mooing noises down the phone at me. Or he would suddenly start speaking in some ridiculous indeterminate foreign accent. To hear his voice was to receive a long-distance cuddle. Simply to be Simon's sister was to walk through life with an arm round your shoulder and a kiss on your cheek.

You've come here today to show respect, admiration and affection for your colleague, mentor and friend. But I've come here to tell you this: 'No one ever had a brother like my Herschel.'

Mayor Boris Johnson's tribute to Sir Simon Milton at his memorial service at Westminster Abbey

Anyone who came to a meeting in the Mayor's office in City Hall would be familiar with Simon Milton's genius for cutting the cackle. I would have spent about half an hour windily extemporising what I thought was a brilliant scheme for the betterment of London while the deputy mayor sat in marmoreal silence, like a Buddha; and then just as I had reached my peroration his eyes would open. He would interrupt me with a small cough, and then he would tersely sum up – in about fifty words – what I had been trying to say. He would inform everyone what needed to be done and he would announce that the meeting was over.

So, it is not perhaps surprising that since last April some of the commentary has focused on this super Sir Humphrey aspect of his personality, the unflappable technocrat, the details man. And yet that is wildly to underestimate his achievement and I think it misjudges his personality, because from his very earliest schooldays Simon was a showman.

He was a performer, and he was a leader. His school contemporaries remember a stellar performance in *Oh What A Lovely War* in which he interpreted the role of Sir John French, playing opposite the teenage Imogen Stubbs with a budding Dean Godson in the supporting cast. When he was elected to the presidency of the Cambridge Union – unopposed, since his enemies had either been painlessly liquidated or had concluded that resistance was futile – he did not campaign with Thatcherite speeches. He had no particular manifesto that his friends can recall. He was simply the funniest and most charismatic student politician of the year, with impeccable comic timing and a fund of gags that he apparently collated in a famous Blue File, in the manner of Bob Monkhouse.

In other words, there was a paradox at work in Simon. He was the show pony who converted himself into the most prodigious workhorse. He was a natural gossip who became the soul of discretion. He was the university funster who became one of the most admired politicians in London – across the political spectrum. There are students of his success who believe that the transformation took place during his time helping to manage Sharaton's, the family chain of patisseries. I have spoken to at least one former employee of Sharaton's, and she has confirmed that the Miltons were excellent and kindly bosses, and that long before the days of the Social Chapter or the 48-hour week, they could expect to be pampered with extra squishy cream buns to take home at the end of the day.

Simon also ran Milton's restaurant, another family venture; and there are some of his friends who think it was this experience that gave him the managerial skill that was to serve

Boris giving his eulogy at Simon's Memorial Service.

him so well in his career, that flair for exactly when to dish out and when to withhold the squishy cream bun; and he turned those skills to the service of this city.

However you look at the story, the reputation of Westminster Council had suffered a bad knock in the homes for votes affair. As leader of Westminster, Simon turned it round, and the council became one of the most successful in the country – with the highest levels of satisfaction and among the lowest council taxes. He saw that educational standards were too low, and he decided to do something about it, and the expansion of the first academies programme was very largely thanks to his vision and his drive.

So, if you ask yourself how and why this performer and extrovert turned himself into this supremely effective administrator, I think there are many sides to the answer. It was his business experience that gave him the flair for the manipulation of the squishy bun; it was his immersion in local government that showed him how much you can do; indeed, as Ronald Reagan once pointed out, there is no limit to what you can achieve in politics, as long as you are happy not to take the credit; and Simon understood that. I think that after his first brush with leukaemia, so long ago now, he understood how fleeting life is, and that may have given an urgency to his work.

I also think he loved London. He saw how much the city had given to him, and to his family – to his father Clive, who arrived on the Kindertransport from Germany – and he wanted to give something back; and he did, on an extraordinary scale. In five, ten, fifty years' time our city will be landmarked with things that he either inspired or encouraged – from Paddington basin to new academies to a cable car across the river to the new London Plan.

He was one of only two Tories to be knighted in the reign of Tony Blair – which was a tribute to his political skill – and yet he fully deserved it. He never put on airs. He was no respecter of persons, and I remember when Prince Andrew came to lunch at City Hall and discussed the future of Battersea power station he said 'Even if it is listed, can't we just knock it down?' To which Simon replied 'The same could be said of Buckingham Palace'.

He was utterly devoted to his sister Lisa, to his mother Ruth and of course to Robert, and it is desperately sad that we will not now see him complete his progression to a ministry in the Lords. He was a great public servant who has left the city richer for his work, and if anyone finds Simon Milton's Blue File of gags, they should know they are handling the work of a master.

Boris's eulogy reminded me of an amusing joke he made about himself and Simon which appeared the day after Simon's death, in an article Boris wrote about Simon in the *Evening Standard*:

> He and I were once watching some unfortunate footage of me (Boris) falling into a river in Catford. Simon turned to me and said 'I've got the *Standard* their headline – River crisis – Mayor steps in!'

The Dean of Westminster and me at Simon's memorial service.

That said everything about Simon's dry sense of humour.

On the evening of the memorial service, the *Evening Standard* carried a double page article about Simon following an extensive interview I gave them a few days earlier. The national press all covered the service and *The Times* and *The Telegraph* carried the full list of those attending, taking up half a page in doing so. The gossip columns ran stories about those attending for weeks afterwards.

When I managed to sit down that evening, I thought about what happened that day. A service in Westminster Abbey, the most important religious place in our country and of course the Royal church. I was very proud of what I had organised to celebrate Simon's life

The Evening Standard *article published on the day of the Memorial Service.*

and very proud of Simon and the respect so many people had for him. He was truly a very special person. I love him dearly and missed him terribly. And I was now alone!

A few weeks later, I was entering the lift in City Hall to go up to my office when an officer of the Council joined me. It was just us two in the lift. I did not know the officer. We were going through a reorganisation of one of the council's departments which would result in several redundancies. So, when the officer broke the silence and asked me if I was Councillor Davis, I hesitated before responding, thinking he was going to have a go at me about this issue. But instead, he said he had been a great fan of Simon's.

He went on to say that in all his (the officer's) long service for the council, Simon had been the best Leader of the Council by far and that although he did not agree with everything Simon did, at least you knew what his views were, you could work with those policies and he just felt that the council would get it right and be respected for doing so. He ended by saying that Simon's death was a real tragedy.

I am afraid I was not expecting that. When I frequently spoke about Simon and others did too, I would brace myself and be strong. But these kind words from someone I did not know, just blew me apart. I burst into tears. I do not know who was more embarrassed, the officer or me. But it said everything about Simon and the loss I felt.

Just short of a year after Simon's death, in accordance with Jewish tradition, we held his Stone Setting Ceremony when a rabbi consecrated our tombstone. Simon was buried in a double plot, so that in time I can be buried next to him. After the service, a number of our friends and relatives including Boris, joined us at a reception in a nearby hotel.

People deal with grief in different ways. I love talking about Simon and his achievements and ensuring his name lives on. My two homes have photos of Simon everywhere, as did my offices in my law firm and in City Hall. Simon may have died but he lives on in my heart, in my memory and through his work, his legacy and the memorials we have established in his name.

Boris, Ruth and me at the reception following the stone setting.

Chapter 34

In Simon's Memory

I call it the Marilyn Monroe Syndrome. When Marilyn Monroe died young, at the height of her career, she became an icon for decades after her death. Similarly, James Dean, an undistinguished but handsome actor died young but at the height of his film career and he too became a legend. However, when a really great Hollywood legend such as Olivia de Haviland, Jane Russell or Doris Day die in old age, after the obligatory obituaries they are forgotten by the current generation.

My partner Sir Simon Milton was a great politician, a great leader and a great orator but had he survived many further years of service in local government, retiring with me to Mallorca and dying in his eighties he would have been the recipient of barely six inches of obituaries and then forgotten. But dying as he did at 49, at the height of his powers as the senior Deputy Mayor of London and Chief of Staff to the then Mayor of London Boris Johnson and having served as a well-respected chairman of the Local Government Association (which represents all the councils in England and Wales and which negotiates on behalf of local government with national government) and as an award-winning Leader of Westminster Council, his untimely death was heralded as a major catastrophe for London and Boris in particular, as much as it was for me and his immediate family and friends. The result was a number of initiatives that will ensure his legacy and, more particularly, his name will live on for many years to come.

The Sir Simon Milton Foundation

After his death, I received a number of requests to honour his memory in different sorts of way. Christabel Flight, one of my council colleagues, was in the process of setting up a charity for the council and it was not long before she approached me, asking if the new charity could be called the Sir Simon Milton Foundation.

More details about how we set it up and what it does are given in the next chapter so I will not describe its work further at this stage.

Potter's Field

Shortly after Simon's death, Tony Pidgley, the founder and chairman of one of the largest house-building companies, Berkeley Homes, came to see me. Our paths had crossed a few times but I did not know him well. Tony explained to me that he had been a great fan of Simon's and told me stories of how as Deputy Mayor for London, Simon had helped him resolve numerous issues.

Although Tony knew Boris well, whenever he saw Boris about an issue, Boris referred it to someone else or never followed through despite offering help. But at one such meeting, he brought in Simon to assist and within days the problem had been resolved. Thereafter, whenever Tony had an issue, he went straight to Simon and very soon the issue had been resolved or at least Simon explained how he had tried to help but for some special reason could not, but always suggesting a compromise instead.

Shocked by Simon's sudden death, Tony wanted to do something to recognise his contribution to London. He explained that he was building a major residential and leisure complex adjacent to Potter's Fields, which is itself next to the Mayor of London's City Hall. He therefore thought it appropriate to do something on that site, bearing in mind its proximity to the seat of London government. He suggested a statue of Simon. I loved the idea.

During further discussions, I was invited to suggest a sculptor. I suggested Philip Jackson, in my view the greatest living life sculptor working in the UK at the moment. His work included the Mozart statue in Orange Square and the majestic statue of the Queen Mother in the Mall. But to be honest, in suggesting Philip, I either thought it was not a prestigious enough commission for him to accept or he would be too expensive for Tony. But Tony loved the idea and Philip was very keen to do it.

Philip came up with some ideas and particularly favoured Simon sitting on a regal chair reading some official papers. A clay maquette was prepared and Tony and I both approved it. A few months later, we were invited down to Sussex to Philip's studio to see a life-sized

The statue of Simon in Philip Jackson's studio prior to some final changes.

clay model. As Philip opened the door to his main studio, I gasped. There was my Simon, sitting there in front of me. It was uncanny. It could have been Simon himself. I was shocked and, for a change, I was speechless and had to stop myself bursting into tears. That is why Philip is so highly recognised.

It was perfect.

After studying it for a while, we agreed on some minor changes, particularly to the documents in his hand, but the face was Simon. It was also massive, about one and a half times life-size. What was so impressive was that Philip had never met Simon and worked merely from a set of photos I had provided.

Once approved it was cast in bronze and awaited the partial completion of the Berkeley development next to the Mayor of London's City Hall. A position for the statue was agreed in the development

Boris Johnson, Philip Jackson, me, Tony Pidgley and Greg Clark in front of Simon's statue.

looking onto Potter's Field and on 4th April 2016 the finished statue was unveiled by Boris Johnson, then the Mayor of London, and Greg Clark, the then Secretary of State for Communities and Local Government (and a former Westminster councillor under Simon's leadership) in front of about 150 invited guests from Simon's life.

Piccadilly Circus

About two years before Simon's death, I was chairing a planning committee meeting considering an application by the Crown Estate for the redevelopment of a large site bounded by Piccadilly, Eagle Pace and Jermyn Street (near Piccadilly Circus) then called the Gateway Scheme. When I first met Simon in the spring of 1988, he was living in a flat above one of his father's shops on this site. As a joke, I said in my summing up,

Ruth (Simon's mother), Ronald (Simon's stepfather) and me in front of Philip Jackson's statue of Simon.

that I wanted to add a planning condition to require the building to be called Milton Towers in recognition of the fact that the Deputy Mayor of London once lived there.

I thought nothing further until a few months after Simon's death, when David Shaw and James Cooksey, two of the senior executives at the Crown Estate said that they wanted to do something on the site to commemorate Simon's leadership of Westminster Council. After discussions, it was agreed that they would commission a carved stone sculpture of Simon to adorn the corner of the site facing down Piccadilly.

Simon's bust in Piccadilly Circus.

The development's architect, Eric Parry, prepared some plans with proposals of where it would go and how it would fit in with the existing proposals. The concept was that the bust of Simon would be carved from stone and to carve this he brought in Alan Micklethwaite, one of the country's finest stone carvers. More used to carving gargoyles for cathedrals, Alan came up with a proposal in clay. When Lisa (Simon's sister) and I met Alan and Eric, I came up with the idea of showing in the background carved images of certain buildings that had played a major part in Simon's life.

The final piece shows the Gate of Honour, the beautiful Elizabethan gate at Simon's (and my) Cambridge college (Gonville & Caius College) carved out of stone over Simon's right shoulder with the Westminster Council House in Marylebone behind it while the sphere-like home of the Mayor of London sits carved in stone behind his left shoulder. To add some fun, I asked Alan to carve at the bottom left-hand side of the piece, a chocolate éclair and a slice of gateau, to represent Simon's family business, Sharaton patisseries.

Boris unveiled the sculpture in a ceremony which also revealed a plaque at eye level explaining who Simon was and the fact that he once lived on the site.

Boris (and bike), Lisa (Simon's sister), Ruth (Simon's mother) and me after the unveiling of Simon's bust at Piccadilly Circus on the site where he lived for several years.

Paddington

I was touched when another developer approached me with an idea for a statue of Simon. Richard Banks, the chief executive of European Land, the developers of a large part of Paddington Basin, adjacent to the Regent's Canal and Paddington Station, said that his shareholders, the Reuben brothers, had asked him to work with me to commemorate Simon on their site, as Simon had been very helpful to them. The suggestion was another statue.

I was not sure how to respond, bearing in mind the Piccadilly bust and the Potter's Field statue which were both at that stage still on the drawing board. But after some thought, it occurred to me that one or even both of the earlier offers may never come to fruition, so another proposed statue may mean that at least one of the three would actually be installed and if all three saw the light of day, they would all be different and in very different parts of London. That is exactly what happened.

Again, I was asked to suggest a sculptor. I had an idea. One of Simon's school friends from St Paul's School, who kept in touch with Simon and had remained friends with me after Simon's death was Tim Cohen.

Tim's partner was a contemporary sculptor and I therefore suggested, bearing in mind the connection, that Bruce Denny be invited to do it. Richard approved after meeting Bruce and he soon set to work. The statue was going to be positioned adjacent to an amphitheatre in the public realm of the Paddington Basin site and it was therefore decided that instead of standing on a plinth in the traditional way, Simon would be life sized and be positioned sitting on one of the benches around the amphitheatre with the ability for the public to sit next to him while watching performances or just to be photographed next to him.

Bruce and Tim suggested that I might like a bust of Simon for myself, which would be taken from the same cast of the full-bodied statue at a nominal cost. I liked the idea and in fact ordered two. One I kept and the other I donated to Westminster City Hall.

This originally sat in the ground floor reception but after the refurbishment of City Hall, it was moved to the main reception floor. My copy sits in pride of place in my Mallorcan flat.

The Denny statue of Simon was unveiled on 11th September 2014 by the Rt Hon (now Lord) Eric Pickles, then Secretary of State for Communities and Local Government. I frequently walk past the

The Bruce Denny statue of Simon at Paddington.

Eric Pickles Secretary of State for Local Government (now Lord Pickles) unveils the Bruce Denny sculpture of Simon at Paddington.

statue, which is close to my home, and see tourists and visitors sitting next to Simon being photographed or taking selfies with him. Only recently when visiting with friends, I had to queue up to have my photo taken sitting next to Simon.

The Chelsea Flower Show Garden

In 2016, the Sir Simon Milton Foundation decided to sponsor a small garden for the world-famous Chelsea Flower Show. We persuaded the Victoria Business Improvement District to sponsor it and we employed Lee Bestall, a well-known garden designer, to design it for us. On our first attempt, the Sir Simon Milton Garden won a silver medal. I spent most of the week in the garden, dishing out leaflets about the plants in the garden and answering questions from visitors, even though I frequently had to bluff the answers.

At the time, I was in my first relationship since Simon's death, with an expert in orchids who not only wrote books about them but also propagated new versions. I was therefore delighted when he offered to create a Sir Simon Milton orchid – a Dactylorhiza. This is a hybrid hardy orchid which in the UK flourishes outdoors. It was featured in our Chelsea Flower Show garden that year and through contacts I have at Buckingham Palace, it was arranged for me and the creator of the orchid to present it personally to Her Majesty The Queen during her annual visit to the Flower Show.

Every year at 4 pm on the Monday of the show, everyone is asked to leave apart from a representative from each garden or display while the Royal Family arrive en masse, each member of the family bringing a small party of friends.

We stood in the designated place awaiting the Royal arrival. It was shortly after The Queen's 90th birthday, so we had prepared a birthday card from the Sir Simon Milton Foundation, which sat neatly in the large bowl which contained four of the orchids in full bloom.

*Presenting The Queen with the Sir Simon Milton
orchid at the Chelsea Flower Show 2016.*

All of a sudden, we saw a whole gaggle of paparazzi approaching and knew the arrival was imminent. And then in Fortnum & Mason blue, The Queen arrived. As she walked towards us, her entourage stayed twenty feet behind and she approached us alone. We bowed and I explained that we had created this new orchid named after Simon and wished to present her with some. She asked us a number of questions about the orchids. I then said that we would arrange for the large basket containing the orchids to be delivered to the Palace the following day as it was rather heavy. I did not want to actually hand it to her as I had visions of her dropping it. But she said she would be happy to take it with her and called someone to take it from us. As it was being removed, she noticed the card sitting in the basket. She quickly took it, saying 'I think that is for me'. She opened her handbag and placed the card inside. She then turned to me and with a smile said 'I will open it later'. And at that, she shook our hands and walked off. I had visions of her sitting in bed that night, opening her bag, taking out the birthday card and reading it. A few days later, I received a letter from the Palace on behalf of The Queen thanking us for the orchids and advising us that they had been planted in the Buckingham Palace gardens.

Following the success of the show, we decided to do another Sir Simon Milton Foundation Garden the following year. This time we took a larger, more central plot and with sponsorship from CapCo, the company that owns most of Covent Garden, Lee Bestall again designed the garden. This time it was based on the old apple orchards that once stood where Covent Garden is now. Surrounding the garden were miniature green iron arches that reflected those found in the Floral Hall, now part of the Royal Opera House but once home to the Covent Garden flower market.

Without trying to push our luck too far, we used our Palace connections again to see if we could arrange for The Queen to visit our garden on her tour. With a day to go, we received

Explaining to Her Majesty about the Covent Garden styled garden at the Chelsea Flower Show 2017.

notification that we would be included on her tour. It was agreed that I would be at the garden to receive Her Majesty with Lee Bestall and a representative from our sponsors. Neither of them had met her before and were really nervous.

I spent some time beforehand explaining what would happen and the protocol for being presented to her, from bowing and curtseying to what to call her (Your Majesty at first and then Ma'am – as in jam – thereafter).

This time in a floral dress and blue jacket, The Queen arrived and I presented my colleagues and explained the theme of the garden. Lee then talked about the planting. The Queen asked some pertinent questions including why the apple trees were in bloom so early. Lee explained that they had been forced to flower for the show. Her Majesty laughed, saying she had expected so. After at least five minutes with us, she said goodbye and moved on. Hoping to improve on the previous year's silver medal and proud of this year's design, we were a little disappointed to receive another silver medal.

Having decided to do another garden in 2018, we chose a different designer, Kate Gould. She proposed a larger garden which would be given a more prominent site right in front of the Royal Hospital. It was to be sponsored by a number of Westminster Business Improvement Districts.

We did not ask for a Royal visit, having been rewarded twice in two years, as we thought it too cheeky to try our luck a third time. However, this time, we were rewarded with a gold medal and were delighted.

Nova – Victoria

I had been involved in the redevelopment of the Victoria area as had Simon when he was Leader of the Council. In fact, when *GQ* magazine was publishing its special 25th anniversary edition, it chose to include a profile on the reformation of Victoria as an area which it titled 'The new Victorians'. Most of the main sites along Victoria Street are owned by Land Securities, the largest private property company in the country. The *GQ* article included a double page photograph of the ten individuals who had been central to Victoria's transformation and I was honoured when I was asked to be included.

The 'new Victorians' – part of the photograph that appeared in the 25th anniversary edition of GQ *magazine.*

After a full afternoon being photographed in different positions as a group and individually, little me eventually appeared in a centre spread of *GQ* magazine.

A few weeks later, I received a call from Rob Noel, the Chief Executive of Land Securities, advising me that the major development scheme opposite Victoria Station to be known as Nova, was about a year away from completion. He explained that through the middle of the development they were creating a new T-shaped street surrounded by bars, restaurants and cafes with the public realm full of al fresco dining. He told me that they would like to call this new street Sir Simon Milton Square and requested my permission to do so. I told him that I would be delighted, subject to approval from Simon's mother and sister.

On my 60th birthday (27th September 2017), I unveiled the new street signs that surround the square (or streets) together with a number of green plaques that describe who Simon was. When I subsequently went to a restaurant there for dinner, I almost burst into tears when I noticed that on the bill was the address of the restaurant, No 2 Sir Simon Milton Square.

Of all the statues and other memorials, this one is the seen and noticed by most people who report back to me. Many tell me that they have been there and seen Simon's name everywhere. A great memorial to him and his impact on Westminster and London. I was very proud (as you can tell) to have been his husband.

Unveiling the street signs and plaque in Sir Simon Milton Square on my 60th birthday – 27th September 2017.

Chapter 35

My Charitable and Voluntary Work

At the time of writing this book, I am deeply involved with four separate charities and a historic society although I have also in the past supported several others over my many years in public life. This chapter tells you a little about each of them.

The Sir Simon Milton Foundation

The one closest to my heart is of course the Sir Simon Milton Foundation, which was set up following Simon's death in 2011. The 2008 financial crisis resulted in the amount of money given to the council by central government diminishing as part of its austerity programme. My colleague Christabel Flight argued that we had many wealthy residents in Westminster who would contribute towards a charitable arm of the council to support some of the services we would otherwise be cutting and that accordingly we should set up an arms-length charity to enable us to continue to support these services.

Christabel decided that before a charity could be set up, we needed expert advice in how to do so effectively. Meetings were held with a variety of organisations and charities and with the help of a number of senior officers of the council, steps were taken to start setting up the charity on a formal basis. At this stage I was not involved but as Deputy Leader I was kept fully informed of what was developing. Christabel's original name for the new charity was 'Westminster First'.

Then Simon died very suddenly. A few weeks later, Christabel approached me to say that she and a number of other senior councillors (Nickie Aiken in particular) wanted to name the new charity after Simon.

I was honoured and touched and my immediate response was that I would be delighted but on one condition. At that stage, I was still working all the hours available to me, either being a busy solicitor or as Deputy Leader and Cabinet Member for the Built Environment (which included planning). I was also chairing the council's main Planning Committee. Added to this were my existing other outside interests and charities including the full-on job of chairing the London Mayors' Association. The last thing I needed was more responsibility and a larger workload. My one condition was that I was not asked to take on any responsibility for the new charity, let alone for raising money for it.

Christabel assured me that she was happy to agree to that condition. I laugh now, because the opposite happened and I have become not only immensely involved in the running of the Foundation but deputy chairman and the principal fundraiser!

The Sir Simon Foundation was formally established by deed in 2012 with Lisa (Simon's sister) and I becoming life trustees. Julia Corkey (Director of Communications and Policy at the council), Sir Peter Rogers (Chief Executive of Westminster when Simon was Leader and in 2012 the Mayor of London's Economic Adviser) and, of course, Christabel were appointed the other founding trustees. We asked Peter to be Chairman and he was delighted to accept.

The Foundation had one overriding aim, which was to build on the success of Simon's pioneering One City initiative when Leader of Westminster Council that sought to provide young people with jobs and training and to ensure that older residents were looked after in a community that valued their contribution.

From the outset, we established that the Foundation would continue Simon's vision of a society in which 'communities care, the young aspire and older people thrive'. This developed into our mission, to 'provide opportunities in education and training for the young' and to 'address isolation and loneliness among older people'.

We recruited further trustees including several Westminster Council colleagues and friends of Simon, namely Daniel Astaire, Sarah Richardson and Danny Chalkley, his former LGA colleague Baroness (Margaret) Eaton, Baroness (Anne) Jenkin, wife of Simon's close friend from his Cambridge days, Sir Bernard Jenkin MP, former councillor Lady (Gillian) Rees-Mogg (mother of Jacob Rees-Mogg) and former Westminster Council Deputy Chief Executive during Simon's tenure as Leader, Julie Jones, and developer (and friend of Simon's) Tony Pidgley, chairman of Berkeley Homes.

The Foundation has been extremely successful. Its achievements include:

- Running our flagship project Silver Sunday which celebrates older people and addresses their isolation and loneliness.
- Holding an annual Tea Dance in December each year for over 1,000 older people in the Great Room of the Grosvenor House Hotel in Park Lane. Numerous cadets are invited to dance with the guests.
- Distributing over 500 Christmas hampers to the most isolated, disadvantaged and impoverished people in the city. We have started distributing Christmas hampers to carers too.

The annual Tea Dance.

- In 2020, because of the consequences of Covid, we also distributed £50 vouchers to looked-after children (orphans and children in care) and to 'young carers', £75 vouchers to 'care leavers' (children recently having left care and moving on into the 'big wide world') and £100 supermarket vouchers to 'Families in Need'.

- We funding over thirty separate scholarships and bursaries to students at university, including a specific bursary for undergraduates at Gonville & Caius College, Cambridge, Simon's and my college at Cambridge, thereby helping them to afford to live and eat while they can concentrate on studying.

The Sir Simon Milton Westminster University Technical College

During the early days of the Foundation, Christabel came up with an idea. Why not sponsor the creation of a new style of secondary school as part of the Foundation's work to support young people? University Technology Colleges (UTCs) were the brainchild of Lord (Kenneth) Baker, the former Secretary of State for Education. The concept was that young people finding an academic life at school challenging would be able to transfer at the age of fourteen to a school that specialised in some form of practical training. Once there, they would spend the next four years learning a trade and about two days a week working in the industry they were training for.

Christabel had heard all about these new type of schools from Lord Baker and after having visited a couple already operating, she was keen that the Foundation set up a UTC in Westminster in Simon's name.

When she first told me of her idea, my immediate view was that this was too big a project for us to undertake, just as we were establishing the Foundation itself. But when the council's Education Department said that they would support the opening of a new specialist school, I agreed we should go ahead. The council's full resources were put at our disposal and within a few weeks, a site was found. The council owned a former Victorian school building in Pimlico, on the boundary of the railway lines leading out of Victoria Station. The school had left the site years before and in more recent times the building had been occupied by the council's Adult Education Service. They had in turn moved to new premises and the building was now vacant.

The council's Property Department came up with an idea. They believed that the council could carry out a mixed-use development by building a large block of private flats for sale and include within the site a new school for the UTC to occupy. The council's Planning Department waived the usual obligations to provide affordable housing onsite as the planning gain would instead be the creation of a new school. Consequently, the costs of building the UTC and fitting it out would be paid from the sale of the luxury flats within the development.

The council's property team also thought that some vacant land at the side of the site could be incorporated into the development, but the land in question was owned by Network Rail and was adjacent to the railway lines going into Victoria Station. Negotiations started with Network Rail whereby the development would incorporate part of the railway sidings and in return the UTC would specialise in engineering, with Network Rail becoming a major partner in the UTC and providing engineering work experience for the students.

The UTC now had a specialist subject, as we all thought training young people (both male and female) to become engineers was just what the Foundation should be supporting. We would find other engineering partners to offer support and work experience. These were British Telcom Fleet (its engineering division) and Land Securities, the largest property company in the country. As a University Technology College, we had to have a university partner, hence the name. Our existing connections with the University of Westminster (formerly the Polytechnic of Central London and the first Polytechnic in the UK) opened the door to seeking their support and partnership. They were very supportive and became a key partner in delivering the UTC.

In the meantime, after further consideration, Network Rail advised us that they could not in fact release any of the land adjacent to the council's site, as it was required by Network Rail for operational reasons. But they would continue to be a partner and offer work experience and other avenues of support.

We put together a proposal for the government. If successful, the government (through the Department for Education) would fund the day-to-day costs of running the school.

After a controversial planning process, whereby a handful of residents living opposite the site opposed the scheme, as they did not want screaming kids annoying them nor a tall block of flats obstructing their view (views are not protected in planning law), planning permission was finally granted and a developer partner found to build the scheme at their expense.

Christabel (then Lord Mayor), Peter Rogers and I were honoured to dig the first spadeful of soil, as construction began.

The ground breaking of the new school.

With literally minutes to spare, the building works and fitting out finished just in time for the Sir Simon Milton Westminster University Technology School to open for its first intake of pupils in September 2017.

The Philip Jackson sculpture of Simon on the wall of the school.

Outside the Sir Simon Milton Westminster University Technical College.

On one of the internal walls of the ground floor lobby, the council erected a large bronze relief of Simon's face commissioned from Philip Jackson, who had created Simon's statue at Potter's Field.

The Foundation has supported the funding of the school, such as paying for the Principal for four terms before the UTC actually opened as well as paying the salary of the Head of Marketing and the annual cost of promoting the UTC among feeder schools. We have also funded equipment and sourced inspirational leaders of the community to speak to the students.

However, the school has faced a number of issues, principally revolving around the working of a UTC and the fact that the Department for Education now no longer supports the concept of UTCs. Our UTC, like many others created around the country, has failed to attract enough pupils to make it viable. As I write, it has been agreed by the government to close the UTC, but the Foundation will continue to ensure that whatever emerges, such as a different form of educational establishment, it will continue to be associated with Simon.

Silver Sunday and the Tea Dance
The flagship project we run is Silver Sunday. This was something conceived by Christabel and, rather like Mother's Day or Father's Day, is held annually, on the first Sunday in October each year. It is a day on which we want people to recognise older people and to address their loneliness and isolation. We encourage and coordinate others to organise a series of events to entertain the older residents of their area. This includes tea dances, recitals, shows, gym-style sessions and numerous other events and activities. Originally

based just in Westminster, Christabel has brilliantly expanded Silver Sunday across the nation and in 2019 over twelve hundred events were held not just on Silver Sunday itself but over the entire weekend.

In December each year, we also organise a Tea Dance for all the older residents of Westminster (well, those who apply on a first come first served basis, as it sells out very quickly – although the tickets are free). The event is held in the Great Room of the Grosvenor House Hotel in Park Lane. The guests arrive in their Sunday best, with some in their furs (real or artificial). It is rewarding to see the mix of those attending, from the wealthy widows of St John's Wood, to the pensioners from the council estates of Westminster.

Dancing at the annual Tea Dance.

The hotel provides a full traditional English afternoon tea, with crust-free dainty sandwiches, scones, jam and cream and then cakes and pastries. With the support of nearly a hundred police cadets, the guests are encouraged to dance to the band playing the music of the 1940s and 1950s. Most guests do not need any persuasion.

We receive many thank you letters from those attending the Tea Dance and these include:

'I had such a lovely time; I didn't realise that growing old can also be fun.'

'As I suffer from depression it does help me feel part of the community, a special tea dance like this. Thank you very much.'

'My husband has developed lots of illnesses in the past three years and this is a very good occasion for him to get out and be around people. Thank you.'

'It is the only time I meet up with people and socialise otherwise I pace up and down indoors.'

Christabel spends much of her time as a trustee, organising and expanding Silver Sunday and the Tea Dance, while I have found myself the principal fundraiser. I have helped to organise a number of fundraising events, such as a Quiz Night in the ME Hotel in the Aldwych and a dinner and cabaret evening in the Matcham Theatre within the London Hippodrome. The largest fundraising event is the Gala Dinner, which has raised substantial funds for the Foundation.

The Open Air Theatre in Regent's Park

In 1985, with the abolition of the Greater London Council (GLC) on the horizon, Shirley Porter, the Leader of Westminster Council, asked me to draft the council's Arts Policy which we would then adopt in order to fill the gap left by the GLC's abolition. The GLC had taken the lead on the arts in London and had financially supported many West End arts venues. Much of the criticism levelled at the Thatcher government regarding abolition was the consequential loss of support to the arts sector. Shirley, as a lover of the arts herself, was keen to prove that the loss of the GLC would not affect the arts world, in Westminster at least.

I spent a few months drafting the policy and in due course it was endorsed by the council. One of the main new policies I proposed was that in return for the council providing financial support to any theatre or other arts organisations, we would demand a seat on their Board of Trustees. As a consequence, my colleague Roger Bramble took up directorships of the English National Opera and English National Ballet companies, while I became a trustee of the Open Air Theatre in Regent's Park and joined the board in time for the 1986 summer season.

I loved my time on the board and found myself surrounded by some of the greatest names in the world of theatre. When I first joined, fellow board members included the actors Michael Denison and Robert Lang together with broadcaster Benny Green, former

Pride and Prejudice *(2013) at Regent's Park Open Air Theatre.*

Arts Minister Baroness (Alma) Birk and actress Dame Judi Dench. Just being in the room with these icons from the world of theatre was exciting and I learnt so much from listening to them and chatting to them about their careers. At the time I joined the board, David Conville (who had founded the company in the early 1960s) had just retired as chief executive and artistic director to become chairman while Ian Talbot, a well-known actor and director, took his place.

As years went by, the amount Westminster Council gave to the theatre started diminishing over time. So, when cuts started to be enforced on local government, the arts were the top of the list for reduced funding, as they found it difficult to compete with social services and education.

After a few years, David Conville advised me that as the council's funding was now just a few thousand pounds a year, he did not believe that warranted a position on the board and so he was sacking me as the council's representative.

However, after my heart sank, he immediately said that he wanted to invite me to join the board in my own right, rather than as the council's representative. I was pleased and honoured and of course accepted.

I continued my support and trusteeship of the theatre for many years and just before David Conville's retirement, William Village took over as chief executive and Tim Sheader became artistic director, with both of them having equal status within the company.

In 2009, the person who had taken over as chairman of the board from David Conville (who had become Honorary President) a couple of years earlier decided to resign, and I was shocked but delighted when William told me that he and other members of the board wanted me to take over as chairman.

In the audience of the Open Air Theatre in Regent's Park.

One of the first things I did was to invite my friend and former colleague Sir Peter Rogers to join the board. I was conscious that my fellow board members were brilliant actors and theatre experts but no one was particularly financially astute. Peter had been Director of Finance at Westminster and Chief Executive of the London Development Agency and so I thought he would be perfect to chair a Finance Sub-Committee, which he was happy to do. He brought rigorous financial scrutiny to the operation and, with his expertise in human resource management and running major organisations, I asked him to take the lead on negotiating the annual bonus and other employment issues relating to both the chief executive and artistic director.

The framed dress from Evita *with a scene from the Open Air Theatre's production in 2019 showing the dress being worn.*

We also brought in new governance rules requiring trustees to serve a maximum of six years with certain exceptions, such as the chairman who could serve nine years. Pushing this a little, I eventually retired as chairman after ten years at the end of 2019 and on my retirement the theatre threw a 'thank you' dinner party for me at the Ivy with all the trustees and senior staff attending with their partners.

After the usual speeches, I was presented with the iconic dress worn by Evita in the award-winning show that had broken box office records that summer. The dress was not for me to wear, of course!! It was framed with an inscription thanking me for my thirty-three years on the board and ten years as chairman. This hangs proudly on the wall of my TV room at home.

But my connection with the theatre did not end there. During my tenure as chairman, we established three subsidiary companies, one to run our catering operation, the second was our production company while the third was our touring company. I was a director of all three of these companies. Only the principal company was a registered charity and had to comply with governance guidelines recommended by the Charity Commission to limit trustees' tenures. There were no governance rules on time limits for directors of these subsidiaries and I was therefore invited to remain a director of these companies and, as such, was invited to continue to attend the board meetings of the main company in an observer role.

Holding the Olivier Award won by the Theatre for Crazy for You.

The Savoy Educational Trust

During my time as a councillor, I met and got to know the then General Manager of the Four Seasons Hotel just off Park Lane in Mayfair, Ramon Pajares. In 1990, just a few years after retiring as Lord Mayor, I received a call from Ramon, who was now chief executive of the Savoy Hotel Group, asking me if I would like to become a trustee of the Savoy Educational Trust. I did not know anything about it. But I said I would do some homework and revert when I knew more about the Trust.

The Trustees in 2011 including Ramon Pajares sitting on the right.

The Savoy Educational Trust (or SET) was established by the directors of the Savoy Hotel in 1961 to support training in the hospitality industry. The Savoy Hotel donated a number of shares in the parent group to the Trust and the annual income in dividends from those shares was in the early 1990s worth about £100,000 (in today's value). The Trust would then distribute the income to applicants including colleges and universities, teaching and training those entering the industry or already working in the industry but seeking promotion and advancement.

Then in 1998, the Savoy Hotel Group was bought by the American private equity house, the Blackstone Group and all the shares in the Savoy Hotel Group had to be sold to them including those held by SET.

Young students benefitting from grants from the Savoy Educational Trust.

The trustees were shocked to discover that the resulting proceeds from the sale of the shares was forty million pounds. With prudent investment those shares are now worth about sixty million pounds producing an annual income from dividends of about one and a half million pounds, which we use to support a wide range of training activities within the hospitality industry.

The trustees provide grants for new or refurbished training kitchens or pay for the cost of new equipment and uniforms in schools and colleges. Other recipients include organisations that support those in the hospitality industry such as those groups helping chefs suffering from alcohol and drug abuse. The Trust also supports a number of industry competitions as well as the 'Junior Chefs Academy', which teaches children how to cook.

The Trust now also supports various charitable causes that take people who are on the fringes of society, with little training and prospects and financially supports them by funding training through working in community cafés, hoping that they would be encouraged to undertake further training and pursue a career in hospitality.

I accepted Ramon's invitation and have served as a trustee for more than twenty years becoming the longest-serving trustee of SET. I have been the only trustee over this period who has not spent my working life in the hospitality industry, but the other trustees keep reminding me that they like the fact that my independent, legal and political mind enables me to give good advice to the board. In turn, I have learnt a lot about the hospitality industry and this was able to support me as a senior councillor working with the hospitality industry within Westminster.

Mousetrap Theatre Projects

I first met Susan Whiddington, an American married to an English solicitor, during my term as Lord Mayor when she was a senior officer at the (then named) Society of West End Theatres or 'SWET' (now renamed the Society of London Theatres).

In 1994, Sir Stephen Waley-Cohen had become producer of Agatha Christie's long-running whodunnit *The Mousetrap* on the retirement of Peter Saunders, the previous producer. A few years later, in 1997, Stephen decided to create a charity called Mousetrap Theatre Projects. The original idea behind the charity was to bring disadvantaged young people into the West End to experience theatre as well as to run educational development programmes about theatre.

On setting up the charity, he coaxed Susan away from SWET to act as chief executive of his new charity and in 2011 Susan invited me to become a trustee and I have served on the board ever since.

Although initially funded from the profits of *The Mousetrap* (hence the name), the work of the project has expanded so much, that it now relies on a wide range of other grants from a variety of charities, commercial companies and individuals. It also organises a series of fundraising events throughout the year including a biannual gala dinner and show, supported by many famous actors and celebrities.

During my term on the board, I have been joined by numerous fellow trustees well known in the theatre world. These have included Matthew Pritchard, Agatha Christie's grandson, to whom she left the rights to *The Mousetrap* in her will, Johnathan Burke, one of the creators, writers and stars of *The Play That Goes Wrong* series, Phyllida Lloyd, the director of *Mamma Mia!* and *The Iron Lady* and many other films and shows, Raymond Gubbay, the famous impresario, and Ed Snape, the renowned theatre producer. And Sir Stephen has been Chairman of the Board since its inception.

The most important project it undertakes, is to sell tickets to the top West End shows (from serious plays to the big musicals) at prices that everyone can afford. For example, Mousetrap will either be donated or will buy (say) one hundred tickets to see *Hamilton* and then resell them to families from council estates or families on low incomes for between £5

A trip to the Theatre for two young Mousetrappers.

and £10 each (depending on the particular programme). Family First Nights, for example, is one programme where we have sold £6.00 tickets to 10,000 disadvantaged families. Most of them will never have been to the theatre at all, let alone a West End show. Another programme, Theatre Openers, takes students from around one hundred and fifty schools in London, to see modern plays and classical theatre, again at affordable prices. They are also given further insight into the production through pre-show sessions and Q & A's with the cast and creative teams.

One thousand children with special needs are not only (through their parents and carers) sold cheap tickets to attend shows but are able to develop their confidence and skills through a series of bespoke creative learning projects.

My favourite programme is our annual Relaxed Performance. Families with a child with autism cannot go to the theatre with the entire family, as the autistic child may annoy and disturb other audience members as well as the cast on stage. Mousetrap therefore buys all the tickets for an entire show and then resells them at an affordable cost to families with an autistic child, so the entire audience comprises such families. So, if an autistic child starts shouting or running around, it does not matter. Everyone understands and the actors are fully aware of what to expect and just ignore it, something they would not do during a normal performance.

One year, I attended a Mousetrap Relaxed Performance of *Mamma Mia!* and sat next to a young man aged about twelve, who was attending with his parents and siblings. At first, he kept jumping up, shouting and running out to the aisle in front of me and the others sitting in our row and then after a few minutes, ran back to his seat again, all the time shouting and moaning. But after about half an hour, he was mesmerised by the show (the first he had seen) and by the second act, just sat there glued to what was happening on stage. It was a moving experience watching him change.

After each Relaxed Performance, Mousetrap receives hundreds of letters from delighted parents who talk of it being their first or only visit to the theatre with their whole family and how their children (autistic or not) do not stop talking about their experience for days afterwards.

The Soho Theatre

I served on the board of the Soho Theatre from 1986 to 1996, latterly as its vice chairman. When I joined the board, it was known as the 'Soho Poly' Theatre, as it occupied the basement of part of the then Polytechnic of Central London (PCL), now known as Westminster University, in Riding House Street in east Marylebone. It produced and presented new works and nurtured new writings. For example, Sue Townsend of *Adrian Mole* fame started by writing for the theatre as did Hanif Kureishi (of *My Beautiful Launderette* fame).

I loved the plays that they produced in that claustrophobic and small basement where the audience sat inside the set. For example, if the play was set in the lounge of a rundown council flat, the entire black box of the basement would be decorated like the flat with the audience sitting in chairs in the middle of the room and the action taking place all around them. It was immersive theatre at its best.

I joined the board in 1986 (at the same time as I joined the Board of the Open Air Theatre) following the Council taking over responsibility for funding the arts on the demise of the GLC and my report making it a condition of our making a grant that a councillor should become a member of the board.

Within a few years, we faced eviction. PCL decided they wanted the basement back for use as another lecture theatre. I knew the vice chancellor of PCL and so asked if he would see me. He readily agreed and at the meeting I persuaded PCL to give us another two years on the basis that we would sign a lease outside the security of tenure provisions of the Landlord and Tenant Act 1954 and so we would have to leave when the new lease term expired but that would give us the time to find new premises.

In my legal capacity, I negotiated the terms of the new lease, which we signed and completed. But after eighteen months of looking, we had still not found anywhere to move to. But in my role as a councillor, I was on a tour of the Church Street Estate in Marylebone, when I was shown the Cockpit Theatre, which housed the Drama Department of the City of Westminster College, a further education college. Again, I knew the Principal and so went to see him and persuaded him to allow us to share the theatre, so that the students could use it during the day but at 6 pm each weekday and on Saturday evenings, we would come in and open to the public with one of our shows.

It allowed us to move in after the temporary lease of the Riding House Street basement expired. But after several months in our new premises, conflicts started to arise between the theatre and the students using in it the daytime. When we were due to take over the theatre to prepare for a show, the college students and their teaching staff would often overrun their classes and refuse us access, frequently causing us to keep the public waiting to see our show that night. So, after a while we decided to vacate and, without a home, hired different theatres and spaces to put on our work. That did not work either and we started talking about winding up the company. And then the National Lottery came to our rescue.

Just after the National Lottery was launched in November 1994, we learnt that they were keen to support major cultural projects. We sought advice from their team to see whether they would support the acquisition or development of a new theatre building for us to occupy. They told us that they would be interested so we started the search for premises.

We soon found the ideal building. The Soho Synagogue in Dean Street was seeing a declining congregation with some Saturday services being attended by too few men to make a minyan, which in Jewish law prevented services taking place unless at least ten men are present. They were negotiating to amalgamate with another West End synagogue and were therefore looking to sell their building in the heart of Soho. An agent introduced us and we soon realised that it was perfect. We appointed an architect to come up with some ideas and plans. We concluded that we needed to demolish what was there and build a new purpose-built theatre, with a raked auditorium, offices, rehearsal rooms and enough front of house to make the theatre commercial.

The plans included a separate, independently accessed restaurant at ground floor and basement level which could also be used and accessed directly from the theatre, with a bar on the ground floor, so audience members could buy drinks from the restaurant's bar. The rental income from the restaurant would support the work of the theatre. Above the new theatre would be flats which would be sold on the open market and the net receipts would support the building costs.

The National Lottery were supportive, so an application was made and before too long we were awarded a substantial grant which, with the projected income from the sale of the flats, allowed us to buy the building and rebuild it as planned. Further fundraising from supporters paid for doors, seats and other fixtures and fittings.

As vice chairman of the board during this period, I played a central role but by the time the building was complete and being fitted out, I was Lord Mayor and so, to reduce some of my commitments, I retired from the board to allow others to take the theatre through the next stage of its life. The theatre has now gone on to be very successful and continues to specialise in new writing. I am proud to have played a small part.

Westminster Guide Lecturers' Association

I was approached in 2006 by my friend Christine Peters to help her establish a new Association. I knew Christine through her sister Councillor Heather Johnson who had twice been Mayor of Camden. During Heather's first term as mayor, Christine had acted as her consort and both had been active members of the London Mayors' Association, which I chaired.

It appeared that a number of Blue Badge Guides (those who had undertaken an appropriate course, passed an exam and then qualified as an official guide for tourists in London) wanted to establish a Westminster Guides' Association. This would involve a year-long course studying the history of Westminster and its buildings and if they passed the end-of-year exam, they could then call themselves a qualified Westminster guide and lecturer.

The issue on which they had sought help from me was to obtain the council's official endorsement for the Association and to allow them to use a slightly varied version of the Westminster Council coat of arms as their logo and on their official badge. This badge would be green rather than the standard blue of the London wide blue badge. As someone keen on the history of Westminster, I was happy to help and use my position to get them all the necessary consents that were required.

When they subsequently established the City of Westminster Guide Lecturers' Association (although they are now called 'Westminster Guides'), they kindly invited me to become their inaugural President, which required me to preside at their Annual General Meeting and at their annual badge awarding ceremony at which those successful in their exams were awarded the green badge to enable them to claim they were appropriately qualified and obtain work as a green badge guide.

For the first two years, the year-long course (one or two evenings a week) was undertaken at a college in Islington, but after the second intake had completed their year, the college decided that they no longer wanted to host the course any more. The chairman, in despair, sought my help. At a meeting in my office, he asked me if there was any way I could help as otherwise the Association may have to consider closing, so soon after it had been established. I had the solution. I explained that I was a friend of the vice chancellor of the University of Westminster, Dr Geoffrey Copeland, and that I would be happy to speak to him to see if he would take over the course. The chairman thought it was a brilliant idea, so with the chairman still sitting in my office, I phoned Geoffrey and explained what we needed and he jumped at the opportunity to run such a course in his university. That relationship continues to this day.

By 2017, I had served as President for ten years and in line with my attempt to reduce my workload, I offered my retirement, but instead of leaving them in the lurch, I suggested they ask my friend and colleague Steve Summers, who had just stood down as Lord Mayor of Westminster, to be my successor. They were delighted and he was honoured to be asked. He remains President to today and, on my retirement, I was awarded honorary membership, which I graciously accepted.

The New West End Company

In 1999, Ian Henderson, the then chief executive of the country's largest property company, Land Securities Plc and Vittorio Radice, the then managing director of Selfridges, got together with the chief executives of several other major retail stores and major landowners with businesses and properties on Oxford Street, Regent's Street and Bond Street, to set up an organisation which would represent them in an endeavour to work with the council to improve the public realm, keep the streets clean and promote them as the centre of retail in the UK.

The result was the establishment of the New West End Company (NWEC) and with financial support from its members, they immediately recruited a chief executive. This was before statutory Business Improvement Districts (BIDs) had been introduced in to the UK but was based on a similar concept being used in New York City.

Their first attempt to work with the council was frustrated by negative responses to the idea. As I had been a supporter of the Oxford Street Association for many years, they sought my help, but I struggled to change the views of some of my colleagues. And then, everything changed.

My partner Simon Milton became Leader of the Council and on my suggestion, he not only formally recognised NWEC and said that they had his and the council's full support but that he would ask me, his Chief Whip to sit on the main board of NWEC. They were delighted and from then, officers from the council started to work with them on joint projects.

Simon subsequently flew to New York with a number of other London politicians and political thinkers, to see how BIDs worked there. He was impressed with what he saw and returned to London to lobby the government to introduce legislation to give BIDs formal status and enable them to compulsorily levy an additional business rate from all occupiers of shops whose rateable value was above an agreed threshold.

Originally, only retailers contributed. Office and other uses are still not part of BIDs but landowners subsequently became statutorily included. However, in the early days of NWEC, a number of the major landowners in the area made voluntary contributions and participated at board level, as they saw the benefits to the area that would arise, notwithstanding there being no legal obligation to do so.

When legislation was eventually introduced, a BID needed to win a referendum of potential contributing retailers (and/or landowners) and if passed by a simple majority, then the BID would be established and the council would collect the levy from each retailer (and/or landowner) with the normal business rates demand and then pass the levy to the BID.

NWEC became one of the first to become a statutory BID and remains the largest in the UK. Cities and towns across the country now have BIDs and Westminster has about seven.

NWEC has in my view been very successful in promoting the West End at a time of serious competition from the Westfield shopping centres in both the west and east of London and from elsewhere. Its 'Shop West End' promotion has benefitted the area and, working in tandem with the council and myself, we jointly introduced a number of public realm schemes to improve the area, such as the new streetscape schemes in Bond Street and Hanover Square.

NWEC also pays for a supplementary cleaning service with its own liveried team of street sweepers. Added to this are the wardens that patrol the streets within NWEC's district in a distinct uniform, helping visitors as guides and reporting issues such as broken pavements or street lighting.

NWEC has also brought additional funding into the area as a result of its members contributing towards the numerous new major public realm schemes that we were implementing. Without this support, the council would never have been able to afford the works let alone the high-quality materials required for these premier shopping streets.

At Christmas, NWEC puts up the Christmas lights in Oxford Street and Bond Street and arranges grand lights turning-on ceremonies, which are broadcast live on national TV. Because Regent's Street is owned by the Crown Estate, it arranges its own Christmas lights and defrays the cost through the service charges levied on its tenants.

During this period, I acted as the liaison between NWEC and the City Council, sitting ex officio on its board. I was proud to do so, as I have always seen the West End as one of the jewels of our city.

Then a problem arose in 2012. The Leader of Westminster had a disagreement with the then chairman of NWEC and unilaterally decided to withdraw the council's representative on the NWEC board. That meant that I had to resign from the board. I was given a farewell luncheon in my honour to thank me for my service to NWEC and presented with a gift of a beautiful briefcase, which I still have. However, despite not being on the board, I continued to support them in a variety of ways.

Several years later, in 2017, I became the cabinet member responsible for BIDs and suggested to all of them that I be invited to join each of their boards. Most of them were delighted and this included NWEC, where I started attending their board meetings again. I checked that I did not have to return my briefcase! I remained on their boards until I stood down from the council in 2018.

The Past Overseers' Society of Saint Margaret and Saint John the Evangelist

Every year the Lord Mayor is the guest of honour at the annual dinner of the Past Overseers' Society, so my first encounter with this unique body was in 1996. It has an intriguing history. In the early 18th century, the responsibility for looking after the poor of Westminster rested with the 'Overseers of the Poor' who were the governors of the local workhouse for the destitute, which provided lodgings, employment and food. Think of the workhouse where Dickens finds little Oliver Twist at the beginning of his book. The Overseers also had the power to levy a local tax to pay for the workhouse (an early version of council tax).

The Past Overseers' Society was originally founded as a dining society for retired Overseers of the Westminster workhouse. They would meet from time to time in a local tavern to discuss parochial affairs and to dine together. As was traditional in those days, after dinner, the members would smoke pipes of tobacco. In 1713, one of its members, a

Mr Henry Monck (Monck Street in Victoria is named after him), presented to the Society on his retirement as an Overseer, for use at their dinners, a simple horn tobacco box which held three ounces of tobacco. It had been bought by Monck at the Charlton Horn Fair and would be passed around the members to allow them to take some tobacco for their pipes.

When Monck died, the members, concerned that the box was in poor condition, had it repaired and in doing so added a silver rim and on the lid, they engraved details of Monck's gift and the date of his death. It then became a tradition that each year the box would be passed on to a new custodian responsible for looking after the tobacco box until the next annual dinner and when returning it he was

The original Monck Tobacco Box.

expected to add a further inscription or engraving on the silver rim of one or two events that had happened during the intervening year. If the Custodian failed to return the box at the next annual dinner, the rules of the Society required him to pay a fine of five guineas (a lot of money in the mid-18th century).

Once the silver rim was full, the Custodian was also expected to add an additional silver plaque with the new inscriptions. The inside of the lid to the Monck box has a 1746 engraving commemorating the Battle of Culloden of 1745, supposedly engraved by William Hogarth.

An example of the engravings.

In 1783, when the Monck tobacco box had no more room for additional inscriptions, the Society bought a second silver tobacco box which the original fitted inside. And once that was full, a further silver tobacco box was purchased. The other two fitted into the third just like Russian dolls. Eventually further tobacco boxes were bought and each one enclosed the others and became fully adorned with inscriptions and in some years pictorial engravings too.

By the end of the 19th century, the Victorian tobacco box, with a mini statue of Queen Victoria made of silver sitting on top, was added, standing about five feet tall with all the earlier boxes fitting inside it. In 1935, when the Victorian box was itself full, Sir Edwin Lutyens designed a large Tudor Rose Dish on which the annual citations were engraved. When that too was complete, three further Rose Dishes were acquired. All four fitted into the base of the Victorian box.

In 1998, the fourth dish was complete and so in 1999, Sir Bernard Weatherill, the recently retired Speaker (and a member of the Society), donated to the Society a thimble, which he had carried with him when Speaker, to remind him that he had come from humble origins, as a tailor.

The thimble carried a design of the Speaker's mace. It was placed in a Perspex candlestick and silver engravings were placed around the base. The following year, a wooden case was constructed in which the candlestick could be placed or on top of which it could stand. Inside the pentagonal box were five large silver plates on which the inscriptions for the following ten years were engraved.

Speaker Weatherill's thimble.

When this in turn was complete, a silver dish was made to cater for the following few years.

2012 was a special year which commemorated not only the Queen's Diamond Jubilee but the London Olympics, and so a special one-off piece was created – the Jubilee Shard of silver.

Then in 2013, three hundred years after Henry Monck's original gift, a new small horn box was donated to the Society by the Horner's Livery Company and it was placed in a silver surround for the 2013 inscriptions. For the period 2014 to 2019, a silver stand for the 2013 box was made on which the inscriptions for those years were engraved. My good friend, sculptor Lee Simmons has designed a new uniquely shaped silver piece that should allow engravings for the next eight years.

This historic Society continues to exist today. More than a century after the abolition of the Poor Laws, the Society's membership now comprises members and officers (current and former) of Westminster Council, senior members of the College of Westminster Abbey and the Abbey's Honorary Stewards as well as other persons involved with the day-to-day life of the City of Westminster, from parliamentarians to property developers.

The Society currently has a membership of about one hundred and meets once a year for its annual dinner in November. At the annual dinner, all the silver is displayed for members to view and after dinner the formal ceremony takes place when the outgoing Senior and Junior Custodians responsible for the silver, retire and the outgoing Junior Custodian becomes the Senior Custodian and a new Junior Custodian takes up office. The new engravings for that year are then announced and the silver with the engravings inscribed on are presented to the members to inspect.

In my year a Lord Mayor, when I attended the annual dinner for the first time, they were still using the Tudor Rose Dishes and one of the inscriptions that year described the dissolution of the marriage of Prince Charles and Princess Diana. As I read aloud the inscription, as it is the job of the Lord Mayor to do, I noticed a spelling error in the engraving. It said 'The marriage of the Prince and Princess of Wales was sadley dissolved'. I pointed out the spelling error to the chairman who announced that it was too late to change it and so it would become one of the stories behind the many engravings.

One of the Tudor Rose Bowls – including the 'sadley' engraving.

As someone who loves the history of Westminster, I was enthralled by the Society and the story of the boxes and so was delighted to accept their invitation to become a member.

Over the years, I rose through the ranks and in 2004 became the Junior Custodian and then in 2005 the Senior Custodian. As a Custodian, I became a member of the Standing Committee and continue to be a member to this day.

When the silver is not on display at the annual dinner, instead of being kept by the Custodians, as the rules of the Society require, it is held by Westminster City Council. Until the temporary move of City Hall to 5 Strand in 2017, the silver was displayed in the council's Plate Room on the 18th floor together with the council's own silver and historic objects, behind an eighteen-inch-thick metal safe door.

In 2005, while I was Chief Whip and Simon was Leader, we persuaded Peter Rogers, the then Chief Executive, to find the money to refurbish the Plate Room. (Peter subsequently became a member and continues to attend the annual dinner, long after his retirement from Westminster.)

Until then, the Plate Room was literally behind closed doors. Access was only permitted by invitation from the Lord Mayor or a senior councillor. As part of the redesign, a plate glass window was inserted into the wall, allowing everyone walking along the adjacent corridor to look in and see the silver on display. All the silver was also arranged and labelled by a museum display specialist. For the rest of my time on the council, I took charge of the Plate Room and what was displayed in it and would regularly give tours describing in detail the full history of all the displayed items.

The London New Year's Day Parade

For over thirty years I have been an active supporter of the London Parade and Festival which takes place on New Year's Day each year. The parade is run by Bob Bone through his company Destination Events. He has been running parades in Westminster since 1st January 1987 and although the routes have changed over the years, the parade has got bigger and bigger each year.

The parade and accompanying choral and orchestral concert series is now the biggest event of its kind in the world, beating Macy's Thanksgiving Day Parade and the Pasadena Rose Parade in terms of the numbers participating.

Since the London Parade's inception, Westminster had always supported it and lent its name to it. Originally, it was called the Lord Mayor of Westminster's New Year's Day Parade, but as it got bigger, Bob brought in all the other London boroughs and renamed it the London New Year's Day Parade and, when the concerts were added, it became the London New Year's Day Parade and Festival.

The Parade itself comprises many different participants from Chinese lions to veteran cars, from historic police vehicles to Shetland ponies and massive balloons depicting cartoon characters to miniature steam engines.

Participants in the London Parade.

An American marching band.

Many of the London boroughs participate with floats competing for the inter-borough trophy and a large sum for the winning mayor's charity. But the backbone of the parade is the large number of American participating marching bands from a variety of schools and universities throughout the United States and some from further afield including Mexico.

Each December, Bob and his team would bring to London over ten thousand Americans to participate in and watch the parade and concerts. This would include members of the

Participants in the London Parade.

Another American marching band performing at the judging area in Whitehall.

marching bands, the teachers and support staff, the parents and siblings as well as local supporters and sponsors from up to twenty different US high schools from right across the United States. The money they spend in London (and Westminster in particular) is a boost to the local economy, specifically at a time when central London is usually very quiet.

In the USA, most high schools have marching bands to entertain the crowds during the numerous breaks in American football matches. The standard of the bands is very high and certainly beats those of their British equivalents. The students take it very seriously and practise early mornings before school, during school, after school and at weekends. They are also well supported by their parents.

Students have to pay for their trip. But in return, they are given a fantastic week in London. For many, it will be their first visit abroad and for the majority, probably their last. With their families and supporting team, they are flown over from the US on Boxing Day, put up in four-star hotels throughout central London, given tours of all the famous sights such as the Tower of London, Westminster Abbey, Windsor Castle and Stratford-upon-Avon as well as provided with meals and given free time to discover London for themselves.

The young students are then given the opportunity to perform in the parade itself, along some of the most iconic streets in the world, marching through Piccadilly Circus, Trafalgar Square, Whitehall (past 10 Downing Street – where one year the then Prime Minister came out to watch) and ending up in Parliament Square where the parade finishes under Big Ben. Millions watch the parade throughout the world, live on syndicated TV broadcasts.

For pupils who cannot afford the cost, their band's fundraising committee (called the Boosters) made up of mums and dads and other relatives, run numerous fundraising events to raise the money. They also seek sponsorship from local businesses.

Although it is a commercial venture run by Bob and his family, it does bring with it massive benefits to Westminster. Over half a million people turn out on the streets of Westminster to watch it and the City of Westminster is seen as the official host. Live worldwide TV coverage brings the streets of Westminster to millions of homes.

It's a win-win for Westminster, receiving all the kudos and benefits while costing the council (and the local taxpayers) nothing and with the council assuming no risks. Added to this is the business that is brought to shopkeepers, restaurants and hotels by the participants, supporters and spectators. Westminster's Lord Mayor, as host, receives a large sum for his or her mayoral charity from the parade organisers.

Trips to the United States in Support of the Parade

To persuade the Americans to participate and bring over as many participants as possible, together with teachers, families and supporters, Bob tours the States several times a year, visiting the schools to sell them the excitement, experience and honour of being invited to attend and participate. If the school does not have a band, but an orchestra or choir, then they are still encouraged to attend in order to perform in the concert series.

Three or four times a year, Bob would take with him a former Lord Mayor of Westminster, who would deliver a formal invitation to attend the Parade. The former Lord Mayors would wear the red robes worn by past Lord Mayors and their past Lord Mayor's badge.

I was one of those who undertook this trip. When I did, the Lord Mayor's office would loan me the Lady Mayoress's chains to wear on the red robes. The others who undertook similar trips included Roger Bramble (Lord Mayor 1985–1986), Cathy Longworth (2004–2005), Duncan Sandys (2009–2010) and Steve Summers (2016–2017). In addition, many incumbent Lord Mayors undertook a similar trip during their year of office.

The trips were enjoyable but also hard work. We would have to be up each morning at about 6 am in order to travel to a school, so that we could address them shortly after the school day started. After an introduction by Bob about me and the parade, I would give a speech all about the City of Westminster and our amazing history and include details of the parade by referencing all the famous historic buildings that line the route.

There would then be a handover of gifts including the official invitation to participate in the parade or concerts. The large invite would be presented in a frame and I would also present the school with a silver plate engraved with details of the invitation.

Presenting a school's band with their formal invitation to participate
in the New Year's Day Parade.

In addition, the school Principal would receive an enamelled dinner-sized plate from the Buckingham Palace gift shop, while the band director, local mayor and other dignitaries would receive Westminster cufflinks and brooches.

In exchange, I would usually be given a wicker basket containing a variety of local products, such as soap, mugs, candy, scarves, table mats and t-shirts with the school's emblem on them plus books and even umbrellas.

On a couple of occasions, I received a teddy bear wearing the uniform of the marching band.

After the formal ceremony was over, I would meet and chat to all the young people, who would queue up to meet me and take selfies and photos with me in my robes. This would often take over ninety minutes, if not longer, as I made sure I took the opportunity to chat with everyone who was queuing. I certainly obliged on the photo front, frequently borrowing one of the children's instruments and pretending to play it in the

With my teddy bear band member.

photo. We would then be off to the next school where I would go through the same format.

Auditioning for the band.

Sometimes the next school required a further flight and hours of travel. Several times during the week, we would fit in three schools in different states each day. We would then arrive in our next hotel about 6 pm and after a shower and a change of clothes, Bob and I would jointly host a dinner for invited guests and I would give yet another speech. By the time I got to my bed, I was shattered and would fall immediately asleep before being awoken by my alarm at 5 am the next morning in order to be ready to repeat the process.

After seven days, it was time to return home, in need of a well-earned break. So, although the trips look exciting, they were exhausting. But I did love these trips and in particular meeting all these immensely talented children, their teachers and families.

The Westminster Parade Float

I would also organise the Westminster Council entry in the inter-borough competition for the best float in each year's parade. The council would provide the administrative support. I would choose the theme and with help from the council officer designated to work with me on the project, I would write to a number of stakeholders, seeking sponsorship to pay for the cost of building the float, hiring the flatback lorry, the costumes and the make-up artists.

Our themes over the years included *Mary Poppins, Alice in Wonderland, Oliver,*

Feeling uncomfortable in a bra and high heels as Mary Poppins on the Westminster Float in 2017.

My appearance in the 2011 London Parade as the Mad Hatter from Alice in Wonderland.

With friends and colleagues (including Nickie Aiken) on the Westminster Float in the 2016 London Parade as Thenardier in Les Misérables.

As one of the ugly sisters with Nickie Aiken (then Leader of Westminster Council and now MP for the Cities of London and Westminster) as Cinderella standing in front of Westminster's pantomime-themed Float in 2018.

Peter Pan and *Thunderbirds*. For several years, we won first prize with about £20,000 going to the Lord Mayor's charity each year.

One of the most important elements for me was to include my fellow councillors as well as senior officers. It became a fun corporate event with fellow councillors and senior directors all dressing up in some amazing and some hysterical costumes with professional make-up added, to give the right finishing touch.

Lady Penelope played by my colleague Angela Harvey and myself as Parker from Thunderbirds, *the Westminster Council entry in the 2014 London Parade.*

Westminster's Thunderbirds float in the 2014 London Parade.

Chapter 36

Honours and Recognition

My thirty-seven years in public life has been recognised by several honours and awards. These are some of them.

Deputy Lieutenant

The Lord-Lieutenant of a county is the Monarch's personal representative in that county. Historically, each Lord-Lieutenant was responsible for organising the county's militia, but in 1871 this responsibility was removed. The Lord-Lieutenant is now an honorary position usually awarded to a notable person in the county.

The principal role of Her Majesty's Lord-Lieutenant is to 'uphold the dignity of the Crown' and to follow the example of The Queen by providing the residents of the county with a focus for national identity, unity and pride.

In practice, the modern responsibilities of a Lord-Lieutenant include:

- Arranging visits of members of the Royal Family and during those visits escorting the Royal visitors;
- Presenting medals and awards on behalf of the sovereign and advising on honours nominations;
- Participating in civic, voluntary and social activities within the area covered by the lieutenancy;
- Acting as liaison with local units of the Royal Navy, Royal Marines, Army, Royal Air Force and their associated cadet forces;
- Leading the local magistracy as chairman of the Advisory Committee on Justices of the Peace.

Each Lord-Lieutenant is supported by a Vice Lord-Lieutenant and a number of Deputy Lieutenants that he or she appoints. A Deputy Lieutenant is entitled to use the initials DL after their name.

The DL's role is to stand in for the Lord-Lieutenant or his Vice Lord-Lieutenant when they cannot attend an event. In London, however, the Lord-Lieutenant appoints a specific DL known as a Representative DL or Rep DL to take responsibility for each of the thirty-two boroughs. [The City of London has its own separate lieutenancy.] It is the Rep DL in a borough that has a day-to-day relationship with the council and the mayor in particular, attending civic events in the borough to represent the lieutenancy. DLs tend to be those

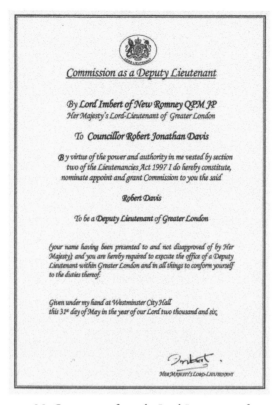

*My Commission from the Lord-Lieutenant of
Greater London as a Deputy Lieutenant.*

who have either served their local community or have a history of public service in other fields.

I was therefore honoured when in early 2006, Lord Imbert, the former Metropolitan Police Commissioner and then Lord-Lieutenant of Greater London invited me to become a DL. I was touched and after my nomination was 'not disapproved by Her Majesty The Queen' I received my Commission on 31st May 2006 and I was thenceforth allowed to use the letters DL after my name.

Order of the British Empire

I was equally honoured when I received a letter from 10 Downing Street in late April 2015, requesting my permission for the Prime Minister (David Cameron) to put my name forward to Her Majesty The Queen to be made a member of the Order of the British Empire (an MBE) for my 'services to local government and planning'.

I was delighted and although I had drafted my response accepting, work pressure meant that the envelope containing the acceptance letter was still in my briefcase, when just a week later, I was having breakfast with a friend in the café in Sotheby's, Bond Street, when my mobile phone rang. It was about 8.30 am. I answered and was advised that it was No 10 on the phone and they were wondering if I was going to accept my honour, as they had not heard back from me. I apologised for the delay (only a few days) and told them that I would be delighted to accept and promised to post the letter later that day.

The Honours List was published on the Queen's Official Birthday in June 2015 and I received numerous messages, emails and letters congratulating me. One congratulatory note I received was from Prince Charles. I had assumed everyone being honoured received

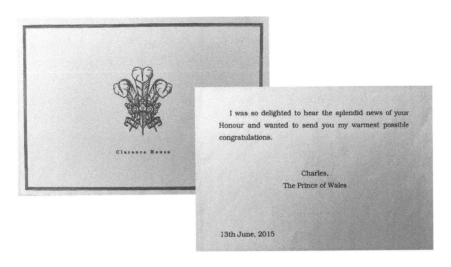

I was so delighted to hear the splendid news of your Honour and wanted to send you my warmest possible congratulations.

Charles,
The Prince of Wales

Clarence House

13th June, 2015

The message from the Prince of Wales.

one, but on talking to other recipients, I discovered that only I had. I was touched.

A few months later, I received an invitation to attend Buckingham Place for the investiture itself. However, it was on the Thursday prior to Christmas and I was to be in Mallorca for the holiday season. I called the Palace and asked if I could attend on a different day. They were happy to move it to Thursday 4th February 2016.

When the day arrived, I woke up excited but nervous. I already had my mayoral morning suit to wear and wore the green tie I had worn at my wedding to Simon. I was allowed three guests and as my mother-in-law Ruth and sister-in-law had both attended Simon's investiture, I had no qualms in inviting my two nieces Cassie and Jessica and my brother-in-law Bradley (my late sister's husband).

We met up in my flat and I drove the four of us to the Palace in my car as I had a permit to park in the Quadrangle within the centre of the Palace. Neither Cassie, Jessica nor Bradley had been inside the Palace before and they were equally excited.

Having entered through the Grand Entrance and walking up the Grand Staircase, we were separated, with Bradley, Cassie and Jessica being ushered towards the ballroom while I was ushered to the Picture Gallery where the other recipients were waiting, drinking the tea and coffee on offer. As I entered the Picture Gallery, I was required to register at a desk and once my name was ticked off, one of the Palace team affixed a special hoop onto my jacket to allow the Honour to be simply slipped on me rather than the fiddling of trying to pin the MBE on my jacket.

Three friends were coincidently also receiving their MBEs the same day and so we all met up chatting over coffee. They were Rosemarie MacQueen, who had been the Director of Planning under my tenure as Cabinet Member for Planning, Matthew Bennet a leading member of the Soho Society and Michael Salter who had been David Cameron's Political Head of Broadcasting at 10 Downing Street.

With ten minutes until the investiture was due to start, the Comptroller of the Lord Chamberlain's Office, Sir Andrew Ford KCVO addressed us all and explained the procedure and how and where we should stand, bow (or curtsy) and move to.

Our names were then called in batches of about fifteen and we were led in single file through the back of the ballroom to the waiting area. With two recipients in front of me, I moved to my position at the entrance to the ballroom where I waited for the signal from the usher standing at the doorway. I saw his nod and it was my turn.

I walked slowly up to the next usher who was standing in front of the dais while the person in front of me received his MBE. He bowed, having been invested and moved off. It was me now! The Lord Chamberlain announced my name together with the citation. I walked slowly to the middle of the dais, turned and faced His Royal Highness the Prince of Wales. I was delighted. I knew that Her Majesty rarely undertook investitures now, so I was pleased that I would receive my MBE from Prince Charles, who knew me and my work in planning as he had a particular interest in architecture.

Receiving the MBE from the Prince of Wales at Buckingham Palace.

The Prince of Wales had sought my help a few years earlier, when he was horrified by the proposed designs for the new buildings to be built on the site of the former Chelsea Barracks adjacent to the Royal Hospital. The site was on the edge of the city, but very much a Westminster responsibility. The development was being funded by the site's owner, Qatari Diar, the property company ultimately owned by the Emir of Qatar, but the development itself was being led by their joint venture partners, the Candy Brothers. The very modern design was favoured by the officers at Westminster who had recommended approval in the relevant committee papers to be considered at the forthcoming planning committee. I was not actually chairing that committee. My deputy Cabinet Member Councillor Alastair Moss had been leading on this application and was to chair the sub-committee meeting considering it.

The Prince's Private Secretary called my office to invite Simon (who was then Deputy Mayor of London for Planning) and me to meet the Prince in Poundbury, the experimental new town that the Prince had masterminded in Dorset. At that stage, we did not know the reason but after a couple of hours on a train, we were met by a member of the Prince's staff and taken to a community hall at the centre of the town. There were a number of other guests there and we were all given a lecture about the history of the town and the Prince's involvement. The Prince then arrived and spoke to us all about his vision.

We were then invited on a walk around the town with the Prince as guide. Halfway around, we were tipped off by a member of his staff that we should approach him as he wanted to talk to us privately. So, we moved forward and after some initial small talk, the Prince raised his concern about the proposed Chelsea Barracks application and the officer's recommendations. Simon explained that this was really a matter for me, as the Mayor's Office was not yet involved. I explained that the application had gone too far and there was no way I could interfere with the officer's recommendations or the committee's consideration of the application. However, I explained there was one solution. I said that the only person who could stop the process was the Emir himself and that the Prince should contact the Emir personally and suggest he withdraws the application. The Prince thanked me and agreed that this was indeed the only sensible way and we then changed the subject and started a different discussion about Poundbury.

A few days later, I heard from reading *The Times* that the application had suddenly and surprisingly been withdrawn prior to it being considered by the planning sub-committee on instructions from Qatar. I can only surmise, but it appears that my advice had been followed.

A few weeks later, I was asked to attend a day-long seminar on planning and heritage issues chaired by the Prince at St James's Palace. During the course of the morning, I was again presented to the Prince when he thanked me for my earlier advice. He said nothing more and moved on.

So, there I was, a number of years later, bowing before him in my morning coat in the grandeur of the ballroom in Buckingham Palace. I moved forward as instructed, bowed again and the Prince hooked the MBE medal onto the clip on my jacket breast.

He then said to me 'Congratulations Robert, I am surprised it has taken so long'. I was taken back by this remark and without much thought replied 'And so am I, Sir'.

He then asked me about the amount of development going on in Westminster at the time and we exchanged words for a few moments before he reached out to shake my hand and in doing so gave me a polite push away, indicating (as I had been warned at the earlier run through) that my time was over. I walked backwards still facing him for a few feet, bowed again and then turned to my right and walked out of the ballroom to my right. I was now a member of the Order of the British Empire.

In the ante-room, the Comptroller, Sir Andrew Ford, shook my hand and a page took off the medal and the hook and placed the medal in its official box and returned it to me. I was then ushered into the back of the ballroom to watch the remaining recipients receive their honours.

About a year prior to my investiture, the Sir Simon Milton Foundation had employed a new Chief Executive, Major General Matthew Sykes, who was also a (part-time) Member of the Royal Household, acting as an usher at many State and Royal occasions. He very kindly arranged for me to be entertained with my family at a private drinks party held in Her Majesty's Equerry's office for the senior members of the Household after the investiture had concluded. So, on meeting up with Bradley, Cassie and Jessica, we were escorted through the private areas of the Palace to the small reception, while everyone else left to go and celebrate elsewhere.

We were the only guests there and chatted with the senior members of the Royal Household about the ceremony. After about half an hour, one of the Household present suggested we go and have our photos taken by the professional photographers outside in the Quadrangle.

The official photo in the Quadrangle of the Palace with my brother-in-law Bradley and my nieces Cassie and Jessica.

My MBE.

A team of professional photographers is on duty so that all the recipients of honours can have official photographs taken within the Palace grounds (private cameras not being allowed). Escorted by a member of the Household, we jumped the long queue of recipients and their guests and went straight to the front.

After the photographs had been taken, we got into my car and drove over to Mayfair. I had arranged a lunch for sixty close friends and family at '34', the restaurant just off Grosvenor Square. I had booked the private room on the first floor and when we got there, many friends had already arrived, all keen to hear all about the morning's investiture. Others arrived and we enjoyed pre-lunch drinks around the bar area before being ushered to the six tables of ten for lunch.

After a delicious three-course meal, I thanked everyone for coming and spoke about how much their presence meant to me. Then to my surprise, my guests started standing up, one after the other to say such lovely things about me and their connection with me. That took about forty-five minutes as everyone seemed to want to say something. Eventually, the lunch was over and a wonderful day was coming to an end.

What made my MBE very special was the fact that I was the only councillor during my 36-year tenure on the council who had received such an honour for service as a Westminster councillor. Many others had received honours but they were for what they had achieved or undertaken outside the council. The only exceptions were Shirley Porter and her damehood and Simon's knighthood, both for being Leader. That made me very proud.

Addressing my guests at my MBE luncheon party.

Simon's Knighthood

Although not an honour that I personally received, I cannot fail to mention Simon's knighthood of which I was so very proud. Simon was Leader of Westminster Council and had led it from a struggling council with a bad reputation to Council of the Year in 2004. He was also recognised for the way in which he had handled the situation after the 7th July bombings and his introduction of the 'One City' programme and the establishment of the 'All Faiths Forum'.

At the same time, he was also chairman of the Innovation Committee of the Local Government Association (LGA) which brought him into regular contact with government ministers. At that time, Tony Blair was Prime Minister and John Prescott Deputy Prime Minister and Secretary of State for Local Government.

The first I knew that there was something in the offing was one day at work, when I received a telephone call from Peter Rogers, the council's chief executive. It appeared that he had just received a call from the private secretary to the Deputy Prime Minister (John Prescott) and that the Deputy PM wanted to nominate Simon for a knighthood for his services to local government but needed a full citation to be prepared and wanted Peter to write it. Peter had made a first attempt at drafting it but wanted me (on a strictly private and confidential basis) to check it and add anything else I could think of and in particular reference to his health battles. With little delay, I made the necessary amendments and additions and returned the document to Peter, not mentioning anything to Simon of course.

We then heard nothing for months. With the New Year's Honours List in 2005 just a month away, I assumed that Simon had missed out that year. But on 1st December the letter arrived and Simon opened it and we were both delighted to see the offer of a knighthood. The letter makes it clear that Simon had to keep it secret until the full list was published on 30th December. But we wanted his mother, sister and stepfather to know beforehand.

Each year, Simon and I would spend Christmas abroad and return just before New Year's Eve, so we could attend the London New Year's Day Parade. By tradition, Ruth and Ronald would visit London before we left and with Lisa we would have a family dinner to exchange gifts before our departure. This year, I booked a French restaurant in St John's Wood. I had brought Christmas presents from Simon and me. After we had all ordered, I instigated the exchange of presents, which were opened and thanks were bandied about. Then as the used wrapping paper and gifts were put away to allow the dinner to arrive, I said I had one more gift for everyone. I then produced from my jacket three envelopes with each of their names on. I handed out. They all looked suspicious.

Ruth managed to rip open hers first and as she read the photocopy of the letter from No 10 Downing Street, she let out a deafening scream as if she had been stabbed! Everyone in the restaurant stopped talking and looked over at us. By this time the others had read their copies of the letter too and Ruth had to assure all the other restaurant guests that she had shrieked with joy and apologised for upsetting them all.

The questions then started about, why, when, etc. We told them that they must keep it secret until 30th December. But Ruth later told us that the following morning Ronald had phoned his aged parents and told them he had been told a fantastic secret but could not tell them what it was. They were furious that he would not tell them, leading to much speculation. Ronald had kept his promise in a strict sense, but tantalising his parents was not clever.

The Investiture was held a few months later and Simon invited Ruth, Lisa and me to join him at the Palace. I have described earlier the procedure at the Palace. Ruth, Lisa and I were seated in the third row, right behind the family of the English cricket team, there to pick up a series of medals.

Having been instructed by Palace officials what knee to use, Simon told us afterwards that because he was so nervous, he initially went down on the wrong knee and had to quickly correct this, hoping Her Majesty hadn't noticed. As he did so, he felt the sword tap his shoulder and so as instructed, he stood up as Sir Simon Milton.

On our subsequent civil partnership, I therefore became Lady Milton!

After the ceremony and the photos in the Quadrangle, we went to the Ritz Hotel, where we were joined for lunch by Ronald (Ruth's husband), Margaret Eaton (then just Margaret as it was prior to her peerage) and Leader of the Conservative Group on the LGA together with Dean Godson (now Lord Godson), Simon's closest friend, and Peter Rogers (subsequently knighted too), who had assisted in getting Simon the knighthood.

Simon being knighted by The Queen.

David Cameron with Ronald and Simon at Simon's knighthood party.

The following week, Simon hosted a celebratory drinks reception in the Lord Mayor's Reception Rooms for all his family, friends and colleagues as well as members of his ward committee. David Cameron, then Leader of the Opposition, attended resulting in numerous comments in the national newspaper's gossip columns. But the other guests were impressed and delighted and queued up to say hello and to be photographed with Cameron.

Asian Voice

I was surprised as well as honoured when in early 2014, I received a phone call from my friend the Rt Hon. Keith Vaz, a well-known Labour MP and former government Minister. Keith and I had been friends at Caius College during our time as undergraduates at Cambridge. We not only lived in the same court in both our first and third years but in adjacent houses when we were required to live in lodgings during our second year. He qualified as a solicitor but in 1987 became one of the first BAME MPs.

Keith had called to advise me that I had been voted 'Conservative Councillor of the Year' by the widely read *Asian Voice* newspaper as part of their annual 'Political and Public Life Awards' and that I would receive the award from Betty Boothroyd, the former

My Asian Voice Award.

426

Speaker of the House of Commons at a reception in one of the state rooms of the Houses of Parliament.

When it came for me to receive the award, Betty Boothroyd remembered me. We had met when I had been Lord Mayor and she was Speaker, frequently sitting next to each other at dinners. We also had a mutual friend, the famous photographer Gemma Levine, who had often entertained us both.

Visit London Awards

In 2009 Simon and I were invited to the Visit London Award Ceremony and dinner at the Westfield Shopping Centre in Shepherd's Bush. It was a black-tie dinner and we were excited because West End Live had been nominated in two categories. After the dinner, we waited in anticipation as each award was announced. The first one for us was the Consumer Event of the Year Award. We came third and I went up and received the bronze award. We were delighted that the event had been recognised.

Then after a few more awards, came the big one the Kiss 100's Hottest Music Event and after the announcement of the bronze and silver awards, I presumed that was it. To my surprise, they announced West End Live as the winner. I jumped up and cheered and made my way to the stage to receive the splendid (heavy) award. I was very proud, as I stood with the award held above my head, like footballers do on receiving the FA cup after winning the trophy at Wembley. I was chuffed.

London First 20th Anniversary Awards

In 2012, I was contacted by Baroness (Jo) Valentine, who had worked with Simon both as Leader of Westminster but also at the GLA. She explained that London First, a not-for-profit organisation representing the leaders of major London businesses which campaigns for investment in London, was celebrating its 20th anniversary and was therefore hosting a black-tie dinner and award ceremony. Jo told me that the judges had wanted to award the Lifetime Contribution to London award to Simon posthumously and wanted me to accept it on his behalf. I was honoured and delighted to do so. I took as my guest, Ruth, Simon's mother, and we sat on the top table next to Michael Portillo, who was going to present the award. After Michael told the guests why Simon deserved the award, I came up on to the stage to receive the large ceramic jug with details of the award inscribed on it. I gave a short speech of thanks. Both Ruth and I were very proud.

Simon's Lifetime Contribution to London Award which I received on his behalf after he had died.

Chapter 37

My Downfall ...
or What Goes Up Must Come Down

This has been the most difficult chapter to write and covers the most challenging period of my political career.

You will have seen throughout this book how I have dedicated my life to Westminster and the City Council. Rightfully or wrongfully, it had taken over my life, particularly in the years after Simon died. I lived and breathed Westminster and was often described by friends and colleagues as 'Mr Westminster'. All I endeavoured to do was to make Westminster a better place and to support those who lived, worked and visited our great city. I gave up my job as a partner in a West End firm of solicitors to spend every morning, day and evening on council affairs, even taking a wheelie case full of council papers to read on holidays. I was often one of the first to arrive on our floor at City Hall in the mornings and the last to leave.

But that life and what I would describe as dedication to public service for thirty-six years came to a grinding halt when in February 2018, the *Guardian* newspaper splashed a story over its entire front page, accusing me of being the 'most schmoozed politician in Britain'. That in itself was an exaggeration as I am sure there were many other politicians including members of both Houses of Parliament who enjoyed greater hospitality, but after all, the facts should not get in the way of a good story!

The story that did emerge led to my resignation as Deputy Leader and cabinet member and, a few months later, from the council itself. The story of what exactly happened is complicated and so to put it all in context, it is important to describe a number of parallel stories as well as explaining a little about life in local government while emphasising the political atmosphere in Westminster as we headed towards elections in May 2018, with fears that control of Westminster Council could be lost.

Life in the Fast Lane

Anyone who knows me will tell you that I am an outgoing person who loves socialising and meeting people. Therefore, in my position as a councillor, I was delighted to accept invitations to a variety of different events. All councillors, but particularly those in the majority party and those with responsibilities within the administration, were frequently invited to represent the council at numerous events.

Meetings with stakeholders would take place over dinner at a West End restaurant or hotel. As an example (without trying to highlight them in particular), the Crown Estate would regularly entertain the Leader, myself as Deputy Leader and three or four cabinet members with responsibilities that intersected with the Crown Estate's own work, at dinner in a restaurant in Regent's Street to discuss a variety of issues. This is the way we did business and officers would, more often than not, join us at these lunches or dinners. In fact, these meetings were very fruitful, as the council and the city would benefit from such open and frank exchanges of views.

Invitations

Simon and I did everything together – well, almost everything! We were always there for each other and we loved each other's company. So, when Simon died, one of the ways I dealt with the consequential loneliness, was to accept any invitation that I was offered. It kept me away from the empty flat, which I hated returning to at night. When Simon was alive, I would decline many invitations to spend time with him. I now no longer needed to ... or wanted to.

The Lord Mayor of Westminster is the civic and ceremonial head of Westminster City Council and in this ambassadorial role, the Lord Mayor is entertained throughout the city at the expense of the relevant host, whether it is an ambassador, a community organisation or a local business. In doing so, the Lord Mayor undertakes about nine hundred engagements throughout the year – about 80% of which involve receiving hospitality. However, the role of Lord Mayor is non-political and so when being entertained, the Lord Mayor is not supposed to discuss political issues or anything about the running of the council.

On the other hand, the Leader and Deputy Leader of the Council are not only responsible for running the council but also act in a quasi-ambassadorial role, particularly when stakeholders want to meet the political leadership to discuss the council's services, its policies or to raise wider concerns about the city.

Both Philippa Roe and Nickie Aiken, when Leaders of the Council, were mothers of relatively young children and both had working husbands and so they frequently declined invitations, especially in the evenings, wanting to be at home to spend time with their families. This left much of the ambassadorial role of political leadership to the Deputy Leader. And I had the time and interest to carry out this political ambassadorial role. I was popular and so found myself frequently invited to represent the council.

So, not only before Simon's death in 2011 but also more intensely afterwards, I was out most evenings at council meetings and events or representing the council at a variety of receptions and dinners. Moreover, when working full time as a solicitor, the only time during the working day when I could meet people concerning council matters, was at lunch time, so meeting up over a bite to eat, was the most convenient way of doing this.

When I retired from Freeman Box in 2015, I was able to squeeze more of my council meetings into the daytime, giving me even more time in the evening to attend events and dinners.

My diary was organised by my diary secretary based in my office in City Hall. Cabinet members all benefitted from an assistant who organised their diaries, chased officers and provided appropriate briefings. Most shared a PA between two of them while the Leader and Deputy Leader each had a diary secretary and a policy assistant. My diary secretary arranged all my meetings, lunches and dinners and, where I did arrange them myself, the details would be added to my official diary.

In later years, in order for the Cabinet and senior officers to work together more effectively, a weekly grid would be circulated which would contain a schedule of many of the meetings, lunches and dinners that cabinet members were attending that week. If other leading members or officers wanted a cabinet member to raise an issue with the people they were meeting, they could do so. My detailed diary was also circulated widely to senior councillors and officers. So, for years, everyone knew what I was doing.

In fact, one of the most senior female officers of the council would regularly ask me if I required a 'plus one' to attend some of the more glamourous events I was attending. More frequently, officers or indeed councillors would invite me to raise issues or make a request of my dining companion.

To put it simply, everyone in the upper echelons of the council knew about my busy life. There were no secret meetings and no clandestine entertainment. Added to this was my compliance with the council's standing orders by fully and publicly disclosing every single one of these events and all the hospitality I enjoyed, tea and biscuits included. I did so for over ten years with the register available for public inspection on the council's website, without anyone raising an issue until the summer of 2017, more of which later. And what is more, I was scrupulous in doing so.

The rules required a disclosure within 28 days of any entertainment or hospitality received, of a value of more than £25. But how do you prove three years later that the meal you were seen having at a restaurant cost your host £23 and so fell below the limit, when someone wants to know why you did not declare the hospitality? I therefore took a decision to declare everything, even if it was costing less than ten pounds. In this way, I thought, I could not be accused of failing to make the necessary declaration, as to fail to do so was a criminal offence. I did not believe that over-declaring would be a problem. How wrong could I be.

With regard to gifts worth over £25, these too had to be declared. Again, I would frequently be given nominal gifts. A book about a country from a visiting mayor or an ambassador, books from architects keen to show off their work, a cheap *objet d'art* such as a glass bowl from a museum director after a tour of their new exhibition. When Americans visited, they frequently gave one boxes of candy or even soap bars and tea-towels with their football teams emblazoned on them.

Most gifts were worth much less than £25. The only exceptions were a handful of silver trowels, shovels and silver bricks which were given when I either topped out a new building or dug the first shovel full of mud when works started on construction of a new building. It is part of the tradition of such ceremonies that such gifts are given to about five or six of the people instrumental in the construction of the building. This would take place years after the planning process had ended.

At Christmas, constituents and people I had dealt with during the year would frequently send me gifts of champagne or boxes of wine. I am not a drinker, so the gifts were of no interest to me personally. I thought it rude to return them, so instead I donated them either to a charity I was working with at the time or gave them to staff in City Hall. But I still declared them … every one of them.

Benefitting the City

When invited to join a stakeholder for lunch or dinner, I usually took the opportunity to seek benefits for the council. For example, I was invited by the new general manager of a hotel in Westminster, to meet him and tour the hotel. He had been told that I was the man at Westminster who he should get to know. After the tour of some of the hotel's refurbished rooms, he invited me to join him for lunch in their restaurant. At the time, I was the Cabinet Member for Business which included responsibility for employment. We had set up a team, working with those finding it difficult to find and stay in employment, to help them to obtain jobs. We would train them for interviews, assist in ensuring they dressed appropriately, make sure they turned up on time and if they got the job, ensure they stuck with it by continuing to mentor them for months after they started. What we needed, however, were companies who were prepared to employ them.

Over lunch with the hotel general manager, I described the service we offered and he agreed to take on about thirty of our residents in various jobs in his hotel from doormen, to cleaners, kitchen porters and chambermaids. Yes, I received a free meal from this. But in reality, it cost my host nothing. The cost of the meal would be lost in the day's expenses in operating the hotel. My host certainly did not pay for the meal. But of course I declared the lunch in the Register of Hospitality and while a free lunch in a five-star hotel looks luxurious, it was a working lunch that gave thirty of our unemployed a step into work. A win-win for us all. Well, so you would think!

My Colleagues Came Too

With regard to the numerous receptions I attended, I was rarely the only councillor present. As Deputy Leader, I was often the guest of honour and was required to give a speech, but that comes with holding high office and being perceived as influential and powerful. For many of the events, lunches and dinners that I attended, I was just one of many councillors and officers also enjoying the hospitality. Although again, you would not have realised that if you had read the newspapers interpretation of my hospitality record.

MIPIM

MIPIM is the world's largest international property event hosted each year in Cannes, in the south of France. Tens of thousands of people interested in property attend from around the world. London has its own pavilion with displays and exhibitions from many property companies, trade organisations and local councils. Councils from other parts of the UK host their own pavilion and even the national government is represented. Much business is undertaken at the week-long convention.

For example, the City of London Corporation takes a massive stand and at least ten common councillors from the city attend at their council's expense. Westminster was one of the only London councils which did not attend or send any representatives. This would be frequently criticised, especially by groups and companies operating in Westminster.

In 2015, Westminster decided to accept the criticism levelled against it and send representation. Philippa Roe as Leader decided that she and I should attend with the Chief Executive and the Director of Planning. But when we were discussing this at a cabinet meeting, many of our colleagues thought it wrong for the council to pay for members and officers to attend. They thought it would attract bad publicity.

Philippa and the Chief Executive argued in favour, citing the good PR it would bring among the property industry. But they eventually conceded defeat and a compromise was suggested. I would be deputed to attend alone to represent the council. We would then ask the Westminster Property Association (a group representing most of the larger property companies operating in Westminster) to pay my travel and hotel costs. They were happy to do so. Therefore, the costs were not borne by

Speaking at a lunch at MIPIM with Jules Pipe (the Deputy Mayor for London on the left) and James Cooksey (of the Crown Estate on the right).

council taxpayers or any individual property owner.

I flew out and spent the three days in back-to-back meetings, giving speeches about Westminster and its planning policies. I was also invited to attend a number of functions, lunches and dinners each day, at which I was expected to give a speech about the council's work with the property industry.

In between these events, I would go to a series of receptions with hundreds of others attending the convention. I am not a drinker so while attending I rarely consumed any of the alcohol on offer.

At MIPIM with Jace Tyrrell, Liz Peace and Susan Freeman.

Westminster's presence was favourably commented upon and I found myself in great demand. The success of that first year resulted in the industry inviting me to MIPIM again over the following two years. Although the *Guardian* (more of which later) accused me of all-expenses-paid holidays in Cannes, it was hard work, exhausting and involved long hours. No sunbathing involved. But a lot of good PR for the council.

Being interviewed at MIPIM.

Westminster Restaurants

In Westminster, when entertained by the chief executive of a company or by a stakeholder, it is inevitable that the places they would normally entertain their guests included some of the best restaurants and hotels in the capital. They would think nothing of lunching at the Ivy, the Wolseley or at the restaurant in the Ritz Hotel or even the Goring Hotel. That is where they would probably dine regularly in any event. Some of my hosts were the owners of the restaurants, clubs and hotels where I dined, so the costs would have been lost in the day-to-day running costs. The type of people I was meeting would not go to Wagamama or a Pizza Hut for lunch.

So, when it was suggested by the press that I was being entertained at some of the most fashionable restaurants and hotels in the country, it was not surprising, if you understood the context.

But I do accept that from an outsider's point of view, it would seem extravagant. If you are a councillor in Wigan, you probably do get entertained at a Nando's – but I was operating in Westminster, which is a very different city. I can also understand that it would seem extravagant to someone living on benefits, but that is the reality of how business at a certain level is conducted in central London.

Hospitality in Context

Set in context, you will see that while I was the recipient of much hospitality, many gifts and the occasional foreign trip, it was because I was a full-time councillor, working hard for the people of Westminster and delivering numerous initiatives for the benefit of all Londoners. Whether it be raising funds to finance the Hanover Square public realm renovation project or persuading a company director to employ some unemployed youths from our council estates, it was all to support the work I was doing to make Westminster a better place.

Everyone at the council knew what I was doing and many fellow councillors were in receipt of hospitality and gifts too. Yes, I did receive more than others, but I was Deputy

Leader with a wide-ranging portfolio and seen externally as a key person to represent the council. I was in great demand to open conferences, seminars and events as well as a sought-after speaker at breakfast briefings, business lunches and dinners, expected to talk during and after the food, about the work of the council and our plans for the future. That came with the role but being alone following Simon's untimely death, I took up these responsibilities with relish.

Planning Committee Declarations

To me, transparency was important as was being honest and open. So, when chairing the council's senior Planning Committee, at the beginning of each meeting I would make a series of verbal declarations detailing any connection I had with any applicant or their agents. Even if I only knew the person because they attended meetings with me, I still declared that I knew them.

I liked putting applicants and their advisers at ease at meetings by starting off with a general chit chat. For example, a famous architect would come and see me on several occasions with different clients/applicants on a number of totally independent projects. Inevitably, after a while, I would get to know him and among the small talk at such meetings I would chat about his work and matters generally.

At the Planning Committee meeting, where the architect's application was being considered, I would declare that I 'knew' him. This did not mean that I was his best friend, but just that I knew him. Conscious of the fact that the people sitting in the public gallery may be concerned by the fact that I knew so many people associated with the applications, I would try and put this in context by always reading out a statement at the beginning of the meeting before making my declarations.

This statement included (inter alia) the following:

> In my capacity as Deputy Leader and Cabinet Member for Planning it is inevitable and part of my role that I get to know, meet and talk to leading members of the planning and property industry including landowners and developers and their professional teams such as architects, surveyors, planning consultants, lawyers and public affairs advisers as well as residents, residents' associations and amenity groups. It does not mean that they are my personal friends or that I had a pecuniary interest but merely that I had worked with them in my capacity as Cabinet Member for Planning.

It is appreciated that a number of members of the public attending their first council meeting in the public gallery may have been surprised by my declarations, but my preamble tried to put it in context.

I felt that I would be a narrow-minded cabinet member for planning if I did not meet any developer or their architects and agents and thereby understand the workings of the industry.

Local Newspaper Headlines

In September 2017, when the local free newspaper that covered the Soho, Mayfair and St James's area included an article about the long list of declarations of hospitality made by my colleague Jonathan Glanz and myself, I did not give it much thought. Jonathan was in a long-running battle with a colleague and we assumed that the colleague in question may have given the paper the story about Jonathan's long list of hospitality declarations. His was about a third of the length of mine, but of course he was only a backbencher at the time. It is my view, that having been referred to Jonathan's online Declaration of Hospitality, the paper's reporter also looked at the declaration of all the other councillors and came across my lengthy list.

When the article appeared, I was not too bothered as I had done nothing wrong. In fact, the opposite. I had declared absolutely everything and so clearly had not broken any laws. Not to have declared anything was unlawful.

Following the article appearing in the West End newspaper, I sought a meeting with the council's Head of Legal Services. She came to my office and we discussed the article. Her advice was that I had done nothing wrong. As she explained, it was a criminal offence not to make a declaration but not unlawful to over-declare. On further discussions about the detailed declarations made, she did suggest that I did not need to declare so much, as many were worth under £25 in value or were of a total private nature. I took note and amended my future declarations accordingly. I thought nothing more and within a few weeks the article and the issue were forgotten.

Elections Approaching

At the beginning of 2018 with just four months before the local elections, the divisions over Brexit were seriously damaging the Conservatives, and the Prime Minister, Theresa May, was under siege.

The Labour Party in Westminster were convinced they would, for the first time ever, win control of Westminster Council in the coming local elections. It was rumoured that the Leader of the Opposition had already given notice to his employer of his intention to resign from his job to become Leader of the Council on a full-time basis, once they had gained control.

At the same time, the Conservative group on the council (led by Nickie Aiken) were announcing a whole range of exciting new initiatives and programmes and receiving a lot of positive responses. Added to this was Nickie's enthusiasm and love of campaigning together with her ability to motivate the Conservative troops to get out and canvas.

Nickie put pressure on all the Conservative councillors to join a mammoth canvas each Saturday morning, backed up by a series of street stalls distributing Tory literature. In each ward, several local members together with friends of the ward councillors would meet up on a street corner in the ward to start the canvassing sessions. Before we began, we would all be photographed holding 'Vote Conservative' posters. The photo would then be heavily circulated on social media to boost the morale of our canvassing teams.

The Labour Party started to respond, but they only comprised a handful of canvassers in each photo and they were often the same ones.

Nationally, the Brexiteers v Remainers divide was still damaging the Conservative Party and, in the referendum, Westminster had voted predominantly to remain in the EU and so many felt the Conservatives would be punished by the Remainers in the local elections. In addition, the statistics showed that in the 2017 general election, the once-safe Cities of London and Westminster seat had become a marginal, with Mark Field only just hanging on to the seat. The swing away from the Conservative Party in London made Westminster Council a target for Labour in the pending elections.

The Labour Party, feeling that the momentum was in their favour, were however concerned that the Conservatives, led by Nickie were gaining too much ground and so they had to pull a card out of the box to give their campaign a boost.

And that card was me!

Targeted

My understanding, from whispers coming out of the Labour group, was that they wanted to 'get me' as probably the most prominent councillor on the Conservative side, apart from the Leader. Added to this was their view that I had become too powerful and had to be brought down a peg or two. I am sure that this view was also shared by some of my own colleagues, feeling that not only had I become too powerful, with my large office and my cabinet responsibilities covering a wide range of high-profile areas of the council's work, but that I had been doing this for too long.

I had been a part of the leadership team for almost eighteen years (Deputy Leader for almost ten and Chief Whip – number three in the council hierarchy – for eight years). Most senior councillors never stayed in the cabinet longer than five or six years and yet I had been in the cabinet for nearly eighteen. Jealousy is rooted in politics just as much as it is in everyday life.

Journalistic Enquiries

It was late morning on Monday 19th February 2018 when it kicked off. I was at City Hall (as I was most days) and in between meetings when I decided to go to the toilet. Walking to the Gents on my floor, I started to check my emails on my mobile phone. There was an email from a journalist on the national newspaper, the *Guardian*, asking me a number of questions about my Declarations of Hospitality.

I was pretty annoyed that something I thought had been dealt with was now back again. After returning to my office, I read it carefully. But as I was doing so, I was called into my next meeting with the Leader and some guests. However, I could not concentrate and just thought about how I would respond to the journalist who was imposing a one-hour deadline for my response.

When the meeting ended, I returned to my office to find the council's Head of Press waiting for me. He too had been contacted. The Leader and the Director of Communications soon joined us and we discussed how I should respond. They were all confident that this was a non-story. It was agreed that the council would issue a formal statement on my behalf.

After a few drafts, I was satisfied with the statement and it was sent to the journalist within his self-imposed deadline. I had accepted in my mind that the piece would probably appear on page twenty of the next day's *Guardian* and that the issue would disappear over the next few days, very much as the similar article had done when published a few months earlier in the West End freebie. The Head of Legal Services had already assured me, months earlier, that I had done nothing wrong and since then I had only been declaring hospitality and gifts that exceeded the threshold and were properly declarable.

The Story Breaks

Relieved that the matter had been satisfactorily dealt with, I went home to change and freshen up, as I was due to attend my cousin Sally-Anne Stein's birthday party at Harry's Bar in Mayfair. I was a little worried about attending as I would only know a few people but was delighted when I found that I did in fact know many of the guests and others were very friendly, so I had lots of people to talk to.

During the dessert, I was in deep conversation with my neighbour when my mobile phone rang. I discreetly looked at the phone to see that it was my sister-in-law Lisa calling. Lisa rarely rang me and if she did it was usually an emergency because she was feeling unwell. Making my excuses, I went into a neighbouring room to take the call.

Lisa assured me that she was fine, but that she had been watching Sky News and they had discussed the next morning's newspapers. In doing so, they proceeded to show the front page of the *Guardian*. Most of the front page was the story about me with a massive photo of me (taken at the Chelsea Flower Show the previous year). This was not at all what I had expected.

I thought no one would notice, let alone read, a small piece in the middle pages of the left-wing *Guardian* newspaper and so the story would be quickly forgotten. But the front page – and almost the whole of it! This was a game changer.

The front page of the Guardian *on
20th February 2018.*

Lisa explained that as it was front page, the studio guests had discussed it, adding fuel to the fire. There was nothing I could do at 11 pm on that Monday night, so I tried to return to the dinner party and enjoy myself, but I must admit, I was quite distracted and so after a short while, I made my excuses and left.

The Next Morning

At the time, City Hall in Victoria Street was undertaking a major refurbishment which required us to move out for two years. For a temporary period, our main office was in the Strand overlooking Trafalgar Square but although the building was very prestigious and perfect for the council's member and officer leadership to occupy, it was not big enough and so we also rented three floors at Portland House in Victoria for several of our departments to occupy during this period.

Nickie Aiken, the Leader of the Council, felt that it was important to show the officers who were occupying Portland House that we did not think they were second-class citizens and so she decided that she would hold all her meetings on a Tuesday in Portland House rather than in the Strand. Likewise, the Chief Executive, who hosted his Senior Management Team's weekly meeting on a Tuesday, would also meet with his team in Portland House that day each week. During Nickie's leadership, she and I would attend the first forty-five minutes of the weekly Senior Management Team (which is attended by all the top tier of officers) to go through the major issues in each of the departments that week. In Nickie's absence, I would chair this meeting.

As the *Guardian* article was published on the Tuesday morning, I woke up early and made my way to Portland House to attend the Senior Management Team, picking up three copies of the *Guardian* on the way. When I got there, I sat in my car and read the piece several times. It was certainly a hatchet job and took everything out of context and certainly sexed up the entertainment side of things.

The Guardian Story

The article read:

> Westminster city council's deputy leader has emerged as a contender for the title of the most schmoozed politician in Britain, receiving entertainment, meals and gifts more than 500 times in the last three years.
>
> From tickets to the hottest West End shows to exclusive dinners in London's finest restaurants and trips to the south of France, the official declarations reveal an extraordinary lifestyle that included one day in Mallorca, when Robert Davis managed two lunches, the first at the home of Andrew Lloyd Webber and the second at the home of the Earl of Chichester.
>
> Davis, the Conservative deputy leader of the central London borough and until last year the chairman of its powerful planning committee, was entertained by and received gifts from property industry figures at least 150 times since the start of 2015 – a rate of almost once a week.

After listing many of the people who had hosted me for lunches and dinners, the article quoted at length from Labour councillors:

> Labour said the extent of Davis's register of interests was evidence of a 'broken culture at Westminster council' and said there was a 'clear perception that senior Conservative councillors have a very close relationship with developers. It has accused the council of letting developers get away with building far fewer 'affordable' homes than required under Westminster's planning policy.
>
> Adam Hug, leader of the Labour group on Westminster council, said residents needed to be reassured 'that their representatives are fighting for them rather than dining out on developers' expense accounts'.
>
> Labour believes that such an approach does not help build public trust that the council will put the needs of residents before those of property developers and business interests,' he said. 'They have pushed through controversial schemes and promoted an approach to architecture based on the whims of senior councillors.

The article did try and balance the piece by setting out my and the council's response by saying:

> Davis added: 'As planning chairman it was an important part of my job to meet groups ranging from developers to residents, property agents, heritage associations, arts groups and trade organisations. These meetings were all properly declared and open to anyone to examine. Their sole purpose was to ensure and encourage the right kind of development in Westminster and ensure that anything put before the council was going to benefit the city as a whole.'

The article then stated:

> The records show Davis also dined with several planning consultancy companies whose job it is to help their clients secure planning consent. When he was chairman of the planning committee, he was given breakfast at the Carlton Club in St James by the consultancy Thorncliffe which boasts on its website: 'We get clients planning committee approval.'

This was ironic. The breakfast at the Carlton Club was to give a speech to Thorncliffe's clients about planning issues. First of all, I was speaking so much that I did not actually eat anything and so the breakfast meeting should not have been declared at all. Furthermore, I only accepted the invitation because one of the Labour councillors worked for Thorncliffe and I thought I would get some brownie points from him for doing so!

But the article did make it clear that:

> There is no suggestion that Davis breached any rules. There is no suggestion of wrongdoing on the part of Davis or any other named individual.

But that was hidden at the very end of the article, probably inserted at the insistence of their lawyers. But the hatchet was well and truly in my back.

The Conclave

After the first part of the Senior Management Team meeting finished, Nickie asked the Chief Executive to suspend the rest of his meeting so that he, Nickie and Julia Corkey (the Director of Communications) could join me in a private meeting to discuss the *Guardian* story.

They were sympathetic to me but they were extremely concerned about the perception among Westminster residents who would not understand the full picture. However, I was assured that they all agreed that I had done nothing wrong. It just looked bad, despite the *Guardian* making it clear at the end of the lengthy article that I had done nothing wrong or illegal.

We agreed that the council would issue a further statement, in case other media picked up on the story. My friend Steve Summers (a fellow councillor) rang to offer his support and agreed to join the meeting to assist in the drafting of the statement. Daniel Astaire, a solicitor and another friend and colleague, also assisted by email and by phone.

During the meeting, someone called to advise us that there was an army of photographers, journalists and TV cameras waiting for me outside City Hall in the Strand. They were clearly not aware that on Tuesday mornings we all decamped to Victoria!

The Chief Executive suggested that in his view it would be sensible to kill the story, by me resigning as Deputy Leader. But Nickie would have none of it and defended me, saying that we would get through it, recognising it was a deliberate political act with the Westminster Labour Party probably behind the story.

It was suggested that I should go home and fly out to my flat in Mallorca the next day until all the publicity had died down. Rather distraught, I left for my flat to pack and book a flight.

That evening I put on the London local TV News only to see my story as the headline. Not only had they filmed outside my flat (presumably, while I was in the earlier meeting in Victoria) but the TV journalist presenting the story was filmed talking to the camera in front of the Ritz Hotel. Great drama at my expense. A similar story was shown on the other stations with another presenter standing outside the Ivy restaurant. The story was repeated again after the 10 O'clock news on both main channels. I was having my fifteen minutes of fame or infamy.

The National Press Takes up the Story

The following day, on the way to the airport, I picked up copies of all the morning papers. I was featured in all of them. Not just a small column on page 36 but a half or whole page including half a page in *The Times* and half a page near the front in the *Daily Mail*. All included photos of me, some of which made me look quite handsome while in others, I looked a bit seedy. All the articles included photos of the Ritz, the Ivy or other restaurants I had frequented.

I was pleased I was getting out of town. I made it to Mallorca without any hassle and, out of sight and out of mind, the story started to fade. Of course, I had the weekly and monthly periodicals to look forward to but the only one that went to town was *Private Eye*. I had previously had my run-ins with them and so was expecting the worst and they did not disappoint.

After a week away I returned to find the world had moved on. The *Guardian* with me on the front page was now being used for fish and chips. I was relieved. Over the next week or so life went back to normal although I quietened down both my social life and my need to make appropriate declarations.

Group Apology

With our next group meeting approaching, Nickie suggested that I tackle the issue head on, by giving an apology to the group before colleagues raised the issue. I prepared a carefully worded statement, making it clear that I had never intended to embarrass the group or the council and apologising profusely. I read out the statement at the beginning of the meeting and Nickie moved straight on to another issue before anyone could make any mischief.

While I had many friends among the councillors, I had annoyed several with policies on such matters as the pedestrianisation of Oxford Street (which at the behest of both Nickie and, before her, Philippa, I had led as a project) as well as my support of the development industry. Others were jealous of my power and influence over an eighteen-year period. Many had only served on the council during a period when I had continuously been part of the leadership team and they wanted change, if not an opportunity to hold many of the positions I held on the council including that of Deputy Leader, a post which I had held through three leaders and for just short of ten years. Politicians are by their nature ambitious and if someone clogs up the hierarchy by clinging on to the top jobs for a long time, this prevents others from climbing up Disraeli's greasy pole. I was therefore conscious of how some of my colleagues might react. But thanks to Nickie's handling of the meeting, she seemed to kick the issue into the long grass. Or so I thought!

Stepping Aside

Having got through the group meeting, life again returned to normal. The issue was rarely discussed or raised again.

Well, that was until the morning of Wednesday 7th March 2018, when the council's press office received a call from the same *Guardian* journalist, who had written that first article. He told them that he was intending to run another article that week, raising new issues and would continue to do so until I resigned. This was a shock. It was clearly now a personal vendetta against me.

As soon as Nickie heard, she came into my office with Tim Mitchell, the Chief Whip, and explained that she was concerned that this would dominate our election campaign and that we could not afford to lose control of the council because of this ongoing hatchet job against me. She assured me that she was convinced I had done nothing wrong, but suggested that it was in the best interest of the Conservative group and of the council, that I 'stepped aside' (as she put it) as Deputy Leader and as a Cabinet Member. The last thing I wanted was to be the cause of our losing control of the council, so I accepted the inevitable.

Nickie went on to suggest that I self-refer myself to the council's Monitoring Officer (the council's Head of Legal Services) and request that she set up an enquiry into whether I had indeed done anything illegal or broken the council's Member's Code of Conduct. Nickie referred to a close friend of hers who was a member of Parliament, who had been involved in a scandal that had been exposed by the press and to clear his name, had referred the matter to the parliamentary equivalent of our Monitoring Officer to undertake an investigation. In doing so, he resigned as a government junior minister. After the enquiry cleared him, he returned to government in another senior governmental role. Nickie argued that my referral of the matter to an internal investigation would hopefully formally clear me in a matter of weeks, allowing me to return to high office in the council in the future. How naïve I was!

I had little choice. With the withdrawal of Nickie's support, I (as she put it) 'stood aside' as Deputy Leader and as a Cabinet Member. My mind was in a spin. Everything I had worked for, for years, was coming to an abrupt end. I had given up my job as a partner at Freeman Box to be a full-time Deputy Leader. I had worked all the hours given to me (often eighteen hours a day and certainly seven days a week including public holidays) working on council matters and with the interests of Westminster at the forefront of my mind. All gone in just a few minutes.

Although Nickie dangled the possibility of a return to the front bench, it was clearly not going to be as Deputy Leader as the leadership and deputy leadership elections would shortly follow the local elections, and it was unlikely I would be in a position to stand or even get re-elected as Deputy Leader. Giving up my lovely office was probably the saddest part for me.

As Nickie hugged me, she was in tears, saying that she had no choice, which I accepted. I asked if I could clear my office (which was full of my photos covering every inch of the walls as well as mementos and souvenirs) the following weekend, when no one was around to see me doing so. She readily agreed.

At this stage, Julia Corkey, our Director of Communications and Policy, joined the meeting and said how sorry she was but that it was in everyone's best interest including my own. She also emphasised that I needed to obtain proper independent professional legal advice in respect of my referral of the matter to the council's Monitoring Officer and should not rely on only my own judgement and advice or that of friends. I agreed.

We also agreed that Nickie would announce my resignation at that night's full council meeting. I told her that I did not want to attend the meeting. She understood but it was our intention to have a series of photographs taken of all the councillors on the steps of the Council House where the meeting was being held, to immortalise the 2014–2018 councillors.

The final photo of the Conservative councillors in March 2018.

It was customary to have this group photo taken at the last council meeting before local elections, as many colleagues were not standing again or would fail to win re-election and so it would be a record of the councillors elected during the outgoing four-year term. Nickie insisted I be in the photo. I was happy to do so.

I went to the Council House at 6 pm that night with my robes, jabot, gloves and past Lord Mayor's badge. No one except a handful of people knew that I had resigned at that stage. As Deputy Leader I stood next to the Lord Mayor, on his other side from Nickie. As soon as the photos had been taken, everyone disrobed and went up to have supper before the main council meeting which was to start at 7 pm. I stood around chatting until they had all gone up to supper and discreetly left, without anyone noticing. The meeting started in my absence and at the beginning, Nickie stood up and announced my decision. A huge part of my life was now officially over.

Legal Advice

When I returned home, I immediately phoned Susan Freeman. Susan was the wife of Jeremy Freeman, who had been one of my partners in my law firm Freeman Box. Susan was a senior partner in the well-known law firm Mishcon. I knew that Mishcon frequently represented clients on such highly political issues and in discussing my case with Susan, she confirmed that they had a whole department specialising in what they called 'Reputation Management'. This sounded perfect.

But I explained that I was concerned about cost. And how right I was to be worried. She reassured me that I would benefit from mates rates. I agreed to instruct her firm and in turn she said she would arrange for the head of the Reputation Management department to call me the following day.

One of the reasons I eventually pulled the plug on my political life was when my legal costs hit nearly £60,000, with about another £20,000 required to take the matter further with no assurance that I would ever be returned to the front bench.

Further Story

I must mention that the *Guardian's* threat of publishing a further story in the paper, was thwarted by the council giving the story of my resignation to the *Evening Standard* which covered it the following day. The *Guardian* journalist phoned the council's press office complaining, emphasising that they were furious that the *Evening Standard* had been given the story ahead of them.

In any event, they proceeded to publish the 'new' story the following day but when we all read it, it contained nothing new at all, but merely repeated the same story as had been in the earlier front page piece. This threat to keep publishing new stories was just to get me to resign, which I am told was their intention from day one. Not exactly fair journalism at its best.

The Enquiry

A couple of days later, the council's Monitoring Officer informed us (that's me and my lawyer Harry Eccles-Williams) that because she was conflicted in having already advised me that I was doing nothing wrong following the local West End paper covering a similar story the previous September, she had brought in a QC to conduct the enquiry. He was James Goudie QC, an experienced senior silk specialising in administrative and public law and local government law. I thought this acceptable, although it did seem to be going over the top, as I had assumed it would be dealt with swiftly and internally but I did understand her reasons for going to an independent barrister.

A couple of weeks later, I mentioned this to my friend Terry Neville, the former senior legal adviser to John Lewis and before that the City Solicitor at Westminster Council and a former legal adviser to the London Boroughs Association. Terry was now a well-respected conservative councillor in Enfield. He knew of Goudie straight away and was horrified. He explained that James Goudie was well known to him and that he was known to have previously been active in the Labour Party.

My own subsequent research revealed that his wife (Baroness Goudie) was a Labour peer in the House of Lords and that Goudie had himself stood for Parliament in the 1974 general elections for the Labour Party in Brent North, albeit unsuccessfully. He had also served as Labour Leader of Brent Council between 1977–1978. In addition, he had been chairman of the Society of Labour Lawyers and was in chambers with Tony Blair's friend and Lord Chancellor, Lord Irvine. *The Telegraph* in December 2001 described Goudie as 'Labour's most powerful lawyer'. He was also adviser to the Labour Party's National Executive Committee.

I was horrified. I assumed that like the *Guardian*, the Council officers were now determined to get me and instead of this so-called 'independent enquiry' being a way of quickly moving on and allowing me to return to the fold, I was being set up. After given up my life for the council, I was now about to be hung out to dry. I spoke to Nickie, who I had thought was supporting me, but she advised me that she did not want to get involved.

My lawyer then wrote to the council's Monitoring Officer, raising our concerns at their choice of Goudie. Almost by return, we received a brusque response, making it clear that it was the monitoring officer's decision and reminding us that as a QC, Goudie would be acting with absolute integrity and indicating annoyance that we were challenging her decision. After discussing the surprisingly aggressive response with me, Harry called her and tried to explain our concern. Her response was equally sharp as she explained that she was not prepared to change her mind and if I wanted to pursue the issue, this would not help my case.

After a further discussion, Harry and I agreed that we would have to proceed with Goudie if we were to prevent the council's team turning nasty. We would have to rely on Goudie's honour as a QC to give me a fair hearing.

In a call with the Monitoring Officer, Harry discussed a timetable. It was suggested that before the enquiry started, I would put together a detailed written case in my defence. This I was keen to do. But as I was keen on fighting the forthcoming local elections, I asked if they could wait until after the election for me to start work on my case, with a deadline of producing this by the end of June. This was acceptable to the council. Accordingly, everything was put on hold for a few months.

Elections

Over the following few months, I put everything into canvassing and running my election campaign, as it was essential that I was re-elected in the May local elections. I knew that the Labour Party were determined to defeat me and make mischief in doing so. I also had to prove that my electorate supported me, notwithstanding this stupid story.

When I set my mind to something, I put my whole heart into it. In fact, I put my whole life into it. I wanted to run the election campaign like a military battle. The first thing I did at the beginning of 2018 was to persuade a friend, who owned an empty office in my ward, to loan me the office to run our campaign from.

In previous elections, we had used a ward committee member's front room for the entire campaign but this caused the host inconvenience and also they frequently were not available to let us in, when we wanted access to our election material or the canvas sheets. Our own dedicated campaign room was essential if we were to start the campaign properly and professionally.

However, we could only use this office for the period before the official election campaign started. After that legal date, when all expenses have to be accounted for, we had no choice but vacate the office and revert to the ward vice-chairman's front room for our headquarters.

I loaned the campaign office my spare computer and printer together with a kettle, mugs and a tea towel and we were in business. We printed off thousands of canvas cards. These were sheets listing everyone on the electoral register with their address and giving details of their past canvassing preferences.

Canvassing in my ward – April 2018.

For a given name, it would tell us not only who they had pledged to vote for in the last nine elections but whether they had actually voted. To find a person who had pledged to vote Conservative in the past nine elections (local and national) and who had actually voted in all those nine elections, was more important to find and see if they would pledge a Conservative vote again, than someone who had pledged to vote Conservative during the past nine elections but had never voted. A promised vote is useless if someone does not

Canvassing in my ward with Susie Burbridge and Daniel Astaire.

have a record of actually voting. Of course, if we did find them in, and they pledged to vote Conservative, then the canvasser's job was to emphasise the importance of actually voting and either persuade them to obtain a postal vote (and we would have the forms with us) or ensure they would be in the country on election day.

I recruited a number of friends and persuaded them to commit to a few days canvassing with me, each month. With a number of elderly members of my ward committee who did not like canvassing running the office, we were ready for business.

Now I was free of responsibilities at the council and therefore with an empty diary for the first time in decades, I diarised to go canvassing between 10 am and noon, between 2 pm and 4 pm and then again from 6 pm to 8 pm each weekday with further canvassing at 10 am to 1 pm on Saturdays. Sunday I took off to recharge my batteries.

Although friends and colleagues would join me on most occasions, I still went out regularly by myself when there was no one available, as I was determined to keep to the rota and by doing so, ensure that we got to as many people as we could. The weather was irrelevant, hot or cold, dry or wet, snowy or sunny, I still went out on cue.

For those of you not acquainted with canvassing, the secret is not to waste time converting someone to vote Conservative, but to find out where your vote is and then, having recorded where your supporters live, you must then ensure that they come out to vote on election day itself.

As an experienced canvasser and one of three local long-term councillors, I knew the area well and my experience told me that if I felt that I was meeting someone who might vote for me and my colleagues after some persuasion, I would (despite the general rule not to waste my time) spend a little time with them, hoping I would succeed in getting them to vote for us. And sometimes it worked.

The Labour Party thought my case a big election winner and so extracts from the *Guardian* and my photo appeared on the front page of all their literature, not only in my ward but throughout Westminster. At first, I was extremely upset, thinking my little issue was going to affect the election result and I was really concerned I would single-handedly lose us the election. But within a few days, the Party's intelligence feedback was that me and my 'issue' were rarely mentioned on the doorstep.

Despite canvassers in all the wards out in force and knocking on thousands of doors, only a handful of people were mentioning me and of those who did, half were supportive of me and saw it as a non-issue and a deliberate Labour Party ploy. Of those who did mention it adversely, most were clearly non-Tories. I started feeling a little more optimistic.

About six weeks before the election day, the Labour Party started canvassing my ward hard. In all the eight previous elections that I had fought in the ward, being such a safe Conservative seat meant that we rarely saw a Labour Party canvasser. The candidates standing against me were usually just paper candidates (that is, they did not think they would win, but were just standing to make up numbers). But this time, hordes of young Momentum supporters swamped the ward with over thirty young canvassers covering street after street. But my feedback was that this back-fired because as soon as

With friends and colleagues out canvassing in my Lancaster Gate ward.

anyone asked them a question about Westminster or the local area, the canvassers had no idea how to respond.

In each ward, three councillors would be elected and so each of the main parties would put up three candidates. Historically, in Lancaster Gate, all three Conservatives always won. But in some other wards in Westminster, the voting was so close that two Conservative candidates would win with the third seat going to the Labour Party. I had a persistent fear that my two colleagues Susie Burbridge and Andrew Smith would win and I would do well but not well enough and one of the Labour Party candidates would beat me.

To make this scenario more plausible, one of the Labour Party candidates had stood against me unsuccessfully numerous times and so had name recognition. She also lived in my ward and had been the headteacher of a local school. I feared that she would pick up sufficient personal votes to beat me.

Councillor Susie Burbridge

One of my two ward colleagues was Susie Burbridge. She is also one of my closest friends. She had originally been elected for the Maida Vale ward in 1998 but after disagreements with one of her ward colleagues, she decided to look for another ward in time to fight the 2002 elections. At that time, Simon was Leader and I was Chief Whip. Simon and I were the two councillors for Lancaster Gate and our third colleague was Richard Tallboys – a former British Ambassador but not a very effective councillor. He spent most of his time on cruise ships lecturing and so had decided to retire from the council.

Susie was determined to get selected in Bryanston and Dorset Square ward where there were two vacancies and she had been working hard to do so. Simon and I recognised her as a hard-working councillor, so wanted her to find a new seat. We were both members of the Bryanston and Dorset Square ward selection committee, but there was going to be a fight between four strong candidates. One of the councillors was seeking re-selection, namely Angela Hooper (also a close friend of mine and an excellent councillor).

The third candidate was a former councillor who had stood down four years earlier having represented St James's ward, only to have regretted standing down and so wanted to return. Carolyn Keen had been my Deputy Lord Mayor during my mayoralty. She too was highly regarded as a councillor.

The fourth candidate was Audrey Lewis, a former high-profile chairman of the Marylebone Association (the local residents society) and she lived in the ward (which Susie and Angela did not).

Despite four excellent candidates, we could only select three. But which one would we drop?

After each candidate was interviewed, from the ensuing discussions, it became clear from chatter in the selection committee room that Angela would be the unsuccessful one, even though she was the only current councillor for that ward and furthermore, was a member of Simon's Cabinet.

Susie Burbridge as Lord Mayor with me.

Audrey and Carolyn as the two who lived in the ward appeared to be the frontrunners. Susie had performed well. Simon whispered to me that we should make sure Angela was selected as the third candidate, as Susie would be better off being selected in our own ward, where we were still trying to find a candidate to become our third colleague in Lancaster Gate ward. Simon told the selection committee that Susie was the one not to select, but on the basis that he hoped he would help her find a seat elsewhere. On that advice, the other three were duly selected.

Susie was furious and when we took her aside to explain that she would be better off with us in Lancaster Gate, she made it clear that she disagreed and had her heart set on winning the Bryanston selection. She stormed off.

But a few weeks later, she appeared before the Lancaster Gate ward selection committee meeting and won the selection unanimously with Simon and my backing. From then on, we worked extremely well as a team and became close friends. I am sure she now accepts that she fitted in much better in Lancaster Gate than had she been elected in Marylebone.

Election Day Approaches
The election was to take place on Thursday 3rd May 2018. On the previous Friday night, we were all out canvassing when one of my supporters found pushed through some letter boxes, a leaflet about me. He gave me a copy. It contained a large photo of me with the headline: 'Don't vote for this man' and merely contained the link to the *Guardian* website revealing the original article about me.

I was not sure how to react. I was upset, but maybe I just had to accept that I was going down and would fail in my attempt to be re-elected to the council. Maybe this was for the best? But overnight, I gathered my strength and decided to try and ignore it and keep going. We realised that the leaflet had been distributed throughout my ward but our team managed to remove as many as we could following a blitz around all the streets.

We referred the leaflet to the council's Returning Office and to our agent, as the leaflet was illegal as it failed to include an imprint confirming who had published it, as was required by election law. But I knew they would do nothing about it and indeed that's what happened.

I believed I knew who was behind this document. I have no proof and can only surmise that it was her. A constituent of mine hated me and had over a period of time launched a one-person campaign against me, criticising me as frequently as she could in print and in letters of complaint to the council's Chief Executive. The reason for this hatred stemmed from her opposition to a planning application near to her home. I had chaired the planning committee that had granted the consent in question, but despite it being a committee decision, she blamed me, notwithstanding that the officers had recommended the application for approval as it satisfied all the council's policies.

I could not prove that it was her or someone else I had upset. One of the Labour Party candidates in my ward took me aside and assured me that it was not the Labour Party and

Telling early on election day morning outside the polling station in St Petersburgh Place.

informed me that they thought it had gone too far. Failing to leave an imprint of who had published any document in an election was a very serious criminal offence and I did not believe that the Labour Party would risk breaking the law and getting found out, as this misdemeanour was more serious than the accusations against me.

Over the next few days, it started to appear that the distribution of this leaflet had upset many constituents, who thought it nasty. I was stopped in the street on numerous occasions to be told that they were voting for me despite the leaflet and how disgraceful they thought it was. Several called it a deliberate political character assassination. Many cited my long history of dedicated work in the ward.

On the day itself, as usual I was telling outside one of my polling stations at 7 am for the opening of the polls. Telling was usually undertaken by the older members of my committee who did not like going out door to door. The three candidates always did the telling outside the three polling stations in my ward from 7 am to 9 am at each election.

Tellers stood or sat outside the polling station (often next to the opposition's own tellers) and asked the voters entering or leaving the polling station for their electoral register number. Everyone is given a registration number which is printed on the voting card everyone is sent before the election confirming they can vote and where to vote.

Every hour, the tellers would change over and the list of numbers would be taken to our committee HQ where they were added to the computer database confirming who had voted. By 4 pm we could then start 'knocking-up'.

The computer prints out lists of those constituents that we had canvassed over the past four months who had promised us that they would vote Conservative but who had not voted yet. Those who had voted and had given their electoral number to the tellers would have been deleted, so we would not waste our time and theirs knocking on their door. It was not a perfect system, as often we would knock on doors where we had no details of their having voted but where the elector advised us that they had. But it was a good way (used by all the parties) of getting ones vote out. Elections are won not by promises of votes but in getting out to actually vote, those who had promised to do so.

Voting in the first two hours, during my telling stint, was brisk and many voters recognised me and wished me well. At 4 pm, with knocking-up started, I was swamped by numerous friends coming to help and knock-up for me. We kept going until 10 pm, when the polling stations closed.

I returned home exhausted. After a shower and change of clothes, I drove to the count. The suspense was immense. I had been so preoccupied all day with my own ward that I had no idea what was happening elsewhere in Westminster. It appears that things were not going well. At one stage during the day, the leadership were concerned that we would lose both West End ward and St James's ward. Bad signs were coming from Maida Vale ward and Bayswater ward. My friend Jonathan Glanz, the councillor for West End ward, told me it was guaranteed he had lost. I was told colleagues were also concerned that I was going to lose too.

I sat and watched the votes being counted in my own ward. It was fascinating. The Conservative vote seemed to be holding up and although Labour were doing well, their vote did not look as strong as ours. The counters first went through all the ballot papers and placed them in appropriately coloured boxes where the ballot sheets showed all three of the votes being cast for the same party (known as voting for the 'Ticket'). Where there was cross-voting between parties then the ballot papers were put in a fourth box while those voting for less than three candidates or for more, or those where the voter's intention was unclear or the ballot paper was defaced were put in another box to allow individual judgement on each ballot.

This reminds me of the count at an earlier election, where again I was watching the votes being counted. One ballot paper that required adjudication from the returning officer had no crosses against any of the names. The voter had merely written across the ballot paper, in large thick capital letters – **A B C D**.

And next to each letter the following:

> **A**nyone
> **B**ut
> **C**ouncillor
> **D**avis

That's when I realised that not everyone loved me! I am pleased to say that the voting slip was deemed a defaced vote and not counted.

Returning to the 2018 count, when it got to the box of cross-voters, when people had not voted for a ticket, many of the voters were voting for two of the Labour candidates AND me. I was shocked. That nasty leaflet had in fact helped me.

I knew Susie would come top of the poll. She always did, even when Simon was Leader and standing in the same ward. Susie is an amazing local councillor, spending hours in the ward looking after many constituents. She visits many of them regularly and has got to know their families and would help them with a range of matters that were far outside the responsibility of councillors. We all knew that she had a great personal following. This was particularly the case on Hallfield, our large council estate, where she had been battling for the residents over the poor quality of workmanship carried out by the council's contractors. She would earn top place.

When it came to those who had voted for just a single candidate, again my personal vote held up and I was only just pipped by Susie's personal vote. And then the count was over and we were kept in the dark for about half an hour. We could guess at the results by seeing the bundles of votes but it was a guess.

As we waited, the bad news started to leak out. We had lost two seats in Maida Vale (we had lost the third four years earlier) and had lost a seat in Bayswater which would have a mixed ward.

Then our vote was announced. The results were:

Baring	Liberal Democrat	456
Burbridge	**Conservative**	**1,318**
Davis	**Conservative**	**1,226**
Gray	Liberal Democrat	376
Piddock	Labour	992
Smith	**Conservative**	**1,223**
Ubilava	Liberal Democrat	321
Whitmore	Labour	967
Wyatt	Labour	852

I had been re-elected and to give me hope, I had come second (albeit by just three votes) but it was vindication. Bearing in mind what I had been through and that nasty circular, I had feared that even if I were re-elected, I would come a poor third, hundreds of votes behind Susie and Andrew. Well, I did not. I came second. I left the count with my head held high. I flew to Mallorca the next day to recover and start work on preparing my case.

The victorious re-elected councillors for Lancaster Gate ward immediately after the results were announced.

My Case

I did take a couple of days off to relax and recover after the campaign but on the Monday I sat at my computer and started preparing my case. I had two jobs to do. Firstly, I had to prepare a document setting out justification for all the hospitality I had received. The second job was to go through and schedule each of the 621 hospitality and gift declarations made between 5th January 2015 and March 2018 and provide details, such as the name of the host or donor, details of all planning applications made by the host/donor and whether any planning committee chaired by me and considering any applications made by the host/donor, had overturned the officer's recommendation. The schedule also addressed whether the hospitality or gift should have been declared at all.

This involved me in substantial research as I was required to look back (through the council's website) to every planning committee I had chaired since 2000 and download, save and read the committee reports, to assess whether I had supported the officer's recommendation. Copies of all the relevant applications, committee reports and committee minutes were not only downloaded but saved and collated.

It took me about six weeks to complete and once I was happy with the documents I had prepared and collated, they comprised six lever arch files. I duly presented them to Harry, my lawyer at Mishcon. I must add that I also gave him a USB with everything carefully filed in sub-directories on it.

The Substance of My Case

I should mention at this stage that my review as to whether I should have declared every one of the 621 declarations concluded that:

I should have declared:	344 of them	55%
I should NOT have declared:	277 of them	45%

I thought I was being open and transparent by declaring everything. But that was my big

453

mistake. I should have been more select as clearly my colleagues had been, as many of them privately admitted to me.

I also obtained character references from over forty friends and colleagues such as Sir David Brewer, the former Lord-Lieutenant of Greater London, the Rt Hon. Lord Deben (John Selwyn Gummer), the former Secretary of State for Local Government, the Very Revd John Hall, Dean of Westminster Abbey, Lord Lloyd Webber (Andrew Lloyd Webber), composer, producer and theatre owner, Valerie Shawcross CBE, the former (Labour) Deputy Mayor of London as well as William Shawcross CVO, Royal biographer and former chairman of the Charites Commission.

I was touched and honoured to read such glowing references and in fact, in the final report issued by the council, they commented on the impressive references submitted on my behalf.

My lawyer, Harry, spent considerable time going through everything, rewriting sections and editing the report. Once I had approved it, I was very happy, believing that it made a persuasive case in my favour.

The Enquiry Itself

While I was working on my case, James Goudie requested a brief conference with my lawyer and me to discuss the parameters of his investigation. We therefore attended on him at his chambers and were joined by the council's Monitoring Officer and her assistant.

James Goudie made it clear at the start that he had given my case an initial review (and before seeing the case that I was working on), he believed that I had done nothing illegal and so would not investigate that at all. His view was that his role was to see whether I had broken the council's Code of Conduct and in this respect only two of the numerous codes were in his view relevant.

These were:

1. A councillor must not place themselves under a financial or other obligation to any individual or organisation that might seek to influence them in the performance of their official duties (para 2.2 of the Code of Conduct)

2. [A councillor must ...] promote and support high standards of conduct through leadership and by example (para 2.10 of the Code of Conduct)

In addition, he would consider whether my actions were 'inappropriate from a point of view of Westminster City Council's reputation'.

My QC's Opinion

On the issue as to whether I had breached that part of the Code which said a councillor must 'promote and support high standards of conduct through leadership and by example', Harry suggested we seek the advice of our own QC. At great expense (over £6,000 for his short written opinion), we instructed Richard Drabble QC.

Drabble's written legal Opinion argued that:

1. Councillor Davis has undertaken a comprehensive assessment of his declarations and his participation in planning decisions. This assessment reveals no evidence at all of Councillor Davis placing himself under a financial or other obligation to any individual or organisation that might seek to influence him in the performance of his official duties. It must be borne in mind that this is a very specific requirement in the Code. The mere receipt of hospitality or gifts does not constitute the imposition of any obligation. The witness statement of Councillor Davis points out that there was no reason for him to place himself under an obligation, being well-off financially and a man of high reputation.

   Councillor Davis felt under no financial or other obligation to anyone in relation to the declarations he made (or otherwise), nor was he influenced by any hospitality he received. It is (therefore) submitted that there is no evidential basis upon which to conclude that:

   (1) Councillor Davis has placed himself under any obligation;

   (2) Allowed himself to be influenced in the performance of his duties.

   It follows that Councillor Davis has not breached paragraph 2.2 of the Code.

2. It is submitted that the evidence is clear that Councillor Davis has – throughout the relevant period – promoted and supported high standards of conduct through his leadership and by example. In particular:

   a. He has been scrupulously and meticulously transparent in his registration of gifts and hospitality, beyond what was strictly required of him by the Code. He has done this in the public interest of transparency, ensuring full disclosure to other members, WCC officers including the Monitoring Officer, and the public. This sets an example of good practice for other members.

   b. At the beginning of every planning committee meeting he chaired, he would read a declaration setting out his connections, if any, with the applicant in question. This too is a model of transparency and openness.

   c. His record of public service is extensive, and indicates that Councillor Davis has devoted a significant amount of his career to serving WCC. He left his job as a partner at law firm Freeman Box in 2015 to further concentrate on his work at WCC. His attendance at events as an ambassador for WCC is a material part of this service.

   d. His decision to refer himself to the Monitoring Officer is also an indication of his integrity and willingness to fully participate in resolving the allegations made against him.

   e. His full co-operation with the investigation, including the provision of a comprehensive review of declarations and planning decisions, is a commendable approach for the holder of a public office to take.

   f. The written testimonials speak consistently to the high standard of his conduct in public office, and reject the allegations made against him.

[therefore…] it is submitted that there is no breach of paragraph 2.10 (if it is justiciable at all).

Counsel concluded by stating that in his view:

It is submitted that there is no prima facie case for Councillor Davis to answer. On this basis, the investigation should be concluded as soon as practicable with a full exoneration of Councillor Davis and without the matter being referred to the Standards Committee. There is no legally sustainable basis for such a reference, which should only be made where there is at least a prima facie case.

The Interview

In the meantime, I had planned to be in my flat in Mallorca over the summer and I was flying out in mid-July with the intention of not returning until mid-September, although I had booked to return to London for 48 hours in mid-August to check on my London flat and visit the Open Air Theatre to see the season's musical, as I was chairman of the board of directors.

A few days after I had arrived in the sunshine, I received a call from Harry, my solicitor. Hazel, the assistant Monitoring Officer, had phoned him to require our attendance at a meeting in Goudie's chambers on Tuesday 24th July. But I would be in Mallorca on that day and it was only a few weeks before my planned return. I asked Harry to see if we could do the meeting on one of the two days I had already planned to be in London. Hazel refused. She insisted Harry and I appear before them on the original date. I had no choice but to arrange another return journey to do so. It was very costly. The end of July is the height of the holiday season with schools just having broken up and so the return plane tickets cost over twice the usual amount.

I asked Harry to find out how long the meeting would be so that I could plan to either return to Mallorca that same evening or the following morning. Hazel's response was that I should expect to be in the meeting all day. Accordingly, I booked my return trip for the Wednesday morning.

My final case with all its bundles had been delivered by Harry to both the Monitoring Officer and Mr Goudie a few days before the meeting. On the day itself, having arrived back late the previous evening, I met Harry in his office at 8 am to allow us to run through my case, before we left for the meeting in Mr Goudie's chambers in the Temple at 10 am.

We arrived at chambers and waited in the waiting room, as we were told by the receptionist that Mr Goudie was already in a pre-meeting with the Monitoring Officer and her assistant Hazel. After about fifteen minutes, we were ushered in to the meeting. I was obviously nervous as I had never been subject to cross-examination before. But Mr Goudie was very gracious. He stood and walked towards Harry and me and shook our hands, welcoming us and apologising to me for bringing me back from Mallorca. We acknowledged the others and sat down to allow the meeting to start.

Goudie continued the casual chat asking me about Mallorca and telling us that he was soon off to his home in Cape Cod, Massachusetts. In the meantime, the monitoring Officer and Hazel sat there, saying nothing.

Goudie then advised us that he had read all my papers and that they were very impressive and made a good case in my favour. He then asked me if I wanted to add anything. I said no, as the documents supplied had contained everything I wanted to say.

He then, to my horror, said that he had no questions either, as everything he wanted to ask was in the papers we had supplied and so thanked me for coming and asked if I had any questions that I wanted to ask him before I left.

I was stunned! I had come back from Mallorca at great expense, delayed my return by twenty-four hours to ensure I could be interviewed all day and yet the meeting was over in ten minutes and could have been conducted over the phone.

I composed myself and asked when we should expect his decision. He replied without consulting the Monitoring Officer that he was off to Cape Cod in a week and would have it delivered to Westminster before he left! Harry said he had no questions and so we all stood and said our goodbyes and Harry and I left.

As we stood in the courtyard outside Goudie's chambers, I turned to Harry and said 'what the fxxk was that all about??' We had been in the meeting no more than fifteen minutes, most of which had been spent discussing our summer holidays.

I returned to Mallorca the next day and life continued.

The Leader Visits

About a year earlier, while still Deputy Leader, I had invited Nickie Aiken to join me in Mallorca for a weekend in my flat. Weeks before the Goudie meeting, we had arranged that she would fly to Mallorca with Daniel Astaire, a good friend of both of ours on a particular weekend. A few weeks after the election, Nickie and Daniel arrived and I picked them up at the airport and we had a very enjoyable weekend. I showed them the sights of Palma and we had a number of great dinners and lunches in my favourite restaurants.

We sunbathed on my roof terrace, while we gossiped and chatted. I never raised the issue of the enquiry. I felt it inappropriate. They then returned to London a few days later. What was important to me was Nickie's faith in me, in wanting to join me in Mallorca despite what had happened. It gave a positive signal to others that she was backing me despite the issues I was having to address.

With Nickie Aiken in Mallorca – June 2018.

The Long Wait

As the summer in Mallorca progressed, I was concerned that I had heard nothing and this was despite Goudie telling me at that July meeting that his report would only take a week to finalise. I then received a telephone call from a senior officer at the council who was a supporter of mine. The officer told me that they had overheard a conversation where a very senior officer had been alleged to have said that the leadership (although they did not say whether they meant officers or members) were extremely concerned that I was going to be cleared by the investigation and that the consequences of me being cleared was that the Labour Party and the *Guardian* would turn their attention to the council's leadership and accuse them of a whitewash. It was claimed that the council were therefore keen to find some grounds to find me guilty of breaching the council's Code of Conduct so that this would deflect any accusations against them. This seemed to explain why the report was taking months to finalise instead of the promised weeks.

The Standards Committee

I should point out at this stage that the Monitoring Officer's final report (which would incorporate the findings of Goudie's investigation) would merely contain details of her finding of fact and then contain a recommendation to the council's Standards Committee. She had no powers to take action against me herself. That was the responsibility of the Standards Committee which comprised seven councillors from both political parties. This included two Labour Party members and was chaired by Judith Warner, who had been a colleague of mine since 1983. She was the second longest-serving councillor after me. We had got on well for many years, but I was not sure how she would handle the Monitoring Officer's recommendation. While some of the Conservative members on the committee were good friends, others were just colleagues and I was therefore not confident as to how they would deal with the matter.

In any event, it should also be recognised that the Standards Committee had only limited powers and penalties to impose should the Monitoring officer have declared that I had breached the council's Code of Conduct and they endorsed that view. The most severe penalty was to suspend me as a councillor for a few months.

They could have removed me from office or service on a committee but at that stage, I was a backbencher with no committees or jobs. Or they could just reprimand me. But they could also decide that they disagreed with the Monitoring Officer's views and clear me.

The London New Year's Day Parade

This is where the story gets even more complicated. To put you fully in the picture, we have to go back in time. I described earlier my association with the London New Year's Day Parade and Festival run by Bob Bone of Destination Events and how, like several other former Lord Mayors, I had travelled to the United States to invite American marching bands to fly to London to participate in either the parade or the accompanying concert series.

I had done so every September for five years with the full support of the then officer and member leadership of the council and this included taking with me formal invitations signed by the Lord Mayor and with the Lord Mayor's office loaning me one of the mayoral chains to wear with my past Lord Mayor's badge over my red robes and jabot, when visiting the schools to present the invitation.

A Change in Policy

In March 2018, at one of the regular Monday morning leadership meetings attended by the Leader, me (as Deputy Leader), the Chief Whip, the Chief Executive and a number of senior officers, the London Parade was raised by an officer who had never been a fan of it. However, as Deputy Leader and a great supporter of the London Parade, I had up to then sidelined this officer's opposition and until that morning I thought that the parade had the full support of my colleagues including the Leader (and her predecessors), many of whom had dressed up and participated in the Westminster float in the parade, as well as from senior officers. Even the Chief Executive had himself dressed up as the Emperor of Japan from Aladdin, just a few weeks earlier.

The issue raised by the officer was that the parade was a commercial venture. The officer took the view that this was unacceptable and that any profits from running the event should be shared with the council because of their use of our streets and our name. I did point out that as Cabinet Member for Special Events, we had obtained counsel's advice as to whether the council could profit from events on our streets by making a charge or even demanding a share of the profits. But counsel had advised that it was illegal for the council to do so.

I also reminded the meeting that the parade was not the only organisation arranging events on our streets that were commercial. The London Marathon, for example, although donating millions to charity, was also run by a private company. Other events such as a Formula One extravaganza in Trafalgar Square was run as a commercial venture. All these companies including the London Parade had to pay a number of charges, such as for parking suspensions and cleaning up after the event. But my arguments were dismissed.

The meeting was taking place a fortnight after the *Guardian* story had hit the headlines. I was in a weak position to argue back or kick up a fight.

To my total surprise, both Nickie and the Chief Executive backed the officer. Nickie then announced that henceforth the council would no longer support the London Parade. She also ordered that the Lord Mayor, who was intending to fly out to the USA with Bob Bone a few weeks later for a five-day visit to tour a number of schools and formally invite them to the 2019 Parade, would not be allowed to go.

My fate was then sealed. Nickie and the officer in question then claim that they turned to me to instruct me not to go on my annual trip to the USA with Bob later that year. I am afraid that despite racking my brain on frequent occasions, I have no recollection of them doing so.

Over the next few months, after I had briefed Bob on the council's strange and unbelievable change in policy towards the London Parade after over thirty years of a very successful partnership, he undertook a series of meetings with officers to address the council's concerns. He was of the view that as a result of these positive meetings, the council were more relaxed about the parade continuing to take place. However, Bob and I believed that the council did not have the power to stop the parade in any event, in the same way that it cannot stop protesters from marching through the streets of Westminster.

Later that summer, I called Nickie from Mallorca and during the conversation I asked her what her latest stance was on the London Parade, as I told her that I understood that there had been numerous meetings between Bob and officers and I believed that matters had now been resolved. Nickie said they were and that the parade would go ahead again but she wanted to have a discussion with Bob about how his operation worked. I took this as a green light that all was now well and there would be no problem with me going with Bob to the USA on the usual annual trip in September.

Visit to the United States

By mid-September, I had still not heard from the council about the enquiry even though Mr Goudie had said in July he would have his report finished within a week. It did occur to me that a week was not a long time to consider all the evidence and arguments that I had made, but his lack of questions at our late July meeting seemed to suggest he was happy with my defence. Harry, my solicitor, agreed with me and whenever I asked him whether he had heard anything, he assured me not to worry and that the summer holidays had probably delayed things.

I flew to Atlanta with Bob and his colleague, Johnny, and we began the tour of schools. The tour went very well until we attended a school fifty miles to the north-west of Atlanta, where they kept calling me Lord Mayor Davis.

Meeting members of the marching band of a school in Georgia in September 2018

In the United States, once you have a title, you have it forever. For example, President Clinton is still called President Clinton even though he is no longer President. I kept telling them that I was not the Lord Mayor, merely a former one and that it was not appropriate to still call me Lord Mayor. They accepted this and, on my insistence, referred to me as Robert.

But it appears that no one told the schools press office which tweeted a photo of me speaking to the school in my red robes (as I had done on these trips for years – as had the other former Lord Mayors on their own tours of the US) with the caption 'Lord Mayor of Westminster Davis visits school'.

460

When I saw it, I was horrified but hoped that no one would see a tweet from a small-town school in suburban Georgia. How wrong I was. Of course, with social media the story soon travelled around the world and some bright young trainee in the Westminster press office's monitoring service picked it up and included it in the following day's press briefing for councillors and officers.

The next morning I woke in my hotel room about 5.30 am as we had an early start. I sat up in bed and turned on my iPad to find an email from the council's Chief Executive. I read it three times, as I could not believe what I was being accused of. He was claiming that I was touring the US 'masquerading as the Lord Mayor'.

As the one councillor who was well known for upholding the traditions and protocols of the Lord Mayoralty, I was the last person who would ever do this. I knew what the rules were and I was doing nothing different from what other colleagues had done in the past nor different from what I had done for the last five years. Everyone I met knew I was a 'former' Lord Mayor and not the current one. I then realised he must have seen the press coverage from the one school that called me Lord Mayor. I wrote back immediately defending what I was doing and explaining why the school had issued the photo with an incorrect description and suggested we meet up on my return to discuss it further. This whole episode put a dampener on the rest of the trip.

Back in London – The Final Curtain

I returned to London the following Monday to find a message from Nickie's personal assistant asking me to attend a meeting with her at her flat in Pimlico on the Wednesday.

When I arrived, Tim Mitchell, the Chief Whip, was already there. I was invited to take a seat. I was then told by Nickie that she was furious that I had travelled to the United States with Bob Bone, as the council no longer wanted to be associated with the London Parade and that she had told me earlier that year (in the meeting described earlier) that I was not to go to the States.

I apologised profusely, saying that I had no recollection of her saying at that meeting that I could not go, merely that the Lord Mayor could not go. I understood that the Lord Mayor going was one thing, as she would have attended as the council's official representative/ambassador. But I was going in a very different capacity, although I was still a serving councillor and I was a former Lord Mayor. Although the troublesome tweet calling me Lord Mayor was an error, I explained that Americans continue to call retired post holders with their former title and used the President as an example.

I further emphasised that I had made it clear in all my speeches that I was there in my own right supporting the London Parade and I never once gave any indication that I was officially representing the council. I knew that she would indicate her disapproval but as we had been such close friends for years and I had been (as she constantly told other people) 'her rock' when I served as her Deputy Leader, she would just give me a severe telling off and allow us all to move on.

I ended the discussion by not only apologising but emphasising that there had clearly been a misunderstanding but I had done no harm, in that all I was doing was promoting an event that brought great credit to both the city and the council and the London Parade brought much foreign investment by bringing thousands of visitors to our city.

Added to this was the council's constant support for the London Parade stretching back over thirty years. I then concluded my plea with the fact that Nickie and I had been close friends. She had only recently come to stay at my flat in Mallorca. Why would I want to deliberately disobey her order or do something to antagonise her?

I had been a loyal deputy and had been totally loyal to the Conservative Group on the council for over 36 years without any blemish on my record or performance. I had been recognised as one of the hardest working councillors and was highly respected, hence the award of an MBE several years earlier, something rarely bestowed on a Westminster councillor. I rested my case.

Tim then intervened for the first time. He became quite aggressive in the way he spoke, which surprised me. We had also been good friends and he was usually mildly spoken. He brought up the Goudie Enquiry and said that his sources had told him that the Monitoring Officer was 'going to throw the book at me' and bring disgrace on me and the council. I was horrified that he knew more about the Enquiry than me or my lawyer. The Monitoring Officer had assured us that the work they were carrying out was highly confidential and would not be discussed with senior members or anyone else at City Hall. She later assured my solicitor that this was indeed the case and no one knew what was in the draft report let alone how the investigation and enquiry were proceeding.

Nickie then took back control of the meeting and told me that, having discussed me with her cabinet colleagues, she had decided to suspend me from the council's Conservative group, for going to America without her consent. However, the Conservative group rules (which coincidentally I had drafted some seventeen years earlier when I was Chief Whip under Simon's leadership) only allowed the Leader to unilaterally suspend a member until the next group meeting, when she would be required to put her decision to the full group to vote on as to whether the suspension would be upheld. She went on to remind me that the group was meeting a week later and she proposed to put this to the group meeting to endorse and that I would be allowed five minutes to set out my case.

I was horrified. After my 36 years' service on the council, eighteen of those in the leadership and a member of the council's cabinet (and before that the chairman's group) almost consistently for 32 years without a single blemish on my service and after my loyal support to her and her two predecessors as Deputy Leader, I was being given the harshest of penalties. Not only was the suspension painful enough, but the shame would be even greater.

I had been Chief Whip for eight years under Simon's leadership and in charge of the group's discipline. I had also been jointly responsible for group discipline under Philippa's leadership (as she frequently asked me to take on this responsibility). And yet, in all those years and in fact over my entire 36 years on the Council, no Conservative member of the

In happier times, with Nickie Aiken launching the council's City for All campaign when we were Leader and Deputy Leader of Westminster Council.

council had ever been suspended from the group for any period at all. Over the years, we had had to deal with numerous colleagues who had misbehaved, voted against the whip, not turned up at meetings or done something very inappropriate. But none of them had ever been suspended. Yes, we removed them from a committee or did not promote them. Often, we just gave them a severe telling off or warning. But never a suspension.

So here I was, having committed the so-called 'crime' of going to America with Bob Bone to promote the London Parade, promoting Westminster as a city and in doing so, bringing investment to Westminster – as I and others had been doing without any issue for several years – and I was being given the most severe punishment ever given to a member of the group in all my 36 years on the Council, despite my otherwise perfect record as a councillor and a member of the leadership team for eighteen years. I was stunned.

Nickie made it quite clear that this was her decision and it was backed by her entire Cabinet. It was clear to me that this was a 'stitch up'. It was my conclusion that she wanted me out of the Conservative group before the publication of the Monitoring Officer's report, so that she could distance herself from me and ensure she did not get any backlash. There was no other rational explanation. Why else punish me so severely for such a minor misdemeanour, where there had in my view been a simple misunderstanding. If I had been a problem councillor for years, then that was something. But I had behaved without blemish over many years and had been extremely loyal to her and had also been her close friend. Yet I was being thrown to the wolves.

I made it clear that I was shocked but that I realised she was determined to proceed with her intentions. I was then told that I should prepare my case to appear before the full group of Conservative councillors the following week. This kangaroo court would then determine my future. I said in response that I had no choice but to consider whether I wanted to remain a councillor at all. I then stood up to leave. Nickie then burst into tears, saying she was so sorry that it had ended this way. I said and did nothing. I just left and returned home.

As I drove north towards my home, like, it is said, a dying man seeing his life flash before him, I too saw highlights of my amazing civic life flash through my mind as I drove past many of the streets, buildings and monuments that had provided the historic backdrop to so many important and fascinating events in my life.

My Resignation

On arriving home, I immediately phoned Harry and told him what happened. He then told me that he had just heard from Hazel, the assistant Monitoring Officer, to say that the report was now in its final version and would be sent to us on a confidential basis, for us to correct any errors.

Having thought further about the forthcoming trial before my peers on the journey home, I realised that this was going to be a charade. A third of the group were new councillors, elected a few months earlier and all very ambitious. I had recalled the numerous elections when I was Chief Whip or Deputy Leader, with the newly elected councillors all trying to impress me and attempting to get in to my good books, hoping I would help them get an early promotion. I knew that all the new councillors would support whatever the Leader proposed. Whatever I said in my defence would not be listened to and they would all support Nickie. Other members of the group had fallen out with me over the years on a variety of different policy issues. As Chief Whip and Deputy Leader, I had used my position to discipline many of them or had failed to promote them, so I already had a small army of those who wanted my powers curtailed, once and for all.

Did I really want to be humiliated by putting my case to my colleagues and then finding most of them supporting Nickie against me? And yet, only six months earlier, I was Deputy Leader, with everyone respecting me. Was it really worth the time I would require to put into preparing my case? And if I sought help from Harry, it would substantially increase my already high legal costs. Food for thought.

It was also clear that even if I returned to the council, having been punished or not, Nickie would never offer me a job in her administration again. Did I want to be a backbencher when I had had a taste of the leadership for eighteen years? It would never be the same.

The Monitoring Officer's Report

Later that night, my decision was made for me when Harry sent me (on a confidential basis) the draft reports from the monitoring officer. This confirmed my worst fear.

The summary of the Monitoring Officers conclusion was as follows:

> I find that the number of gifts and hospitality recorded is not in dispute. I also find that Cllr Davis has followed the Code of Conduct in registering his gifts and hospitality appropriately.

I am of the view that the acceptance of gifts and hospitality is not unlawful provided that gifts and hospitality over £25 is registered.

I am also of the view that the acceptance of a large number of gifts and hospitality is not in itself unlawful. There is no precise limit set on the numbers of gifts and hospitality.

The instances where Cllr Davis has accepted gifts and hospitality from developers/agents before or after planning decisions is not of itself evidence of any inappropriate conduct by Cllr Davis but I find that it also does not rule out a conclusion that he has placed himself in a position where people might seek to influence him in the performance of his duties (paragraph 2.2 of the Code of Conduct)

I am satisfied that Cllr Davis was given advice which did not affect his conduct until after September 2017.

More importantly, it is my view that the Code of Conduct imposes the obligations on members individually. It is Cllr Davis' judgement that is in question and this is relevant to paragraph 2.10 of the Code.

I find that by accepting the large scale of gifts and hospitality Cllr Davis has not promoted and supported high standards of conduct through leadership and by example. His conduct has attracted media and public attention which has an impact on the council as a whole.

The Independent Member (an independent person appointed by the council to oversee all Standards questions) was asked his view on reading the Monitoring Officer's draft report and his conclusion was set out in the final draft as follows:

I have read the report prepared by Hazel Best on the case of Cllr Robert Davis.

I agree that Cllr Davis has properly followed the Code of Conduct in registering gifts and hospitality of which he has been the beneficiary, even though he may in practice have registered unnecessarily some of those occasions; and I agree that acceptance of a large number of gifts and hospitality is not in itself unlawful.

I take the view that Cllr Davis's acceptance of gifts and hospitality from developers before or after a planning decision may thereby have placed him in a position in which people might seek to influence him in the performance of his duties. But I have seen no evidence that this did in fact happen.

The core of this matter is the issue of Cllr Davis's judgement in accepting such a volume of gifts and hospitality, notwithstanding his personal circumstances.

My conclusion is that this could, of itself, lay open his reputation, and therefore that of the council, to a perception – fairly or unfairly – that called into question his personal responsibility to promote high standards of conduct.

It is, however, important to put this conclusion properly into its context. If Cllr Davis's judgement in this respect has been wanting, it is against the background of his deep commitment over many years to the work and effectiveness of Westminster City Council.

It was clear to me that although they found that I had not done anything illegal and there was no evidence at all that I had put myself in a position whereby I was influenced in the performance of my duties, the Monitoring Officer had concluded that I did, however, put myself in a position in which people 'might' seek to influence me in the performance of my duties – even if (as they confirmed) there was no evidence that anyone had. And, as such, I did not 'promote and support high standards of conduct through leadership and by example'.

I had done nothing wrong. In fact, they complimented me on my honesty, transparency and dedication over many years of service to the council and referred to the fact that my case had been supported by 'impressive references'. Yet they used a strict and partial interpretation of two strands of the Code of Conduct to suggest that I had breached them. Despite my QC making very cogent and detailed arguments to the contrary. Why was I surprised? I had been warned!

The next stage was for me to confirm that there were no errors of fact and then the council would formally release the report to the public a few days later. The case would then be referred to the Standards Committee, where the councillors would consider the report and decided whether they agreed or not and if they did, what the sanctions would be.

To take it to this next stage, I would have to prepare a new case to put to the Standards Committee, addressing head on the findings of the Monitoring Officer. The Standards Committee would act as a quasi-judicial court of Law and I would have to instruct Mishcon to represent me at the hearing and of course I would have to ask them to help me to prepare the case.

To date, my legal costs had already reached nearly £60,000. Would it be sensible to spend another £20,000 on my lawyer's fees, only to have the Standards Committee finding against me whatever I said in my defence? And if I won, Nickie had made it clear that I was now not only persona non grata but I would be excluded from the Conservative group for about six months and I would not be given another job in her administration.

I had no difficulty in deciding what I had to do, however painful that decision was. I had to resign and do so immediately without incurring further costs and start a new life away from local government. I had spent all my adult life as a councillor, but there had to be a world out there.

I felt in my heart that all my friends on the council and outside knew that I was an honest person and I was well liked, so would have no difficulty moving on. At least I would get my weekends, evenings and holidays back and would not have to spend every waking moment on council matters or reading council papers. There was simply no choice.

I phoned Harry and told him my decision. He agreed to write a first draft of my resignation statement which would be released to the press and sent to Nickie and the Chief Executive. However, we decided not to do so until the following Wednesday, a few hours before the group meeting that was to consider my suspension.

Further Advice

I called my close friend Steve Summers, who had retired from the council after a successful year as Lord Mayor of Westminster and who was a public affairs consultant. He told me that before I did anything, I needed advice from a media adviser and he recommended his former colleague Jamie Lyons of MHP Communications. Jamie was an experienced political journalist having been deputy political editor of the *News of the World*. Jamie agreed to take on my case for a mates rates fee, which I must admit was still eye watering and more than I had intended to spend. I explained to him that my resignation had to be handled sensitively and be as low key as possible, as I did not want national headlines again.

It was agreed that he would be helped by his colleague, Ian Kirby, who would handle press enquiries on the day itself and in the days afterwards. Ian would also help in the drafting of my resignation statement and letters.

We met and agreed a strategy to minimise the coverage. The *Evening Standard* would be given the story first. But it would be sent to them too late to make their printed edition that day. Although it would get on their website, by the following day it would be old news so would not appear in print. With regard to the dailies, the press release was to be given to them later in the afternoon and it was hoped that they would include it in a small piece in their middle pages, if at all.

It was agreed that I would send Nickie my letter of resignation at midday and then send a copy to the Chief Executive. It was my letter to the Chief Executive that would be the legal letter of resignation. Once sent, it could not be revoked.

In drafting my statement and resignation letters, Harry had included reference to the conclusion of the Monitoring Officer's report, even though this had not been published and was still a confidential document. I raised concern that we were breaching the confidentiality rules on which we had been sent the document. He dismissed this, saying we were not directly quoting from the report, just summarising the conclusions. As he was an experienced lawyer on such matters, I deferred to his judgement.

My Resignation Statement

My resignation statement read as follows:

> I am today announcing my resignation from Westminster City Council with immediate effect. I am very proud of my 36 years' service in local government during which I made a major contribution to the wellbeing of the city and its people.
>
> Earlier this year there was some press coverage concerning the hospitality I received during the course of my duties. To avoid this becoming an issue in this year's elections, I agreed to refer myself to the Monitoring Officer, and stand aside as Deputy Leader while an investigation was carried out.
>
> My approach to declarations has always been to be honest, open and transparent. I have nothing to hide. I registered all my hospitality and it was posted by officers on the council's website. I have been making such declarations since 2007 when the requirement

was first introduced. I also declared any relevant interests at the beginning of every planning committee I chaired during this time.

I have acted with the utmost transparency and probity at all times and have only ever taken decisions on the basis of what I thought was best for Westminster.

An inquiry has been completed by the council. They have confirmed that none of the declarations I made or hospitality I received influenced decisions I took as a councillor and that nothing I did was unlawful.

However, they have concluded my actions nevertheless created a perception that was negative to the council. While I dispute this, I wish to draw a line under the matter. It is now time for me to move on to the next stage in my life, and for the next generation of councillors to lead Westminster.

I do not propose to make any further statements.

You will note that I made no reference to the issue of my American trip nor to my pending suspension from the Westminster Council Conservative group.

However, as I had resigned from the council, I was automatically no longer a member of the group, so my suspension being considered that night was no longer relevant. Furthermore, as I was no longer a councillor, neither the Standards Committee nor the Monitoring Officer had any jurisdiction over me and so their investigations came to an abrupt halt.

The Council's Response

In response, and I now gather, in anger at my leaking the conclusions of the draft report, the council did two things. Firstly, it issued a statement to the press basically saying they were pleased that I had resigned and that it was best for the council that I was no longer a member.

When government ministers resign, for whatever reason, the prime minister issues a statement to thank the departing minister for all his work and referring to all the resigning minister's achievements in office. This is standard practice, even though everyone knows the prime minister hated the minister and/or forced his resignation. But with me, they made no reference to a single achievement of mine, despite a record-breaking thirty-six years on the council and having served in most of the top offices including Lord Mayor, Deputy Leader and Chief Whip. But that is politics for you!

If that was not enough, a few days later, the council's press office gave a story to the *Evening Standard* about me, claiming that I had been to the United States without consent posing in 'fake Lord Mayor's robes' and implying that I was selling myself in the US as the incumbent Lord Mayor.

I have explained exactly what happened earlier. However, this made a big splash in the lunchtime editions of the paper but as soon as I got wind of the story, Ian Kirby (my PR adviser) managed to set the *Standard* right and the article was reduced in size in later editions with half the revised article giving my side of the story.

Meanwhile, I started my new life, free of all those meetings, all that paperwork and backstabbing.

Post Resignation

I was inundated with hundreds of messages of support. You certainly learn who your friends are and those who you thought were friends and who cut you off.

One of my best friends on the council, who I regularly socialised with, never contacted me after my resignation and did not do so for several years. I had been his mentor and helped him get all his promotions within the council. Clearly that counted for nothing. That said it all. Others who I did not think liked me contacted me to say really nice things and to say that they regretted what had happened. It was quite overwhelming.

Just recently, a former Labour councillor who had frequently attacked me in council meetings, stopped me in the street to apologise and say they were just doing their job and that in reality, they had really respected me for what I did for Westminster, for my expert handling of the planning brief and for my impressive legacy of buildings, public realm and public art throughout the city. I was touched and almost burst into tears.

Kind Words from Boris

A few weeks after my resignation, I received a handwritten letter from Boris Johnson. The letter (inter alia) read as follows:

> I just wanted to say that although I of course no longer have any standing on the matter, I believe you have been a SUPERB servant of our great capital, a fine colleague and of course you have been a great friend not just to me but to Ann Sindall and many others. I didn't follow the stupid left-wing campaign against you, but I am sure you will come through it all with your reputation SPOTLESS.
>
> All the best, love Boris
>
> [*the capitals were as Boris wrote and Ann Sindall is Boris's personal private assistant and a good friend of both Simon and mine. Her and Simon's desks flanked the entrance to Boris's office as Mayor of London]

This meant a lot to me.

Boris and me in Leicester Square when Boris as Mayor of London opened the refurbished gardens in May 2012.

Chapter 38

Moving On

Shortly after the 2018 local elections and a few months after I had stepped aside as Deputy Leader, a friend of mine introduced me to a friend who had just arrived in London. Çağatay Yilmaz (pronounced 'chart-eye') was Turkish and from the capital city of Ankara. He had come to the UK to undertake a Master's degree in Business Administration (an MBA) at the London campus of the University of West of Scotland. New to London, our mutual friend suggested that I was the best person to give him a tour of London, particularly as I was newly unemployed. Apart from working on my case for the forthcoming Enquiry, I had little to do, so was delighted to accept as I love showing people around London and describing its rich history. I was, of course, an honorary member of the Westminster Guides Association!

We got on well and within a few weeks, we became more than good friends and Çağatay moved in with me. Çağatay successfully completed his MBA degree at Easter 2019 and was allowed to stay in London for a further three months during which he was allowed

Çağatay and me in the gardens of Westminster Abbey.

to work. I helped him find a job assisting a friend running a small business with the intention that the employer would apply for a visa for Çağatay to stay working for him in London. Alas, no application was made and in mid-July, concerned not to overstay his visa, so he could apply in the future to return without any blemish on his record, he returned to live with his parents in Ankara.

Back in Turkey and with professional support, he put together a business plan for the small enterprise that he proposed setting up and applied to the British Embassy in Ankara for an entrepreneurial visa under the 1963 Ankara Agreement. After lengthy delays in his application being processed because of Covid, in the autumn of 2020 he was granted a visa and returned to live with me in London.

My Family Now

Although I have lost most of my family, I now have a new growing family. My late sister, Susan, had two beautiful daughters who are now in their thirties. Cassie, the eldest, was married in 2015 to Daniel Krendel, who by coincidence is the grandson of a friend of my own father. Their wedding was a splendid occasion and they are now blessed with two lovely children, Sadie (born in April 2017) and Eden (born in March 2020). Jessica, my youngest

Jessica, Daniel, Cassie and me at Cassie and Daniel's wedding.

Sadie, aged four, and me.

Eden, aged one, and me.

Ronald and Ruth with me in the Sir Simon Milton Garden
at the Chelsea Flower Show.

niece, is not yet married. I am also still very close to my brother-in-law Bradley and his new partner Ruth and my family give me great pleasure as I watch them mature and grow.

And I have Simon's family. I am close to Simon's mother, Ruth, and her husband, Ronald, as well as his sister, Lisa. Ronald and Ruth of course now live in Mallorca in the same development as me and so I see a lot of them while I am there and we have many friends in common on the island.

Conclusion of a Difficult Period in my Life

I think my record of achievements stands for itself as a testament of what I delivered over the thirty-six years I served the residents of Westminster.

I am still invited by many of the stakeholders of Westminster to events such as the opening of new buildings for which I had given consent and I have been told that without my support and vision they would never have been built.

An officer who had worked in many local authorities before moving to Westminster to work with me, called me to tell me how sorry he was that I had resigned and that I was the most inspiring and motivating councillor he had ever worked for and that his department had achieved so much under my leadership. I was touched.

It was a great period of my life.

Enjoying life in Mallorca.

Chapter 39

A Life of Ups and Downs – A Reflection

I have had a rollercoaster of a life. The ups and the downs. The tantrums, the joys, the falls and the loves. But at the end of my political career, I can look back with genuine pride at what I achieved in public life and my numerous legacies.

I sometimes wonder what life would have been like had that butterfly on the other side of the world not flapped its wings in 1982. I would certainly not have been elected to the council in May 1982. I could have spent my time just being a lawyer, playing golf or bridge in my spare time. I would never have met Simon or many of my friends. Fate has certainly had its impact on me and my life.

I did not choose my political exit and would have preferred to have retired on my own terms, but few successful political lives end well. Just look at Margaret Thatcher, David Cameron and Theresa May and their departures from Downing Street. But if you are going to make a difference in public life and not sit back and be lobby-fodder, then you will cause resentment, envy, upset and even hatred.

But, as I look back at my political life, I am confident that those who really know me and what I have achieved over thirty-six years in public life, respect me and admire me for all that I did. I know this from what those people I worked with inside and outside the council have said directly to me or to others (which has been reported back to me). I am well aware that many people in Westminster disliked me and do not like what I did or achieved, but many of those have either partial views or do not really know me and just think they do. But everyone, I hope, knows and appreciates that what I did was (in my view anyway) for the benefit of Westminster, the greatest city in the world and in the interest of the city and its people (whether residents, visitors or businesses).

I was honoured and humbled when on my retirement after seventeen years as a cabinet member and chairman for planning, a number of senior respected figures in the property industry, held a 'thank you' party for me in a series of historic rooms in the Royal Academy in Piccadilly.

Over three hundred people attended including almost the entire leadership of the London property world together with numerous colleagues and friends as well as many I had worked with on a variety of projects over the years.

Speeches about me were given by Sir Stuart Lipton (the doyen of the property industry), Gerald Ronson (another doyen of the property world), Steve Norris (former

*Gerald Ronson speaking at my farewell party as chairman of
planning in the Royal Academy – 2017.*

government minister and London mayoral candidate), Tony Travers (LSE Professor and expert on London local government) and Nica Burns (one of the leading theatre owners and producers). Even I was impressed with what they said about me!

Who would have thought that from a simple sheltered Jewish family up bringing in north-west London, a boy who only just got into a grammar school and with few friends before going to university, would not only end up as the youngest Lord Mayor of Westminster, but also become the longest serving Deputy Leader and be rewarded with an MBE for a record-breaking leadership of planning in Westminster as well as being personally recognised by the entire central London property industry? As they say: 'who would have thought?'

Whatever happens now and whatever regrets I have had, I have had a great life and I have made a difference. In doing so, I have made many lifelong friends.

I quote again from my letter of resignation as a councillor:

> I am very proud of my 36 years' service to Westminster, 18 of which were spent in senior leadership positions, and the numerous legacies I have left. I worked tirelessly for the people of Westminster. We had an excellent team and achieved a lot over this period, and I was very honoured to be awarded an MBE for my services.
>
> It is now time for me to move on to the next stage in my life, and for the next generation of councillors to lead Westminster.

I was also lucky to have spent over twenty years sharing my life with an amazing man who I loved and adored and continue to worship, long after his untimely death. It has been a good life and I look forward to moving on to the next chapter not only of my life but the next chapter of a future edition of this autobiography.

Postscript

After completing the final draft of this book in January 2022, I received some devastating personal news. I was diagnosed with aggressive prostate cancer. Cancer has killed three of the people I loved the most in this world. Fortunately, mine is curable. As this book goes to the printers, I am booked in for prostate surgery and very much hope that by the time you read this, I will have been given the all-clear by my doctors. I am lucky. Since I inherited the BCRA gene, I have been tested regularly. If it had not been for one of those regular MRI scans, this silent cancer would not have been detected.

Robert Davis

Index

Numerals in *italic* refer to photograph captions

2i's Club, 194
9/11, fallout from, 334–6
'34' restaurant, Mayfair, 423

Abbott, Diane, 118
Abrahams, Harold, 93–4
Ahmed, Mehfuz, 279
Aiken, Nickie, 186, 238, *239*, *332*, 391, *415*, 435,
    440, *441*, 442–3, *457*, 459–62, *463*, *464*,
Alexandra, Princess, 165, 256, 257
Allford Hall Monaghan Morris, 214
Allford, Simon, 214–5
Allibone, David, 101
Allott, Nick, 211, 223, 226
Almacantar, 199
Althasen, Paul, 369
Ambassador Theatre Group (ATG), 212–3
Amess, (Sir) David, 167
Amusement Arcade Action Group (AAAG), 142
amusement arcades, 141–4
Anderson, Lindsay, 95, 97
Andrew, Prince, 165–7, *286*, 287, 378
Annabel's, 211–2
Annan, Kofi, 169
Anne, Princess, 14, *175*, 194, 287
APCO, 51, 179, 183, 250, 359, 373
Apollo Theatre, 212
Archbishop of Canterbury, 269
Argar, Ed, 331
Arthur, (Sir) Gavyn, 102
Ashe, Anna Maria, *171*, 172–3
Asian Voice, 426–7
Asprey's, 14
Astaire, Daniel, 238, *239*, 392, 440, *446*, 457
Astoria Theatre, 214–6
Attallah, Naim, 293
Avery, David, 128
Avis, 308–9

Babbage, Charles, 194
Baker, Lord (Kenneth), 393–4
Baldwin, Peter, 208
Ball, Stephen, 93
Banksy, 295–6

Banqueting House, Whitehall, 299
Barden, Ronnie, 244, 246
Barker, Ronnie, 202
Barlow, Gary, 343
Barnes, Melvyn, 119
Barnett (nee Goldstein), Frances, 24
Barrow, Colin, 186, 189–90, 240–1, 328, *329*, 330
Barter, Freda, 264–5
Baskin family, 48
Baskin, Geoffrey, 38
Bassey, Dame Shirley, 165, 180, 342
Bather, Dr Leslie, 18
Battersea footbridge, 294–5
Batt, Steve, *268*, 269
Batty, Pamela, 109–11
Baylis, Vic, 184
BBC, 58–60, 86, 135, 143, 148, 157, 182, 221, 286,
    309, 310, 330, 363
BCRA 1 gene mutation, 52–3, 475
Beale, Simon Russell, 311–2
Beatles, 317
Beaumont Hotel, Mayfair, 327
Bennet, Matthew, 420
Bennett, Alan, 91, 210
Bennett, Douglas, 60, *64*, 64–5, 81
Bennett, Lesley, 37–8
Bennett, Tony, 342
Benn, Tony, 302
Berglas, Marvin, 224, 227
Berkeley Square, 220–1, 226
Berwick Street Market, 25
Bestall, Lee, 386–8
Best, Hazel, 456, *457*, 464, 465
Bianco, Jenny, 51, 251–2
Biggins, Christopher, 60–1, 224
Bingham of Cornhill, Lord, 371
Bingle, Peter, 141
Bird, Julian, 226
Birk, Baroness Alma, 398
Bishop (nee Smart), Christine, 84, 108
Bishop, Mark, 84
Black, Cilla, *58–62*, 105, 202, 208, 317
Blackshaw, Carole, 101–2
Blair government, 255, 338

Blair, (Sir) Tony, 15, 121, 140, 378, 424, 444
Blakemore, Sir Colin, 296
Blandford Street, 354
Bloomberg, Michael, 290–1
Blue, 224
Blue Man Group, 224
Blue Peter, 285–6
Blur, 279
Bone, Bob, 249–50, 254, 288, 369, 410–14, 458–61
    and Geri, 369
Boothroyd, Baroness (Betty), 426–7
Bottomley, Sir Peter, 86, 303–5, *303*
Bottomley, Baroness (Virginia), 165
Boxall, Stephen, 204
Box, Trevor, 11, 102–7, 318
Bracket, Dame Hilda, *306*
Bradford, Earl, *149*
Bradley, Alan, 51, 120, 153–4, 367
Brahams, Michael and Stephanie, 236, 369
Bramall, Lord, 13
Bramble, Roger, 230, 344, 397, 413
Bray, Angie, 179
Breakfast TV, 147–8
breast cancer, 53
Brent Cross Shopping Centre, 123
Brent Walker, 123
Breuer-Weil, David, 196
Brewer, Sir David, 454
Brexit, 369, 435–6
British Telcom Fleet, 394
Brittain, Vera, *194*
Brittan, Leon, 86
Broadway, New York, 223
Brown, Keith, 88
Brown, Michael, 302
Brown, Roy, 344–5
Brown, Tina, 291
Bruce-Lockhart, Lord, 203
Buckingham Palace, 13–7, 161, 165, 167, 174, 185,
    189, 216, 256, 291, 340–50, 378, 386, 414, 420–1
    State Banquet, 14–6
    Diplomatic Reception, 340–2
    Jubilee concerts, 342–3
    Master of the Household, 343–4
    receptions and garden parties, 345–8, *346*
    Privileged Bodies ceremony, 348, *349*, 350
Building Stable Communities (BSC), 129–31,
    134–40, 157, 180
Bull, John, 260
Burbridge, Susie, 198, *349*, 353, 446–53, *446, 449,*
    453

Burke, Jonathan, 401
Burnand, Jacqueline, *233*
Burns, Alfred, 29–30, 34
Burns (nee Lee), Dorothy (RD's maternal great-aunt),
    29–30, 34, 36
Burns, Frank (RD's cousin), *30*, 46, 52, 290, *291*
Burns, Jeremy (RD's cousin), 30
Burns, John, 216
Burns, Nica, 7, 212, *213*, 215, 216, 226, 474
Burns, Suzanne, 52, 290, *291*
Business Improvement Districts (BIDs), 406
Butler, Lord (Rab), 91–2

Cadbury, 221
Caius, Dr John, 68, 70
Callaghan government, 110
Callaghan, James, 10, 305
Cambridge Tory Reform Group (TRG), 85–9, 90,
    112–4, 300
Cambridge University, 15, 67–100, *74*, 108, 155, 300
    Conservatives Association (CUCA), 71, 74,
        81–92, *85, 92*, 374
    Footlights, 210
    Gonville & Caius College, 15, 67, *68*, 69, 70, *71*,
        72, 74, *75*, 76, *77*, 78, 79, 87, 93–5, *96*, 97,
        195, 311–2, 367, 384, 393, 426
    'My Oscar', 93–100
    sexual awakening, 80
    Union Society, 71, 74, *75*, 83, 93, 94, 374, 377
Cameron, David, 84, 147, 205, 331, 347, 373, 418,
    420, *426*, 473
Cameron government, 111, 339
Cameron Markby, 101–2
Can't Stand the Heat, 171–3
canvassing, 11, 89, 90, 112, 114, 279, 435–6, 445–7,
    449
CapCo, 288–90, 387
Caplan, Melvyn, 153–4, 179–80, 183–4, 219
Carlton Club, 439
Carlton, Eva and Jack, 40
Carlton Tavern, Maida Vale, 324
Carnaby Street, 320
Carter Ruck, 319
Castle, Ronnie, 43–4
Cathcart, Alison, 205, 277
Cats, 194
Cawdor, Catherine, Countess of, 230
Caxton Hall, 124
Chalker, Baroness (Lynda), 87, 88
Chalkley, Danny, 392
Chariots of Fire, 93–100, *95, 99*

Charles, Prince, 66, 105, 410, *419*, *420*, 420–2
Chelsea Barracks application, 421
Chelsea FC, 43
Chelsea Flower Show, 386–8
Chicago, 224
Chichester, (Earl of), John and June, 369, 438
Chihuly, Dale, 196, 199
childhood, 40–57
Chinatown, 337–9
Christie, Agatha, 318, 401
Christmas lights, Oxford and Regent Street, 280–2
Chronic Lymphocytic Leukaemia (CLL), 183, 359,
    378 – *see also* Milton, Sir Simon
Chubb, Rosemary, 86
Churchill, Sir Winston, 124
Cinnamon Club, The, 119
City of London Corporation, 432
City of Westminster, 11, 16, 82, 140, 152, 157–8,
    190, 242–3, 267–8, 293, 349, 350, 403, 405, 409,
    412, 413
City of Westminster – a celebration of people and place,
    The, 293
Clark, Greg, *383*
Cleese, John, 210
Clegg, Sir Nick, 194
Close, Glenn, 307
Clutton, Gareth, 352
Cobbold, David, 116–8, 120
Cockpit Theatre, 403
Coe, Robert, 180
Cohen, (Sir) Jack, 116, 139
Cohen, Melvin, 111, 186
Cohen, Tim, 385
College of Law, 108–9
Collins, Nick, 72
Comedy About a Bank Robbery, The, 228
Comptroller of the Lord Chamberlain's Department,
    256
Conan Doyle, Sir Arthur, 194
Condon (Lord), Paul (previously Sir Paul), 13
Conrad, Jess, *369*, 370
Conservative Central Office, 11, 304
Conservative group, Westminster City Council, 131,
    134, 153, 328, 435, 442, *443*, 462–4, 466, 468
Conservative Party, 10, 81–5, 89, 91, 110–1, 114,
    125, 130, 150, 154, 178, 180–1, 203, 206, 278–9,
    303–4, 367, 436
Conservative Party Conference, 84–5, 178
Conservatives, Young, 81, 88
Conservative Trade Unionists (CTU), 303–5
Conville, David, 398

Cook, Peter, 210
Cooksey, James, 384, 432
Cooper, Robin, 267–9
Copeland, Dr Geoffrey, 405
Corbin, Chris, 308
Corbyn, Jeremy, 118
Corinthia Hotel, Whitehall, 327
Corkey, Julia, 219, 392, 440, 442
Coronation Street, 208
Cotton, Terry, 184
Covid, 392, 470
Cow Parade, 274
Crazy for You, 399
Crick, Francis, 195
Crispy Duck restaurant, 337–9
Criterion, 228
Cromwell, Oliver, 267
Cross, Ben, 95
Crossman, Richard, 19
Crossrail, 214
Crown Estate, 212–3, 223, 282, 383, 407, 428–9
Culloden, Battle of, 197
Cumberland, Duke of, 197
Curtis, Sarah Jane, 288–9

Dahl, Roald, 276
Daily Mail, 262, 440
Danse Gwenedour (sculpture), *198*
Davies, Councillor Robert, 318–9
Davis, Bernard, 43
Davis (formerly Pevovar), Gerald (RD's father), 20–9,
    24, 37–9, *39*, 40–57, *54*, *55*, *56*, *57*, 63, 67, 69,
    76, 104, 105, 171, 221, 272, 297, 359, 368,
    471
Davis, Gerald and Pamela (RD's parents), 20, *38*, *39*,
    50, *123*, 154, *159*, 203, 347, 357
Davis (nee Lee), Pamela (RD's mother) 11, 20–4,
    34–5, *35*, 37–9, 40–57, *49*, *57*, 59, 74, 76, 105,
    115, 144, 153–4, 165, *166*, 171, 209, 236, 290,
    296–7, 357, 359
Davis, Paul, 43
Dean of Westminster, 158, *160*, 200, 201, 231, 256,
    311, 371, 379, 454
Deane, Phyllis, *76*
Deben, Lord (John Selwyn Gummer), 301, 454
Decaux, JC, 187, *188*, 189, 351, 479
De La Renta, Oscar, 291
Delaunay restaurant, 295
Delfont Mackintosh (Cameron Mackintosh), 212
De Luca, Nick, 183
Dench, Dame Judi, 398

De Niro, Robert, 288–90, *289*
Denison, Michael, 397
Denny, Bruce, *385, 386*
Department for Education, 394–95
Deputy Mayor of London, 134, 186, 347, 365, 381, 384, 421, 454
Derwent London, 214–6
Deuchar, Patrick, 211
de Walden Estate, Howard, 200
Diana, Princess, 252, 410
Diplomatic Corps, 341
Diplomatic Reception, 340–2
Disneyland, 230
District Auditor, 131–2, 136–9, 157–8, 180
Ditlev-Simonsen, Per, 284–7
Dixon, Sir Jeremy, *202*
Dobson, Frank, 302
Dolphin Square, 294
Domingo, Plácido, *227*
Donn, Harry, 38
Dorchester Hotel, 196
Drabble QC, Richard, 454–6
Drukier, Ian, 289
Duchess Theatre, 228
Dunamis (sculpture), *198*
Dunford, Neil and Gill, 369
Dutt, Michael, 136–7

Eaton, Baroness (Margaret), 392, 425
Eberhard, Urs, 233–5, 237–8, 248
Eccles-Williams, Harry, 444–5, 453, 456, 460, 464, 467
Edinburgh, Duke of, 13, 15, 161, 257, *259*, 341, 343, 348, 349
education:
    Brooklands primary school, 47, 131
    Kerem House School, 57, 72–73
    Christ's College, Finchley, *18*, 63–5, *66*, 67–72, 209–10, 244
    see also Cambridge University
Edward, Prince, *221*
elections, local, 37
    (1978) 10, 112
    (1982) 10–11, 89, 93, 112–15
    (1986) 125–30, *127*
    (2002) 448
    (2018) *279*, 428, 435, 445, *446, 447*, 448, 450
Elgar, Sir Edward, 194
Eliot, TS, 194
Elizabeth, Queen, the Queen Mother, 15
Elizabeth I, Queen, 70

Elizabeth II, Queen, 13–16, 61, 82, 91, 105, 118, 135, 154, 159, 161–5, *169, 170*, 174, 189, 195, 218, 221, 257, *258, 259*, 260, 286, 292, *333, 334*, 340–50, 355, 386, *387, 388*, 417–8, 420, 422, *425*
    Diamond Jubilee, 195, 343, 348–50, 409
    Golden Jubilee, 221, *342*, 355
'Emily's Travels', 45
Enfield Council, 142
Engel, Robin and Robyn, 370
English Baroque choir, 224
English Heritage, 194
English National Ballet, 220, 397
English National Opera, 223, 397
Epstein, Brian, 62
Essendine Primary School, Maida Vale, 177
Eton College, 96–7
Etzin, Justin, 372
European Land, 385
Evans, Dr Gerard, *77*
Evans, (Sir) Harold, 291
Evening Standard, 156, *204*, 206, 211, 293, 329, 379, 444, 467, 468
Everage, Dame Edna, 342
Evita, 399

Fairbairn, (Sir) Nicholas, 86
Fair in the Square, 219–21
Fakhoury, Bushra, *198*
Falkland Islands, 10, 114
family and heritage, 20–39, *22*
    bar mitzvah, *27*
    see also Burns, Davis, Goldstein, Grundman, Lee, Pevovar, Schuveck
Farish III, William Stamps, 334–5
Farnham, Lady Diana, 344
Faulkner, Lord (Richard), 142
Favre, Michel, 234
Federman, Katie, *226*
Ferrari, Nick, 256, 325, *326*
Fiddian-Green, Nic, *190*
Field, Mark, 436
Fight for Life, 296
Finchley Conservative Association, 81
Five Guys Named Moe, 193
Flach, Elizabeth and Robert, 232, *273*
Flight, Lady (Christabel), 190, 238, *239*, 381, 391–6
Flight, Lord (Howard), 238, *239*
Footloose, 224
Ford, Sir Andrew, 420, 422
Forsyth, (Sir) Bruce, 202
Forte, Lord (Charles), 135

Foster, Norman, 189, 351

Franco, Carole (RD's Lady Mayoress), 14–17, 50, 72, *79*, 101, 102, 154, *155*, 156–7, *159–60*, 164–6, 174, 233–4, 236, 244–5, *284*, *286*, 288, 295–9, *300*, 305, 306, *314*, 340, *341*, 342, 347

Fraser, John, 179

Freeland, Stephen, 83–4

Freeman Box, 48, 98, 101–7, *104*, 265, 429, 443

Freeman, Jeremy, 11, 102–8, 443

Freeman, Susan, *432*, 443–4

Fry, Stephen, 98, 210

Fyffe, Patrick, 305–6

Galloway, Mark, *69*, 93

Galloway, Stephen, 91, 93–94, 97, 210

Galtieri, General Leopoldo, 10–11, 114

Garden Bridge project, 294–5

Garland, Judy, 202

G-A-Y nightclub, 214

Gee Dee Textiles, 27–8

George Tupou V of Tonga, King, *195*

Ghost of Jerry Bundler, The, 209

Gielgud, Sir John, 105, *195*

Gilbert and Sullivan, 317

Gilmour, Lord (Ian), 86

Glanz, Jonathan, 435, 451

Glickman, David, 67

Gloucester, Duke of, 195

Godson, Lord (Dean), 367, 377, 425

Golders Green Hippodrome, 208

Goldstein (nee Messer), Becky (RD's great aunt), 24

Goldstein, Mark and Emily (RD's great-great-grandparents), 30–1

Goldstein, Mottle, 24

Goldstein, Stanley, 24, 37–8

Goldwin (nee Goldstein), Rosemary, 24

Gonville & Caius – *see* Cambridge University

Gonville, Edmund, 70

Gore, Al, *51*

Goring Hotel, 343, 347, 433

Gormley, Sir Antony, 308

Goudie Enquiry, 462

Goudie QC, James, 444–5, 454, 456–8, 460

Gould, Kate, 388

Govinda, Ravi, 141

GQ magazine, 388, *389*

graffiti, 150, 191, 295, 296

Graham, Sammy, 108

Granville, Howard, 105

Gray, Michael, 262

Greater London Authority (GLA), 226, 255

Greater London Council (GLC), 116, 126, 128, 135, 180, 397, 403

Great North Museum, 270

Great Ormond Street Hospital, 41

Green, Benny, 397

Greenwich Hotel, New York, 288–9

Greer, Ian, 178–9

Griffiths, Bill, 176

Gross, Ronald (Simon's step-father), 203, *358*, 359, 361–3, 366, 368–9, *383*, 424–6, *472*

Gross, Ruth (Simon's mother), 203, 345, *358*, 360–9, 371, 373, 378, *380*, *383*, *384*, 419, 424–5, 427, *472*

Grosvenor Estate, 308

Grundman, Arnold, *159*

Grundman, Bradley (RD's brother in law), 47, 52, 154, *159*, 419, *422*, 472

Grundman, Jessica (RD's niece), 22, 52, 53, *159*, *281*, 419, *422*, 471

Grundman, Marie, *159*

Grundman (nee Davis), Susan (RD's sister), 20–3, 26, *27*, 36, 37, 40–57, *40*, *42*, *46*, 49, 58–9, *159*, 170, 203, 205, 221, 297, 357, 471

Guardian, The, 428, 433, 436, *437*, 438–40, 444–5, 447, 449, 458, 459

Gubbay, Raymond, 401

Guys and Dolls, 224

Habeas Corpus, 91, 210

Hall, Dr John (Dean of Westminster), *201*, 311–12, 371, 454

Hallfield Estate, 112, *113*, 114, 452

Hampshire, Susan, 194

Harry Potter and the Half Blood Prince, 225

Harry's Bar, 437

Harsant, Major Gerry, 264

Hartley, Peter, 102, 117, 120, 121, 127, 131, 134, 137, 151

Hartnell, Sir William, 50

Harvey, Angela, 98, 332, *416*

Harvey, Ian, 110

Haselden, Ron, 354

Hatton, Derek, 140

Heatherwick, Thomas, 294

Heath, (Sir) Ted, 82, 300, 303, 305

Henderson, Ian, 405

Henry IV, King, 311–12

Heywood, Neil, 10, 112, 125

Hicks, Andy, 289

Hinge and Bracket, 306

Historic England, 324–5

Hitler, Adolf, 168, 216
Holland, Graham, 254
Home Office, 255
honours and recognition, 417–27
    Deputy Lieutenant, 417–8
    MBE, 418–23, *420*, *422*, *423*, 474
Hooper, Angela, 52, 233–7, 448
Hooper, Baroness (Gloria), 233, *237*
Hope, Bob, 202
Horne, Jonathan and Nadine, 369
Horner's Livery Company, 409
Household Cavalry, 13, 14, 110, 256
House of Commons, 81, 108, 109, 267, 268, 331,
    427
House of Lords, 18, 137, 138, 140, 147, 244, 267,
    301, 331
Hudson, Hugh, 95, 98, 100
Hug, Adam, 439
Hungarian Jews, 168
Hurd, Lord (Douglas), 143, 161
Hussey, Mike, 199
Hyams, Louise, 192–93, *237*, *239*, 350, 368

Iacobescu, Sir George, 335
Idle, Eric, 210
If, 95, 97
Imbert, Lord, 265, 418
Inner London Education Authority (ILEA), 184
IRA, 36
Irvine, Lord, 445
Isaacs, Sir Jeremy, 202
Ivy Club 212
Ivy restaurant, 194, 433, 440

Jackson, Philip, 169, *382*, *383*, 394–5
James, Clive, 210
James, Duncan, 224
James, Ken, 65, 69–70
Jeffery, Beryl, *259*
Jenkin, Baroness Anne, 392
Jenkin, Sir Bernard, 98, 392
Jenkins, (Sir) Simon, 293
Jersey Boys, 225
Jerusalem Chamber, 311–12
John, (Sir) Elton, 342
Johnson, Boris, 7, 139, 225, 262, *263*, 277, *278*,
    290–1, 294–5, 295, *356*, 360, 363, 365–7, 372,
    374, 376–8, *379*, *380*, 381–2, *383*, *384*, *469*
    eulogy at Simon Milton's memorial, 377, *378*, 379
Johnson, Heather, 404
Johnson, Marina, 262–3, 277

Jones, Julie, 392
Jowell, Baroness (Tessa), 310
Jubilee Walkway Trust, 355
July 2005 London bombings, 309–10

Kaldor, Lord, 86
Kanawa, Dame Kiri Te, 165
Katz, Rabbi Stephen, 371
Kearney, Wing Commander Bill, 110
Keen, Carolyn, 448
Kensington and Chelsea Council, 142, 256–7
Khan, Genghis, 197
Khan, Sadiq, 295
Killick, Angela, 120
Kindertransport, 177, 222, 378
King, Jeremy, 295, 308
King's Speech, The, 194
Kirby, Ian, 467, 468
Kirwan, Patricia, 120, 127, 134, 135, 151
Knapman, Dr Paul, 269
Knight, Ted, 140
Kraus, Margery, 51, *179*, 250
Krendel (nee Grundman), Cassie (RD's niece), 22, 36,
    52, 53, *159*, *281*, 419, *422*, *471*
    and Eden and Sadie, *471*
Krendel, Daniel, *281*, *471*
Kunz, Albert, 146–7, 229, *230*, 233, 238, 240, *242*
Kureishi, Hanif, 403
Kutner, Bernard, 38
Kutner, Diana, 48, 359
Kuwaiti Ambassador, 340

Labour Party, 127, 128, 130, 140, 156, 279, 338, 435,
    436, 440, 444, 445, 447, 448, 450, 458
Lancaster Gate, 108, 109, 125, 126, 127, 129, 131,
    134–5, 151, 195, 353, 447–9, 453
Land Securities, 223, 388–9, 394, 405
Landa, Clive, 87, 88
Lang, Robert, 397
Lasdun, (Sir) Denys, 113
Laurie, Hugh, 210
Lavin, Dagmar, 177
LBC, 325–327, 367
Leckie, Bill, 319
Lee, Anne (nee Schuveck) (RD's maternal
    grandmother), 30–31, *31*, *32*, *33*, *34*, *35*, 36–39,
    39, 40–1, 51, *57*, *159*, *206*, 214, 297
Lee, Arnold (RD's maternal grandfather), *29*, 29–31,
    34, 34–9, 45, 271
Lee (formerly Levy), Joe and Jane (RD's maternal
    great-grandparents), 29

Lee, Stanley (RD's maternal uncle), 34, *35*, *39*, 43, 76–7, *159*
   and Caroline, *159*
Lees, Lois, 141
Leicester Square, 222–6, 229–30, 240–1, 327
Leicester Square funfair, 314–5
Les Misérables, 226
Levan, Cyril, 38
Levan family, 48
Levine, Gemma, *292*, *293*, 427
Lewis, Audrey, 15, 315, *316*, *317*, 448–9
LGBT rainbow flag, 312–3
Libby, Melinda, 151
Liberal Democratic Party, 176
Liberal Party, 194
Licensing Act 2003, 337
licensing, alcohol, 337–9
Liddle, Eric, 93
Lidington, (Sir) David, 92
Lion King, The, 224
Lipton, Sir Stuart, 367, 473
Livingstone, Ken, 116, 135, 139, 310, 312–3
Lloyd, Phyllida, 401
Lloyd Webber, (Lord) Andrew, 201, *211*, 212–3, 218, 226, 306, 438, 454
Lloyd Webber, (Lady) Madeleine, 306
Local Government Association (LGA), 185, *185–6*, 203, 309, 331, 360, 365, 373, 374, 381, 392, 424
Loftus, Richard, 157
Logan, George, 306
Logue, Lionel, 194
London Clinic, 52, 364, *364–6*
London Film Festival, 305
London Hippodrome, 355–6, 396
London Marathon, 459
London Mayors' Association (RD Chairman 1997– 2016), 6, 87, 111, 174, 243, *243–68*, 271, 274, 294, 316, 326, 361, 363, 373, 391, 404
   annual dinner, 256–7, 260–3
   Centenary Reception at St James's Palace, 257–60, *260*
   Civic Service, 251, *252*
   civic trips to Amsterdam, 248; Brussels, 243–5; Edinburgh, 249; Madrid, 249–50; Oslo, 248; US and further afield, 250; Warsaw, 248
   Diplomatic Dinner, 251
   newsletter, 247, 267–9
   Protocol, 254–6
   retirement as chairman, 265, *266*
   Rifle Shoot, 264
   Whittington, in the footsteps of, *253*, 254

London Palladium, 201, 208, 211
London Parade and Festival, 410–16, 458–62
London Tonight, 142, 157, 171
London Zoo, 353
Londoner Hotel, Leicester Square, 327–8
Longworth, Cathy, 413
Lord Chamberlain, 165, 256, 257, 347, 420
Lord-Lieutenant, 13, 14, 195, 252, 255, 256, 265, 310, 417, 418, 454
Low, Martin, 190, *336*
Lubetkin, Berthold, 112
Luff, (Sir) Peter, 300–302
Lumley, (Dame) Joanna, 294, *295*
Lutyens, Sir Edwin, 409
LW Theatres (Andrew Lloyd Webber), 212
Lyons, Jamie, 467
Lyric Theatre, 212

Mabey, Simon, 10, 112, 125, 126
Macbeth, 209, *209–10*
maces, ceremonial, 267–9
Mackintosh, Sir Cameron, 193, 211, 213, 215, 223, 367
Macon Cherry Blossom Festival, 50–1
MacQueen, Rosemarie, 420
Madame Tussauds, 220, 221
Magill, John, 136–7
Major government, 10
Major, (Sir) John, 13, 15, 165
Major, (Dame) Norma, *147*
Mallinson, Anne, 109–10
Mallinson, Lawrence, 84, 108–9
Mallinson, Terrence, 109
Mallorca, 201, 212, 213–14, 271, 273, 277, 306, 357–70, 440, 456–8, *472*
   childhood visits, 357
   holidays with Ronald and Ruth, *358*
   visiting with Simon, 357–8
   flat-hunting and Bendinat, 360–3, *363*
   friends, 369–70
Majorca Daily Bulletin, 369–70
Malthouse, Kit, 139
Mamatsashvili, Teimuraz and Irina, 298
Mamma Mia!, 223–4, 402
Mandarin Oriental, Hanover Square, 327
Mandela, Nelson, 13–17, *17*, 50, 161, *163*, 165, *166*, 167, 340, 355
Marble Arch island, refurbishing of, 189–93, 196, 198
Marble Arch Tower, 199, 202
Marble Arch United Synagogue, 50
Margaretha of Sweden, Princess, 169
Margaret, Princess, 169

Markham, Nick, 164
Marylebone Association, 315
Mary Poppins, 223
Mason, Sam and Edna (nee Levy/Lee), 30, 35–6
Matcham, Frank, 355–6
Matcham Theatre, 355, 356, 396
Maude, Lord (Francis), 10, 111
May, Brian, 342–3
May, Lady (Theresa), 435, 473
Mayfair security, 334–9
Maygar, Chaimi, 32–3
Mayor of London 102, 134, 139, 186, 226, 253, 255,
    255–256, 256, 262, 263, 277, 290, 310, 312, 347,
    356, 360, 365, 372–4, 381–4, 392, 421, 454, 469
McAleer and Rushe, 240–241
McAlpine, Lord, 304
McCartney, Paul, 342
McKenzie, Alice, 30–1
McKenzie, Robert, 86
Meaden, Deborah, 143
Meaden, Sonia, 143
Meekyoung Shin, 197
Messer, Jo (RD's maternal great-grandfather), 23
MHP Communications, 467
Michael of Kent, Princess, 296–300, *297*, *299*
Micklethwaite, Alan, 384
Middlesex Hospital, 296
Midsummer Night's Dream, A, 209, 225
Millbank Tower, 372
Miller, Jonathan, 210
Mills, Chris, 105
Milton, Clive (Simon's father), *177*, 178, 180, 378
Milton, Lisa (RD's sister-in-law), 205, 360, 365–7,
    371, 374, 376–7, *384*, 392, 424, 437–8, 472
Milton, Sir Simon (RD's long-term partner), 9, 11, 51,
    61–2, 80, 84, 100, 106, 135, *152*, 153–4, 157,
    175, *178*, 196, 223, 225, 227, *237*, 250, 270, 275,
    293, 301
    Cornell University, 177–8, 374, 376
    Milton's restaurant, *151*, 177–8
    career move, 178
    Councillor, Lancaster Gate Ward (1988–2008),
        151–2, 353
    Deputy Leader, Westminster Council (1999–
        2000), 176, 179
    Leader, Westminster Council (2000–08), 134,
        139, 183–6, 203–7, 211, 213, 221, 226, 240,
        278–9, 292–3, 309–10, 312–3, 327, 334–5,
        342, 365, 374, 378, 380, 384, 406, 448–9
    Chairman, Local Government Association
        (2007–08), 203, 331
    knighthood (2006), 134, *186*, 424–6, *425*, *426*
    Deputy Mayor of London (2008–11) and Chief
        of Staff to Boris Johnson (2009–11), 134,
        189, 225, 240, 262–3, 277, *278*, 290–1, 294,
        347–8, 365, 381–2, 469
    Mallorca, flat hunting (2011), 360–3
    Mallorca, holidays in, 357, *358*, 359
    illness and funeral, 219, 359–60, 363–4, *365*,
        366–8
    memorials and monuments,
        memorial service, 371–80
        Stone Setting ceremony, 380
        seated statue, Potter's Field, 381, *382*, 383
        portrait bust, Piccadilly Circus, 383, *384*
        seated statue, Paddington Basin, *385*, 386
        Milton Square, Victoria, Sir Simon, 388, 389,
            390
        Lifetime Contribution to London award, *427*
    relationship with RD:
        dedication, 9
        'the day that changed my life', 151–2
        marriage and wedding (2007), 93, 203–7,
            205–7
        eulogy, 374–6, *375*
Milton Foundation, Sir Simon, 293, 319, 356, 381,
    386, 387, 391–6, 422
    Chelsea Flower Show garden 386, *388*, *472*
    Sir Simon Milton orchid, *386*
    Silver Sunday and the Tea Dance, 392, 395, *396*
    Westminster University Technical College 393,
        394, *395*
MIPIM, 431–3
Mishcon, 443–4, 453
Miss Saigon, 226
Mitchell, Andrew, 84–5, 92
Mitchell, Tim, *239*, 332, 441, 461–2
Molloy, Phil, 63, *64*, 65–6, 73
Monck, Sir Henry, 408
Monroe, Marilyn, 381
Montcalm Hotel, 170
Moore, Peter, 260–1
Mothersdale, Tony, 279
Mousetrap, The, 401
Mousetrap Theatre Projects, 401–3
Much Ado about Nothing, 210
Munro, Alexander, 293
Murdoch, Rupert, 291
Museum of London, 223

Nagle, Fred and Mildred, 44
Namdakov, Dashi, *196*, 197

National Gallery, 223
National Lottery, 404
National Portrait Gallery, 220, 223
Neagle, Anna, 194
'Near Beer' bars, 127
Neil, Andrew, 256
Nemeth, Cyril, 153–4, 157, 364, 365
Network Rail, 393–4
Neville, Terry, 142–4, *143*, 444
New College, Oxford, 179
Newman, Margaret, 275
News of the World, 467
New West End Company (NWEC), 222, 405–7
New Year's Day Parade, London, 249, 254, 288, 344, 410–6, 424, 458, *458*–62
New York, 46
New York, Mayor of, 255
Nicholas, Anna, 370
Nimax Theatres, 212
Noble, Andrew, 98, 162, 164
Noel, Rob, 389
Norman Shaw (North) Building, 302–3
Norris, Steve, 473
North Finchley Hospice, 52
Norton, Matthew, 271–2
Norwegian Christmas Tree, 284–7

O'Connor, Des, 201
Ogilvy and Mather, 179
Olivier Award dinners, 213
Olympics, London, 93, 98, 196, 294, 330, 409
Open Air Theatre, Regent's Park, 175, 225, 306, *397, 398, 399*
Other Palace, The, 216–8
ovarian cancer, 20, 48, 52, 53, 165, 176
Oxford Street, 351–2, 441

Paddington Basin, 385
Paddington Cube, 323–4
'Paddington Pole', 320–4
Paddington Recreation Ground (Pad Rec), 219
Paddington redevelopment, 320–4
Pajares, Ramon, 400–1
Palmer, Lord (Munroe) and Lady (Suzette), 244
Panorama, 135
Panter, Sir Howard, 212–4
Parking Committee for London, 244
Parry, Eric, 384
Parsons, Nicholas, 67
Past Overseers' Society, 407–10
Patten, Marguerite, 222

Perrucchetti, Mauro, *196*
Peace, Liz, *432*
Peltz, Lois, 127–8
Peninsula Hotel, Hyde Park Corner, 327
Penny, Dr Leith, 145
Peterlee New Town Development Corporation, 301
Peters, Christine, 404–5
Peters, Clarke, 193
Pevovar, Abraham (Alf) (RD's paternal grandfather), 22–9, *22, 23, 25*
Pevovar, David and Raisa (RD's great-grandparents), 23
Pevovar (nee Messer), Jane (Jenny) (RD's paternal grandmother), 23–9, *24, 25, 26, 28*, 38, *42*, 148, *149*
Pevovar, Phyllis (RD's paternal aunt), 24, *25, 26*, 27, *28, 39*, 42, 47, 76
Peyton, Oliver, 135
Phantom of the Opera, 226
Phillips, Bill, 137
Piano, Renzo, 321–2
Pickles, Lord (Eric), 323, 347, 385, *386*
Pidgley, Tony, 381, *383*, 392
Pipe, Jules, *432*
Playboy Club, 67
Play that Goes Wrong, The, 228
Polizzi, Alex and Olga, 135
Pollock, Benjamin, 208
Pollock's Toy Theatre, *208*, 209
Polytechnic of Central London (PCL), 403
Porchester Centre (formerly Porchester Hall and Baths), 11, 38, 114–5, *122*, 122–6
Porter, Dame Shirley, 116–22, 127–8, *129*, 130–43, 145, 147, 149–50, 157–8, 176, 180, 194, 301, 397, 423
Porter, Sir Leslie, 139
Portillo, Michael, 427
Portland Street Library, Little, 121–2, 128
Portman Estate, 352
Poundbury, 421
Povey, Chris, 105–6
Pow, Eddie and Ivy, 123–5
Prendergast, Tony, 118, 135
Prescott, Lord (John), 203, 424
Prescott, Michael, 209
Princess Grace Hospital, 48–50
Prince's Trust, 66
Pringle, Derek, 98
Pritchard, Matthew, 401
Private Eye, 203, 319, 338–9, 441
Privileged Bodies, 348–50

Producers, The, 224
prostate cancer, 53, 475
Puttnam, Lord (David), 93–4, 98
Puttnam, Lady (Patty), 100

Qatar, Emir of, 421
Qatari Diar, 421
Quatro, Susi, 370
Queen Mother's Sports Centre, Victoria, 310
Queen (the band), 342
Quinn, Anthony and Lorenzo, 196
Quintero, Javier Moreno, *369*

Radice, Vittorio, 405
Raffles Hotel, Whitehall, 327
Rampazzi, Aldo and Miriam, 235–6
Raoul's, 183
Reagan, Ronald, 378
Rees-Mogg, Lady Gillian, 392
Reeve, (Sir) Anthony, 161
Rhodes James, (Sir) Robert, 88
Richard, Sir Cliff, 194, 201, 342
Richardson, Sarah, 392
Ripper, Jack the, 31
Rittson-Thomas, Hugo, 332, *333*
Ritz Hotel, 204, 204–7, 272, 316, 425, 433, 440
Robathan, Rachael, 186, 200, 238, *239*, 332
Roberts, Glenys, 142
Rodgers, Duncan, 69
Roe, Philippa (Baroness Couttie), 322, 331–2, 343, 432, 441, 462
Rogers, Sir Peter, 184, 309, 392, 394, 398, 410, 424, 425
Romani people, 191–3
Ronson, Gerald, 326, 367, 472, *474*
    and (Dame) Gail, 326, 327
Ronson, Lisa, 369
Roots, Bill, *158*
Rosenbaum, Alice, 293
Rosenfeld, Lionel, 50, 157
Rosewell, Roger, 178
Rossetti, Michel, 233
Ross, Sir Malcolm, 165, 257
Rossi, (Sir) Hugh, 176
Rossi, Marie Louise, 176
Rotary Club, 260
Rowntree, Dave, 279
Royal Academy of Arts, 220
Royal Albert Hall, 211, 286–7
Royal Marsden Hospital, 53
Royal Opera House, 202, 227

Royal Warrant Holders Association, 348

Sacks, Rabbi Jonathan, 169
St Albans Hospital, 136
St James's Palace, 161–2, 174, 257–60, 341, 421
St John's and Elizabeth Hospice, 51
St Mary's Hospital, Paddington, 28, 55, 321–3
St Paul's School, 367, 374, 385
St Petersburg Place Synagogue, 157
Sale of the Century, 67
Salter, Michael, 420
Sandford, Sandy, 126
Sandys, Duncan, 51, 247, 413
SANE (Schizophrenia: A National Emergency), 296
Savill, Dame Rosalind, 296, *299*
Savoy Educational Trust, 7, 309, 327, *400*, 400–01
Savoy Hotel, 194, 272, 300, 309, 400
Schaverien caterers, 123
Schuveck, Betty (nee Foule) (RD's maternal great-grandmother), 31, *32*, *33*, *57*
Schuveck, Mark (RD's maternal great uncle), *32*
Schuveck, Solomon (RD's maternal great-grandfather), 31, *32*
Science Museum, 223
Scottish Sun, 318–9
Scott's, Ronnie, 224
Seacole, Mary, 194
security, 132, 164, 182, 192, 297, 298, 314, 334–6, 403
Selfridges, 42–3, 351, 405
Sellar, Irvine, 320–4
Sellar, James, 324
Seward, Ingrid, 342
sex industry, 127
Seymour Place, 352
Shand, Mark, 274–5
Sharaton Patisserie chain, 177–8, 209, 374, 377, 384
Shard, 320–4
Sharpe, Tom, 87, *88*
Shawcross, Valerie, 454
Shawcross, William, 135, 454
Shaw, David, 213, 384
Sheader, Tim, 398
Shebbeare, (Lady) Cynthia, 66
Shebbeare, Sir Tom, 66
Shepherd, Giles, 272

Silver, Martin, 38
Simmons, Lee, 199, *200*, *201*, 202, 409
Simon, Paul, 72
Sindall, Ann, 469

Slater Walker, 301
Slick Wear, 35–6
Smith, Andrew, 448, 452, *453*
Smith, Bill, 244–5
Snape, Ed, 401
Snow, Ann, Dan and Peter, 99
Social Democratic Party (SDP), 114
Society of London Theatres (SOLT), 213, 226
Soho, 25, 36, 127, 128, 182, 194, 312–3, 337–8, 403–4, 420, 435
Soho Theatre, 403–4
solicitor, career as, – *see* Freeman Box (1983–2015)
Sonn (nee Lee), Rose, 29, 36
Sonya of Norway, Queen, *286–7*
Sound of Music, The, 306
South African High Commission, 165, 167
Spencer, Raine, Countess, *206*, 252
Spiegeltent, 192–3
Sporle, Syd, 351
Squire, Dame Rosemary, 212–4
Stadler, Laura, *369*
Stadler, Michael, 369
Standards Board for England, 338–9
Steele, Sir Tommy, 201
Stein, Sally-Anne, 437
Sternberg, Sir Sigmund, 167–9, 252
Stevenson, Lord (Dennis), 301
Stewart, Bill, 202
Strathclyde, Lord, 147, *148*
Stringfellow, Peter, 356
Stubbs, Imogen, 377
suits, 271–3
Sullivan QC, Jeremy, 137
Summers, Steve, 238, *239*, 270, 316–7, 331, 345, 347, 368, 405, 413, 440, 467
Sunday Times, The, 209, 332–33
Sunset Boulevard, 306–7
Sutherland, Dame Joan, 371
Swedish Embassy, 168
swimming, 43–4, 48
Swiss Banking Corporation, 230, 240
Swiss Centre, 229, 229–32, *239*, 240
    Glockenspiel clock 230–2, 240–2
Swiss Tourist Office, 229
Switzerland Tourism, 233
Sykes, Major General Matthew, 422

Tabor, Ashley, 325–6
Tallboys, Richard, 448
Tallis, Mr, 71
Tarbuck, Jimmy, 201

Tate Britain, 252
Taylor, Kevin, 61
Taylor, (Sir) Teddy, 86
Telegraph, The, 367, 379, 445
Tesco, 116, 139–40
Thames Water, 190
Thatcher government, 112, 203, 397
Thatcher, Margaret, 10–11, 63, 74, 81, *82*, 89, 110, 112, 114, 126, 140, 203, 244, 300, 301, 304–5, 473
theatre, 208–18
Thomas, Simon, *356*
Thompson, Emma, 210
Thorncliffe, 439
Thorneycroft, Peter (Lord), 304–5
Thyssen, Baron, 232
Times Square, New York, 223
Times, The, 335, 379, 421, 440
Timewaster Letters, The, 267–9
Tory Reform Group, 85, 90, 112, 300, 302, 303
Totty, Peter, 101
Touche Ross, 136
Townsend, Sue, 403
Trafalgar Square, 226
Trafalgar Theatre, Whitehall, 213
Travers, Tony, 302, 474
Treasure, Julian, 70–1
Trotter, Joe, 352
Turner, Lord (Adair), 15, 83, 92
Tuttle, Robert, *251*, 335, *336*
Tyburn Stone, 199
Tyrrell, Jace, *432*

Underbelly, 192–3
United States Embassy, 334–9
University College Hospital, 359–60
University of Westminster, 394, 405
University Technology Colleges (UTCs), 393

Vaizey, Lord (Ed), 270
Valentine, Baroness (Jo), 427
Vanger, Lilah, 54, *55*, 56, 359
Van Straubenzee, Sir William, 86
Vaz, Keith, 155, 426
Venice, 46
Veolia, 223
Vertex, 185
Vickers, Hugo, 355
Victoria Business Improvement District, 386
Vidaeff, Anca, 335
Village, William, 398

Villefranche-sur-Mer, 48
Vincent, Tim, 285, 286
Viner, Brigadier, 127–8
Viñoly, Rafael, 199
Visit London Awards, 427

Waddington Games, 302
Wade, Gerry, 88
Walden Estate, Howard de, 200
Waldorf Astoria Hotel, Admiralty Arch, 327
Waley-Cohen, Sir Stephen, 401
Walker, Annie, 275
Walker, Air Marshal Sir David, 343–5, 347–8, 350
Walker, George, 123
Walker, John, 239, 294, 320–3
Walker, Lord (Peter), 300–2
Walker, Robin, 111
Walker-Smith, Sir Jonah, 117, 120
Wallace Collection, 223, 296–7, 343
Wallenberg, Raoul, 167–70
Walsh JP, Simon, 255
Walthamstow Market, 24, 26
Wandsworth Council, 141, 245, 294, 328
Warner, Judith, 136, 458
Watkins, Millicent (Micky), 19
Watson, Helen, 257–8, 264
Watson, John, 302
Weatherall, Vice-Admiral Sir James, 340–1
Weatherhead, Doreen, 256
Weatherill, Sir Bernard, *409*
Weeks, David, 117, 120, *129*, 137, 139, 150, 176, *187*, 187, *188*, 189
Weitzenhoffer, Max, 212
Weizman, Ezer, 167–60, *170*, 292
Wellington Hospital, 55
Wessex, Countess of, 221
West End Live, 192, 219–28, 427
West End, supporting the, 222–6
Western Marble Arch Synagogue, 50, 157, 168
Westfield, 222–3, 406, 427
Westminster Abbey, 7, 16, 157–61, 163, 221, 231, 251, 268, 311–312, 316–7, 332, 348, 355, 371–80, 373, 374, 376, 377, 379, 409, 454, 470
Westminster City Council, 10, 11, 25, 37, 38, 89, 100, 102, 108–16, 120, 124, 126, 128, 130, 134, 142–3, 161, 163, 184, 186, 200, 203, 211, 213, 219, 221, 226, 229–30, 243, 247, 249, 257, 268, 273–4, 277, 301–2, 319, 324, 326, 331, 336, 338, 342, 348, 356, 372–4, 378, 381, 384, 392, 397, 398, 405, 409–10, 415–6, 424, 428–9, 435–6, 444, 454, 463, 465, 467–8

RD'S ROLES
Councillor (1982–2018): 10, 21, 38, 66, 84, 97, 108–15, 116–29, 130–40, 153, 164, 171, 176, 202, 216, 267, 271, 273, 297, 299, 315, 319, 336, 339, 351, 356, 380, 400, 403, 423, 426, 428, 433, 436, 455–6, 458, 461–4, 466, 468, 472
Deputy Chief Whip (1986–7), 128–9, 138
Lord Mayor of Westminster (1996–7), 12–7, 21, 28, 37, 49, 60–1, 78, 100, 102, 141, 144, 153–8, 161–75, 211, 233–6, 243–6, 284–7, 292, 296–300, 305–6, 314, 333, 340–2, 410, 429
Chief Whip (2000–08), 118, 184, 186, 211, 221, 272, 313, 406, 410, 436, 448, 459, 462, 464, 468
Deputy Leader (2008–18), 100, 186, 265, 267, 301, 316–7, 319, 329–32, 336, 349, 356, 368, 391, 428–31, 433–4, 436, 438, 440–3, 457, 459, 461–4, 467–8, 470, 474
downfall and resignation 428–69
Arts Policy, 397
Brighter Subway and Loo Initiative, 354
cemeteries, sale of the, 131–4
Chairman's Group, 120–1, 129
Chief Executive, 118, 137, 158, 162, 184, 297, 309, 349, 370, 392, 410, 432, 438, 440, 450, 459, 461, 466, 467
Citizen Task Forces, 145–6
'Civic Renewal', 374
civic trips to Macon, Georgia, USA, 50–51; Switzerland, 229–242
Code of Conduct, 442, 454, 458, 464–6
Considerate Builders/Hoteliers/Restaurants Scheme, 149
Council of the Year 2004, 424
Cow Parade, 274
Chief Whip, 109–10, 117, 332, 441, 461
Deputy Leader, 117, 120, 134, 137, 139, 176, 179–80, 183, 186–7, 429–30, 433, 442, 467, 474
'Don't drink and drive at Christmas' poster campaign, 303
Dream Jar, 276–7
Egg Parade, 275
Elephant Parade, 274–5
Environment Committee, 121, 134, 145, 176
Eros Snowflake sphere, 283
'Exhaust Watch', 149
Fayre in the Square, 221
Festival of Sculpture, 196–7

Finance Committee, 176
Flyposting SWAT Team, 150
General Purposes Committee, 117–8, 141
gifts and hospitality, receiving and disclosing,
    429–31, 433–35, 453–4, 464–6
'Greening the City' programme, 146–7
Highways Committee, 116, 118
Hospitality, Register of, 431, 436
Housing Committee, 131, 136, 183, 219
Information Technology Committee, 181
Leader of the Council, 116, 150, 153, 176, 184,
    187, 189, 219, 292, 301, 309, 322, 327, 343,
    380, 388, 406, 429, 435, 438
Leisure Committee, 120–22, 128, 229
Libraries Review, 119–20
Library Service, 119–22
Licensing Committee, 337–9
Millennium events, 219
Monitoring Officer, 444–5, 454–8, 462–6
'One City' initiative, 374, 392
Paddington Bears, 275–6
Parking fiasco, 328–30
Personnel Committee, 118
Planning and Transportation Committee (RD
    Chairman, 1991–5), 150, 154, 167, 169, 176,
    179, 180, 187, 202, 351, 355
Planning Committee (RD Chairman, 2000–17),
    212–3, 230, 295, 312–3, 319–24, 391, 434,
    450, 453
    declarations, 434
plaques, 194–5, 351–6
Policy Review Sub-Committee, 117–8
scandals at City Hall, 130–40
Standards Committee, 301, 458–9, 466, 468
Traffic and Works Committee, 303
wards, Baker Street, 181; Bayswater, 126, 451–2;
    Belgravia, 125; Bryanston and Dorset Square,
    448; Cavendish, 127; Church Street, 278–9;
    Lancaster Gate, 126–7, 445–53; Maida Vale,
    325, 448, 451–2; Pimlico, 294; West End,
    127, 142
West End at War, 222
Westminster Initiative, the, 145–50
Westminster City Hall, 5, 50, 60, 61, 98, 102, 106,
    107, 118, 125, 126, 128, 130–1, 133, 135, 137,
    139, 150, 154–6, 164, 200, 201, 231, 233, 243,
    251, 254, 271, 275–7, 284, 286, 297–8, 309, 319,
    331, 343, 349, 364, 366–7, 373, 377–8, 380, 382,
    385, 410, 428–9, 431, 436, 438, 440, 462
Westminster, Duke of, 334
Westminster Guide Lecturers' Association, 404–5

Westminster Literary, Scientific and Mechanics'
    Institution, 119
Westminster, Palace of, 81, 174, 220
Westminster Property Association, 432
Westminster restaurants, 433
Westminster School, 252
Westminster Theatre, 216–7
Whalley, Chris, 83
Wheeler, (Sir) John, *112*
Whelan, Clare, 266
Whiddington, Susan, 401
Whitelaw, Lord (William), 82
Whittington, Diana, 264
Whittington, Dick, 253
Whittington Hospital, 253
Wicked, 227
Wilcox, Herbert, 194
Wilde, Oscar, 194
Wilder, Ian, 180–4, *180*
Willetts, Lord (David), 302
Williams, Professor Sir David, 77, *78*
Williams, Paul, 215
Williams, Pharrell, 317
Williams, Robbie, 270
Williams, Baroness (Shirley), *194*
Willis, Bobby, 60–2
Wilson, Angela, 76
Wilson's Funfairs, Bob, 314–5
Wilson, William and Emily, 314–5
Windsor, (Dame) Barbara, *351*
Winer, Rabbi Mark, *205*
Winter of Discontent, 10, 305
Wiseman, David, 59
Wise, Peter, 38
Withers, Pat, 297
Witty, David, 118
Wizard of Oz, The, 211
Wolseley restaurant, 308, 433
Woody Herman Orchestra, 224
World Jewish Congress, 168

Xavier, Michael, 306, *307*

Yad Vashem, Israel, 177
Yilmaz, Çağatay, *470*
Young, Miles, 153, 179, *187*, 188
Young, Sylvia, 224, 261
    Theatre School, 205, 224, *261*

Zamit, John, 353